Part of P9-DVY-811

Top 100

CAREERS

Without a Four-Year Degree™

Your Complete Guidebook to Major Jobs in Many Fields

EIGHTH EDITION

jist Works®

America's Career Publisher

Michael Farr

Top 100 Careers Without a Four-Year Degree, Eighth Edition
Your Complete Guidebook to Major Jobs in Many Fields

Previous edition was titled *America's Top 101 Jobs for People Without a Four-Year Degree*

© 2007 by JIST Publishing, Inc.

Published by JIST Works, an imprint of JIST Publishing, Inc.
8902 Otis Avenue
Indianapolis, IN 46216-1033
Phone: 1-800-648-JIST   Fax: 1-800-JIST-FAX
E-mail: info@jist.com   Web site: www.jist.com

Some books by Michael Farr:
Best Jobs for the 21st Century
Overnight Career Choice
Same-Day Resume
Next-Day Job Interview
The Quick Resume & Cover Letter Book
The Very Quick Job Search

JIST's Top Careers™ Series:
Top 300 Careers
Top 100 Health-Care Careers
100 Fastest-Growing Jobs
Top 100 Careers Without a Four-Year Degree
Top 100 Careers for College Graduates
Top 100 Computer and Technical Careers

Visit www.jist.com for free job search information, book excerpts, and ordering information on our many products. For free information on 14,000 job titles, visit www.careeroink.com.

Quantity discounts are available for JIST products. Have future editions of JIST books automatically delivered to you on publication through our convenient standing order program. Please call 1-800-648-JIST or visit www.jist.com for a free catalog and more information.

Acquisitions Editor: Susan Pines
Development Editors: Stephanie Koutek, Jill Mazurczyk
Database Work: Laurence Shatkin
Cover Photo: Michael Duerinckx/ImageState/Fotosearch
Cover Layout: Trudy Coler
Interior Design and Layout: Marie Kristine Parial-Leonardo
Proofreaders: Linda Seifert, Jeanne Clark

Printed in the United States of America

09 08 07 06   9 8 7 6 5 4 3 2 1

Library of Congress Cataloging-in-Publication Data

Farr, J. Michael.
   Top 100 careers without a four-year degree : your complete guidebook to major jobs in many fields /
Michael Farr. -- 8th ed.
      p. cm. -- (Jist's top careers series)
   Includes bibliographical references and index.
   ISBN-13: 978-1-59357-319-5 (alk. paper)
   ISBN-10: 1-59357-319-7 (alk. paper)
   1. Vocational guidance--United States. 2. Occupations--United States. 3. Job hunting--United States. 4. Employment forecasting--United States. 5. Résumés (Employment) 6. Vocational qualifications. I. Title. II. Title: Top one hundred careers without a four-year degree.
HF5382.5.U5F375 2006
331.702--dc22
                                                              2006031974

ISBN-13: 978-1-59357-319-5
ISBN-10: 1-59357-319-7

Relax. You Don't Have to Read This Whole Book!

You don't need to read this entire book. I've organized it into easy-to-use sections so you can get just the information you want. You will find everything you need to

★ Learn about the 100 top careers that don't require a four-year college degree, including their daily tasks, pay, outlook, and required education and skills.

★ Match your personal skills to the careers.

★ Take seven steps to land a good job in less time.

To get started, simply scan the table of contents to learn more about these sections and to see a list of the jobs described in this book. Really, this book is easy to use, and I hope it helps you.

Who Should Use This Book?

This is more than a book of job descriptions. I've spent quite a bit of time thinking about how to make its contents useful for a variety of situations, including

★ **Exploring career options.** The job descriptions in Part II give a wealth of information on many of the most desirable jobs in the labor market. The assessment in Part I can help you focus your career options.

★ **Considering more education or training.** The information helps you avoid costly mistakes in choosing a career or deciding on additional training or education—and it increases your chances of planning a bright future.

★ **Job seeking.** This book helps you identify new job targets, prepare for interviews, and write targeted resumes. The advice in Part III has been proven to cut job search time in half.

★ **Career planning.** The job descriptions help you explore your options, and Parts III and IV provide career planning advice and other useful information.

Source of Information

The job descriptions come from the good people at the U.S. Department of Labor, as published in the most recent edition of the *Occupational Outlook Handbook*. The *OOH* is the best source of career information available, and the descriptions include the most current, accurate data on jobs. Thank you to all the people at the Department of Labor who gather, compile, analyze, and make sense of this information. It's good stuff, and I hope you can make good use of it.

Mike Farr

Mike Farr

Contents

Summary of Major Sections

Introduction. Provides an explanation of the job descriptions, how best to use the book, and other details. *Begins on page 1.*

Part I: Using the Job-Match Grid to Choose a Career. Match your skills and preferences to the jobs in this book. *Begins on page 15.*

Part II: Descriptions of the Top 100 Careers Without a Four-Year Degree. Presents thorough descriptions of the top 100 careers that don't require a four-year degree. Education and training requirements for these jobs vary from on-the-job training to less than a four-year degree. Each description gives information on the nature of the work, working conditions, employment, training, other qualifications, advancement, job outlook, earnings, related occupations, and sources of additional information. The jobs are presented in alphabetical order. The page numbers where specific descriptions begin are listed in the detailed contents. *Begins on page 31.*

Part III: *Quick Job Search—Seven Steps to Getting a Good Job in Less Time.* This relatively brief but important section offers results-oriented career planning and job search techniques. It includes tips on identifying your key skills, defining your ideal job, using effective job search methods, writing resumes, organizing your time, improving your interviewing skills, and following up on leads. The last part of this section features professionally written and designed resumes for some of the top jobs that don't require a four-year degree. *Begins on page 285.*

Part IV: Important Trends in Jobs and Industries. This section includes three well-written articles on labor market trends. The articles are worth your time. Titles of the articles are "Tomorrow's Jobs," "Employment Trends in Major Industries," and "Job Outlook for People Who Don't Have a Bachelor's Degree." *Begins on page 343.*

Detailed Contents

Introduction

This book is about improving your life, not just about selecting a job. The career you choose will have an enormous impact on how you live your life.

A huge amount of information is available on occupations, but most people don't know where to find accurate, reliable facts to help them make good career decisions—or they don't take the time to look. Important choices such as what to do with your career or whether to get additional training or education deserve your time.

If you are considering more training or education—whether additional coursework, an apprenticeship, or a two-year degree—this book will help with solid information. Training or education beyond high school is now typically required to get better jobs, and the education and training needed for the jobs in this book vary enormously. This book is designed to give you facts to help you explore your options.

A certain type of work or workplace may interest you as much as a certain type of job. If your interests and values lead you to work in health care, for example, you can do this in a variety of work environments, in a variety of industries, and in a variety of jobs. For this reason, I suggest you begin exploring alternatives by following your interests and finding a career path that allows you to use your talents doing something you enjoy.

Also, remember that money is not everything. The time you spend in career planning can pay off in higher earnings, but being satisfied with your work—and your life—is often more important than how much you earn. This book can help you find the work that suits you best.

Keep in Mind That Your Situation Is *Not* "Average"

Projected employment growth and earnings trends are quite positive for many occupations and industries. Keep in mind, however, that the averages in this book will not be true for many individuals. Within any field, many people earn more and many earn less than the average.

My point is that *your* situation is probably not average. Some people do better than others, and some are willing to accept less pay for a more desirable work environment. Earnings vary enormously in different parts of the country, in different occupations, and in different industries. But this book's solid information is a great place to start. Good information will give you a strong foundation for good decisions.

Four Important Labor Market Trends That Will Affect Your Career

Our economy has changed in dramatic ways over the past 10 years, with profound effects on how we work and live. Part IV of this book provides more information on labor market trends, but in case you don't read it, here are four trends that you simply *must* consider.

1. Education Pays

I'm sure you won't be surprised to learn that people with higher levels of education and training have higher average earnings. The data that follows comes from the U.S. Department of Labor. I've selected data to show you the median earnings for people with various levels of education. (The median is the point where half earn more and half earn less.) Based on this information, I computed the earnings advantage of people at various education levels over those who did not graduate from high school. I've also included information showing the average percentage of people at that educational level who are unemployed.

Earnings for Year-Round, Full-Time Workers Age 25 and Over, by Educational Attainment

Level of Education	Median Annual Earnings	Premium Over High School Dropouts	Unemployment Rate
Master's degree	$53,200	$33,400	2.9
Bachelor's degree	45,000	25,200	3.3
Associate degree	33,600	13,800	4.0
Some college, no degree	31,100	11,300	5.2
High school graduate	27,700	7,900	5.5
High school dropout	19,800		8.8

Source: Bureau of Labor Statistics

As you can see in the table, the earnings difference between someone who holds an associate degree and someone with a high school education is $5,900 a year, money that could be used toward a car, a down payment on a house, or even a vacation. As you see, over a lifetime, this earnings difference will make an enormous difference in lifestyle.

The table makes it very clear that those with more training and education earn more than those with less and experience lower levels of unemployment. Jobs that require education and training beyond high school are projected to grow significantly faster than jobs that do not. People with higher levels of education and training are less likely to be unemployed, and when they are, they remain unemployed for shorter periods of time. There are always exceptions, but it is quite clear that more education results in higher earnings and lower rates of unemployment.

2. Knowledge of Computer and Other Technologies Is Increasingly Important

As you look over the list of jobs in the table of contents, you may notice that many require computer or technical skills. Even jobs that do not appear to be technical often call for computer literacy. Agricultural managers, for example, are often expected to understand and use scheduling and estimating software.

In all fields, those without job-related technical and computer skills will have a more difficult time finding good opportunities because they are competing with those who have these skills. Older workers, by the way, often do not have the computer skills that younger workers do. Employers tend to hire people who have the skills they need, and people without these abilities won't get the best jobs. So, whatever your age, consider upgrading your job-related computer and technology skills if you need to—and plan to stay up to date on your current and future jobs.

3. Ongoing Education and Training Are Essential

School and work once were separate activities, and most people did not go back to school after they began working. But with rapid changes in technology, most people are now required to learn throughout their work lives. Jobs are constantly upgraded, and today's jobs often cannot be handled by people who have only the knowledge and skills that were adequate for workers a few years ago.

To remain competitive, you will need to constantly upgrade your technology and other job-related skills. This may include taking formal courses, reading work-related magazines at home, signing up for on-the-job training, or participating in other forms of education. Upgrading your work-related skills on an ongoing basis is no longer optional for most jobs, and you ignore doing so at your peril.

4. Good Career Planning Is More Important Than Ever

Most people spend more time watching TV in a week than they spend on career planning during an entire year. Yet most people will change their jobs many times and make major career changes five to seven times. For this reason, it is important for you to spend time considering your career options and preparing to advance.

While you probably picked up this book for its information on jobs, it also provides a great deal of information on career planning. For example, Part III gives good career and job search advice, and Part IV has useful information on labor market trends. I urge you to read these and related materials because career-planning and job-seeking skills are the keys to surviving in this new economy.

Tips on Using This Book

This book is based on information from a variety of government sources and includes the most up-to-date and accurate data available. The entries are well written and pack a lot of information into short descriptions. *Top 100 Careers Without a Four-Year Degree* can be used in many ways, and I've provided tips for these four major uses:

★ For people exploring career, education, or training alternatives

★ For job seekers

★ For employers and business people

★ For counselors, instructors, and other career specialists

Tips for People Exploring Career, Education, or Training Alternatives

Top 100 Careers Without a Four-Year Degree is an excellent resource for anyone exploring career, education, or training alternatives. Many people do not have a good idea of what they want to do in their careers. They may be considering additional training or education but may not know what sort they should get. If you are one of these people, this book can help in several ways. Here are a few pointers.

Review the list of jobs. Trust yourself. Research studies indicate that most people have a good sense of their interests. Your interests can be used to guide you to career options you should consider in more detail.

Begin by looking over the occupations listed in the table of contents. Look at all the jobs, because you may identify previously overlooked possibilities. If other people will be using this book, please don't mark in it. Instead, on a separate sheet of paper, list the jobs that interest you. Or make a photocopy of the table of contents and use it to mark the jobs that interest you.

Next, look up and carefully read the descriptions of the jobs that most interest you in Part II. A quick review will often eliminate one or more of these jobs based on pay, working conditions, education required, or other considerations. After you have identified the three or four jobs that seem most interesting, research each one more thoroughly before making any important decisions.

Match your skills to the jobs in this book using the Job-Match Grid. Another way to identify possible job options is to answer questions about your skills and job preferences in Part I, "Using the Job-Match Grid to Choose a Career." This section will help you focus your job options and concentrate your research on a handful of job descriptions.

Study the jobs and their training and education requirements. Too many people decide to obtain additional training or education without knowing much about the jobs the training will lead to. Reviewing the descriptions in this book is one way to learn more about an occupation before you enroll in an education or training program. If you are currently a student, the job descriptions in this book can also help you decide on a major course of study or learn more about the jobs for which your studies are preparing you.

Do not be too quick to eliminate a job that interests you. If a job requires more education or training than you currently have, you can obtain this training in many ways.

Don't abandon your past experience and education too quickly. If you have significant work experience, training, or education, these should not be abandoned too quickly. Many times, after people carefully consider what they want to do, they change careers and find that the skills they have can still be used.

Top 100 Careers Without a Four-Year Degree can help you explore career options in several ways. First, carefully review descriptions for jobs you have held in the past. On a separate sheet of paper, list the skills needed in those jobs. Then do the same for jobs that interest you now. By comparing the lists, you will be able to identify skills you used in previous jobs that you could also use in jobs that interest you for the future. These "transferable" skills form the basis for moving to a new career.

You can also identify skills you have developed or used in nonwork activities, such as hobbies, family responsibilities, volunteer work, school, military, and extracurricular interests. If you want to stay with your current employer, the job descriptions can also help. For example, you may identify jobs within your organization that offer more rewarding work, higher pay, or other advantages over your present job. Read the descriptions related to these jobs, as you may be able to transfer into another job rather than leave the organization.

Tips for Job Seekers

You can use the job descriptions in this book to give you an edge in finding job openings and in getting job offers—even when you are competing with people who have better credentials. Here are some ways *Top 100 Careers Without a Four-Year Degree* can help you in the job search.

Identify related job targets. You may be limiting your job search to a small number of jobs for which you feel qualified, but by doing so you eliminate many jobs you could do and enjoy. Your search for a new job should be broadened to include more possibilities.

Go through the entire list of jobs in the table of contents and check any that require skills similar to those you have. Look at all the jobs, as doing so sometimes helps you identify targets you would otherwise overlook.

You may want to answer questions about your skills and job preferences in Part I, "Using the Job-Match Grid to Choose a Career." Your results can help you identify career options that may suit you.

Many people are not aware of the many specialized jobs related to their training or experience. The descriptions in *Top 100 Careers Without a Four-Year Degree* are for major job titles, but a variety of more-specialized jobs may require similar skills. The "Other Major Career Information Sources" section later in this introduction lists sources you can use to find out about more-specialized jobs.

The descriptions can also point out jobs that interest you but that have higher responsibility or compensation levels. While you may not consider yourself qualified for such jobs now, you should think about seeking jobs that are above your previous levels but within your ability to handle.

Prepare for interviews. This book's job descriptions are an essential source of information to help you prepare for interviews. If you carefully review the description of a job before an interview, you will be much better prepared to emphasize your key skills. You should also review descriptions for past jobs and identify skills needed in the new job.

Negotiate pay. The job descriptions in this book will help you know what pay range to expect. Note that local pay and other details can differ substantially from the national averages in the descriptions.

Tips for Employers and Business People

Employers, human resource professionals, and other business users can use this book's information to write job descriptions, study pay ranges, and set criteria for new employees. The information can also help you conduct more-effective interviews by providing a list of key skills needed by new hires.

Tips for Counselors, Instructors, and Other Career Specialists

Counselors, instructors, and other career specialists will find this book helpful for their clients or students exploring career options or job targets. My best suggestion to professionals is to get this book off the shelf and into the hands of the people who need it. Leave it on a table or desk and show people how the information can help them. Wear this book out—its real value is as a tool used often and well.

Additional Information About the Projections

For more information about employment change, job openings, earnings, unemployment rates, and training requirements by occupation, consult *Occupational Projections and Training Data,* published by the Bureau of Labor Statistics. For occupational information from an industry perspective, including some occupations and career paths that *Top 100 Careers Without a Four-Year Degree* does not cover, consult another BLS publication, *Career Guide to Industries.* This book is also available from JIST with enhanced content under the title *40 Best Fields for Your Career.*

Information on the Major Parts of This Book

This book was designed to be easy to use. The table of contents provides brief comments on each section, and that may be all you need. If not, here are some additional details you may find useful in getting the most out of this book.

Part I: Using the Job-Match Grid to Choose a Career

Part I features an assessment with checklists and questions to match your skills and preferences to the jobs in this book. The seven skills covered in the assessment are artistic, communication, interpersonal, managerial, mathematics, mechanical, and science. The five job characteristics covered in the assessment are economically sensitive, geographically concentrated, hazardous conditions, outdoor work, and physically demanding.

Part II: Descriptions of the 100 Top Careers Without a Four-Year Degree

Part II is the main part of the book and probably the reason you picked it up. It contains brief, well-written descriptions for 100 major jobs typically held by people without a four-year degree. A list of the jobs is provided in the table of contents. The content for each of these job descriptions comes from the U.S. Department of Labor and is considered by many to be the most accurate and up-to-date data available. These jobs are presented in alphabetical order.

Together, the jobs in Part II provide enormous variety at all levels of earnings and interest. One way to explore career options is to go to the table of contents and identify those jobs that seem interesting. If you are interested in medical jobs, for example, you can quickly spot those you will want to learn more about. You may also see other jobs that look interesting, and you should consider these as well.

Next, read the descriptions for the jobs that interest you and, based on what you learn, identify those that *most* interest you. These are the jobs you should consider, and Parts III and IV will give you additional information on how you might best do so.

How the 100 Jobs Were Selected

The jobs included in this book are selected from the nearly 270 jobs covered in detail by the *Occupational Outlook Handbook,* published by the U.S. Department of Labor. They are jobs that normally require less education than a bachelor's degree and that had a workforce of more than 200,000 people in 2004. (The largest had a workforce of over 10 million.) Any job that employs at least one-fifth of a million people is going to account for a lot of job openings and therefore is worth your consideration. Even if overall employment in the job is shrinking, you can expect many job opportunities because of retirements and turnover.

Details on Each Section of the Job Descriptions

Each occupational description in this book follows a standard format, making it easier for you to compare jobs. The following overview describes the kinds of information found in each part of a description and offers tips on how to interpret the information.

Job Title

This is the title used for the job in the *Occupational Outlook Handbook*.

*O*NET Codes*

This section of each job description lists one or more code numbers (for example: 11-9031.00, 11-9032.00) for related jobs in a major occupational information system used by the U.S. Department of Labor. This system, named the Occupational Information Network (or O*NET), is used by a variety of state and federal programs to classify applicants and job openings and by a variety of career information systems. You can use the O*NET code numbers to get additional information on the related O*NET titles on the Internet at www.onetcenter.org or at www.careeroink.com. Reference books that provide O*NET descriptions include the *O*NET Dictionary of Occupational Titles* and the *Enhanced Occupational Outlook Handbook*, both published by JIST Publishing. Your librarian can help you find these books.

Significant Points

The bullet points in this part of a description highlight key characteristics for each job, such as recent trends or education and training requirements.

Nature of the Work

This part of the description discusses what workers typically do in a particular job. Individual job duties may vary by industry or employer. For instance, workers in larger firms tend to be more specialized, whereas those in smaller firms often have a wider variety of duties. Most occupations have several levels of skills and responsibilities through which workers may progress. Beginners may start as trainees performing routine tasks under close supervision. Experienced workers usually undertake more difficult tasks and are expected to perform with less supervision.

In this part of a description, you will also find information about the influence of technological advancements on the way work is done. For example, customer service representatives may now help customers over the Internet. This part also discusses emerging specialties.

Working Conditions

This part of the description identifies the typical hours worked, the workplace environment, physical activities, risk of injury, special equipment, and the extent of travel required. For example, construction equipment operators are susceptible to injury, while paralegals and legal assistants have high job-related stress. Radiologic technologists and technicians may wear protective clothing or equipment; carpenters do physically demanding work; and truck drivers and driver/sales workers travel frequently.

In many occupations, people work regular business hours—40 hours a week, Monday through Friday. In other occupations, they do not. For example, licensed practical and licensed vocational nurses often work evenings and weekends. The work setting can range from a hospital to a mall to an off-shore oil rig.

Information on various worker characteristics, such as the average number of hours worked per week, is obtained from the Current Population Survey (CPS), a survey of households conducted by the U.S. Census Bureau for the Bureau of Labor Statistics (BLS).

Training, Other Qualifications, and Advancement

After finding out what a job is all about, you probably want to understand how to train for it. This section describes the most significant sources of education and training, including the education or training preferred by employers, the typical length of training, and the possibilities for advancement. Job skills sometimes are acquired through high school, informal on-the-job training, formal training (including apprenticeships), the U.S. Armed Forces, home study, hobbies, or previous work experience. For example, sales experience is particularly important for many sales jobs. Many professional and technical jobs, on the other hand, require formal postsecondary education.

This section also mentions desirable skills, aptitudes, and personal characteristics. For some entry-level jobs, personal characteristics are more important than formal training. Employers generally seek people who read, write, and speak well; compute accurately; think logically; learn quickly; get along with others; and demonstrate dependability.

Some occupations require certification or licensing to enter the field, to advance in the occupation, or to practice independently. Certification or licensing generally involves completing courses and passing examinations. Many occupations increasingly are requiring workers to participate in continuing education or training in relevant skills, either to keep up with the changes in their jobs or to improve their advancement opportunities.

Employment

This section reports the number of jobs the occupation recently provided, the key industries where these jobs are found, and the number or proportion of self-employed workers in the occupation, if significant. Self-employed workers accounted for about 8 percent of the workforce in 2004; however, they were concentrated in a small number of occupations, such as farmers and ranchers, childcare workers, lawyers, health practitioners, and the construction trades.

When significant, the geographic distribution of jobs and the proportion of part-time (less than 35 hours a week) workers in the occupation are mentioned.

Job Outlook

In planning for the future, you need to consider potential job opportunities. This section describes the factors that will result in employment growth or decline. A number of factors are examined in developing employment projections. One factor is job growth or decline in industries that employ a significant percentage of workers in the occupation. If workers are concentrated in a rapidly growing industry, their employment will likely also grow quickly.

Demographic changes, which affect what services are required, can influence occupational growth or decline. For example, an aging population demands more healthcare workers, from licensed practical and vocational nurses to pharmacy technicians. Technological change is another key factor. New technology can either create new job opportunities or eliminate jobs by making workers obsolete. The Internet has increased the demand for workers in the computer and information technology fields, such as computer support specialists and systems administrators. However, the Internet also has adversely affected travel agents, because many people now book tickets, hotels, and rental cars online.

Another factor affecting job growth or decline is changes in business practices, such as the outsourcing of work or the restructuring of businesses. In the past few years, insurance carriers have been outsourcing sales and claims adjuster jobs to large 24-hour call centers, sometimes in other countries, in order to reduce costs. Corporate restructuring also has made many organizations "flatter," resulting in fewer middle management positions.

The substitution of one product or service for another can affect employment projections. For example, consumption of plastic products has grown as they have been substituted for metal goods in many consumer and manufactured products in recent years. The process is likely to continue and should result in stronger demand for machine operators in plastics than in metal.

Competition from foreign trade usually has a negative impact on employment. Often, foreign manufacturers can produce goods more cheaply than they can be produced in the United States, and the cost savings can be passed on in the form of lower prices with which U.S. manufacturers cannot compete.

In some cases, this book mentions that an occupation is likely to provide numerous job openings or, in others, that an occupation likely will afford relatively few openings. This information reflects the projected change in employment, as well as replacement needs. Large occupations that have high turnover generally provide the most job openings, reflecting the need to replace workers who transfer to other occupations or stop working.

Some job descriptions discuss the relationship between the number of job seekers and the number of job openings. In some occupations, there is a rough balance between job seekers and job openings, resulting in good opportunities. In other occupations, employers may report difficulty finding qualified applicants, resulting in excellent job opportunities. Still other occupations are characterized by a surplus of applicants, leading to keen competition for jobs. On the one hand, limited training facilities, salary regulations, or undesirable aspects of the work—as in the case of private household workers—can result in an insufficient number of entrants to fill all job openings. On the other hand, glamorous or potentially high-paying occupations, such as actors or musicians, generally have surpluses of job seekers. Variation in job opportunities by industry, educational attainment, size of firm, or geographic location also may be discussed. Even in crowded fields, job openings do exist. Good students or highly qualified individuals should not be deterred from undertaking training for, or seeking entry into, those occupations.

Key Phrases Used in the Descriptions

This table explains how to interpret the key phrases that describe projected changes in employment. It also explains the terms for the relationship between the number of job openings and the number of job seekers.

Changing Employment Between 2004 and 2014

If the statement reads	Employment is projected to
Grow much faster than average	Increase 27 percent or more
Grow faster than average	Increase 18 to 26 percent
Grow about as fast as average	Increase 9 to 17 percent
Grow more slowly than average	Increase 0 to 8 percent
Decline	Decrease any amount

Opportunities and Competition for Jobs

If the statement reads	Job openings compared to job seekers may be
Very good to excellent opportunities	More numerous
Good or favorable opportunities	In rough balance
May face or can expect keen competition	Fewer

Earnings

This section discusses typical earnings and how workers are compensated—by means of annual salaries, hourly wages, commissions, piece rates, tips, or bonuses. Within every occupation, earnings vary by experience, responsibility, performance, tenure, and geographic area. Information on earnings in the major industries in which the occupation is employed may be given. Some statements contain additional earnings data from non-BLS sources. Starting and average salaries of federal workers are based on 2005 data from the U.S. Office of Personnel Management. A few statements contain additional earnings information from other sources, such as unions, professional associations, and private companies. These data sources are cited in the text.

Benefits account for a significant portion of total compensation costs to employers. Benefits such as paid vacation, health insurance, and sick leave may not be mentioned because they are so widespread. Although not as common as traditional benefits, flexible hours and profit-sharing plans may be offered to attract and retain highly qualified workers. Less-common benefits also include childcare, tuition for dependents, housing assistance, summers off, and free or discounted merchandise or services. For certain occupations, the percentage of workers affiliated with a union is listed.

Related Occupations

Occupations involving similar duties, skills, interests, education, and training are listed here. This allows you to look up these jobs if they also interest you.

Sources of Additional Information

No single publication can describe all aspects of an occupation. Thus, this section lists the mailing addresses of associations, government agencies, unions, and other organizations that can provide occupational information. In some cases, toll-free telephone numbers and Internet addresses also are listed. Free or relatively inexpensive publications offering more information may be mentioned; some of these publications also may be available in libraries, in school career centers, in guidance offices, or on the Internet.

Part III: *Quick Job Search—Seven Steps to Getting a Good Job in Less Time*

For more than 25 years, I've been helping people find better jobs in less time. If you have ever experienced unemployment, you know it is not pleasant. Unemployment is something most people want to get over quickly—in fact, the quicker the better. Part III will give you some techniques to help.

I know that most of you who read this book want to improve yourselves. You want to consider career and training options that lead to a better job and life in whatever way you define this—better pay, more flexibility, work that is more enjoyable or more meaningful, proving to your mom that you really can do anything you set your mind to, and other reasons. That is why I include advice on career planning and job search in Part III. It's a short section, but it includes the basics that are most important in planning your career and in reducing the time it takes to get a job. I hope it will make you think about what is important to you in the long run.

The second section of Part III showcases professionally written resumes for some of America's top jobs for people without a four-year degree. Use these as examples when creating your own resume.

I know you will resist completing the activities in Part III, but consider this: It is often not the best person who gets the job, but the best job seeker. People who do their career planning and job search homework often get jobs over those with better credentials, because they have these distinct advantages:

1. **They get more interviews,** including many for jobs that will never be advertised.

2. **They do better in interviews.**

People who understand what they want and what they have to offer employers present their skills more convincingly and are much better at answering problem questions. And, because they have learned more about job search techniques, they are likely to get more interviews with employers who need the skills they have.

Doing better in interviews often makes the difference between getting a job offer and sitting at home. And spending time planning your career can make an enormous difference to your happiness and lifestyle over time. So please consider reading Part III and completing its activities. I suggest you schedule a time right now to at least read Part III. An hour or so spent there can help you do just enough better in your career planning, job seeking, and interviewing to make the difference.

One other thing: If you work through Part III and it helps you in some significant way, I'd like to hear from you. Please write or e-mail me via the publisher, whose contact information appears elsewhere in this book.

Part IV: Important Trends in Jobs and Industries

This section is made up of three very good articles on labor market trends. These articles come directly from U.S. Department of Labor sources and are interesting, well written, and short. One is on overall trends, with an emphasis on occupational groups; another is on trends in major industry groups; and the third discusses the job outlook for people without a bachelor's degree. I know they sound boring, but the articles are quick reads and will give you a good idea of factors that will impact your career in the years to come.

The first article is titled "Tomorrow's Jobs." It highlights many important trends in employment and includes information on the fastest-growing jobs, jobs with high pay at various levels of education, and other details.

The second article is titled "Employment Trends in Major Industries." I included this information because you may find that you can use your skills or training in industries you have not considered. The article provides a good review of major trends with an emphasis on helping you make good employment decisions. This information can help you seek jobs in industries that offer higher pay or that are more likely to interest you. Many people overlook one important fact—the industry you work in is as important as the occupation you choose.

The third article is called "Job Outlook for People Who Don't Have a Bachelor's Degree." It identifies high-paying and high-growth career options for people who don't complete four years of college. It includes tables with facts about specific careers, including the typical entry route—which may be as quick as short-term on-the-job training or as long as an associate degree program.

Some Additional Jobs to Consider

Here is a list of additional jobs that may not require a four-year degree that you may want to consider. Their descriptions are not included in this book, but you can find them in the *Occupational Outlook Handbook*, *Top 300 Careers*, or the *Enhanced Occupational Outlook Handbook* or online at www.careeroink.com or www.bls.gov.

- ★ Advertising Sales Agents
- ★ Air Traffic Controllers
- ★ Aircraft Pilots and Flight Engineers
- ★ Animal Care and Service Workers
- ★ Announcers
- ★ Appraisers and Assessors of Real Estate
- ★ Athletes, Coaches, Umpires, and Related Workers
- ★ Boilermakers
- ★ Bookbinders and Bindery Workers
- ★ Brickmasons, Blockmasons, and Stonemasons
- ★ Broadcast and Sound Engineering Technicians and Radio Operators
- ★ Brokerage Clerks
- ★ Cardiovascular Technologists and Technicians
- ★ Cargo and Freight Agents
- ★ Carpet, Floor, and Tile Installers and Finishers
- ★ Cement Masons, Concrete Finishers, Segmental Pavers, and Terrazzo Workers
- ★ Coin, Vending, and Amusement Machine Servicers and Repairers
- ★ Computer Control Programmers and Operators
- ★ Computer Operators
- ★ Construction and Building Inspectors
- ★ Cost Estimators
- ★ Couriers and Messengers
- ★ Court Reporters
- ★ Credit Authorizers, Checkers, and Clerks
- ★ Dancers and Choreographers
- ★ Demonstrators, Product Promoters, and Models
- ★ Dental Hygienists
- ★ Desktop Publishers
- ★ Diagnostic Medical Sonographers
- ★ Electronic Home Entertainment Equipment Installers and Repairers
- ★ Elevator Installers and Repairers
- ★ Emergency Medical Technicians and Paramedics
- ★ Fishers and Fishing Vessel Operators
- ★ Fitness Workers
- ★ Flight Attendants
- ★ Floral Designers
- ★ Forest, Conservation, and Logging Workers

* ★ Funeral Directors
* ★ Gaming Cage Workers
* ★ Glaziers
* ★ Hazardous Materials Removal Workers
* ★ Heavy Vehicle and Mobile Equipment Service Technicians and Mechanics
* ★ Home Appliance Repairers
* ★ Hotel, Motel, and Resort Desk Clerks
* ★ Human Resources Assistants, Except Payroll and Timekeeping
* ★ Industrial Production Managers
* ★ Insulation Workers
* ★ Interpreters and Translators
* ★ Library Assistants, Clerical
* ★ Library Technicians
* ★ Lodging Managers
* ★ Massage Therapists
* ★ Medical Records and Health Information Technicians
* ★ Medical Transcriptionists
* ★ Medical, Dental, and Ophthalmic Laboratory Technicians
* ★ Meter Readers, Utilities
* ★ Millwrights
* ★ Nuclear Medicine Technologists
* ★ Occupational Therapist Assistants and Aides
* ★ Opticians, Dispensing
* ★ Pest Control Workers
* ★ Pharmacy Aides
* ★ Photographic Process Workers and Processing Machine Operators

* ★ Physical Therapist Assistants and Aides
* ★ Plasterers and Stucco Masons
* ★ Power Plant Operators, Distributors, and Dispatchers
* ★ Precision Instrument and Equipment Repairers
* ★ Private Detectives and Investigators
* ★ Procurement Clerks
* ★ Radiation Therapists
* ★ Rail Transportation Occupations
* ★ Respiratory Therapists
* ★ Roofers
* ★ Semiconductor Processors
* ★ Sheet Metal Workers
* ★ Small Engine Mechanics
* ★ Stationary Engineers and Boiler Operators
* ★ Structural and Reinforcing Iron and Metal Workers
* ★ Surgical Technologists
* ★ Surveyors, Cartographers, Photogrammetrists, and Surveying Technicians
* ★ Taxi Drivers and Chauffeurs
* ★ Television, Video, and Motion Picture Camera Operators and Editors
* ★ Tool and Die Makers
* ★ Travel Agents
* ★ Veterinary Technologists and Technicians
* ★ Water and Liquid Waste Treatment Plant and System Operators
* ★ Water Transportation Occupations
* ★ Weighers, Measurers, Checkers, and Samplers, Recordkeeping

Other Major Career Information Sources

The information in this book will be very useful, but you may want or need additional information. Keep in mind that the job descriptions here cover major jobs and not the many more-specialized jobs that are often related to them. Each job description in this book provides some sources of information related to that job, but here are additional resources to consider.

Occupational Outlook Handbook (or the *OOH*): Updated every two years by the U.S. Department of Labor, this book provides descriptions for almost 270 major jobs covering more than 85 percent of the workforce. The *OOH* is the source of the job descriptions used in this book, and the book *Top 300 Careers* includes all the *OOH* content plus additional information.

The *Enhanced Occupational Outlook Handbook:* Includes all descriptions in the *OOH* plus descriptions of more than 6,300 more-specialized jobs that are related to them.

The *O*NET Dictionary of Occupational Titles:* The only printed source of the more than 900 jobs described in the U.S. Department of Labor's Occupational Information Network database (O*NET).

The *New Guide for Occupational Exploration:* An important career reference that allows you to explore all major O*NET jobs based on your interests.

www.careeroink.com: This Web site provides more than 14,000 job descriptions, including those mentioned in the previous books, and a variety of useful ways to explore them.

Best Jobs for the 21st Century: Includes descriptions for the 500 jobs (out of more than 1,100) with the best combination of earnings, growth, and number of openings. Useful lists make jobs easy to explore (examples: highest-paying jobs by level of education or training; best jobs overall; and best jobs for different ages, personality types, interests, and many more).

Exploring Careers—A Young Person's Guide to 1,000 Jobs: For youth exploring career and education opportunities, this book covers 1,000 job options in an interesting and useful format.

Using the Job-Match Grid to Choose a Career

By the Editors at JIST

This book describes so many occupations—how can you choose the best job for you? This section is your answer! It can help you to identify the jobs where your abilities will be valued, and you can rule out jobs that have certain characteristics you'd rather avoid. You will respond to a series of statements and use the Job-Match Grid to match your skills and preferences to the most appropriate jobs in this book.

So grab a pencil and get ready to mark up the following sections. Or, if someone else will be using this book, find a sheet of paper and get ready to take notes.

Thinking About Your Skills

Everybody knows that skills are important for getting and keeping a job. Employers expect you to list relevant skills on your resume. They ask about your skills in interviews. And they expect you to develop skills on the job so that you will remain productive as new technologies and new work situations emerge.

But maybe you haven't thought about how closely skills are related to job satisfaction. For example, let's say you have enough communication skills to hold a certain job where these skills are used heavily, but you wouldn't really *enjoy* using them. In that case, this job probably would be a bad choice for you. You need to identify a job that will use the skills that you *do* enjoy using.

That's why you need to take a few minutes to think about your skills: the ones you're good at and the ones you like using. The checklists that follow can help you do this. On each of the seven skills checklists that follow, use numbers to indicate how much you agree with each statement:

3 = I strongly agree

2 = I agree

1 = There's some truth to this

0 = This doesn't apply to me

Artistic Skills

_____ I am an amateur artist.

_____ I have musical talent.

(continued)

(continued)

_____ I enjoy planning home makeovers.

_____ I am good at performing onstage.

_____ I enjoy taking photos or shooting videos.

_____ I am good at writing stories, poems, articles, or essays.

_____ I have enjoyed taking ballet or other dance lessons.

_____ I like to cook and plan meals.

_____ I can sketch a good likeness of something or somebody.

_____ Playing music or singing is a hobby of mine.

_____ I have a good sense of visual style.

_____ I have participated in amateur theater.

_____ I like to express myself through writing.

_____ I can prepare tasty meals better than most people.

_____ I have a flair for creating attractive designs.

_____ I learn new dance steps or routines easily.

_____ **Total for Artistic Skills**

A note for those determined to work in the arts: Before you move on to the next skill, take a moment to decide whether working in some form of art is essential to you. Some people have exceptional talent and interest in a certain art form and are unhappy unless they are working in that art form—or until they have given their best shot at trying to break into it. If you are that kind of person, the total score shown above doesn't really matter. In fact, you may have given a 3 to just *one* of the statements above, but if you care passionately about your art form, you should toss out ordinary arithmetic and change the total to 100.

Communication Skills

_____ I am good at explaining complicated things to people.

_____ I like to take notes and write up minutes for meetings.

_____ I have a flair for public speaking.

_____ I am good at writing directions for using a computer or machine.

_____ I enjoy investigating facts and showing other people what they indicate.

_____ People consider me a good listener.

_____ I like to write letters to newspaper editors or political representatives.

_____ I have been an effective debater.

_____ I like developing publicity fliers for a school or community event.

_____ I am good at making diagrams that break down complex processes.

_____ I like teaching people how to drive a car or play a sport.

_____ I have been successful as the secretary of a club.

_____ I enjoy speaking at group meetings or worship services.

_____ I have a knack for choosing the most effective word.

_____ I enjoy tutoring young people.

_____ Technical manuals are not hard for me to understand.

_____ **Total for Communication Skills**

Interpersonal Skills

_____ I am able to make people feel that I understand their point of view.

_____ I enjoy working collaboratively.

_____ I often can make suggestions to people without sounding critical of them.

_____ I enjoy soliciting clothes, food, and other supplies for needy people.

_____ I am good at "reading" people to tell what's on their minds.

_____ I have a lot of patience with people who are doing something for the first time.

_____ People consider me outgoing.

_____ I enjoy taking care of sick relatives, friends, or neighbors.

_____ I am good at working out conflicts between friends or family members.

_____ I enjoy serving as a host or hostess for houseguests.

_____ People consider me a team player.

_____ I enjoy meeting new people and finding common interests.

_____ I am good at fundraising for school groups, teams, or community organizations.

_____ I like to train or care for animals.

_____ I often know what to say to defuse a tense situation.

_____ I have enjoyed being an officer or advisor for a youth group.

_____ **Total for Interpersonal Skills**

Managerial Skills

_____ I am good at inspiring people to work together toward a goal.

_____ I tend to use time wisely and not procrastinate.

_____ I usually know when I have enough information to make a decision.

_____ I enjoy planning and arranging programs for school or a community organization.

_____ I am not reluctant to take responsibility when things turn out wrong.

_____ I have enjoyed being a leader of a scout troop or other such group.

_____ I often can figure out what motivates somebody.

_____ People trust me to speak on their behalf and represent them fairly.

_____ I like to help organize things at home, such as shopping lists and budgets.

(continued)

(continued)

_____ I have been successful at recruiting members for a club or other organization.

_____ I have enjoyed helping run a school or community fair or carnival.

_____ People find me persuasive.

_____ I enjoy buying large quantities of food or other products for an organization.

_____ I have a knack for identifying abilities in other people.

_____ I am able to get past details and look at the big picture.

_____ I am good at delegating authority rather than trying to do everything myself.

_____ **Total for Managerial Skills**

Mathematics Skills

_____ I have always done well in math classes.

_____ I enjoy balancing checkbooks for family members.

_____ I can make mental calculations quickly.

_____ I enjoy calculating sports statistics or keeping score.

_____ Preparing family income tax returns is not hard for me.

_____ I like to tutor young people in math.

_____ I have taken or plan to take courses in statistics or calculus.

_____ I enjoy budgeting the family expenditures.

_____ **Subtotal for Mathematics Skills**

x 2   **Multiply by 2**

_____ **Total for Mathematics Skills**

Mechanical Skills

_____ I have a good sense of how mechanical devices work.

_____ I like to tinker with my car or motorcycle.

_____ I can understand diagrams of machinery or electrical wiring.

_____ I enjoy installing and repairing home stereo or computer equipment.

_____ I like looking at the merchandise in a building-supply warehouse store.

_____ I can sometimes fix household appliances when they break down.

_____ I have enjoyed building model airplanes, automobiles, or boats.

_____ I can do minor plumbing and electrical installations in the home.

_____ **Subtotal for Mechanical Skills**

x 2   **Multiply by 2**

_____ **Total for Mechanical Skills**

Science Skills

_____ Some of my best grades have been in science classes.

_____ I enjoy tweaking my computer's settings to make it run better.

_____ I have a good understanding of the systems and organs of the human body.

_____ I have enjoyed performing experiments for a science fair.

_____ I have taken or plan to take college-level courses in science.

_____ I like to read about new breakthroughs in science and technology.

_____ I know how to write programs in a computer language.

_____ I enjoy reading medical or scientific magazines.

_____ **Subtotal for Science Skills**

x 2   **Multiply by 2**

_____ **Total for Science Skills**

Finding Your Skills on the Job-Match Grid

Okay, you've made a lot of progress so far. Now it's time to review what you've said about skills so you can use these insights to sort through the jobs listed on the Job-Match Grid.

Look at your totals for the seven skills listed previously. Enter your totals in the left column on this scorecard:

Total	Skill	Rank
_____	Artistic	_____
_____	Communication	_____
_____	Interpersonal	_____
_____	Managerial	_____
_____	Mathematics	_____
_____	Mechanical	_____
_____	Science	_____

Next, enter the rank of each skill in the right column—that is, the highest-scored skill gets ranked #1, the next-highest #2, and so forth. **Important:** Keep in mind that *the numbers in the Total column are only a rough guideline. If you feel that a skill should be ranked higher or lower than its numerical total would suggest, go by your impressions rather than just by the numbers.*

Now turn to the Job-Match Grid and find the columns for your #1-ranked and #2-ranked skills. Move down through the grid, going from page to page, and notice what symbols appear in those columns. If a row of the grid has a black circle (●) in *both* columns, circle the occupation name—or, if someone else will be using this book, jot down the name on a piece of paper. These occupations use a high level of both skills, or the skills are essential to these jobs.

Go through the Job-Match Grid a second time, looking at the column for your #3-ranked skill. If a *job you have already circled* has a black circle (●) or a bull's-eye (◉) in the column for your #3-ranked skill, put a check mark next to the occupation name. If none of your selected jobs has a black circle or a bull's-eye in this column, look for a white circle (○) and mark these jobs with check marks.

A second note for those determined to work in the arts: If a *particular* art form is essential for you to work in, you almost certainly know which occupations involve that art form and which don't. So not every job that has a black circle (●) in the "Artistic" column is going to interest you. Circle only the jobs that have a black circle in this column that *are* related to your art form (if you're not sure, look at the description of the occupation in this book) and that also have a symbol of some kind (●, ◉, or ○) in the column for your #2-ranked skill. As you circle each job, also give it a check mark, because there will be so few of them that you won't need to go through the Job-Match Grid a second time. If you have a more general interest in the arts, follow the general instructions.

Your Hot List of Possible Career Matches

Now that you have made a first and second cut of the jobs on the Job-Match Grid, you can focus on the occupations that look most promising at this point. Write the names of the occupations that are both *circled* and *checked:*

_____   _____

_____   _____

_____   _____

_____   _____

_____   _____

_____   _____

This is your Hot List of occupations that you are going to explore in detail *if* they are not eliminated by certain important job-related factors that you'll consider next.

Thinking About Other Job-Related Factors

Next, you need to consider four other job-related factors:

- ★ Economic sensitivity
- ★ Outdoor work
- ★ Physically demanding work
- ★ Hazardous conditions

Economic Sensitivity

You've read about how our nation's economy has gone up and down over the years. When the economy is on an upswing, there are more job openings, but when it veers downward toward recession, jobs are harder to find.

Are you aware that these trends affect some occupations more than others? For example, during an economic upswing, people do more vacation traveling and businesses send more workers on business trips. This keeps travel agencies very busy, so they need to hire more travel agents. When the economy is going down, people cut back on their vacation travel, businesses tell their workers to use teleconferencing instead of business trips, and travel agents are not in demand. Some may be laid off, and people who want to enter this field may find very few openings. By contrast, most jobs in the health-care field are not sensitive to the economy, and automotive mechanics are just as busy as ever during economic slowdowns because people want to keep their old cars running.

So this issue of economic sensitivity (and its opposite, job security) is one that may affect which occupation you choose. Some people want to avoid economically sensitive occupations because they don't want to risk losing their job (or having difficulty finding a job) during times of recession. Other people are willing to risk being in an economically sensitive occupation because they want to profit from the periods when both the economy and the occupation are booming.

> How important is it to you to be in an occupation that *doesn't* go through periods of boom and bust along with the nation's economy? Check one:
>
> _____ It doesn't matter to me.
>
> _____ It's not important, but I'd consider it.
>
> _____ It's somewhat important to me.
>
> _____ It's very important to me.

If you answered "It doesn't matter to me," skip to the next section, "Outdoor Work." Otherwise, turn back to the Job-Match Grid and find the column for "Economically Sensitive."

If you answered "It's not important, but I'd consider it," see whether any of the jobs on your Hot List have a black circle (●) in this column. If so, cross them off and write an "E" next to them.

If you answered "It's somewhat important to me," see whether any of the jobs on your Hot List have a black circle (●) or a bull's-eye (◉) in this column. If so, cross them off and write an "E" next to them.

If you answered "It's very important to me," see whether any of the jobs on your Hot List have *any* symbol (●, ◉, or ○) in this column. If so, cross them off and write an "E" next to them.

Outdoor Work

Some people prefer to work indoors in a climate-controlled setting, such as an office, a classroom, a factory floor, a laboratory, or a hospital room. Other people would rather work primarily in an outdoor setting, such as a forest, an athletic field, or a city street. And some would enjoy a job that alternates between indoor and outdoor activities.

> What is *your* preference for working indoors or outdoors? Check one:
>
> _____ It's very important to me to work **indoors.**
>
> _____ I'd prefer to work mostly **indoors.**
>
> _____ Either indoors or outdoors is okay with me.
>
> _____ I'd prefer to work mostly **outdoors.**
>
> _____ It's very important to me to work **outdoors.**

If you answered "Either indoors or outdoors is okay with me," skip to the next section, "Physically Demanding Work." Otherwise, turn to the Job-Match Grid and find the column for "Outdoor Work."

If you answered "It's very important to me to work **indoors,**" see whether any of the jobs on your Hot List have *any* symbol (●, ◉, or ○) in this column. If so, cross them off and write an "O" next to them.

If you answered "I'd prefer to work mostly **indoors,**" see whether any of the jobs on your Hot List have a black circle (●) in this column. If so, cross them off and write an "O" next to them.

If you answered "I'd prefer to work mostly **outdoors,**" see whether any of the jobs on your Hot List have *no* symbol—just a blank—in this column. If so, cross them off and write an "O" next to them. All the jobs remaining on your Hot List should have some kind of symbol (●, ◉, or ○) in this column.

If you answered "It's very important to me to work **outdoors**," see whether any of the jobs on your Hot List have either *no* symbol or just a white circle (○) in this column. If so, cross them off and write an "O" next to them. All the jobs remaining on your Hot List should have either a black circle (●) or a bull's-eye (◉) in this column.

Physically Demanding Work

Jobs vary by how much muscle power they require you to use. Some jobs require a lot of lifting heavy loads, standing for long times, climbing, or stooping. On other jobs, the heaviest thing you lift is a notebook or telephone handset, and most of the time you are sitting. Still other jobs require only a moderate amount of physical exertion.

What is *your* preference for the physical demands of work? Check one:

_____ I don't care whether my work requires heavy or light physical exertion.

_____ I want my work to require only light physical exertion.

_____ I want my work to require no more than occasional moderate physical exertion.

_____ I want my work to require moderate physical exertion, with occasional heavy exertion.

_____ I want my work to require a lot of heavy physical exertion.

If you answered "I don't care whether my work requires heavy or light physical exertion," skip to the next section, "Hazardous Conditions." Otherwise, turn to the Job-Match Grid and find the column for "Physically Demanding Work."

If you answered "I want my work to require only light physical exertion," see whether any of the jobs on your Hot List have *any* symbol (●, ◉, or ○) in this column. If so, cross them off and write a "P" next to them.

If you answered "I want my work to require no more than occasional moderate physical exertion," see whether any of the jobs on your Hot List have either a black circle (●) or a bull's-eye (◉) in this column. If so, cross them off and write a "P" next to them.

If you answered "I want my work to require moderate physical exertion, with occasional heavy exertion," see whether any of the jobs on your Hot List have either a black circle (●), a white circle (○), or *no* symbol in this column. If so, cross them off and write a "P" next to them. All the jobs remaining on your Hot List should have a bull's-eye (◉) in this column.

If you answered "I want my work to require a lot of heavy physical exertion," see whether any of the jobs on your Hot List have either *no* symbol or just a white circle (○) or a bull's-eye (◉) in this column. If so, cross them off and write a "P" next to them. All the jobs remaining on your Hot List should have a black circle (●) in this column.

Hazardous Conditions

Every day about 9,000 Americans sustain a disabling injury on the job. Many workers have jobs that require them to deal with hazardous conditions, such as heat, noise, radiation, germs, toxins, or dangerous machinery. These workers need to wear protective clothing or follow safety procedures to avoid injury.

What is *your* preference regarding hazardous conditions on the job? Check one:

_____ I want hazardous workplace conditions to be very unlikely.

_____ I want hazardous conditions to be unlikely or minor.

_____ I am willing to accept some major workplace hazards.

If you answered "I am willing to accept some major workplace hazards," skip to the section "Geographically Concentrated Jobs." Otherwise, turn to the Job-Match Grid and find the column for "Hazardous Conditions."

If you answered "I want hazardous workplace conditions to be very unlikely," see whether any of the jobs on your Hot List have *any* symbol (●, ◉, or ○) in this column. If so, cross them off and write an "H" next to them.

If you answered "I want hazardous conditions to be unlikely or minor," see whether any of the jobs on your Hot List have a black circle (●) in this column. If so, cross them off and write an "H" next to them.

If Every Job on Your Hot List Is Now Crossed Off

It's possible that you have crossed off *all* the occupations on your Hot List. If so, consider these two options:

★ You may want to relax some of your requirements. Maybe you were too hasty in crossing off some of the jobs. Take another look at the four job-related factors and decide whether you could accept work that doesn't meet the requirements you set previously—for example, work that is not as much indoors or outdoors as you specified. If you change your mind now, you can tell by the letters in the margin which jobs you crossed off for which reasons.

★ You may want to add to your Hot List by considering additional skills. So far you have considered only occupations that involve your top three skills. You may want to add jobs that have a black circle (●) or a bull's-eye (◉) in the column for your #4-ranked skill and possibly for your #5-ranked skill. If you do add any jobs, be sure to repeat your review of the four job-related factors.

Evaluating Occupations Described in This Book

You are now ready to make the jump from the checklists to the detailed information about jobs in this book. The first detailed issue you need to consider is whether you will be able to find work in your area or have to relocate.

Geographically Concentrated Jobs

Turn to the Job-Match Grid one more time and find the column for "Geographically Concentrated." Look at all the occupations on your Hot List that haven't been crossed off. If there is a symbol in this column, especially a bull's-eye (◉) or a black circle (●), it means that employment for this occupation tends to be concentrated in certain geographic areas. For example, most acting jobs are found in big cities because that's where you'll find most theaters, TV studios, and movie studios. Most water transportation jobs are found on the coasts and beside major lakes and rivers.

If a symbol shows that a Hot List occupation *is* geographically concentrated, the location of the jobs may be obvious, as in the examples of acting and water transportation. If it's not clear to you where the jobs may be found, find the occupation in "The Job Descriptions" section and look for the facts under the heading "Employment" in the description. Once you understand where most of the jobs are, you have to make some decisions:

★ **Are most of the job openings in a geographic location where I am now or would enjoy living?** If you answered "yes" to this question, repeat this exercise for all the other occupations still on your Hot List. Then jump to the next heading, "Nature of the Work." If you answered "no," proceed to the next bulleted question.

★ **If most of the job openings are in a distant place where I don't want to relocate, am I willing to take a chance and hope to be one of the few workers who get hired in an *uncommon* location?** If you answered "yes," take a good look at the Job Outlook information in the job description. If the outlook for the occupation is very good and if you expect to have some of the advantages mentioned there (such as the right training, in some cases), taking a chance on being hired in an unusual location may be a reasonable decision. On the other hand, if the outlook is only so-so or not good and if you have no special qualifications, you probably are setting yourself up for disappointment. You should seriously consider changing your mind about this decision. At least speak to people in your area who are knowledgeable about the occupation to determine whether you have any chance of success. If you answered "no"—you are not willing to take a chance—cross off this occupation and write a "G" next to it. (If you now have no jobs left on your Hot List, see the previous section titled "If Every Job on Your Hot List Is Now Crossed Off.")

Nature of the Work

When you read the job description for an occupation on your Hot List, you will see that the "Nature of the Work" section discusses what workers do on the job, what tools and equipment they use, and how closely they are supervised. Keep in mind that this is an overview of a diverse collection of workers, and in fact few workers perform the full set of tasks itemized here. In fact, in many cases the work force covered by the job description is so diverse that it actually divides into several occupational specialties, which are italicized.

Here are some things to think about as you read this section:

★ Note the kinds of problems, materials, and tools you will encounter on the job. Are these a good match for your interests?

★ Also note the work activities mentioned here. Do you think they will be rewarding? Are there many that stand out as unpleasant or boring?

Working Conditions

This section in each job description identifies the typical hours worked, the workplace environment (both physical and psychological), physical activities and susceptibility to injury, special equipment, and the extent of travel required. If conditions vary between the occupational specialties, that is mentioned here. Here are some things to look for in the Working Conditions section:

★ If you have a disability, note the physical requirements that are mentioned here and consider whether you can meet these requirements with or without suitable accommodations.

★ If you're bothered by conditions such as heights, stress, or a cramped workspace, see whether this section mentions any conditions that would discourage you.

★ Note what this section says about the work schedule and the need for travel, if any. This information may be good to know if you have pressing family responsibilities or, on the other hand, a desire for unusual hours or travel.

★ If you find a working condition that bothers you, be sure to check the wording to see whether it *always* applies to the occupation or whether it only *may* apply. Even if it seems to be a condition that you cannot avoid, find out for sure by talking to people in the occupation or educators who teach related courses. Maybe you can carve out a niche that avoids the unappealing working condition.

Training, Other Qualifications, and Advancement

In the "Training, Other Qualifications, and Advancement" section, you can see how to prepare for the occupation and how to advance in it. It identifies the significant entry routes—those that are most popular and that are preferred by employers. It mentions any licensure or certification that may be necessary for entry or advancement. It also identifies the particular skills, aptitudes, and work habits that employers value. Look for these topics in this section:

★ Compare the entry requirements to your background and to the educational and training opportunities that are available to you. Be sure to consider nontraditional and informal entry routes, if any are possible, as well as the formal routes. Ask yourself, Am I willing to get the additional education or training that will be necessary? Do I have the time, money, ability, interest, and commitment?

★ Maybe you're already partway down the road to job entry. In general, you should try to use your previous education, training, and work experience rather than abandon it. Look for specifics that are already on your resume—educational accomplishments, skills, work habits—that will meet employers' expectations. If you have some of these qualifications already, this occupation may be a better career choice than some others.

Employment

The "Employment" section in the job description reports how many jobs the occupation currently provides, the industries that provide the most jobs, and the number or proportion of self-employed or part-time workers in the occupation, if significant. In this section, you'll want to pay attention to these facts:

★ Note the industries that provide most of the employment for the occupation. This knowledge can help you identify contacts who can tell you more about the work, and later it can help in your job hunting.

★ If you're interested in self-employment or part-time work, see whether these work arrangements are mentioned here.

Job Outlook

The "Job Outlook" section describes the economic forces that will affect future employment in the occupation. Here are some things to look for in this section:

★ The information here can help you identify occupations with a good job outlook so that you will have a better-than-average chance of finding work. Be alert for any mention of an advantage that you may have over other job seekers (for example, a college degree) or any other factor that might make your chances better or worse.

★ If you are highly motivated and highly qualified for a particular occupation, don't be discouraged by a bad employment outlook. Job openings occur even in shrinking or overcrowded occupations, and with exceptional talent or good personal connections, you may go on to great success.

★ These projections are the most definitive ones available, but they are not foolproof and apply only to a 10-year time span. No matter what occupation you choose, you will need to adapt to changes.

Earnings

The "Earnings" section discusses the wages for the occupation. Here are some things to keep in mind:

★ The wage figures are national averages. Actual wages in your geographic region may be considerably higher or lower. Also, an average figure means that half of the workers earn more and half earn less, and the actual salary any one worker earns can vary greatly from that average.

★ Remember to consider *all* the pluses and minuses of the job. Not every day of the work week is payday, so make your choice based on the whole occupation, not just the paycheck.

Related Occupations

The "Related Occupations" section identifies occupations that are similar to the one featured in the job description in terms of tasks, interests, skills, education, or training. You may find this section interesting for these reasons:

★ If you're interested in an occupation but not strongly committed to pursuing it, this section may suggest another occupation with similar rewards that may turn out to be a better fit. Try to research these related occupations, but keep in mind that they may not all be included in this book.

★ You may want to choose one of these occupations as your Plan B goal if your original goal should not work out. In that case, it helps to identify an occupation that involves similar kinds of problems and work settings but requires *less* education or training.

Sources of Additional Information

This section in each job description lists several sources and resources you can turn to for more information about the occupation. Try to consult at least some of these sources. This book should be only the beginning of your career decision-making process. You need more detailed information from several viewpoints to make an informed decision.

Don't rely entirely on the Web sites listed here. You especially need to talk to and observe individual workers to learn what their workdays are like, what the workers enjoy and dislike about the job, how they got hired, and what effects the job has had on other aspects of their lives. Maybe you can make contact with local workers through the local chapter of an organization listed here.

Narrowing Down Your Choices

The information in the job descriptions should help you cross more jobs off your Hot List. And what you learn by turning to other resources should help you narrow down your Hot List jobs to a few promising choices and maybe one best bet. Here are some final considerations: Have I talked to people who are actually doing this work? Am I fully aware of the pluses and minuses of this job? If there are aspects of the job that I don't like, how do I expect to avoid them or overcome them? If the odds of finding a job opening are not good, why do I expect to beat the odds? What is my Plan B goal if I lose interest in my original goal or don't succeed at it?

The Job-Match Grid

The grid on the following pages provides information about the personal skills and job characteristics for occupations covered in this book. Use the directions and questions that start at the beginning of this section to help you get the most from this grid.

Below is what the symbols on the grid represent. If a job has no symbol in a column, it means that the skill or job characteristic is not important or relevant to the job.

Personal Skills

● Essential or high skill level

◉ Somewhat essential or moderate skill level

○ Basic skill level

Job Characteristics

● Highly likely

◉ Somewhat likely

○ A little likely

Job-Match Grid

	Personal Skills							Job Characteristics				
	Artistic	Communication	Interpersonal	Managerial	Mathematics	Mechanical	Science	Economically Sensitive	Outdoor Work	Physically Demanding Work	Hazardous Conditions	Geographically Concentrated
Actors, producers, and directors	●	●	●	◉		◉	○	○	○	●		●
Agricultural workers		○	○	○	○	●	○		●	●	◉	●
Aircraft and avionics equipment mechanics and service technicians		○	○		◉	●	◉	◉	●	◉	○	◉
Armed forces		◉	◉	◉	○	○	○		◉	●	◉	◉
Artists and related workers	●	○	○	○	○	◉	○	◉	○	○		
Assemblers and fabricators	○	○			○	●	○	○		◉		
Automotive body and related repairers	○	○	○		○	●	○		○	◉	○	
Automotive service technicians and mechanics		○	○		○	●	◉		○	◉	○	
Barbers, cosmetologists, and other personal appearance workers	●	◉	○		○	◉	○	◉			○	○
Bill and account collectors		○	●		●			◉				
Billing and posting clerks and machine operators		○	○		○	○		○				
Bookkeeping, accounting, and auditing clerks		○	○		●			○				
Building cleaning workers	○	○			○	●		○		●	○	
Bus drivers		○	○		○				○	◉	●	
Carpenters	◉	○	○		◉	●	○	●	◉	●	●	
Cashiers		○	◉		◉			◉		●		
Chefs, cooks, and food preparation workers	●	◉	◉	●	○	◉	○	●		◉	○	
Child care workers	○	◉	●	○	○	○			○	◉		
Claims adjusters, appraisers, examiners, and investigators		◉	○	◉	◉	◉	○		◉			
Clinical laboratory technologists and technicians		◉	○	○	●	●	●				○	○
Communications equipment operators		◉	◉		◉	◉	○	◉				
Computer scientists and database administrators		◉	○	○	●		●	○				
Computer support specialists and systems administrators		◉	◉	○	◉	●	◉	○				
Computer, automated teller, and office machine repairers		○	○		○	●	○		○	○		
Construction equipment operators		○	○		○	●	○	●	●	●	●	
Construction laborers	○	○	○		○	●	○	●	◉	●	●	
Correctional officers		◉	○	○	○	○				◉	●	
Counter and rental clerks		○	◉		◉			◉		◉		
Customer service representatives		●	●		◉		○	○				

(continued)

Personal Skills: ●—Essential or high skill level; ◉—Somewhat essential or moderate skill level; ○—Basic skill level
Job Characteristics: ●—Highly likely; ◉—Somewhat likely; ○—A little likely

(continued)

	Personal Skills							Job Characteristics				
	Artistic	Communication	Interpersonal	Managerial	Mathematics	Mechanical	Science	Economically Sensitive	Outdoor Work	Physically Demanding Work	Hazardous Conditions	Geographically Concentrated
Data entry and information processing workers		○	○		○	◉		●				
Dental assistants		◉	◉	○	○	●	◉			◉	◉	
Diesel service technicians and mechanics		○	○		○	●	◉	◉	○	◉	○	
Dispatchers		◉	○	◉	○							
Drafters	●	◉	○		◉	●	○	◉				
Drywall installers, ceiling tile installers, and tapers	○	○	○		○	●	○	●	○	●	○	
Electrical and electronics installers and repairers		○	○		◉	●	○				○	◉
Electricians		○	○		◉	●	◉	●	○	◉	●	
Engineering technicians	○	◉	○		●	●	●	○	○	○		
Farmers, ranchers, and agricultural managers		●	●	●	◉	●	◉	○	●	◉	◉	●
File clerks		○	○		○							
Fire fighting occupations		●	○	○	○	●	○			●	●	●
Food and beverage serving and related workers	○	◉	●		○			●	○	●		
Food processing occupations		○			○	●				●	●	
Food service managers	◉	●	●	●	◉	◉	○	◉		○		
Gaming services occupations	○	◉	●	●	○	○		◉		●		●
Grounds maintenance workers	◉	○			○	●	○	○	●	●	◉	
Heating, air conditioning, and refrigeration mechanics and installers		○	○		○	●	○	◉	○	◉	○	
Industrial mechanics and maintenance workers		○			○	●	○	○		◉	◉	○
Inspectors, testers, sorters, samplers, and weighers	○	◉	○		◉	●	◉			○		
Interviewers		●	◉	◉	○		○	○				
Jewelers and precious stone and metal workers	●	○	○		○	●	◉	●		○		
Licensed practical and licensed vocational nurses		◉	●	○	○	●	●			◉	◉	
Line installers and repairers		○			◉	●	○	○	●	◉	◉	
Machine setters, operators, and tenders—metal and plastic		○			●	●	◉	○		◉	◉	
Machinists	◉	○			●	●	◉	○		◉	◉	
Maintenance and repair workers, general		○	○		○	●	○		◉	◉	◉	
Material moving occupations		○				●		●	●	●	●	
Medical assistants		◉	◉	○	◉	●	●			◉	◉	
Musicians, singers, and related workers	●	◉	◉	○		○	○			○		○
Nursing, psychiatric, and home health aides		◉	◉	○	○	◉	○			●	●	
Office and administrative support worker supervisors and managers		●	●	●	◉	○		○				

Personal Skills: ●—Essential or high skill level; ◉—Somewhat essential or moderate skill level; ○—Basic skill level
Job Characteristics: ●—Highly likely; ◉—Somewhat likely; ○—A little likely

	Personal Skills							Job Characteristics				
	Artistic	Communication	Interpersonal	Managerial	Mathematics	Mechanical	Science	Economically Sensitive	Outdoor Work	Physically Demanding Work	Hazardous Conditions	Geographically Concentrated
Office clerks, general		○	◉		○			◉				
Order clerks		○	○		◉			◉				
Painters and paperhangers	◉	○	○			●	○	●	●	●	○	
Painting and coating workers, except construction and maintenance	○	○			○	●		○		◉	◉	
Paralegals and legal assistants		●	●	○	○		○	◉				
Payroll and timekeeping clerks		○	○		◉			○				
Personal and home care aides		◉	●	○	○		○			●	◉	
Pharmacy technicians		◉	◉	○	◉	◉	◉			○		
Photographers	●	○	○	○	○	●	○	◉	◉	◉		
Pipelayers, plumbers, pipefitters, and steamfitters		○	○		○	●	◉	●	○	●	○	
Police and detectives		●	○	◉	○	●	○		●	●	●	
Postal Service workers		○	○	○	○	○			●	●		
Prepress technicians and workers	◉	◉	○		◉	◉	○	○		○		
Printing machine operators		○			○	●	○	○		●	◉	
Production, planning, and expediting clerks		◉	○	○	◉		○	○				
Purchasing managers, buyers, and purchasing agents		●	●	●	◉		○	○				
Radio and telecommunications equipment installers and repairers		○	○		◉	●	◉	○	●	◉		◉
Radiologic technologists and technicians		◉	◉	○	●	●	◉			◉	◉	
Real estate brokers and sales agents	○	●	●	◉	◉			◉	○			
Receptionists and information clerks		●	●		◉	◉		○				
Registered nurses		●	●	◉	●	●	●			◉	◉	
Reservation and transportation ticket agents and travel clerks		○	●		◉			●				
Retail salespersons	○	◉	●		○			◉				
Sales representatives, wholesale and manufacturing	○	●	●		◉		○	●				
Sales worker supervisors	○	●	●	●	◉	○	○	◉				
Science technicians	○	◉	○		●	●	●	◉	○	○	○	
Secretaries and administrative assistants	○	●	●	○	○			○				
Security guards and gaming surveillance officers		○	○	○		○		○	◉	○	●	
Shipping, receiving, and traffic clerks		○	○		○	◉		○				
Social and human service assistants		◉	●				○					
Stock clerks and order fillers		○	○		○	○		○		◉		
Teacher assistants	◉	●	●	◉	○		◉					
Teachers—self-enrichment education	◉	●	●	●	◉		◉					

(continued)

Personal Skills: ●—Essential or high skill level; ◉—Somewhat essential or moderate skill level; ○—Basic skill level
Job Characteristics: ●—Highly likely; ◉—Somewhat likely; ○—A little likely

(continued)

	Personal Skills							Job Characteristics				
	Artistic	Communication	Interpersonal	Managerial	Mathematics	Mechanical	Science	Economically Sensitive	Outdoor Work	Physically Demanding Work	Hazardous Conditions	Geographically Concentrated
Tellers		◉	●		●			○				
Textile, apparel, and furnishings occupations	◉	○			○	●		◉		●	○	◉
Truck drivers and driver/sales workers		○				○		●	○	●	●	
Welding, soldering, and brazing workers	○	○			○	●	○	○	◉	●	●	
Woodworkers	◉	○			◉	●	○	◉		○	◉	
Writers and editors	●	●	●	○	○		○					

Personal Skills: ●—Essential or high skill level; ◉—Somewhat essential or moderate skill level; ○—Basic skill level
Job Characteristics: ●—Highly likely; ◉—Somewhat likely; ○—A little likely

Descriptions of the Top 100 Careers Without a Four-Year Degree

This is the book's main section. It contains helpful descriptions of the 100 major occupations that don't require a four-year college degree. To learn a job's ranking, see the introduction.

The jobs are arranged in alphabetical order. Refer to the table of contents for a list of the jobs and the page numbers where their descriptions begin. Review the table of contents to discover occupations that interest you and then find out more about them in this section. If you are interested in medical careers, for example, you can go through the list and quickly pinpoint those you want to learn more about. Or use the assessment in Part I to identify several possible career matches.

While the job descriptions in this part are easy to understand, the introduction provides additional information for interpreting them. Keep in mind that the descriptions present information that is average for the country. Conditions in your area and with specific employers may be quite different.

Also, you may come across jobs that sound interesting but require more education and training than you have or are considering. Don't eliminate them too soon. There are many ways to obtain education and training, and most people change careers many times. You probably have more skills than you realize that can transfer to new jobs. People often have more opportunities than barriers. Use the descriptions to learn more about possible jobs and look into the suggested resources to help you take the next step.

Actors, Producers, and Directors

(O*NET 27-2011.00, 27-2012.01, 27-2012.02, 27-2012.03, 27-2012.04, and 27-2012.05)

Significant Points

■ Actors endure long periods of unemployment, intense competition for roles, and frequent rejections in auditions.

■ Formal training through a university or acting conservatory is typical; however, many actors, producers, and directors find work on the basis of their experience and talent alone.

■ Because earnings for actors are erratic, many supplement their incomes by holding jobs in other fields.

Nature of the Work

Actors, producers, and directors express ideas and create images in theater, film, radio, television, and other performing arts media. They interpret a writer's script to entertain, inform, or instruct an audience. Although the most famous actors, producers, and directors work in film, network television, or theater in New York or Los Angeles, far more work in local or regional television studios, theaters, or film production companies preparing advertising, public-relations, or independent small-scale movie productions.

Actors perform in stage, radio, television, video, or motion picture productions. They also work in cabarets, nightclubs, theme parks, commercials, and "industrial" films produced for training and educational purposes. Most actors struggle to find steady work; only a few ever achieve recognition as stars. Some well-known, experienced performers may be cast in supporting roles. Others work as "extras," with no lines to deliver, or make brief cameo appearances, speaking only one or two lines. Some actors do voiceover and narration work for advertisements, animated features, books on tape, and other electronic media, including computer games. They also teach in high school or university drama departments, acting conservatories, or public programs.

Producers are entrepreneurs, overseeing the business and financial decisions of a motion picture, made-for-television feature, or stage production. They select scripts, approve the development of ideas for the production, arrange financing, and determine the size and cost of the endeavor. Producers hire or approve the selection of directors, principal cast members, and key production staff members. They also negotiate contracts with artistic and design personnel in accordance with collective bargaining agreements and guarantee payment of salaries, rent, and other expenses. Television and radio producers determine which programs, episodes, or news segments get aired. They may research material, write scripts, and oversee the production of individual pieces. Producers in any medium coordinate the activities of writers, directors, managers, and agents to ensure that each project stays on schedule and within budget.

Directors are responsible for the creative decisions of a production. They interpret scripts, express concepts to set and costume designers, audition and select cast members, conduct rehearsals, and direct the work of cast and crew. They approve the design elements of a production, including the sets, costumes, choreography, and music. Assistant directors cue the performers and technicians to make entrances or to make light, sound, or set changes.

Working Conditions

Actors, producers, and directors work under constant pressure. Many face stress from the continual need to find their next job. To succeed, actors, producers, and directors need patience and commitment to their craft. Actors strive to deliver flawless performances, often while working under undesirable and unpleasant conditions. Producers and directors organize rehearsals and meet with writers, designers, financial backers, and production technicians. They experience stress not only from these activities, but also from the need to adhere to budgets, union work rules, and production schedules.

Acting assignments typically are short term—ranging from 1 day to a few months—which means that actors frequently experience long periods of unemployment between jobs. The uncertain nature of the work results in unpredictable earnings and intense competition for even the lowest-paid jobs. Often, actors, producers, and directors must hold other jobs in order to sustain a living.

When performing, actors typically work long, irregular hours. For example, stage actors may perform one show at night while rehearsing another during the day. They also might travel with a show when it tours the country. Movie actors may work on location, sometimes under adverse weather conditions, and may spend considerable time in their trailers or dressing rooms waiting to perform their scenes. Actors who perform in a television series often appear on camera with little preparation time because scripts tend to be revised frequently or even written moments before taping. Those who appear live or before a studio audience must be able to handle impromptu situations and calmly ad lib, or substitute, lines when necessary.

Evening and weekend work is a regular part of a stage actor's life. On weekends, more than one performance may be held per day. Actors and directors working on movies or television programs—especially those who shoot on location—may work in the early morning or late evening hours to film night scenes or tape scenes inside public facilities outside of normal business hours.

Actors should be in good physical condition and have the necessary stamina and coordination to move about theater stages and large movie and television studio lots. They also need to maneuver about complex technical sets while staying in character and projecting their voices audibly. Actors must be fit to endure heat from stage or studio lights and the weight of heavy costumes. Producers and directors ensure the safety of actors by conducting extra rehearsals on the set so that the actors can learn the layout of set pieces and props, by allowing time for warmups and stretching exercises to guard against physical and vocal injuries, and by providing an adequate number of breaks to prevent heat exhaustion and dehydration.

Training, Other Qualifications, and Advancement

Persons who become actors, producers, and directors follow many paths. Employers generally look for people with the creative instincts, innate talent, and intellectual capacity to perform. Actors should possess a passion for performing and enjoy entertaining others. Most aspiring actors participate in high school and college plays, work in college radio stations, or perform with local community theater groups. Local and regional theater experience and work in summer stock, on cruise lines, or in theme parks helps many young actors hone their skills and earn qualifying credits toward membership in one of the actors' unions. Union membership and work experience in smaller communities may lead to work in larger cities, notably New York or Los Angeles. In television and film, actors and directors typically start in smaller television markets or with independent movie production companies and then work their way up to larger media markets and major studio productions. Intense competition, however, can be expected at each level, because ever more applicants will be vying for increasingly fewer numbers of available positions.

Formal dramatic training, either through an acting conservatory or a university program, generally is necessary, but some people successfully enter the field without it. Most people studying for a bachelor's degree take courses in radio and television broadcasting, communications, film, theater, drama, or dramatic literature. Many continue their academic training and receive a Master of Fine Arts (MFA) degree. Advanced curricula may include courses in stage speech and movement, directing, playwriting, and design, as well as intensive acting workshops. The National Association of Schools of Theatre accredits 135 programs in theater arts. A few people go into acting following successful careers in other fields, such as broadcasting or announcing.

Actors, regardless of experience level, may pursue workshop training through acting conservatories or mentoring by a drama coach. Actors also research roles so that they can grasp concepts quickly during rehearsals and understand the story's setting and background. Sometimes actors learn a foreign language or train with a dialect coach to develop an accent to make their characters more realistic.

Actors need talent, creativity, and training that will enable them to portray different characters. Because competition for parts is fierce, versatility and a wide range of related performance skills, such as singing, dancing, skating, juggling, or miming, are especially useful. Experience in horseback riding, fencing, or stage combat also can lift some actors above the average and get them noticed by producers and directors. Actors must have poise, stage presence, the capability to affect an audience, and the ability to follow direction. Modeling experience also may be helpful. Physical appearance, such as possessing the right size, weight, or features, often is a deciding factor in being selected for particular roles.

Many professional actors rely on agents or managers to find work, negotiate contracts, and plan their careers. Agents generally earn a percentage of the pay specified in an actor's contract. Other actors rely solely on attending open auditions for parts. Trade publications list the times, dates, and locations of these auditions.

To become a movie extra, one usually must be listed by a casting agency, such as Central Casting, a no-fee agency that supplies extras to the major movie studios in Hollywood. Applicants are accepted only when the numbers of persons of a particular type on the list—for example, athletic young women, old men, or small children—falls below the foreseeable need. In recent years, only a very small proportion of applicants have succeeded in being listed.

There are no specific training requirements for producers. They come from many different backgrounds. Talent, experience, and business acumen are important determinants of success for producers. Actors, writers, film editors, and business managers commonly enter the field. Also, many people who start out as actors move into directing, while some directors might try their hand at acting. Producers often start in a theatrical management office, working for a press agent, managing director, or business manager. Some start in a performing arts union or service organization. Others work behind the scenes with successful directors, serve on boards of directors, or promote their own projects. No formal training exists for producers; however, a growing number of colleges and universities now offer degree programs in arts management and in managing nonprofits.

As the reputations and box-office draw of actors, producers, and directors grow, they might work on bigger-budget productions, on network or syndicated broadcasts, or in more prestigious theaters. Actors may advance to lead roles and receive star billing. A few actors move into acting-related jobs, such as drama coaches or directors of stage, television, radio, or motion picture productions. Some teach drama privately or in colleges and universities.

Employment

In 2004, actors, producers, and directors held about 157,000 jobs, primarily in motion picture and video, performing arts, and broadcast industries. Because many others were between jobs, the total number of actors, producers, and directors available for work was higher. Employment in the theater, and other performing arts companies, is cyclical—higher in the fall and spring seasons—and concentrated in New York and other major cities with large commercial houses for musicals and touring productions. Also, many cities support established professional regional theaters that operate on a seasonal or year-round basis. About one-fourth of actors, producers, and directors were self-employed.

Actors, producers, and directors may find work in summer festivals, on cruise lines, and in theme parks. Many smaller, nonprofit professional companies, such as repertory companies; dinner theaters; and theaters affiliated with drama schools, acting conservatories, and universities, provide employment opportunities for local amateur talent and professional entertainers. Auditions typically are held in New York for many productions across the country and for shows that go on the road.

Employment in motion pictures and in films for television is centered in New York and Hollywood. However, small studios are located throughout the country. Many films are shot on location and may employ local professional and nonprofessional actors. In television, opportunities are concentrated in the network centers of New York and Los Angeles, but cable television services and local television stations around the country also employ many actors, producers, and directors.

A growing number of actors and other entertainers appear on the payrolls of firms who do accounting and payroll work. Frequently, film production companies will hire actors through casting agencies or contract out their payroll services to accounting firms. Similarly, many actors arrange with a company in this industry to collect their pay from producers or entrepreneurs; make the appropriate deductions for taxes, union dues, and benefits payments; and pay them their net earnings for each job. The result of these increasingly more common payroll arrangements is that many actors appear to be working for accounting offices rather than for the theatrical production companies or studios where they actually perform.

Job Outlook

Employment of actors, producers, and directors is expected to grow about as fast as the average for all occupations through 2014. Although a growing number of people will aspire to enter these professions, many will leave the field early because the work—when it is available—is hard, the hours are long, and the pay is low. Competition for jobs will be stiff, in part because the large number of highly trained and talented actors auditioning for roles generally exceeds the number of parts that become available. Only performers with the most stamina and talent will find regular employment.

Expanding cable and satellite television operations; increasing production and distribution of major studio and independent films; and continued growth and development of interactive media, such as direct-for-Web movies and videos, should increase demand for actors, producers, and directors. However, greater emphasis on national, rather than local, entertainment productions may restrict employment opportunities in the broadcasting industry.

Venues for live entertainment, such as Broadway and off-Broadway theaters, touring productions, and repertory theaters in many major metropolitan areas, as well as theme parks and resorts, are expected to offer many job opportunities. However, prospects in these venues are more variable because they fluctuate with economic conditions.

Earnings

Median hourly earnings of actors were $11.28 in May 2004. The middle 50 percent earned between $7.75 and $30.76. The lowest 10 percent earned less than $6.63, and the highest 10 percent earned more than $56.48. Median annual earnings were $15.20 in performing arts companies and $9.27 in motion picture and video industries. Annual earnings data for actors were not available because of the wide variation in the number of hours worked by actors and the short-term nature of many jobs, which may last for 1 day or 1 week; it is extremely rare for actors to have guaranteed employment that exceeded 3 to 6 months.

Minimum salaries, hours of work, and other conditions of employment are covered in collective bargaining agreements between the producers and the unions representing workers. The Actors' Equity Association (Equity) represents stage actors; the Screen Actors Guild (SAG) covers actors in motion pictures, including television, commercials, and films; and the American Federation of Television and Radio Artists (AFTRA) represents television and radio studio performers. Some actors who regularly work in several media find it advantageous to join multiple unions, while SAG and AFTRA may share jurisdiction for work in additional areas, such as the production of training or educational films not slated for broadcast, tel-

evision commercial work, and interactive media. While these unions generally determine minimum salaries, any actor or director may negotiate for a salary higher than the minimum.

Under terms of a joint SAG and AFTRA contract covering all unionized workers, motion picture and television actors with speaking parts earned a minimum daily rate of $716, or $2,483 for a 5-day week, as of October 1, 2005. Actors also receive contributions to their health and pension plans and additional compensation for reruns and foreign telecasts of the productions in which they appear.

According to Equity, the minimum weekly salary for actors in Broadway productions as of June 30, 2005, was $1,422. Actors in Off-Broadway theaters received minimums ranging from $493 to $857 a week as of October 23, 2005, depending on the seating capacity of the theater. Regional theaters that operate under an Equity agreement pay actors $531 to $800 per week. For touring productions, actors receive an additional $777 per week for living expenses ($819 per week in higher-cost cities). New terms were negotiated under an "experimental touring program" provision for lower-budget musicals that tour to smaller cities or that perform for fewer performances at each stop. In an effort to increase the number of paid workweeks while on tour, actors may be paid less than the full production rate for touring shows in exchange for higher per diems and profit participation.

Some well-known actors—stars—earn well above the minimum; their salaries are many times the figures cited, creating the false impression that all actors are highly paid. For example, of the nearly 100,000 SAG members, only about 50 might be considered stars. The average income that SAG members earn from acting—less than $5,000 a year—is low because employment is sporadic. Therefore, most actors must supplement their incomes by holding jobs in other occupations.

Many actors who work more than a qualifying number of days or weeks per year or earn over a set minimum pay are covered by a union health, welfare, and pension fund, which includes hospitalization insurance to which employers contribute. Under some employment conditions, Equity and AFTRA members receive paid vacations and sick leave.

Median annual earnings of salaried producers and directors were $52,840 in May 2004. The middle 50 percent earned between $35,550 and $87,980. Median annual earnings were $75,200 in motion picture and video industries and $43,890 in radio and television broadcasting.

Many stage directors belong to the Society of Stage Directors and Choreographers (SSDC), and film and television directors belong to the Directors Guild of America. Earnings of stage directors vary greatly. According to the SSDC, summer theaters offer compensation, including "royalties" (based on the number of performances), usually ranging from $2,500 to $8,000 for a 3- to 4-week run. Directing a production at a dinner theater generally will pay less than directing one at a summer theater, but has more potential for generating income from royalties. Regional theaters may hire directors for longer periods, increasing compensation accordingly. The highest-paid directors work on Broadway and commonly earn $50,000 per show. However, they also receive payment in the form of royalties—a negotiated percentage of gross box office receipts—that can exceed their contract fee for long-running box office successes.

Stage producers seldom get a set fee; instead, they get a percentage of a show's earnings or ticket sales.

Related Occupations

People who work in performing arts occupations that may require acting skills include announcers; dancers and choreographers; and musicians, singers, and related workers. Others working in film- and theater-related occupations are makeup artists, theatrical and performance; fashion designers; set and exhibit designers; and writers and authors. Producers share many responsibilities with those who work as top executives.

Sources of Additional Information

For general information about theater arts and a list of accredited college-level programs, contact

▸ National Association of Schools of Theater, 11250 Roger Bacon Dr., Suite 21, Reston, VA 20190. Internet: http://nast.arts-accredit.org

For general information on actors, producers, and directors, contact any of the following organizations:

▸ Actors Equity Association, 165 West 46th St., New York, NY 10036. Internet: http://www.actorsequity.org

▸ Screen Actors Guild, 5757 Wilshire Blvd., Los Angeles, CA 90036-3600. Internet: http://www.sag.org

▸ American Federation of Television and Radio Artists—Screen Actors Guild, 4340 East-West Hwy., Suite 204, Bethesda, MD 20814-4411. Internet: http://www.aftra.org or http://www.sag.org

Agricultural Workers

(O*NET 45-2011.00, 45-2021.00, 45-2041.00, 45-2091.00, 45-2092.01, 45-2092.02, 45-2093.00, and 45-2099.99)

Significant Points

■ Duties and working conditions vary widely, from raising plants in greenhouses to harvesting crops and tending to livestock outdoors to inspecting agricultural products at border crossings.

■ Farmworkers learn through short-term on-the-job training; agricultural inspectors and animal breeders require work experience or a college degree.

■ Most farmworkers receive low pay and perform strenuous work outdoors in all kinds of weather, but many enjoy the rural lifestyle.

■ Employment is projected to decline slightly.

Nature of the Work

Agricultural workers play a large role in getting food, plants, and other agricultural products to market. Working mostly on farms or ranches or in nurseries, slaughterhouses, or ports of entry, these workers have numerous and diverse duties. Among their activities are planting and harvesting crops, installing irrigation, delivering animals, and making sure that our food is safe.

More than 8 out of 10 agricultural workers are farmworkers and laborers. *Farmworkers and laborers, crop, nursery, and greenhouse* perform numerous activities related to growing and harvesting grains, fruits, vegetables, nuts, fiber, trees, shrubs, and other crops. Among their activities are planting and seeding, pruning, irrigating, harvesting, and packing and loading crops for shipment. Farmworkers also apply pesticides, herbicides, and fertilizers to crops; repair fences; and help with irrigation. Nursery and greenhouse workers prepare land or greenhouse beds for growing horticultural products, such as trees, plants, flowers, and sod. Their duties include planting, watering, pruning, weeding, and spraying the plants. They may cut, roll, and stack sod; stake trees; tie, wrap, and pack plants to fill orders; and dig up or move field-grown and containerized shrubs and trees.

Farmworkers, farm and ranch animals care for live farm, ranch, or aquacultural animals that may include cattle, sheep, swine, goats, horses, poultry, finfish, shellfish, and bees. The animals are usually raised to supply such products as meat, fur, skins, feathers, eggs, milk, and honey. The farmworkers' duties may include feeding, watering, herding, grazing, castrating, branding, debeaking, weighing, catching, and loading animals. On dairy farms, farmworkers operate milking machines. They also may maintain records on animals; examine animals to detect diseases and injuries; assist in delivering animals at their birth; and administer medications, vaccinations, or insecticides as appropriate. Daily duties of such farmworkers include cleaning and maintaining animal housing areas.

Other farmworkers known as *agricultural equipment operators* operate a variety of farm equipment used in plowing, sowing, maintaining, and harvesting agricultural products. The equipment may include tractors, fertilizer spreaders, haybines, raking equipment, balers, combines, and threshers, as well as trucks. These farmworkers also operate machines used in moving and treating crops after their harvest, such as conveyor belts, loading machines, separators, cleaners, and dryers. In addition, they may make adjustments and minor repairs to equipment. When not operating machines, agricultural equipment operators may perform other farm duties that are not typical of other farmworkers.

Agricultural inspectors, another type of agricultural worker, are employed by federal and state governments to ensure compliance with laws and regulations governing the health, quality, and safety of agricultural commodities. Inspectors also make sure that the facilities and equipment used in processing the commodities meet quality standards. Meat safety is one of their prime responsibilities, and they try to ensure that the meat we eat is free of harmful ingredients or bacteria. In meat-processing facilities, inspectors may collect samples of suspected diseased animals or materials and send the samples to a laboratory for identification and analysis. They also may inspect livestock to help determine the effectiveness of medication and feeding programs. Some inspectors are stationed at export and import sites to weigh and inspect agricultural shipments leaving and entering the country to ensure the quality and quantity of the shipments. A few work at logging sites, making sure that safety regulations are enforced.

Graders and sorters of agricultural products examine agricultural commodities being prepared to be packed for market and classify them according to quality or size guidelines. They grade, sort, or classify unprocessed food and other agricultural products by size, weight, color, or condition and discard inferior or defective products. For example, graders sort eggs by color and size and also examine the fat content, or marbling, of beef, assigning a grade of "Prime," "Choice," or something else as appropriate. The grade that is assigned determines the price at which the commodity may be sold.

Animal breeders select and breed animals, using their knowledge of genetics and animal science to produce offspring with desired traits and characteristics, such as chickens that lay more eggs, pigs that produce leaner meat, and sheep with more desirable wool. Animal breeders also raise and breed animals simply to sell their offspring for money, including cats and dogs and other household pets. The larger and more expensive animals that are bred, such as horses and cattle, are usually bred through artificial insemination, which requires the taking of semen from the male and the insemination of the female with it. Using this process insures better results and also enables one prized male to sire many more offspring than through conventional mating. To know when and which animals to breed, breeders keep detailed records, including the health of the animal, its size and weight, and the amount and quality of the product produced by the animal. They also keep track of the traits of the offspring. Some breeders work as consultants for a number of farmers, while others breed and raise their own animals for eventual sale or breeding. Breeders that raise animals may also have to care and clean animal shelters, feed and water the animals, and oversee their day-to-day health or supervise others that perform these jobs. Additionally, animal breeders read journals and newsletters to remain current with the latest information on animal breeding and veterinary advice.

Working Conditions

Working conditions for agricultural workers vary widely. Much of the work of farmworkers and laborers on farms and ranches takes place outdoors in all kinds of weather and is physical in nature. Harvesting fruits and vegetables, for example, may require much bending, stooping, and lifting. Workers may lack adequate sanitation facilities while working in the field, and their drinking water may be limited. The year-round nature of much livestock production work means that ranch workers must be out in the heat of summer as well as the cold of winter. While some of these workers enjoy the day-to-day variability of the work, the rural setting, working on the land, and raising animals, the work hours are generally uneven and often long and work cannot be delayed when crops must be planted and harvested or when animals must be sheltered and fed. Weekend work is common, and farmworkers may work a 6- or 7-day week during planting and harvesting seasons. Because much of the work is seasonal in nature, many workers also obtain other jobs during slow seasons. Migrant farmworkers, who move from location to location as crops ripen, live an unsettled lifestyle, which can be stressful.

Work also is seasonal for farmworkers in nurseries; spring and summer are the busiest times of the year. Greenhouse workers enjoy relatively comfortable working conditions while tending to plants indoors. However, during the busy seasons when landscape contractors need plants, work schedules may be more demanding, requiring weekend work. Moreover, the transition from warm weather to cold weather means that nursery workers might have to work overtime with little notice given in order to move plants indoors to protect them from a frost.

Federal meat inspectors may work in highly mechanized plants or with poultry or livestock in confined areas with extremely cold temperatures and slippery floors. The duties often require working with sharp knives, moderate lifting, and walking or standing for long periods. Many inspectors work long and often irregular hours. Inspectors may find themselves in adversarial roles when the organization or individual being inspected objects to the inspection or its potential consequences. Some inspectors travel frequently to visit farms and processing facilities. Others work at ports, inspecting cargo on the docks or on boats.

Graders and sorters may work with similar products for an entire shift, or they may be assigned a variety of items. They may be on their feet all day and may have to lift heavy objects, whereas others may sit during most of their shift and do little strenuous work. Some graders work in clean, air-conditioned environments suitable for carrying out controlled tests. Some may work evenings or weekends because of the perishable nature of the products. Overtime may be required to meet production goals.

Animal breeders spend most of their time outdoors around animals, but can also work in offices or in laboratories. If consulting, breeders may have to travel from farm to farm. If they need to sell the offspring, breeders may have to travel to attend shows and to meet with potential buyers. While tending to the animals, breeders may be bitten or kicked.

Farmworkers in crop production risk exposure to pesticides and other hazardous chemicals sprayed on crops or plants. However, exposure is relatively minimal if safety procedures are followed. Those who work on mechanized farms must take precautions to avoid injury when working with tools and heavy equipment. Those who work directly with animals risk being bitten or kicked.

Training, Other Qualifications, and Advancement

Farmworkers learn through short-term on-the-job training. Most do not have a high school diploma. Workers without a high school diploma are particularly common in the crop production sector, where there are more labor-intensive establishments employing migrant farmworkers.

In nurseries, entry-level workers must be able to follow directions and learn proper planting procedures. If driving is an essential part of a job, employers look for applicants with a good driving record and some experience driving a truck. Workers who deal directly with customers must get along well with people. Employers also look for responsible, self-motivated individuals because nursery workers sometimes work with little supervision.

For graders and sorters, training requirements vary on the basis of their responsibilities. For those who perform tests on various agricultural products, a high school diploma is preferred and may be required. Simple jobs requiring mostly visual inspection may be filled by beginners provided with short-term on-the-job training.

Becoming an agricultural inspector requires relevant work experience or some college course work in a field such as biology or agricultural science. Inspectors are trained in the applicable laws or inspection procedures through some combination of classroom and on-the-job training. In general, people who want to enter this occupation should be responsible, like detailed work, and be able to communicate well. Federal government inspectors whose job performance is satisfactory advance through a career ladder to a specified full-performance level. For positions above this level—usually supervisory positions—advancement is competitive and based on agency needs and individual merit. Advancement opportunities in state and local governments and in the private sector often are similar to those in the federal government.

The education and training requirements for animal breeders vary with the type of breeding they do. For those whose primary activity is breeding—particularly livestock and other large or expensive animals—rather than raising animals, a bachelor's degree or higher in the animal sciences is recommended, with courses in genetics, animal breeding, and animal physiology. For those with experience raising animals or those who are breeding their own animals, an associate's degree or other postsecondary training in animal breeding is recommended. Experience working around animals, especially on a farm, is helpful, even for those getting a degree.

Advancement of agricultural workers depends on motivation and experience. Farmworkers who work hard and quickly, have good communication skills, and take an interest in the business may advance to crew leader or other supervisory positions. Some agricultural workers may aspire to become farm, ranch, and other agricultural managers or farmers or ranchers themselves. (Farmers, ranchers, and agricultural managers are discussed elsewhere in this book.) In addition, their knowledge of raising and harvesting produce may provide an excellent background for becoming purchasing agents and buyers of farm products. Knowledge of working a farm as a business can help agricultural workers become farm and home management advisors. Those who earn a college degree in agricultural science could become agricultural and food scientists.

Employment

Agricultural workers held about 834,000 jobs in 2004. Of these, farmworkers were the most numerous, holding about 690,000 jobs. Graders and sorters held about 45,000 jobs, agricultural inspectors 14,000 jobs, agricultural equipment operators 60,000 jobs, and animal breeders 12,000 jobs. More than 66 percent of all agricultural workers worked for crop and livestock producers, while more than 5 percent worked for agricultural service providers, mostly farm labor contractors.

Job Outlook

Overall employment of agricultural workers is projected to decline slightly over the 2004–2014 period, primarily reflecting the outlook for farmworkers in crops, nurseries, and greenhouses, who make up the large majority of all agricultural workers. Low wages, the physical demands of the work, and the large numbers of workers who leave these jobs for other occupations should result in abundant job opportunities, however.

Continued consolidation of farms and technological advancements in farm equipment that make farmworkers both more efficient and less needed will cause fewer of them to be hired. Farmworkers will increasingly work for farm labor contractors rather than being hired directly by the farm. The agriculture industry also is expected to undergo increased competition from foreign countries and rising imports, particularly from Central America, owing to the passing of a free trade agreement with that region. Nursery and greenhouse workers should experience some growth in this period, reflecting the increasing demand for landscaping services.

Slower-than-average employment growth is anticipated for agricultural inspectors. Governments at all levels are not expected to hire significant numbers of new inspectors, choosing to leave more of the routine inspection to businesses. Slower-than-average growth also is expected for graders and sorters, while employment of agricultural equipment operators is expected to decline slightly, reflecting the agriculture industry's continuing ability to produce more with fewer workers. Animal breeders also will grow more slowly than the average as large commercial farmers continue to attempt to breed the perfect animal. However, because the occupation is so small, there will be few job openings.

Earnings

Median hourly earnings in May 2004 for each of the occupations found in this statement are as follows:

Agricultural inspectors $14.92
Animal breeders 13.55
Agricultural workers, all other 10.15
Agricultural equipment operators 8.88
Farmworkers, farm and ranch animals.......................8.31
Graders and sorters, agricultural products 7.90
Farmworkers and laborers, crop, nursery,
and greenhouse 7.70

Few agricultural workers are members of unions.

Related Occupations

The duties of farmworkers who perform outdoor labor are related to the work of fishers and operators of fishing vessels; forest, conservation, and logging workers; and grounds maintenance workers. Farmworkers who work with farm and ranch animals perform work related to that of animal care and service workers. Animal breeders may perform some duties related to those of veterinary technologists or veterinarians.

Sources of Additional Information

Information on agricultural worker jobs is available from

▸ National FFA Organization, The National FFA Center, Attention: Career Information Requests, P.O. Box 68690, Indianapolis, IN, 46268-0960. Internet: http://www.ffa.org

Information on farmworker jobs is available from

▸ Growing New Farmers Consortium, c/o New England Small Farm Institute, P.O. Box 11, Belchertown, MA 01007.

Information on obtaining positions as an agricultural inspector with the federal government is available from the Office of Personnel Management through USAJOBS, the federal government's official employment information system. This resource for locating and applying for job opportunities can be accessed through the Internet at http://www.usajobs.opm.gov or through an interactive voice response telephone system at (703) 724-1850 or TDD (978) 461-8404. These numbers are not toll free, and charges may result.

Aircraft and Avionics Equipment Mechanics and Service Technicians

(O*NET 49-2091.00, 49-3011.01, 49-3011.02, and 49-3011.03)

Significant Points

■ Most workers learn their job in 1 of about 170 schools certified by the Federal Aviation Administration (FAA).

■ Job opportunities should be excellent for persons who have completed an aircraft mechanic training program, but keen competition is likely for the best-paying airline jobs.

■ Job opportunities are likely to be the best at small commuter and regional airlines, at FAA repair stations, and in general aviation.

Nature of the Work

To keep aircraft in peak operating condition, aircraft and avionics equipment mechanics and service technicians perform scheduled maintenance, make repairs, and complete inspections required by the Federal Aviation Administration (FAA).

Many aircraft mechanics, also called airframe mechanics, power plant mechanics, and avionics technicians, specialize in preventive maintenance. They inspect aircraft engines; landing gear; instruments; pressurized sections; accessories—brakes, valves, pumps, and air-conditioning systems, for example—and other parts of the aircraft and do the necessary maintenance and replacement of parts. They also maintain records related to the maintenance performed on the aircraft. Mechanics and technicians conduct inspections following a schedule based on the number of hours the aircraft has flown, calendar days since the last inspection, cycles of operation, or a combination of these factors. In large, sophisticated planes equipped with aircraft monitoring systems, mechanics can gather valuable diagnostic information from electronic boxes and consoles that monitor the aircraft's basic operations. In planes of all sorts, aircraft mechanics examine engines by working through specially designed openings while standing on ladders or scaffolds or by using hoists or lifts to remove the entire engine from the craft. After taking an engine apart, mechanics use precision instruments to measure parts for wear and use X-ray and magnetic inspection equipment to check for invisible cracks. They repair or replace worn or defective parts. Mechanics also may repair sheet metal or composite surfaces; measure the tension of control cables; and check for corrosion, distortion, and cracks in the fuselage, wings, and tail. After completing all repairs, they must test the equipment to ensure that it works properly.

Mechanics specializing in repair work rely on the pilot's description of a problem to find and fix faulty equipment. For example, during a preflight check, a pilot may discover that the aircraft's fuel gauge does not work. To solve the problem, mechanics may troubleshoot the electrical system, using electrical test equipment to make sure that no wires are broken or shorted out, and replace any defective electrical or electronic components. Mechanics work as fast as safety permits so that the aircraft can be put back into service quickly.

Some mechanics work on one or many different types of aircraft, such as jets, propeller-driven airplanes, and helicopters. Others specialize in one section of a particular type of aircraft, such as the engine, hydraulics, or electrical system. *Airframe mechanics* are authorized to work on any part of the aircraft except the instruments, power plants, and propellers. *Powerplant mechanics* are authorized to work on engines and do limited work on propellers. *Combination airframe-and-powerplant mechanics*—called A&P mechanics—work on all parts of the plane except the instruments. Most mechanics working on civilian aircraft today are A&P mechanics. In small, independent repair shops, mechanics usually inspect and repair many different types of aircraft.

Avionics systems are now an integral part of aircraft design and have vastly increased aircraft capability. *Avionics technicians* repair and maintain components used for aircraft navigation and radio communications; weather radar systems; and other instruments and computers that control flight, engine, and other primary functions. These duties may require additional licenses, such as a radiotelephone license issued by the U.S. Federal Communications Commission (FCC). Because of the increasing use of technology, more time is spent repairing electronic systems, such as computerized controls. Technicians also may be required to analyze and develop solutions to complex electronic problems.

Working Conditions

Mechanics usually work in hangars or in other indoor areas. When hangars are full or when repairs must be made quickly, they can work outdoors, sometimes in unpleasant weather. Mechanics often work under time pressure to maintain flight schedules or, in general aviation, to keep from inconveniencing customers. At the same time, mechanics have a tremendous responsibility to maintain safety standards, and this can cause the job to be stressful.

Frequently, mechanics must lift or pull objects weighing more than 70 pounds. They often stand, lie, or kneel in awkward positions and occasionally must work in precarious positions, such as on scaffolds or ladders. Noise and vibration are common when engines are being tested, so ear protection is necessary. Aircraft mechanics usually work 40 hours a week on 8-hour shifts around the clock. Overtime work is frequent.

Training, Other Qualifications, and Advancement

Most mechanics who work on civilian aircraft are certified by the FAA as an "airframe mechanic" or a "powerplant mechanic." Mechanics who also have an inspector's authorization can certify work completed by other mechanics and perform required inspections. Uncertified mechanics are supervised by those with certificates.

The FAA requires at least 18 months of work experience for an airframe or powerplant certificate. For a combined A&P certificate, at least 30 months of experience working with both engines and airframes is required. Completion of a program at an FAA-certified mechanic school can substitute for the work experience requirement. Applicants for all certificates also must pass written and oral tests and demonstrate that they can do the work authorized by the certificate. To obtain an inspector's authorization, a mechanic must have held an A&P certificate for at least 3 years, with 24 months of hands-on experience. Most airlines require that mechanics have a high school diploma and an A&P certificate.

Although a few people become mechanics through on-the-job training, most learn their job in 1 of about 170 trade schools certified by the FAA. About one-third of these schools award 2-year and 4-year degrees in avionics, aviation technology, or aviation maintenance management.

FAA standards established by law require that certified mechanic schools offer students a minimum of 1,900 actual class hours. Coursework in schools normally lasts from 18 to 24 months and provides training with the tools and equipment used on the job. Aircraft trade schools are placing more emphasis on technologies such as turbine engines, composite materials—including graphite, fiberglass, and boron—and aviation electronics, which are increasingly being used in the construction of new aircraft. Additionally, employers prefer mechanics who can perform a variety of tasks.

Some aircraft mechanics in the Armed Forces acquire enough general experience to satisfy the work experience requirements for the FAA certificate. With additional study, they may pass the certifying exam. In general, however, jobs in the military services are too specialized to provide the broad experience required by the FAA. Most Armed Forces mechanics have to complete the entire training program, although a few receive some credit for the material they learned in the service. In any case, military experience is a great advantage when seeking employment; employers consider applicants with formal training to be the most desirable applicants.

Courses in mathematics, physics, chemistry, electronics, computer science, and mechanical drawing are helpful because they demonstrate many of the principles involved in the operation of aircraft, and knowledge of these principles is often necessary to make repairs. Courses that develop writing skills also are important because mechanics are often required to submit reports.

FAA regulations require current work experience to keep the A&P certificate valid. Applicants must have at least 1,000 hours of work experience in the previous 24 months or take a refresher course. As new and more complex aircraft are designed, more employers are requiring mechanics to take ongoing training to update their skills. Recent technological advances in aircraft maintenance necessitate a strong background in electronics—both for acquiring and for retaining jobs in this field. FAA certification standards also make ongoing training mandatory. Every 24 months, mechanics are required to take at least 16 hours of training to keep their certificate. Many mechanics take courses offered by manufacturers or employers, usually through outside contractors.

Aircraft mechanics must do careful and thorough work that requires a high degree of mechanical aptitude. Employers seek applicants who are self-motivated, hard working, enthusiastic, and able to diagnose and solve complex mechanical problems. Agility is important for the reaching and climbing necessary to do the job. Because they may work on the tops of wings and fuselages on large jet planes, aircraft mechanics must not be afraid of heights.

Advances in computer technology, aircraft systems, and the materials used to manufacture airplanes have made mechanics' jobs more highly technical. Aircraft mechanics must possess the skills necessary to troubleshoot and diagnose complex aircraft systems. They also must continually update their skills with, and knowledge of, new technology and advances in aircraft technology.

As aircraft mechanics gain experience, they may advance to lead mechanic (or crew chief), inspector, lead inspector, or shop supervisor positions. Opportunities are best for those who have an aircraft inspector's authorization. In the airlines, where promotion often is determined by examination, supervisors sometimes advance to executive positions. Those with broad experience in maintenance and overhaul might become inspectors with the FAA. With additional business and management training, some open their own aircraft maintenance facilities. Mechanics learn many different skills in their training that can be applied to other jobs, and some transfer to other skilled repairer occupations or electronics technician jobs. Mechanics with the necessary pilot licenses and flying experience may take the FAA examination for the position of flight engineer, with opportunities to become pilots.

Employment

Aircraft and avionics equipment mechanics and service technicians held about 142,000 jobs in 2004; about 5 in 6 of these workers were aircraft mechanic and service technicians. More than half of aircraft and avionics equipment mechanics and service technicians worked for air transportation companies. About 18 percent worked for the federal government, and about 14 percent worked for aerospace products and parts manufacturing firms. Most of the rest worked for companies that operate their own planes to transport executives and cargo. Few mechanics and technicians were self-employed.

Most airline mechanics and service technicians work at major airports near large cities. Civilian mechanics employed by the U.S. Armed Forces work at military installations. Mechanics who work for aerospace manufacturing firms typically are located in California or in Washington State. Others work for the FAA, many at the facilities in Oklahoma City, Atlantic City, Wichita, or Washington, DC. Mechanics for independent repair shops work at airports in every part of the country.

Job Outlook

Opportunities for aircraft and avionics equipment mechanics and service technicians should be excellent for who have completed aircraft mechanic training programs. Employment is expected to increase about as fast as the average for all occupations through the year 2014, and large numbers of additional job openings should arise from the need to replace experienced mechanics who retire.

Reduced passenger traffic—resulting from a weak economy and the events of September 11, 2001—forced airlines to cut back flights and take aircraft out of service. However, over the next decade, passenger traffic is expected to increase as the result of an expanding economy and a growing population, and the need for aircraft mechanics and service technicians will grow accordingly. Furthermore, if the number of graduates from aircraft mechanic training programs continues to fall short of employer needs, opportunities for graduates of mechanic training programs should be excellent.

Most job openings for aircraft mechanics through the year 2014 will stem from replacement needs. Many mechanics are expected to retire over the next decade and create several thousand job openings per year. In addition, others will leave to work in related fields, such as automobile repair, as their skills are largely transferable to other maintenance and repair occupations. Also contributing to favorable future job opportunities for mechanics is the long-term trend toward fewer students entering technical schools to learn skilled maintenance and repair trades. Many of the students who have the ability and aptitude to work on planes are choosing to go to college, work in computer-related fields, or go into other repair and maintenance occupations with better working conditions. If the trend continues, the supply of trained aviation mechanics will not be able to keep up with the needs of the air transportation industry.

Job opportunities are likely to be the best at small commuter and regional airlines, at FAA repair stations, and in general aviation. Commuter and regional airlines are the fastest-growing segment of the air transportation industry, but wages in these companies tend to be lower than those in the major airlines, so they attract fewer job applicants. Also, some jobs will become available as experienced mechanics leave for higher-paying jobs with the major airlines or transfer to another occupation. At the same time, general aviation aircraft are becoming increasingly sophisticated, boosting the demand for qualified mechanics. Mechanics will face more competition for jobs with large airlines because the high wages and travel benefits that these jobs offer generally attract more qualified applicants than there are openings. Also, there is an increasing trend for large airlines to outsource aircraft and avionics equipment mechanic jobs overseas; however, most airline companies prefer that maintenance work done on aircraft be performed in the U.S. because of safety and regulation issues of overseas contractors.

In spite of these factors, job opportunities with the airlines are expected to be better than they have been in the past. But, in general, prospects will be best for applicants with experience. Mechanics who keep abreast of technological advances in electronics, composite materials, and other areas will be in greatest demand. Also, mechanics who are mobile and willing to relocate to smaller rural areas will have better job opportunities. The number of job openings for aircraft mechanics in the federal government should decline as the government increasingly contracts out service and repair functions to private repair companies.

Job opportunities for avionics technicians who are prepared to master the intricacies of the aircraft and work with A&P mechanics are expected to be good. Technicians who are cross-trained and able to work with complex aircraft systems should have the best job prospects. Additionally, technicians with licensing that enables them to work on the airplane, either removing or reinstalling equipment, are expected to be in especially high demand.

Earnings

Median hourly earnings of aircraft mechanics and service technicians were about $21.77 in May 2004. The middle 50 percent earned between $17.82 and $27.18. The lowest 10 percent earned less than $13.99, and the highest 10 percent earned more than $33.84. Median hourly earnings in the industries employing the largest numbers of aircraft mechanics and service technicians in May 2004 were

Scheduled air transportation $27.37

Federal government 21.67

Nonscheduled air transportation 20.88

Aerospace product and parts manufacturing 20.60

Support activities for air transportation 18.70

Median hourly earnings of avionics technicians were about $21.30 in May 2004. The middle 50 percent earned between $18.12 and $25.12. The lowest 10 percent earned less than $14.63, and the highest 10 percent earned more than $27.85.

Mechanics who work on jets for the major airlines generally earn more than those working on other aircraft. Airline mechanics and their immediate families receive reduced-fare transportation on their own and most other airlines.

About 4 in 10 aircraft and avionics equipment mechanics and service technicians are members of unions or covered by union agreements. The principal unions are the International Association of Machinists and Aerospace Workers and the Transport Workers Union of America. Some mechanics are represented by the International Brotherhood of Teamsters.

Related Occupations

Workers in some other occupations that involve similar mechanical and electrical work are electricians, electrical and electronics installers and repairers, and elevator installers and repairers.

Sources of Additional Information

Information about jobs with a particular airline can be obtained by writing to the personnel manager of the company.

For general information about aircraft and avionics equipment mechanics and service technicians, contact

▸ Professional Aviation Maintenance Association, 717 Princess St., Alexandria, VA 22314. Internet: http://www.pama.org

For information on jobs in a particular area, contact employers at local airports or local offices of the state employment service.

Information on obtaining positions as aircraft and avionics equipment mechanics and service technicians with the federal government is available from the Office of Personnel Management through USAJOBS, the federal government's official employment information system. This resource for locating and applying for job opportunities can be accessed through the Internet at http://www.usajobs.opm.gov or through an interactive voice response telephone system at (703) 724-1850 or TDD (978) 461-8404. These numbers are not toll free, and charges may result.

Armed Forces

(O*NET 55-1011.00, 55-1012.00, 55-1013.00, 55-1014.00, 55-1015.00, 55-1016.00, 55-1017.00, 55-1019.99, 55-2011.00, 55-2012.00, 55-2013.00, 55-3011.00, 55-3012.00, 55-3013.00, 55-3014.00, 55-3015.00, 55-3016.00, 55-3017.00, 55-3018.00, and 55-3019.99)

Significant Points

- Some training and duty assignments are hazardous, even in peacetime; hours and working conditions can be arduous and vary substantially.

- Enlisted personnel need at least a high school diploma or its equivalent, while officers need a bachelor's or an advanced degree.

- Opportunities should be good in all branches of the Armed Forces for applicants who meet designated standards.

Nature of the Work

Maintaining a strong national defense encompasses such diverse activities as running a hospital, commanding a tank, programming computers, operating a nuclear reactor, or repairing and maintaining a helicopter. The military provides training and work experience in these and many other fields for more than 2.6 million people. More than 1.4 million people serve in the active Army, Navy, Marine Corps, and Air Force, and more than 1.2 million serve in their Reserve components and the Air and Army National Guard. The Coast Guard, which is also discussed in this description, is now part of the U.S. Department of Homeland Security.

The military distinguishes between enlisted and officer careers. Enlisted personnel, who make up about 85 percent of the Armed Forces, carry out the fundamental operations of the military in areas such as combat, administration, construction, engineering, health care, and human services. Officers, who make up the remaining 15 percent of the Armed Forces, are the leaders of the military, supervising and managing activities in every occupational specialty of the Armed Forces.

The sections that follow discuss the major occupational groups for enlisted personnel and officers.

Enlisted occupational groups

Administrative careers include a wide variety of positions. The military must keep accurate information for planning and managing its operations. Both paper and electronic records are kept on personnel and on equipment, funds, supplies, and all other aspects of the military. Administrative personnel record information, type reports, maintain files, and review information to assist military officers. Personnel may work in a specialized area such as finance, accounting, legal affairs, maintenance, supply, or transportation.

Combat specialty occupations refer to enlisted specialties, such as infantry, artillery, and special forces, whose members operate weapons or execute special missions during combat. Persons in these occupations normally specialize by the type of weapon system or combat operation. These personnel maneuver against enemy forces and position and fire artillery, guns, and missiles to destroy enemy positions. They also may operate tanks and amphibious assault vehicles in combat or scouting missions. When the military has difficult and dangerous missions to perform, they call upon special forces teams. These elite combat forces maintain a constant state of readiness to strike anywhere in the world on a moment's notice. Team members from the special forces conduct offensive raids, demolitions, intelligence, search-and-rescue missions, and other operations from aboard aircraft, helicopters, ships, or submarines.

Construction occupations in the military include personnel who build or repair buildings, airfields, bridges, foundations, dams, bunkers, and the electrical and plumbing components of these structures. Personnel in construction occupations operate bulldozers, cranes, graders, and other heavy equipment. Construction specialists also may work with engineers and other building specialists as part of military construction teams. Some personnel specialize in areas such as plumbing or electrical wiring. Plumbers and pipefitters install and repair the plumbing and pipe systems needed in buildings and on aircraft and ships. Building electricians install and repair electrical-wiring systems in offices, airplane hangars, and other buildings on military bases.

Electronic and electrical equipment repair personnel repair and maintain electronic and electrical equipment used in the military. Repairers normally specialize by type of equipment, such as avionics, computer, optical, communications, or weapons systems. For example, electronic instrument repairers install, test, maintain, and repair a wide variety of electronic systems, including navigational controls and biomedical instruments. Weapons maintenance technicians maintain and repair weapons used by combat forces; most of these weapons have electronic components and systems that assist in locating targets and in aiming and firing the weapon.

Engineering, science, and technical personnel in the military require specific knowledge to operate technical equipment, solve complex problems, or provide and interpret information. Personnel normally specialize in one area, such as space operations, information technology, environmental health and safety, or intelligence. Space operations specialists use and repair ground-control command equipment having to do with spacecraft, including electronic systems that track the location and operation of a craft. Information technology specialists develop software programs and operate computer systems. Environmental health and safety specialists inspect military facilities and food supplies for the presence of disease, germs, or other conditions hazardous to health and the environment. Intelligence specialists gather and study information by means of aerial photographs and various types of radar and surveillance systems.

Health care personnel assist medical professionals in treating and providing services for men and women in the military. They may work as part of a patient-service team in close contact with doctors, dentists, nurses, and physical therapists to provide the necessary support functions within a hospital or clinic. Health care specialists normally specialize in a particular area—emergency medical treatment, the operation of diagnostic tools such as X-ray and ultrasound equipment, laboratory testing of tissue and blood samples, or maintaining pharmacy supplies or patients' records, among others.

Dental and optical laboratory technicians construct and repair dental equipment and eyeglasses for military personnel.

Human resources development specialists recruit and place qualified personnel and provide the training programs necessary to help people perform their jobs effectively. Personnel in this career area normally specialize by activity. For example, recruiting specialists provide information about military careers to young people, parents, schools, and local communities and explain the Armed Service's employment and training opportunities, pay and benefits, and service life. Personnel specialists collect and store information about the people in the military, including information on their previous and current training, job assignments, promotions, and health. Training specialists and instructors teach classes and give demonstrations to provide military personnel with the knowledge they need to perform their jobs.

Machine operator and production personnel operate industrial equipment, machinery, and tools to fabricate and repair parts for a variety of items and structures. They may operate engines, turbines, nuclear reactors, and water pumps. Often, they specialize by type of work performed. Welders and metalworkers, for instance, work with various types of metals to repair or form the structural parts of ships, submarines, buildings, or other equipment. Survival equipment specialists inspect, maintain, and repair survival equipment such as parachutes and aircraft life support equipment.

Media and public affairs personnel deal with the public presentation and interpretation of military information and events. They take and develop photographs; film, record, and edit audio and video programs; present news and music programs; and produce graphic artwork, drawings, and other visual displays. Other public affairs specialists act as interpreters and translators to convert written or spoken foreign languages into English or other languages.

Protective service personnel include those who enforce military laws and regulations and provide emergency response to natural and human-made disasters. These personnel normally specialize by function. For example, military police control traffic, prevent crime, and respond to emergencies. Other law enforcement and security specialists investigate crimes committed on military property and guard inmates in military correctional facilities. Fire fighters put out, control, and help prevent fires in buildings, on aircraft, and aboard ships.

Support service personnel provide subsistence services and support the morale and well-being of military personnel and their families. Food service specialists prepare all types of food in dining halls, hospitals, and ships. Counselors help military personnel and their families deal with personal issues. They work as part of a team that may include social workers, psychologists, medical officers, chaplains, personnel specialists, and commanders. Religious program specialists assist chaplains with religious services, religious education programs, and related administrative duties.

Transportation and material handling specialists ensure the safe transport of people and cargo. Most personnel within this occupational group are classified according to mode of transportation, such as aircraft, motor vehicle, or ship. Aircrew members operate equipment on board aircraft during operations. Vehicle drivers operate all types of heavy military vehicles, including fuel or water tank trucks, semi-trailers, heavy troop transports, and passenger buses. Quartermasters and boat operators navigate and pilot many types of small watercraft, including tugboats, gunboats, and barges. Cargo specialists load and unload military supplies, using equipment such as forklifts and cranes.

Vehicle and machinery mechanics conduct preventive and corrective maintenance on aircraft, automotive and heavy equipment, heating and cooling systems, marine engines, and powerhouse station equipment. These workers typically specialize by the type of equipment that they maintain. For example, aircraft mechanics inspect, service, and repair helicopters and airplanes. Automotive and heavy equipment mechanics maintain and repair vehicles such as humvees, trucks, tanks, self-propelled missile launchers, and other combat vehicles. They also repair bulldozers, power shovels, and other construction equipment. Heating and cooling mechanics install and repair air-conditioning, refrigeration, and heating equipment. Marine engine mechanics repair and maintain gasoline and diesel engines on ships, boats, and other watercraft. They also repair shipboard mechanical and electrical equipment. Powerhouse mechanics install, maintain, and repair electrical and mechanical equipment in power-generating stations.

Officer occupational groups

Combat specialty officers plan and direct military operations, oversee combat activities, and serve as combat leaders. This category includes officers in charge of tanks and other armored assault vehicles, artillery systems, special forces, and infantry. Combat specialty officers normally specialize by the type of unit that they lead. Within the unit, they may specialize by the type of weapon system. Artillery and missile system officers, for example, direct personnel as they target, launch, test, and maintain various types of missiles and artillery. Special-operations officers lead their units in offensive raids, demolitions, intelligence gathering, and search-and-rescue missions.

Engineering, science, and technical officers have a wide range of responsibilities based on their area of expertise. They lead or perform activities in areas such as space operations, environmental health and safety, and engineering. These officers may direct the operations of communications centers or the development of complex computer systems. Environmental health and safety officers study the air, ground, and water to identify and analyze sources of pollution and its effects. They also direct programs to control safety and health hazards in the workplace. Other personnel work as aerospace engineers to design and direct the development of military aircraft, missiles, and spacecraft.

Executive, administrative, and managerial officers oversee and direct military activities in key functional areas such as finance, accounting, health administration, international relations, and supply. Health services administrators, for instance, are responsible for the overall quality of care provided at the hospitals and clinics they operate. They must ensure that each department works together to provide the highest quality of care. As another example, purchasing and contracting managers negotiate and monitor contracts for the purchase of the billions of dollars worth of equipment, supplies, and services that the military buys from private industry each year.

Health care officers provide health services at military facilities on the basis of their area of specialization. Officers who examine, diagnose, and treat patients with illness, injury, or disease include physicians, registered nurses, and dentists. Other health care officers provide therapy, rehabilitative treatment, and additional services for patients. Physical and occupational therapists plan and administer therapy to help patients adjust to disabilities, regain independence, and return to work. Speech therapists evaluate and treat patients with hearing and speech problems. Dietitians manage food service facilities and plan meals for hospital patients and for outpatients who need special diets. Pharmacists manage the purchase, storage, and dispensation of drugs and medicines. Physicians and surgeons in this occupational group provide the majority of medical services to the military and their families. Dentists treat diseases and disorders of the mouth. Optometrists treat vision problems by prescribing eyeglasses or contact lenses. Psychologists provide mental health care and also conduct research on behavior and emotions.

Human resource development officers manage recruitment, placement, and training strategies and programs in the military. They normally specialize by activity. Recruiting managers direct recruiting efforts and provide information about military careers to young people, parents, schools, and local communities. Personnel managers direct military personnel functions such as job assignment, staff promotion, and career counseling. Training and education directors identify training needs and develop and manage educational programs designed to keep military personnel current in the skills they need to perform their jobs.

Media and public affairs officers oversee the development, production, and presentation of information or events for the public. These officers may produce and direct motion pictures, videotapes, and television and radio broadcasts that are used for training, news, and entertainment. Some plan, develop, and direct the activities of military bands. Public information officers respond to inquiries about military activities and prepare news releases and reports to keep the public informed.

Protective service officers are responsible for the safety and protection of individuals and property on military bases and vessels. Emergency management officers plan and prepare for all types of natural and human-made disasters. They develop warning, control, and evacuation plans to be used in the event of a disaster. Law enforcement and security officers enforce all applicable laws on military bases and investigate crimes when the law has been broken.

Support services officers manage food service activities and perform services in support of the morale and well-being of military personnel and their families. Food services managers oversee the preparation and delivery of food services within dining facilities located on military installations and vessels. Social workers focus on improving conditions that cause social problems such as drug and alcohol abuse, racism, and sexism. Chaplains conduct worship services for military personnel and perform other spiritual duties covering the beliefs and practices of all religious faiths.

Transportation officers manage and perform activities related to the safe transport of military personnel and material by air and water. These officers normally specialize by mode of transportation or area of expertise because, in many cases, they must meet licensing and certification requirements. Pilots in the military fly various types of specialized airplanes and helicopters to carry troops and equipment and to execute combat missions. Navigators use radar, radio, and other navigation equipment to determine their position and plan their route of travel. Officers on ships and submarines work as a team to manage the various departments aboard their vessels. Ship engineers direct engineering departments aboard ships and

submarines, including engine operations, maintenance, repair, heating, and power generation.

Training, Other Qualifications, and Advancement

Enlisted personnel. In order to join the services, enlisted personnel must sign a legal agreement called an enlistment contract, which usually involves a commitment to 8 years of service. Depending on the terms of the contract, 2 to 6 years are spent on active duty, and the balance is spent in the National Guard or Reserves. The enlistment contract obligates the service to provide the agreed-upon job, rating, pay, cash bonuses for enlistment in certain occupations, medical and other benefits, occupational training, and continuing education. In return, enlisted personnel must serve satisfactorily for the period specified.

Requirements for each service vary, but certain qualifications for enlistment are common to all branches. In order to enlist, one must be between 17 and 35 years old for active service, be a U.S. citizen or an alien holding permanent resident status, not have a felony record, and possess a birth certificate. Applicants who are aged 17 must have the consent of a parent or legal guardian before entering the service. Coast Guard enlisted personnel must enter active duty before their 28th birthday, whereas Marine Corps enlisted personnel must not be over the age of 29. Applicants must both pass a written examination—the Armed Services Vocational Aptitude Battery—and meet certain minimum physical standards, such as height, weight, vision, and overall health. All branches of the Armed Forces require high school graduation or its equivalent. In 2004, more than 9 out of 10 recruits were high school graduates.

People thinking about enlisting in the military should learn as much as they can about military life before making a decision. Doing so is especially important if you are thinking about making the military a career. Speaking to friends and relatives with military experience is a good idea. Find out what the military can offer you and what it will expect in return. Then, talk to a recruiter, who can determine whether you qualify for enlistment, explain the various enlistment options, and tell you which military occupational specialties currently have openings. Bear in mind that the recruiter's job is to recruit promising applicants into his or her branch of military service, so the information that the recruiter gives you is likely to stress the positive aspects of military life in the branch in which he or she serves.

Ask the recruiter for the branch you have chosen to assess your chances of being accepted for training in the occupation of your choice, or, better still, take the aptitude exam to see how well you score. The military uses this exam as a placement exam, and test scores largely determine an individual's chances of being accepted into a particular training program. Selection for a particular type of training depends on the needs of the service, your general and technical aptitudes, and your personal preference. Because all prospective recruits are required to take the exam, those who do so before committing themselves to enlist have the advantage of knowing in advance whether they stand a good chance of being accepted for training in a particular specialty. The recruiter can schedule you for the Armed Services Vocational Aptitude Battery without any obligation. Many high schools offer the exam as an easy way for students to explore the possibility of a military career, and the test also affords an insight into career areas in which the student has demonstrated aptitudes and interests.

If you decide to join the military, the next step is to pass the physical examination and sign an enlistment contract. Negotiating the contract involves choosing, qualifying for, and agreeing on a number of enlistment options, such as the length of active-duty time, which may vary according to the option. Most active-duty programs have first-term enlistments of 4 years, although there are some 2-, 3-, and 6-year programs. The contract also will state the date of enlistment and other options—for example, bonuses and the types of training to be received. If the service is unable to fulfill any of its obligations under the contract, such as providing a certain kind of training, the contract may become null and void.

All branches of the Armed Services offer a delayed entry program (DEP) by which an individual can delay entry into active duty for up to 1 year after enlisting. High school students can enlist during their senior year and enter a service after graduation. Others choose this program because the job training they desire is not currently available, but will be within the coming year, or because they need time to arrange their personal affairs.

Women are eligible to enter most military specialties; for example, they may become mechanics, missile maintenance technicians, heavy-equipment operators, and fighter pilots, or they may enter into medical care, administrative support, and intelligence specialties. Generally, only occupations involving direct exposure to combat are excluded.

People planning to apply the skills gained through military training to a civilian career should first determine how good the prospects are for civilian employment in jobs related to the military specialty that interests them. Second, they should know the prerequisites for the related civilian job. Because many civilian occupations require a license, certification, or minimum level of education, it is important to determine whether military training is sufficient for a person to enter the civilian equivalent or, if not, what additional training will be required. Other descriptions in this book discuss the job outlook, training requirements, and other aspects of civilian occupations for which military training and experience are helpful. Additional information often can be obtained from school counselors.

Following enlistment, new members of the Armed Forces undergo initial-entry training, better known as "basic training" or "boot camp." Through courses in military skills and protocol recruit training provides a 6-week to 13-week introduction to military life. Days and nights are carefully structured and include rigorous physical exercise designed to improve strength and endurance and build each unit's cohesion.

Following basic training, most recruits take additional training at technical schools that prepare them for a particular military occupational specialty. The formal training period generally lasts from 10 to 20 weeks, although training for certain occupations—nuclear power plant operator, for example—may take as long as a year. Recruits not assigned to classroom instruction receive on-the-job training at their first duty assignment.

Many service people get college credit for the technical training they receive on duty, which, combined with off-duty courses, can lead to an associate degree through programs in community colleges such as the Community College of the Air Force. In addition to on-duty training, military personnel may choose from a variety of educational programs. Most military installations have tuition assistance programs for people wishing to take courses during off-duty hours. The courses may be correspondence courses or courses in degree programs offered by local colleges or universities. Tuition assistance pays up to 100 percent of college costs up to a credit-hour and annual limit. Each branch of the service provides opportunities for full-time study to a limited number of exceptional applicants. Military personnel accepted into these highly competitive programs—in law or medicine, for example—receive full pay, allowances, tuition, and related fees. In return, they must agree to serve an additional amount of time in the service. Other highly selective programs enable enlisted personnel to qualify as commissioned officers through additional military training.

Warrant officers. Warrant officers are technical and tactical leaders who specialize in a specific technical area; for example, Army aviators make up one group of warrant officers. The Army Warrant Officer Corps constitutes less than 5 percent of the total Army. Although the Corps is small in size, its level of responsibility is high. Its members receive extended career opportunities, worldwide leadership assignments, and increased pay and retirement benefits. Selection to attend the Warrant Officer Candidate School is highly competitive and restricted to those who meet rank and length-of-service requirements. The only exception is the Army aviator warrant officer, which has no prior military service requirements (table 1).

Officers. Officer training in the Armed Forces is provided through the federal service academies (Military, Naval, Air Force, and Coast Guard); the Reserve Officers Training Corps (ROTC) program offered at many colleges and universities; Officer Candidate School (OCS) or Officer Training School (OTS); the National Guard (State Officer Candidate School programs); the Uniformed Services University of Health Sciences; and other programs. All are highly selective and are good options for those wishing to make the military a career. Persons interested in obtaining training through the federal service academies must be single to enter and graduate, while those seeking training through OCS, OTS, or ROTC need not be single. Single parents with one or more minor dependents are not eligible to become commissioned officers.

Federal service academies provide a 4-year college program leading to a bachelor-of-science degree. Midshipmen or cadets are provided free room and board, tuition, medical and dental care, and a monthly allowance. Graduates receive regular or reserve commissions and have a 5-year active-duty obligation, or more if they are entering flight training.

To become a candidate for appointment as a cadet or midshipman in one of the service academies, applicants are required to obtain a nomination from an authorized source, usually a member of Congress. Candidates do not need to know a member of Congress personally to request a nomination. Nominees must have an academic record of the requisite quality, college aptitude test scores above an established minimum, and recommendations from teachers or school officials; they also must pass a medical examination. Appointments are made from the list of eligible nominees. Appointments to the Coast Guard Academy, however, are based strictly on merit and do not require a nomination.

ROTC programs train students in about 575 Army, 130 Navy and Marine Corps, and 300 Air Force units at participating colleges and universities. Trainees take 3 to 5 hours of military instruction a week in addition to regular college courses. After graduation, they may serve as officers on active duty for a stipulated period. Some may serve their obligation in the Reserves or National Guard. In the last 2 years of a ROTC program, students typically receive a monthly allowance while attending school, as well as additional pay for summer training. ROTC scholarships for 2, 3, and 4 years are available on a competitive basis. All scholarships pay for tuition and have allowances for textbooks, supplies, and other costs.

College graduates can earn a commission in the Armed Forces through OCS or OTS programs in the Army, Navy, Air Force, Marine Corps, Coast Guard, and National Guard. These officers generally must serve their obligation on active duty. Those with training in certain health professions may qualify for direct appointment as officers. In the case of persons studying for the health professions, financial assistance and internship opportunities are available from the military in return for specified periods of military service. Prospective medical students can apply to the Uniformed Services University of Health Sciences, which offers a salary and free tuition in a program leading to a doctor-of-medicine (M.D.) degree. In return, graduates must serve for 7 years in either the military or the U.S. Public Health Service. Direct appointments also are available for those qualified to serve in other specialty areas, such as the judge advocate general (legal) or chaplain corps. Flight training is available to commissioned officers in each branch of the Armed Forces. In addition, the Army has a direct enlistment option to become a warrant officer aviator.

Each service has different criteria for promoting personnel. Generally, the first few promotions for both enlisted and officer personnel come easily; subsequent promotions are much more competitive. Criteria for promotion may include time in service and in grade, job performance, a fitness report (supervisor's recommendation), and passing scores on written examinations. Table 1 shows the officer, warrant officer, and enlisted ranks by service.

Employment

In 2005, more than 2.6 million people served in the Armed Forces. More than 1.4 million were on active duty in the Armed Forces—about 487,000 in the Army, 350,000 in the Navy, 356,000 in the Air Force, and 185,000 in the Marine Corps. In addition, more than 1.2 million people served in their Reserve components, and the Air and Army National Guard. In addition, 33,000 individuals served in the Coast Guard, which is now part of the U.S. Department of Homeland Security. Table 2 shows the occupational composition of the 1.2 million active-duty enlisted personnel in February 2005; table 3 presents similar information for the 216,000 active-duty officers.

Military personnel are stationed throughout the United states and in many countries around the world. About half of all military jobs in the U.S. are located in California, Texas, North Carolina, Virginia, Florida, and Georgia. Approximately 169,000 service members were deployed to Operation Iraqi Freedom either in or around Iraq in June 2005. An additional 278,000 individuals were stationed outside the United states , including 21,000 assigned to ships at sea. About 106,000 were stationed in Europe, mainly in Germany, and another 81,000 were assigned to East Asia and the Pacific area, mostly in Japan and the Republic of Korea.

Table 1. Military rank and employment for active duty personnel, January 2005

Grade	Army	Navy	Air Force	Marine Corps	Employment Total
Commissioned officers:					
O-10	General	Admiral	General	General	34
O-9	Lieutenant General	Vice Admiral	Lieutenant General	Lieutenant General	125
O-8	Major General	Rear Admiral Upper	Major General	Major General	276
O-7	Brigadier General	Rear Admiral Lower	Brigadier General	Brigadier General	439
O-6	Colonel	Captain	Colonel	Colonel	11,483
O-5	Lieutenant Colonel	Commander	Lieutenant Colonel	Lieutenant Colonel	28,378
O-4	Major	Lieutenant Commander	Major	Major	43,846
O-3	Captain	Lieutenant	Captain	Captain	70,500
O-2	1st Lieutenant	Lieutenant (JG)	1st Lieutenant	1st Lieutenant	30,853
O-1	2nd Lieutenant	Ensign	2nd Lieutenant	2nd Lieutenant	24,948
Warrant officers:					
W-5	Chief Warrant Officer	Chief Warrant Officer	—	Chief Warrant Officer	540
W-4	Chief Warrant Officer	Chief Warrant Officer	—	Chief Warrant Officer	2,180
W-3	Chief Warrant Officer	Chief Warrant Officer	—	Chief Warrant Officer	4,618
W-2	Chief Warrant Officer	Chief Warrant Officer	—	Chief Warrant Officer	6,227
W-1	Warrant Officer	Warrant Officer	—	Warrant Officer	2,193

(continued)

(continued)

Grade	Army	Navy	Air Force	Marine Corps	Employment Total
Enlisted personnel:					
E-9	Sergeant Major ....Master Chief Petty	Officer	Chief Master Sergeant	Sergeant Major/Master Gunnery Sergeant 10,704	
E-8	1st Sergeant/ Master Sergeant	Senior Chief Petty Officer	Senior Master Sergeant	1st Sergeant/ Master Sergeant 27,229	
E-7	Sergeant First Class .....Chief Petty Officer ....Master Sergeant ....Gunnery Sergeant.............100,458				
E-6	Staff Sergeant..............Petty Officer 1st Class.......Technical Sergeant ......Staff Sergeant 174,467				
E-5	Sergeant.....................Petty Officer 2nd Class .....Staff Sergeant ....Sergeant........................249,816				
E-4	Corporal ....Petty Officer 3rd Class.......Senior Airman ....Corporal 260,631				
E-3	Private First Class ....Seaman ....Airman 1st Class..........Lance Corporal..................216,321				
E-2	Private......................Seaman Apprentice...........Airman ....Private 1st Class 82,008				
E-1	Private.......................Seaman Recruit ....Airman Basic ....Private.............................48,818				

SOURCE: U.S. Department of Defense

Table 2. Military enlisted personnel by broad occupational category and branch of military service, February 2005

Occupational Group - Enlisted	Army	Air Force	Coast Guard	Marine Corps	Navy	Total, all services
Administrative occupations	14,016	25,008	2,241	9,612	25,923	76,800
Combat specialty occupations	113,689	398	851	52,256	6,264	173,458
Construction occupations	15,544	6,407	—	5,147	5,085	32,183
Electronic and electrical repair occupations	39,601	40,083	3,045	15,586	58,992	157,307
Engineering, science, and technical occupations.....................................	35,482	50,732	986	23,656	41,951	152,807
Health care occupations	27,031	17,924	682	—	26,614	72,251
Human resource development occupations	15,908	12,468	—	6,803	4,822	40,001
Machine operator and precision work occupations.......................................	4,103	7,409	1,548	2,439	12,274	27,773
Media and public affairs occupations...............	4,867	6,453	121	2,258	5,047	18,746
Protective service occupations	23,270	31,716	2,695	5,733	12,215	75,629
Support services occupations	13,438	1,667	1,146	2,264	10,699	29,214
Transportation and material handling occupations	53,349	34,588	10,549	22,825	42,860	164,171
Vehicle machinery mechanic occupations	48,577	50,532	5,538	18,076	50,020	172,743
Total, by service	**408,875**	**285,385**	**29,402**	**166,655**	**302,766**	**1,193,083**

SOURCE: U.S. Department of Defense, Defense Manpower Data Center

Table 3. Military officer personnel by broad occupational category and branch of service, February 2005

Occupational Group - Officer	Army	Air Force	Coast Guard	Marine Corps	Navy	Total, all services
Combat specialty occupations	18,835	6,007	—	4,662	5,463	34,967
Engineering, science, and technical occupations	19,137	17,503	1,576	3,576	9,778	51,087
Executive, administrative, and managerial occupations	11,262	10,395	282	2,582	7,450	31,971
Health care occupations	9,792	9,413	43	—	6,983	26,231
Human resource development occupations	2,128	2,418	213	299	3,258	8,316
Media and public affairs occupations...............	224	500	20	44	282	1,070
Protective service occupations	2,237	1,410	104	309	890	4,950

Occupational Group - Officer	Army	Air Force	Coast Guard	Marine Corps	Navy	Total, all services
Support services occupations	1,525	830	—	38	1,003	3,396
Transportation occupations	13,216	19,729	2,250	7,082	11,975	54,252
Total, by service	78,356	68,205	4,005	18,592	47,082	216,240

SOURCE: U.S. Department of Defense, Defense Manpower Data Center

Job Outlook

Opportunities should be good for qualified individuals in all branches of the Armed Forces through 2014. Many military personnel retire with a pension after 20 years of service, while they still are young enough to start a new career. About 170,000 personnel must be recruited each year to replace those who complete their commitment or retire. Since the end of the draft in 1973, the military has met its personnel requirements with volunteers. When the economy is good and civilian employment opportunities generally are more favorable, it is more difficult for all the services to meet their recruitment quotas. It is also more difficult to meet these goals during times of war, when recruitment goals typically rise.

America's strategic position is stronger than it has been in decades. Despite reductions in personnel due to the elimination of the threats of the Cold War, the number of active-duty personnel is expected to remain roughly constant through 2014. However, recent conflicts and the resulting strain on the Armed Forces may lead to an increasing number of active-duty personnel. The Armed Forces' current goal is to maintain a sufficient force to fight and win two major regional conflicts at the same time. Political events, however, could lead to a significant restructuring with or without an increase in size.

Educational requirements will continue to rise as military jobs become more technical and complex. High school graduates and applicants with a college background will be sought to fill the ranks of enlisted personnel, while virtually all officers will need at least a bachelor's degree and, in some cases, an advanced degree as well.

Earnings

The earnings structure for military personnel is shown in table 4. Most enlisted personnel started as recruits at Grade E-1 in 2004; however, those with special skills or above-average education started as high as Grade E-4. Most warrant officers had started at Grade W-1 or W-2, depending upon their occupational and academic qualifications and the branch of service of which they were a member, but warrant officer typically is not an entry-level occupation and, consequently, most of these individuals had previous military service. Most commissioned officers started at Grade O-1; some with advanced education started at Grade O-2, and some highly trained officers—for example, physicians and dentists—started as high as Grade O-3. Pay varies by total years of service as well as rank. Because it usually takes many years to reach the higher ranks, most personnel in higher ranks receive the higher pay rates awarded to those with many years of service.

In addition to receiving their basic pay, military personnel are provided with free room and board (or a tax-free housing and subsistence allowance), free medical and dental care, a military clothing allowance, military supermarket and department store shopping privileges, 30 days of paid vacation a year (referred to as leave), and travel opportunities. In many duty stations, military personnel may receive a housing allowance that can be used for off-base housing. This allowance can be substantial, but varies greatly by rank and duty station. For example, in fiscal year 2005, the average housing allowance for an E-4 with dependents was $958 per month; for a comparable individual without dependents, it was $752. The allowance for an O-4 with dependents was $1,645 per month; for a comparable individual without dependents, it was $1,428. Other allowances are paid for foreign duty, hazardous duty, submarine and flight duty, and employment as a medical officer. Athletic and other facilities—such as gymnasiums, tennis courts, golf courses, bowling centers, libraries, and movie theaters—are available on many military installations. Military personnel are eligible for retirement benefits after 20 years of service.

The Veterans Administration (VA) provides numerous benefits to those who have served at least 24 months of continuous active duty in the Armed Forces. Veterans are eligible for free care in VA hospitals for all service-related disabilities, regardless of time served; those with other medical problems are eligible for free VA care if they are unable to pay the cost of hospitalization elsewhere. Admission to a VA medical center depends on the availability of beds, however. Veterans also are eligible for certain loans, including loans to purchase a home. Veterans, regardless of health, can convert a military life insurance policy to an individual policy with any participating company upon separation from the military. In addition, job counseling, testing, and placement services are available.

Veterans who participate in the Montgomery GI Bill Program receive education benefits. Under this program, Armed Forces personnel may elect to deduct up to $100 a month from their pay during the first 12 months of active duty, putting the money toward their future education. In fiscal year 2005, veterans who served on active duty for 3 or more years or who spent 2 years in active duty plus 4 years in the Selected Reserve received $1,004 a month in basic benefits for 36 months of full-time institutional training. Those who enlisted and serve less than 3 years received $816 a month for 36 months for the same. In addition, each service provides its own contributions to the enlistee's future education. The sum of the amounts from all these sources becomes the service member's educational fund. Upon separation from active duty, the fund can be used to finance educational costs at any VA-approved institution. Among those institutions which are approved by the VA are many vocational, correspondence, certification, business, technical, and flight-training schools; community and junior colleges; and colleges and universities.

Table 4. Military basic monthly pay by grade for active duty personnel, January 2005

Grade	Less than 2	Over 4	Over 8	Over 12	Over 16	Over 20
O-10	—	—	—	—	—	$12,963.00
O-9	—	—	—	—	—	11,337.90
O-8	$8,022.30	$8,508.30	$9,089.40	$9,519.00	$9,915.30	10,742.40
O-7	6,666.00	6,233.00	7,642.50	8,113.50	9,089.40	9,714.60
O-6	4,940.70	5,784.00	6,054.90	6,087.90	7,045.50	7,763.40
O-5	4,118.70	5,021.40	5,341.80	5,799.00	6,431.10	6,793.20
O-4	3,553.80	4,449.60	4,977.60	5,582.70	5,872.20	5,933.70
O-3	3,124.50	4,168.20	4,586.70	4,962.00	5,083.20	5,083.20
O-2	2,699.40	3,660.90	3,736.20	3,736.20	3,736.20	3,736.20
O-1	2,343.60	2,948.10	2,948.10	2,948.10	2,948.10	2,948.10
W-5	—	—	—	—	—	5,548.20
W-4	3,228.60	3,671.40	4,007.10	4,341.00	4,779.00	5,117.40
W-3	2,948.40	3,238.80	3,522.30	3,918.90	4,285.50	4,509.30
W-2	2,593.50	2,965.50	3,268.20	3,564.00	3,771.30	3,977.40
W-1	2,290.20	2,684.40	3,030.90	3,275.40	3,438.30	3,659.70
E-9	—	—	—	3,989.70	4,232.40	4,575.90
E-8	—	—	3,193.50	3,442.10	3,640.50	3,949.20
E-7	2,220.00	2,638.80	2,899.50	3,084.60	3,332.40	3,458.70
E-6	1,920.30	2,296.50	2,604.30	2,779.20	2,888.70	2,908.20
E-5	1,759.50	2,060.70	2,329.80	2,450.70	2,450.70	2,450.70
E-4	1,612.80	1,877.70	1,957.80	1,957.80	1,957.80	1,957.80
E-3	1,456.20	1,641.00	1,641.00	1,641.00	1,641.00	1,641.00
E-2	1,384.50	1,384.50	1,384.50	1,384.50	1,384.50	1,384.50
E-1 4mos+	1,235.10	1,235.10	1,235.10	1,235.10	1,235.10	1,235.10
E-1 <4mos	1,142.70	—	—	—	—	—

SOURCE: U.S. Department of Defense, Defense Finance and Accounting Service

Sources of Additional Information

Each of the military services publishes handbooks, fact sheets, and pamphlets describing entrance requirements, training and advancement opportunities, and other aspects of military careers. These publications are widely available at all recruiting stations, at most state employment service offices, and in high schools, colleges, and public libraries. Information on educational and other veterans' benefits is available from VA offices located throughout the country.

In addition, the Defense Manpower Data Center, an agency of the U.S. Department of Defense, publishes *Military Career Guide Online*, a compendium of military occupational, training, and career information designed for use by students and jobseekers. This information is available on the Internet: http://www.todaysmilitary.com

Artists and Related Workers

(O*NET 27-1011.00, 27-1012.00, 27-1013.01, 27-1013.02, 27-1013.03, 27-1013.04, and 27-1014.00)

Significant Points

■ About 63 percent of artists and related workers are self-employed.

■ Keen competition is expected for both salaried jobs and freelance work; the number of qualified workers exceeds the number of available openings because the arts attract many talented people with creative ability.

■ Artists usually develop their skills through a bachelor's degree program or other postsecondary training in art or design.

■ Earnings for self-employed artists vary widely; some well-established artists earn more than salaried artists, while others find it difficult to rely solely on income earned from selling art.

Nature of the Work

Artists create art to communicate ideas, thoughts, or feelings. They use a variety of methods—painting, sculpting, or illustration—and an assortment of materials, including oils, watercolors, acrylics, pastels, pencils, pen and ink, plaster, clay, and computers. Artists' works may be realistic, stylized, or abstract and may depict objects, people, nature, or events.

Artists generally fall into one of four categories. *Art directors* formulate design concepts and presentation approaches for visual communications media. *Craft artists* create or reproduce handmade objects for sale or exhibition. *Fine artists,* including *painters, sculptors, and illustrators,* create original artwork, using a variety of media and techniques. *Multi-media artists and animators* create special effects, animation, or other visual images on film, on video, or with computers or other electronic media.

Art directors develop design concepts and review material that is to appear in periodicals, newspapers, and other printed or digital media. They decide how best to present the information visually so that it is eye catching, appealing, and organized. Art directors decide which photographs or artwork to use and oversee the layout design and production of the printed material. They may direct workers engaged in artwork, layout design, and copywriting.

Craft artists hand-make a wide variety of objects that are sold either in their own studios, in retail outlets, or at arts-and-crafts shows. Some craft artists may display their works in galleries and museums. Craft artists work with many different materials—ceramics, glass, textiles, wood, metal, and paper—to create unique pieces of art, such as pottery, stained glass, quilts, tapestries, lace, candles, and clothing. Many craft artists also use fine-art techniques—for example, painting, sketching, and printing—to add finishing touches to their art.

Fine artists typically display their work in museums, commercial art galleries, corporate collections, and private homes. Some of their artwork may be commissioned (done on request from clients), but most is sold by the artist or through private art galleries or dealers. The gallery and the artist predetermine how much each will earn from the sale. Only the most successful fine artists are able to support themselves solely through the sale of their works. Most fine artists have at least one other job to support their art careers. Some work in museums or art galleries as fine-arts directors or as curators, planning and setting up art exhibits. A few artists work as art critics for newspapers or magazines or as consultants to foundations or institutional collectors. Other artists teach art classes or conduct workshops in schools or in their own studios. Some artists also hold full-time or part-time jobs unrelated to the art field and pursue fine art as a hobby or second career.

Usually, fine artists specialize in one or two art forms, such as painting, illustrating, sketching, sculpting, printmaking, and restoring. *Painters, illustrators, cartoonists, and sketch artists* work with two-dimensional art forms, using shading, perspective, and color to produce realistic scenes or abstractions.

Illustrators typically create pictures for books, magazines, and other publications and for commercial products such as textiles, wrapping paper, stationery, greeting cards, and calendars. Increasingly, illustrators are working in digital format, preparing work directly on a computer.

Medical and *scientific illustrators* combine drawing skills with knowledge of biology or other sciences. Medical illustrators draw illustrations of human anatomy and surgical procedures. Scientific illustrators draw illustrations of animal and plant life, atomic and molecular structures, and geologic and planetary formations. The illustrations are used in medical and scientific publications and in audiovisual presentations for teaching purposes. Medical illustrators also work for lawyers, producing exhibits for court cases.

Cartoonists draw political, advertising, social, and sports cartoons. Some cartoonists work with others who create the idea or story and write the captions. Most cartoonists have comic, critical, or dramatic talents in addition to drawing skills.

Sketch artists create likenesses of subjects with pencil, charcoal, or pastels. Sketches are used by law enforcement agencies to assist in identifying suspects, by the news media to depict courtroom scenes, and by individual patrons for their own enjoyment.

Sculptors design three-dimensional artworks, either by molding and joining materials such as clay, glass, wire, plastic, fabric, or metal or by cutting and carving forms from a block of plaster, wood, or stone. Some sculptors combine various materials to create mixed-media installations. Some incorporate light, sound, and motion into their works.

Printmakers create printed images from designs cut or etched into wood, stone, or metal. After creating the design, the artist inks the surface of the woodblock, stone, or plate and uses a printing press to roll the image onto paper or fabric. Some make prints by pressing the inked surface onto paper by hand or by graphically encoding and processing data, using a computer. The digitized images are then printed on paper with the use of a computer printer.

Painting restorers preserve and restore damaged and faded paintings. They apply solvents and cleaning agents to clean the surfaces of the paintings, they reconstruct or retouch damaged areas, and they apply preservatives to protect the paintings. Restoration is highly detailed work and usually is reserved for experts in the field.

Multi-media artists and animators work primarily in motion picture and video industries, advertising, and computer systems design services. They draw by hand and use computers to create the large series of pictures that form the animated images or special effects seen in movies, television programs, and computer games. Some draw storyboards for television commercials, movies, and animated features. Storyboards present television commercials in a series of scenes similar to a comic strip and allow an advertising agency to evaluate commercials proposed by the company doing the advertising. Storyboards also serve as guides to placing actors and cameras on the television or motion picture set and to other details that need to be taken care of during the production of commercials.

Working Conditions

Many artists work in fine- or commercial-art studios located in office buildings, warehouses, or lofts. Others work in private studios in their homes. Some fine artists share studio space, where they also may exhibit their work. Studio surroundings usually are well lighted and ventilated; however, fine artists may be exposed to fumes from glue, paint, ink, and other materials and to dust or other residue from filings, splattered paint, or spilled fluids. Artists who sit at drafting tables or who use computers for extended periods may experience back pain, eyestrain, or fatigue.

Artists employed by publishing companies, advertising agencies, and design firms generally work a standard workweek. During busy periods, they may work overtime to meet deadlines. Self-employed artists can set their own hours, but may spend much time and effort selling their artwork to potential customers or clients and building a reputation.

Training, Other Qualifications, and Advancement

Postsecondary training is recommended for all artist specialties. Although formal training is not strictly required, it is very difficult to become skilled enough to make a living without some training. Many colleges and universities offer programs leading to the bachelor's or master's degree in fine arts. Courses usually include core subjects such as English, social science, and natural science in addition to art history and studio art.

Independent schools of art and design also offer postsecondary studio training in the craft, fine, and multi-media arts leading to a certificate in the specialty or to an associate's or bachelor's degree in fine arts. Typically, these programs focus more intensively on studio work than do the academic programs in a university setting. The National Association of Schools of Art and Design accredits about 250 postsecondary institutions with programs in art and design; most award a degree in art.

Formal educational programs in art also provide training in computer techniques. Computers are used widely in the visual arts, and knowledge and training in computer graphics and other visual display software are critical elements of many jobs in these fields.

Medical illustrators must have both a demonstrated artistic ability and a detailed knowledge of living organisms, surgical and medical procedures, and human and animal anatomy. A bachelor's degree combining art and premedical courses usually is required. However, most medical illustrators also choose to pursue a master's degree in medical illustration. This degree is offered in five accredited schools in the United States.

Art directors usually begin as entry-level artists in advertising, publishing, design, and motion picture production firms. Artists are promoted to art director after demonstrating artistic and leadership abilities. Some art schools offer coursework in art direction as part of postsecondary training. Depending on the scope of their responsibilities, some art directors also may pursue a degree in art administration, which teaches nonartistic skills such as project management and communication.

Those who want to teach fine arts at public elementary or secondary schools must have a teaching certificate in addition to a bachelor's degree. An advanced degree in fine arts or arts administration is necessary for management or administrative positions in government or in foundations or for teaching in colleges and universities.

Evidence of appropriate talent and skill, displayed in an artist's portfolio, is an important factor used by art directors, clients, and others in deciding whether to hire an individual or to contract out work. The portfolio is a collection of handmade, computer-generated, photographic, or printed samples of the artist's best work. Assembling a successful portfolio requires skills usually developed through postsecondary training in art or visual communications. Internships also provide excellent opportunities for artists to develop and enhance their portfolios.

Artists hired by firms often start with relatively routine work. While doing this work, however, they may observe and practice their skills on the side. Many artists freelance on a part-time basis while continuing to hold a full-time job until they are established. Others freelance part time while still in school to develop experience and to build a portfolio of published work.

Freelance artists try to develop a set of clients who regularly contract for work. Some freelance artists are widely recognized for their skill in specialties such as cartooning or children's book illustration. These artists may earn high incomes and can choose the type of work they do.

Craft and fine artists advance professionally as their work circulates and as they establish a reputation for a particular style. Many of the most successful artists continually develop new ideas, and their work often evolves over time.

Employment

Artists held about 208,000 jobs in 2004. Sixty-three percent were self-employed. Employment was distributed as follows:

Multi-media artists and animators	94,000
Art directors	71,000
Fine artists, including painters, sculptors, and illustrators	29,000
Artists and related workers, all other	8,500
Craft artists	6,100

Of the artists who were not self-employed, many worked in advertising and related services; newspaper, periodical, book, and software publishers; motion picture and video industries; specialized design services; and computer systems design and related services. Some self-employed artists offered their services to advertising agencies, design firms, publishing houses, and other businesses on a contract or freelance basis.

Job Outlook

Employment of artists and related workers is expected to grow about as fast as average for all occupations through the year 2014. However, the competition for jobs is expected to be keen for both salaried and freelance jobs in all specialties because the number of qualified workers exceeds the number of available openings. Also, because the arts attract many talented people with creative ability, the number of aspiring artists continues to grow. Employers in all industries should be able to choose from among the most qualified candidates.

Art directors work in a variety of industries, such as advertising, public relations, publishing, and design firms. Despite an expanding number of opportunities, they should experience keen competition for the available openings.

Craft and fine artists work mostly on a freelance or commission basis and may find it difficult to earn a living solely by selling their artwork. Only the most successful craft and fine artists receive major commissions for their work. Competition among artists for the privilege of being shown in galleries is expected to remain acute, and grants from sponsors such as private foundations, state and local arts councils, and the National Endowment for the Arts should remain competitive. Nonetheless, studios, galleries, and individual clients are always on the lookout for artists who display outstanding talent, creativity, and style. Among craft and fine artists, talented individuals who have developed a mastery of artistic techniques and skills will have the best job prospects.

The growth in computer graphics packages and stock art Web sites is making it easier for writers, publishers, and art directors to create their own illustrations. As the use of this technology grows, there will be fewer opportunities for illustrators. One exception is the small number of medical illustrators, who will be in greater demand to illustrate journal articles and books as medical research continues to grow.

Salaried cartoonists will have fewer job opportunities because many newspapers and magazines are increasingly relying on freelance work. In addition, many cartoonists are opting to post their work on political Web sites and online publications. As online posting of cartoons increases, many are creating animated or interactive images to satisfy readers' demands for more sophisticated cartoons.

Multi-media artists and animators should have better job opportunities than other artists, but still will experience competition. Demand for these workers will increase as consumers continue to demand more realistic video games, movie and television special effects, and 3-D animated movies. Additional job openings will arise from an increasing demand for Web site development and for computer graphics adaptation from the growing number of mobile technologies. Job opportunities for animators of lower-technology, two-dimensional television cartoons could be hampered as these jobs continue to be outsourced overseas.

Earnings

Median annual earnings of salaried art directors were $63,840 in May 2004. The middle 50 percent earned between $47,890 and $88,120. The lowest 10 percent earned less than $35,500, and the highest 10 percent earned more than $123,320. Median annual earnings were $66,900 in advertising and related services.

Median annual earnings of salaried craft artists were $23,520 in May 2004. The middle 50 percent earned between $17,950 and $32,980. The lowest 10 percent earned less than $14,740, and the highest 10 percent earned more than $44,490.

Median annual earnings of salaried fine artists, including painters, sculptors, and illustrators, were $38,060 in May 2004. The middle 50 percent earned between $25,990 and $51,730. The lowest 10 percent earned less than $17,390, and the highest 10 percent earned more than $68,860. According to the Association of Medical Illustrators, the median earnings in 2005 for salaried medical illustrators were $59,000.

Median annual earnings of salaried multi-media artists and animators were $50,360 in May 2004. The middle 50 percent earned between $37,980 and $70,730. The lowest 10 percent earned less than $29,030, and the highest 10 percent earned more than $94,260. Median annual earnings were $67,390 in motion picture and video industries and $46,810 in advertising and related services.

Earnings for self-employed artists vary widely. Some charge only a nominal fee while they gain experience and build a reputation for their work. Others, such as well-established freelance fine artists and illustrators, can earn more than salaried artists. Many, however, find it difficult to rely solely on income earned from selling paintings or other works of art. Like other self-employed workers, freelance artists must provide their own benefits.

Related Occupations

Other workers who apply art skills include architects, except landscape and naval; archivists, curators, and museum technicians; commercial and industrial designers; fashion designers; floral designers; graphic designers; interior designers; jewelers and precious stone and metal workers; landscape architects; photographers; and woodworkers. Some workers who use computers extensively, including computer software engineers and desktop publishers, may require art skills.

Sources of Additional Information

For general information about art and design and a list of accredited college-level programs, contact

▸ National Association of Schools of Art and Design, 11250 Roger Bacon Dr., Suite 21, Reston, VA 20190-5248. Internet: http://nasad.arts-accredit.org

For information on careers in the craft arts and for a list of schools and workshops, contact

▸ American Craft Council Library, 72 Spring St., 6th Floor, New York, NY 10012-4019. Internet: http://www.craftcouncil.org

For information on careers in illustration, contact

▸ Society of Illustrators, 128 E. 63rd St., New York, NY 10021-7303. Internet: http://www.societyillustrators.org

For information on careers in medical illustration, contact

▸ Association of Medical Illustrators, 245 First St., Suite 1800, Cambridge, MA 02142. Internet: http://www.ami.org

For information on workshops, scholarships, internships, and competitions for art students interested in advertising careers, contact

▸ Art Directors Club, 106 W. 29th St., New York, NY 10001. Internet: http://www.adcglobal.org

Assemblers and Fabricators

(O*NET 51-2011.01, 51-2011.02, 51-2011.03, 51-2021.00, 51-2022.00, 51-2023.00, 51-2031.00, 51-2041.01, 51-2041.02, 51-2091.00, 51-2092.00, 51-2093.00, and 51-2099.99)

Significant Points

■ More than half of all assemblers are team assemblers.

■ Work areas may be noisy, and many assemblers may have to sit or stand for long periods.

■ A high school diploma is preferred for most positions, but specialized training is required for some assembly jobs.

Nature of the Work

Assemblers and fabricators play an important role in the manufacturing process. They are responsible for putting together finished and semifinished goods—assembling the pieces of components of a product and then joining the components into a whole product. The products they produce range from entire airplanes to intricate timing devices. They fabricate and assemble household appliances, automobiles, and automobile engines and parts, as well as computers and other electronic devices.

Assemblers begin by reading detailed schematics or blueprints that show how to assemble complex machines. After determining how parts should connect, they often need to use hand or power tools to trim, shim, cut, and make other adjustments to make components fit together and align properly. Once the parts are properly aligned, they connect parts with bolts and screws or by welding or soldering pieces together. Careful quality control is important throughout the assembly process, so assemblers look for both mistakes in the assembly process and faulty components. They try to help fix problems before more defective products are produced.

Changes in technology have transformed the manufacturing and assembly process. Automated manufacturing systems now use robots, computers, programmable motion control devices, and various sensing technologies. These systems change the way in which goods are made and affect the jobs of those who make them. The more advanced assemblers must be able to work with these new technologies and be comfortable using them to produce goods.

Manufacturing techniques are evolving away from traditional assembly line systems towards "lean" manufacturing systems, which is causing the nature of assemblers' work to change. Lean manufacturing involves using teams of workers within "cells" to produce entire products or components. *Team assemblers* perform all of the assembly tasks assigned to their teams, rotating through the different tasks rather than specializing in a single task as would be done on an assembly line. The team also may decide how the work is to be assigned and how different tasks are to be performed. This worker flexibility helps companies to cover for absent workers, improves productivity, and increases their ability to respond to changes in demand by shifting labor from one product line to another. For example, if demand for a product drops, companies may reduce the number of workers involved, while individual workers perform more stages of the assembly process. Some aspects of lean production, such as rotating tasks and seeking worker input on improving the assembly process, are common to all assembly and fabrication occupations.

Although more than half of all assemblers and fabricators are classified as "team assemblers," others specialize in producing one type of product or perform the same or similar functions throughout the assembly process. These workers are classified according to the type of products they assemble or produce. *Electrical and electronic equipment assemblers* build products such as electric motors, batteries, computers, electronic control devices, and sensing equipment. *Electromechanical equipment assemblers* assemble and modify electromechanical devices such as household appliances, dynamometers, actuators, or vending machines. *Coil winders, tapers, and finishers* wind wire coil used in resistors, transformers, generators, and electric motors. *Engine and other machine assemblers* construct, assemble, or rebuild engines and turbines and machines used in almost all manufacturing industries, including agriculture; construction; mining; rolling mills; and textile, paper, and food processing. *Aircraft structure, surfaces, rigging, and systems assemblers* assemble, fit, fasten, and install parts of airplanes, space vehicles, or missiles, such as the tails and wings, landing gear, and heating and ventilation systems. *Structural metal fabricators and fitters* cut, align, and fit together structural metal parts according to detailed specifications prior to welding or riveting. *Fiberglass laminators and fabricators* create products made of fiberglass,

mainly boat decks and hulls and automobile body parts. *Timing device assemblers, adjusters, and calibrators* perform precision assembling or adjusting of timing devices within very narrow tolerances.

Involving assemblers and fabricators in product development has become more common. Designers and engineers consult manufacturing workers during the design stage to improve product reliability and manufacturing efficiency. For example, an assembler may tell a designer that the dash of a new car design will be too difficult to install quickly and consistently. The designer could then redesign the dash to make it easier to install.

Some experienced assemblers work with designers and engineers to build prototypes or test products. These assemblers read and interpret complex engineering specifications from text, drawings, and computer-aided drafting systems. They also may use a variety of tools and precision measuring instruments.

Working Conditions

The working conditions for assemblers and fabricators vary from plant to plant and from industry to industry. They may even vary within a plant. One consistent trend is increasingly improving working conditions. Many physically difficult tasks, such as manually tightening massive bolts or moving heavy parts in position, have been made much easier through the use of hydraulic and electromechanical equipment. Most factories today are generally clean, well-lit, and well-ventilated, and depending on what type of work is being performed, they may also need to be dirt- and dust-free. Electronic and electromechanical assemblers particularly must work in environments free of dust that could affect the operation of the products they build. Some assemblers may also come into contact with potentially harmful chemicals or fumes, but ventilation systems and other safety precautions normally minimize any harmful effects. Other assemblers may come in contact with oil and grease, and their working areas may be quite noisy.

Most full-time assemblers work a 40-hour week, although overtime and shift work is fairly common in some industries. Work schedules of assemblers may vary at plants with more than one shift.

Training, Other Qualifications, and Advancement

New assemblers and fabricators are normally considered entry-level employees. The ability to do accurate work at a rapid pace and to follow detailed instructions are key job requirements. A high school diploma is preferred for most positions. Following detailed assembly instructions requires basic reading skills, although many instructions rely on pictures and diagrams.

Applicants need specialized training for some assembly jobs. For example, employers may require that applicants for electrical, electronic, or aircraft assembler jobs be technical school graduates or have equivalent military training. Other positions require only on-the-job training, sometimes including employer-sponsored classroom instruction, in the broad range of assembly duties that employees may be required to perform. Many new assemblers are hired as temporary workers, often through employment services firms.

Good eyesight, with or without glasses, is required for assemblers and fabricators who work with small parts. Plants that make electrical and electronic products may test applicants for color vision, because many of their products contain many differently colored wires. Manual dexterity and the ability to carry out complex, repetitive tasks quickly and methodically also are important.

As assemblers and fabricators become more experienced, they may progress to jobs that require greater skill and be given more responsibility. Experienced assemblers may become product repairers if they have learned the many assembly operations and understand the construction of a product. These workers fix assembled articles that operators or inspectors have identified as defective. Assemblers also can advance to quality control jobs or be promoted to supervisor. Experienced assemblers and fabricators also may become members of research and development teams, working with engineers and other project designers to design, develop, and build prototypes and test new product models. In some companies, assemblers can become trainees for one of the skilled trades, such as machinist. Those with a background in math, science, and computers may advance to become programmers or operators of more highly automated production equipment.

Employment

Assemblers and fabricators held nearly 2 million jobs in 2004. They were found in almost every industry, but the vast majority, nearly 3 out of 4, were found in manufacturing. In addition, 9 percent of workers were employed by employment services firms, mostly as temporary workers. In all likelihood, many of these temporary workers were assigned to manufacturing plants. Wholesale and retail trade firms employed the next highest number of assemblers and fabricators. Team assemblers, the largest specialty, accounted for 62 percent of assembler and fabricator jobs. The distribution of employment among the various types of assemblers was as follows:

Team assemblers 1,200,000

All other assemblers and fabricators 268,000

Electrical and electronic equipment
    assemblers 221,000

Structural metal fabricators and fitters 90,000

Electromechanical equipment assemblers 52,000

Engine and other machine assemblers 46,000

Fiberglass laminators and fabricators 31,000

Coil winders, tapers, and finishers 28,000

Aircraft structure, surfaces, rigging,
    and systems assemblers 19,000

Timing device assemblers, adjusters,
    and calibrators 3,300

Within the manufacturing sector, assembly of transportation equipment, such as aircraft, autos, trucks, and buses, accounted for 19 percent of all jobs. Assembly of computers and electronic products accounted for another 11 percent of all jobs. Other industries that employ many assemblers and fabricators were machinery manufacturing (heating and air-conditioning equipment; agriculture, construction, and mining machinery; and engine, turbine, and power transmission equipment); electrical equipment, appliance, and component manufacturing (lighting, household appliances, and electrical equipment); and fabricated metal products.

The following tabulation shows wage and salary employment in manufacturing industries employing the most assemblers and fabricators in 2004.

Transportation equipment manufacturing.............387,000

Computer and electronic product manufacturing 225,000

Machinery manufacturing 193,000

Fabricated metal product manufacturing 143,000

Electrical equipment, appliance, and
    component manufacturing 139,000

Job Outlook

Employment of assemblers and fabricators is expected to grow more slowly than average through the year 2014, reflecting growth in mainly nonmanufacturing industries. The largest increase in the number of assemblers and fabricators is projected to be in the employment services industry, which supplies temporary workers to the various industries. Temporary workers are gaining in importance in the manufacturing sector and elsewhere as companies strive for a more flexible workforce to meet the fluctuations in the market. There will also be more jobs for assemblers and fabricators in the wholesale and retail sectors of the economy. As more goods come unassembled from foreign countries to save on shipping costs, it is increasingly up to wholesalers and retailers to provide assembly of products to their customers.

Within the manufacturing sector, employment of assemblers and fabricators is expected to grow mainly in motor vehicle and motor vehicle parts manufacturing, furniture manufacturing, and food processing due to increasing sales of these products. In many other manufacturing industries, assemblers and fabricators have been negatively affected by increasing automation, improving productivity, and the shift of assembly to countries with lower labor costs. In addition to new jobs stemming from growth in this occupation, many job openings will result from the need to replace workers leaving this large occupational group.

The effects of automation will be felt more among some types of assemblers and fabricators than among others. Automated manufacturing systems are expensive, and a large volume of repetitive work is required to justify their purchase. Also, where the assembly parts involved are irregular in size or location, new technology only now is beginning to make inroads. For example, much assembly in the aerospace industry is done in hard-to-reach locations—inside airplane fuselages or gear boxes, for example—which are unsuited to robots; as a result, aircraft assemblers will not be easily replaced by automated processes.

The use of team production techniques has been a success in the manufacturing sector, boosting productivity and improving the quality of goods. Workers collaborate to decide how to best perform assembly tasks. Team assemblers are often consulted during the design phase of production to make sure that the product is easy to assemble. Through continued efforts to improve the assembly process, most manufacturing companies have significantly reduced the amount of labor needed to assemble a product. By boosting productivity, companies are better able to compete with low-wage companies. Thus, while the number of assemblers overall will decline in manufacturing, the number of team assemblers will remain stable.

Many producers have sent their assembly functions to countries where labor costs are lower. Decisions by American corporations to move assembly to other nations should limit employment growth for assemblers in some industries, but a free trade environment also may lead to growth in the export of goods assembled in the United States.

Earnings

Earnings vary by industry, geographic region, skill, educational level, and complexity of the machinery operated. Median hourly earnings of team assemblers were $11.42 in May 2004. The middle 50 percent earned between $9.12 and $14.60. The lowest 10 percent earned less than $7.56, and the highest 10 percent earned $18.80. Median hourly earnings in the manufacturing industries employing the largest numbers of team assemblers in May 2004 are shown here:

Motor vehicle manufacturing	$22.45
Motor vehicle parts manufacturing	12.91
Other wood product manufacturing	10.90
Plastics product manufacturing	10.54
Employment services	8.66

Median hourly earnings of electrical and electronic equipment assemblers were $11.68 in May 2004. The middle 50 percent earned between $9.54 and $14.84. The lowest 10 percent earned less than $8.01, and the highest 10 percent earned more than $18.64. Median hourly earnings in the manufacturing industries employing the largest numbers of electrical and electronic equipment assemblers in May 2004 are shown here:

Computer and peripheral equipment manufacturing	$12.80
Navigational, measuring, electromedical, and control instruments manufacturing	12.61
Electrical equipment manufacturing	12.55
Communications equipment manufacturing	11.61
Semiconductor and other electronic component manufacturing	11.02

In May 2004, other assemblers and fabricators had the following median hourly earnings:

Aircraft structure, surfaces, rigging, and systems assemblers	$17.79
Engine and other machine assemblers	16.73
Structural metal fabricators and fitters	14.34
Timing device assemblers, adjusters, and calibrators	13.76
Electromechanical equipment assemblers	12.71
Coil winders, tapers, and finishers	12.24
Fiberglass laminators and fabricators	12.18
Assemblers and fabricators, all other	11.90

Many assemblers and fabricators are members of labor unions. These unions include the International Association of Machinists and Aerospace Workers; the United Electrical, Radio, and Machine Workers of America; the United Automobile, Aerospace, and Agricultural Implement Workers of America; the International Brotherhood of Electrical Workers; and the United Steelworkers of America.

Related Occupations

Other occupations that involve operating machines and tools and assembling products include welding, soldering, and brazing workers and machine setters, operators, and tenders—metal and plastic. Assemblers and fabricators also are responsible for some quality control and product testing, as is the case for inspectors, testers, sorters, samplers, and weighers.

Sources of Additional Information

Information about employment opportunities for assemblers is available from local offices of the state employment service and from locals of the unions mentioned earlier.

Automotive Body and Related Repairers

(O*NET 49-3021.00 and 49-3022.00)

Significant Points

- To become a fully skilled automotive body repairer, formal training followed by on-the-job instruction is recommended because repair of newer automobiles requires more advanced skills to fix their new technologies and new body materials.

- Repairers need good reading ability and basic mathematics and computer skills in order to follow instructions and diagrams in print and computer-based technical manuals.

Nature of the Work

While running errands or driving to and from work, we sometimes observe traffic accidents. Most of the vehicle damage resulting from these collisions can be repaired and the vehicle refinished to once again look and drive like new. Automotive body repairers, also often called collision repair technicians, straighten bent bodies, remove dents, and replace crumpled parts that cannot be fixed. They repair all types of vehicles, and although some work on large trucks, buses, or tractor-trailers, most work on cars and small trucks.

Automotive body repairers use special equipment to restore damaged metal frames and body sections. Repairers chain or clamp frames and sections to alignment machines that use hydraulic pressure to align damaged components. "Unibody" vehicles—designs built without frames—must be restored to precise factory specifications for the vehicle to operate correctly. To do so, repairers use benchmark systems to make accurate measurements of how much each section is out of alignment and hydraulic machinery to return the vehicle to its original shape.

Body repairers remove badly damaged sections of body panels with a pneumatic metal-cutting gun or by other means and then weld in replacement sections. Repairers pull out less-serious dents with a hydraulic jack or hand-prying bar or knock them out with hand tools or pneumatic hammers. They smooth out small dents and creases in the metal by holding a small anvil against one side of the damaged area while hammering the opposite side. Repairers also remove very small pits and dimples with pick hammers and punches in a process called metal finishing. Body repairers use plastic or solder to fill small dents that cannot be worked out of plastic or metal panels. On metal panels, they file or grind the hardened filler to the original shape and clean the surface with a media blaster before repainting the damaged portion of the vehicle.

Body repairers also repair or replace the plastic body parts that are increasingly being used on new-model vehicles. They remove damaged panels and identify the type and properties of the plastic used on the vehicle. With most types of plastic, repairers can apply heat from a hot-air welding gun or by immersion in hot water and press the softened panel back into its original shape by hand. They replace plastic parts that are badly damaged or very difficult to repair. A few body repairers specialize in repairing fiberglass car bodies.

The advent of assembly-line repairs in large shops enables the establishment to move away from the one-vehicle, one-repairer method to a team approach that allows body repairers to specialize in one type of repair, such as straightening frames, repairing doors and fenders, or painting and refinishing. In most shops, automotive painters do the painting. However, in small shops, workers often do both body repairing and painting. Some body repairers specialize in installing and repairing glass in automobiles and other vehicles. *Automotive glass installers and repairers* remove broken, cracked, or pitted windshields and window glass. Glass installers apply a moisture-proofing compound along the edges of the glass, place the glass in the vehicle, and install rubber strips around the sides of the windshield or window to make it secure and weatherproof.

Body repair work has variety and challenges: Each damaged vehicle presents a different problem. Using their broad knowledge of automotive construction and repair techniques, repairers must develop appropriate methods for each job. They usually work alone, with only general directions from supervisors. In some shops, helpers or apprentices assist experienced repairers.

Working Conditions

Most automotive body repairers work a standard 40-hour week, although some, including the self-employed, work more than 40 hours a week. Repairers work indoors in body shops that are noisy with the clatters of hammers against metal and the whine of power tools. Most shops are well ventilated in order to disperse dust and paint fumes. Body repairers often work in awkward or cramped positions, and much of their work is strenuous and dirty. Hazards include cuts from sharp metal edges, burns from torches and heated metal, injuries from power tools, and fumes from paint. However, serious accidents usually are avoided when the shop is kept clean and orderly and safety practices are observed.

Training, Other Qualifications, and Advancement

Automotive technology is rapidly increasing in sophistication, and most training authorities strongly recommend that persons seeking automotive body repair and related jobs complete a formal training program in automotive body repair or refinishing. Programs are offered in high school or in postsecondary vocational schools and community colleges, but these programs provide only a portion of the training needed to become fully skilled. Most new repairers receive primarily on-the-job training, supplemented with short-term training sessions given by vehicle, parts, and equipment manufacturers, when available. Training is necessary because advances in technology have greatly changed the structure, components, and materials used in automobiles. As a result, proficiency in new repair techniques is necessary. For example, the bodies of automobiles are usually a combination of materials—traditional steel, aluminum, and a growing variety of metal alloys and plastics. Each of these materials or composites requires the use of somewhat different techniques to reshape parts and smooth out dents and small pits.

Fully skilled automotive body repairers must have good reading ability and basic mathematics and computer skills. Restoring unibody automobiles to their original form requires body repairers to follow instructions and diagrams in technical manuals in order to make precise three-dimensional measurements of the position of one body section relative to another.

New repairers begin by assisting experienced body repairers in tasks such as removing damaged parts, sanding body panels, and installing repaired parts. Novices learn to remove small dents and to make other minor repairs. They then progress to more difficult tasks, such as straightening body parts and returning them to their correct alignment. Generally, to become skilled in all aspects of body repair requires 3 to 4 years of on-the-job training.

Certification by the National Institute for Automotive Service Excellence (ASE), although voluntary, is the recognized industry credential for automotive body repairers. Repairers may take from one to four ASE Master Collision Repair and Refinish Exams. Repairers who pass at least one exam and have 2 years of hands-on work experience earn ASE certification. The completion of a postsecondary program in automotive body repair may be substituted for 1 year of work experience. Those who pass all four exams become ASE Master Collision Repair and Refinish Technicians. Automotive body repairers must retake the examination at least every 5 years to retain their certification. While the ASE designations are the most widely recognized, many vehicle manufacturers and paint manufacturers also have product certification programs available for body repairers.

Continuing education is required throughout a career in automotive body repair. Automotive parts, body materials, and electronics continue to change and to become more complex and technologically advanced. To keep up with the technological advances, repairers must continue to gain new skills, read technical manuals, and attend seminars and classes. Many companies within the automotive body repair industry provide ongoing training for workers.

As beginners increase their skills, learn new techniques, and complete work more rapidly, their pay increases. An experienced automotive body repairer with managerial ability may advance to shop supervisor. Some workers even open their own body repair shops. Others become automobile damage appraisers for insurance companies.

Employment

Automotive body and related repairers held about 223,000 jobs in 2004; about 1 in 10 specialized in automotive glass installation and repair. Most repairers worked for automotive repair and maintenance shops or automobile dealers. Others worked for organizations that maintain their own motor vehicles, such as trucking companies. A small number worked for wholesalers of motor vehicles, parts, and supplies. More than 1 automotive body repairer in 5 was self-employed, more than double the proportion for all installation, maintenance, and repair occupations.

Job Outlook

Employment of automotive body repairers is expected to grow as fast as the average for all occupations through the year 2014. The need to replace experienced repairers who transfer to other occupations or who retire or stop working for other reasons will account for the majority of job openings. Opportunities will be best for persons with formal training in automotive body repair and refinishing. Those without formal training in automotive body refinishing or collision repair will face competition for these jobs.

Demand for qualified body repairers will increase as the number of motor vehicles in operation continues to grow in line with the nation's population. With each rise in the number of motor vehicles in use, the number of vehicles damaged in accidents also will grow. New automobile designs increasingly have body parts made of steel alloys, aluminum, and plastics—materials that are more difficult to work with than traditional steel body parts. In addition, new automotive designs of lighter weight are prone to greater collision damage than are older, heavier designs, so more time is consumed in repair.

However, increasing demand due to growth in the number of vehicles in operation will be somewhat tempered by improvements in the quality of vehicles and technological innovations that enhance safety and reduce the likelihood of accidents. Also, more body parts are simply being replaced rather than repaired. Larger shops also are instituting productivity enhancements, such as employing a team approach to repairs to decrease repair time and expand their volume of work. In addition, demand for automotive body repair services will be constrained as more vehicles are declared a total loss after accidents. In many such cases, the vehicles are not repaired because of the high cost of replacing the increasingly complex parts and electronic components and fixing the extensive damage that results when airbags deploy. Employment growth will continue to be concentrated in automotive body, paint, interior, and glass repair shops. Automobile dealers will employ a smaller portion of this occupation as the equipment needed for collision repair becomes more specialized and expensive to operate and maintain.

Experienced body repairers are rarely laid off during a general slowdown in the economy. Automotive repair business is not very sensitive to changes in economic conditions because major body damage must be repaired if a vehicle is to be restored to safe operating condition. However, repair of minor dents and crumpled fenders often can be deferred when drivers' budgets become tight.

Earnings

Median hourly earnings of automotive body and related repairers, including incentive pay, were $16.68 in May 2004. The middle 50 percent earned between $12.55 and $22.04 an hour. The lowest 10 percent earned less than $9.42, and the highest 10 percent earned more than $28.45 an hour. In May 2004, median hourly earnings of automotive body and related repairers were $17.73 in automobile dealers and $16.44 in automotive repair and maintenance.

Median hourly earnings of automotive glass installers and repairers, including incentive pay, were $13.45 in May 2004. The middle 50 percent earned between $10.36 and $17.04 an hour. The lowest 10 percent earned less than $8.53, and the highest 10 percent earned more than $20.63 an hour. Median hourly earnings in automotive repair and maintenance shops, the industry employing most automotive glass installers and repairers, were $13.43.

The majority of body repairers employed by independent repair shops and automotive dealers are paid on an incentive basis. Under this method, body repairers are paid a predetermined amount for various tasks, and earnings depend on the amount of work assigned to the repairer and how fast it is completed. Employers frequently guarantee workers a minimum weekly salary. Body repairers who work for trucking companies, bus lines, and other organizations that maintain their own vehicles usually receive an hourly wage.

Helpers and trainees typically earn from 30 percent to 60 percent of the earnings of skilled workers. Helpers and trainees usually receive an hourly rate until they are skilled enough to be paid on an incentive basis.

Related Occupations

Repairing damaged motor vehicles often involves working on mechanical components as well as vehicle bodies. Automotive body repairers often work closely with individuals in several related occupations, including automotive service technicians and mechanics; diesel service technicians and mechanics; auto damage insurance appraisers; and painting and coating workers, except construction and maintenance.

Sources of Additional Information

Additional details about work opportunities may be obtained from automotive body repair shops, automobile dealers, or local offices of your state employment service. State employment service offices also are a source of information about training programs.

For general information about automotive body repairer careers, contact any of the following sources:

▸ Automotive Service Association, P.O. Box 929, Bedford, TX 76095-0929. Internet: http://www.asashop.org

▸ National Automobile Dealers Association, 8400 Westpark Dr., McLean, VA 22102. Internet: http://www.nada.org

▸ Inter-Industry Conference On Auto Collision Repair Education Foundation (I-CAR), 5125 Trillium Blvd., Hoffman Estates, IL 60192. Telephone (toll free): 800-422-7872.

▸ Automotive Jobs Today, 8400 Westpark Drive, MS #2, McLean, VA 22102. Internet: http://www.autojobstoday.org

For general information about careers in automotive glass installation and repair, contact

National Glass Association. 8200 Greensboro Dr., Suite 302, McLean, VA 22102-3881. Internet: http://www.glass.org

For information on how to become a certified automotive body repairer, write to

▶ National Institute for Automotive Service Excellence (ASE), 101 Blue Seal Dr. SE, Suite 101, Leesburg, VA 20175. Internet: http://www.asecert.org

For a directory of certified automotive body repairer programs, contact

▶ National Automotive Technician Education Foundation, 101 Blue Seal Dr. SE, Suite 101, Leesburg, VA 20175. Internet: http://www.natef.org

For a directory of accredited private trade and technical schools that offer training programs in automotive body repair, contact

▶ Accrediting Commission of Career Schools and Colleges of Technology, 2101 Wilson Blvd., Suite 302, Arlington, VA 22201. Internet: http://www.accsct.org

Automotive Service Technicians and Mechanics

(O*NET 49-3023.01 and 49-3023.02)

Significant Points

- Formal automotive technician training is the best preparation for these challenging technology-based jobs.

- Opportunities should be very good for automotive service technicians and mechanics with diagnostic and problem-solving skills, knowledge of electronics and mathematics, and mechanical aptitude.

- Automotive service technicians and mechanics must continually adapt to changing technology and repair techniques as vehicle components and systems become increasingly sophisticated.

Nature of the Work

Anyone whose car or light truck has broken down knows the importance of the jobs of automotive service technicians and mechanics. The ability to diagnose the source of a problem quickly and accurately requires good reasoning ability and a thorough knowledge of automobiles. Many technicians consider diagnosing hard-to-find troubles one of their most challenging and satisfying duties.

The work of automotive service technicians and mechanics has evolved from mechanical repair to a high-technology job. As a result, these workers are now usually called "technicians" in automotive services and the term "mechanic" is falling into disuse. Today, integrated electronic systems and complex computers run vehicles and measure their performance while on the road. Technicians must have an increasingly broad base of knowledge about how vehicles' complex components work and interact, as well as the ability to work with electronic diagnostic equipment and computer-based technical reference materials.

Automotive service technicians use their high-tech skills to inspect, maintain, and repair automobiles and light trucks that run on gasoline; ethanol; and other alternative fuels, such as electricity. The increasing sophistication of automotive technology now requires workers who can use computerized shop equipment and work with electronic components while maintaining their skills with traditional hand tools. (Service technicians who work on diesel-powered trucks, buses, and equipment are discussed in the description of diesel service technicians and mechanics. Motorcycle technicians—who repair and service motorcycles, motor scooters, mopeds, and, occasionally, small all-terrain vehicles—are discussed in the description of small engine mechanics.)

When mechanical or electrical troubles occur, technicians first get a description of the symptoms from the owner or, if they work in a large shop, from the repair service estimator or service advisor who wrote the repair order. To locate the problem, technicians use a diagnostic approach. First, they test to see whether components and systems are proper and secure. Then, they isolate the components or systems that could not logically be the cause of the problem. For example, if an air-conditioner malfunctions, the technician's diagnostic approach can pinpoint a problem as simple as a low coolant level or as complex as a bad drive-train connection that has shorted out the air conditioner. Technicians may have to test-drive the vehicle or use a variety of testing equipment, such as onboard and hand-held diagnostic computers or compression gauges, to identify the source of the problem. These tests may indicate whether a component is salvageable or whether a new one is required to get the vehicle back in working order.

During routine service inspections, technicians test and lubricate engines and other major components. In some cases, the technician may repair or replace worn parts before they cause breakdowns that could damage critical components of the vehicle. Technicians usually follow a checklist to ensure that they examine every critical part. Belts, hoses, plugs, brake and fuel systems, and other potentially troublesome items are among those closely watched.

Service technicians use a variety of tools in their work—power tools, such as pneumatic wrenches to remove bolts quickly; machine tools like lathes and grinding machines to rebuild brakes; welding and flame-cutting equipment to remove and repair exhaust systems; and jacks and hoists to lift cars and engines. They also use common hand tools, such as screwdrivers, pliers, and wrenches, to work on small parts and in hard-to-reach places.

Computers also have become commonplace in modern repair shops. Service technicians compare the readouts from computerized diagnostic testing devices with the benchmarked standards given by the manufacturer of the components being tested. Deviations outside of acceptable levels are an indication to the technician that further attention to an area is necessary. A shop's computerized system provides automatic updates to technical manuals and unlimited access to manufacturers' service information, technical service bulletins, and other databases that allow technicians to keep current on problem spots and to learn new procedures.

Automotive service technicians in large shops have increasingly become specialized. For example, *transmission technicians and rebuilders* work on gear trains, couplings, hydraulic pumps, and other parts of transmissions. Extensive knowledge of computer controls, the ability to diagnose electrical and hydraulic problems, and other specialized skills are needed to work on these complex components, which employ some of the most sophisticated technology used in vehicles. *Tuneup technicians* adjust the ignition timing and valves and adjust or replace spark plugs and other parts to ensure efficient engine performance. They often use electronic testing equipment to isolate and adjust malfunctions in fuel, ignition, and emissions control systems.

Automotive air-conditioning repairers install and repair air conditioners and service their components, such as compressors, condensers, and controls. These workers require special training in federal and state regulations governing the handling and disposal of refrigerants. *Front-end mechanics* align and balance wheels and repair steering mechanisms and suspension systems. They frequently use special alignment equipment and wheel-balancing machines. *Brake repairers* adjust brakes, replace brake linings and pads, and make other repairs on brake systems. Some technicians specialize in both brake and front-end work. Even though electronics and electronic systems in automobiles were a specialty in the past, electronics are now so common that it is essential for all types of service technicians to be familiar with at least the basic principles of electronics.

Working Conditions

Nearly half of automotive service technicians work more than 40 hours a week. Some may also work evenings and weekends to satisfy customer service needs. Generally, service technicians work indoors in well-ventilated and -lighted repair shops. However, some shops are drafty and noisy. Although some problems can be fixed with simple computerized adjustments, technicians frequently work with dirty and greasy parts and in awkward positions. They often lift heavy parts and tools. Minor cuts, burns, and bruises are common, but technicians can usually avoid serious accidents if the shop is kept clean and orderly and safety practices are observed.

Training, Other Qualifications, and Advancement

Automotive technology is rapidly increasing in sophistication, and most training authorities strongly recommend that persons seeking automotive service technician and mechanic jobs complete a formal training program in high school or in a postsecondary vocational school or community college. However, some service technicians still learn the trade solely by assisting and learning from experienced workers. Courses in automotive repair, electronics, physics, chemistry, English, computers, and mathematics provide a good educational background for a career as a service technician.

High school programs, while an asset, vary greatly in scope. Some aim to equip graduates with enough skills to get a job as a technician's helper or trainee technician. Other programs offer only an introduction to automotive technology and service for the future consumer or hobbyist. Some of the more extensive programs participate in Automotive Youth Education Service (AYES), which has about 500 participating schools and more than 4000 participating dealers. Students who complete these programs receive an AYES certification and upon high school graduation are better prepared to enter entry-level technician positions or to advance their technical education.

Postsecondary automotive technician training programs vary greatly in format, but normally provide intensive career preparation through a combination of classroom instruction and hands-on practice. Some trade and technical school programs provide concentrated training for 6 months to a year, depending on how many hours the student attends each week, and award a certificate. Community college programs normally award an associate degree or certificate and usually spread the training over 2 years by supplementing the automotive training with instruction in English, basic mathematics, computers, and other subjects. Some students earn repair certificates in one particular skill and opt to leave the program to begin their career before graduation. Recently, some programs have added to their curriculums training on employability skills such as customer service and stress management. Employers find that these skills help technicians handle the additional responsibilities of dealing with the customers and parts vendors.

The various automobile manufacturers and their participating dealers sponsor 2-year associate degree programs at postsecondary schools across the nation. The Accrediting Commission of Career Schools and Colleges of Technology (ACCSCT) currently certifies a number of automotive and diesel technology schools. Schools update their curriculums frequently to reflect changing technology and equipment. Students in these programs typically spend alternate 6- to 12-week periods attending classes full time and working full time in the service departments of sponsoring dealers. At these dealerships, students get practical experience while assigned to an experienced worker who provides hands-on instruction and timesaving tips.

The ASE certification is a nationally recognized standard for programs offered by high schools, postsecondary trade schools, technical institutes, and community colleges that train automobile service technicians. Some automotive manufacturers provide ASE-certified instruction programs with service equipment and current-model cars on which students practice new skills and learn the latest automotive technology. While ASE certification is voluntary, it does signify that the program meets uniform standards for instructional facilities, equipment, staff credentials, and curriculum. To ensure that programs keep up with ever-changing technology, repair techniques, and ASE standards, the certified programs are subjected to periodic compliance reviews and mandatory recertification, as are the ASE standards themselves. In 2004, about 2000 high school and postsecondary automotive service technician training programs had been certified by ASE.

For trainee automotive service technician jobs, employers look for people with strong communication and analytical skills. Technicians need good reading, mathematics, and computer skills to study technical manuals and to keep abreast of new technology and learn new service and repair procedures and specifications. Trainees also must possess mechanical aptitude and knowledge of how automobiles work. Most employers regard the successful completion of a vocational training program in automotive service technology as the best preparation for trainee positions. Experience working on motor vehicles in the Armed Forces or as a hobby also is valuable. Because of the complexity of new vehicles, a growing number of employers require completion of high school and additional postsecondary training.

Many new cars have several onboard computers that operate everything from the engine to the radio. Engine controls and dashboard instruments were among the first components to use electronics, but today most automotive systems, such as braking, transmission, and steering systems, are controlled primarily by computers and electronic components. Some of the more advanced vehicles have global positioning systems, Internet access, and other high-tech features integrated into the functions of the vehicle. The training in electronics is vital because electrical components, or a series of related components, account for nearly all malfunctions in modern vehicles.

In addition to electronics and computers, automotive service technicians will have to learn and understand the science behind the alternate-fuel vehicles that have begun to enter the market. The fuel for these vehicles will come from the dehydrogenization of water, electric fuel cells, natural gas, solar power, and other non-petroleum-based sources. Hybrid vehicles, for example, use the energy from braking to recharge batteries that power an electric motor, which supplements a gasoline engine. As vehicles with these new technologies become more common, technicians will need additional training to learn the science and engineering that makes them possible. Currently, the manufacturers of these alternate-fuel vehicles are providing the necessary training. However, as the warrantees begin to expire, technicians in all industries will need to be trained to service these vehicles. As the number of these automobiles on the road increases, some technicians will likely specialize in the service and repair of these vehicles.

Those new to automotive service usually start as trainee technicians, technicians' helpers, or lubrication workers and gradually acquire and practice their skills by working with experienced mechanics and technicians. With a few months' experience, beginners perform many routine service tasks and make simple repairs. While some graduates of postsecondary automotive training programs are often able to earn promotion to the journey level after only a few months on the job, it typically takes 2 to 5 years of experience to become a journey-level service technician, who is expected to quickly perform the more difficult types of routine service and repairs. An additional 1 to 2 years of experience familiarizes technicians with all types of repairs. Complex specialties, such as transmission repair, require another year or two of training and experience. In contrast, brake specialists may learn their jobs in considerably less time because they do not need a complete knowledge of automotive repair.

At work, the most important possessions of technicians are their hand tools. Technicians usually provide their own tools, and many experienced workers have thousands of dollars invested in them. Employers typically furnish expensive power tools, engine analyzers, and other diagnostic equipment, but technicians accumulate hand tools with experience. Some formal training programs have alliances with tool manufacturers that help entry-level technicians accumulate tools during their training period.

Employers increasingly send experienced automotive service technicians to manufacturer training centers to learn to repair new models or to receive special training in the repair of components such as electronic fuel injection or air conditioners. Motor vehicle dealers and other automotive service providers also may send promising beginners to manufacturer-sponsored technician training programs; most employers periodically send experienced technicians to manufacturer-sponsored technician training programs for additional training to maintain or upgrade employees' skills and thus increase the employees' value to the employer. Factory representatives also visit many shops to conduct short training sessions.

Voluntary certification by the National Institute for Automotive Service Excellence (ASE) has become a standard credential for automotive service technicians. Certification is available in 1 or more of 8 different areas of automotive service, such as electrical systems, engine repair, brake systems, suspension and steering, and heating and air conditioning. For certification in each area, technicians must have at least 2 years of experience and pass the examination. Completion of an automotive training program in high school, vocational or trade school, or community or junior college may be substituted for 1 year of experience. For ASE certification as a master automobile technician, technicians must be certified in all eight areas. Technicians must retake each examination once every 5 years to maintain their certifications.

Experienced technicians who have leadership ability sometimes advance to shop supervisor or service manager. Those who work well with customers may become automotive repair service estimators. Some with sufficient funds open independent repair shops.

Employment

Automotive service technicians and mechanics held about 803,000 jobs in 2004. The majority worked for automotive repair and maintenance shops; automobile dealers; and retailers and wholesalers of automotive parts, accessories, and supplies. Others found employment in gasoline stations; home and auto supply stores; automotive equipment rental and leasing companies; federal, state, and local governments; and other organizations. More than 16 percent of service technicians were self-employed, more than twice the proportion for all installation, maintenance, and repair occupations.

Job Outlook

Job opportunities in this occupation are expected to be very good for persons who complete automotive training programs in high school, vocational and technical schools, or community colleges, as employers report difficulty in finding workers with the right skills. Persons with good diagnostic and problem-solving abilities, and whose training includes basic electronics and computer courses, should have the best opportunities. For well-prepared people with a technical background, automotive service technician careers offer an excellent opportunity for good pay and the satisfaction of highly skilled work with vehicles incorporating the latest in advanced technology. However, persons without formal automotive training are likely to face competition for entry-level jobs.

Employment of automotive service technicians and mechanics is expected to increase as fast as the average through the year 2014. Over the 2004–2014 period, demand for technicians will grow as the number of vehicles in operation increases, reflecting continued growth in the number of multi-car families. Growth in demand will be offset somewhat by slowing population growth and the continuing increase in the quality and durability of automobiles, which will require less frequent service. Additional job openings will be due to the need to replace a growing number of retiring technicians, who tend to be the most experienced workers.

Most persons who enter the occupation can expect steady work, even through downturns in the economy. While car owners may postpone maintenance and repair on their vehicles when their budgets become strained, and employers of automotive technicians may cutback hiring new workers, changes in economic conditions generally have minor effects on the automotive service and repair business.

Employment growth will continue to be concentrated in automobile dealerships and independent automotive repair shops. Many new jobs also will be created in small retail operations that offer after-warranty repairs, such as oil changes, brake repair, air-conditioner service, and other minor repairs generally taking less than 4 hours to complete. Employment of automotive service technicians and mechanics in gasoline service stations will continue to decline as fewer stations offer repair services.

Earnings

Median hourly earnings of automotive service technicians and mechanics, including commission, were $15.60 in May 2004. The middle 50 percent earned between $11.31 and $20.75 per hour. The lowest 10 percent earned less than $8.70, and the highest 10 percent earned more than $26.22 per hour. Median annual earnings in the industries employing the largest numbers of service technicians in May 2004 were as follows:

Local government	$38,160
Automobile dealers	38,060
Automotive repair and maintenance	28,810
Gasoline stations	28,030
Automotive parts, accessories, and tire stores	27,180

Many experienced technicians employed by automobile dealers and independent repair shops receive a commission related to the labor cost charged to the customer. Under this method, weekly earnings depend on the amount of work completed. Employers frequently guarantee commissioned technicians a minimum weekly salary.

Some automotive service technicians are members of labor unions such as the International Association of Machinists and Aerospace Workers; the International Union, United Automobile, Aerospace, and Agricultural Implement Workers of America; the Sheet Metal Workers' International Association; and the International Brotherhood of Teamsters.

Related Occupations

Other workers who repair and service motor vehicles include automotive body and related repairers, diesel service technicians and mechanics, and small engine mechanics.

Sources of Additional Information

For more details about work opportunities, contact local automobile dealers and repair shops or local offices of the state employment service. The state employment service also may have information about training programs.

A list of certified automotive service technician training programs can be obtained from

▶ National Automotive Technicians Education Foundation, 101 Blue Seal Dr. SE, Suite 101, Leesburg, VA 20175. Internet: http://www.natef.org

For a directory of accredited private trade and technical schools that offer programs in automotive service technician training, contact

▶ Accrediting Commission of Career Schools and Colleges of Technology, 2101 Wilson Blvd., Suite 302, Arlington, VA 22201. Internet: http://www.accsct.org

Information on automobile manufacturer-sponsored programs in automotive service technology can be obtained from

▶ Automotive Youth Educational Systems (AYES), 100 W. Big Beaver, Suite 300, Troy, MI 48084. Internet: http://www.ayes.org

Information on how to become a certified automotive service technician is available from

▶ National Institute for Automotive Service Excellence (ASE), 101 Blue Seal Dr. SE, Suite 101, Leesburg, VA 20175. Internet: http://www.asecert.org

For general information about a career as an automotive service technician, contact

▶ National Automobile Dealers Association, 8400 Westpark Dr., McLean, VA 22102. Internet: http://www.nada.org

▶ Automotive Retailing Today, 8400 Westpark Dr., MS #2, McLean, VA 22102. Internet: http://www.autoretailing.org

▶ Automotive Jobs Today, 8400 Westpark Dr., MS #2, McLean, VA 22102. Internet: http://www.autojobstoday.org

▶ Career Voyages, U.S. Department of Labor, 200 Constitution Ave. NW, Washington DC 20210. Internet: http://www.careervoyages.gov/automotive-main.cfm

Barbers, Cosmetologists, and Other Personal Appearance Workers

(O*NET 39-5011.00, 39-5012.00, 39-5091.00, 39-5092.00, 39-5093.00, and 39-5094.00)

Significant Points

■ Job opportunities generally should be good, but competition is expected for jobs and clients at higher-paying salons; opportunities will be best for those licensed to provide a broad range of services.

■ A state license is required for barbers, cosmetologists, and most other personal appearance workers, with the exception of shampooers; qualifications vary by state.

■ About 48 percent of workers are self-employed; many also work flexible schedules.

Nature of the Work

Barbers and cosmetologists, also called *hairdressers* and *hairstylists*, provide hair care services to enhance the appearance of consumers. Other personal appearance workers, such as *manicurists and pedicurists*, *shampooers*, and *skin care specialists* provide specialized services that help clients look and feel their best.

Barbers cut, trim, shampoo, and style hair. They also fit hairpieces and offer scalp treatments and facial shaving. In many states, barbers are licensed to color, bleach, or highlight hair and to offer permanent-wave services. Many barbers also provide skin care and nail treatments.

Hairdressers, hairstylists, and cosmetologists offer beauty services, such as shampooing, cutting, coloring, and styling hair. They may advise clients on how to care for their hair, how to straighten their hair or give it a permanent wave, or how to lighten or darken their hair color. In addition, cosmetologists may be trained to give manicures, pedicures, and scalp and facial treatments; provide makeup analysis; and clean and style wigs and hairpieces.

A number of workers offer specialized services. *Manicurists and pedicurists*, called *nail technicians* in some states, work exclusively on nails and provide manicures, pedicures, coloring, and nail extensions to clients. Another group of specialists is *skin care specialists*, or *estheticians*, who cleanse and beautify the skin by giving facials, full-body treatments, and head and neck massages and by removing hair through waxing. *Electrologists* use an electrolysis machine to remove hair. Finally, in some larger salons, *shampooers* specialize in shampooing and conditioning hair.

In addition to working with clients, personal appearance workers are expected to maintain clean work areas and sanitize all their work instruments. They may make appointments and keep records of hair color and permanent-wave formulas used by their regular clients. A growing number actively sell hair care products and other cosmetic supplies. Barbers, cosmetologists, and other personal appearance workers who operate their own salons have managerial duties that may include hiring, supervising, and firing workers, as well as keeping business and inventory records, ordering supplies, and arranging for advertising.

Working Conditions

Barbers, cosmetologists, and other personal appearance workers usually work in clean, pleasant surroundings with good lighting and ventilation. Good health and stamina are important because these workers are on their feet for most of their shift. Prolonged exposure to some hair and nail chemicals may cause irritation, so protective clothing, such as plastic gloves or aprons, may be worn.

Most full-time barbers, cosmetologists, and other personal appearance workers put in a 40-hour week, but longer hours are common, especially among self-employed workers. Work schedules may include evenings and weekends, the times when beauty salons and barbershops are busiest. Barbers and cosmetologists generally work on weekends and during lunch and evening hours; as a result, they may arrange to take breaks during less busy times. About 32 percent of cosmetologists and 17 percent of barbers work part time, and 14 percent of cosmetologists and 17 percent of barbers have variable schedules.

Training, Other Qualifications, and Advancement

All states require barbers, cosmetologists, and most other personal appearance workers, with the exception of shampooers, to be licensed; however, qualifications for a license vary by state. Gener-

ally, a person must have graduated from a state-licensed barber or cosmetology school and be at least 16 years old. A few states require applicants to pass a physical examination. Some states require graduation from high school, while others require as little as an eighth-grade education. In a few states, the completion of an apprenticeship can substitute for graduation from a school, but very few barbers or cosmetologists learn their skills in this way. Applicants for a license usually are required to pass a written test and demonstrate an ability to perform basic barbering or cosmetology services.

Some states have reciprocity agreements that allow licensed barbers and cosmetologists to obtain a license in a different state without additional formal training. Such agreements are uncommon, however, and most states do not recognize training or licenses obtained from a different state. Consequently, persons who wish to work in a particular state should review the laws of that state before entering a training program.

Public and private vocational schools offer daytime or evening classes in barbering and cosmetology. Full-time programs in barbering and cosmetology usually last 9 to 24 months, but training for manicurists and pedicurists, skin care specialists, and electrologists requires significantly less time. An apprenticeship program can last from 1 to 3 years. Shampooers generally do not need formal training or a license. Formal training programs include classroom study, demonstrations, and practical work. Students study the basic services—cutting and styling hair, chemically treating hair, shaving customers, and giving hair and scalp treatments—and, under supervision, practice on customers in school "clinics." Students attend lectures on the use and care of instruments, sanitation and hygiene, chemistry, anatomy, physiology, and the recognition of simple skin ailments. Instruction also is provided in communication, sales, and general business practices. Experienced barbers and cosmetologists may take advanced courses in hairstyling, coloring, the sale and service of wigs and hairpieces, and sales and marketing.

After graduating from a training program, students can take a state licensing examination, which consists of a written test and, in some cases, a practical test of styling skills based on established performance criteria. A few states include an oral examination in which applicants are asked to explain the procedures they are following while taking the practical test. In many states, cosmetology training may be credited toward a barbering license, and vice versa. A few states combine the two licenses into one hairstyling license. Many states require separate licensing examinations for manicurists, pedicurists, and skin care specialists.

For many barbers, cosmetologists, and other personal appearance workers, formal training and a license are only the first steps in a career that requires years of continuing education. Personal appearance workers must keep abreast of the latest fashions and beauty techniques as hairstyles change, new products are developed, and services expand to meet clients' needs. They attend training at salons, cosmetology schools, or industry trade shows. Through workshops and demonstrations of the latest techniques, industry representatives introduce cosmetologists to a wide range of products and services. As retail sales become an increasingly important part of salons' revenue, the ability to be an effective salesperson becomes ever more vital for salon workers.

Successful personal appearance workers should have an understanding of fashion, art, and technical design. They should enjoy working with the public and be willing and able to follow clients' instructions. Communication, image, and attitude play an important role in career success. Some cosmetology schools consider "people skills" to be such an integral part of the job that they require coursework in that area. Business skills are important for those who plan to operate their own salons.

During their first months on the job, new workers are given relatively simple tasks or are assigned the simplest procedures. Once they have demonstrated their skills, they are gradually permitted to perform more complicated tasks, such as coloring hair or applying permanent waves. As they continue to work in the field, more training usually is required to learn the techniques particular to each salon and to build on the basics learned in cosmetology school.

Advancement usually takes the form of higher earnings as barbers and cosmetologists gain experience and build a steady clientele. Some barbers and cosmetologists manage large salons, lease booth space in salons, or open their own salons after several years of experience. Others teach in barber or cosmetology schools or provide training through vocational schools. Still others advance to become sales representatives, image or fashion consultants, or examiners for state licensing boards.

Employment

Barbers, cosmetologists, and other personal appearance workers held about 790,000 jobs in 2004. Of these, barbers, hairdressers, hairstylists, and cosmetologists held 670,000 jobs, manicurists and pedicurists 60,000, skin care specialists 30,000, and shampooers 27,000.

Most of these workers are employed in beauty salons or barber shops, but they also are found in nail salons, day and resort spas, department stores, nursing and other residential care homes, and drug and cosmetics stores. Nearly every town has a barbershop or beauty salon, but employment in this occupation is concentrated in the most populous cities and states.

About 48 percent of all barbers, cosmetologists, and other personal appearance workers are self-employed. Many own their own salon, but a growing number lease booth space or a chair from the salon's owner.

Job Outlook

Job opportunities generally should be good. However, competition is expected for jobs and clients at higher-paying salons as applicants compete with a large pool of licensed and experienced cosmetologists for these positions. Opportunities will be best for those with previous experience and for those licensed to provide a broad range of services.

Overall employment of barbers, cosmetologists, and other personal appearance workers is projected to grow about as fast as the average for all occupations through 2014 because of an increasing population, rising incomes, and growing demand for personal appearance services. In addition to those arising from job growth, numerous job openings will come about from the need to replace workers who transfer to other occupations, retire, or leave the labor force for other reasons.

Employment trends are expected to vary among the different occupational specialties. On the one hand, slower-than-average growth is expected in employment of barbers because of the large number of retirements expected over the 2004–2014 projection period and because of the relatively small number of cosmetology school graduates opting to obtain barbering licenses. On the other hand, employment of hairdressers, hairstylists, and cosmetologists should grow about as fast as the average for all workers because many now cut and style both men's and women's hair and because the demand for hair treatment by teens and aging baby boomers is expected to remain steady or even grow.

Continued growth in the number of nail salons and full-service day spas will generate numerous job openings for manicurists, pedicurists, skin care specialists, and shampooers. Employment of manicurists, pedicurists, and skin care specialists will grow faster than the average, while employment of shampooers will grow about as fast as the average. Nail salons specialize in providing manicures and pedicures. Day spas typically provide a full range of services, including beauty wraps, manicures and pedicures, facials, and massages.

Earnings

A number of factors, including the size and location of the salon, clients' tipping habits, and competition from other barber shops and salons, determine the total income of barbers, cosmetologists, and other personal appearance workers. They may receive commissions based on the price of the service or a salary based on the number of hours worked, and many receive commissions on the products they sell. In addition, some salons pay bonuses to employees who bring in new business. A cosmetologist's or barber's initiative and ability to attract and hold regular clients also are key factors in determining his or her earnings. Earnings for entry-level workers are usually low; however, for those who stay in the profession, earnings can be considerably higher.

Although some salons offer paid vacations and medical benefits, many self-employed and part-time workers in this occupation do not enjoy such benefits.

Median annual earnings in May 2004 for salaried hairdressers, hairstylists, and cosmetologists, including tips and commission, were $19,800. The middle 50 percent earned between $15,480 and $26,600. The lowest 10 percent earned less than $12,920, and the highest 10 percent earned more than $35,990.

Median annual earnings in May 2004 for salaried barbers, including tips, were $21,200. The middle 50 percent earned between $15,380 and $30,390. The lowest 10 percent earned less than $12,950, and the highest 10 percent earned more than $43,170.

Among skin care specialists, median annual earnings, including tips, were $24,010, for manicurists and pedicurists $18,500, and for shampooers $14,610.

Related Occupations

Other workers who provide a personal service to clients and usually must be professionally licensed or certified include massage therapists and fitness workers.

Sources of Additional Information

A list of licensed training schools and licensing requirements for cosmetologists may be obtained from

▸ National Accrediting Commission of Cosmetology Arts and Sciences, 4401 Ford Ave., Suite 1300, Alexandria, VA 22302. Internet: http://www.naccas.org

Information about a career in cosmetology is available from

▸ National Cosmetology Association, 401 N. Michigan Ave., 22nd Floor, Chicago, IL 60611. Internet: http://www.ncacares.org

For details on state licensing requirements and approved barber or cosmetology schools, contact the state boards of barber or cosmetology examiners in your state.

Bill and Account Collectors

(O*NET 43-3011.00)

Significant Points

■ About 1 in 5 collectors works for collection agencies; others work in banks, retail stores, government, physicians' offices, hospitals, and other institutions that lend money and extend credit.

■ Most jobs in this occupation require only a high school diploma, though many employers prefer workers with some postsecondary training.

■ Faster-than-average employment growth is expected as companies focus more efforts on collecting unpaid debts.

Nature of the Work

Bill and account collectors, called simply *collectors*, keep track of accounts that are overdue and attempt to collect payment on them. Some are employed by third-party collection agencies, while others—known as "in-house collectors"—work directly for the original creditors, such as department stores, hospitals, or banks.

The duties of bill and account collectors are similar in the many different organizations in which they are employed. First, collectors are called upon to locate and notify customers of delinquent accounts, usually over the telephone, but sometimes by letter. When customers move without leaving a forwarding address, collectors may check with the post office, telephone companies, credit bureaus, or former neighbors to obtain the new address. The attempt to find the new address is called "skip tracing." New computer systems assist in tracing by automatically tracking when customers change their address or contact information on any of their open accounts.

Once collectors find the debtor, they inform him or her of the overdue account and solicit payment. If necessary, they review the terms of the sale, service, or credit contract with the customer. Collectors also may attempt to learn the cause of the delay in payment. Where feasible, they offer the customer advice on how to pay off the debts, such as by taking out a bill consolidation loan. However, the collector's prime objective is always to ensure that the customer pays the debt in question.

If a customer agrees to pay, collectors record this commitment and check later to verify that the payment was indeed made. Collectors may have authority to grant an extension of time if customers ask for one. If a customer fails to respond, collectors prepare a statement indicating the customer's action for the credit department of the establishment. In more extreme cases, collectors may initiate repossession proceedings, disconnect the customer's service, or hand the account over to an attorney for legal action. Most collectors handle other administrative functions for the accounts assigned to them, including recording changes of addresses and purging the records of the deceased.

Collectors use computers and a variety of automated systems to keep track of overdue accounts. Typically, collectors work at video display terminals that are linked to computers. In sophisticated predictive dialer systems, a computer dials the telephone automatically, and the collector speaks only when a connection has been made. Such systems eliminate time spent calling busy or nonanswering numbers. Many collectors use regular telephones, but others wear headsets like those used by telephone operators.

Working Conditions

In-house bill and account collectors typically are employed in an office environment, while those who work for third-party collection agencies may work in a call-center environment. Workers spend most of their time on the phone tracking down and contacting people with debts. The work can be stressful, as some customers can be confrontational when pressed about their debts, although some appreciate assistance in resolving their outstanding debt. Collectors may also feel pressured to meet targets for the amount of debt they are expected to recover in a certain period.

Bill and account collectors often have to work evenings and weekends, when it usually is easier to reach people. As a result, it is not uncommon for workers to work part time or on flexible work schedules, though the majority work 40 hours per week.

Training, Other Qualifications, and Advancement

Most bill and account collectors are required to have at least a high school diploma. However, employers prefer workers who have completed some college or who have experience in other occupations that involve contact with the public. Workers should have good communication skills and be computer literate; experience with advanced telecommunications equipment is also useful.

Once hired, workers usually receive on-the-job training. Under the guidance of a supervisor or some other senior worker, new employees learn company procedures. Some formal classroom training also may be necessary, such as training in specific computer software. Additional training topics usually include telephone techniques and negotiation skills. Workers are also instructed in the laws governing the collection of debt as mandated by the Fair Debt Collection Practices Act (FDCPA), which applies to all third party and some in-house collectors.

Workers usually advance by taking on more duties in the same occupation for higher pay or by transferring to a closely related occupation. Many companies fill supervisory positions by promoting individuals from within the organization, and workers who acquire additional skills, experience, and training improve their advancement opportunities.

Employment

Bill and account collectors held about 456,000 jobs in 2004. About 1 in 5 collectors works for collection agencies. Many others work in banks, retail stores, government, physician's offices, hospitals, and other institutions that lend money and extend credit.

Job Outlook

Employment of bill and account collectors is expected to grow faster than the average for all occupations through 2014. Cash flow is becoming increasingly important to companies, which are now placing greater emphasis on collecting unpaid debts sooner. Thus, the workload for collectors is expected to continue to increase as they seek to collect not only debts that are relatively old, but ones that are more recent. Also, as more companies in a wide range of industries get involved in lending money and issuing their own credit cards, they will need to hire collectors because debt levels will likely continue to rise. In addition to job openings from employment growth, a significant number of openings will result from the high level of turnover in the occupation. As a result, job opportunities should be favorable.

Hospitals and physicians' offices are two of the fastest-growing industries requiring collectors. With insurance reimbursements not keeping up with cost increases, the health care industry is seeking to recover more money from patients. Government agencies also are making more use of collectors to collect on everything from parking tickets to child-support payments and past-due taxes. Finally, the Internal Revenue Service (IRS) is looking into outsourcing the collection of overdue federal taxes to third-party collection agencies. If the IRS does outsource, more collectors will be required for this large job.

Despite the increasing demand for bill collectors, employment growth may be limited due to an increased use of third-party debt collectors, who are generally more efficient than in-house collectors. Also, some firms are beginning to use offshore collection agencies, whose lower cost structures allow them to collect debts that are too small for domestic collection agencies. Contrary to the pattern in most occupations, employment of bill and account collectors tends to rise during recessions, reflecting the difficulty that many people have in meeting their financial obligations. However, collectors usually have more success at getting people to repay their debts when the economy is good.

Earnings

Median hourly earnings of bill and account collectors were $13.20 in May 2004. The middle 50 percent earned between $10.87 and $16.28. The lowest 10 percent earned less than $9.22, and the highest 10 percent earned more than $20.10. In addition to a basic rate of pay, many bill and account collectors earn commissions based on the amount of debt they recover.

Related Occupations

Bill and account collectors review and collect information on accounts. Other occupations with similar responsibilities include credit authorizers, checkers, and clerks; loan officers; and interviewers.

Sources of Additional Information

Career information on bill and account collectors is available from

▷ ACA International, The Association of Credit and Collection Professionals, P.O. Box 390106, Minneapolis, MN 55439. Internet: http://www.acainternational.org

Billing and Posting Clerks and Machine Operators

(O*NET 43-3021.01, 43-3021.02, and 43-3021.03)

Significant Points

■ The health care industry employs 1 out of 3 workers.

■ Most jobs in this occupation require only a high school diploma; however, many employers prefer to hire workers who have completed some college courses or a degree.

■ Slower-than-average employment growth is expected as increased automation of billing services reduces the need for billing clerks.

Nature of the Work

Billing and posting clerks and machine operators, commonly called *billing clerks*, compile records of charges for services rendered or goods sold, calculate and record the amounts of these services and goods, and prepare invoices to be mailed to customers.

Billing clerks review purchase orders, sales tickets, hospital records, or charge slips to calculate the total amount due from a customer. They must take into account any applicable discounts, special rates, or credit terms. A billing clerk for a trucking company often needs to consult a rate book to determine shipping costs of machine parts, for example. A hospital's billing clerk may need to contact an insurance company to determine what items will be reimbursed and for how much. In accounting, law, consulting, and similar firms, billing clerks calculate client fees based on the actual time required to perform the task. They keep track of the accumulated hours and dollar amounts to charge to each job, the type of job performed for a customer, and the percentage of work completed.

After billing clerks review all necessary information, they compute the charges, using calculators or computers. They then prepare itemized statements, bills, or invoices used for billing and recordkeeping purposes. In one organization, the clerk might prepare a bill containing the amount due and the date and type of service; in another, the clerk would produce a detailed invoice with codes for all goods and services provided. This latter form might list the items sold; the terms of credit; the date of shipment or the dates services were provided; a salesperson's or doctor's identification, if necessary; and the sales total.

Computers and specialized billing software allow many clerks to calculate charges and prepare bills in one step. Computer packages prompt clerks to enter data from handwritten forms and to manipulate the necessary entries of quantities, labor, and rates to be charged. Billing clerks verify the entry of information and check for errors before the computer prints the bill. After the bills are printed, billing clerks check them again for accuracy. Computer software also allows bills to be sent electronically if both the biller and the customer prefer not to use paper copies; this, coupled with the prevalence of electronic payment options, allows a completely paperless billing process. In offices that are not automated, *billing machine operators* run off the bill on a billing machine to send to the customer.

In addition to producing invoices, billing clerks may be asked to handle follow-up questions from customers and resolve any discrepancies or errors. Finally, all changes must be entered in the accounting records.

Working Conditions

Billing clerks typically are employed in an office environment, although a growing number—particularly medical billers—work at home. Most billing clerks work 40 hours per week during regular business hours, though about one in seven works part time. Because billing clerks use computers on a daily basis, workers may have to sit for extended periods and also may experience eye and muscle strain, backaches, headaches, and repetitive motion injuries.

Training, Other Qualifications, and Advancement

Most billing clerks need at least a high school diploma. However, many employers prefer to hire workers who have completed some college courses or a degree. Workers with an associate or bachelor's degree are likely to start at higher salaries and advance more easily than those without degrees. Employers also seek workers who are computer literate and in particular those who have experience with billing software programs.

Billing clerks usually receive on-the-job training from their supervisor or some other senior worker. Some formal classroom training also may be necessary, such as training in the specific computer software used by the company. Workers must be careful, orderly, and detail-oriented with an aptitude for working with numbers in order to avoid making errors and to recognize errors made by others. Workers also should be discreet and trustworthy because they frequently come in contact with confidential material. Medical billers in particular need to understand and follow the regulations of the Health Insurance Portability and Accountability Act (HIPAA), which were enacted to maintain the confidentiality of patient medical records.

A number of community and career colleges offer certificate programs in medical billing. Courses typically cover basic biology, anatomy, and physiology in addition to training on coding and computer billing software.

Billing clerks usually advance by taking on more duties in the same occupation for higher pay or by transferring to a closely related occupation. Most companies fill office and administrative support supervisory and managerial positions by promoting individuals from within the organization. Workers who acquire additional skills, experience, and training improve their advancement opportunities. With appropriate experience and education, some billing clerks may become accountants, human resource specialists, or buyers.

Employment

In 2004, billing and posting clerks and machine operators held about 523,000 jobs. Although all industries employ billing clerks, the health care industry employs the most, about a third of all billing clerks. The wholesale and retail trade industries also employ a large number of billing clerks. Third-party billing companies—companies that provide billing services for other companies—are employing a growing number of billing clerks. Industries that are providing this service are the accounting, tax preparation, bookkeeping, and payroll services industry and the office administrative and business support services industries. These industries currently employ around 5 percent of the occupation, although a portion of clerks in these industries are performing the function on their own accounts. Another 3 percent—mostly medical billers—were self employed.

Job Outlook

Employment of billing and posting clerks and machine operators is expected to grow more slowly than the average for all occupations through the year 2014. Automated and electronic billing processes are greatly simplifying billing and allowing companies to send out bills faster without hiring additional workers. In addition, as the billing process becomes simplified, other people, particularly accounting and bookkeeping clerks, are taking on the billing function. Strong growth in the health care industry, which employs many billing clerks due to the complicated nature of medical billing, will generate some jobs for billing clerks in the future. Although growth will be limited, many job openings will occur as workers transfer to other occupations or leave the labor force. Turnover in the occupation is relatively high, characteristic of an entry-level occupation that typically requires only a high school diploma.

Employment growth will occur in the expanding health care industries, but growth will be limited as more hospitals and physicians' offices use contract billing companies. Contract billing companies generally have much more sophisticated technology and software, enabling them to produce more bills per person. In all industries, including health care, the billing function is becoming increasingly automated and invoices and statements are automatically generated upon delivery of the service or shipment of goods. Bills also will increasingly be delivered electronically over the Internet, eliminating the production and mailing of paper bills.

Earnings

Median hourly earnings of billing and posting clerks and machine operators were $13.00 in May 2004. The middle 50 percent earned between $10.76 and $15.86. The lowest 10 percent earned less than $9.12, and the highest 10 percent earned more than $18.88.

Related Occupations

Billing clerks process and send records of transactions for payment; other occupations with similar responsibilities include payroll and timekeeping clerks; bookkeeping, auditing, and accounting clerks; tellers; and order clerks.

Sources of Additional Information

Information on employment opportunities for billing clerks is available from local offices of the state employment service.

Bookkeeping, Accounting, and Auditing Clerks

(0*NET 43-3031.00)

Significant Points

- Bookkeeping, accounting, and auditing clerks held more than 2 million jobs in 2004 and are employed in every industry.

- Employment is projected to grow more slowly than average as the spread of office automation lifts worker productivity.

- The large size of this occupation ensures plentiful job openings, including many opportunities for temporary and part-time work; those who can carry out a wider range of bookkeeping and accounting activities will be in greater demand than specialized clerks.

Nature of the Work

Bookkeeping, accounting, and auditing clerks are an organization's financial recordkeepers. They update and maintain one or more accounting records, including those which tabulate expenditures, receipts, accounts payable and receivable, and profit and loss. They represent a wide range of skills and knowledge from full-charge bookkeepers who can maintain an entire company's books to accounting clerks who handle specific accounts. All of these clerks make numerous computations each day and increasingly must be comfortable using computers to calculate and record data.

In small establishments, *bookkeeping clerks* handle all financial transactions and recordkeeping. They record all transactions, post debits and credits, produce financial statements, and prepare reports and summaries for supervisors and managers. Bookkeepers also prepare bank deposits by compiling data from cashiers; verifying and balancing receipts; and sending cash, checks, or other forms of payment to the bank. They also may handle payroll, make purchases, prepare invoices, and keep track of overdue accounts.

In large offices and accounting departments, *accounting clerks* have more specialized tasks. Their titles, such as accounts payable clerk or accounts receivable clerk, often reflect the type of accounting they do. In addition, their responsibilities vary by level of experience. Entry-level accounting clerks post details of transactions, total accounts, and compute interest charges. They also may monitor loans and accounts to ensure that payments are up to date.

More advanced accounting clerks may total, balance, and reconcile billing vouchers; ensure the completeness and accuracy of data on accounts; and code documents according to company procedures. These workers post transactions in journals and on computer files and update the files when needed. Senior clerks also review computer printouts against manually maintained journals and make necessary corrections. They may review invoices and statements to ensure that all the information appearing on them is accurate and complete, and they may reconcile computer reports with operating reports.

Auditing clerks verify records of transactions posted by other workers. They check figures, postings, and documents to ensure that they are correct, mathematically accurate, and properly coded. They also correct or note errors for accountants or other workers to adjust.

As organizations continue to computerize their financial records, many bookkeeping, accounting, and auditing clerks are using specialized accounting software on personal computers. With manual posting to general ledgers becoming obsolete, these clerks increasingly are posting charges to accounts on computer spreadsheets and databases. They now enter information from receipts or bills into computers, and the information is then stored either electronically or as computer printouts (or both). The widespread use of computers also has enabled bookkeeping, accounting, and auditing clerks to take on additional responsibilities, such as payroll, procurement, and billing. Many of these functions require these clerks to write letters, make phone calls to customers or clients, and interact with colleagues. Therefore, good communication skills are becoming increasingly important in the occupation.

Working Conditions

Bookkeeping, accounting, and auditing clerks work in an office environment. They may experience eye and muscle strain, backaches, headaches, and repetitive motion injuries as a result of using computers on a daily basis. Clerks may have to sit for extended periods while reviewing detailed data.

Many bookkeeping, accounting, and auditing clerks work regular business hours and a standard 40-hour week. A substantial number work just part time. Full-time and part-time clerks may work some evenings and weekends. Bookkeeping, accounting, and auditing clerks may work longer hours to meet deadlines at the end of the fiscal year, during tax time, or when monthly or yearly accounting audits are performed. Those who work in hotels, restaurants, and stores may put in overtime during peak holiday and vacation seasons.

Training, Other Qualifications, and Advancement

Most bookkeeping, accounting, and auditing clerks are required to have a high school degree at a minimum. However, having some college is increasingly important, and an associate degree in business or accounting is required for some positions. Although a college degree is rarely required, graduates may accept bookkeeping, accounting, and auditing clerk positions to get into a particular company or to enter the accounting or finance field with the hope of eventually being promoted to professional or managerial positions.

Experience in a related job and working in an office environment also is recommended. Employers prefer workers who are computer-literate; knowledge of word-processing and spreadsheet software is especially valuable.

Once hired, bookkeeping, accounting, and auditing clerks usually receive on-the-job training. Under the guidance of a supervisor or other senior worker, new employees learn company procedures. Some formal classroom training also may be necessary, such as training in specific computer software. Bookkeeping, accounting, and auditing clerks must be careful, orderly, and detail-oriented in order to avoid making errors and to recognize errors made by others. These workers also should be discreet and trustworthy because they frequently come in contact with confidential material. In addition, all bookkeeping, accounting, and auditing clerks should have a strong aptitude for numbers.

Bookkeepers, particularly those who handle all the recordkeeping for companies, may find it beneficial to become certified. The Certified Bookkeeper designation, awarded by the American Institute of Professional Bookkeepers, assures employers that individuals have the skills and knowledge required to carry out all the bookkeeping and accounting functions up through the adjusted trial balance, including payroll functions. For certification, candidates must have at least 2 years of bookkeeping experience, pass three tests, and adhere to a code of ethics. More than 100 colleges and universities offer a preparatory course for certification and another 150 offer a course online. The Universal Accounting Center offers the Professional Bookkeeper designation. Bookkeeping, accounting, and auditing clerks usually advance by taking on more duties in the same occupation for higher pay or by transferring to a closely related occupation. Most companies fill office and administrative support supervisory and managerial positions by promoting individuals from within their organizations, so clerks who acquire additional skills, experience, and training improve their advancement opportunities. With appropriate experience and education, some bookkeeping, accounting, and auditing clerks may become accountants or auditors.

Employment

Bookkeeping, accounting, and auditing clerks held more than 2 million jobs in 2004. They are found in all industries and at all levels of government. Local government and the accounting, tax preparation, bookkeeping, and payroll services industry are among the individual industries employing the largest numbers of these clerks. A growing number work for employment services firms, the result of an increase in outsourcing of this occupation. About 1 out of 4 bookkeeping, accounting, and auditing clerks worked part time in 2004.

Job Outlook

Employment of bookkeeping, accounting, and auditing clerks is projected to grow more slowly than the average for all occupations through 2014. More job openings will stem from replacement needs than from job growth. Each year, numerous jobs will become available as these clerks transfer to other occupations or leave the labor force. The large size of this occupation ensures plentiful job openings, including many opportunities for temporary and part-time work.

Although a growing economy will result in more financial transactions and other activities that require these clerical workers, the continuing spread of office automation will lift worker productivity and contribute to the slower-than-average increase in employment. In addition, organizations of all sizes will continue to downsize and consolidate various recordkeeping functions, thus reducing the demand for bookkeeping, accounting, and auditing clerks. Furthermore, some work performed by these workers will be outsourced to lower-wage foreign countries. Those who can carry out a wider range of bookkeeping and accounting activities will be in greater demand than specialized clerks. Demand for full-charge bookkeepers is expected to increase because they are called upon to do much of the work of accountants as well as perform a wider variety of financial transactions, from payroll to billing. Certified bookkeepers and those with several years of accounting or bookkeeper experience will have the best job prospects.

Earnings

In May 2004, the median wage and salary annual earnings of bookkeeping, accounting, and auditing clerks were $28,570. The middle half of the occupation earned between $22,960 and $35,450. The top 10 percent of bookkeeping, accounting, and auditing clerks earned more than $43,570, and the bottom 10 percent earned less than $18,580.

Related Occupations

Bookkeeping, accounting, and auditing clerks work with financial records. Other clerks who perform similar duties include bill and account collectors; billing and posting clerks and machine operators; brokerage clerks; credit authorizers, checkers, and clerks; payroll and timekeeping clerks; procurement clerks; and tellers.

Sources of Additional Information

For information on the Certified Bookkeeper designation, contact

▶ American Institute of Professional Bookkeepers, 6001 Montrose Rd., Suite 500, Rockville, MD 20852. Internet: http://www.aipb.org

For information on the Professional Bookkeeper designation, contact

▶ Universal Accounting Center, 5250 South Commerce Dr., Salt Lake City, UT 84107.

Building Cleaning Workers

(O*NET 37-1011.01, 37-1011.02, 37-2011.00, and 37-2012.00)

Significant Points

■ This very large occupation requires few skills to enter and has one of the largest numbers of job openings of any occupation each year.

■ Most job openings result from the need to replace the many workers who leave these jobs because of their limited opportunities for training or advancement, low pay, and high incidence of only part-time or temporary work.

■ Most new jobs will occur in businesses providing janitorial and cleaning services on a contract basis.

Nature of the Work

Building cleaning workers—including janitors, maids, housekeeping cleaners, window washers, and rug shampooers—keep office buildings, hospitals, stores, apartment houses, hotels, and residences clean, sanitary, and in good condition. Some do only cleaning, while others have a wide range of duties.

Janitors and cleaners perform a variety of heavy cleaning duties, such as cleaning floors, shampooing rugs, washing walls and glass, and removing rubbish. They may fix leaky faucets, empty trash cans, do painting and carpentry, replenish bathroom supplies, mow lawns, and see that heating and air-conditioning equipment works properly. On a typical day, janitors may wet- or dry-mop floors, clean bathrooms, vacuum carpets, dust furniture, make minor repairs, and exterminate insects and rodents. They also clean snow or debris from sidewalks in front of buildings and notify management of the need for major repairs. While janitors typically perform most of the duties mentioned, cleaners tend to work for companies that specialize in one type of cleaning activity, such as washing windows.

Maids and housekeeping cleaners perform any combination of light cleaning duties to keep private households or commercial establishments such as hotels, restaurants, hospitals, and nursing homes clean and orderly. In hotels, aside from cleaning and maintaining the premises, maids and housekeeping cleaners may deliver ironing boards, cribs, and rollaway beds to guests' rooms. In hospitals, they also may wash bed frames, brush mattresses, make beds, and disinfect and sterilize equipment and supplies with germicides and sterilizing equipment.

Janitors, maids, and cleaners use many kinds of equipment, tools, and cleaning materials. For one job they may need standard cleaning implements; another may require an electric polishing machine and a special cleaning solution. Improved building materials, chemical cleaners, and power equipment have made many tasks easier and less time consuming, but cleaning workers must learn the proper use of equipment and cleaners to avoid harming floors, fixtures, and themselves.

Cleaning supervisors coordinate, schedule, and supervise the activities of janitors and cleaners. They assign tasks and inspect building areas to see that work has been done properly; they also issue supplies and equipment and inventory stocks to ensure that supplies on hand are adequate. They also screen and hire job applicants; train new and experienced employees; and recommend promotions, transfers, or dismissals. Supervisors may prepare reports concerning the occupancy of rooms, hours worked, and department expenses. Some also perform cleaning duties.

Cleaners and servants in private households dust and polish furniture; sweep, mop, and wax floors; vacuum; and clean ovens, refrigerators, and bathrooms. They also may wash dishes, polish silver, and change and make beds. Some wash, fold, and iron clothes; a few wash windows. General houseworkers also may take clothes and laundry to the cleaners, buy groceries, and perform many other errands.

Building cleaning workers in large office and residential buildings, and more recently in large hotels, often work in teams consisting of workers who specialize in vacuuming, picking up trash, and cleaning restrooms, among other things. Supervisors conduct inspections to ensure that the building is cleaned properly and the team is functioning efficiently. In hotels, one member of the team is responsible for reporting electronically to the supervisor when rooms are cleaned.

Working Conditions

Because most office buildings are cleaned while they are empty, many cleaning workers work evening hours. Some, however, such as school and hospital custodians, work in the daytime. When there is a need for 24-hour maintenance, janitors may be assigned to shifts. Most full-time building cleaners work about 40 hours a week. Part-time cleaners usually work in the evenings and on weekends.

Building cleaning workers usually work inside heated, well-lighted buildings. However, they sometimes work outdoors, sweeping walkways, mowing lawns, or shoveling snow. Working with machines can be noisy, and some tasks, such as cleaning bathrooms and trash rooms, can be dirty and unpleasant. Janitors may suffer cuts, bruises, and burns from machines, hand tools, and chemicals. They spend most of their time on their feet, sometimes lifting or pushing heavy furniture or equipment. Many tasks, such as dusting or sweeping, require constant bending, stooping, and stretching. As a result, janitors also may suffer back injuries and sprains.

Training, Other Qualifications, and Advancement

No special education is required for most janitorial or cleaning jobs, but beginners should know simple arithmetic and be able to follow instructions. High school shop courses are helpful for jobs involving repair work.

Most building cleaners learn their skills on the job. Beginners usually work with an experienced cleaner, doing routine cleaning. As they gain more experience, they are assigned more complicated tasks. In some cities, programs run by unions, government agencies, or employers teach janitorial skills. Students learn how to clean buildings thoroughly and efficiently; how to select and safely use various cleansing agents; and how to operate and maintain machines, such as wet and dry vacuums, buffers, and polishers. Students learn to plan their work, to follow safety and health regulations, to interact positively with people in the buildings they clean, and to work without supervision. Instruction in minor electrical, plumbing, and other repairs also may be given. Those who come in contact with the public should have good communication skills. Employers usually look for dependable, hard-working individuals who are in good health, follow directions well, and get along with other people.

Building cleaners usually find work by answering newspaper advertisements, applying directly to organizations where they would like to work, contacting local labor unions, or contacting state employment service offices.

Advancement opportunities for workers usually are limited in organizations where they are the only maintenance worker. Where there is a large maintenance staff, however, cleaning workers can be promoted to supervisor or to area supervisor or manager. A high school diploma improves the chances for advancement. Some janitors set up their own maintenance or cleaning businesses.

Supervisors usually move up through the ranks. In many establishments, they are required to take some inservice training to improve their housekeeping techniques and procedures and to enhance their supervisory skills.

A small number of cleaning supervisors and managers are members of the International Executive Housekeepers Association, which offers two kinds of certification programs for cleaning supervisors and managers: Certified Executive Housekeeper (CEH) and Registered Executive Housekeeper (REH). The CEH designation is offered to those with a high school education, while the REH designation is offered to those who have a 4-year college degree. Both designations are earned by attending courses and passing exams, and both must be renewed every 2 years to ensure that workers keep abreast of new cleaning methods. Those with the REH designation usually oversee the cleaning services of hotels, hospitals, casinos, and other large institutions that rely on well-trained experts for their cleaning needs.

Employment

Building cleaning workers held more than 4 million jobs in 2004. More than 6 percent were self-employed.

Janitors and cleaners work in nearly every type of establishment and held about 2.4 million jobs. They accounted for more than 58 percent of all building cleaning workers. More than 29 percent worked for firms supplying building maintenance services on a contract basis, more than 20 percent were employed in public or private educational services, and 2 percent worked in hotels or motels. Other employers included hospitals; restaurants; religious institutions; manufacturing firms; government agencies; and operators of apartment buildings, office buildings, and other types of real estate.

First-line supervisors of housekeeping and janitorial workers held about 236,000 jobs. Approximately 23 percent worked in firms supplying building maintenance services on a contract basis, while approximately 13 percent were employed in hotels or motels. More than 20 percent worked for state and local governments, primarily at schools and colleges. Others worked for hospitals, nursing homes, and other residential care facilities.

Maids and housekeepers held about 1.4 million jobs. Private households employed the most maids and housekeepers—almost 28 percent—while hotels, motels, and other traveler accommodations employed the second most—almost 27 percent. Hospitals, nursing homes, and other residential care facilities employed large numbers, also. Although cleaning jobs can be found in all cities and towns, most are located in highly populated areas where there are many office buildings, schools, apartment houses, nursing homes, and hospitals.

Job Outlook

Overall employment of building cleaning workers is expected to grow as fast as average for all occupations through 2014, as more office complexes, apartment houses, schools, factories, hospitals,

and other buildings requiring cleaning are built to accommodate a growing population and economy. As many firms reduce costs by contracting out the cleaning and maintenance of buildings, businesses providing janitorial and cleaning services on a contract basis are expected to have the greatest number of new jobs in this field. Although there have been some improvements in productivity in the way buildings are cleaned and maintained—using teams of cleaners, for example, and better cleaning supplies—cleaning still is very much a labor-intensive job. Faster-than-average growth is expected among janitors and cleaners and among cleaning supervisors, but average growth is projected for maids and housekeeping cleaners. In addition to job openings arising due to growth, numerous openings should result from the need to replace those who leave this very large occupation each year. Limited promotion potential, low pay, and the fact that many jobs are part-time and temporary induce many to leave the occupation, thereby contributing to the number of job openings and the need to replace these workers.

Much of the growth in these occupations will come from cleaning residential properties. As families become more pressed for time, they increasingly are hiring cleaning and handyman services to perform a variety of tasks in their homes. Also, as the population ages, older people will need to hire cleaners to help maintain their houses. In addition, housekeeping cleaners will be needed to clean the growing number of residential care facilities for the elderly. These facilities, including assisted-living residences, generally provide housekeeping services as part of the rent.

Earnings

Median annual earnings of janitors and cleaners, except maids and housekeeping cleaners, were $18,790 in May 2004. The middle 50 percent earned between $15,320 and $24,420. The lowest 10 percent earned less than $13,010 and the highest 10 percent earned more than $31,780. Median annual earnings in 2004 in the industries employing the largest numbers of janitors and cleaners, except maids and housekeeping cleaners, were as follows:

Elementary and secondary schools	$22,910
Local government	22,860
Colleges, universities, and professional schools	21,860
Lessors of real estate	21,050
Services to buildings and dwellings	16,820

Median annual earnings of maids and housekeepers were $16,900 in May 2004. The middle 50 percent earned between $14,570 and $20,570. The lowest 10 percent earned less than $12,530, and the highest 10 percent earned more than $25,220. Median annual earnings in 2004 in the industries employing the largest numbers of maids and housekeepers were as follows:

General medical and surgical hospitals	$18,770
Services to buildings and dwellings	17,130
Community care facilities for the elderly	17,010
Nursing care facilities	16,960
Traveler accommodation	16,250

Median annual earnings of first-line supervisors and managers of housekeeping and janitorial workers were $29,510 in May 2004. The middle 50 percent earned between $22,720 and $38,790. The lowest 10 percent earned less than $18,550, and the highest 10 percent earned more than $49,230. Median annual earnings in May 2004 in the industries employing the largest numbers of first-line supervisors and managers of housekeeping and janitorial workers were as follows:

Local government	$34,780
Elementary and secondary schools	33,760
Nursing care facilities	28,370
Services to buildings and dwellings	27,760
Traveler accommodation	24,310

Related Occupations

Workers who specialize in one of the many job functions of janitors and cleaners include pest control workers; general maintenance and repair workers; and grounds maintenance workers.

Sources of Additional Information

Information about janitorial jobs may be obtained from state employment service offices.

For information on certification in executive housekeeping, contact

▸ International Executive Housekeepers Association, Inc., 1001 Eastwind Dr., Suite 301, Westerville, OH 43081-3361. Internet: http://www.ieha.org

Bus Drivers

(O*NET 53-3021.00 and 53-3022.00)

Significant Points

■ Opportunities should be good, particularly for school bus driver jobs; applicants for higher-paying public transit bus driver positions may encounter competition.

■ State and federal governments establish bus driver qualifications and standards, which include a commercial driver's license.

■ Work schedules vary considerably among various types of bus drivers.

■ Bus drivers must possess strong customer service skills, including communication skills and the ability to manage large groups of people with varying needs.

Nature of the Work

Bus drivers provide transportation for millions of people every year, from commuters to school children to vacationers. There are two major kinds of bus drivers: *transit and intercity bus drivers*, who transport people between regions of a state or of the country, along routes run within a metropolitan area or county, or on chartered excursions and tours; and *school bus drivers*, who take children to and from schools and related events.

Bus drivers pick up and drop off passengers at bus stops, stations, or—in the case of students—at regularly scheduled neighborhood locations, all according to strict time schedules. Drivers must operate vehicles safely, especially in heavy traffic. They cannot let light traffic put them ahead of schedule so that they miss passengers. Bus drivers drive a range of vehicles, from 15-passenger buses to 60-foot articulated buses that can carry more than 100 passengers.

Local-transit and *intercity bus drivers* report to their assigned terminal or garage, where they stock up on tickets or transfers and prepare trip report forms. In some transportation firms, maintenance departments are responsible for keeping vehicles in good condition; in others, drivers may be expected to check their vehicle's tires, brakes, windshield wipers, lights, oil, fuel, and water supply before beginning their routes. Drivers usually verify that the bus has safety equipment, such as fire extinguishers, first aid kits, and emergency reflectors.

During the course of their shift, local-transit and intercity bus drivers collect fares; answer questions about schedules, routes, and transfer points; and sometimes announce stops. Intercity bus drivers may make only a single one-way trip to a distant city or a round trip each day. They may stop at towns just a few miles apart or only at large cities hundreds of miles apart. Local-transit bus drivers may make several trips each day over the same city and suburban streets, stopping as frequently as every few blocks.

Local-transit bus drivers submit daily trip reports with a record of trips, significant schedule delays, and mechanical problems. Intercity drivers who drive across state or national boundaries must comply with U.S. Department of Transportation regulations. These include completing vehicle inspection reports and recording distances traveled and the periods they spend driving, performing other duties, and off duty.

Some intercity drivers operate motor coaches which transport passengers on chartered trips and sightseeing tours. Drivers routinely interact with customers and tour guides to make the trip as comfortable and informative as possible. They are directly responsible for keeping to strict schedules, adhering to the guidelines of the tour's itinerary, and ensuring the overall success of the trip. These drivers act as customer service representative, tour guide, program director, and safety guide. Trips frequently last more than a day. The driver may be away for more than a week if assigned to an extended tour. As with all commercial drivers who drive across state or national boundaries, motor coach drivers must comply with U.S. Department of Transportation and state regulations.

School bus drivers usually drive the same routes each day, stopping to pick up pupils in the morning and return them to their homes in the afternoon. Some school bus drivers also transport students and teachers on field trips or to sporting events. In addition to driving, some school bus drivers work part time in the school system as janitors, mechanics, or classroom assistants when not driving buses.

Bus drivers must be alert to prevent accidents, especially in heavy traffic or in bad weather, and to avoid sudden stops or swerves that jar passengers. School bus drivers must exercise particular caution when children are getting on or off the bus. They must maintain order on their bus and enforce school safety standards by allowing only students to board. In addition, they must know and enforce the school system's rules regarding student conduct.

School bus drivers do not always have to report to an assigned terminal or garage. In some cases, they have the choice of taking their bus home or parking it in a more convenient area. School bus drivers do not collect fares. Instead, they prepare weekly reports on the number of students, trips or "runs," work hours, miles, and fuel consumption. Their supervisors set time schedules and routes for the day or week.

Working Conditions

Driving a bus through heavy traffic while dealing with passengers is more stressful and fatiguing than physically strenuous. Many drivers enjoy the opportunity to work without direct supervision, with full responsibility for their bus and passengers. To improve working conditions and retain drivers, many bus lines provide ergonomically designed seats and controls for drivers. Many bus companies use Global Positioning Systems to help dispatchers manage their bus fleets and help drivers navigate.

Intercity bus drivers may work nights, weekends, and holidays and often spend nights away from home, during which they stay in hotels at company expense. Senior drivers with regular routes have regular weekly work schedules, but others do not have regular schedules and must be prepared to report for work on short notice. They report for work only when called for a charter assignment or to drive extra buses on a regular route. Intercity bus travel and charter work tend to be seasonal. From May through August, drivers may work the maximum number of hours per week that regulations allow. During winter, junior drivers may work infrequently, except for busy holiday travel periods, and may be furloughed at times.

School bus drivers work only when school is in session. Many work 20 hours a week or less, driving one or two routes in the morning and afternoon. Drivers taking field or athletic trips, or who also have midday kindergarten routes, may work more hours a week. As more students with a variety of physical and behavioral disabilities assimilate into mainstream schools, school bus drivers must learn how to accommodate their special needs.

Regular local-transit bus drivers usually have a 5-day workweek; Saturdays and Sundays are considered regular workdays. Some drivers work evenings and after midnight. To accommodate commuters, many work "split shifts"—for example, 6 a.m. to 10 a.m. and 3 p.m. to 7 p.m., with time off in between.

Intercity bus drivers operating tour and charter buses may work any day and all hours of the day, including weekends and holidays. Their hours are dictated by the destinations, schedules, and itineraries of chartered tours. Like all commercial drivers, their weekly hours must be consistent with the Department of Transportation's rules and regulations concerning hours of service. For example, drivers may drive for 10 hours and work for up to 15 hours—including driving and nondriving duties—before having 8 hours off duty. Drivers may not drive after having worked for 60 hours in the past 7 days or 70 hours in the past 8 days. Most drivers are required to document their time in a logbook.

Training, Other Qualifications, and Advancement

Many employers prefer high school graduates and require a written test of ability to follow complex bus schedules. Many intercity and public transit bus companies prefer applicants who are at least 24 years of age; some require several years of experience driving a bus

or truck. In some states, school bus drivers must pass a background investigation to uncover any criminal record or history of mental problems.

Bus driver qualifications and standards are established by state and federal regulations. All drivers must comply with federal regulations and with any state regulations that exceed federal requirements. Federal regulations require drivers who operate commercial motor vehicles in excess of 26,000 pounds gross vehicle weight rating or designed to carry 16 or more persons, including the driver, to hold a commercial driver's license (CDL) with the appropriate endorsements from the state in which they live.

To qualify for a CDL, applicants must pass a knowledge test on rules and regulations and then demonstrate in a skills test that they can operate a bus safely. A national databank records all driving violations incurred by persons who hold commercial licenses, and a state may not issue a CDL to a person who has already had a license suspended or revoked in another state. To be issued a CDL, a driver must surrender all other driver's licenses. A driver with a CDL must accompany trainees until the trainees get their own CDL. In addition to having a CDL, all bus drivers must have a "passenger" endorsement for their CDL, which requires passing a knowledge test and demonstrating the necessary skills in a vehicle of the same type as the one they would be driving in their duties. Information on how to apply for a CDL and each type of endorsement can be obtained from state motor vehicle administrations.

While many states allow those who are 18 years of age and older to drive buses within state borders, the Department of Transportation establishes minimum qualifications for bus drivers engaged in interstate commerce. Federal Motor Carrier Safety Regulations require drivers to be at least 21 years old and to pass a physical examination once every 2 years. The main physical requirements include good hearing, at least 20/40 vision with or without glasses or corrective lenses, and a 70-degree field of vision in each eye. Drivers cannot be colorblind. They must be able to hear a forced whisper in one ear at not less than 5 feet, with or without a hearing aid. Drivers must have normal blood pressure as well as normal use of their arms and legs. They may not use any controlled substances unless prescribed by a licensed physician. Persons with epilepsy or with diabetes controlled by insulin are not permitted to be interstate bus drivers. Federal regulations also require employers to test their drivers for alcohol and drug use as a condition of employment and require periodic random tests of the drivers while they are on duty. In addition, a driver must not have been convicted of a felony involving the use of a motor vehicle, a crime involving drugs, driving under the influence of drugs or alcohol, refusing to submit to an alcohol test required by a state or its implied consent laws or regulations, leaving the scene of a crime, or causing a fatality through negligent operation of a commercial vehicle. All drivers must be able to read and speak English well enough to read road signs, prepare reports, and communicate with law enforcement officers and the public. In addition, drivers must take a written examination on the Motor Carrier Safety Regulations of the U.S. Department of Transportation.

Because bus drivers deal with passengers, they must be courteous. They need an even temperament and emotional stability because driving in heavy, fast-moving, or stop-and-go traffic and dealing with passengers can be stressful. Drivers must have strong customer service skills, including communication skills and the ability to coordinate and manage large groups of people.

Most intercity bus companies and local-transit systems give driver trainees 2 to 8 weeks of classroom and behind-the-wheel instruction. In the classroom, trainees learn Department of Transportation and company work rules, safety regulations, state and municipal driving regulations, and safe driving practices. They also learn to read schedules, determine fares, keep records, and deal courteously with passengers.

School bus drivers also are required to obtain a CDL from the state in which they live. They must additionally have a "school bus" endorsement for their CDL. To receive this endorsement, they must pass a written test and demonstrate necessary skills. The skills portion of the test is taken in a bus of the same type that they would be driving on their route. Both of these tests are specific to school buses and are in addition to the testing required to receive a CDL and the "passenger" endorsement. Many persons who become school bus drivers have never driven any vehicle larger than an automobile. They receive between 1 and 4 weeks of driving instruction and classroom training on state and local laws, regulations, and policies of operating school buses; safe driving practices; driver-pupil relations; first aid; special needs of disabled and emotionally troubled students; and emergency evacuation procedures. School bus drivers also must be aware of the school system's rules for discipline and conduct for bus drivers and the students they transport.

During training, bus drivers practice driving on set courses. They practice turns and zigzag maneuvers, backing up, and driving in narrow lanes. Then, they drive in light traffic and, eventually, on congested highways and city streets. They also make trial runs without passengers to improve their driving skills and learn the routes. Local-transit trainees memorize and drive each of the runs operating out of their assigned garage. New drivers make regularly scheduled trips with passengers, accompanied by an experienced driver who gives helpful tips, answers questions, and evaluates the new driver's performance. Most bus drivers get brief supplemental training at regular periods to keep abreast of safety issues and regulatory changes.

New intercity and local-transit drivers usually are placed on an "extra" list to drive chartered runs, extra buses on regular runs, and special runs (for example, during morning and evening rush hours and to sports events). They also substitute for regular drivers who are ill or on vacation. New drivers remain on the extra list and may work only part time, perhaps for several years, until they have enough seniority to be given a regular run.

Senior drivers may bid for the runs that they prefer, such as those with more work hours, lighter traffic, weekends off, or—in the case of intercity bus drivers—higher earnings or fewer workdays per week.

Opportunities for promotion are generally limited. However, experienced drivers may become supervisors or dispatchers—assigning buses to drivers, checking whether drivers are on schedule, rerouting buses to avoid blocked streets or other problems, and dispatching extra vehicles and service crews to scenes of accidents and breakdowns. In transit agencies with rail systems, drivers may become train operators or station attendants. Opportunities exist for bus drivers to become either instructors of new bus drivers or master-instructors, who train new instructors. A few drivers become

managers. Promotion in publicly owned bus systems is often determined by competitive civil service examination. Some motor coach drivers purchase their own equipment and open their own business.

Employment

Bus drivers held about 653,000 jobs in 2004. About 35 percent worked part time. Around 71 percent of all bus drivers were school bus drivers working primarily for school systems or for companies providing school bus services under contract. Most of the remainder worked for private and local government transit systems; some also worked for intercity and charter bus lines.

Job Outlook

Persons seeking jobs as bus drivers likely will encounter many opportunities. Individuals who have good driving records and who are willing to work a part-time or irregular schedule probably will have the best job prospects. School bus driving jobs, particularly in rapidly growing suburban areas, should be easiest to acquire because most are part-time positions with high turnover and less training required than for other bus-driving jobs. Those seeking higher-paying public transit bus driver positions may encounter competition. Opportunities for intercity driving positions should be good, although employment prospects for motor coach drivers will depend on tourism which fluctuates with the cyclical nature of the economy.

Employment of bus drivers overall is expected to increase about as fast as the average for all occupations through the year 2014, primarily to meet the transportation needs of the growing general population and the school-aged population. Most job openings are expected to occur each year because of the need to replace workers who take jobs in other occupations or who retire or leave the occupation for other reasons.

The number of school bus drivers is expected to increase as fast as average over the next 10 years, although at a decreasing rate. School enrollments are projected to increase in 30 states and to decrease in 20 states. The net effect will be a slowdown in school enrollment and, therefore, in employment growth of school bus drivers. This, as well as the part-time nature of the occupation, will result in most openings for school bus drivers being to replace those who leave the occupation.

Employment growth for local-transit bus drivers is expected to be faster than the average for all occupations through 2014 and will likely be the result of the increasing popularity of mass transit due to congestion and rising fuel prices, as well as the demand for transit services in expanding portions of metropolitan areas. There may be competition for positions with more regular hours and steady driving routes.

Competition from other modes of transportation—airplane, train, or automobile—will temper job growth among intercity bus drivers. Most growth in intercity bus transportation will occur in group charters to locations not served by other modes of transportation. Like automobiles, buses have a far greater number of possible destinations than airplanes or trains. Since they offer greater cost savings and convenience over automobiles, buses usually are the most economical option for tour groups traveling to out-of-the-way destinations.

Full-time bus drivers rarely are laid off during recessions. If the number of passengers decreases, however, employers might reduce the hours of part-time local-transit and intercity bus drivers since fewer extra buses would be needed. Seasonal layoffs are common. Many intercity bus drivers with little seniority, for example, are furloughed during the winter when regularly scheduled and charter business declines, while school bus drivers seldom work during the summer or school holidays.

Earnings

Median hourly earnings of transit and intercity bus drivers were $14.30 in May 2004. The middle 50 percent earned between $10.74 and $19.31 an hour. The lowest 10 percent earned less than $8.66, and the highest 10 percent earned more than $23.53 an hour. Median hourly earnings in the industries employing the largest numbers of transit and intercity bus drivers in May 2004 were as follows:

Local government $17.10

Interurban and rural bus transportation 15.86

Urban transit systems 13.49

Charter bus industry 10.81

Other transit and ground passenger transportation....10.74

Median hourly earnings of school bus drivers were $11.18 in May 2004. The middle 50 percent earned between $8.10 and $13.92 an hour. The lowest 10 percent earned less than $6.23, and the highest 10 percent earned more than $16.81 an hour. Median hourly earnings in the industries employing the largest numbers of school bus drivers in May 2004 were as follows:

School and employee bus transportation................$11.97

Elementary and secondary schools 10.74

Other transit and ground passenger
    transportation 10.62

Child day care services...9.28

Individual and family services.................................8.75

The benefits bus drivers receive from their employers vary greatly. Most intercity and local-transit bus drivers receive paid health and life insurance, sick leave, vacation leave, and free bus rides on any of the regular routes of their line or system. School bus drivers receive sick leave, and many are covered by health and life insurance and pension plans. Because they generally do not work when school is not in session, they do not get vacation leave.

Many intercity and local-transit bus drivers are members of the Amalgamated Transit Union. Local-transit bus drivers in New York and several other large cities belong to the Transport Workers Union of America. Some drivers belong to the United Transportation Union or to the International Brotherhood of Teamsters.

Related Occupations

Other workers who drive vehicles on highways and city streets include taxi drivers and chauffeurs and truck drivers and driver/sales workers.

Sources of Additional Information

For information on employment opportunities, contact local-transit systems, intercity bus lines, school systems, or the local offices of the state employment service.

General information on school bus driving is available from

▶ National School Transportation Association, 113 South West St., 4th Floor, Alexandria, VA 22314.

▶ National Association of State Directors of Pupil Transportation Services, 6298 Rock Hill Road, The Plains, VA 20198-1916.

General information on motor coach driving is available from

▶ United Motorcoach Association, 113 South West St., 4th Floor, Alexandria, VA 22314.

▶ American Bus Association, 700 13th Street NW, Suite 575, Washington, DC 20005.

Carpenters

(O*NET 47-2031.01, 47-2031.02, 47-2031.03, 47-2031.04, 47-2031.05, and 47-2031.06)

Significant Points

■ About one-third of all carpenters—the largest construction trade—were self-employed.

■ Job opportunities should be excellent for those with the most training and all-around skills.

■ To become a skilled carpenter usually takes between 3 and 4 years of both on-the-job training and classroom instruction.

Nature of the Work

Carpenters are involved in many different kinds of construction activity, from the building of highways and bridges to the installation of kitchen cabinets. Carpenters construct, erect, install, and repair structures and fixtures made from wood and other materials. Depending on the type of work and the employer, carpenters may specialize in one or two activities or may be required to know how to perform many different tasks. Small home builders and remodeling companies may require carpenters to learn about all aspects of building a house—framing walls and partitions, putting in doors and windows, building stairs, installing cabinets and molding, and many other tasks. Large construction contractors or specialty contractors, however, may require their carpenters to perform only a few regular tasks, such as framing walls, constructing wooden forms for pouring concrete, or erecting scaffolding. Carpenters also build tunnel bracing, or brattices, in underground passageways and mines to control the circulation of air through the passageways and to worksites.

Each carpentry task is somewhat different, but most involve the same basic steps. Working from blueprints or instructions from supervisors, carpenters first do the layout—measuring, marking, and arranging materials—in accordance with local building codes. They cut and shape wood, plastic, fiberglass, or drywall, using hand and power tools, such as chisels, planes, saws, drills, and sanders. They then join the materials with nails, screws, staples, or adhesives. In the final step, carpenters check the accuracy of their work with levels, rules, plumb bobs, framing squares, or electronic versions of these tools and make any necessary adjustments. When working with prefabricated components, such as stairs or wall panels, the carpenter's task is somewhat simpler because it does not require as much layout work or the cutting and assembly of as many pieces. Prefabricated components are designed for easy and fast installation and generally can be installed in a single operation.

Carpenters who remodel homes and other structures need a broad range of carpentry skills because they must be able to perform any of the many different tasks these jobs may require. Since they are so well-trained, these carpenters often can switch from residential building to commercial construction or remodeling work, depending on which offers the best work opportunities.

Carpenters employed outside the construction industry perform a variety of installation and maintenance work. They may replace panes of glass, ceiling tiles, and doors as well as repair desks, cabinets, and other furniture. Depending on the employer, carpenters install partitions, doors, and windows; change locks; and repair broken furniture. In manufacturing firms, carpenters may assist in moving or installing machinery. (For more information on workers who install machinery, see the description of industrial machinery installation, repair, and maintenance workers, except millwrights, elsewhere in this book.)

Working Conditions

As is true of other building trades, carpentry work is sometimes strenuous. Prolonged standing, climbing, bending, and kneeling often are necessary. Carpenters risk injury working with sharp or rough materials, using sharp tools and power equipment, and working in situations where they might slip or fall. Although many carpenters work indoors, those that work outdoors are subject to variable weather conditions.

Some carpenters change employers each time they finish a construction job. Others alternate between working for a contractor and working as contractors themselves on small jobs, depending on where the work is available.

Training, Other Qualifications, and Advancement

Carpenters learn their trade through formal and informal training programs. To become a skilled carpenter usually takes between 3 and 4 years of both classroom and on-the-job training. While there are a number of different ways to obtain this training, in general, the more formalized the process, the more skilled you will become and the more in demand by employers you will be. For some, this training can begin in a high school, where classes in English, algebra, geometry, physics, mechanical drawing, blueprint reading, and general shop are recommended. After high school, there are a number of different avenues that one can take to obtain the necessary training. One of the ways is to obtain a job with a contractor who will then provide on-the-job training. Entry-level workers generally start as helpers, assisting more experienced workers. During this time, the carpenter's helper may elect to attend a trade or vocational school or community college to receive further trade-related training.

Some employers, particularly large nonresidential construction contractors with union membership, offer employees formal apprenticeships. These programs combine on-the-job training with related classroom instruction. Apprenticeship applicants usually must be at least 18 years old and meet local requirements; some union locals, for example, test an applicant's aptitude for carpentry. Apprenticeship programs are usually 3 to 4 years in length, but vary with the apprentice's skill. The number of apprenticeship programs is limited, however, so only a small proportion of carpenters learn their trade through these programs, mostly those working for commercial and industrial building contractors.

On the job, apprentices learn elementary structural design and become familiar with common carpentry jobs, such as layout, form building, rough framing, and outside and inside finishing. They also learn to use the tools, machines, equipment, and materials of the trade. Apprentices receive classroom instruction in safety, first aid, blueprint reading, freehand sketching, basic mathematics, and various carpentry techniques. Both in the classroom and on the job, they learn the relationship between carpentry and the other building trades.

Some persons aiming for carpentry careers choose to obtain their classroom training before seeking a job. There are a number of public and private vocational-technical schools and training academies affiliated with the unions and contractors that offer training to become a carpenter. Employers often look favorably upon these students and usually start them at a higher level than those without the training.

Some skills needed to become a carpenter include manual dexterity, eye-hand coordination, physical fitness, and a good sense of balance. The ability to solve arithmetic problems quickly and accurately also is required. In addition, a good work history or military service is viewed favorably by contractors.

Carpenters usually have greater opportunities than most other construction workers to become general construction supervisors because carpenters are exposed to the entire construction process. For those who would like to advance, it is increasingly important to be able to communicate in both English and Spanish in order to relay instructions and safety precautions to workers with limited understanding of English; Spanish-speaking workers make up a large part of the construction workforce in many areas. Carpenters may advance to carpentry supervisor or general construction supervisor positions. Others may become independent contractors. Supervisors and contractors need good communication skills to deal with clients and subcontractors and should be able to identify and estimate the quantity of materials needed to complete a job and accurately estimate how long a job will take to complete and at what cost.

Employment

Carpenters are employed throughout the country in almost every community and make up the largest building trades occupation. They held about 1.3 million jobs in 2004. About one-third worked in building construction and about one-fifth worked for special trade contractors. Most of the rest of the wage and salary workers worked for manufacturing firms, government agencies, retail establishments, and a wide variety of other industries. About one-third of all carpenters were self-employed.

Job Outlook

Job opportunities for carpenters are expected to be excellent over the 2004–2014 period, particularly for those with the most skills. Employment of carpenters is expected to increase about as fast as the average for all occupations through 2014, and turnover also creates a large number of openings each year. Contractors report having trouble finding skilled carpenters to fill many of their openings, due in part to the fact that many jobseekers are not inclined to go into construction, preferring work that is less strenuous with more comfortable working conditions. Also, many people with limited skills take jobs as carpenters but eventually leave the occupation because they dislike the work or cannot find steady employment.

The need for carpenters is expected to grow as construction activity increases in response to demand for new housing, office and retail space and for modernizing and expanding schools and industrial plants. A strong home remodeling market also will create a large demand for carpenters.

Some of the demand for carpenters, however, will be offset by expected productivity gains resulting from the increasing use of prefabricated components and improved fasteners and tools. Prefabricated wall panels, roof assemblies, and stairs and prehung doors and windows can be installed very quickly. Instead of having to be built on the worksite, prefabricated walls, partitions, and stairs can be lifted into place in one operation; beams—and, in some cases, entire roof assemblies—are lifted into place using a crane. As prefabricated components become more standardized, builders will use them more often. In addition, improved adhesives are reducing the time needed to join materials, and lightweight, cordless, and pneumatic tools—such as nailers and drills—will all continue to make carpenters more efficient. New and improved tools, equipment, techniques, and materials also have vastly increased carpenter versatility.

Carpenters with all-around skills will have better opportunities for steady work than carpenters who can perform only a few relatively simple, routine tasks. Carpenters can experience periods of unemployment because of the short-term nature of many construction projects, winter slowdowns in construction activity in northern areas, and the cyclical nature of the construction industry. During economic downturns, the number of job openings for carpenters declines. Building activity depends on many factors that vary with the state of the economy—interest rates, availability of mortgage funds, government spending, and business investment.

Job opportunities for carpenters also vary by geographic area. Construction activity parallels the movement of people and businesses and reflects differences in local economic conditions. The areas with the largest population increases will also provide the best job opportunities for carpenters and apprenticeship opportunities for persons seeking to enter carpentry.

Earnings

In May 2004, median hourly earnings of carpenters were $16.78. The middle 50 percent earned between $12.91 and $22.62. The lowest 10 percent earned less than $10.36, and the highest 10 percent earned more than $28.65. Median hourly earnings in the industries employing the largest numbers of carpenters in May 2004 were as follows:

Nonresidential building construction	$18.70
Building finishing contractors	17.51
Residential building construction	16.48
Foundation, structure, and building exterior contractors	16.40
Employment services	13.94

Earnings can be reduced on occasion because carpenters lose work time in bad weather and during recessions when jobs are unavailable.

Some carpenters are members of the United Brotherhood of Carpenters and Joiners of America.

Related Occupations

Carpenters are skilled construction workers. Other skilled construction occupations include brickmasons, blockmasons, and stonemasons; cement masons, concrete finishers, segmental pavers, and terrazzo workers; electricians; pipelayers, plumbers, pipefitters, and steamfitters; and plasterers and stucco masons.

Sources of Additional Information

For information about carpentry apprenticeships or other work opportunities in this trade, contact local carpentry contractors, locals of the union mentioned earlier, local joint union-contractor apprenticeship committees, or the nearest office of the state employment service or apprenticeship agency. You can also find information on the registered apprenticeship system with links to state apprenticeship programs on the U.S. Department of Labor's Web site: http://www.doleta.gov/atels_bat

For information on training opportunities and carpentry in general, contact

- ▸ Associated Builders and Contractors, 4250 North Fairfax Dr., 9th Floor, Arlington, VA 22203. Internet: http://www.trytools.org
- ▸ Associated General Contractors of America, Inc., 2300 Wilson Blvd., Suite 400, Arlington, VA 22201. Internet: http://www.agc.org
- ▸ National Center for Construction Education and Research, P.O. Box 141104, Gainesville, FL 32614-1104. Internet: http://www.nccer.org
- ▸ National Association of Home Builders, Home Builders Institute, 1201 15th St. NW, Washington, DC 20005. Internet: http://www.hbi.org
- ▸ United Brotherhood of Carpenters and Joiners of America, Carpenters Training Fund, 6801 Placid St., Las Vegas, NV 89119. Internet: http://www.carpenters.org

Cashiers

(O*NET 41-2011.00 and 41-2012.00)

Significant Points

■ Cashiers are trained on the job; this occupation provides opportunities for many young people with no previous work experience.

■ Nearly one-half of all cashiers work part time.

■ Despite projected slower-than-average employment growth, good employment opportunities are expected because of the large number of workers who leave this occupation each year.

■ Many cashiers start at minimum wage.

Nature of the Work

Supermarkets, department stores, gasoline service stations, movie theaters, restaurants, and many other businesses employ cashiers to register the sale of their merchandise. Most cashiers total bills, receive money, make change, fill out charge forms, and give receipts.

Although specific job duties vary by employer, cashiers usually are assigned to a register at the beginning of their shifts and are given drawers containing a specific amount of money with which to start—their "tills." They must count their tills to ensure that they contain the correct amount of money and adequate supplies of change. Cashiers also handle returns and exchanges. They must ensure that returned merchandise is in good condition and determine where and when it was purchased and what type of payment was used.

After entering charges for all items and subtracting the value of any coupons or special discounts, cashiers total the customer's bill and take payment. Acceptable forms of payment include cash, personal checks, credit cards, and debit cards. Cashiers must know the store's policies and procedures for each type of payment the store accepts. For checks and charges, they may request additional identification from the customer or call in for an authorization. They must verify the age of customers purchasing alcohol or tobacco. When the sale is complete, cashiers issue a receipt to the customer and return the appropriate change. They may also wrap or bag the purchase.

At the end of their shifts, they once again count the drawers' contents and compare the totals with sales data. An occasional shortage of small amounts may be overlooked but, in many establishments, repeated shortages are grounds for dismissal. In addition to counting the contents of their drawers at the end of their shifts, cashiers usually separate and total charge forms, return slips, coupons, and any other noncash items.

Most cashiers now use scanners and computers, but some establishments still require price and product information to be entered manually. In a store with scanners, a cashier passes a product's Universal Product Code over the scanning device, which transmits the code number to a computer. The computer identifies the item and its price. In other establishments, cashiers manually enter codes into computers, and descriptions of the items and their prices appear on the screen.

Depending on the type of establishment, cashiers may have other duties as well. In many supermarkets, for example, cashiers weigh produce and bulk food as well as return unwanted items to the shelves. In convenience stores, cashiers may be required to know how to use a variety of machines other than cash registers and how to furnish money orders and sell lottery tickets. Operating ticket-dispensing machines and answering customers' questions are common duties for cashiers who work at movie theaters and ticket agencies. In casinos, *gaming change persons* and *booth cashiers* exchange coins and tokens and may issue payoffs. They may also operate a booth in the slot-machine area and furnish change persons with a money bank at the start of the shift or count and audit money in drawers.

Working Conditions

Nearly one-half of all cashiers work part time. Hours of work often vary depending on the needs of the employer. Generally, cashiers are expected to work weekends, evenings, and holidays to accommodate customers' needs. However, many employers offer flexible schedules. Because the holiday season is the busiest time for most retailers, many employers restrict the use of vacation time from Thanksgiving through the beginning of January.

Most cashiers work indoors, usually standing in booths or behind counters. In addition, they often are unable to leave their workstations without supervisory approval because they are responsible for large sums of money. The work of cashiers can be very repetitious, but improvements in workstation design are being made to combat problems caused by repetitive motion. In addition, the work can sometimes be dangerous; cashiers' risk from robberies and homicides is much higher than that of the total workforce, although more safety precautions are being taken to help deter robbers.

Gaming change persons and booth cashiers can expect a safer work environment than cashiers in other industries. However, casinos are not without their hazards, such as exposure to fumes from cigarettes, cigars, and pipes and noise from slot machines.

Training, Other Qualifications, and Advancement

Cashier jobs tend to be entry-level positions requiring little or no previous work experience. Although there are no specific educational requirements, employers filling full-time jobs often prefer applicants with high school diplomas. Gaming change persons and booth cashiers are required to obtain a license and background check from their state's gaming board and must meet a certain age requirement, usually set at 21 years old.

Nearly all cashiers are trained on the job. In small businesses, an experienced worker often trains beginners. The trainee spends the first day observing the operation and becoming familiar with the store's equipment, policies, and procedures. After this, trainees are assigned to a register—frequently under the supervision of an experienced worker. In larger businesses, trainees spend several days in classes before being placed at cash registers. Topics typically covered in class include a description of the industry and the company, store policies and procedures, equipment operation, and security.

Training for experienced workers is not common except when new equipment is introduced or when procedures change. In these cases, the employer or a representative of the equipment manufacturer trains workers on the job.

Persons who want to become cashiers should be able to do repetitious work accurately. They also need basic mathematics skills and good manual dexterity. Because cashiers deal constantly with the public, they should be neat in appearance and able to deal tactfully and pleasantly with customers. In addition, some businesses prefer to hire persons who can operate specialized equipment or who have business experience, such as typing, selling, or handling money. Advancement opportunities for cashiers vary. For those working part time, promotion may be to a full-time position. Others advance to head cashier or cash-office clerk. In addition, this job offers a good opportunity to learn about an employer's business and can serve as a stepping-stone to a more responsible position.

Employment

Cashiers held about 3.5 million jobs in 2004. Of these, 29,000 were employed as gaming change persons and booth cashiers. Although cashiers are employed in almost every industry, 27 percent of all jobs were in food and beverage stores. Gasoline stations, department stores, other retail establishments, and restaurants also employed large numbers of these workers. Outside of retail establishments, many cashiers worked in amusement, gambling, and recreation industries; local government; and personal and laundry services. Because cashiers are needed in businesses and organizations of all types and sizes, job opportunities are found throughout the country.

Job Outlook

Opportunities for full-time and part-time cashier jobs should continue to be good because of employment growth and the need to replace the large number of workers who transfer to other occupations or leave the labor force. There is substantial movement into and out of the occupation because education and training requirements are minimal and the predominance of part-time jobs is attractive to people seeking a short-term source of income rather than a full-time career. Historically, workers under the age of 25 have filled many of the openings in this occupation—in 2004, almost fifty percent of all cashiers were 24 years of age or younger. Some establishments have begun hiring elderly and disabled persons to fill some of their job openings.

Cashier employment is expected to grow more slowly than average for all occupations through the year 2014. The rising popularity of purchasing goods online may reduce the employment growth of cashiers, although many customers still prefer the traditional method of purchasing goods at stores. Also, the growing use of self-service check-out systems in retail trade, especially at grocery stores, should have an adverse effect on employment of cashiers. These self-checkout systems may outnumber checkouts with clerks in the future in many establishments. The impact on employment growth of cashiers will largely depend on the public's acceptance of the new self-service technology.

Job opportunities may vary from year to year because the strength of the economy affects demand for cashiers. Companies tend to hire more persons for such jobs when the economy is strong. Seasonal demand for cashiers also causes fluctuations in employment.

Opportunities will be strong for gaming cashiers as more states legalize casinos and gaming becomes more popular. An increasing number of gaming venues and high turnover in this occupation will generate many job openings. However, many casinos are finding ways to use less cash in their operations, particularly the slot machines, which now generate tickets that can be accepted by other slot machines.

Earnings

Many cashiers start at the federal minimum wage, which was $5.15 an hour in 2005. Some state laws set the minimum wage higher, and establishments must pay at least that amount. Wages tend to be higher in areas in which there is intense competition for workers.

Median hourly earnings of cashiers, except gaming, in May 2004 were $7.81. The middle 50 percent earned between $6.72 and $9.10 an hour. The lowest 10 percent earned less than $5.91, and the highest 10 percent earned more than $11.30 an hour. Median hourly earnings in the industries employing the largest numbers of cashiers in May 2004 were

Grocery stores	$7.90
Department stores	7.89
Other general merchandise stores	7.85
Health and personal care stores	7.68
Gasoline stations	7.54

Median hourly earnings for gaming cashiers in May 2004 were $9.87. The middle 50 percent earned between $8.23 and $11.74 an hour. The lowest 10 percent earned less than $7.07, and the highest 10 percent earned more than $13.51 an hour.

Benefits for full-time cashiers tend to be better than those for cashiers working part time. In addition to typical benefits, those working in retail establishments often receive discounts on purchases, and cashiers in restaurants may receive free or low-cost meals. Some employers also offer employee stock-option plans and education-reimbursement plans.

Related Occupations

Cashiers accept payment for the purchase of goods and services. Other workers with similar duties include tellers, counter and rental clerks, food and beverage serving and related workers, Postal Service workers, and retail salespersons, all of whom are discussed elsewhere in this book.

Sources of Additional Information

General information on retailing is available from

▸ National Retail Federation, 325 7th St. NW, Suite 1100, Washington, DC 20004.

General information on careers in grocery stores is available from

▸ Food Marketing Institute, 655 15th St. NW, Washington, DC 20005.

For information about employment opportunities as a cashier, contact

▸ National Association of Convenience Stores, 1605 King St., Alexandria, VA 22314-2792.

▸ United Food and Commercial Workers International Union, Education Office, 1775 K St. NW, Washington, DC 20006-1502.

Chefs, Cooks, and Food Preparation Workers

(O*NET 35-1011.00, 35-2011.00, 35-2012.00, 35-2013.00, 35-2014.00, 35-2015.00, and 35-2021.00)

Significant Points

■ Many young people work as cooks and food preparation workers—almost 19 percent are between 16 and 19 years old.

■ More than 2 out of 5 food preparation workers are employed part time.

■ Job openings are expected to be plentiful because many of these workers transfer to other occupations with higher earnings or burn out from the fast work pace and pressure to fill orders quickly.

Nature of the Work

Chefs, cooks, and food preparation workers prepare, season, and cook a wide range of foods—from soups, snacks, and salads to entrees, side dishes, and desserts—in a variety of restaurants and other food services establishments. Chefs and cooks create recipes and prepare meals, while food preparation workers peel and cut vegetables, trim meat, prepare poultry, and perform other duties such as keeping work areas clean and monitoring temperatures of ovens and stovetops.

In general, *chefs* and *cooks* measure, mix, and cook ingredients according to recipes, using a variety of pots; pans; cutlery; and other equipment, including ovens, broilers, grills, slicers, grinders, and blenders. Chefs and head cooks also are responsible for directing the work of other kitchen workers, estimating food requirements, and ordering food supplies.

Larger restaurants and food services establishments tend to have varied menus and larger kitchen staffs. They often include several chefs and cooks, sometimes called assistant or line cooks, along with other lesser-skilled kitchen workers, such as *food preparation workers*. Each chef or cook works an assigned station that is equipped with the types of stoves, grills, pans, and ingredients needed for the foods prepared at that station. Job titles often reflect the principal ingredient prepared or the type of cooking performed—*vegetable cook, fry cook,* or *grill cook.*

Executive chefs and *head cooks* coordinate the work of the kitchen staff and direct the preparation of meals. They determine serving sizes, plan menus, order food supplies, and oversee kitchen operations to ensure uniform quality and presentation of meals. The terms chef and cook often are used interchangeably, but generally reflect the different types of chefs and the organizational structure of the kitchen staff. For example, an *executive chef* is in charge of all food service operations and also may supervise the many kitchens of a hotel, restaurant group, or corporate dining operation. A *chef de cui-*

sine reports to an executive chef and is responsible for the daily operations of a single kitchen. A *sous chef*, or sub chef, is the second-in-command and runs the kitchen in the absence of the chef. Chefs tend to be more highly skilled and better trained than cooks. Many chefs earn fame both for themselves and for their kitchens because of the quality and distinctive nature of the food they serve.

The specific responsibilities of most cooks are determined by a number of factors, including the type of restaurant in which they work. *Institution and cafeteria cooks*, for example, work in the kitchens of schools, cafeterias, businesses, hospitals, and other institutions. For each meal, they prepare a large quantity of a limited number of entrees, vegetables, and desserts. *Restaurant cooks* usually prepare a wider selection of dishes, cooking most orders individually. *Short-order cooks* prepare foods in restaurants and coffee shops that emphasize fast service and quick food preparation. They grill and garnish hamburgers, prepare sandwiches, fry eggs, and cook French fries, often working on several orders at the same time. *Fast-food cooks* prepare a limited selection of menu items in fast-food restaurants. They cook and package batches of food, such as hamburgers and fried chicken, to be kept warm until served. (*Combined food preparation and service workers,* who both prepare and serve items in fast-food restaurants, are included with the material on food and beverage serving and related workers elsewhere in this book.)

Some cooks do not work in restaurant or food service kitchens. *Private household cooks* (or *personal chefs*) plan and prepare meals in private homes according to the client's tastes or dietary needs. They order groceries and supplies, clean the kitchen, and wash dishes and utensils. They also may serve meals. *Research chefs* combine culinary skills with knowledge of food science to develop recipes and test new formulas; experiment with flavors and eye appeal of prepared foods; and test new products and equipment for chain restaurants, food growers and processors, and manufacturers and marketers.

Food preparation workers perform routine, repetitive tasks such as readying ingredients for complex dishes, slicing and dicing vegetables, and composing salads and cold items under the direction of chefs and cooks. They weigh and measure ingredients, go after pots and pans, and stir and strain soups and sauces. Food preparation workers may cut and grind meats, poultry, and seafood in preparation for cooking. Their responsibilities also include cleaning work areas, equipment, utensils, dishes, and silverware.

The number and types of workers employed in kitchens depends on the type of establishment. For example, fast-food establishments offer only a few items, which are prepared by fast-food cooks. Small, full-service restaurants offering casual dining often feature a limited number of easy-to-prepare items supplemented by short-order specialties and ready-made desserts. Typically, one cook prepares all the food with the help of a short-order cook and one or two other kitchen workers.

Grocery and specialty food stores employ chefs, cooks, and food preparation workers to develop recipes and prepare meals for customers to carry out. Typically, entrees, side dishes, salads, or other items are prepared in large quantities and stored at an appropriate temperature. Servers portion and package items according to customer orders for serving at home.

Working Conditions

Many restaurant and institutional kitchens have modern equipment, convenient work areas, and air conditioning, but kitchens in older and smaller eating places are often not as well designed. Kitchens must be well ventilated, appropriately lit, and properly equipped with sprinkler systems to protect against fires. Kitchen staffs invariably work in small quarters against hot stoves and ovens. They are under constant pressure to prepare meals quickly while ensuring that quality is maintained and safety and sanitation guidelines are observed.

Working conditions vary with the type and quantity of food prepared and the local laws governing food service operations. Workers usually must withstand the pressure and strain of standing for hours at a time, lifting heavy pots and kettles, and working near hot ovens and grills. Job hazards include slips and falls, cuts, and burns, but injuries are seldom serious.

Work hours in restaurants may include early mornings, late evenings, holidays, and weekends. Work schedules of chefs, cooks, and other kitchen workers in factory and school cafeterias may be more regular. In 2004, about 40 percent of cooks and 46 percent of food preparation workers had part-time schedules, compared to 16 percent of workers throughout the economy. Work schedules in fine-dining restaurants, however, tend to be longer because of the time required to prepare ingredients in advance. Many executive chefs regularly work 12-hour days because they oversee the delivery of foodstuffs early in the day, plan the menu, and start preparing those menu items that take the greatest amount of preparation time or skill.

The wide range in dining hours and the need for fully-staffed kitchens during all open hours creates work opportunities for individuals seeking supplemental income, flexible work hours, or variable schedules. For example, almost 19 percent of cooks and food preparation workers were 16–19 years old in 2004, and almost 11 percent had variable schedules. Kitchen workers employed by schools may work during the school year only, usually for 9 or 10 months. Similarly, resort establishments usually only offer seasonal employment.

Training, Other Qualifications, and Advancement

Most fast-food or short-order cooks and food preparation workers require little education or training; most skills are learned on the job. Training generally starts with basic sanitation and workplace safety subjects and continues with instruction on food handling, preparation, and cooking procedures.

A high school diploma is not required for beginning jobs, but it is recommended for those planning a career as a cook or chef. High school or vocational school programs may offer courses in basic food safety and handling procedures and general business and computer classes for those who want to manage or open their own place. Many school districts, in cooperation with state departments of education, provide on-the-job training and summer workshops for cafeteria kitchen workers who aspire to become cooks. Large corporations in the food services and hospitality industries also offer paid internships and summer jobs to those just starting out in the field. Internships provide valuable experience and can lead to placement in more formal chef training programs.

Executive chefs and head cooks who work in fine-dining restaurants require many years of training and experience and an intense desire to cook. Some chefs and cooks may start their training in high school or post–high school vocational programs. Others may receive formal training through independent cooking schools, professional culinary institutes, or 2- or 4-year college degree programs in hospitality or culinary arts. In addition, some large hotels and restaurants operate their own training and job-placement programs for chefs and cooks. Most formal training programs require some form of apprenticeship, internship, or outplacement program jointly offered by the school and affiliated restaurants. Professional culinary institutes, industry associations, and trade unions also may sponsor formal apprenticeship programs in coordination with the U.S. Department of Labor. Many chefs are trained on the job, receiving real work experience and training from chef mentors in the restaurants where they work.

People who have had courses in commercial food preparation may start in a cook or chef job without spending a lot of time in lower-skilled kitchen jobs. Their education may give them an advantage when looking for jobs in better restaurants. Some vocational programs in high schools may offer training, but employers usually prefer training given by trade schools, vocational centers, colleges, professional associations, or trade unions. Postsecondary courses range from a few months to 2 years or more. Degree-granting programs are open only to high school graduates. Chefs also may compete and test for certification as master chefs. Although certification is not required to enter the field, it can be a measure of accomplishment and lead to further advancement and higher-paying positions. The U.S. Armed Forces also are a good source of training and experience.

Although curricula may vary, students in formal culinary training programs spend most of their time in kitchens learning to use the appropriate equipment and to prepare meals through actual practice. They learn good knife techniques, safe food-handling procedures, and proper use and care of kitchen equipment. Training programs often include courses in nutrition, menu planning, portion control, purchasing and inventory methods, proper food storage procedures, and use of leftover food to minimize waste. Students also learn sanitation and public health rules for handling food. Training in food service management, computer accounting and inventory software, and banquet service are featured in some training programs.

The number of formal and informal culinary training programs continues to increase to meet demand. Formal programs, which may offer training leading to a certificate or a 2- or 4-year degree, are geared more for training chefs for fine-dining or upscale restaurants. They offer a wider array of training options and specialties, such as advanced cooking techniques; cooking for banquets, buffets, or parties; and cuisines and cooking styles from around the world.

The American Culinary Federation accredits more than 100 formal training programs and sponsors apprenticeship programs around the country. Typical apprenticeships last three years and combine classroom training and work experience. Accreditation is an indication that a culinary program meets recognized standards regarding course content, facilities, and quality of instruction. The American Culinary Federation also certifies pastry professionals, personal chefs, and culinary educators in addition to various levels of chefs. Certification standards are based primarily on experience and formal training.

Vocational or trade-school programs typically offer more basic training in preparing food, such as food handling and sanitation procedures; nutrition; slicing and dicing methods for various kinds of meats and vegetables; and basic cooking methods, such as baking, broiling, and grilling.

Important characteristics for chefs, cooks, and food preparation workers include working well as part of a team, having a keen sense of taste and smell, and working efficiently to turn out meals rapidly. Personal cleanliness is essential because most states require health certificates indicating that workers are free from communicable diseases. Knowledge of a foreign language can be an asset because it may improve communication with other restaurant staff, vendors, and the restaurant's clientele.

Advancement opportunities for chefs, cooks, and food preparation workers depend on their training, work experience, and ability to perform more responsible and sophisticated tasks. Many food preparation workers, for example, may move into assistant or line cook positions. Chefs and cooks who demonstrate an eagerness to learn new cooking skills and to accept greater responsibility may move up within the kitchen and take on responsibility for training or supervising newer or lesser-skilled kitchen staff. Others may move from one kitchen or restaurant to another.

Some chefs and cooks go into business as caterers or personal chefs or they open their own restaurant. Others become instructors in culinary training programs. A number of cooks and chefs advance to executive chef positions or food service management positions, particularly in hotels; clubs; or larger, more elegant restaurants where they may oversee operations in a number of kitchens or restaurants. (See the description of food service managers elsewhere in this book.)

Employment

Chefs, cooks and food preparation workers held nearly 3.1 million jobs in 2004. The distribution of jobs among the various types of chefs, cooks, and food preparation workers was as follows:

Food preparation workers	889,000
Cooks, restaurant	783,000
Cooks, fast food	662,000
Cooks, institution and cafeteria	424,000
Cooks, short order	230,000
Chefs and head cooks	125,000
Cooks, private household	9,200

Nearly two-thirds of all chefs, cooks, and food preparation workers were employed in restaurants and other food services and drinking places. Almost one-fifth worked in institutions such as schools, universities, hospitals, and nursing care facilities. Grocery stores, hotels, gasoline stations with convenience stores, and other organizations employed the remainder.

Job Outlook

Job openings for chefs, cooks, and food preparation workers are expected to be plentiful through 2014; however, competition should be keen for jobs in the top kitchens of higher-end restaurants. While job growth will create new positions, primarily due to the expansion of family-casual dining, the overwhelming majority of job openings will stem from the need to replace workers who leave this large occupational group. Many chef, cook, and food preparation worker jobs are attractive to people seeking first-time or short-term employment, additional income, or a flexible schedule. Employers typically hire a large number of part-time workers and require minimal education and training for these lesser-skilled entry-level positions. Many of these workers transfer to other occupations or stop working, creating numerous openings for those entering the field.

Overall employment of chefs, cooks, and food preparation workers is expected to increase about as fast as the average for all occupations over the 2004–2014 period. Employment growth will be spurred by increases in population, household income, and leisure time that will allow people to more often dine out and take vacations. In addition, the large number of two-income households will lead more families to opt for the convenience of dining out.

Projected employment growth, however, varies by specialty. The number of higher-skilled chefs and cooks working in full-service restaurants—those that offer table service and more varied menus—is expected to increase about as fast as the average. Much of the increase in this segment, however, will come from job growth in more casual dining rather than upscale full-service restaurants. Dining trends suggest increasing numbers of meals eaten away from home and growth in family dining restaurants but greater limits on expense-account meals. Similarly, employment of food preparation workers will grow faster than the average, reflecting diners' desires for convenience as they shop for carryout meals in a greater variety of places—full-service restaurants, limited-service eating places, or grocery stores.

Employment of fast-food cooks is expected to grow about as fast as the average. Duties of cooks in fast-food restaurants are limited; most workers are likely to be combined food preparation and serving workers rather than fast-food cooks. Employment of short-order cooks is expected to increase about as fast as the average. Short-order cooks may work a grill or sandwich station in a full-line restaurant but also may work in lunch counters or coffee shops that specialize in meals served quickly.

Employment of institution and cafeteria chefs and cooks will show little or no growth. Their employment will not keep pace with the rapid growth in the educational and health services industries where their employment is concentrated. In an effort to make "institutional food" more attractive to office workers, students, staff, visitors, and patients, offices, schools, and hospitals increasingly contract out their food services. Employment of cooks, private household, however, is projected to decline, reflecting the general decline in private household service employment.

Employment of chefs, cooks, and food preparation workers who prepare meals to go, such as those who work in the prepared foods sections of grocery or specialty food stores, should increase much faster than the average as people continue to demand quality meals and convenience. Similarly, much-faster-than-average growth also is expected among those who work in contract food service establishments, such as those that provide catering services and those who support employee dining rooms or staff hotel restaurants on a contract basis. These changes reflect a continuing trend among large establishments to contract out food services so they may better focus on their core business of running a hospital, hotel, factory, or school. Also, there is a growing consumer desire for healthier, made-from-scratch meals without sacrificing the convenience of pre-packaged prepared foods or fast-food dining.

Earnings

Wages of chefs, cooks, and food preparation workers vary greatly according to region of the country and the type of food services establishment in which they work. Wages usually are highest in elegant restaurants and hotels, where many executive chefs are employed, and in major metropolitan areas.

Median hourly earnings of chefs and head cooks were $14.75 in May 2004. The middle 50 percent earned between $10.71 and $20.28. The lowest 10 percent earned less than $8.28, and the highest 10 percent earned more than $26.75 per hour. Median hourly earnings in the industries employing the largest number of chefs and head cooks in May 2004 were

```
Other amusement and recreation industries ...........$19.27
Traveler accommodations ......................................18.25
Special food services ...........................................15.06
Full-service restaurants ........................................13.57
Limited-service eating places ...............................12.00
```

Median hourly earnings of cooks, private household were $9.42 in May 2004. The middle 50 percent earned between $7.08 and $12.79. The lowest 10 percent earned less than $6.01, and the highest 10 percent earned more than $16.55 per hour.

Median hourly earnings of restaurant cooks were $9.39 in May 2004. The middle 50 percent earned between $7.79 and $11.13. The lowest 10 percent earned less than $6.76, and the highest 10 percent earned more than $13.37 per hour. Median hourly earnings in the industries employing the largest numbers of restaurant cooks in May 2004 were

```
Traveler accommodations ...................................$10.69
Other amusement and recreation industries..............10.55
Special food services ...........................................10.00
Full-service restaurants ........................................9.34
Drinking places (alcoholic beverages) ....................9.27
Limited-service eating places ...............................8.25
```

Median hourly earnings of institution and cafeteria cooks were $9.10 in May 2004. The middle 50 percent earned between $7.20 and $11.22. The lowest 10 percent earned less than $6.08, and the highest 10 percent earned more than $13.72 per hour. Median hourly earnings in the industries employing the largest numbers of institution and cafeteria cooks in May 2004 were

```
General medical and surgical hospitals .................$10.38
Special food services ...........................................10.11
```

```
Community care facilities for the elderly ..................9.60
Nursing care facilities ..........................................9.33
Elementary and secondary schools...........................8.06
```

Median hourly earnings of short-order cooks were $8.11 in May 2004. The middle 50 percent earned between $6.90 and $9.92. The lowest 10 percent earned less than $5.97, and the highest 10 percent earned more than $11.50 per hour. Median hourly earnings in the industries employing the largest number of short-order cooks in May 2004 were

```
Full-service restaurants ........................................$8.53
Drinking places (alcoholic beverages) .....................8.08
Other amusement and recreation industries...............7.79
Limited-service eating places .................................7.21
Gasoline stations .................................................6.99
```

Median hourly earnings of food preparation workers were $8.03 in May 2004. The middle 50 percent earned between $6.89 and $9.78. The lowest 10 percent earned less than $5.97, and the highest 10 percent earned more than $11.90 per hour. Median hourly earnings in the industries employing the largest number of food preparation workers in May 2004 were

```
Elementary and secondary schools .........................$9.04
Grocery stores ....................................................8.54
Nursing care facilities ..........................................8.10
Full-service restaurants ........................................7.94
Limited-service eating places .................................7.27
```

Median hourly earnings of fast-food cooks were $7.07 in May 2004. The middle 50 percent earned between $6.20 and $8.22. The lowest 10 percent earned less than $5.68, and the highest 10 percent earned more than $9.63 per hour. Median hourly earnings in the industries employing the largest number of fast-food cooks in May 2004 were

```
Grocery stores.....................................................$8.26
Special food services ...........................................7.97
Gasoline stations .................................................7.18
Full-service restaurants ........................................7.16
Limited-service eating places .................................7.02
```

Some employers provide employees with uniforms and free meals, but federal law permits employers to deduct from their employees' wages the cost or fair value of any meals or lodging provided, and some employers do so. Chefs, cooks, and food preparation workers who work full time often receive typical benefits, but part-time workers usually do not.

In some large hotels and restaurants, kitchen workers belong to unions. The principal unions are the Hotel Employees and Restaurant Employees International Union and the Service Employees International Union.

Related Occupations

Workers who perform tasks similar to those of chefs, cooks, and food preparation workers include food processing occupations, such as butchers and meat cutters, and bakers. Others who work closely with these workers include food service managers and food and beverage serving and related workers.

Sources of Additional Information

Information about job opportunities may be obtained from local employers and local offices of the state employment service.

Career information about chefs, cooks, and other kitchen workers, as well as a directory of 2- and 4-year colleges that offer courses or programs that prepare persons for food service careers, is available from

▸ National Restaurant Association, 1200 17th St. NW, Washington, DC 20036-3097. Internet: http://www.restaurant.org

For information on the American Culinary Federation's apprenticeship and certification programs for cooks, as well as a list of accredited culinary programs, send a self-addressed, stamped envelope to

▸ American Culinary Federation, 180 Center Place Way, St. Augustine, FL 32095. Internet: http://www.acfchefs.org

For information about becoming a personal chef, contact

▸ American Personal Chef Association, 4572 Delaware St., San Diego, CA 92116.

For general information on hospitality careers, contact

▸ International Council on Hotel, Restaurant, and Institutional Education, 2613 North Parham Rd., 2nd Floor, Richmond, VA 23294. Internet: http://www.chrie.org

Child Care Workers

(O*NET 39-9011.00 and 39-9011.01)

Significant Points

■ About 1 out of 3 child care workers are self-employed; most of these are family child care providers.

■ Training requirements vary from a high school diploma to a college degree, although a high school diploma and little or no experience are adequate for many jobs.

■ Many workers leave these jobs every year, creating good job opportunities.

Nature of the Work

Child care workers nurture and care for children who have not yet entered formal schooling and also work with older children in before- and after-school situations. These workers play an important role in a child's development by caring for the child when parents are at work or away for other reasons. In addition to attending to children's basic needs, child care workers organize activities that stimulate children's physical, emotional, intellectual, and social growth. They help children explore individual interests, develop talents and independence, build self-esteem, and learn how to get along with others.

Child care workers generally are classified in three different groups, depending on the setting in which they work: workers who care for children at the children's home, called private household workers; those who care for children in their own home, called family child care providers; and those that work at separate child care centers and centers that provide preschool services to 3- and 4-year-old children.

Private household workers who are employed on an hourly basis usually are called *babysitters*. These child care workers bathe, dress, and feed children; supervise their play; wash their clothes; and clean their rooms. Babysitters also may put children to bed and wake them, read to them, involve them in educational games, take them for doctors' visits, and discipline them. Those who are in charge of infants, sometimes called *infant nurses*, also prepare bottles and change diapers. *Nannies* work full or part time for a single family. They generally take care of children from birth to age 10 or 12, tending to the child's early education, nutrition, health, and other needs, and also may perform the duties of a housekeeper, including cleaning and laundry.

Family child care providers often work alone with a small group of children, though some work in larger settings with multiple adults. Child care centers generally have more than one adult per group of children; in groups of older children, a child care worker may assist a more experienced preschool teacher.

Most child care workers perform a combination of basic care and teaching duties, but the majority of their time is spent on caregiving activities. Workers whose primary responsibility is teaching are classified as preschool teachers. However, many basic care activities also are opportunities for children to learn. For example, a worker who shows a child how to tie a shoelace teaches the child while also providing for that child's basic care needs. Child care programs help children learn about trust and gain a sense of security.

Child care workers spend most of their day working with children. However, they do maintain contact with parents or guardians through informal meetings or scheduled conferences to discuss each child's progress and needs. Many child care workers keep records of each child's progress and suggest ways in which parents can stimulate their child's learning and development at home. Some child care centers and before- and after-school programs actively recruit parent volunteers to work with the children and participate in administrative decisions and program planning.

Young children learn mainly through play. Child care workers recognize this and capitalize on children's play to further language development (storytelling and acting games), improve social skills (working together to build a neighborhood in a sandbox), and introduce scientific and mathematical concepts (balancing and counting blocks when building a bridge or mixing colors when painting). Often a less-structured approach is used to teach young children, including small-group lessons; one-on-one instruction; and creative activities such as art, dance, and music. Child care workers play a vital role in preparing children to build the skills they will need in school.

Child care workers in child care centers or family child care homes greet young children as they arrive, help them to remove outer garments, and select an activity of interest. When caring for infants, they feed and change them. To ensure a well-balanced program, child care workers prepare daily and long-term schedules of activities. Each day's activities balance individual and group play, as well as quiet and active time. Children are given some freedom to participate in activities in which they are interested.

Concern over school-aged children being home alone before and after school has spurred many parents to seek alternative ways for their children to constructively spend their time. The purpose of before- and after-school programs is to watch over school-aged children during the gap between school hours and their parents' work hours. These programs also may operate during the summer and on weekends. Workers in before- and after-school programs may help students with their homework or engage them in other extracurricular activities. These activities may include field trips, learning about computers, painting, photography, and participating in sports. Some child care workers may be responsible for taking children to school in the morning and picking them up from school in the afternoon. Before- and after-school programs may be operated by public school systems, local community centers, or other private organizations.

Helping keep young children healthy is an important part of the job. Child care workers serve nutritious meals and snacks and teach good eating habits and personal hygiene. They ensure that children have proper rest periods. They identify children who may not feel well and, in some cases, may help parents locate programs that will provide basic health services. Child care workers also watch for children who show signs of emotional or developmental problems and discuss these matters with their supervisor and the child's parents. Early identification of children with special needs—such as those with behavioral, emotional, physical, or learning disabilities—is important to improve their future learning ability. Special education teachers often work with these preschool children to provide the individual attention they need.

Working Conditions

Helping children grow, learn, and gain new skills can be very rewarding. Child care workers help to improve children's communication, learning, and other personal skills. The work is sometimes routine; however, new activities and challenges mark each day. Child care can be physically and emotionally taxing, as workers constantly stand, walk, bend, stoop, and lift to attend to each child's interests and problems.

To ensure that children in child care centers receive proper supervision, state or local regulations may require a certain ratio of workers to children. The ratio varies with the age of the children. Child development experts generally recommend that a single caregiver be responsible for no more than 3 or 4 infants (less than 1 year old), 5 or 6 toddlers (1 to 2 years old), or 10 preschool-aged children (between 2 and 5 years old). In before- and after-school programs, workers may be responsible for many school-aged children at a time.

Family child care providers work out of their own homes. While this arrangement provides convenience, it also requires that their homes be accommodating to young children. Private household workers usually work in the pleasant and comfortable homes or apartments of their employers. Most are day workers who live in their own homes and travel to work, though some live in the home of their employer, generally with their own room and bath. They often become part of their employer's family and may derive satisfaction from caring for the family.

The work hours of child care workers vary widely. Child care centers usually are open year round, with long hours so that parents can drop off and pick up their children before and after work. Some centers employ full-time and part-time staff with staggered shifts to cover the entire day. Some workers are unable to take regular breaks during the day due to limited staffing. Public and many private preschool programs operate during the typical 9- or 10-month school year, employing both full-time and part-time workers. Family child care providers have flexible hours and daily routines, but they may work long or unusual hours to fit parents' work schedules. Live-in nannies usually work longer hours than do those who have their own homes. However, although nannies may work evenings or weekends, they usually get other time off.

Training, Other Qualifications, and Advancement

The training and qualifications required of child care workers vary widely. Each state has its own licensing requirements that regulate caregiver training; these range from a high school diploma to community college courses to a college degree in child development or early childhood education. State requirements are generally higher for workers at child care centers than for family child care providers; child care workers in private settings who care for only a few children often are not regulated by states at all. Child care workers generally can obtain some form of employment with a high school diploma and little or no experience, but certain private firms and publicly funded programs have more demanding training and education requirements.

Some employers prefer to hire child care workers who have earned a nationally recognized Child Development Associate (CDA) credential or the Certified Childcare Professional designation, have taken secondary or postsecondary courses in child development and early childhood education, or have work experience in a child care setting. Other employers require their own specialized training. An increasing number of employers require an associate degree in early childhood education.

Child care workers must anticipate and prevent problems, deal with disruptive children, provide fair but firm discipline, and be enthusiastic and constantly alert. They must communicate effectively with the children and their parents, as well as with other teachers and child care workers. Workers should be mature, patient, understanding, and articulate and have energy and physical stamina. Skills in music, art, drama, and storytelling also are important. Self-employed child care workers must have business sense and management abilities.

Opportunities for advancement are limited. However, as child care workers gain experience, some may advance to supervisory or administrative positions in large child care centers or preschools. Often, these positions require additional training, such as a bachelor's or master's degree. Other workers move on to work in resource and referral agencies, consulting with parents on available child services. A few workers become involved in policy or advocacy work related to child care and early childhood education. With a bachelor's degree, workers may become preschool teachers or become certified to teach in public or private schools. Some workers set up their own child care businesses.

Employment

Child care workers held about 1.3 million jobs in 2004. Many worked part time. About 1 out of 3 child care workers were self-employed; most of these were family child care providers.

Seventeen percent of all child care workers are found in child day care services, and about 21 percent work for private households. The remainder worked primarily in local government educational services; nursing and residential care facilities; religious organizations; amusement and recreation industries; private educational services; civic and social organizations; individual and family services; and local government, excluding education and hospitals. Some child care programs are for-profit centers; some of these are affiliated with a local or national chain. Religious institutions, community agencies, school systems, and state and local governments operate non-profit programs. A very small percentage of private industry establishments operate onsite child care centers for the children of their employees.

Job Outlook

High replacement needs should create good job opportunities for child care workers. Qualified persons who are interested in this work should have little trouble finding and keeping a job. Many child care workers must be replaced each year as they leave the occupation temporarily to fulfill family responsibilities, to study, or for other reasons. Others leave permanently because they are interested in pursuing other occupations or because of dissatisfaction with hours, low pay and benefits, and stressful conditions.

Employment of child care workers is projected to increase about as fast as the average for all occupations through the year 2014. The number of women in the labor force of childbearing age (widely considered to be ages 15 to 44) and the number of children under 5 years of age are both expected to rise over the next 10 years. Also, the proportion of children being cared for exclusively by parents or other relatives is likely to continue to decline, spurring demand for additional child care workers. Concern about the behavior of school-aged children during nonschool hours also should increase demand for before- and after-school programs and child care workers to staff them.

The growth in demand for child care workers will be moderated, however, by an increasing emphasis on early childhood education programs. While only a few states currently provide targeted or universal preschool programs, many more are considering or currently implementing such programs. There also is likely to be a rise in enrollment in private preschools as the value of formal education before kindergarten becomes more widely accepted. Since the majority of workers in these programs are classified as preschool teachers, this growth in preschool enrollment will mean that relatively fewer child care workers will be needed for children old enough to participate in preschool.

Earnings

Pay depends on the educational attainment of the worker and the type of establishment. Although the pay generally is very low, more education usually means higher earnings. Median hourly earnings of wage and salary child care workers were $8.06 in May 2004. The middle 50 percent earned between $6.75 and $10.01. The lowest 10 percent earned less than $5.90, and the highest 10 percent earned more than $12.34. Median hourly earnings in the industries employing the largest numbers of child care workers in 2004 were as follows:

Other residential care facilities	$9.66
Elementary and secondary schools	9.22
Civic and social organizations	7.62
Other amusement and recreation industries	7.58
Child day care services	7.34

Earnings of self-employed child care workers vary depending on the hours worked, the number and ages of the children, and the location.

Benefits vary, but are minimal for most child care workers. Many employers offer free or discounted child care to employees. Some offer a full benefits package, including health insurance and paid vacations, but others offer no benefits at all. Some employers offer seminars and workshops to help workers learn new skills. A few are willing to cover the cost of courses taken at community colleges or technical schools. Live-in nannies receive free room and board.

Related Occupations

Child care work requires patience; creativity; an ability to nurture, motivate, teach, and influence children; and leadership, organizational, and administrative skills. Others who work with children and need these qualities and skills include teacher assistants; teachers—preschool, kindergarten, elementary, middle, and secondary; and teachers—special education.

Sources of Additional Information

For an electronic question-and-answer service on child care, information on becoming a child care provider, and other resources, contact

▸ National Child Care Information Center, 243 Church St. NW, 2nd Floor, Vienna, VA 22180. Internet: http://www.nccic.org

For information on becoming a family child care provider, send a stamped, self-addressed envelope to

▸ The Children's Foundation, 725 15th St. NW, Suite 505, Washington, DC 20005-2109. Internet: http://www.childrensfoundation.net

For eligibility requirements and a description of the Child Development Associate credential, contact

▸ Council for Professional Recognition, 2460 16th St. NW, Washington, DC 20009-3575. Internet: http://www.cdacouncil.org

For eligibility requirements and a description of the Certified Childcare Professional designation, contact

▸ National Child Care Association, 1016 Rosser St., Conyers, GA 30012. Internet: http://www.nccanet.org

For information about a career as a nanny, contact

▸ International Nanny Association, 191 Clarksville Rd., Princeton Junction, NJ 08550-3111. Telephone (toll free): 888-878-1477. Internet: http://www.nanny.org

State departments of human services or social services can supply state regulations and training requirements for child care workers.

Claims Adjusters, Appraisers, Examiners, and Investigators

(O*NET 13-1031.01, 13-1031.02, and 13-1032.00)

Significant Points

■ Adjusters and examiners investigate insurance claims, negotiate settlements, and authorize payments; appraisers assess the cost or value of an insured item; investigators deal with claims about which there is a question of liability and where fraud or criminal activity is suspected.

■ Licensing and continuing education requirements vary by state.

■ College graduates have the best opportunities; competition will be keen for jobs as investigators because this occupation attracts many qualified people.

Nature of the Work

Individuals and businesses purchase insurance policies to protect against monetary losses. In the event of a loss, policyholders submit claims, or requests for payment, seeking compensation for their loss. Adjusters, appraisers, examiners, and investigators work primarily for property and casualty insurance companies, for whom they handle a wide variety of claims alleging property damage, liability, or bodily injury. Their main role is to investigate the claims, negotiate settlements, and authorize payments to claimants, all the while mindful not to violate the claimant's rights under federal and state privacy laws. They must determine whether the customer's insurance policy covers the loss and how much of the loss should be paid to the claimant. Although many adjusters, appraisers, examiners, and investigators have overlapping functions and may even perform the same job, the insurance industry generally assigns specific roles to each of these claims workers.

Adjusters plan and schedule the work required to process a claim that would follow, for example, an automobile accident or damage to one's home caused by a storm. They investigate claims by interviewing the claimant and witnesses, consulting police and hospital records, and inspecting property damage to determine the extent of the company's liability. Adjusters may consult with other professionals, such as accountants, architects, construction workers, engineers, lawyers, and physicians, who can offer a more expert evaluation of a claim. The information gathered, including photographs and written or audiotaped or videotaped statements, is set down in a report that is then used to evaluate the associated claim. When the policyholder's claim is legitimate, the claims adjuster negotiates with the claimant and settles the claim. When claims are contested, adjusters will work with attorneys and expert witnesses to defend the insurer's position.

Many companies centralize claims adjustment in a claims center, where the cost of repair is determined and a check is issued immediately. More complex cases, usually involving bodily injury, are referred to senior adjusters. Some adjusters work with multiple types of insurance; however, most specialize in homeowner claims, business losses, automotive damage, or workers' compensation.

Claimants can opt not to rely on the services of their insurance company's adjuster and may instead choose to hire a public adjuster. These workers assist clients in preparing and presenting claims to insurance companies and in trying to negotiate a fair settlement. They perform the same services as adjusters who work directly for companies; however, they work in the best interests of the client rather than the insurance company.

Claims examiners within property and casualty insurance firms may have duties similar to those of an adjuster, but often their primary job is to review the claims submitted in order to ensure that proper guidelines have been followed. They may assist adjusters with complex and complicated claims or when a disaster suddenly greatly increases the volume of claims. Most claims examiners work for life or health insurance companies. In health insurance companies, examiners review health-related claims to see whether costs are reasonable on the basis of the diagnosis. The examiners are provided with guides that supply information on the average period of disability, the expected treatments, and the average hospital stay for patients with the various ailments for which a claim may be submitted. Examiners check claim applications for completeness and accuracy, interview medical specialists, and consult policy files to verify the information reported in a claim. Examiners will then either authorize the appropriate payment or refer the claim to an investigator for a more thorough review. Claims examiners usually specialize in group or individual insurance plans and in hospital, dental, or prescription drug claims.

In life insurance, claims examiners review the causes of death, particularly in the case of an accident, because most life insurance policies pay additional benefits if a death is accidental. Claims examiners also may review new applications for life insurance to make sure that the applicants have no serious illnesses that would make them a high risk to insure and thus disqualify them from obtaining insurance.

Another occupation that plays an important role in the accurate settlement of claims is that of the *appraiser*, whose role is to assess the cost or value of an insured item. The majority of appraisers employed by insurance companies and independent adjusting firms are *auto damage appraisers*. These appraisers inspect damaged vehicles after an accident and estimate the cost of repairs. This information is then relayed to the adjuster, who incorporates the appraisal into the settlement. Auto damage appraisers are valued by insurance companies because they can provide an unbiased judgment of repair costs. Otherwise, the companies would have to rely on auto mechanics' estimates, which might be unreasonably high.

Many claims adjusters and auto damage appraisers are equipped with laptop computers from which they can download the necessary forms and files from insurance company databases. Many adjusters and appraisers use digital cameras, which allow photographs of the damage to be sent to the company via the Internet. Many also input information about the damage directly into their computers, where software programs produce estimates of damage on standard forms. These new technologies allow for faster and more efficient processing of claims.

When adjusters or examiners suspect fraud, they refer the claim to an investigator. *Insurance investigators* in an insurance company's special investigative unit handle claims in which the company suspects fraudulent or criminal activity, such as arson, falsified workers' disability claims, staged accidents, or unnecessary medical treatments. The severity of insurance fraud cases can vary greatly, from claimants simply overstating the damage to a vehicle to complicated fraud rings responsible for many claimants and supported by dishonest doctors, lawyers, and even insurance personnel.

Investigators usually start with a database search to obtain background information on claimants and witnesses. Investigators can access certain personal information and identify Social Security numbers, aliases, driver's license numbers, addresses, phone numbers, criminal records, and past claims histories to establish whether a claimant has ever attempted insurance fraud. Then, investigators may visit claimants and witnesses to obtain a recorded statement, take photographs, and inspect facilities such as doctors' offices to determine whether the doctors have a proper license. Investigators often consult with legal counsel and can be expert witnesses in court cases.

Often, investigators also perform surveillance work. For example, in a case involving fraudulent workers' compensation claims, an investigator may covertly observe the claimant for several days or even weeks. If the investigator observes the subject performing an activity that is ruled out by injuries stated in a workers' compensation claim, the investigator will take video or still photographs to document the activity and report it to the insurance company.

Working Conditions

Working environments of claims adjusters, appraisers, examiners, and investigators vary greatly. Most claims examiners employed by life and health insurance companies work a standard 5-day, 40-hour week in a typical office environment. Many claims adjusters and auto damage appraisers, however, often work outside the office, inspecting damaged buildings and automobiles. Adjusters who inspect damaged buildings must be wary of potential hazards such as collapsed roofs and floors as well as weakened structures.

In general, adjusters are able to arrange their work schedules to accommodate evening and weekend appointments with clients. This accommodation sometimes results in adjusters working irregular schedules or more than 40 hours a week, especially when they have a lot of claims to investigate. Some report to the office every morning to get their assignments, while others simply call in from home and spend their days traveling to claim sites. New technology, such as laptop computers and cellular telephones, is making telecommuting easier for claims adjusters and auto damage appraisers. Many adjusters work inside their office only a few hours a week, while others conduct their business entirely out of their home and automobile. Occasionally, experienced adjusters must be away from home for days—for example, when they travel to the scene of a disaster such as a tornado, hurricane, or flood—to work with local adjusters and government officials. Adjusters often are called to work in the event of such emergencies and may have to work 50 or 60 hours a week until all claims are resolved.

Insurance investigators often work irregular hours because of the need to conduct surveillance and contact people who are not available during normal working hours. Early morning, evening, and weekend work is common. Some days, investigators will spend all day in the office, searching databases, making telephone calls, and

writing reports. Other times, they may be away, performing surveillance activities or interviewing witnesses. Some of the work can involve confrontation with claimants and others involved in a case, so the job can be stressful and dangerous.

Training, Other Qualifications, and Advancement

Training and entry requirements vary widely for claims adjusters, appraisers, examiners, and investigators. Although many in these occupations do not have a college degree, most companies prefer to hire college graduates. No specific college major is recommended, but a variety of backgrounds can be an asset. A claims adjuster who, for example, has a business or an accounting background might specialize in claims of financial loss due to strikes, breakdowns of equipment, or damage to merchandise. College training in architecture or engineering is helpful in adjusting industrial claims, such as those involving damage from fires or other accidents. Some claims adjusters and examiners apply expertise acquired through specialized professional training to adjust claims. A legal background can be beneficial to someone handling workers' compensation and product liability cases. A medical background is useful for those examiners working on medical and life insurance claims.

Because they often work closely with claimants, witnesses, and other insurance professionals, claims adjusters and examiners must be able to communicate effectively with others. Knowledge of computer applications also is extremely helpful. In addition, a valid driver's license and a good driving record are required for workers for whom travel is an important aspect of their job. Some companies require applicants to pass a series of written aptitude tests designed to measure their communication, analytical, and general mathematical skills.

Licensing requirements for these workers vary by state. Some states have very few requirements, while others require either the completion of prelicensing education or a satisfactory score on a licensing exam. Fulfilling the requirements for earning a voluntary professional designation may, in some cases, be substituted for completing the exam. In some states, claims adjusters employed by insurance companies can work under the company license and need not become licensed themselves. Separate or additional requirements may apply for public adjusters. For example, some states require public adjusters to file a surety bond.

Continuing education in claims is very important for claims adjusters, appraisers, examiners, and investigators because federal and state laws and court decisions affect how claims are handled or who is covered by insurance policies. Also, examiners working on life and health claims must be familiar with new medical procedures and prescription drugs. Some states that require licensing also require a certain number of continuing education credits per year in order to renew the license. These credits can be obtained from a number of sources. Many companies offer training sessions to inform their employees of industry changes. A number of schools and associations give courses and seminars on various topics having to with claims. Correspondence courses via the Internet are making long-distance learning possible. Workers also can earn continuing education credits by writing articles for claims publications or by giving lectures and presentations. In addition, numerous adjusters and examiners choose to earn professional certifications and designations for independent recognition of their professional expertise. Although requirements for these designations vary, many entail at least 5 to 10 years of experience in the claims field and the successful completion of an examination; in addition, a certain number of continuing education credits must be earned each year to retain the designation.

For auto damage appraiser jobs, insurance companies and independent adjusting firms typically prefer to hire persons with experience as an estimator for, or manager of, an auto body repair shop. An appraiser must know how to repair vehicles in order to identify and estimate damage, and technical skills are essential. While auto damage appraisers do not require a college education, most companies prefer to hire persons with formal training. Many vocational colleges offer 2-year programs in auto body repair on how to estimate and repair damaged vehicles. Some states require auto damage appraisers to be licensed, and certification also may be required or preferred. Basic computer skills are an important qualification for many auto damage appraiser positions. As with adjusters and examiners, continuing education is important because of the continual introduction of new car models and repair techniques.

Most insurance companies prefer to hire former law enforcement officers or private investigators as insurance investigators. Many experienced claims adjusters or examiners also become investigators. Licensing requirements vary among states. Most employers look for individuals with ingenuity who are persistent and assertive. Investigators should not be afraid of confrontation, should communicate well, and should be able to think on their feet. Good interviewing and interrogation skills also are important and usually are acquired in earlier careers in law enforcement.

Beginning claims adjusters, appraisers, examiners, and investigators work on small claims under the supervision of an experienced worker. As they learn more about claims investigation and settlement, they are assigned larger, more complex claims. Trainees are promoted as they demonstrate competence in handling assignments and progress in their coursework. Employees who demonstrate competence in claims work or administrative skills may be promoted to more responsible managerial or administrative jobs. Similarly, claims investigators may rise to supervisor or manager of the investigations department. Once they achieve a certain level of expertise, many choose to start their own independent adjusting or auto damage appraising firms.

Employment

Adjusters, appraisers, examiners, and investigators held about 263,000 jobs in 2004. Only 5 percent of these jobs were held by auto damage insurance appraisers. Insurance carriers, agencies, brokerages, and related industries—such as private claims adjusting companies—employed more than 8 out of 10 claims adjusters, appraisers, examiners, and investigators. Relatively few adjusters, appraisers, examiners, and investigators were self-employed.

Job Outlook

Employment of claims adjusters, appraisers, examiners, and investigators is expected to grow about as fast as average for all occupations over the 2004–2014 period. College graduates have the best opportunities. Numerous job openings also will result from the need to replace workers who transfer to other occupations or leave the labor force.

Many insurance carriers are downsizing their claims staff in an effort to contain costs. Larger companies are relying more on customer service representatives in call centers to handle the recording of the necessary details of the claim, allowing adjusters to spend more of their time investigating claims. New technology is reducing the amount of time it takes for an adjuster to complete a claim, thereby increasing the number of claims that one adjuster can handle. However, as long as more insurance policies are being sold to accommodate a growing population, there will be a need for adjusters, appraisers, examiners, and investigators. Further, as the elderly population increases, there will be a greater need for health care, resulting in more health insurance claims.

Despite recent gains in productivity resulting from technological advances, these jobs are not easily automated. Adjusters still are needed to contact policyholders, inspect damaged property, and consult with experts. Although the number of claims in litigation and the number and complexity of insurance fraud cases are expected to increase over the next decade, demand for insurance investigators is not expected to grow significantly, because technology such as the Internet, which reduces the amount of time it takes to perform background checks, will allow investigators to handle more cases. Competition for investigator jobs will remain keen because the occupation attracts many qualified people, including retirees from law enforcement and military careers, as well as experienced claims adjusters and examiners who choose to get their investigator license.

As with claims adjusters, examiners, and investigators, employment of auto damage appraisers should grow about as fast as the average for all occupations. Insurance companies and agents continue to sell growing numbers of auto insurance policies, leading to more claims being filed that require the attention of an auto damage appraiser. The work of this occupation is not easily automated, because most appraisals require an onsite inspection. However, employment growth will be limited by downsizing in the insurance industry and by the implementation of new technology that is making auto damage appraisers more efficient. In addition, some insurance companies are opening their own repair facilities, which may reduce the need for auto damage appraisers.

Earnings

Earnings of claims adjusters, appraisers, examiners, and investigators vary significantly. Median annual earnings were $44,220 in May 2004. The middle 50 percent earned between $33,900 and $57,410. The lowest 10 percent earned less than $27,220, and the highest 10 percent earned more than $72,620.

Many claims adjusters, especially those who work for insurance companies, receive additional bonuses or benefits as part of their job. Adjusters often are furnished a laptop computer, a cellular telephone, and a company car or are reimbursed for the use of their own vehicle for business purposes.

Median annual earnings of auto damage insurance appraisers were $45,330 in May 2004. The middle 50 percent earned between

$37,210 and $54,280. The lowest 10 percent earned less than $29,550, and the highest 10 percent earned more than $63,220.

Related Occupations

Property-casualty insurance adjusters and life and health insurance examiners must determine the validity of a claim and negotiate a settlement. They also are responsible for determining how much to reimburse the client. Occupations similar to those of claims adjusters, appraisers, examiners, and investigators include cost estimators; bill and account collectors; medical records and health information technicians; billing and posting clerks; credit authorizers, checkers, and clerks; and bookkeeping, accounting, and auditing clerks.

In determining the validity of a claim, insurance adjusters must inspect the damage in order to assess the magnitude of the loss. Workers who perform similar duties include fire inspectors and investigators and construction and building inspectors.

To ensure that company practices and procedures are followed, property and casualty examiners review insurance claims to which a claims adjuster has already proposed a settlement. Others in occupations that review documents for accuracy and compliance with a given set of rules and regulations are tax examiners, collectors, and revenue agents, as well as accountants and auditors.

Insurance investigators detect and investigate fraudulent claims and criminal activity. Their work is similar to that of private detectives and investigators.

Like automotive body and related repairers and automotive service technicians and mechanics, auto damage appraisers must be familiar with the structure and functions of various automobiles and their parts.

Sources of Additional Information

General information about a career as a claims adjuster, appraiser, examiner, or investigator is available from the home offices of many insurance companies.

Information about licensing requirements for claims adjusters may be obtained from the department of insurance in each state.

For information about professional designation and training programs, contact any of the following organizations:

▸ American Institute for Chartered Property Casualty Underwriters and the Insurance Institute of America, 720 Providence Rd., P.O. Box 3016, Malvern, PA 19355–0716. Internet: http://www.aicpcu.org

▸ American College, 270 South Bryn Mawr Ave., Bryn Mawr, PA 19010–2196. Internet: http://www.theamericancollege.edu

▸ International Claim Association, 1255 23rd St. NW, Washington, DC 20037. Internet: http://www.claim.org

Information on careers in auto damage appraising can be obtained from

▸ Independent Automotive Damage Appraisers Association, P.O. Box 12291, Columbus, GA 31917–2291. Internet: http://www.iada.org

Clinical Laboratory Technologists and Technicians

(O*NET 29-2011.00 and 29-2012.00)

Significant Points

■ Faster-than-average employment growth is expected as the volume of laboratory tests continues to increase with both population growth and the development of new types of tests.

■ Clinical laboratory technologists usually have a bachelor's degree with a major in medical technology or in one of the life sciences; clinical laboratory technicians generally need either an associate degree or a certificate.

■ Job opportunities are expected to be excellent.

Nature of the Work

Clinical laboratory testing plays a crucial role in the detection, diagnosis, and treatment of disease. Clinical laboratory technologists, also referred to as clinical laboratory scientists or medical technologists and clinical laboratory technicians, also known as medical technicians or medical laboratory technicians, perform most of these tests.

Clinical laboratory personnel examine and analyze body fluids and cells. They look for bacteria, parasites, and other microorganisms; analyze the chemical content of fluids; match blood for transfusions; and test for drug levels in the blood to show how a patient is responding to treatment. Technologists also prepare specimens for examination, count cells, and look for abnormal cells in blood and body fluids. They use automated equipment and computerized instruments capable of performing a number of tests simultaneously, as well as microscopes, cell counters, and other sophisticated laboratory equipment. Then they analyze the results and relay them to physicians. With increasing automation and the use of computer technology, the work of technologists and technicians has become less hands-on and more analytical.

The complexity of tests performed, the level of judgment needed, and the amount of responsibility workers assume depend largely on the amount of education and experience they have.

Clinical laboratory technologists perform complex chemical, biological, hematological, immunologic, microscopic, and bacteriological tests. Technologists microscopically examine blood and other body fluids. They make cultures of body fluid and tissue samples to determine the presence of bacteria, fungi, parasites, or other microorganisms. Clinical laboratory technologists analyze samples for chemical content or a chemical reaction and determine concentrations of compounds such as blood glucose and cholesterol levels. They also type and cross-match blood samples for transfusions.

Clinical laboratory technologists evaluate test results, develop and modify procedures, and establish and monitor programs to ensure the accuracy of tests. Some technologists supervise clinical laboratory technicians.

Technologists in small laboratories perform many types of tests, whereas those in large laboratories generally specialize. Technologists who prepare specimens and analyze the chemical and hormonal contents of body fluids are called clinical chemistry technologists. Those who examine and identify bacteria and other microorganisms are microbiology technologists. Blood bank technologists, or immunohematology technologists, collect, type, and prepare blood and its components for transfusions. Immunology technologists examine elements of the human immune system and its response to foreign bodies. Cytotechnologists prepare slides of body cells and examine these cells microscopically for abnormalities that may signal the beginning of a cancerous growth. Molecular biology technologists perform complex protein and nucleic acid testing on cell samples.

Clinical laboratory technicians perform less-complex tests and laboratory procedures than technologists perform. Technicians may prepare specimens and operate automated analyzers, for example, or they may perform manual tests in accordance with detailed instructions. Like technologists, they may work in several areas of the clinical laboratory or specialize in just one. Histotechnicians cut and stain tissue specimens for microscopic examination by pathologists, and phlebotomists collect blood samples. They usually work under the supervision of medical and clinical laboratory technologists or laboratory managers.

Working Conditions

Hours and other working conditions of clinical laboratory technologists and technicians vary with the size and type of employment setting. In large hospitals or in independent laboratories that operate continuously, personnel usually work the day, evening, or night shift and may work weekends and holidays. Laboratory personnel in small facilities may work on rotating shifts rather than on a regular shift. In some facilities, laboratory personnel are on call several nights a week or on weekends in case of an emergency.

Clinical laboratory personnel are trained to work with infectious specimens. When proper methods of infection control and sterilization are followed, few hazards exist. Protective masks, gloves, and goggles are often necessary to ensure the safety of laboratory personnel.

Laboratories usually are well lighted and clean; however, specimens, solutions, and reagents used in the laboratory sometimes produce fumes. Laboratory workers may spend a great deal of time on their feet.

Training, Other Qualifications, and Advancement

The usual requirement for an entry-level position as a clinical laboratory technologist is a bachelor's degree with a major in medical technology or in one of the life sciences, although it is possible to qualify through a combination of education, on-the-job, and specialized training. Universities and hospitals offer medical technology programs.

Bachelor's degree programs in medical technology include courses in chemistry, biological sciences, microbiology, mathematics, and statistics, as well as specialized courses devoted to knowledge and skills used in the clinical laboratory. Many programs also offer or require courses in management, business, and computer applications. The Clinical Laboratory Improvement Act requires technologists who perform highly complex tests to have at least an associate degree.

Medical and clinical laboratory technicians generally have either an associate degree from a community or junior college or a certificate from a hospital, a vocational or technical school, or one of the U.S. Armed Forces. A few technicians learn their skills on the job.

The National Accrediting Agency for Clinical Laboratory Sciences (NAACLS) fully accredits 469 programs for medical and clinical laboratory technologists, medical and clinical laboratory technicians, histotechnologists and histotechnicians, cytogenetic technologists, and diagnostic molecular scientists. NAACLS also approves 57 programs in phlebotomy and clinical assisting. Other nationally recognized accrediting agencies that accredit specific areas for clinical laboratory workers include the Commission on Accreditation of Allied Health Education Programs and the Accrediting Bureau of Health Education Schools.

Some states require laboratory personnel to be licensed or registered. Information on licensure is available from state departments of health or boards of occupational licensing. Certification is a voluntary process by which a nongovernmental organization, such as a professional society or certifying agency, grants recognition to an individual whose professional competence meets prescribed standards. Widely accepted by employers in the health care industry, certification is a prerequisite for most jobs and often is necessary for advancement. Agencies certifying medical and clinical laboratory technologists and technicians include the Board of Registry of the American Society for Clinical Pathology, the American Medical Technologists, the National Credentialing Agency for Laboratory Personnel, and the Board of Registry of the American Association of Bioanalysts. These agencies have different requirements for certification and different organizational sponsors.

Clinical laboratory personnel need good analytical judgment and the ability to work under pressure. Close attention to detail is essential because small differences or changes in test substances or numerical readouts can be crucial for patient care. Manual dexterity and normal color vision are highly desirable. With the widespread use of automated laboratory equipment, computer skills are important. In addition, technologists in particular are expected to be good at problem solving.

Technologists may advance to supervisory positions in laboratory work or may become chief medical or clinical laboratory technologists or laboratory managers in hospitals. Manufacturers of home diagnostic testing kits and laboratory equipment and supplies seek experienced technologists to work in product development, marketing, and sales. A graduate degree in medical technology, one of the biological sciences, chemistry, management, or education usually speeds advancement. A doctorate is needed to become a laboratory director; however, federal regulation allows directors of moderately complex laboratories to have either a master's degree or a bachelor's degree, combined with the appropriate amount of training and experience. Technicians can become technologists through additional education and experience.

Employment

Clinical laboratory technologists and technicians held about 302,000 jobs in 2004. More than half of jobs were in hospitals. Most of the remaining jobs were in offices of physicians and in medical and diagnostic laboratories. A small proportion was in educational services and in all other ambulatory health care services.

Job Outlook

Job opportunities are expected to be excellent because the number of job openings is expected to continue to exceed the number of job seekers. Employment of clinical laboratory workers is expected to grow faster than the average for all occupations through the year 2014 as the volume of laboratory tests continues to increase with both population growth and the development of new types of tests.

Technological advances will continue to have two opposing effects on employment. On the one hand, new, increasingly powerful diagnostic tests will encourage additional testing and spur employment. On the other hand, research and development efforts targeted at simplifying routine testing procedures may enhance the ability of non-laboratory personnel—physicians and patients in particular—to perform tests now conducted in laboratories. Although hospitals are expected to continue to be the major employer of clinical laboratory workers, employment is expected to grow faster in medical and diagnostic laboratories, offices of physicians, and all other ambulatory health care services.

Although significant, job growth will not be the only source of opportunities. As in most occupations, many openings will result from the need to replace workers who transfer to other occupations, retire, or stop working for some other reason.

Earnings

Median annual earnings of medical and clinical laboratory technologists were $45,730 in May 2004. The middle 50 percent earned between $38,740 and $54,310. The lowest 10 percent earned less than $32,240, and the highest 10 percent earned more than $63,120. Median annual earnings in the industries employing the largest numbers of medical and clinical laboratory technologists in May 2004 were as follows:

General medical and surgical hospitals	$46,020
Medical and diagnostic laboratories	45,840
Offices of physicians	41,070

Median annual earnings of medical and clinical laboratory technicians were $30,840 in May 2004. The middle 50 percent earned between $24,890 and $37,770. The lowest 10 percent earned less than $20,410, and the highest 10 percent earned more than $45,680. Median annual earnings in the industries employing the largest numbers of medical and clinical laboratory technicians in May 2004 were as follows:

Colleges, universities, and professional schools	$32,410
General medical and surgical hospitals	31,830

Offices of physicians	29,620
Medical and diagnostic laboratories	29,220
Other ambulatory health care services	28,130

According to the American Society for Clinical Pathology, median hourly wages of staff clinical laboratory technologists and technicians in 2003 varied by specialty and laboratory type as follows:

	Hospital	Private clinic	Physician office laboratory
Cytotechnologist	$24.70	$24.07	$25.66
Histotechnologist	19.88	19.22	20.50
Medical technologist	20.40	19.00	18.00
Histotechnician	16.97	16.13	20.00
Medical laboratory technician	16.12	15.00	14.75
Phlebotomist	11.13	10.57	10.50

Related Occupations

Clinical laboratory technologists and technicians analyze body fluids, tissue, and other substances, using a variety of tests. Similar or related procedures are performed by chemists and materials scientists, science technicians, and veterinary technologists and technicians.

Sources of Additional Information

For a list of accredited and approved educational programs for clinical laboratory personnel, contact

▶ National Accrediting Agency for Clinical Laboratory Sciences, 8410 W. Bryn Mawr Ave., Suite 670, Chicago, IL 60631. Internet: http://www.naacls.org

Information on certification is available from

▶ American Association of Bioanalysts, Board of Registry, 906 Olive St., Suite 1200, St. Louis, MO 63101-1434. Internet: http://www.aab.org

▶ American Medical Technologists, 710 Higgins Rd., Park Ridge, IL 60068.

▶ American Society for Clinical Pathology, 2100 West Harrison St., Chicago, IL 60612. Internet: http://www.ascp.org

▶ National Credentialing Agency for Laboratory Personnel, P.O. Box 15945, Lenexa, KS 66285. Internet: http://www.nca-info.org

Additional career information is available from

▶ American Association of Blood Banks, 8101 Glenbrook Rd., Bethesda, MD 20814-2749. Internet: http://www.aabb.org

▶ American Society for Clinical Laboratory Science, 6701 Democracy Blvd., Suite 300, Bethesda, MD 20817. Internet: http://www.ascls.org

▶ American Society for Cytopathology, 400 West 9th St., Suite 201, Wilmington, DE 19801. Internet: http://www.cytopathology.org

▶ Clinical Laboratory Management Association, 989 Old Eagle School Rd., Suite 815, Wayne, PA 19087. Internet: http://www.clma.org

Communications Equipment Operators

(O*NET 43-2011.00, 43-2021.01, 43-2021.02, and 43-2099.99)

Significant Points

■ Switchboard operators hold 4 out of 5 jobs.

■ Workers train on the job.

■ Employment is expected to decline.

Nature of the Work

Most communications equipment operators work as *switchboard operators* for a wide variety of businesses, such as hospitals, hotels, telephone call centers, and government agencies. Switchboard operators use private branch exchange (PBX) or voice over Internet protocol (VoIP) switchboards to relay incoming, outgoing, and interoffice calls, usually for a single organization. They also may handle other clerical duties, such as supplying information, taking messages, and announcing visitors. Technological improvements have automated many of the tasks handled by switchboard operators. New systems automatically connect outside calls to the correct destination or automated directories, and voice-mail systems take messages without the assistance of an operator.

Some communications equipment operators work as *telephone operators*, assisting customers in making telephone calls. Although most calls are connected automatically, callers sometimes require the assistance of an operator. *Central office operators* help customers to complete local and long-distance calls, usually under special circumstances. *Directory assistance operators* provide customers with information such as telephone numbers or area codes.

When callers dial "0," they usually reach a central office operator, also known as a *local*, *long-distance*, or *call completion operator*. Most of these operators work for telephone companies, and many of their responsibilities have been automated. For example, callers can make international, collect, and credit card calls without the assistance of a central office operator. Other tasks previously handled by these operators, such as billing calls to third parties and monitoring the cost of a call, also have been automated.

Callers still need a central office operator for a limited number of tasks, including placing person-to-person calls or interrupting busy lines if an emergency warrants the disruption. When natural disasters such as storms or earthquakes occur, central office operators provide callers with emergency phone contacts. They also assist callers who are having difficulty with automated phone systems. An operator monitoring an automated system that aids a caller in placing collect calls, for example, may intervene if a caller needs assistance with the system.

Directory assistance operators provide callers with information such as telephone numbers or area codes. Most directory assistance operators work for telephone companies; increasingly, they also work for companies that provide business services. Automated systems now handle many of the responsibilities once performed by directory

assistance operators. The systems prompt callers for a listing and may even connect the call after providing the telephone number. However, directory assistance operators monitor many of the calls received by automated systems. The operators listen to recordings of the customer's request and then key information into electronic directories to access the correct telephone numbers. Directory assistance operators also provide personal assistance to customers having difficulty using the automated system.

Other communications equipment operators include workers who operate satellite communications equipment, telegraph equipment, and a wide variety of other communications equipment.

Working Conditions

Most communications equipment operators work in pleasant, well-lighted surroundings. Because telephone operators spend much time seated at keyboards and video monitors, employers often provide workstations designed to decrease glare and other physical discomforts. Such improvements reduce the incidence of eyestrain, back discomfort, and injury due to repetitive motion.

Switchboard operators generally work the same hours as other clerical employees at their company. In most organizations, full-time operators work regular business hours over a 5-day workweek. Work schedules are more irregular in hotels, hospitals, and other organizations that require round-the-clock operator services. In these companies, switchboard operators may work in the evenings and on holidays and weekends.

Central office and directory assistance operators must be accessible to customers 24 hours a day; therefore, they work a variety of shifts. Some operators work split shifts, coming on duty during peak calling periods in the late morning and early evening and going off duty during the intervening hours. Telephone companies normally assign shifts by seniority, allowing the most experienced operators first choice of schedules. As a result, entry-level operators may have less desirable schedules, including late evening, split-shift, and weekend work. Telephone company operators may work overtime during emergencies.

Approximately 1 in 6 communications equipment operators works part time. Because of the irregular nature of telephone operator schedules, many employers seek part-time workers for those shifts that are difficult to fill.

An operator's work may be quite repetitive and the pace hectic during peak calling periods. To maintain operators' efficiency, supervisors at telephone companies often monitor their performance, including the amount of time they spend on each call. The rapid pace of the job and frequent monitoring may cause stress.

Training, Other Qualifications, and Advancement

Switchboard operators usually receive informal on-the-job training lasting only a few days or weeks. Because they are often the first contact with the public or client, switchboard operators often receive some training in customer service. Training may also vary by place of employment—a switchboard operator in a hospital would need training on how to handle different emergencies. Since switchboard operators' duties may include clerical work, basic computer skills training may also be required.

Entry-level central office and directory assistance operators at telecommunications companies may receive both classroom and on-the-job instruction that can last several weeks. These operators may be paired with experienced personnel who provide hands-on instruction.

New employees in both occupations are trained in the operation of their equipment and in procedures designed to maximize efficiency. They are familiarized with company policies, including the expected level of customer service. Instructors monitor both the time and quality of trainees' responses to customer requests. Supervisors may continue to monitor new employees closely after they complete their initial training session.

Employers generally require a high school diploma. Applicants should have clear speech; good hearing; and strong reading, spelling, and numerical skills. Computer literacy and typing skills also are important, and familiarity with a foreign language is helpful for some positions because of the increasing diversity of the population. Candidates for positions may be required to take an examination covering basic language and math skills. Most companies emphasize customer service and seek operators who will remain courteous to customers while working at a fast pace.

After 1 or 2 years on the job, communications equipment operators may advance to other positions within a company. Many enter clerical occupations in which their operator experience is valuable, such as customer service representative, dispatcher, and receptionist. (See the descriptions of these occupations elsewhere in this book.) Operators interested in more technical work may take training classes and advance into positions having to do with installing and repairing equipment. (See the descriptions of radio and telecommunications equipment installers and repairers and line installers and repairers elsewhere in this book.) Promotion to supervisory positions also is possible.

Employment

Communications equipment operators held about 256,000 jobs in 2004. About 4 out of 5 worked as switchboard operators. Employment was distributed as follows:

Switchboard operators, including
  answering service 213,000
Telephone operators..39,000
All other communications equipment operators 4,200

Switchboard operators work in almost all industries, but are concentrated in telephone call centers, hospitals, and hotels. Many work as temporary employees in the employment services industry.

Job Outlook

Employment of communications equipment operators is projected to decline through 2014, due largely to new labor-saving communications technologies; the movement of jobs to foreign countries; and consolidation of telephone operator jobs into fewer locations, often staffed by temporary or contract workers. Virtually all job openings will result from the need to replace communications

equipment operators who transfer to other occupations or leave the labor force.

Developments in communications technologies—in particular, voice recognition systems that are accessible and easy to use—will continue to have a significant impact on the demand for communications equipment operators. Voice recognition technology allows automated telephone systems to recognize human speech. Callers speak directly to the system, which interprets the speech and then connects the call. Because voice recognition systems do not require callers to input data through a telephone keypad, they are easier to use than touch-tone systems. Voice recognition systems are increasingly able to understand sophisticated vocabulary and grammatical structures; however, many companies will continue to employ operators so that those callers who do have problems can access a "live" employee if they desire.

The proliferation of cell phones has negatively affected both switchboard operators and telephone operators. By allowing for direct communication between persons, cell phones have eliminated the need for operators to transfer calls in certain situations. Cell phones have reduced the demand for directory assistance and collect calls and have resulted in decreasing use of pay phones that often required operators to assist with the call. The increasing use of cell phones also has reduced demand for switchboard operators in hotels because hotel guests now use in-room phones less frequently.

Electronic communication through the Internet or e-mail provides alternatives to telephone communication and requires no operators. Internet directory assistance services are reducing the need for directory assistance operators. Local telephone companies currently have the most reliable telephone directory data; however, Internet services provide information such as addresses and maps in addition to telephone numbers. As the functions of telephones and computers converge, the convenience of Internet directory assistance is expected to attract many customers, reducing the need for telephone operators to provide this service.

As communications technologies have improved and the price of long-distance service has fallen, companies are finding other ways to reduce costs by consolidating operator jobs in low-cost locations. Increasingly, this has entailed the movement of telephone operator jobs offshore to other lower-wage countries in order to reduce costs.

Earnings

Median hourly earnings of switchboard operators, including answering service, were $10.38 in May 2004. The middle 50 percent earned between $8.69 and $12.64. The lowest 10 percent earned less than $7.35, and the highest 10 percent earned more than $15.13. Median hourly earnings in the industries employing the largest numbers of switchboard operators in May 2004 are

Offices of physicians $10.54
General medical and surgical hospitals 10.47
Traveler accommodation.......................................10.25
Automobile dealers 9.60
Business support services......................................8.91

Median hourly earnings of telephone operators in May 2004 were $13.65. The middle 50 percent earned between $10.28 and $19.32.

The lowest 10 percent earned less than $8.91, and the highest 10 percent earned more than $21.32.

Some telephone operators working at telephone companies are members of the Communications Workers of America or the International Brotherhood of Electrical Workers. For these operators, union contracts govern wage rates, wage increases, and the time required to advance from one pay step to the next. It normally takes 4 years to rise from the lowest-paying nonsupervisory operator position to the highest. Contracts call for extra pay for work beyond the normal 6-1/2 to 7-1/2 hours a day or 5 days a week, for Sunday and holiday work, and for bilingual positions. A pay differential also is guaranteed for night work and split shifts. Many contracts provide for a 1-week vacation after 6 months of service, 2 weeks after 1 year, 3 weeks after 7 years, 4 weeks after 15 years, and 5 weeks after 25 years. Holidays range from 9 to 11 days a year.

Median hourly earnings of communication equipment operators, all other, in May 2004 were $15.23. The middle 50 percent earned between $12.27 and $18.99. The lowest 10 percent earned less than $10.23, and the highest 10 percent earned more than $22.70.

Related Occupations

Other workers who provide information to the general public include dispatchers; hotel, motel, and resort desk clerks; customer service representatives; receptionists and information clerks; and reservation and transportation ticket agents and travel clerks.

Sources of Additional Information

For more details about employment opportunities, contact a telephone company or temporary help agency or write to either of the following unions:

▸ Communications Workers of America, 501 3rd St. NW, Washington, DC 20001.

▸ International Brotherhood of Electrical Workers, Telecommunications Department, 1125 15th St. NW, Room 807, Washington, DC 20005.

For more information on training in customer service and customer relations, contact

▸ International Association of Administrative Professionals, 10502 NW Ambassador Dr., PO Box 20404, Kansas City, MO 64195-0404.

Computer Scientists and Database Administrators

(O*NET 15-1011.00, 15-1061.00, and 15-1099.99)

Significant Points

■ Education requirements range from an associate degree to a doctoral degree.

■ Employment is expected to increase much faster than the average as organizations continue to adopt increasingly sophisticated technologies.

■ Job prospects are favorable.

Nature of the Work

The rapid spread of computers and information technology has generated a need for highly trained workers proficient in various job functions. These workers—computer scientists, database administrators, and network systems and data communication analysts—include a wide range of computer specialists. Job tasks and occupational titles used to describe these workers evolve rapidly, reflecting new areas of specialization or changes in technology as well as the preferences and practices of employers.

Computer scientists work as theorists, researchers, or inventors. Their jobs are distinguished by the higher level of theoretical expertise and innovation they apply to complex problems and the creation or application of new technology. Those employed by academic institutions work in areas ranging from complexity theory to hardware to programming-language design. Some work on multidisciplinary projects, such as developing and advancing uses of virtual reality, extending human–computer interaction, or designing robots. Their counterparts in private industry work in areas such as applying theory; developing specialized languages or information technologies; or designing programming tools, knowledge-based systems, or even computer games.

With the Internet and electronic business generating large volumes of data, there is a growing need to be able to store, manage, and extract data effectively. *Database administrators* work with database management systems software and determine ways to organize and store data. They identify user requirements, set up computer databases, and test and coordinate modifications to the computer database systems. An organization's database administrator ensures the performance of the system, understands the platform on which the database runs, and adds new users to the system. Because they also may design and implement system security, database administrators often plan and coordinate security measures. With the volume of sensitive data generated every second growing rapidly, data integrity, backup systems, and database security have become increasingly important aspects of the job of database administrators.

Because networks are configured in many ways, *network systems and data communications analysts* are needed to design, test, and evaluate systems such as local area networks (LANs), wide area networks (WANs), the Internet, intranets, and other data communications systems. Systems can range from a connection between two offices in the same building to globally distributed networks, voice mail, and e-mail systems of a multinational organization. Network systems and data communications analysts perform network modeling, analysis, and planning; they also may research related products and make necessary hardware and software recommendations. *Telecommunications specialists* focus on the interaction between computer and communications equipment. These workers design voice and data communication systems, supervise the installation of the systems, and provide maintenance and other services to clients after the systems are installed.

The growth of the Internet and the expansion of the World Wide Web (the graphical portion of the Internet) have generated a variety of occupations related to the design, development, and maintenance of Web sites and their servers. For example, *Webmasters* are responsible for all technical aspects of a Web site, including performance issues such as speed of access, and for approving the content of the site. *Internet developers* or W*eb developers*, also called W*eb designers*, are responsible for day-to-day site creation and design.

Working Conditions

Computer scientists and database administrators normally work in offices or laboratories in comfortable surroundings. They usually work about 40 hours a week—the same as many other professional or office workers do. However, evening or weekend work may be necessary to meet deadlines or solve specific problems. With the technology available today, telecommuting is common for computer professionals. As networks expand, more work can be done from remote locations through modems, laptops, electronic mail, and the Internet.

Like other workers who spend long periods in front of a computer terminal typing on a keyboard, computer scientists and database administrators are susceptible to eyestrain, back discomfort, and hand and wrist problems such as carpal tunnel syndrome or cumulative trauma disorder.

Training, Other Qualifications, and Advancement

Rapidly changing technology requires an increasing level of skill and education on the part of employees. Companies look for professionals with an ever-broader background and range of skills including not only technical knowledge, but also communication and other interpersonal skills. While there is no universally accepted way to prepare for a job as a network systems analyst, computer scientist, or database administrator, most employers place a premium on some formal college education. A bachelor's degree is a prerequisite for many jobs; however, some jobs may require only a 2-year degree. Relevant work experience also is very important. For more technically complex jobs, persons with graduate degrees are preferred.

For database administrator positions, many employers seek applicants who have a bachelor's degree in computer science, information science, or management information systems (MIS). MIS programs usually are part of the business school or college and differ considerably from computer science programs, emphasizing business and management-oriented coursework and business computing courses. Employers increasingly seek individuals with a master's degree in business administration (MBA), with a concentration in information systems, as more firms move their business to the Internet. For some network systems and data communication analysts, such as Webmasters, an associate degree or certificate is sufficient, although more advanced positions might require a computer-related bachelor's degree. For computer and information scientists, a doctoral degree generally is required because of the highly technical nature of their work.

Despite employers' preference for those with technical degrees, persons with degrees in a variety of majors find employment in these occupations. The level of education and the type of training that employers require depend on their needs. One factor affecting these needs is changes in technology. Employers often scramble to find workers capable of implementing new technologies. Workers with formal education or experience in information security, for example, are in demand because of the growing need for their skills and

services. Employers also look for workers skilled in wireless technologies as wireless networks and applications have spread into many firms and organizations.

Most community colleges and many independent technical institutes and proprietary schools offer an associate's degree in computer science or a related information technology field. Many of these programs may be geared more toward meeting the needs of local businesses and are more occupation-specific than are 4-year degree programs. Some jobs may be better suited to the level of training that such programs offer. Employers usually look for people who have broad knowledge and experience related to computer systems and technologies, strong problem-solving and analytical skills, and good interpersonal skills. Courses in computer science or systems design offer good preparation for a job in these computer occupations. For jobs in a business environment, employers usually want systems analysts to have business management or closely related skills, while a background in the physical sciences, applied mathematics, or engineering is preferred for work in scientifically oriented organizations. Art or graphic design skills may be desirable for Webmasters or Web developers.

Jobseekers can enhance their employment opportunities by participating in internship or co-op programs offered through their schools. Because many people develop advanced computer skills in a non-computer occupation and then transfer those skills to a computer occupation, a background in the industry in which the person's job is located, such as financial services, banking, or accounting, can be important. Others have taken computer science courses to supplement their study in fields such as accounting, inventory control, or other business areas.

Computer scientists and database administrators must be able to think logically and have good communication skills. Because they often deal with a number of tasks simultaneously, the ability to concentrate and pay close attention to detail is important. Although these computer specialists sometimes work independently, they frequently work in teams on large projects. They must be able to communicate effectively with computer personnel, such as programmers and managers, as well as with users or other staff who may have no technical computer background.

Computer scientists employed in private industry may advance into managerial or project leadership positions. Those employed in academic institutions can become heads of research departments or published authorities in their field. Database administrators may advance into managerial positions, such as chief technology officer, on the basis of their experience managing data and enforcing security. Computer specialists with work experience and considerable expertise in a particular subject or a certain application may find lucrative opportunities as independent consultants or may choose to start their own computer consulting firms.

Technological advances come so rapidly in the computer field that continuous study is necessary to keep one's skills up to date. Employers, hardware and software vendors, colleges and universities, and private training institutions offer continuing education. Additional training may come from professional development seminars offered by professional computing societies.

Certification is a way to demonstrate a level of competence in a particular field. Some product vendors or software firms offer certification and require professionals who work with their products to be certified. Many employers regard these certifications as the industry standard. For example, one method of acquiring enough knowledge to get a job as a database administrator is to become certified in a specific type of database management. Voluntary certification also is available through various organizations associated with computer specialists. Professional certification may afford a jobseeker a competitive advantage.

Employment

Computer scientists and database administrators held about 507,000 jobs in 2004, including about 66,000 who were self-employed. Employment was distributed among the detailed occupations as follows:

Network systems and data communication
    analysts 231,000

Database administrators 104,000

Computer and information scientists, research 22,000

Computer specialists, all other............................149,000

Although they are increasingly employed in every sector of the economy, the greatest concentration of these workers is in the computer systems design and related services industry. Firms in this industry provide services related to the commercial use of computers on a contract basis, including custom computer programming services; computer systems integration design services; computer facilities management services, including computer systems or data-processing facilities support services for clients; and other computer-related services, such as disaster recovery services and software installation. Many computer scientists and database administrators are employed by Internet service providers; Web search portals; and data-processing, hosting, and related services firms. Others work for government, manufacturers of computer and electronic products, insurance companies, financial institutions, and universities.

A growing number of computer specialists, such as network and data communications analysts, are employed on a temporary or contract basis; many of these individuals are self-employed, working independently as contractors or consultants. For example, a company installing a new computer system may need the services of several network systems and data communication analysts just to get the system running. Because not all of the analysts would be needed once the system is functioning, the company might contract for such employees with a temporary help agency or a consulting firm or with the network systems analysts themselves. Such jobs may last from several months to 2 years or more. This growing practice enables companies to bring in people with the exact skills they need to complete a particular project instead of having to spend time or money training or retraining existing workers. Often, experienced consultants then train a company's in-house staff as a project develops.

Job Outlook

Computer scientists and database administrators should continue to enjoy favorable job prospects. As technology becomes more sophisticated and complex, however, employers demand a higher level of skill and expertise from their employees. Individuals with an advanced degree in computer science or computer engineering or with an MBA with a concentration in information systems should enjoy favorable employment prospects. College graduates with a bachelor's degree in computer science, computer engineering, information science, or MIS also should enjoy favorable prospects, particularly if they have supplemented their formal education with practical experience. Because employers continue to seek computer specialists who can combine strong technical skills with good interpersonal and business skills, graduates with degrees in fields other than computer science who have had courses in computer programming, systems analysis, and other information technology areas also should continue to find jobs in these computer fields. In fact, individuals with the right experience and training can work in these computer occupations regardless of their college major or level of formal education.

Computer scientists and database administrators are expected to be among the fastest-growing occupations through 2014. Employment of these computer specialists is expected to grow much faster than the average for all occupations as organizations continue to adopt and integrate increasingly sophisticated technologies. Job increases will be driven by very rapid growth in computer systems design and related services, which is projected to be one of the fastest-growing industries in the U.S. economy. Job growth will not be as rapid as during the previous decade, however, as the information technology sector begins to mature and as routine work is increasingly outsourced overseas. In addition to growth, many job openings will arise annually from the need to replace workers who move into managerial positions or other occupations or who leave the labor force.

The demand for networking to facilitate the sharing of information, the expansion of client–server environments, and the need for computer specialists to use their knowledge and skills in a problem-solving capacity will be major factors in the rising demand for computer scientists and database administrators. Moreover, falling prices of computer hardware and software should continue to induce more businesses to expand their computerized operations and integrate new technologies into them. To maintain a competitive edge and operate more efficiently, firms will keep demanding computer specialists who are knowledgeable about the latest technologies and are able to apply them to meet the needs of businesses.

Increasingly, more sophisticated and complex technology is being implemented across all organizations, fueling demand for computer scientists and database administrators. There is growing demand for network systems and data communication analysts to help firms maximize their efficiency with available technology. Expansion of electronic commerce—doing business on the Internet—and the continuing need to build and maintain databases that store critical information on customers, inventory, and projects are fueling demand for database administrators familiar with the latest technology. Also, the increasing importance placed on cybersecurity—the protection of electronic information—will result in a need for workers skilled in information security.

The development of new technologies usually leads to demand for various kinds of workers. The expanding integration of Internet technologies into businesses, for example, has resulted in a growing need for specialists who can develop and support Internet and intranet applications. The growth of electronic commerce means that more establishments use the Internet to conduct their business online. The introduction of the wireless Internet, known as WiFi, creates new systems to be analyzed and new data to be administered. The spread of such new technologies translates into a need for information technology professionals who can help organizations use technology to communicate with employees, clients, and consumers. Explosive growth in these areas also is expected to fuel demand for specialists who are knowledgeable about network, data, and communications security.

Earnings

Median annual earnings of computer and information scientists, research, were $85,190 in May 2004. The middle 50 percent earned between $64,860 and $108,440. The lowest 10 percent earned less than $48,930, and the highest 10 percent earned more than $132,700. Median annual earnings of computer and information scientists employed in computer systems design and related services in May 2004 were $85,530.

Median annual earnings of database administrators were $60,650 in May 2004. The middle 50 percent earned between $44,490 and $81,140. The lowest 10 percent earned less than $33,380, and the highest 10 percent earned more than $97,450. In May 2004, median annual earnings of database administrators employed in computer systems design and related services were $70,530, and for those in management of companies and enterprises, earnings were $65,990.

Median annual earnings of network systems and data communication analysts were $60,600 in May 2004. The middle 50 percent earned between $46,480 and $78,060. The lowest 10 percent earned less than $36,260, and the highest 10 percent earned more than $95,040. Median annual earnings in the industries employing the largest numbers of network systems and data communications analysts in May 2004 are shown here:

Wired telecommunications carriers	$65,130
Insurance carriers	64,660
Management of companies and enterprises	64,170
Computer systems design and related services	63,910
Local government	52,300

Median annual earnings of all other computer specialists were $59,480 in May 2004. Median annual earnings of all other computer specialists employed in computer systems design and related services were $57,430, and, for those in management of companies and enterprises, earnings were $68,590 in May 2004.

According to the National Association of Colleges and Employers, starting offers for graduates with a doctoral degree in computer science averaged $93,050 in 2005. Starting offers averaged $50,820 for graduates with a bachelor's degree in computer science; $46,189 for those with a degree in computer systems analysis; $44,417 for those with a degree in management information systems; and $44,775 for those with a degree in information sciences and systems.

According to Robert Half International, a firm providing specialized staffing services, starting salaries in 2005 ranged from $67,750 to $95,500 for database administrators. Salaries for networking and Internet-related occupations ranged from $47,000 to $68,500 for LAN administrators and from $51,750 to $74,520 for Web developers. Starting salaries for information security professionals ranged from $63,750 to $93,000 in 2005.

Related Occupations

Others who work with large amounts of data are computer programmers, computer software engineers, computer and information systems managers, engineers, mathematicians, and statisticians.

Sources of Additional Information

Further information about computer careers is available from:

▸ Association for Computing Machinery (ACM), 1515 Broadway, New York, NY 10036. Internet: http://www.acm.org

▸ Institute of Electrical and Electronics Engineers Computer Society, Headquarters Office, 1730 Massachusetts Ave. NW, Washington, DC 20036-1992. Internet: http://www.computer.org

▸ National Workforce Center for Emerging Technologies, 3000 Landerholm Circle SE, Bellevue, WA 98007. Internet: http://www.nwcet.org

Computer Support Specialists and Systems Administrators

(O*NET 15-1041.00, 15-1071.00, and 15-1071.01)

Significant Points

■ Rapid job growth is projected over the 2004–2014 period.

■ There are many paths of entry to these occupations.

■ Job prospects should be best for college graduates who are up to date with the latest skills and technologies; certifications and practical experience are essential for persons without degrees.

Nature of the Work

In the last decade, computers have become an integral part of everyday life, used for a variety of reasons at home, in the workplace, and at schools. Of course, almost every computer user encounters a problem occasionally, whether it is the disaster of a crashing hard drive or the annoyance of a forgotten password. The explosive use of computers has created a high demand for specialists to provide advice to users as well as for day-to-day administration, maintenance, and support of computer systems and networks.

Computer support specialists provide technical assistance, support, and advice to customers and other users. This occupational group includes *technical support specialists* and *help-desk technicians.* These troubleshooters interpret problems and provide technical support for hardware, software, and systems. They answer telephone calls, analyze problems by using automated diagnostic programs, and resolve recurring difficulties. Support specialists may work either within a company that uses computer systems or directly for a computer hardware or software vendor. Increasingly, these specialists work for help-desk or support services firms, for which they provide computer support to clients on a contract basis.

Technical support specialists answer telephone calls from their organizations' computer users and may run automatic diagnostics programs to resolve problems. Working on monitors, keyboards, printers, and mice, they install, modify, clean, and repair computer hardware and software. They also may write training manuals and train computer users in how to use new computer hardware and software. In addition, technical support specialists oversee the daily performance of their company's computer systems and evaluate software programs with regard to their usefulness.

Help-desk technicians assist computer users with the inevitable hardware and software questions that are not addressed in a product's instruction manual. Help-desk technicians field telephone calls and e-mail messages from customers who are seeking guidance on technical problems. In responding to these requests for guidance, help-desk technicians must listen carefully to the customer, ask questions to diagnose the nature of the problem, and then patiently walk the customer through the problem-solving steps.

Help-desk technicians deal directly with customer issues, and companies value them as a source of feedback on their products. These technicians are consulted for information about what gives customers the most trouble as well as other customer concerns. Most computer support specialists start out at the help desk.

Network administrators and *computer systems administrators* design, install, and support an organization's local area network (LAN), wide area network (WAN), network segment, Internet, or intranet system. They provide day-to-day onsite administrative support for software users in a variety of work environments, including professional offices, small businesses, government, and large corporations. They maintain network hardware and software, analyze problems, and monitor the network to ensure its availability to system users. These workers gather data to identify customer needs and then use the information to identify, interpret, and evaluate system and network requirements. Administrators also may plan, coordinate, and implement network security measures.

Systems administrators are the information technology employees responsible for the efficient use of networks by organizations. They ensure that the design of an organization's computer site allows all of the components, including computers, the network, and software, to fit together and work properly. Furthermore, they monitor and adjust the performance of existing networks and continually survey the current computer site to determine future network needs. Administrators also troubleshoot problems reported by users and by automated network monitoring systems and make recommendations for enhancements in the implementation of future servers and networks.

In some organizations, *computer security specialists* may plan, coordinate, and implement the organization's information security. These workers may be called upon to educate users about computer security, install security software, monitor the network for security breaches, respond to cyber attacks, and, in some cases, gather data and evidence to be used in prosecuting cyber crime. The responsibilities of computer security specialists have increased in recent years, as there has been a large increase in the number of cyber attacks on data and networks. This and other growing specialty occupations reflect an increasing emphasis on client-server applications, the expansion of Internet and intranet applications, and the demand for more end-user support.

Working Conditions

Computer support specialists and systems administrators normally work in well-lighted, comfortable offices or computer laboratories. They usually work about 40 hours a week, but that may include being "on call" via pager or telephone for rotating evening or weekend work if the employer requires computer support over extended hours. Overtime may be necessary when unexpected technical problems arise. Like other workers who type on a keyboard for long periods, computer support specialists and systems administrators are susceptible to eyestrain, back discomfort, and hand and wrist problems such as carpal tunnel syndrome.

Due to the heavy emphasis on helping all types of computer users, computer support specialists and systems administrators constantly interact with customers and fellow employees as they answer questions and give valuable advice. Those who work as consultants are away from their offices much of the time, sometimes spending months working in a client's office.

As computer networks expand, more computer support specialists and systems administrators may be able to connect to a customer's computer remotely, using modems, laptops, e-mail, and the Internet, to provide technical support to computer users. This capability would reduce or eliminate travel to the customer's workplace. Systems administrators also can administer and configure networks and servers remotely, although this practice is not as common as it is among computer support specialists.

Training, Other Qualifications, and Advancement

Due to the wide range of skills required, there are many paths of entry to a job as a computer support specialist or systems administrator. While there is no universally accepted way to prepare for a job as a computer support specialist, many employers prefer to hire persons with some formal college education. A bachelor's degree in computer science or information systems is a prerequisite for some jobs; however, other jobs may require only a computer-related associate's degree. For systems administrators, many employers seek applicants with bachelor's degrees, although not necessarily in a computer-related field.

A number of companies are becoming more flexible about requiring a college degree for support positions. However, certification and practical experience demonstrating these skills will be essential for applicants without a degree. The completion of a certification training program, offered by a variety of vendors and product makers, may help some people to qualify for entry-level positions. Relevant computer experience may substitute for formal education.

Beginning computer support specialists usually work for organizations that deal directly with customers or in-house users. Then they may advance into more responsible positions in which they use what they have learned from customers to improve the design and efficiency of future products. Job promotions usually depend more on performance than on formal education. Eventually, some computer support specialists become applications developers, designing products rather than assisting users. Computer support specialists at hardware and software companies often enjoy great upward mobility; advancement sometimes comes within months of one's initial employment.

Entry-level network and computer systems administrators are involved in routine maintenance and monitoring of computer systems, typically working behind the scenes in an organization. After gaining experience and expertise, they often are able to advance into more senior-level positions in which they take on more responsibilities. For example, senior network and computer systems administrators may present recommendations to management on matters related to a company's network. They also may translate the needs of an organization into a set of technical requirements based on the available technology. As with support specialists, administrators may become software engineers, actually involved in the designing of the system or network and not just its day-to-day administration.

Persons interested in becoming a computer support specialist or systems administrator must have strong problem-solving, analytical, and communication skills because troubleshooting and helping others are vital parts of the job. The constant interaction with other computer personnel, customers, and employees requires computer support specialists and systems administrators to communicate effectively on paper, via e-mail, or in person. Strong writing skills are useful in preparing manuals for employees and customers.

As technology continues to improve, computer support specialists and systems administrators must keep their skills current and acquire new ones. Many continuing education programs are provided by employers, hardware and software vendors, colleges and universities, and private training institutions. Professional development seminars offered by computing services firms also can enhance one's skills and advancement opportunities.

Employment

Computer support specialists and systems administrators held about 797,000 jobs in 2004. Of these, approximately 518,000 were computer support specialists and around 278,000 were network and computer systems administrators. Although they worked in a wide range of industries, about 23 percent of all computer support specialists and systems administrators were employed in professional, scientific, and technical services industries, principally computer systems design and related services. Other organizations that employed substantial numbers of these workers include administrative and support services companies; banks; government agencies; insurance companies; educational institutions; and wholesale and retail vendors of computers, office equipment, appliances, and home electronic equipment. Many computer support specialists worked for manufacturers of computers, semiconductors, and other electronic components.

Employers of computer support specialists and systems administrators range from startup companies to established industry leaders. With the continued development of the Internet, telecommunications, and e-mail, industries not typically associated with computers—such as construction—increasingly need computer workers. Small and large firms across all industries are expanding or developing computer systems, creating an immediate need for computer support specialists and systems administrators.

Job Outlook

Job prospects should be best for college graduates who are up to date with the latest skills and technologies, particularly if they have supplemented their formal education with some relevant work experience. Employers will continue to seek computer specialists who possess a strong background in fundamental computer skills combined with good interpersonal and communication skills. Due to the demand for computer support specialists and systems administrators over the next decade, those who have strong computer skills but do not have a bachelor's degree should continue to qualify for some entry-level positions. However, certifications and practical experience are essential for persons without degrees.

Employment of computer support specialists is expected to increase faster than the average for all occupations through 2014 as organizations continue to adopt increasingly sophisticated technology and integrate it into their systems. Job growth will continue to be driven by the ongoing expansion of the computer system design and related services industry, which is projected to remain one of the fastest-growing industries in the U.S. economy. Growth will not be as explosive as during the previous decade, however, as the information technology industry matures and some of these jobs are increasingly outsourced overseas.

Job growth among computer support specialists reflects the rapid pace of improved technology. As computers and software become more complex, support specialists will be needed to provide technical assistance to customers and other users. New mobile technologies, such as wireless Internet access, will continue to create a demand for these workers to familiarize and educate computer users. Consulting opportunities for computer support specialists also should continue to grow as businesses increasingly need help managing, upgrading, and customizing ever more complex computer systems. However, growth in employment of support specialists may be tempered somewhat as firms continue to cut costs by shifting more routine work abroad to countries where workers are highly skilled and labor costs are lower. Physical location is not as important for computer support specialists as it is for others because these workers can provide assistance remotely and support services can be provided around the clock.

Employment of systems administrators is expected to increase much faster than the average for all occupations as firms continue to invest heavily in securing computer networks. Companies are looking for workers who are knowledgeable about the function and administration of networks. Such employees have become increasingly hard to find as systems administration has moved from being a separate function within corporations to one that forms a crucial element of business in an increasingly high-technology economy. Also, demand for computer security specialists will grow as businesses and government continue to invest heavily in "cyber security," protecting vital computer networks and electronic infrastructures from attack. The information security field is expected to generate many opportunities over the next decade as firms across all industries place a high priority on safeguarding their data and systems.

The growth of electronic commerce means that more establishments use the Internet to conduct their business online. This growth translates into a need for information technology specialists who can help organizations use technology to communicate with employees, clients, and consumers. Growth in these areas also is expected to fuel demand for specialists who are knowledgeable about network, data, and communications security.

Earnings

Median annual earnings of computer support specialists were $40,430 in May 2004. The middle 50 percent earned between $30,980 and $53,010. The lowest 10 percent earned less than $24,190, and the highest 10 percent earned more than $69,110. Median annual earnings in the industries employing the largest numbers of computer support specialists in May 2004 were as follows:

Software publishers $44,890

Management of companies and enterprises 42,780

Computer systems design and related services 42,750

Colleges, universities, and professional schools 37,940

Elementary and secondary schools 35,500

Median annual earnings of network and computer systems administrators were $58,190 in May 2004. The middle 50 percent earned between $46,260 and $73,620. The lowest 10 percent earned less than $37,100, and the highest 10 percent earned more than $91,300. Median annual earnings in the industries employing the largest numbers of network and computer systems administrators in May 2004 were as follows:

Wired telecommunications carriers $65,120

Computer systems design and related services 63,710

Management of companies and enterprises 61,600

Elementary and secondary schools 51,420

Colleges, universities, and professional schools 51,170

According to Robert Half International, starting salaries in 2005 ranged from $26,250 to $53,750 for help-desk and technical support staff and from $44,500 to $63,250 for more senior technical support specialists. For systems administrators, starting salaries in 2005 ranged from $47,250 to $70,500.

Related Occupations

Other computer specialists include computer programmers, computer software engineers, computer systems analysts, and computer scientists and database administrators.

Sources of Additional Information

For additional information about a career as a computer support specialist, contact the following organizations:

▸ Association of Computer Support Specialists, 333 Mamaroneck Ave., #129, White Plains, NY 10605. Internet: http://www.acss.org

▸ Association of Support Professionals, 122 Barnard Ave., Watertown, MA 02472.

For additional information about a career as a systems administrator, contact

▸ System Administrators Guild, 2560 9th St., Suite 215, Berkeley, CA 94710. Internet: http://www.sage.org

Further information about computer careers is available from

▸ National Workforce Center for Emerging Technologies, 3000 Landerholm Circle SE, Bellevue, WA 98007. Internet: http://www.nwcet.org

Computer, Automated Teller, and Office Machine Repairers

(O*NET 49-2011.01, 49-2011.02, and 49-2011.03)

Significant Points

■ Workers qualify for these jobs by receiving training in electronics from associate degree programs, the military, vocational schools, equipment manufacturers, or employers.

■ Job growth reflects the increasing dependence of businesses and individuals on computers and other sophisticated office machines.

■ Job prospects will be best for applicants with knowledge of electronics as well as repair experience.

Nature of the Work

Computer repairers, also known as *computer service technicians or data-processing equipment repairers,* service mainframe, server, and personal computers; printers; and disc drives. These workers perform primarily hands-on repair, maintenance, and installation of computers and related equipment. Workers who provide technical assistance, in person or by telephone, to computer system users are known as computer support specialists or computer support technicians. (See the description of computer support specialists and systems administrators elsewhere in this book.)

Automated teller machines (ATMs) allow customers to carry out bank transactions without the assistance of a teller. ATMs now also provide a growing variety of other services, including stamp, phone card, and ticket sales. *Automated teller machine servicers* repair and service these machines.

Office machine and cash register servicers work on photocopiers, cash registers, mail-processing equipment, and fax machines. Newer models of office machinery include computerized components that allow them to function more effectively than earlier models.

To install large equipment, such as mainframe computers and ATMs, repairers connect the equipment to power sources and communication lines that allow the transmission of information over computer networks. For example, when an ATM dispenses cash, it transmits the withdrawal information to the customer's bank. Workers also may install operating software and peripheral equipment, checking that all components are configured to function together correctly. The installation of personal computers and other small office machines is less complex and may be handled by the purchaser.

When equipment breaks down, many repairers travel to customers' workplaces or other locations to make the necessary repairs. These workers, known as *field technicians,* often have assigned areas in which they perform preventive maintenance on a regular basis. *Bench technicians* work in repair shops located in stores, factories, or service centers. In small companies, repairers may work both in repair shops and at customer locations.

Computer repairers usually replace subsystems instead of repairing them. Replacement is common because subsystems are inexpensive and businesses are reluctant to shut down their computers for time-consuming repairs. Subsystems commonly replaced by computer repairers include video cards, which transmit signals from the computer to the monitor; hard drives, which store data; and network cards, which allow communication over the network. Defective modules may be given to bench technicians, who use software programs to diagnose the problem and who may repair the modules, if possible.

When ATMs malfunction, computer networks recognize the problem and alert repairers. Common problems include worn magnetic heads on card readers, which prevent the equipment from recognizing customers' bank cards, and "pick failures," which prevent the equipment from dispensing the correct amount of cash. Field technicians travel to the locations of ATMs and usually repair equipment by removing and replacing defective components. Broken components are taken to a repair shop, where bench technicians make the necessary repairs. Field technicians perform routine maintenance on a regular basis, replacing worn parts and running diagnostic tests to ensure that the equipment functions properly.

Office machine repairers usually work on machinery at the customer's workplace; alternatively, if the machines are small enough, customers may bring them to a repair shop for maintenance. Common malfunctions include paper misfeeds caused by worn or dirty parts and poor-quality copy resulting from problems with lamps, lenses, or mirrors. These malfunctions usually can be resolved simply by cleaning the relevant components. Breakdowns also may result from the failure of commonly used parts. For example, heavy use of a photocopier may wear down the print head, which applies ink to the final copy. In such cases, the repairer usually replaces the part instead of repairing it.

Workers use a variety of tools for diagnostic tests and repair. To diagnose malfunctions, they use multimeters to measure voltage, current, resistance, and other electrical properties; signal generators to provide test signals; and oscilloscopes to monitor equipment signals. To diagnose computerized equipment, repairers use software programs. To repair or adjust equipment, workers use hand tools, such as pliers, screwdrivers, soldering irons, and wrenches.

Working Conditions

Repairers usually work in clean, well-lighted surroundings. Because computers and office machines are sensitive to extreme temperatures and to humidity, repair shops usually are air-conditioned and well ventilated. Field repairers must travel frequently to various locations to install, maintain, or repair customers' equipment. ATM repairers may have to perform their jobs in small, confined spaces that house the equipment.

Because computers and ATMs are critical for many organizations to function efficiently, data processing equipment repairers and ATM field technicians often work around the clock. Their schedules may include evening, weekend, and holiday shifts, sometimes assigned on the basis of seniority. Office machine and cash register servicers usually work regular business hours because the equipment they repair is not as critical.

Although their job is not strenuous, repairers must lift equipment and work in a variety of postures. Repairers of computer monitors need to discharge voltage from the equipment to avoid electrocution. Workers may have to wear protective goggles.

Training, Other Qualifications, and Advancement

Knowledge of electronics is necessary for employment as a computer, automated teller, or office machine repairer. Employers prefer workers who are certified as repairers or who have training in electronics from associate degree programs, the military, vocational schools, or equipment manufacturers. Employers generally provide some training to new repairers on specific equipment; however, workers are expected to arrive on the job with a basic understanding of equipment repair. Employers may send experienced workers to training sessions to keep up with changes in technology and service procedures.

Most office machine and ATM repairer positions require an associate degree in electronics. A basic understanding of mechanical equipment also is important, because many of the parts that fail in office machines and ATMs, such as paper loaders, are mechanical. Entry-level employees at large companies normally receive on-the-job training lasting several months. Such training may include a week of classroom instruction, followed by a period of 2 weeks to several months assisting an experienced repairer.

Field technicians work closely with customers and must have good communications skills and a neat appearance. Employers normally require that field technicians have a driver's license.

Various organizations offer certification. To receive certification, repairers must pass qualifying examinations corresponding to their level of training and experience.

Newly hired computer repairers may work on personal computers or peripheral equipment. With experience, they can advance to positions maintaining more sophisticated systems, such as networking equipment and servers. Field repairers of ATMs may advance to bench technician positions responsible for more complex repairs. Experienced workers may become specialists who help other repairers diagnose difficult problems or who work with engineers in designing equipment and developing maintenance procedures. Experienced workers also may move into management positions responsible for supervising other repairers.

Because of their familiarity with equipment, experienced repairers may move into customer service or sales positions. Some experienced workers open their own repair shops or become wholesalers or retailers of electronic equipment.

Employment

Computer, automated teller, and office machine repairers held about 168,000 jobs in 2004. Wholesale trade establishments employed about 35 percent of the workers in this occupation; most of these establishments were wholesalers of professional and commercial equipment and supplies. Many workers also were employed in electronics, appliance, and office supply stores. Others worked in electronic and precision equipment repair shops and computer systems design firms. A small number found employment with computer and peripheral equipment manufacturers, government agencies, and Internet service providers. About 15 percent of computer, automated teller, and office machine repairers were self-employed, which is more than twice the proportion for all installation, maintenance, and repair occupations.

Job Outlook

Employment of computer, automated teller, and office machine repairers is expected to grow more slowly than the average for all occupations through 2014. Limited job growth will be driven by the increasing dependence of business and individuals on computers and other sophisticated office machines. The need to maintain this equipment will create new jobs for repairers. In addition, openings will result from the need to replace repairers who retire or transfer to new occupations.

Job prospects will be best for applicants with knowledge of electronics as well as repair experience. Although computer equipment continues to become less expensive and more reliable, malfunctions still occur and can cause severe problems for users, most of whom lack the knowledge to make repairs. Computers are critical to most businesses today and will become even more so to companies that do business on the Internet and to individuals that bank, pay bills, or make purchases online.

People also are becoming increasingly reliant on ATMs. Besides offering bank and retail transactions, ATMs provide an increasing number of other services, such as employee information processing and distribution of government payments. Improvements in ATM design have increased reliability and simplified repair tasks, reducing the number and extent of repairs. However, opportunities for ATM repairers should still be available; they will arise primarily from the need to replace workers who leave the specialty, rather than from employment growth.

Conventional office machines, such as calculators, are inexpensive and often are replaced instead of repaired. However, digital copiers and other, newer office machines are more costly and complex. This equipment often is computerized, designed to work on a network, and capable of performing multiple functions. The growing need for repairers to service such sophisticated equipment should result in job opportunities for office machine repairers.

Earnings

Median hourly earnings of computer, automated teller, and office machine repairers were $16.90 in May 2004. The middle 50 percent earned between $13.11 and $21.36. The lowest 10 percent earned less than $10.31, and the highest 10 percent earned more than $26.28. Median hourly earnings in the industries employing the largest numbers of computer, automated teller, and office machine repairers in May 2004 are shown here:

Professional and commercial equipment and supplies merchant wholesalers $18.51

Computer systems design and related services 18.08

Office supplies, stationery, and gift stores 15.69

Electronic and precision equipment repair and maintenance 14.95

Electronics and appliance stores 14.04

Related Occupations

Workers in other occupations who repair and maintain electronic equipment include broadcast and sound engineering technicians and radio operators; electronic home entertainment equipment installers and repairers; electrical and electronics installers and repairers; industrial machinery mechanics and maintenance workers; and radio and telecommunications equipment installers and repairers.

Sources of Additional Information

For information on careers and certification, contact

▸ ACES International, 5241 Princess Anne Rd., Suite 110, Virginia Beach, VA 23462. Internet: http://www.acesinternational.org

▸ Electronics Technicians Association International, 5 Depot St., Greencastle, IN 46135.

▸ International Society of Certified Electronics Technicians, 3608 Pershing Ave., Fort Worth, TX 76107-4527. Internet: http://www.iscet.org

Construction Equipment Operators

(O*NET 47-2071.00, 47-2072.00, 47-2073.01, and 47-2073.02)

Significant Points

■ Many construction equipment operators acquire their skills on the job, but formal apprenticeship programs provide more comprehensive training.

■ Job opportunities are expected to be good, with employment growing about as fast as the average for all occupations.

■ Hourly pay is relatively high, but some construction equipment operators cannot work in inclement weather, so total annual earnings may be reduced.

Nature of the Work

Construction equipment operators use machinery to move construction materials, earth, and other heavy materials at construction sites, mines, and sometimes your back yard. They operate equipment that clears and grades land to prepare it for construction of roads, buildings, and neighborhoods. They dig trenches to lay or repair sewer and other pipelines, and they hoist heavy construction materials. They may even work offshore constructing oil rigs. Construction equipment operators also operate machinery that applies asphalt and concrete to roads and other structures.

Operators control equipment by moving levers or foot pedals, operating switches, or turning dials. The operation of much of this equipment is becoming more complex as a result of computerized controls. Global Positioning System (GPS) technology also is being used to help with grading and leveling activities. In addition to controlling the equipment, construction equipment operators also set up and inspect the equipment, make adjustments, and perform some maintenance and minor repairs.

Construction equipment operators include paving, surfacing, and tamping equipment operators; piledriver operators; and operating engineers and other construction equipment operators. *Operating engineers and other construction equipment operators* operate one or several types of power construction equipment. They may operate excavation and loading machines equipped with scoops, shovels, or buckets that dig sand, gravel, earth, or similar materials and load it into trucks or onto conveyors. In addition to the familiar bulldozers, they operate trench excavators, road graders, and similar equipment. Sometimes, they may drive and control industrial trucks or tractors equipped with forklifts or booms for lifting materials or with hitches for pulling trailers. They also may operate and maintain air compressors, pumps, and other power equipment at construction sites. Construction equipment operators who are classified as operating engineers are capable of operating several different types of construction equipment.

Paving and surfacing equipment operators use levers and other controls to operate machines that spread and level asphalt or spread and smooth concrete for roadways or other structures. *Asphalt paving machine operators* turn valves to regulate the temperature and flow of asphalt onto the roadbed. They must take care that the machine distributes the paving material evenly and without voids and make sure that there is a constant flow of asphalt going into the hopper. *Concrete paving machine operators* control levers and turn hand-wheels to move attachments that spread, vibrate, and level wet concrete within forms. They must observe the surface of concrete to identify low spots into which workers must add concrete. They use other attachments to smooth the surface of the concrete, spray on a curing compound, and cut expansion joints. *Tamping equipment operators* operate tamping machines that compact earth and other fill materials for roadbeds. They also may operate machines with interchangeable hammers to cut or break up old pavement and drive guardrail posts into the earth.

Piledriver operators operate piledrivers—large machines, mounted on skids, barges, or cranes, that hammer piles into the ground. Piles are long heavy beams of wood or steel driven into the ground to support retaining walls, bulkheads, bridges, piers, or building foundations. Some piledriver operators work on offshore oil rigs. Piledriver operators move hand and foot levers and turn valves to activate, position, and control the pile-driving equipment.

Working Conditions

Many construction equipment operators work outdoors in nearly every type of climate and weather condition, although in many areas of the country, some types of construction operations must be suspended in winter. Also, during periods of extremely wet weather, grading and leveling activities can be difficult to perform and may be suspended. Bulldozers, scrapers, and especially tampers and piledrivers are noisy and shake or jolt the operator. Operating heavy construction equipment can be dangerous. As with most machinery, accidents generally can be avoided by observing proper operating procedures and safety practices. Construction equipment operators are cold in the winter and hot in the summer and often get dirty, greasy, muddy, or dusty.

Operators may have irregular hours because work on some construction projects continues around the clock or must be performed late at night or early in the morning. Some operators work in remote locations on large construction projects, such as highways and dams, or in factory or mining operations.

Training, Other Qualifications, and Advancement

Construction equipment operators usually learn their skills on the job. They may start by operating light equipment under the guidance of an experienced operator. Later, they may operate heavier equipment, such as bulldozers and cranes. However, it is generally accepted that formal training provides more comprehensive skills. Some construction equipment operators train in formal operating engineer apprenticeship programs administered by union-management committees of the International Union of Operating Engineers and the Associated General Contractors of America. Because apprentices learn to operate a wider variety of machines than do other beginners, they usually have better job opportunities. Apprenticeship programs consist of at least 3 years, or 6,000 hours, of on-the-job training and 144 hours a year of related classroom instruction.

Employers of construction equipment operators generally prefer to hire high school graduates, although some employers may train non-graduates to operate some types of equipment. Technologically advanced construction equipment has computerized controls and improved hydraulics and electronics, requiring more skill to operate. Operators of such equipment may need more training and some understanding of electronics. Mechanical aptitude and high school training in automobile mechanics are helpful because workers may perform some maintenance on their machines. Also, high school courses in science and mechanical drawing are useful. Experience operating related mobile equipment, such as farm tractors or heavy equipment, in the Armed Forces or elsewhere is an asset.

Private vocational schools offer instruction in the operation of certain types of construction equipment. Completion of such programs may help a person get a job as a trainee or apprentice. However, persons considering such training should check the school's reputation among employers in the area and find out if it offers the opportunity to work on actual machines in realistic situations.

Operators need to be in good physical condition and have a good sense of balance, the ability to judge distance, and eye-hand-foot coordination. Some operator positions require the ability to work at heights.

Employment

Construction equipment operators held about 449,000 jobs in 2004. Jobs were found in every section of the country and were distributed among various types of operators as follows:

Operating engineers and other construction
equipment operators 382,000

Paving, surfacing, and tamping equipment
operators 63,000

Pile-driver operators 4,400

About three out of five construction equipment operators worked in the construction industry. Many equipment operators worked in heavy construction, building highways, bridges, or railroads. About one out of five of all construction equipment operators worked in state and local government. Others—mostly grader, bulldozer, and scraper operators—worked in mining. Some also worked in manufacturing and for utility companies. Less than one in twenty construction equipment operators were self-employed.

Job Outlook

Job opportunities for construction equipment operators are expected to be good through 2014. Some potential workers may choose not to enter training programs because they prefer work that has more comfortable working conditions.

Employment of construction equipment operators is expected to increase as fast as the average for all occupations through the year 2014 even with improvements in equipment that are expected to continue to raise worker productivity and to moderate demand for these workers. Employment is expected to increase as population and business growth create a need for new houses, industrial facilities, schools, hospitals, offices, and other structures. More construction equipment operators also will be needed as a result of expected growth in highway, bridge, and street construction. Bridge construction is expected to grow the fastest, due to the need to repair or replace structures before they become unsafe. Highway conditions also will spur demand for highway maintenance and repair. In addition to job growth, many job openings will arise because of the need to replace experienced construction equipment operators who transfer to other occupations, retire, or leave the job for other reasons.

Like that of other construction workers, employment of construction equipment operators is sensitive to fluctuations in the economy. Workers may experience periods of unemployment when the level of construction activity falls.

Earnings

Earnings for construction equipment operators vary. In May 2004, median hourly earnings of operating engineers and other construction equipment operators were $17.00. The middle 50 percent earned between $13.19 and $23.00. The lowest 10 percent earned less than $10.98, and the highest 10 percent earned more than $29.34. Median hourly earnings in the industries employing the largest numbers of operating engineers in May 2004 were

Highway, street, and bridge construction $19.20

Utility system construction....................................18.13

Other specialty trade contractors...........................17.73

Local government 15.20

State government 13.52

Median hourly earnings of paving, surfacing, and tamping equipment operators were $14.42 in May 2004. The middle 50 percent earned between $11.35 and $19.30. The lowest 10 percent earned less than $9.47, and the highest 10 percent earned more than $26.51. Median hourly earnings in the industries employing the largest numbers of paving, surfacing, and tamping equipment operators in May 2004 were as follows:

Other specialty trade contractors $15.03

Highway, street, and bridge construction 14.56

Local government 13.70

In May 2004, median hourly earnings of piledriver operators were $21.29. The middle 50 percent earned between $15.50 and $30.23. The lowest 10 percent earned less than $11.78, and the highest 10 percent earned more than $34.04.

Pay scales generally are higher in large metropolitan areas. Annual earnings of some workers may be lower than hourly rates would indicate because work time may be limited by bad weather.

Related Occupations

Other workers who operate mechanical equipment include agricultural equipment operators; truck drivers, heavy and tractor trailer; logging equipment operators; and a variety of material moving occupations.

Sources of Additional Information

For further information about apprenticeships or work opportunities for construction equipment operators, contact a local of the International Union of Operating Engineers, a local apprenticeship committee, or the nearest office of the state apprenticeship agency or employment service. For general information about the work of construction equipment operators, contact

▸ National Center for Construction Education and Research, P.O. Box 141104, Gainesville, FL 32614-1104. Internet: http://www.nccer.org

▸ Associated General Contractors of America, 2300 Wilson Blvd., Suite 400, Arlington, VA 22201. Internet: http://www.agc.org

▸ International Union of Operating Engineers, 1125 17th St. NW, Washington, DC 20036. Internet: http://www.iuoe.org

Construction Laborers

(O*NET 47-2061.00)

Significant Points

■ Job opportunities should be good.

■ With training and experience, construction laborers can move into other skilled craft occupations.

■ Most construction laborers learn through informal on-the-job training, but formal apprenticeship programs provide more thorough preparation.

■ Like many other construction occupations, employment opportunities are affected by the cyclical nature of the construction industry and can vary greatly by state and locality.

Nature of the Work

Construction laborers can be found on almost all construction sites performing a wide range of tasks from the very easy to the potentially hazardous. They can be found at building, highway, and heavy construction sites; tunnel and shaft excavations; and demolition sites. Many of the jobs they perform require physical strength and some training and experience. Other jobs require little skill and can be learned in a short amount of time. While most construction laborers tend to specialize in a type of construction, such as highway or tunnel construction, they are generalists who perform many different tasks during all stages of construction. However, construction laborers who work in underground construction, such as in tunnels, or in demolition are more likely to specialize in only those areas.

Construction laborers clean and prepare construction sites, which may require them to remove asbestos or lead-based paint from buildings. Laborers also remove trees and debris; tend pumps, compressors, and generators; and build forms for pouring concrete. They erect and disassemble scaffolding and other temporary structures. They load, unload, identify, and distribute building materials to the appropriate location according to project plans and specifications. Laborers also tend machines; for example, they may mix concrete using a portable mixer or tend a machine that pumps concrete, grout, cement, sand, plaster, or stucco through a spray gun for application to ceilings and walls. Construction laborers often help other craftworkers, including carpenters, plasterers, operating engineers, and masons.

Construction laborers are responsible for oversight of the installation and maintenance of traffic control devices and patterns. At heavy and highway construction sites, this work may include clearing and preparing highway work zones and rights of way; installing traffic barricades, cones, and markers; and controlling traffic passing near, in, and around work zones. They also dig trenches; install sewer, water, and storm drain pipes; and place concrete and asphalt on roads. Other highly specialized tasks include operating laser guidance equipment to place pipes; operating air, electric, and pneumatic drills; and transporting and setting explosives for tunnel, shaft, and road construction.

Construction laborers operate a variety of equipment, including pavement breakers; jackhammers; earth tampers; concrete, mortar, and plaster mixers; electric and hydraulic boring machines; torches; small mechanical hoists; laser beam equipment; and surveying and measuring equipment. They may use computers and other high-tech input devices to control robotic pipe cutters and cleaners. To perform their jobs effectively, construction laborers must be familiar with the duties of other craftworkers and with the materials, tools, and machinery they use.

Construction laborers often work as part of a team with other skilled craftworkers, jointly carrying out assigned construction tasks. At other times, construction laborers may work alone, reading and interpreting instructions, plans, and specifications with little or no supervision.

Working Conditions

Most laborers do physically demanding work. They may lift and carry heavy objects and stoop, kneel, crouch, or crawl in awkward positions. Some work at great heights or outdoors in all weather conditions. Some jobs expose workers to harmful materials or chemicals, fumes, odors, loud noise, or dangerous machinery. Some laborers may be exposed to lead-based paint, asbestos, or other hazardous substances during their work, especially when working in confined spaces. To avoid injury, workers in these jobs wear safety clothing, such as gloves; hardhats; protective chemical suits; and devices to protect their eyes, respiratory system, or hearing. While working in underground construction, construction laborers must be especially alert to safely follow procedures and must deal with a variety of hazards.

Construction laborers generally work 8-hour shifts, although longer shifts are common. Overnight work may be required when working on highways. Construction laborers may work only during certain seasons in certain parts of the country. They may also experience weather-related work stoppages at any time of the year.

Training, Other Qualifications, and Advancement

Many construction laborer jobs require few skills, but others require specialized training and experience. Many workers enter the occupation with few skills by obtaining a job with a contractor who will then provide on-the-job training. Entry-level workers generally start as helpers, assisting more experienced workers. A growing route of entry is through temporary help agencies that send laborers to construction sites for short-term work. Beginning laborers perform routine tasks, such as cleaning and preparing the worksite and unloading materials. When the opportunity arises, they learn from experienced construction trades workers how to do more difficult tasks, such as operating tools and equipment. During this time, the construction laborer may elect to attend a trade or vocational school or community college to receive further trade-related training.

The most skilled laborers usually have more formalized training. Some employers, particularly large nonresidential construction contractors with union membership, offer employees formal apprenticeships. These programs include between 2 and 4 years of classroom and on-the-job training. A core curriculum consisting of basic construction skills such as blueprint reading, the correct use of tools and equipment, and knowledge of safety and health procedures comprises the first 200 hours. The remainder of the curriculum consists of specialized skills training in three of the largest segments of the construction industry: building construction; heavy/highway construction; and environmental remediation, such as lead or asbestos abatement and mold or hazardous waste remediation. Workers who use dangerous equipment or handle toxic chemicals usually receive specialized training in safety awareness and procedures. Apprenticeship applicants usually must be at least 18 years old and meet local requirements. Because the number of apprenticeship programs is limited, however, only a small proportion of laborers learn their trade through these programs.

High school classes in English, mathematics, physics, mechanical drawing, blueprint reading, welding, and general shop are recommended. Laborers need manual dexterity, eye-hand coordination, good physical fitness, an ability to work as a member of a team, and a good sense of balance. The ability to solve arithmetic problems quickly and accurately also is required. In addition, a good work

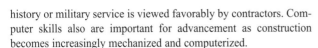

history or military service is viewed favorably by contractors. Computer skills also are important for advancement as construction becomes increasingly mechanized and computerized.

Through training and experience, laborers can move into other construction occupations. Laborers may also advance to become construction supervisors or general contractors. For those who would like to advance, it is increasingly important to be able to communicate in both English and Spanish in order to relay instructions and safety precautions to workers with limited understanding of English; Spanish-speaking workers make up a large part of the construction workforce in many areas. Supervisors and contractors need good English skills in order to deal with clients and subcontractors. Supervisors and contractors should be able to identify and estimate the quantity of materials needed to complete a job and accurately estimate how long a job will take to complete and at what cost.

Employment

Construction laborers held about 1 million jobs in 2004. They worked throughout the country but, like the general population, were concentrated in metropolitan areas. Most construction laborers work in the construction industry, and almost one-third work for special trade contractors. About 15 percent were self-employed in 2004.

Job Outlook

Employment of construction laborers is expected to grow more slowly than the average for all occupations through the year 2014 as the construction industry in general grows more slowly than it has in the recent past. However, job opportunities are expected to be good due to the numerous openings that rise each year as laborers leave the occupation. Opportunities will be best for those with experience and specialized skills and for those willing to relocate to areas with new construction projects. Opportunities will also be good for laborers specializing in lead, asbestos, and other hazardous materials removal.

Although construction will continue to grow, construction laborer jobs will be adversely affected by automation as some jobs are replaced by new machines and equipment that improve productivity and quality. Also, laborers will be increasingly employed by staffing agencies that will contract laborers out to employers on a temporary basis.

Employment of construction laborers, like that of many other construction workers, can be variable or intermittent due to the limited duration of construction projects and the cyclical nature of the construction industry. Employment opportunities can vary greatly by state and locality. During economic downturns, job openings for construction laborers decrease as the level of construction activity declines.

Earnings

Median hourly earnings of construction laborers in May 2004 were $12.10. The middle 50 percent earned between $9.47 and $16.88. The lowest 10 percent earned less than $7.71, and the highest 10 percent earned more than $23.61. Median hourly earnings in the

industries employing the largest number of construction laborers in May 2004 were as follows:

Highway, street, and bridge construction	$13.55
Nonresidential building construction	12.94
Other specialty trade contractors	12.43
Residential building construction	12.18
Foundation, structure, and building exterior contractors	11.90

Earnings for construction laborers can be reduced by poor weather or by downturns in construction activity, which sometimes result in layoffs. Apprentices or helpers usually start at about 50 percent of the wage rate paid to experienced workers. Pay increases as apprentices gain experience and learn new skills.

Some laborers belong to the Laborers' International Union of North America.

Related Occupations

The work of construction laborers is closely related to other construction occupations. Other workers who perform similar physical work include persons in material-moving occupations; forest, conservation, and logging workers; and grounds maintenance workers.

Sources of Additional Information

For information about jobs as construction laborers, contact local building or construction contractors, local joint labor-management apprenticeship committees, apprenticeship agencies, or the local office of your state employment service.

For information on education programs for laborers, contact

▸ Laborers-AGC Education and Training Fund, 37 Deerfield Rd., P.O. Box 37, Pomfret Center, CT 06259. Internet: http://www.laborerslearn.org

▸ National Center for Construction Education and Research, P.O. Box 141104, Gainesville, FL 32614-1104. Internet: http://www.nccer.org

Correctional Officers

(O*NET 33-1011.00, 33-3011.00, and 33-3012.00)

Significant Points

■ The work can be stressful and hazardous.

■ Most correctional officers are employed in state and federal prisons.

■ Job opportunities are expected to be excellent.

Nature of the Work

Correctional officers are responsible for overseeing individuals who have been arrested and are awaiting trial or who have been convicted of a crime and sentenced to serve time in a jail, reformatory, or penitentiary. Correctional officers maintain security and inmate accountability to prevent disturbances, assaults, and escapes. Officers have no law enforcement responsibilities outside the institution where they work. (For more information on related occupations, see the description of police and detectives elsewhere in this book.)

Police and sheriffs' departments in county and municipal jails or precinct station houses employ many correctional officers, also known as *detention officers*. Most of the approximately 3,400 jails in the United States are operated by county governments, with about three-quarters of all jails under the jurisdiction of an elected sheriff. Individuals in the jail population change constantly as some are released, some are convicted and transferred to prison, and new offenders are arrested and enter the system. Correctional officers in local jails admit and process about 12 million people a year, with about 700,000 offenders in jail at any given time. When individuals are first arrested, the jail staff may not know their true identity or criminal record, and violent detainees may be placed in the general population. This is the most dangerous phase of the incarceration process for correctional officers.

Most correctional officers are employed in state and federal prisons, watching over the approximately 1.4 million offenders who are incarcerated there at any given time. Other correctional officers oversee individuals being held by the U.S. Immigration and Naturalization Service pending release or deportation or work for correctional institutions that are run by private for-profit organizations. Although both jails and prisons can be dangerous places to work, prison populations are more stable than jail populations, and correctional officers in prisons know the security and custodial requirements of the prisoners with whom they are dealing.

Regardless of the setting, correctional officers maintain order within the institution and enforce rules and regulations. To help ensure that inmates are orderly and obey rules, correctional officers monitor the activities and supervise the work assignments of inmates. Sometimes officers must search inmates and their living quarters for contraband like weapons or drugs, settle disputes between inmates, and enforce discipline. Correctional officers periodically inspect the facilities, checking cells and other areas of the institution for unsanitary conditions, contraband, fire hazards, and any evidence of infractions of rules. In addition, they routinely inspect locks, window bars, grilles, doors, and gates for signs of tampering. Finally, officers inspect mail and visitors for prohibited items.

Correctional officers report orally and in writing on inmate conduct and on the quality and quantity of work done by inmates. Officers also report security breaches, disturbances, violations of rules, and any unusual occurrences. They usually keep a daily log or record of their activities. Correctional officers cannot show favoritism and must report any inmate who violates the rules. Should the situation arise, they help the responsible law enforcement authorities investigate crimes committed within their institution or search for escaped inmates.

In jail and prison facilities with direct supervision cellblocks, officers work unarmed. They are equipped with communications devices so that they can summon help if necessary. These officers often work in a cellblock alone or with another officer among the 50 to 100 inmates who reside there. The officers enforce regulations primarily through their interpersonal communications skills and through the use of progressive sanctions, such as the removal of some privileges.

In the highest-security facilities, where the most dangerous inmates are housed, correctional officers often monitor the activities of prisoners from a centralized control center with closed-circuit television cameras and a computer tracking system. In such an environment, the inmates may not see anyone but officers for days or weeks at a time and may leave their cells only for showers, solitary exercise time, or visitors. Depending on the offenders' security classification within the institution, correctional officers may have to restrain inmates in handcuffs and leg irons to safely escort them to and from cells and other areas and to see authorized visitors. Officers also escort prisoners between the institution and courtrooms, medical facilities, and other destinations outside the institution.

Bailiffs, also known as *marshals* or *court officers*, are law enforcement officers who maintain safety and order in courtrooms. Their duties, which vary by location, include enforcing courtroom rules, assisting judges, guarding juries from outside contact, delivering court documents, and providing general security for courthouses.

Working Conditions

Working in a correctional institution can be stressful and hazardous. Every year, correctional officers are injured in confrontations with inmates. Correctional officers may work indoors or outdoors. Some correctional institutions are well lighted, temperature controlled, and ventilated, but others are old, overcrowded, hot, and noisy. Correctional officers usually work an 8-hour day 5 days a week on rotating shifts. Because prison and jail security must be provided around the clock, officers work all hours of the day and night, weekends, and holidays. In addition, officers may be required to work paid overtime.

Training, Other Qualifications, and Advancement

Most institutions require correctional officers to be at least 18 to 21 years of age and a U.S. citizen; have a high school education or its equivalent; demonstrate job stability, usually by accumulating 2 years of work experience; and have no felony convictions. Promotion prospects may be enhanced by obtaining a postsecondary education.

The Federal Bureau of Prisons requires entry-level correctional officers to have at least a bachelor's degree or 3 years of full-time experience in a field providing counseling, assistance, or supervision to individuals or a combination of these two requirements.

Correctional officers must be in good health. Candidates for employment are generally required to meet formal standards of physical fitness, eyesight, and hearing. In addition, many jurisdictions use standard tests to determine applicant suitability to work in a correctional environment. Good judgment and the ability to think and act quickly are indispensable. Applicants are typically screened for drug abuse, subject to background checks, and required to pass a written examination.

Federal, state, and some local departments of corrections provide training for correctional officers based on guidelines established by the American Correctional Association and the American Jail Association. Some states have regional training academies that are

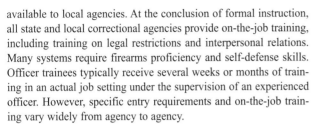

available to local agencies. At the conclusion of formal instruction, all state and local correctional agencies provide on-the-job training, including training on legal restrictions and interpersonal relations. Many systems require firearms proficiency and self-defense skills. Officer trainees typically receive several weeks or months of training in an actual job setting under the supervision of an experienced officer. However, specific entry requirements and on-the-job training vary widely from agency to agency.

Academy trainees generally receive instruction in a number of subjects, including institutional policies, regulations, and operations, as well as custody and security procedures. New federal correctional officers must undergo 200 hours of formal training within the first year of employment. They also must complete 120 hours of specialized training at the U.S. Federal Bureau of Prisons residential training center at Glynco, GA, within 60 days of their appointment. Experienced officers receive annual in-service training to keep abreast of new developments and procedures.

Some correctional officers are members of prison tactical response teams, which are trained to respond to disturbances, riots, hostage situations, forced cell moves, and other potentially dangerous confrontations. Team members practice disarming prisoners wielding weapons, protecting themselves and inmates against the effects of chemical agents, and other tactics.

With education, experience, and training, qualified officers may advance to the position of correctional sergeant. Correctional sergeants supervise correctional officers and usually are responsible for maintaining security and directing the activities of other officers during an assigned shift or in an assigned area. Ambitious and qualified correctional officers can be promoted to supervisory or administrative positions all the way up to warden. Officers sometimes transfer to related jobs, such as probation officers, parole officers, and correctional treatment specialists.

Employment

Bailiffs, correctional officers, and jailers held about 484,000 jobs in 2004. About 3 of every 5 jobs were in state correctional institutions such as prisons, prison camps, and youth correctional facilities. About 16,000 jobs for correctional officers were in federal correctional institutions, and about 15,000 jobs were in privately owned and managed prisons.

Most of the remaining jobs were in city and county jails or in other institutions run by local governments. Some 300 of these jails, all of them in urban areas, are large: They house over 1,000 inmates. Most correctional officers who work in jails, however, work in institutions located in rural areas with smaller inmate populations.

Job Outlook

Job opportunities for correctional officers are expected to be excellent. The need to replace correctional officers who transfer to other occupations, retire, or leave the labor force, coupled with rising employment demand, will generate thousands of job openings each year. In the past, some local and state corrections agencies have experienced difficulty in attracting and keeping qualified applicants, largely because of low salaries, shift work, and the concentration of jobs in rural locations. This situation is expected to continue.

Employment of correctional officers is expected to grow more slowly than the average for all occupations through 2014. Increasing demand for correctional officers will stem from mandatory sentencing guidelines calling for longer sentences and reduced parole for inmates and from expansion and new construction of corrections facilities. However, mandatory sentencing guidelines are being reconsidered in many states because of a combination of budgetary constraints, court decisions, and doubts about their effectiveness. Instead, there may be more emphasis on reducing sentences or putting offenders on probation or in rehabilitation programs in many states. As a result, the prison population, and employment of correctional officers, will probably grow at a slower rate than in the past. Some employment opportunities also will arise in the private sector as public authorities contract with private companies to provide and staff corrections facilities.

Layoffs of correctional officers are rare because of increasing offender populations. While officers are allowed to join bargaining units, they are not allowed to strike.

Earnings

Median annual earnings of correctional officers and jailers were $33,600 in May 2004. The middle 50 percent earned between $26,560 and $44,200. The lowest 10 percent earned less than $22,630, and the highest 10 percent earned more than $54,820. Median annual earnings in the public sector were $44,700 in the federal government, $33,750 in state government, and $33,080 in local government. In the facilities support services industry, where the relatively small number of officers employed by privately operated prisons is classified, median annual earnings were $21,490. According to the Federal Bureau of Prisons, the starting salary for federal correctional officers was about $26,747 a year in 2005. Starting federal salaries were slightly higher in areas where prevailing local pay levels were higher.

Median annual earnings of first-line supervisors/managers of correctional officers were $44,720 in May 2004. The middle 50 percent earned between $33,070 and $60,550. The lowest 10 percent earned less than $27,770, and the highest 10 percent earned more than $70,990. Median annual earnings were $41,080 in state government and $49,470 in local government.

Median annual earnings of bailiffs were $33,870 in May 2004. The middle 50 percent earned between $24,710 and $44,240. The lowest 10 percent earned less than $17,930, and the highest 10 percent earned more than $54,770. Median annual earnings were $30,410 in local government.

In addition to typical benefits, correctional officers employed in the public sector usually are provided with uniforms or a clothing allowance to purchase their own uniforms. Civil service systems or merit boards cover officers employed by the federal government and most state governments. Their retirement coverage entitles correctional officers to retire at age 50 after 20 years of service or at any age with 25 years of service.

Related Occupations

A number of options are available to those interested in careers in protective services and security. Security guards and gaming surveillance officers protect people and property against theft, vandalism, illegal entry, and fire. Police and detectives maintain law and order, prevent crime, and arrest offenders. Probation officers and correctional treatment specialists monitor and counsel offenders and evaluate their progress in becoming productive members of society.

Sources of Additional Information

Further information about correctional officers is available from

▶ American Correctional Association, 4380 Forbes Blvd., Lanham, MD 20706. Internet: http://www.aca.org

▶ American Jail Association, 1135 Professional Ct., Hagerstown, MD 21740.

Information on entrance requirements, training, and career opportunities for correctional officers at the federal level may be obtained from the Federal Bureau of Prisons. Internet: http://www.bop.gov

Information on obtaining a position as a correctional officer with the federal government is available from the Office of Personnel Management through USAJOBS, the federal government's official employment information system. This resource for locating and applying for job opportunities can be accessed through the Internet at http://www.usajobs.opm.gov or through an interactive voice response telephone system at (703) 724-1850 or TDD (978) 461-8404. These numbers are not toll free, and charges may result.

Counter and Rental Clerks

(O*NET 41-2021.00)

Significant Points

■ Jobs primarily are entry level and require little or no experience and minimal formal education.

■ Faster-than-average employment growth is expected as businesses strive to improve customer service.

■ Part-time employment opportunities should be plentiful.

Nature of the Work

Whether renting videos, air compressors, or moving vans or dropping off clothes to be drycleaned or appliances to be serviced, customers rely on counter and rental clerks to handle their transactions efficiently. Although the specific duties of these workers vary by establishment, counter and rental clerks answer questions involving product availability, cost, and rental provisions. Counter and rental clerks also take orders, calculate fees, receive payments, and accept returned merchandise. (Cashiers and retail salespersons, two occupations with similar duties, are discussed elsewhere in this book.)

Regardless of where they work, counter and rental clerks must be knowledgeable about the company's goods and services, policies, and procedures. Depending on the type of establishment, counter and rental clerks use their special knowledge to give advice on a wide variety of products and services ranging from hydraulic tools to shoe repair. For example, in the car rental industry, these workers inform customers about the features of different types of automobiles and about daily and weekly rental costs. They also ensure that customers meet age and other requirements for renting cars, and they indicate when and in what condition the cars must be returned. Those in the equipment rental industry have similar duties but also must know how to operate and care for the machinery rented. In drycleaning establishments, counter clerks inform customers when items will be ready and about the effects, if any, of the chemicals used on garments. In video rental stores, counter clerks advise customers about the use of video and game players and the length of a rental, scan returned movies and games, restock shelves, handle money, and log daily reports.

When taking orders, counter and rental clerks use various types of equipment. In some establishments, they write out tickets and order forms, although most use computers or barcode scanners. Most of these computer systems are user friendly, require very little data entry, and are customized for each firm. Scanners read the product code and display a description of the item on a computer screen. However, clerks must ensure that the data on the screen pertain to the product.

Working Conditions

Firms employing counter and rental clerks usually operate nights and weekends for the convenience of their customers. As a result, many employers offer flexible schedules. Some counter and rental clerks work 40-hour weeks, but about half are on part-time schedules—usually during rush periods, such as weekends, evenings, and holidays.

Working conditions usually are pleasant; most stores and service establishments are clean, well lighted, and temperature controlled. However, clerks are on their feet much of the time and may be confined behind a small counter area or may be required to move, lift, or carry heavy machinery or other equipment. The job requires constant interaction with the public and can be stressful, especially during busy periods.

Training, Other Qualifications, and Advancement

Most counter and rental clerk jobs are entry-level positions that require little or no experience and minimal formal education. However, many employers prefer workers with at least a high school diploma.

In most companies, counter and rental clerks are trained on the job, sometimes through the use of videos, brochures, and pamphlets. Clerks usually learn how to operate a firm's equipment and become familiar with the firm's policies and procedures under the observation of a more experienced worker. However, some employers have formal classroom training programs lasting from a few hours to a few weeks. Topics covered in this training include the nature of the industry, the company and its policies and procedures, operation of equipment, sales techniques, and customer service. Counter and rental clerks also must become familiar with the different products and services rented or provided by their company to give customers the best possible service.

Counter and rental clerks should enjoy working with people and should have the ability to deal tactfully with difficult customers. They also should be able to handle several tasks at once while continuing to provide friendly service. In addition, good oral and written communication skills are essential.

Advancement opportunities depend on the size and type of company. Many establishments that employ counter or rental clerks tend to be small businesses, making advancement difficult. In larger establishments, however, jobs such as counter and rental clerks offer good opportunities for workers to learn about their company's products and business practices. These jobs can lead to more responsible positions. It is common in many establishments to promote counter and rental clerks to event planner, assistant manager, or salesperson. Workers may choose to pursue related positions, such as mechanic, or even establish their own business.

In certain industries, such as equipment repair, counter and rental jobs may be an additional or alternative source of income for workers who are unemployed or semiretired. For example, retired mechanics could prove invaluable at tool rental centers because of their knowledge of, and familiarity with, tools.

Employment

Counter and rental clerks held 451,000 jobs in 2004. About 23 percent of clerks worked in consumer goods rental, which includes video rental stores. Other large employers included drycleaning and laundry services; automotive equipment rental and leasing services; automobile dealers; amusement, gambling, and recreation industries; and grocery stores.

Counter and rental clerks are employed throughout the country but are concentrated in metropolitan areas, where personal services and renting and leasing services are in greater demand.

Job Outlook

Employment of counter and rental clerks is expected to increase faster than the average for all occupations through the year 2014 as all types of businesses strive to improve customer service by hiring more clerks. In addition, some industries employing counter and rental clerks—for example, rental and leasing services and amusement and recreation industries—are expected to grow rapidly. Nevertheless, most job openings will arise from the need to replace experienced workers who transfer to other occupations or leave the labor force. Part-time employment opportunities are expected to be plentiful.

Earnings

Counter and rental clerks typically start at the minimum wage, which, in establishments covered by federal law, was $5.15 an hour in 2004. In some states, the law sets the minimum wage higher, and establishments must pay at least that amount. Wages also tend to be higher in areas where there is intense competition for workers. In addition to wages, some counter and rental clerks receive commissions based on the number of contracts they complete or services they sell.

Median hourly earnings of counter and rental clerks in May 2004 were $8.79. The middle 50 percent earned between $7.21 and $11.99 an hour. The lowest 10 percent earned less than $6.15 an hour, and the highest 10 percent earned more than $16.79 an hour. Median hourly earnings in the industries employing the largest number of counter and rental clerks in May 2004 were as follows:

Automobile dealers	$17.87
Automotive equipment rental and leasing	10.42
Lessors of real estate	9.92
Consumer goods rental	7.78
Drycleaning and laundry services	7.62

Full-time workers typically receive health and life insurance, paid vacation, and sick leave. Benefits for counter and rental clerks who work part time or work for independent stores tend to be significantly less than for those who work full time. Many companies offer discounts to both full-time and part-time employees on the goods or services they provide.

Related Occupations

Counter and rental clerks take orders and receive payment for services rendered. Other workers with similar duties include tellers, cashiers, food and beverage serving and related workers, gaming cage workers, Postal Service workers, and retail salespersons.

Sources of Additional Information

For general information on employment in the equipment rental industry, contact

▸ American Rental Association, 1900 19th St., Moline, IL 61265. Internet: http://www.ararental.org

For more information about the work of counter clerks in drycleaning and laundry establishments, contact

▸ International Fabricare Institute, 14700 Sweitzer Lane, Laurel, MD 20707. Internet: http://www.ifi.org

Customer Service Representatives

(O*NET 43-4051.01 and 43-4051.02)

Significant Points

■ Job prospects are expected to be excellent.

■ Most jobs require only a high school diploma, but educational requirements are rising.

■ Strong verbal communication and listening skills are important.

Nature of the Work

Customer service representatives are employed by many different types of companies throughout the country to serve as a direct point of contact for customers. They are responsible for ensuring that their company's customers receive an adequate level of service or help with their questions and concerns. These customers may be individual consumers or other companies, and the nature of their service needs can vary considerably.

All customer service representatives interact with customers to provide information in response to inquiries about products or services and to handle and resolve complaints. They communicate with customers through a variety of means—by telephone; by e-mail, fax, or regular mail correspondence; or in person. Some customer service representatives handle general questions and complaints, whereas others specialize in a particular area.

Many customer inquiries involve routine questions and requests. For example, customer service representatives may be asked to provide a customer with their credit card balance or to check on the status of an order that has been placed. Obtaining the answers to such questions usually requires simply looking up information on their computer. Other questions are more involved and may call for additional research or further explanation on the part of the customer service representative. In handling customers' complaints, customer service representatives must attempt to resolve the problem according to guidelines established by the company. These procedures may involve asking questions to determine the validity of a complaint; offering possible solutions; or providing customers with refunds, exchanges, or other offers, such as discounts or coupons. In some cases, customer service representatives are required to follow up with an individual customer until a question is answered or an issue is resolved.

Some customer service representatives help people decide what types of products or services would best suit their needs. They may even aid customers in completing purchases or transactions. Although the primary function of customer service representatives is not sales, some may spend a part of their time with customers encouraging them to purchase additional products or services. Customer service representatives also may make changes or updates to a customer's profile or account information. They may keep records of transactions and update and maintain databases of information.

Most customer service representatives use computers and telephones extensively in their work. Customer service representatives frequently enter information into a computer as they are speaking to customers. Often, companies have large amounts of data, such as account information, that can be pulled up on a computer screen while the representative is talking to a customer so that he or she can answer specific questions relating to the account. Customer service representatives also may have access to information such as answers to the most common customer questions or guidelines for dealing with complaints. In the event that they encounter a question or situation to which they do not know how to respond, workers consult with a supervisor to determine the best course of action. Customer service representatives use multiline telephones systems, which often route calls directly to the most appropriate representative. However, at times, the customer service representative must transfer a call to someone who may be better able to respond to the customer's needs.

In some organizations, customer service representatives spend their entire day on the telephone. In others, they may spend part of their day answering e-mails and the remainder of the day taking calls. For some, most of their contact with the customer is face to face. Customer service representatives need to remain aware of the amount of time spent with each customer so that they can fairly distribute their time among the people who require their assistance. This is particularly important for customer service representatives whose primary activities are answering telephone calls and whose conversations often are required to be kept within set time limits. For customer service representatives working in call centers, there usually is very little time between telephone calls; as soon as representatives have finished with one call, they must move on to another. When working in call centers, customer service representatives are likely to be under close supervision. Telephone calls may be taped and reviewed by supervisors to ensure that company policies and procedures are being followed, or a supervisor may listen in on conversations.

Job responsibilities can differ, depending on the industry in which a customer service representative is employed. For example, a customer service representative working in the branch office of a bank may assume the responsibilities of other workers, such as teller or new account clerk, as needed. In insurance agencies, a customer service representative interacts with agents, insurance companies, and policyholders. These workers handle much of the paperwork related to insurance policies, such as policy applications and changes and renewals to existing policies. They answer questions regarding policy coverage, help with reporting claims, and do anything else that may need to be done. Although they must know as much as insurance agents about insurance products, and usually must have credentials equal to those of an agent in order to sell products and make changes to policies, the duties of a customer service representative differ from those of an agent in that customer service representatives are not responsible for actively seeking potential customers. Customer service representatives employed by utilities and communications companies assist individuals interested in opening accounts for various utilities, such as electricity and gas, or for communication services such as cable television and telephone. They explain various options and receive orders for services to be installed, turned on, turned off, or changed. They also may look into and resolve complaints about billing and service provided by utility, telephone, and cable television companies.

Working Conditions

Although customer service representatives can work in a variety of settings, most work in areas that are clean and well lit. Many work in call or customer contact centers. In this type of environment, workers generally have their own workstation or cubicle space equipped with a telephone, headset, and computer. Because many call centers are open extended hours beyond the traditional work day or are staffed around the clock, these positions may require workers to take on early morning, evening, or late night shifts. Weekend or holiday work also may be necessary. As a result, the occupation is well suited to flexible work schedules. Nearly 1 out of 5 customer service representatives work part time. The occupation also offers the opportunity for seasonal work in certain industries, often through temporary help agencies.

Call centers may be crowded and noisy, and work may be repetitious and stressful, with little time between calls. Workers usually must attempt to minimize the length of each call while still providing excellent service. To ensure that these procedures are followed, conversations may be monitored by supervisors, something that can be stressful. Also, long periods spent sitting, typing, or looking at a computer screen may cause eye and muscle strain, backaches, headaches, and repetitive motion injuries.

Customer service representatives working outside of a call center environment may interact with customers through several different means. For example, workers employed by an insurance agency or in a grocery store may have customers approach them in person or contact them by telephone, computer, mail, or fax. Many of these customer service representatives work a standard 40-hour week; however, their hours generally depend on the hours of operation of the establishment in which they are employed. Work environments outside of a call center also vary accordingly. Most customer service representatives work either in an office or at a service or help desk.

For virtually all types of customer service representatives, dealing with difficult or irate customers can be a trying task; however, the ability to resolve customers' problems has the potential to be very rewarding.

Training, Other Qualifications, and Advancement

Most customer service representative jobs require only a high school diploma. However, due to employers demanding a higher-skilled workforce, many customer service jobs now require an associate or bachelor's degree. Basic to intermediate computer knowledge and good interpersonal skills also are important qualities for people who wish to be successful in the field. Because customer service representatives constantly interact with the public, good communication and problem-solving skills are a must. Verbal communication and listening skills are especially important. Additionally, for workers who communicate through e-mail, good typing, spelling, and written communication skills are necessary. High school courses in computers, English, or business are helpful in preparing for a job in customer service.

Customer service representatives play a critical role in providing an interface between customer and company, and for this reason employers seek out people who come across in a friendly and professional manner. The ability to deal patiently with problems and complaints and to remain courteous when faced with difficult or angry people is very important. Also, a customer service representative needs to be able to work independently within specified time constraints. Workers should have a clear and pleasant speaking voice and be fluent in English. However, the ability to speak a foreign language is becoming increasingly necessary, and bilingual skills are considered a plus.

Training requirements vary by industry. Almost all customer service representatives are provided with some training prior to beginning work, and training continues once on the job. This training generally covers customer service and phone skills, products and services and common customer problems with them, the use or operation of the telephone and/or computer systems, and company policies and regulations. Length of training varies, but it usually lasts at least several weeks. Because of a constant need to update skills and knowledge, most customer service representatives continue to receive instruction and training throughout their career. This is particularly true of workers in industries such as banking, in which regulations and products are continually changing.

Although some positions may require previous industry, office, or customer service experience, many customer service jobs are entry-level. Customer service jobs are often good introductory positions into a company or an industry. In some cases, experienced workers can move up within the company into supervisory or managerial positions, or they may move into areas such as product development, in which they can use their knowledge to improve products and services.

Within insurance agencies and brokerages, however, a customer service representative job usually is not an entry-level position. Workers must have previous experience in insurance and are often required by state regulations to be licensed like insurance sales agents. A variety of designations are available to demonstrate that a candidate has sufficient knowledge and skill, and continuing education and training are often offered through the employer. As they gain more knowledge of industry products and services, customer service representatives in insurance may advance to other higher-level positions, such as insurance sales agent.

Employment

Customer service representatives held about 2.1 million jobs in 2004. Although they were found in a variety of industries, about 1 in 4 customer service representatives worked in finance and insurance. The largest numbers were employed by insurance carriers, insurance agencies and brokerages, and banks and credit unions.

About 1 in 8 customer service representatives were employed in administrative and support services. These workers were concentrated in the business support services industry (which includes telephone call centers) and employment services (which includes temporary help services and employment placement agencies). Another 1 in 8 customer service representatives were employed in retail trade establishments such as general merchandise stores, food and beverage stores, or nonstore retailers. Other industries that employ significant numbers of customer service representatives include information, particularly the telecommunications industry; manufacturing, such as printing and related support activities; and wholesale trade.

Although they are found in all states, customer service representatives who work in call centers tend to be concentrated geographically. Four states—California, Texas, Florida, and New York—employ 30 percent of customer service representatives. Delaware, Arizona, South Dakota, and Utah have the highest concentration of workers in this occupation, with customer service representatives comprising over 2 percent of total employment in these states.

Job Outlook

Prospects for obtaining a job in this field are expected to be excellent, with more job openings than jobseekers. Bilingual jobseekers, in particular, may enjoy favorable job prospects. In addition to many new openings occurring as businesses and organizations expand, numerous job openings will result from the need to replace experienced customer service representatives who transfer to other occupations or leave the labor force. Replacement needs are expected to be significant in this large occupation because many young people work as customer service representatives before switching to other jobs. This occupation is well suited to flexible work schedules, and many opportunities for part-time work will continue to be available, particularly as organizations attempt to cut labor costs by hiring more temporary workers.

Employment of customer service representatives is expected to increase faster than the average for all occupations through the year 2014. Beyond growth stemming from expansion of the industries in which customer service representatives are employed, a need for additional customer service representatives is likely to result from heightened reliance on these workers. Customer service is critical to the success of any organization that deals with customers, and strong customer service can build sales and visibility as companies try to distinguish themselves from competitors. In many industries, gaining a competitive edge and retaining customers will be increasingly important over the next decade. This is particularly true in industries such as financial services, communications, and utilities, which already employ numerous customer service representatives. As the trend toward consolidation in industries continues, centralized call centers will provide an effective method for delivering a high level of customer service. As a result, employment of customer service representatives may grow at a faster rate in call centers than in other areas. However, this growth may be tempered: A variety of factors, including technological improvements, make it increasingly feasible and cost-effective for call centers to be built or relocated outside of the United States.

Technology is affecting the occupation in many ways. The Internet and automated teller machines have provided customers with means of obtaining information and conducting transactions that do not entail interacting with another person. Technology also allows for a greater streamlining of processes while at the same time increasing the productivity of workers. The use of computer software to filter e-mails, generating automatic responses or directing messages to the appropriate representative, and the use of similar systems to answer or route telephone inquiries are likely to become more prevalent in the future. Also, with rapidly improving telecommunications, some organizations have begun to position their call centers overseas.

Despite such developments, the need for customer service representatives is expected to remain strong. In many ways, technology has heightened consumers' expectations for information and services, and availability of information online seems to have generated more need for customer service representatives, particularly to respond to e-mail. Also, technology cannot replace human skills. As more sophisticated technologies are able to resolve many customers' questions and concerns, the nature of the inquiries to be handled by customer service representatives is likely to become increasingly complex.

Furthermore, the job responsibilities of customer service representatives are expanding. As companies downsize or take other measures to increase profitability, workers are being trained to perform additional duties such as opening bank accounts or cross-selling products. As a result, employers may increasingly prefer customer service representatives who have education beyond high school, such as some college or even a college degree.

While jobs in some industries, such as retail trade, may be affected by economic downturns, the customer service occupation is generally resistant to major fluctuations in employment.

Earnings

In May 2004, median annual earnings for wage and salary customer service representatives were $27,020. The middle 50 percent earned between $21,510 and $34,560. The lowest 10 percent earned less than $17,680, and the highest 10 percent earned more than $44,160.

Earnings for customer service representatives vary according to level of skill required, experience, training, location, and size of firm. Median annual earnings in the industries employing the largest numbers of these workers in May 2004 are shown here.

Insurance carriers	$29,790
Agencies, brokerages, and other insurance related activities	28,800
Depository credit intermediation	26,140
Employment services	23,100
Business support services	21,390

In addition to receiving an hourly wage, full-time customer service representatives who work evenings, nights, weekends, or holidays may receive shift differential pay. Also, because call centers are often open during extended hours, or even 24 hours a day, some customer service representatives have the benefit of being able to work a schedule that does not conform to the traditional workweek. Other benefits can include life and health insurance, pensions, bonuses, employer-provided training, and discounts on the products and services the company offers.

Related Occupations

Customer service representatives interact with customers to provide information in response to inquiries about products and services and to handle and resolve complaints. Other occupations in which workers have similar dealings with customers and the public are information and record clerks; financial clerks, such as tellers and new-account clerks; insurance sales agents; securities, commodities, and financial services sales agents; retail salespersons; computer support specialists; and gaming services workers.

Sources of Additional Information

State employment service offices can provide information about employment opportunities for customer service representatives.

Data Entry and Information Processing Workers

(O*NET 43-9021.00 and 43-9022.00)

Significant Points

- Employers generally hire high school graduates who meet company requirements for keyboarding speed; for many people, a job as a data entry and information processing worker is their first job after graduating from high school.

- Although overall employment is projected to decline, the need to replace workers who leave this large occupation each year should produce many job openings.

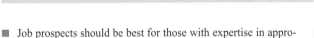

■ Job prospects should be best for those with expertise in appropriate computer software applications.

Nature of the Work

Organizations need to process a rapidly growing amount of information. Data entry and information processing workers help ensure the smooth and efficient handling of information. By keying in text, entering data into a computer, operating a variety of office machines, and performing other clerical duties, these workers help organizations keep up with the rapid changes that are characteristic of today's "Information Age." In addition to the job titles discussed here—such as word processors, typists, and data entry keyers—data entry and information processing workers are known by various other titles, including electronic data processors, keypunch technicians, and transcribers.

Word processors usually set up and prepare reports, letters, mailing labels, and other text material. As entry-level workers, word processors may begin by keying headings on form letters, addressing envelopes, or preparing standard forms on computers. As they gain experience, they often are assigned tasks requiring a higher degree of accuracy and independent judgment. Senior word processors may work with highly technical material, plan and key complicated statistical tables, combine and rearrange materials from different sources, or prepare master copies.

Most keyboarding is now done on computers that normally are connected to a monitor, keyboard, and printer and may have "add-on" capabilities, such as optical character recognition readers. *Word processors* use this equipment to record, edit, store, and revise letters, memos, reports, statistical tables, forms, and other printed materials. Although it is becoming less common, some word-processing workers are employed on centralized word-processing teams that handle transcription and keying for several departments.

In addition to fulfilling the duties mentioned above, word processors often perform other office tasks, such as answering telephones, filing, and operating copiers or other office machines. Job titles of these workers frequently vary to reflect these duties. For example, administrative clerks combine word processing with filing, sorting mail, answering telephones, and other general office work. Note readers transcribe stenotyped notes of court proceedings into standard formats.

Data entry keyers usually input lists of items, numbers, or other data into computers or complete forms that appear on a computer screen. They also may manipulate existing data, edit current information, or proofread new entries into a database for accuracy. Some examples of data sources include customers' personal information, medical records, and membership lists. Usually, this information is used internally by a company and may be reformatted before other departments or customers utilize it.

Keyers use various types of equipment to enter data. Many use a machine that converts the information they type to magnetic impulses on tapes or disks for entry into a computer system. Others prepare materials for printing or publication by using data entry composing machines. Some keyers operate online terminals or personal computers. Increasingly, data entry keyers are working with nonkeyboard forms of data entry, such as scanners and electroni-

cally transmitted files. When using the new character recognition systems, data entry keyers often enter only those data which cannot be recognized by machines. In some offices, keyers also operate computer peripheral equipment such as printers and tape readers, act as tape librarians, and perform other clerical duties.

Working Conditions

Data entry and information processing workers usually work a standard 40-hour week in clean offices. They sit for long periods and sometimes must contend with high noise levels caused by various office machines. These workers are susceptible to repetitive strain injuries such as carpal tunnel syndrome, neck and back injuries, and eyestrain. To help prevent these conditions, many offices have adopted regularly scheduled exercise breaks, ergonomically designed keyboards, and workstations that allow workers to stand or sit as they wish.

Training, Other Qualifications, and Advancement

Employers generally hire high school graduates who meet their requirements for keyboarding speed. Increasingly, employers also are expecting applicants to have training or experience in word-processing or data entry tasks. Spelling, punctuation, and grammar skills are important, as is familiarity with standard office equipment and procedures.

Students acquire skills in keyboarding and in the use of word-processing, spreadsheet, and database management computer software packages through high schools; community colleges; business schools; temporary help agencies; or self-teaching aids such as books, tapes, and Internet tutorials.

For many people, a job as a data entry and information processing worker is their first job after graduating from high school or after a period of full-time family responsibilities. This work frequently serves as a stepping-stone to higher-paying jobs with increased responsibilities. Large companies and government agencies usually have training programs to help administrative employees upgrade their skills and advance to higher-level positions. It is common for data entry and information processing workers to transfer to other administrative jobs, such as secretary, administrative assistant, or statistical clerk, or to be promoted to a supervisory job in a word-processing or data entry center.

Employment

Data entry and information processing workers held about 525,000 jobs in 2004 and were employed in every sector of the economy; 330,000 were data entry keyers and 194,000 were word processors. Some workers telecommute, working from their homes on personal computers linked by telephone lines to those in the main office. This arrangement enables them to key in material at home while still being able to produce printed copy in their offices.

About 1 out of 5 data entry and information processing workers held jobs in firms providing administrative and support services, including temporary help and word-processing agencies, and another 1 in 5 worked for state or local government.

Job Outlook

Overall employment of data entry and information processing workers is projected to decline through 2014. Nevertheless, the need to replace those who transfer to other occupations or leave this large occupation for other reasons will produce numerous job openings each year. Job prospects will be most favorable for those with the best technical skills—in particular, expertise in appropriate computer software applications. Data entry and information processing workers must be willing to upgrade their skills continuously in order to remain marketable.

Although data entry and information processing workers are affected by productivity gains stemming from organizational restructuring and the implementation of new technologies, projected growth differs among these workers. Employment of word processors and typists is expected to decline because of the proliferation of personal computers, which allows other workers to perform duties formerly assigned to word processors and typists. Most professionals and managers, for example, now use desktop personal computers to do their own word processing. However, because technologies affecting data entry keyers tend to be costlier to implement, employment of these workers will decline less than word processors and typists.

Employment growth of data entry keyers will be dampened by productivity gains as various data-capturing technologies, such as barcode scanners, voice recognition technologies, and sophisticated character recognition readers, become more prevalent. These technologies can be applied to a variety of business transactions, such as inventory tracking, invoicing, and placing orders. Moreover, as telecommunications technology improves, many organizations will increasingly take advantage of computer networks that allow data to be transmitted electronically. These networks will permit more data to be entered automatically into computers, reducing the demand for data entry keyers.

In addition to being affected by technology, employment of data entry and information processing workers will be adversely affected by businesses that are increasingly contracting out their work. Many organizations have reduced or even eliminated permanent in-house staff in favor of temporary employment and staffing services firms. Some large data entry and information processing firms increasingly employ workers in nations with relatively lower wages. As international trade barriers continue to fall and telecommunications technology improves, this transfer of jobs will mean reduced demand for data entry keyers in the United States.

Earnings

Median annual earnings of word processors and typists in May 2004 were $28,030. The middle 50 percent earned between $22,850 and $34,900. The lowest 10 percent earned less than $18,960, while the highest 10 percent earned more than $43,190. The salaries of these workers vary by industry and by region. In May 2004, median annual earnings in the industries employing the largest numbers of word processors and typists were as follows:

Legal services $36,890

Local government 29,190

Elementary and secondary schools 27,630

State government 27,210

Employment services 25,450

Median annual earnings of data entry keyers in May 2004 were $23,250. The middle 50 percent earned between $19,630 and $28,150. The lowest 10 percent earned less than $16,480, and the highest 10 percent earned more than $34,410. The following are median annual earnings for May 2004 in the industries employing the largest numbers of data entry keyers:

Insurance carriers $23,980

Accounting, tax preparation, bookkeeping, and
     payroll services..23,120

Depository credit intermediation 21,950

Employment services 21,550

Data-processing, hosting, and related services........20,750

Related Occupations

Data entry and information processing workers must transcribe information quickly. Other workers who deliver information in a timely manner are dispatchers and communications equipment operators. Data entry and information processing workers also must be comfortable working with office technology, and in this regard they are similar to court reporters, medical records and health information technicians, secretaries and administrative assistants, and computer operators.

Sources of Additional Information

For information about job opportunities for data entry and information processing workers, contact the nearest office of the state employment service.

Dental Assistants

(O*NET 31-9091.00)

Significant Points

■ Job prospects should be excellent.

■ Dentists are expected to hire more assistants to perform routine tasks so that they may devote their own time to more complex procedures.

■ Most assistants learn their skills on the job, although an increasing number are trained in dental-assisting programs; most programs take 1 year or less to complete.

Nature of the Work

Dental assistants perform a variety of patient care, office, and laboratory duties. They work chairside as dentists examine and treat patients. They make patients as comfortable as possible in the dental chair, prepare them for treatment, and obtain their dental records. Assistants hand instruments and materials to dentists and keep patients' mouths dry and clear by using suction or other devices. Assistants also sterilize and disinfect instruments and equipment, prepare trays of instruments for dental procedures, and instruct patients on postoperative and general oral health care.

Some dental assistants prepare materials for impressions and restorations, take dental X rays, and process X-ray film as directed by a dentist. They also may remove sutures, apply topical anesthetics to gums or cavity-preventive agents to teeth, remove excess cement used in the filling process, and place rubber dams on the teeth to isolate them for individual treatment.

Those with laboratory duties make casts of the teeth and mouth from impressions, clean and polish removable appliances, and make temporary crowns. Dental assistants with office duties schedule and confirm appointments, receive patients, keep treatment records, send bills, receive payments, and order dental supplies and materials.

Dental assistants should not be confused with dental hygienists, who are licensed to perform different clinical tasks.

Working Conditions

Dental assistants work in a well-lighted, clean environment. Their work area usually is near the dental chair so that they can arrange instruments, materials, and medication and hand them to the dentist when needed. Dental assistants must wear gloves, masks, eyewear, and protective clothing to protect themselves and their patients from infectious diseases. Assistants also follow safety procedures to minimize the risks associated with the use of X-ray machines.

About half of dental assistants have a 35- to 40-hour workweek, which may include work on Saturdays or evenings.

Training, Other Qualifications, and Advancement

Most assistants learn their skills on the job, although an increasing number are trained in dental-assisting programs offered by community and junior colleges, trade schools, technical institutes, or the Armed Forces. Assistants must be a second pair of hands for a dentist; therefore, dentists look for people who are reliable, work well with others, and have good manual dexterity. High school students interested in a career as a dental assistant should take courses in biology, chemistry, health, and office practices.

The Commission on Dental Accreditation within the American Dental Association (ADA) approved 265 dental-assisting training programs in 2005. Programs include classroom, laboratory, and preclinical instruction in dental-assisting skills and related theory. In addition, students gain practical experience in dental schools, clinics, or dental offices. Most programs take 1 year or less to complete and lead to a certificate or diploma. Two-year programs offered in community and junior colleges lead to an associate degree. All programs require a high school diploma or its equivalent, and some require science or computer-related courses for admission. A number of private vocational schools offer 4-month to 6-month courses in dental assisting, but the Commission on Dental Accreditation does not accredit these programs.

Most states regulate the duties that dental assistants are allowed to perform through licensure or registration. Licensure or registration may require passing a written or practical examination. States offering licensure or registration have a variety of schools offering courses—approximately 10 to 12 months in length—that meet their state's requirements. Other states require dental assistants to complete state-approved education courses of 4 to 12 hours in length. Some states offer registration of other dental assisting credentials with little or no education required. Some states require continuing education to maintain licensure or registration. A few states allow dental assistants to perform any function delegated to them by the dentist.

Individual states have adopted different standards for dental assistants who perform certain advanced duties, such as radiological procedures. Completion of the Radiation Health and Safety examination offered by the Dental Assisting National Board (DANB) meets those standards in more than 30 states. Some states require completion of a state-approved course in radiology as well.

Certification is available through DANB and is recognized or required in more than 30 states. Other organizations offer registration, most often at the state level. Certification is an acknowledgment of an assistant's qualifications and professional competence and may be an asset when one is seeking employment. Candidates may qualify to take the DANB certification examination by graduating from an ADA-accredited dental assisting education program or by having 2 years of full-time, or 4 years of part-time, experience as a dental assistant. In addition, applicants must have current certification in cardiopulmonary resuscitation. For annual recertification, individuals must earn continuing education credits.

Without further education, advancement opportunities are limited. Some dental assistants become office managers, dental-assisting instructors, or dental product sales representatives. Others go back to school to become dental hygienists. For many, this entry-level occupation provides basic training and experience and serves as a stepping-stone to more highly skilled and higher-paying jobs.

Employment

Dental assistants held about 267,000 jobs in 2004. Almost all jobs for dental assistants were in offices of dentists. A small number of jobs were in the federal, state, and local governments or in offices of physicians. About 2 out of 5 dental assistants worked part time, sometimes in more than one dental office.

Job Outlook

Job prospects for dental assistants should be excellent. Employment is expected to grow much faster than average for all occupations through the year 2014. In fact, dental assistants is expected to be one of the fastest-growing occupations over the 2004–2014 projection period.

In addition to job openings due to employment growth, numerous job openings will arise out of the need to replace assistants who transfer to other occupations, retire, or leave for other reasons. Many opportunities are for entry-level positions offering on-the-job training.

Population growth and greater retention of natural teeth by middle-aged and older people will fuel demand for dental services. Older dentists, who have been less likely to employ assistants, are leaving the occupation and will be replaced by recent graduates, who are more likely to use one or even two assistants. In addition, as dentists' workloads increase, they are expected to hire more assistants to perform routine tasks so that they may devote their own time to more complex procedures.

Earnings

Median hourly earnings of dental assistants were $13.62 in May 2004. The middle 50 percent earned between $11.06 and $16.65 an hour. The lowest 10 percent earned less than $9.11, and the highest 10 percent earned more than $19.97 an hour.

Benefits vary substantially by practice setting and may be contingent upon full-time employment. According to the American Dental Association (ADA), almost all full-time dental assistants employed by private practitioners received paid vacation time. The ADA also found that 9 out of 10 full-time and part-time dental assistants received dental coverage.

Related Occupations

Other workers supporting health practitioners include medical assistants, occupational therapist assistants and aides, pharmacy aides, pharmacy technicians, and physical therapist assistants and aides.

Sources of Additional Information

Information about career opportunities and accredited dental assistant programs is available from

▶ Commission on Dental Accreditation, American Dental Association, 211 East Chicago Ave., Suite 1814, Chicago, IL 60611. Internet: http://www.ada.org

For information on becoming a Certified Dental Assistant and a list of state boards of dentistry, contact

▶ Dental Assisting National Board, Inc., 676 North Saint Clair St., Suite 1880, Chicago, IL 60611. Internet: http://www.danb.org

For more information on a career as a dental assistant and general information about continuing education, contact

▶ American Dental Assistants Association, 35 East Wacker Dr., Suite 1730, Chicago, IL 60601. Internet: http://www.dentalassistant.org

For more information about continuing education courses, contact

▶ National Association of Dental Assistants, 900 South Washington St., Suite G-13, Falls Church, VA 22046.

Diesel Service Technicians and Mechanics

(O*NET 49-3031.00)

Significant Points

■ A career as a diesel service technician or mechanic can offer relatively high wages and the challenge of skilled repair work.

■ Opportunities are expected to be very good for persons who complete formal training programs.

■ National certification is the recognized standard of achievement for diesel service technicians and mechanics.

Nature of the Work

The diesel engine is the workhorse powering the nation's trucks and buses because it delivers more power, is more efficient, and is more durable than its gasoline-burning counterpart. Diesel-powered engines also are becoming more prevalent in light vehicles, including passenger vehicles, pickups, and other work trucks.

Diesel service technicians and mechanics, which includes *bus and truck mechanics* and *diesel engine specialists*, repair and maintain the diesel engines that power transportation equipment such as heavy trucks, buses, and locomotives. Some diesel technicians and mechanics also work on heavy vehicles and mobile equipment, including bulldozers, cranes, road graders, farm tractors, and combines. Other technicians repair diesel-powered passenger automobiles, light trucks, or boats. (For information on technicians and mechanics working primarily on gasoline-powered automobiles, see this book's descriptions of automotive service technicians and mechanics.)

Technicians who work for organizations that maintain their own vehicles spend most of their time doing preventive maintenance to ensure that equipment will operate safely. These workers also eliminate unnecessary wear on, and damage to, parts that could result in costly breakdowns. During a routine maintenance check on a vehicle, technicians follow a checklist that includes inspecting brake systems, steering mechanisms, wheel bearings, and other important parts. Following inspection, technicians repair or adjust parts that do not work properly or remove and replace parts that cannot be fixed.

Increasingly, technicians must be versatile in order to adapt to customers' needs and new technologies. It is common for technicians to handle all kinds of repairs, from working on a vehicle's electrical system one day to doing major engine repairs the next. Diesel maintenance is becoming increasingly complex as more electronic components are used to control the operation of an engine. For example, microprocessors now regulate and manage fuel timing, increasing the engine's efficiency. Also, new emissions standards are requiring mechanics to retrofit engines to comply with pollution regulations. In modern shops, diesel service technicians use hand-held or laptop computers to diagnose problems and adjust engine functions. Because of continual advances in automotive technology, technicians must regularly learn new techniques to repair vehicles.

Diesel service technicians use a variety of tools in their work, including power tools, such as pneumatic wrenches, to remove bolts quickly; machine tools, such as lathes and grinding machines, to rebuild brakes; welding and flame-cutting equipment to remove and repair exhaust systems; and jacks and hoists to lift and move large parts. Common hand tools—screwdrivers, pliers, and wrenches—are used to work on small parts and get at hard-to-reach places. Diesel service technicians and mechanics also use a variety of computerized testing equipment to pinpoint and analyze malfunctions in electrical systems and engines.

In large shops, technicians generally receive their assignments from shop supervisors or service managers. Most supervisors and managers are experienced technicians who also assist in diagnosing problems and maintaining quality standards. Technicians may work as a team or be assisted by an apprentice or helper when doing heavy work, such as removing engines and transmissions.

Working Conditions

Diesel technicians usually work indoors, although they occasionally make repairs to vehicles on the road. Diesel technicians may lift heavy parts and tools, handle greasy and dirty parts, and stand or lie in awkward positions to repair vehicles and equipment. Minor cuts, burns, and bruises are common, although serious accidents can usually be avoided if the shop is kept clean and orderly and if safety procedures are followed. Technicians normally work in well-lighted, heated, and ventilated areas; however, some shops are drafty and noisy. Many employers provide lockers and shower facilities.

Training, Other Qualifications, and Advancement

Although many persons qualify for diesel service technician and mechanic jobs through years of on-the-job training, authorities on diesel engines recommend the completion of a formal diesel engine training program. Employers prefer to hire graduates of formal training programs because those workers often have a head start in training and are able to advance quickly to the journey level of diesel service.

Many community colleges and trade and vocational schools offer programs in diesel repair. These programs, lasting 6 months to 2 years, lead to a certificate of completion or an associate degree. Programs vary in the degree of hands-on training they provide on equipment. Some offer about 30 hours per week on equipment, whereas others offer more lab or classroom instruction. Training provides a foundation in the latest diesel technology and instruction in the service and repair of the vehicles and equipment that technicians will encounter on the job. Training programs also improve the skills needed to interpret technical manuals and to communicate with co-workers and customers. In addition to the hands-on aspects of the training, many institutions teach communication skills, customer service, basic understanding of physics, and logical thought. Increasingly, employers work closely with representatives of training programs, providing instructors with the latest equipment, techniques, and tools and offering jobs to graduates.

Whereas most employers prefer to hire persons who have completed formal training programs, some technicians and mechanics continue to learn their skills on the job. Unskilled beginners generally are assigned tasks such as cleaning parts, fueling and lubricating vehicles, and driving vehicles into and out of the shop. Beginners usually are promoted to trainee positions as they gain experience and as vacancies become available. In some shops, beginners with experience in automobile service start as trainee technicians.

After a few months' experience, most trainees can perform routine service tasks and make minor repairs. These workers advance to increasingly difficult jobs as they prove their ability and competence. After technicians master the repair and service of diesel engines, they learn to work on related components, such as brakes, transmissions, and electrical systems. Generally, technicians with at least 3 to 4 years of on-the-job experience will qualify as journey-level diesel technicians. The completion of a formal training program speeds advancement to the journey level.

For unskilled entry-level jobs, employers usually look for applicants who have mechanical aptitude and strong problem-solving skills and who are at least 18 years of age and in good physical condition. Nearly all employers require the completion of high school. Courses in automotive repair, electronics, English, mathematics, and physics provide a strong educational background for a career as a diesel service technician or mechanic. Technicians need a state commercial driver's license to test-drive trucks or buses on public roads. Many companies also require applicants to pass a drug test. Practical experience in automobile repair at an automotive service station, in the Armed Forces, or as a hobby is valuable as well.

Employers often send experienced technicians and mechanics to special training classes conducted by manufacturers and vendors in which workers learn the latest technology and repair techniques. Technicians constantly receive updated technical manuals and instructions outlining changes in techniques and standards for repair. It is essential for technicians to read, interpret, and comprehend service manuals in order to keep abreast of engineering changes.

Voluntary certification by the National Institute for Automotive Service Excellence (ASE) is the recognized industry credential for diesel service technicians and mechanics. Diesel service technicians may be certified as master medium/heavy truck technicians, master school bus technicians, or master truck equipment technicians. They may also be ASE-certified in specific areas of truck repair, such as gasoline engines, drivetrains, brakes, suspension and steering, electrical and electronic systems, or preventive maintenance and inspection.

For certification in each area, a technician must pass one or more of the ASE-administered exams and present proof of 2 years of relevant hands-on work experience. Two years of relevant formal training from a high school, vocational or trade school, or community or junior college program may be substituted for up to 1 year of the work experience requirement. To remain certified, technicians must be retested every 5 years. Retesting ensures that service technicians and mechanics keep up with changing technology.

The most important work possessions of technicians and mechanics are their hand tools. Technicians usually provide their own tools, and many experienced workers have thousands of dollars invested in them. Employers typically furnish expensive power tools, computerized engine analyzers, and other diagnostic equipment, but individual workers ordinarily accumulate their own hand tools with experience.

Experienced diesel service technicians and mechanics with leadership ability may advance to shop supervisor or service manager. Technicians and mechanics with sales ability sometimes become sales representatives. Some open their own repair shops.

Employment

Diesel service technicians and mechanics held about 270,000 jobs in 2004. They were employed by almost every industry; in particular, those that use trucks, buses, and equipment to haul, deliver, and transport materials, goods, and people. The largest employer, the truck transportation industry, employed nearly one out of six diesel service technicians and mechanics. Slightly fewer were employed by local governments, mainly to repair school buses, waste removal trucks, and road equipment. About 1 out of 10 was employed by automotive and commercial equipment repair and maintenance facilities. The rest were employed throughout the economy, including construction, manufacturing, retail and wholesale trade, and automotive leasing. A relatively small number were self-employed. Nearly every section of the country employs diesel service technicians and mechanics, although most work in towns and cities where trucking companies, bus lines, and other fleet owners have large operations.

Job Outlook

Employment of diesel service technicians and mechanics is expected to increase about as fast as the average for all occupations through the year 2014. Besides openings resulting from employment growth, opportunities will be created by the need to replace workers who retire or transfer to other occupations.

Employment of diesel service technicians and mechanics is expected to grow as freight transportation by truck increases. Additional trucks will be needed to keep pace with the increasing volume of freight shipped nationwide. Trucks also serve as intermediaries for other forms of transportation, such as rail and air. Due to the greater durability and economy of the diesel engine relative to the gasoline engine, the number of buses, trucks, and passenger vehicles that are powered by diesel engines is expected to increase.

While diesel engines are a more efficient and powerful option, diesel engines tend to produce more pollutants than gasoline-powered engines. As governments have applied emissions-lowering standards to diesel engines, many older diesel engines must be retrofitted to comply. These new emissions control systems, such as emissions filters and catalysts, may create additional jobs for diesel service technicians and mechanics.

Careers as diesel service technicians attract many because they offer relatively high wages and the challenge of skilled repair work. Opportunities should be very good for persons who complete formal training in diesel mechanics at community and junior colleges or vocational and technical schools. Applicants without formal training may face stiffer competition for entry-level jobs.

Most persons entering this occupation can expect relatively steady work because changes in economic conditions have less of an effect on the diesel repair business than on other sectors of the economy. During a downturn in the economy, however, some employers may lay off workers or be reluctant to hire new workers.

Earnings

Median hourly earnings of bus and truck mechanics and diesel engine specialists, including incentive pay, were $17.20 in May 2004. The middle 50 percent earned between $13.73 and $21.13 an hour. The lowest 10 percent earned less than $11.19, and the highest 10 percent earned more than $25.67 an hour. Median hourly earnings in the industries employing the largest numbers of bus and truck mechanics and diesel engine specialists in May 2004 were as follows:

Local government, excluding schools	$20.18
Motor vehicle and motor vehicle parts and supplies merchant wholesalers	17.97
Automotive repair and maintenance	16.65
General freight trucking	16.33
Elementary and secondary schools	15.73

Because many experienced technicians employed by truck fleet dealers and independent repair shops receive a commission related to the labor cost charged to the customer, weekly earnings depend on the amount of work completed. Beginners usually earn from 50 to 75 percent of the rate of skilled workers and receive increases as they become more skilled.

The majority of service technicians work a standard 40-hour week, although some work longer hours, particularly if they are self-employed. A growing number of shops have expanded their hours, either to perform repairs and routine service in a more timely fashion or as a convenience to customers. Those technicians employed by truck and bus firms providing service around the clock may work evenings, nights, and weekends, usually at a higher rate of pay than those working traditional hours.

Many diesel service technicians and mechanics are members of labor unions, including the International Association of Machinists and Aerospace Workers; the Amalgamated Transit Union; the International Union, United Automobile, Aerospace, and Agricultural Implement Workers of America; the Transport Workers Union of America; the Sheet Metal Workers' International Association; and the International Brotherhood of Teamsters.

Related Occupations

Diesel service technicians and mechanics repair trucks, buses, and other diesel-powered equipment. Related technician and mechanic occupations include aircraft and avionics equipment mechanics and service technicians, automotive service technicians and mechanics, heavy vehicle and mobile equipment service technicians and mechanics, and small engine mechanics.

Sources of Additional Information

More details about work opportunities for diesel service technicians and mechanics may be obtained from local employers such as trucking companies, truck dealers, or bus lines; locals of the unions previously mentioned; and local offices of your state employment service. Local state employment service offices also may have information about training programs. State boards of postsecondary career schools have information on licensed schools with training programs for diesel service technicians and mechanics.

For general information about a career as a diesel service technician or mechanic, write

▸ Association of Diesel Specialists, 10 Laboratory Dr., PO Box 13966, Research Triangle Park, NC 27709. Internet: http://www.diesel.org

Information on how to become a certified diesel technician of medium to heavy-duty vehicles or a certified bus technician is available from

▸ National Institute for Automotive Service Excellence (ASE), 101 Blue Seal Dr. SE, Suite 101, Leesburg, VA 20175. Internet: http://www.asecert.org

For a directory of accredited private trade and technical schools with training programs for diesel service technicians and mechanics, contact

▸ Accrediting Commission of Career Schools and Colleges of Technology, 2101 Wilson Blvd., Suite 302, Arlington, VA 22201. Internet: http://www.accsct.org

▸ National Automotive Technicians Education Foundation, 101 Blue Seal Dr. SE, Suite 101, Leesburg, VA 20175. Internet: http://www.natef.org

Dispatchers

(O*NET 43-5031.00 and 43-5032.00)

Significant Points

■ Population growth and economic expansion are expected to spur employment growth for all types of dispatchers.

■ Many dispatchers are at the entry level and do not require more than a high school diploma.

■ Although there are no mandatory licensing or certification requirements, some states require public safety dispatchers to be certified.

Nature of the Work

Dispatchers schedule and dispatch workers, equipment, or service vehicles to carry materials or passengers. They keep records, logs, and schedules of the calls that they receive, the transportation vehicles that they monitor and control, and the actions that they take. They maintain information on each call and then prepare a detailed report on all activities occurring during their shifts. Many dispatchers employ computer-aided dispatch systems to accomplish these tasks. The work of dispatchers varies greatly, depending on the industry in which they work.

Regardless of where they work, all dispatchers are assigned a specific territory and have responsibility for all communications within that area. Many work in teams, especially dispatchers in large communications centers or companies. One person usually handles all dispatching calls to the response units or company drivers, while the other members of the team usually receive the incoming calls and deal with the public.

Police, fire, and ambulance dispatchers, also called public safety dispatchers, monitor the location of emergency services personnel from any one or all of the jurisdiction's emergency services departments. These workers dispatch the appropriate type and number of units in response to calls for assistance. Dispatchers, or call takers, often are the first people the public contacts when emergency assistance is required. If certified for emergency medical services, the dispatcher may provide medical instruction to those on the scene of the emergency until the medical staff arrives.

Police, fire, and ambulance dispatchers work in a variety of settings: a police station, a fire station, a hospital, or, increasingly, a centralized communications center. In many areas, the police department serves as the communications center. In these situations, all emergency calls go to the police department, where a dispatcher handles the police calls and screens the others before transferring them to the appropriate service.

When handling calls, dispatchers question each caller carefully to determine the type, seriousness, and location of the emergency. The information obtained is posted either electronically by computer or, with decreasing frequency, by hand. The request for help is communicated immediately to uniformed or supervisory personnel, who quickly decide on the priority of the incident, the kind and number of units needed, and the location of the closest and most suitable units available. Typically, a team answers calls and relays the information to be dispatched. Responsibility then shifts to the dispatchers, who send response units to the scene and monitor the activity of the public safety personnel answering the dispatched message. During the course of the shift, dispatchers may rotate these functions.

When appropriate, dispatchers stay in close contact with other service providers—for example, a police dispatcher would monitor the response of the fire department when there is a major fire. In a medical emergency, dispatchers keep in close touch not only with the dispatched units, but also with the caller. They may give extensive first-aid instructions before the emergency personnel arrive, while the caller is waiting for the ambulance. Dispatchers continuously give updates on the patient's condition to the ambulance personnel and often serve as a link between the medical staff in a hospital and the emergency medical technicians in the ambulance.

Other dispatchers coordinate deliveries, service calls, and related activities for a variety of firms. *Truck dispatchers,* who work for local and long-distance trucking companies, coordinate the movement of trucks and freight between cities. These dispatchers direct the pickup and delivery activities of drivers, receive customers' requests for the pickup and delivery of freight, consolidate freight orders into truckloads for specific destinations, assign drivers and trucks, and draw up routes and pickup and delivery schedules. *Bus dispatchers* make sure that local and long-distance buses stay on schedule. They handle all problems that may disrupt service, and they dispatch other buses or arrange for repairs in order to restore service and schedules. *Train dispatchers* ensure the timely and efficient movement of trains according to orders and schedules. They must be aware of track switch positions, track maintenance areas, and the location of other trains running on the track. *Taxicab dispatchers,* or starters, dispatch taxis in response to requests for service and keep logs on all road service calls. *Tow-truck dispatchers* take calls for emergency road service. They relay the nature of the problem to a nearby service station or a tow-truck service and see to it that the road service is completed. *Gas and water service dispatchers* monitor gas lines and water mains and send out service trucks and crews to take care of emergencies.

Working Conditions

The work of dispatchers can be very hectic when many calls come in at the same time. The job of public safety dispatcher is particularly stressful because a slow or an improper response to a call can result in serious injury or further harm. Also, callers who are anxious or afraid may become excited and be unable to provide needed information; some may even become abusive. Despite provocations, dispatchers must remain calm, objective, and in control of the situation.

Dispatchers sit for long periods, using telephones, computers, and two-way radios. Much of their time is spent at video display terminals, viewing monitors and observing traffic patterns. As a result of working for long stretches with computers and other electronic equipment, dispatchers can experience significant eyestrain and back discomfort. Generally, dispatchers work a 40-hour week; however, rotating shifts and compressed work schedules are common. Alternative work schedules are necessary to accommodate evening, weekend, and holiday work, as well as 24-hour-per-day, 7-day-per-week operations.

Training, Other Qualifications, and Advancement

Many dispatchers are at the entry level and do not require more than a high school diploma. Employers, however, prefer to hire people familiar with computers and other electronic office and business equipment. Typing, filing, recordkeeping, and other clerical skills also are important.

State or local government civil service regulations usually govern police, fire, emergency medical, and ambulance dispatching jobs. Candidates for these positions may have to pass written, oral, and performance tests. Also, they may be asked to attend training classes and attain the proper certification in order to qualify for advancement.

Workers usually develop the necessary skills on the job. This informal training lasts from several days to a few months, depending on the complexity of the job. Public safety dispatchers usually require the most extensive training. While working with an experienced dispatcher, new employees monitor calls and learn how to operate a variety of communications equipment, including telephones, radios, and various wireless devices. As trainees gain confidence, they begin to handle calls themselves. In smaller operations, dispatchers sometimes act as customer service representatives, processing orders. Many public safety dispatchers also participate in structured training programs sponsored by their employer. Increasingly, public safety dispatchers receive training in stress and crisis management as well as family counseling. This training helps them to provide effective services to others, and, at the same time, it helps them manage the stress involved in their work.

Communication skills and the ability to work under pressure are important personal qualities for dispatchers. Residency in the city or county of employment frequently is required for public safety dispatchers. Dispatchers in transportation industries must be able to deal with sudden influxes of shipments and disruptions of shipping schedules caused by bad weather, road construction, or accidents.

Although there are no mandatory licensing or certification requirements, some states require that public safety dispatchers possess a certificate to work on a state network, such as the Police Information Network. Many dispatchers participate in these programs in order to improve their prospects for career advancement.

Dispatchers who work for private firms, which usually are small, will find few opportunities for advancement. In contrast, public safety dispatchers may become a shift or divisional supervisor or chief of communications, or they may move to higher-paying administrative jobs. Some become police officers or fire fighters.

Employment

Dispatchers held 266,000 jobs in 2004. About 36 percent were police, fire, and ambulance dispatchers, almost all of whom worked for state and local governments—primarily local police and fire departments. About 26 percent of all dispatchers worked in the transportation and warehousing industry, and the rest worked in a wide variety of mainly service-providing industries.

Although dispatching jobs are found throughout the country, most dispatchers work in urban areas, where large communications centers and businesses are located.

Job Outlook

Employment of dispatchers is expected to grow about as fast as the average for all occupations through 2014. In addition to those positions resulting from job growth, many openings will arise from the need to replace workers who transfer to other occupations or leave the labor force.

Population growth and economic expansion are expected to spur employment growth for all types of dispatchers. The growing and aging population will increase demand for emergency services and stimulate employment growth of police, fire, and ambulance dispatchers. Many districts are consolidating their communications centers into a shared area-wide facility. Individuals with computer skills and experience will have a greater opportunity for employment as public safety dispatchers.

Employment of some dispatchers is more adversely affected by economic downturns than employment of other dispatchers. For example, when economic activity falls, demand for transportation services declines. As a result, taxicab, train, and truck dispatchers may experience layoffs or a shortened workweek, and jobseekers may have some difficulty finding entry-level jobs. Employment of tow-truck dispatchers, by contrast, is seldom affected by general economic conditions because of the emergency nature of their business.

Earnings

Median annual earnings of dispatchers, except police, fire, and ambulance, in May 2004 were $30,920. The middle 50 percent earned between $23,480 and $41,040. The lowest 10 percent earned less than $18,820, and the highest 10 percent earned more than $52,440.

Median annual earnings of police, fire, and ambulance dispatchers in 2004 were $28,930. The middle 50 percent earned between $23,060 and $35,970. The lowest 10 percent earned less than $18,710, and the highest 10 percent earned more than $44,520.

Dispatchers usually receive the same benefits as most other workers.

Related Occupations

Other occupations that involve directing and controlling the movement of vehicles, freight, and personnel, as well as distributing information and messages, include air traffic controllers, communications equipment operators, customer service representatives, and reservation and transportation ticket agents and travel clerks.

Sources of Additional Information

For further information on training and certification for police, fire, and emergency dispatchers, contact

▸ Association of Public Safety Communications Officials, International, 351 N. Williamson Blvd., Daytona Beach, FL 32114-1112. Internet: http://www.apco911.org

▸ International Municipal Signal Association (IMSA), PO Box 359, 165 E. Union Street, Newark, NY 14513-0539. Internet: http://www.IMSAsafety.org

Information on job opportunities for police, fire, and emergency dispatchers is available from personnel offices of state and local governments or police departments. Information about work opportunities for other types of dispatchers is available from local employers and state employment service offices.

Drafters

(O*NET 17-3011.01, 17-3011.02, 17-3012.01, 17-3012.02, and 17-3013.00)

Significant Points

■ The type and quality of postsecondary drafting programs vary considerably; prospective students should be careful in selecting a program.

■ Employment is projected to grow more slowly than average.

■ Opportunities should be best for individuals with at least 2 years of postsecondary training in drafting and considerable skill and experience using computer-aided design and drafting (CADD) systems.

■ Demand for drafters varies by specialty and depends on the needs of local industry, particularly architectural and engineering services and manufacturing.

Nature of the Work

Drafters prepare technical drawings and plans used by production and construction workers to build everything from manufactured products such as toys, toasters, industrial machinery, and spacecraft to structures such as houses, office buildings, and oil and gas pipelines. Drafters' drawings provide visual guidelines; show the technical details of the products and structures; and specify dimensions, materials, and procedures. Drafters fill in technical details using drawings, rough sketches, specifications, codes, and calculations previously made by engineers, surveyors, architects, or scientists. For example, drafters use their knowledge of standardized building techniques to draw in the details of a structure. Some use their knowledge of engineering and manufacturing theory and standards to draw the parts of a machine to determine design elements, such as the numbers and kinds of fasteners needed to assemble the machine. Drafters use technical handbooks, tables, calculators, and computers to complete their work.

Traditionally, drafters sat at drawing boards and used pencils, pens, compasses, protractors, triangles, and other drafting devices to prepare a drawing manually. Most drafters now use CADD systems to prepare drawings. Consequently, some drafters may be referred to as *CADD operators*. CADD systems employ computers to create and store drawings electronically that can then be viewed, printed, or programmed directly into automated manufacturing systems. These systems also permit drafters to quickly prepare variations of a design. Although drafters use CADD extensively, it is only a tool. Persons who produce technical drawings with CADD still function as drafters and need the knowledge of traditional drafters in addition to CADD skills. Despite the nearly universal use of CADD systems, manual drafting and sketching still are used in certain applications.

Drafting work has many specialties, and titles may denote a particular discipline of design or drafting.

Aeronautical drafters prepare engineering drawings detailing plans and specifications used in the manufacture of aircraft, missiles, and related parts.

Architectural drafters draw architectural and structural features of buildings and other structures. These workers may specialize in a type of structure, such as residential or commercial, or in a kind of material used, such as reinforced concrete, masonry, steel, or timber.

Civil drafters prepare drawings and topographical and relief maps used in major construction or civil engineering projects, such as highways, bridges, pipelines, flood control projects, and water and sewage systems.

Electrical drafters prepare wiring and layout diagrams used by workers who erect, install, and repair electrical equipment and wiring in communication centers, power plants, electrical distribution systems, and buildings.

Electronics drafters draw wiring diagrams, circuit board assembly diagrams, schematics, and layout drawings used in the manufacture, installation, and repair of electronic devices and components.

Mechanical drafters prepare drawings showing the detail and assembly of a wide variety of machinery and mechanical devices, indicating dimensions, fastening methods, and other requirements.

Process piping or *pipeline drafters* prepare drawings used in the layout, construction, and operation of oil and gas fields, refineries, chemical plants, and process piping systems.

Working Conditions

Most drafters work a standard 40-hour week; only a small number work part time. Drafters usually work in comfortable offices furnished to accommodate their tasks. They may sit at adjustable drawing boards or drafting tables when doing manual drawings, although most drafters work at computer terminals much of the time. Because they spend long periods in front of computer terminals doing detailed work, drafters may be susceptible to eyestrain, back discomfort, and hand and wrist problems.

Training, Other Qualifications, and Advancement

Employers prefer applicants who have completed postsecondary school training in drafting, training that is offered by technical institutes, community colleges, and some 4-year colleges and universities. Employers are most interested in applicants with well-developed drafting and mechanical drawing skills; knowledge of drafting standards, mathematics, science, and engineering technology; and a solid background in CADD techniques. In addition, communication and problem-solving skills are important.

Training and coursework differ somewhat within the drafting specialties. The initial training for each specialty is similar. All incorporate math and communication skills, for example, but coursework relating to the specialty varies. In an electronics drafting program, for example, students learn how to depict electronic components and circuits in drawings.

Many types of publicly and privately operated schools provide some form of training in drafting. Because the kind and quality of programs vary considerably, prospective students should be careful in selecting a program. They should contact prospective employers regarding their preferences and ask schools to provide information about the kinds of jobs that are obtained by the school's graduates, the types and conditions of the instructional facilities and equipment, and the faculty's qualifications.

Technical institutes offer intensive technical training but less general education than do junior and community colleges. Certificates or diplomas based on the completion of a certain number of course hours may be awarded. Many technical institutes offer 2-year associate degree programs, which are similar to, or part of, the programs offered by community colleges or state university systems. Their programs vary considerably in both length and type of courses offered. Some area vocational-technical schools are postsecondary public institutions that serve local students and emphasize the type of training preferred by local employers. Many offer introductory drafting instruction. Most require a high school diploma or its equivalent for admission. Other technical institutes are run by private, often for-profit, organizations sometimes called proprietary schools.

Community colleges offer curricula similar to those in technical institutes but include more courses on theory and liberal arts. Often, there is little or no difference between technical institute and community college programs. However, courses taken at community colleges are more likely than those given at technical institutes to be accepted for credit at 4-year colleges. After completing a 2-year associate degree program, graduates may obtain jobs as drafters or continue their education in a related field at 4-year colleges. Most 4-year colleges usually do not offer training in drafting, but college courses in engineering, architecture, and mathematics are useful for obtaining a job as a drafter.

Technical training obtained in the Armed Forces also can be applied in civilian drafting jobs. Some additional training may be necessary, depending on the technical area or military specialty.

The American Design Drafting Association (ADDA) has established a certification program for drafters. Although employers usually do not require drafters to be certified, certification demonstrates an understanding of nationally recognized practices and standards of knowledge. Individuals who wish to become certified must pass the Drafter Certification Test, which is administered periodically at ADDA-authorized sites. Applicants are tested on their knowledge and understanding of basic drafting concepts, such as geometric construction, working drawings, and architectural terms and standards.

Individuals planning careers in drafting should take courses in mathematics, science, computer technology, design, and computer graphics, as well as any high school drafting courses available. Mechanical ability and visual aptitude are important. Prospective drafters should be able to draw well and perform detailed work accurately and neatly. Artistic ability is helpful in some specialized fields, as is knowledge of manufacturing and construction methods. In addition, prospective drafters should have good interpersonal skills because they work closely with engineers, surveyors, architects, and other professionals and, sometimes, with customers.

Entry-level or junior drafters usually do routine work under close supervision. After gaining experience, they may become intermediate drafters and progress to more difficult work with less supervision. At the intermediate level, they may need to exercise more judgment and perform calculations when preparing and modifying drawings. Drafters may eventually advance to senior drafter, designer, or supervisor. Many employers pay for continuing education, and, with appropriate college degrees, drafters may go on to become engineering technicians, engineers, or architects.

Employment

Drafters held about 254,000 jobs in 2004. Architectural and civil drafters held 43 percent of all jobs for drafters, mechanical drafters held about 32 percent of all jobs, and about 15 percent of jobs were held by electrical and electronics drafters.

About 44 percent of all jobs for drafters were in architectural, engineering, and related services firms that design construction projects or do other engineering work on a contract basis for other industries. Another 27 percent of jobs were in manufacturing industries such as machinery manufacturing, including metalworking and other general machinery; fabricated metal products manufacturing, including architectural and structural metals; computer and electronic products manufacturing, including navigational, measuring, electromedical, and control instruments; and transportation equipment manufacturing, including aerospace products and parts manufacturing, as well as ship and boat building. Most of the rest were employed in construction, government, wholesale trade, utilities, and employment services. Approximately 6 percent were self-employed in 2004.

Job Outlook

Employment of drafters is expected to grow more slowly than the average for all occupations through 2014. Industrial growth and increasingly complex design problems associated with new products and manufacturing processes will increase the demand for drafting services. Further, drafters are beginning to break out of the traditional drafting role and do work traditionally performed by engineers and architects, thus also increasing demand for drafters. However, drafters tend to be concentrated in slowly growing or declining manufacturing industries. CADD systems that are more powerful and easier to use also should limit demand for lesser-skilled drafters as simple tasks are increasingly done quickly and easily by other drafters or other technical professionals, resulting in slower-than-average overall employment growth. Because some drafting work can be done in other locations by using the Internet to send CADD files internationally, the offshoring of some drafting jobs also should dampen growth. Most job openings are expected to arise from the need to replace drafters who transfer to other occupations, leave the labor force, or retire.

Opportunities should be best for individuals with at least 2 years of postsecondary training in a drafting program that provides strong technical skills as well as considerable experience with CADD systems. CADD has increased the complexity of drafting applications while enhancing the productivity of drafters. It also has enhanced the nature of drafting by creating more possibilities for design and drafting. As technology continues to advance, employers will look for drafters with a strong background in fundamental drafting principles, a high level of technical sophistication, and the ability to apply their knowledge to a broader range of responsibilities.

While growth is expected to be greatest for mechanical, architectural, and civil drafters, demand for particular drafting specialties varies throughout the country because employment usually is contingent on the needs of local industry. Employment of drafters remains highly concentrated in industries that are sensitive to cyclical changes in the economy, primarily manufacturing industries. During recessions, drafters may be laid off. However, a growing number of drafters should continue to find employment on a temporary or contract basis as more companies turn to the employment services industry to meet their changing needs.

Earnings

Drafters' earnings vary by specialty, location, and level of responsibility. Median annual earnings of architectural and civil drafters were $39,190 in May 2004. The middle 50 percent earned between $31,460 and $47,800. The lowest 10 percent earned less than $25,670, and the highest 10 percent earned more than $57,670. Median annual earnings for architectural and civil drafters in architectural, engineering, and related services were $38,760.

Median annual earnings of mechanical drafters were $43,000 in May 2004. The middle 50 percent earned between $34,090 and $54,240. The lowest 10 percent earned less than $27,490, and the highest 10 percent earned more than $67,650. Median annual earnings for mechanical drafters in architectural, engineering, and related services were $44,560.

Median annual earnings of electrical and electronics drafters were $43,180 in May 2004. The middle 50 percent earned between $33,920 and $56,110. The lowest 10 percent earned less than $27,600, and the highest 10 percent earned more than $72,050. In architectural, engineering, and related services, median annual earnings for electrical and electronics drafters were $42,200.

Related Occupations

Other workers who prepare or analyze detailed drawings and make precise calculations and measurements include architects, except landscape and naval; landscape architects; commercial and industrial designers; engineers; engineering technicians; science technicians; and surveyors, cartographers, photogrammetrists, and surveying technicians.

Sources of Additional Information

Information on schools offering programs in drafting and related fields is available from

▶ Accrediting Commission of Career Schools and Colleges of Technology, 2101 Wilson Blvd., Suite 302, Arlington, VA 22201. Internet: http://www.accsct.org

Information about certification is available from

▶ American Design Drafting Association, 105 E. Main St., Newbern, TN 38059. Internet: http://www.adda.org

Drywall Installers, Ceiling Tile Installers, and Tapers

(O*NET 47-2081.01, 47-2081.02, and 47-2082.00)

Significant Points

■ Most workers learn the trade on the job by starting as helpers to more experienced workers; additional classroom instruction may also be needed.

■ Job prospects are expected to be good.

■ Inclement weather seldom interrupts work, but workers may be idled when downturns in the economy slow new construction activity.

Nature of the Work

Drywall consists of a thin layer of gypsum between two layers of heavy paper. It is used for walls and ceilings in most buildings today because it is both faster and cheaper to install than plaster.

There are two kinds of drywall workers—installers and tapers—although many workers do both types of work. Installers, also called *applicators* or *hangers*, fasten drywall panels to the inside framework of residential houses and other buildings. *Tapers*, or *finishers*, prepare these panels for painting by taping and finishing joints and imperfections.

Because drywall panels are manufactured in standard sizes—usually 4 feet by 8 or 12 feet—drywall installers must measure, cut, and fit some pieces around doors and windows. They also saw or cut holes in panels for electrical outlets, air-conditioning units, and plumbing. After making these alterations, installers may glue, nail, or screw the wallboard panels to the wood or metal framework. Because drywall is heavy and cumbersome, a helper generally assists the installer in positioning and securing the panel. Workers often use a lift when placing ceiling panels.

After the drywall is installed, tapers fill joints between panels with a joint compound. Using the wide, flat tip of a special trowel, they spread the compound into and along each side of the joint with brush-like strokes. They immediately use the trowel to press a paper tape—used to reinforce the drywall and to hide imperfections—into the wet compound and to smooth away excess material. Nail and screw depressions also are covered with this compound, as are imperfections caused by the installation of air-conditioning vents and other fixtures. On large projects, finishers may use automatic taping tools that apply the joint compound and tape in one step.

Tapers apply second and third coats of the compound, sanding the treated areas where needed after each coat to make them as smooth as the rest of the wall surface. This results in a very smooth and almost perfect surface. Some tapers apply textured surfaces to walls and ceilings with trowels, brushes, or spray guns.

Ceiling tile installers, or *acoustical carpenters*, apply or mount acoustical tiles or blocks, strips, or sheets of shock-absorbing materials to ceilings and walls of buildings to reduce reflection of sound or to decorate rooms. First, they measure and mark the surface according to blueprints and drawings. Then, they nail or screw moldings to the wall to support and seal the joint between the ceiling tile and the wall. Finally, they mount the tile, either by applying a cement adhesive to the back of the tile and then pressing the tile into place or by nailing, screwing, stapling, or wire-tying the lath directly to the structural framework.

Lathers also are included in this occupation. Lathers fasten metal or rockboard lath to walls, ceilings, and partitions of buildings. Lath forms the support base for plaster, fireproofing, or acoustical materials. At one time, lath was made of wooden strips. Now, lathers work mostly with wire, metal mesh, or rockboard lath. Metal lath is used where the plaster application will be exposed to weather or water or for curved or irregular surfaces for which drywall is not a practical material. Using hand tools and portable power tools, lathers nail, screw, staple, or wire-tie the lath directly to the structural framework.

Working Conditions

As in many other construction trades, the work sometimes is strenuous. Drywall installers, ceiling tile installers, and tapers spend most of the day on their feet, either standing, bending, or kneeling. Some tapers use stilts to tape and finish ceiling and angle joints. Installers have to lift and maneuver heavy panels. Hazards include falls from ladders and scaffolds and injuries from power tools and from working with sharp materials. Because sanding a joint compound to a smooth finish creates a great deal of dust, some finishers wear masks for protection.

Training, Other Qualifications, and Advancement

Drywall installers, ceiling tile installers, and tapers learn their trade through formal and informal training programs. To become a skilled drywall installer, ceiling tile installer, or taper, between 3 and 4 years of both classroom and on-the-job training may be required, but many of the skills can be learned within the first year. While there are a number of different ways to obtain this training, in general the more formalized the process, the more skilled the individual becomes and the more in demand they are by employers.

There are a number of different avenues that one can take to obtain the necessary training. The most common entry route is to obtain a job with a contractor who will then provide on-the-job training. Entry-level workers generally start as helpers, assisting more experienced workers. During this time, employers may send the employee to a trade or vocational school or community college to receive further classroom training.

Some employers, particularly large nonresidential construction contractors with union membership, offer employees formal apprenticeships. These programs combine on-the-job training with related classroom instruction. Usually, apprenticeship applicants must be at least 18 years old and meet local requirements. The length of the program, usually 3 to 4 years, varies with the apprentice's skill. Because the number of apprenticeship programs is limited, however, only a small proportion of drywall installers, ceiling tile installers, and tapers learn their trade through these programs.

Other jobseekers may choose to obtain their classroom training before seeking a job. There are a number of public and private vocational-technical schools and training academies affiliated with the unions and contractors that offer training to become a drywall installer, ceiling tile installer, and taper. Employers often look favorably upon these students and usually start them at a higher level than those without the training.

Installer helpers start by carrying materials, lifting and holding panels, and cleaning up debris. They also learn to use the tools, machines, equipment, and materials of the trade. Within a few weeks, they learn to measure, cut, and install materials. Eventually, they become fully experienced workers. Tapers learn their job by taping joints and touching up nail holes, scrapes, and other imperfections. They soon learn to install corner guards and to conceal openings around pipes. At the end of their training, drywall installers, ceiling tile installers, and tapers learn to estimate the cost of installing and finishing drywall.

Training for this profession can begin in high school, where classes in English, math, mechanical drawing, blueprint reading, and general shop are recommended. Some skills needed to become a drywall installer, ceiling tile installer, and taper include manual dexterity, eye-hand coordination, good physical fitness, and a good sense of balance. The ability to solve arithmetic problems quickly and accurately also is required. In addition, a good work history or military service is viewed favorably by contractors.

Drywall installers, ceiling tile installers, and tapers may advance to carpentry supervisor or general construction supervisor positions. Others may become independent contractors. For those who would like to advance, it is increasingly important to be able to communicate in both English and Spanish in order to relay instructions and safety precautions to workers with limited understanding of English; Spanish-speaking workers make up a large part of the construction workforce in many areas. Spanish-speaking workers who want to advance should learn English. Supervisors and contractors need good English skills in order to deal with clients and subcontractors. They also should be able to identify and estimate the quantity of materials needed to complete a job and accurately estimate how long a job will take to complete and at what cost.

Employment

Drywall installers, ceiling tile installers, and tapers held about 196,000 jobs in 2004. Most worked for contractors specializing in drywall and ceiling tile installation; others worked for contractors doing many kinds of construction. About 43,000 were self-employed independent contractors.

Most installers and tapers are employed in populous areas. In other areas, where there may not be enough work to keep a drywall or ceiling tile installer employed full time, carpenters and painters usually do the work.

Job Outlook

Job opportunities for drywall installers, ceiling tile installers, and tapers are expected to be good. Many potential workers are not attracted to this occupation because they prefer work that is less strenuous and has more comfortable working conditions. Experienced workers will have especially favorable opportunities.

Employment is expected to increase more slowly than the average for all occupations over the 2004–2014 period, reflecting the number of new construction and remodeling projects. In addition to jobs involving traditional interior work, drywall workers will find employment opportunities in the installation of insulated exterior wall systems, which are becoming increasingly popular.

Besides those resulting from job growth, many jobs will open up each year because of the need to replace workers who transfer to other occupations or leave the labor force. Some drywall installers, ceiling tile installers, and tapers with limited skills leave the occupation when they find that they dislike the work or fail to find steady employment.

Despite the growing use of exterior panels, most drywall installation and finishing is done indoors. Therefore, drywall workers lose less work time because of inclement weather than do some other construction workers. Nevertheless, they may be unemployed between construction projects and during downturns in construction activity.

Earnings

In May 2004, the median hourly earnings of drywall and ceiling tile installers were $16.36. The middle 50 percent earned between $12.59 and $21.82. The lowest 10 percent earned less than $9.98, and the highest 10 percent earned more than $28.30. The median hourly earnings in the industries employing the largest numbers of drywall and ceiling tile installers in May 2004 were as follows:

Residential building construction	$17.33
Building finishing contractors	16.53
Nonresidential building construction	14.57

In May 2004, the median hourly earnings of tapers were $18.78. The middle 50 percent earned between $14.07 and $24.43. The lowest 10 percent earned less than $10.66, and the highest 10 percent earned more than $28.79.

Some contractors pay these workers according to the number of panels they install or finish per day; others pay an hourly rate. A 40-hour week is standard, but the workweek may sometimes be longer or shorter. Workers who are paid hourly rates receive premium pay for overtime. Trainees usually started at about half the rate paid to experienced workers and received wage increases as they became more highly skilled.

Related Occupations

Drywall installers, ceiling tile installers, and tapers combine strength and dexterity with precision and accuracy to make materials fit according to a plan. Other occupations that require similar abilities include carpenters; carpet, floor, and tile installers and finishers; insulation workers; and plasterers and stucco masons.

Sources of Additional Information

For information about work opportunities in drywall application and finishing and ceiling tile installation, contact local drywall installation and ceiling tile installation contractors, a local joint union-management apprenticeship committee, a state or local chapter of the Associated Builders and Contractors, or the nearest office of the state employment service or apprenticeship agency.

For details about job qualifications and training programs in drywall application and finishing and ceiling tile installation, contact

▸ Associated Builders and Contractors, 4250 North Fairfax Dr., 9th Floor, Arlington, VA 22203. Internet: http://www.trytools.org

▸ National Association of Home Builders, Home Builders Institute, 1201 15th St. NW, Washington, DC 20005. Internet: http://www.hbi.org

▸ Joint Apprenticeship and Training Fund, International Union of Painters and Allied Trades, 1750 New York Ave. NW, Washington, DC 20006. Internet: http://www.jatf.org

▸ National Center for Construction Education and Research, P.O. Box 141104, Gainesville, FL 32614-1104. Internet: http://www.nccer.org

▸ United Brotherhood of Carpenters and Joiners of America, Carpenters Training Fund, 6801 Placid St., Las Vegas, NV 89119. Internet: http://www.carpenters.org

Electrical and Electronics Installers and Repairers

(O*NET 49-2092.01, 49-2092.02, 49-2092.03, 49-2092.04, 49-2092.05, 49-2092.06, 49-2093.00, 49-2094.00, 49-2095.00, and 49-2096.00)

Significant Points

■ Knowledge of electrical equipment and electronics is necessary for employment; many applicants complete 1 to 2 years at vocational schools and community colleges, although some less-skilled repairers may have only a high school diploma.

■ Employment is projected to grow more slowly than average, but prospects vary by occupational specialty.

■ Job opportunities will be best for applicants with a thorough knowledge of electrical and electronic equipment as well as repair experience.

Nature of the Work

Businesses and other organizations depend on complex electronic equipment for a variety of functions. Industrial controls automatically monitor and direct production processes on the factory floor. Transmitters and antennae provide communication links for many organizations. Electric power companies use electronic equipment to operate and control generating plants, substations, and monitoring equipment. The federal government uses radar and missile control systems to provide for the national defense and to direct commercial air traffic. These complex pieces of electronic equipment are installed, maintained, and repaired by electrical and electronics installers and repairers.

Electrical equipment and electronic equipment are two distinct types of industrial equipment, although much equipment contains both electrical and electronic components. In general, electrical portions provide the power for the equipment, while electronic components control the device, although many types of equipment still are controlled with electrical devices. Electronic sensors monitor the equipment and the manufacturing process, providing feedback to the programmable logic control (PLC), which controls the equipment. The PLC processes the information provided by the sensors and makes adjustments to optimize output. To adjust the output, the PLC sends signals to the electrical, hydraulic, and pneumatic devices that power the machine—changing feed rates, pressures, and other variables in the manufacturing process. Many installers and repairers, known as *field technicians*, travel to factories or other locations to repair equipment. These workers often have assigned areas in which they perform preventive maintenance on a regular basis. When equipment breaks down, field technicians go to a customer's site to repair the equipment. *Bench technicians* work in repair shops located in factories and service centers, fixing components that cannot be repaired on the factory floor.

Some industrial electronic equipment is self-monitoring and alerts repairers to malfunctions. When equipment breaks down, repairers first check for common causes of trouble, such as loose connections or obviously defective components. If routine checks do not locate the trouble, repairers may refer to schematics and manufacturers' specifications that show connections and provide instructions on how to locate problems. Automated electronic control systems are increasing in complexity, making diagnosis more challenging. With these systems, repairers use software programs and testing equipment to diagnose malfunctions. Among their diagnostic tools are multimeters, which measure voltage, current, and resistance, and advanced multimeters, which measure capacitance, inductance, and current gain of transistors. Repairers also use signal generators, which provide test signals, and oscilloscopes, which display signals graphically. Finally, repairers use hand tools such as pliers, screwdrivers, soldering irons, and wrenches to replace faulty parts and adjust equipment.

Because repairing components is a complex activity and factories cannot allow production equipment to stand idle, repairers on the factory floor usually remove and replace defective units, such as circuit boards, instead of fixing them. Defective units are discarded or returned to the manufacturer or a specialized shop for repair. Bench technicians at these locations have the training, tools, and parts needed to thoroughly diagnose and repair circuit boards or other complex components. These workers also locate and repair circuit defects, such as poorly soldered joints, blown fuses, or malfunctioning transistors.

Electrical and electronics installers often fit older manufacturing equipment with new automated control devices. Older manufacturing machines are frequently in good working order but are limited by inefficient control systems for which replacement parts are no longer available. Installers replace old electronic control units with new PLCs. Setting up and installing a new PLC involves connecting it to different sensors and electrically powered devices (electric

motors, switches, and pumps) and writing a computer program to operate the PLC. Electronics installers coordinate their efforts with those of other workers who are installing and maintaining equipment. (See the description of industrial machinery mechanics and maintenance workers elsewhere in this book.)

Electrical and electronics installers and repairers, transportation equipment install, adjust, or maintain mobile electronic communication equipment, including sound, sonar, security, navigation, and surveillance systems on trains, watercraft, or other vehicles. *Electrical and electronics repairers, powerhouse, substation, and relay* inspect, test, maintain, or repair electrical equipment used in generating stations, substations, and in-service relays. These workers may be known as powerhouse electricians, relay technicians, or power transformer repairers. *Electric motor, power tool, and related repairers*—such as armature winders, generator mechanics, and electric golf cart repairers—specialize in installing, maintaining, and repairing electric motors, wiring, or switches.

Electronic equipment installers and repairers, motor vehicles have a significantly different job. They install, diagnose, and repair communication, sound, security, and navigation equipment in motor vehicles. Most installation work involves either new alarm or sound systems. New sound systems vary significantly in cost and complexity of installation. Replacing a head unit (radio) with a new CD player is simple, requiring the removal of a few screws and the connection of a few wires. Installing a new sound system with a subwoofer, amplifier, and fuses is far more complicated. The installer builds a fiberglass or wood box designed to hold the subwoofer and to fit inside the unique dimensions of the automobile. Installing sound-deadening material, which often is necessary with more powerful speakers, requires an installer to remove many parts of a car (for example, seats, carpeting, or interiors of doors), add sound-absorbing material in empty spaces, and reinstall the interior parts. The installer also runs new speaker and electrical cables. The new system may require additional fuses, a new electrical line to be run from the battery through a newly drilled hole in the firewall into the interior of the vehicle, or an additional or more powerful alternator or battery. Motor vehicle installers and repairers work with an increasingly complex range of electronic equipment, including DVD players, satellite navigation equipment, passive security systems, and active security systems.

Working Conditions

Many electrical and electronics installers and repairers work on factory floors, where they are subject to noise, dirt, vibration, and heat. Bench technicians work primarily in repair shops, where the surroundings are relatively quiet, comfortable, and well lighted.

Installers and repairers may have to do heavy lifting and work in a variety of positions. They must follow safety guidelines and often wear protective goggles and hardhats. When working on ladders or on elevated equipment, repairers must wear harnesses to avoid falls. Before repairing a piece of machinery, these workers must follow procedures to ensure that others cannot start the equipment during the repair process. They also must take precautions against electric shock by locking off power to the unit under repair.

Motor vehicle electronic equipment installers and repairers normally work indoors in well-ventilated and well-lighted repair shops.

Minor cuts and bruises are common, but serious accidents usually are avoided when safety practices are observed.

Training, Other Qualifications, and Advancement

Knowledge of electrical equipment and electronics is necessary for employment. Many applicants gain this knowledge through programs lasting 1 to 2 years at vocational schools or community colleges, although some less-skilled repairers may have only a high school diploma. Entry-level repairers may work closely with more experienced technicians who provide technical guidance.

Installers and repairers should have good eyesight and color perception to work with the intricate components used in electronic equipment. Field technicians work closely with customers and should have good communication skills and a neat appearance. Employers also may require that field technicians have a driver's license.

Various organizations offer certification. Repairers may specialize—in industrial electronics, for example. To receive certification, repairers must pass qualifying exams corresponding to their level of training and experience.

Experienced repairers with advanced training may become specialists or troubleshooters who help other repairers diagnose difficult problems. Workers with leadership ability may become supervisors of other repairers. Some experienced workers open their own repair shops.

Employment

Electrical and electronics installers and repairers held about 158,000 jobs in 2004. The following tabulation breaks down their employment by occupational specialty:

Electrical and electronics repairers, commercial
and industrial equipment 72,000

Electric motor, power tool, and related
repairers 28,000

Electrical and electronics repairers, powerhouse,
substation, and relay.......................................21,000

Electronic equipment installers and repairers,
motor vehicles...19,000

Electrical and electronics installers and repairers,
transportation equipment..................................18,000

Many repairers worked for utilities; building equipment contractors; machinery and equipment repair shops; wholesalers; the federal government; retailers of automotive parts and accessories; rail transportation companies; and manufacturers of electrical, electronic, and transportation equipment.

Job Outlook

Job opportunities should be best for applicants with a thorough knowledge of electrical equipment and electronics as well as with repair experience. Overall employment of electrical and electronics installers and repairers is expected to grow more slowly than the average for all occupations during the 2004–2014 period, but

prospects vary by occupational specialty. In addition to employment growth, the need to replace workers who transfer to other occupations or leave the labor force will result in many job openings.

Average employment growth is projected for electrical and electronics installers and repairers of commercial and industrial equipment. This equipment will become more sophisticated and will be used more frequently as businesses strive to lower costs by increasing and improving automation. Companies will install electronic controls, robots, sensors, and other equipment to automate processes such as assembly and testing. As prices decline, applications will be found across a number of industries, including services, utilities, and construction, as well as manufacturing. Improved reliability of equipment should not constrain employment growth, however: Companies increasingly will rely on repairers because malfunctions that idle commercial and industrial equipment will continue to be costly.

Employment of motor vehicle electronic equipment installers and repairers also is expected to grow about as fast as the average. However, as motor vehicle manufacturers install more and better sound, security, entertainment, and navigation systems in new vehicles, and as newer electronic systems require progressively less maintenance, employment growth for aftermarket electronic equipment installers will be limited.

Employment of electric motor, power tool, and related repairers is expected to grow more slowly than average. Improvements in electrical and electronic equipment design should limit job growth by simplifying repair tasks. The design of more parts that are easily disposable will further reduce employment growth.

Employment of electrical and electronic installers and repairers of transportation equipment is also expected to grow more slowly than the average because of declining industry employment in railroad rolling stock manufacturing and shipbuilding and boatbuilding.

Employment of electrical and electronics installers and repairers, powerhouse, substation, and relay is expected to decline slightly. Consolidation and privatization in utilities industries should improve productivity, reducing employment. Newer equipment will be more reliable and easier to repair, further limiting employment.

Earnings

Median hourly earnings of electrical and electronics repairers, commercial and industrial equipment were $20.48 in May 2004. The middle 50 percent earned between $16.04 and $25.07. The lowest 10 percent earned less than $12.55, and the highest 10 percent earned more than $28.68. In May 2004, median hourly earnings were $23.79 in the federal government and $17.82 in building equipment contractors, the industries employing the largest numbers of electrical and electronics repairers, commercial and industrial equipment.

Median hourly earnings of electric motor, power tool, and related repairers were $15.54 in May 2004. The middle 50 percent earned between $12.12 and $19.71. The lowest 10 percent earned less than $9.48, and the highest 10 percent earned more than $23.90. In May 2004, median hourly earnings were $15.02 in commercial and industrial machinery and equipment (except automotive and electronic) repair and maintenance, the industry employing the largest number of electronic motor, power tool, and related repairers.

Median hourly earnings of electrical and electronics repairers, powerhouse, substation, and relay were $25.86 in May 2004. The middle 50 percent earned between $22.47 and $29.73. The lowest 10 percent earned less than $18.01, and the highest 10 percent earned more than $33.82. In May 2004, median hourly earnings were $26.37 in electric power generation, transmission, and distribution—the industry employing the largest number of these repairers.

Median hourly earnings of electronics installers and repairers, motor vehicles were $12.79 in May 2004. The middle 50 percent earned between $10.27 and $16.55. The lowest 10 percent earned less than $8.85, and the highest 10 percent earned more than $22.02.

Median hourly earnings of electrical and electronics repairers, transportation equipment were $19.25 in May 2004. The middle 50 percent earned between $15.06 and $23.57. The lowest 10 percent earned less than $11.86, and the highest 10 percent earned more than $27.70.

Related Occupations

Workers in other occupations who install and repair electronic equipment include broadcast and sound technicians and radio operators; computer, automated teller, and office machine repairers; electronic home entertainment equipment installers and repairers; and radio and telecommunications equipment installers and repairers. Industrial machinery mechanics and maintenance workers also install, maintain, and repair industrial machinery.

Sources of Additional Information

For information on careers and certification, contact any of the following organizations:

▸ ACES International, 5241 Princess Anne Rd., Suite 110, Virginia Beach, VA 23462. Internet: http://www.acesinternational.org

▸ Electronics Technicians Association International, 5 Depot St., Greencastle, IN 46135.

▸ International Society of Certified Electronics Technicians, 3608 Pershing Ave., Fort Worth, TX 76107-4527. Internet: http://www.iscet.org

Electricians

(O*NET 47-2111.00)

Significant Points

■ Job opportunities are expected to be good, especially for those with the right skills.

■ Most electricians acquire their skills by completing an apprenticeship program lasting 4 to 5 years.

■ Nearly three-fourths of electricians work for building contractors or are self-employed, but there also will be many job openings for electricians in other industries.

Nature of the Work

Electricity is essential for light, power, air-conditioning, and refrigeration. Electricians install, connect, test, and maintain electrical systems for a variety of purposes, including climate control, security, and communications. They also may install and maintain the electronic controls for machines in business and industry.

Electricians generally specialize in construction or maintenance work, although a growing number do both. Electricians specializing in construction work primarily install wiring systems into new homes, businesses, and factories, but they also rewire or upgrade existing electrical systems as needed. Electricians specializing in maintenance work primarily maintain and upgrade existing electrical systems and repair electrical equipment.

Electricians work with blueprints when they install electrical systems. Blueprints indicate the locations of circuits, outlets, load centers, panel boards, and other equipment. Electricians must follow the National Electrical Code and comply with state and local building codes when they install these systems. Regulations vary depending on the setting and require various types of installation procedures.

When electricians install wiring systems in factories and commercial settings, they first place conduit (pipe or tubing) inside partitions, walls, or other concealed areas as designated by the blueprints. They also fasten to the walls small metal or plastic boxes that will house electrical switches and outlets. They pull insulated wires or cables through the conduit to complete circuits between these boxes. In residential construction, electricians usually install plastic-encased insulated wire, which does not need to be run through conduit. The gauge and number of wires installed in all settings depends upon the load and end use of that part of the electrical system. The greater the diameter of the wire, the higher the voltage and amperage that can flow through it.

Electricians connect all types of wire to circuit breakers, transformers, outlets, or other components. They join the wires in boxes with various specially designed connectors. During installation, electricians use hand tools such as conduit benders, screwdrivers, pliers, knives, hacksaws, and wire strippers, as well as power tools such as drills and saws. After they finish installing the wiring, they use testing equipment, such as ammeters, ohmmeters, voltmeters, and oscilloscopes, to check the circuits for proper connections, ensuring electrical compatibility and safety of components.

Maintenance work varies greatly, depending on where the electrician is employed. Electricians who specialize in residential work perform a wide variety of electrical work for homeowners. They may rewire a home and replace an old fuse box with a new circuit breaker box to accommodate additional appliances, or they may install new lighting and other electric household items, such as ceiling fans. Those who work in large factories may repair motors, transformers, generators, and electronic controllers on machine tools and industrial robots. Those in office buildings and small plants may repair all types of electrical equipment.

Maintenance electricians working in factories, hospitals, and other settings repair electric and electronic equipment when breakdowns occur and install new electrical equipment. When breakdowns occur, they must make the necessary repairs as quickly as possible in order to minimize inconvenience. They may replace items such as circuit breakers, fuses, switches, electrical and electronic components, or wire. Electricians also periodically inspect all equipment to ensure it is operating properly and locate and correct problems before breakdowns occur. Electricians also advise management whether continued operation of equipment could be hazardous. When working with complex electronic devices, they may work with engineers; engineering technicians; line installers and repairers; or industrial machinery installation, repair, and maintenance workers.

Although primarily classified as work for line installers and repairers, electricians also may install low-voltage wiring systems in addition to wiring a building's electrical system. Low-voltage wiring involves voice, data, and video wiring systems, such as those for telephones, computers and related equipment, intercoms, and fire alarm and security systems. Electricians also may install coaxial or fiber-optic cable for computers and other telecommunications equipment and electronic controls for industrial uses.

Working Conditions

Electricians work both indoors and out at construction sites, in homes, and in businesses or factories. Work may be strenuous at times and include bending conduit; lifting heavy objects; and standing, stooping, and kneeling for long periods of time. When working outdoors, they may be subject to inclement weather conditions. Some electricians may have to travel long distances to jobsites. Electricians risk injury from electrical shock, falls, and cuts; they must follow strict safety procedures to avoid injuries.

Most electricians work a standard 40-hour week, although overtime may be required. Those in maintenance work may work nights or weekends and be on call to go to the worksite when needed. Electricians working in industrial settings may also have periodic extended overtime during scheduled maintenance or retooling periods. Companies that operate 24 hours a day may employ three shifts of electricians.

Training, Other Qualifications, and Advancement

Most electricians learn their trade through apprenticeship programs. These programs combine on-the-job training with related classroom instruction. Apprenticeship programs may be sponsored by joint training committees made up of local unions of the International Brotherhood of Electrical Workers and local chapters of the National Electrical Contractors Association; company management committees of individual electrical contracting companies; or local chapters of the Associated Builders and Contractors and the Independent Electrical Contractors Association. Because of the comprehensive training received, those who complete apprenticeship programs qualify to do both maintenance and construction work.

Applicants for apprenticeships usually must be at least 18 years old and have a high school diploma or a G.E.D. They should have good math and English skills, since most instruction manuals are in English. They also may have to pass a test and meet other requirements. Apprenticeship programs usually last 4 years, and each year includes at least 144 hours of classroom instruction and 2,000 hours of on-the-job training. In the classroom, apprentices learn electrical theory and installing and maintaining electrical systems. They also take classes in blueprint reading, mathematics, electrical code requirements, and safety and first aid practices and also may receive specialized training in soldering, communications, fire alarm

systems, and cranes and elevators. On the job, apprentices work under the supervision of experienced electricians. At first, they drill holes, set anchors, and attach conduit. Later, they measure, fabricate, and install conduit, as well as install, connect, and test wiring, outlets, and switches. They also learn to set up and draw diagrams for entire electrical systems. To complete the apprenticeship and become electricians, apprentices must demonstrate mastery of the electrician's work.

Some persons seeking to become electricians choose to obtain their classroom training before seeking a job. Training to become an electrician is offered by a number of public and private vocational-technical schools and training academies in affiliation with local unions and contractor organizations. Employers often hire students who complete these programs and usually start them at a more advanced level than those without the training. A few persons become electricians by first working as helpers, assisting electricians setting up job sites, gathering materials, and doing other non-electrical work, before entering an apprenticeship program.

Skills needed to become an electrician include manual dexterity, eye-hand coordination, physical fitness, and a good sense of balance. The ability to solve arithmetic problems quickly and accurately also is required. Good color vision is needed because workers frequently must identify electrical wires by color. In addition, a good work history or military service is viewed favorably by apprenticeship committees and employers.

Most localities require electricians to be licensed. Although licensing requirements vary from area to area, electricians usually must pass an examination that tests their knowledge of electrical theory, the National Electrical Code, and local electric and building codes. Experienced electricians periodically take courses offered by their employer or union to keep abreast of changes in the National Electrical Code and new materials or methods of installation. For example, classes on installing low-voltage voice, data, and video systems have recently become common as these systems have become more prevalent.

Experienced electricians can advance to jobs as supervisors. In construction, they also may become project managers or construction superintendents. Those with sufficient capital and management skills may start their own contracting business, although this may require an electrical contractor's license. Many electricians also become electrical inspectors. Supervisors and contractors should be able to identify and estimate the correct type and quantity of materials needed to complete a job and accurately estimate how long a job will take to complete and at what cost. For those who seek to advance, it is increasingly important to be able to communicate in both English and Spanish in order to relay instructions and safety precautions to workers with limited understanding of English; Spanish-speaking workers make up a large part of the construction workforce in many areas. Spanish-speaking workers who want to advance in this occupation need very good English skills to understand instruction presented in classes and installation instructions, which are usually written in English and are highly technical.

Employment

Electricians held about 656,000 jobs in 2004. Nearly two-thirds of wage and salary workers were employed in the construction industry, while the remainder worked as maintenance electricians in other industries. In addition, about one in ten electricians were self-employed.

Because of the widespread need for electrical services, electrician jobs are found in all parts of the country.

Job Outlook

Employment of electricians is expected to increase as fast as the average for all occupations through the year 2014. As the population and economy grow, more electricians will be needed to install and maintain electrical devices and wiring in homes, factories, offices, and other structures. New technologies also are expected to continue to stimulate the demand for these workers. For example, buildings need to increasingly accommodate the use of computers and telecommunications equipment. Also, the increasing prevalence in factories of robots and other automated manufacturing systems will require more complex wiring systems to be installed and maintained. Additional jobs will be created as older structures are rehabilitated and retrofitted, which usually requires that they be brought up to meet existing electrical codes.

In addition to jobs created by the increased demand for electrical work, many openings are expected to occur over the next decade as a large number of electricians are expected to retire. This will create good job opportunities for the most qualified jobseekers. Job openings for electricians, though, will vary by area and will be greatest in the fastest-growing regions of the country.

Employment of construction electricians, like that of many other construction workers, is sensitive to changes in the economy. This results from the limited duration of construction projects and the cyclical nature of the construction industry. During economic downturns, job openings for electricians are reduced as the level of construction activity declines. Apprenticeship opportunities also are less plentiful during these periods.

Although employment of maintenance electricians is steadier than that of construction electricians, those working in the automotive and other manufacturing industries that are sensitive to cyclical swings in the economy may be laid off during recessions. Also, opportunities for maintenance electricians may be limited in many industries by an increase in contracting out for electrical services in an effort to reduce operating costs and increase productivity. However, increased job opportunities for electricians in electrical contracting firms should partially offset job losses in other industries.

Earnings

In May 2004, median hourly earnings of electricians were $20.33. The middle 50 percent earned between $15.43 and $26.90. The lowest 10 percent earned less than $12.18, and the highest 10 percent earned more than $33.63. Median hourly earnings in the industries employing the largest numbers of electricians in May 2004 were as follows:

Motor vehicle parts manufacturing	$30.04
Local government	22.24
Nonresidential building construction	19.99
Building equipment contractors	19.76
Employment services	15.62

Apprentices usually start at between 40 and 50 percent of the rate paid to fully trained electricians, depending on experience. As apprentices become more skilled, they receive periodic pay increases throughout the course of their training.

Some electricians are members of the International Brotherhood of Electrical Workers. Among unions representing maintenance electricians are the International Brotherhood of Electrical Workers; the International Union of Electronic, Electrical, Salaried, Machine, and Furniture Workers; the International Association of Machinists and Aerospace Workers; the International Union, United Automobile, Aircraft and Agricultural Implement Workers of America; and the United Steelworkers of America.

Related Occupations

To install and maintain electrical systems, electricians combine manual skill and knowledge of electrical materials and concepts. Workers in other occupations involving similar skills include heating, air-conditioning, and refrigeration mechanics and installers; line installers and repairers; electrical and electronics installers and repairers; electronic home entertainment equipment installers and repairers; and elevator installers and repairers.

Sources of Additional Information

For details about apprenticeships or other work opportunities in this trade, contact the offices of the state employment service, the state apprenticeship agency, local electrical contractors or firms that employ maintenance electricians, or local union-management electrician apprenticeship committees. This information also may be available from local chapters of the Independent Electrical Contractors, Inc.; the National Electrical Contractors Association; the Home Builders Institute; the Associated Builders and Contractors; and the International Brotherhood of Electrical Workers.

For information about union apprenticeship and training programs, contact

▸ National Joint Apprenticeship Training Committee (NJATC), 301 Prince George's Blvd., Upper Marlboro, MD 20774. Internet: http://www.njatc.org

▸ National Electrical Contractors Association (NECA), 3 Metro Center, Suite 1100, Bethesda, MD 20814. Internet: http://www.necanet.org

▸ International Brotherhood of Electrical Workers (IBEW), 1125 15th St. NW, Washington, DC 20005. Internet: http://www.ibew.org

For information about independent apprenticeship programs, contact

▸ Associated Builders and Contractors, Workforce Development Department, 4250 North Fairfax Dr., 9th Floor, Arlington, VA 22203. Internet: http://www.trytools.org

▸ Independent Electrical Contractors, Inc., 4401 Ford Ave., Suite 1100, Alexandria, VA 22302. Internet: http://www.ieci.org

▸ National Association of Home Builders, Home Builders Institute, 1201 15th St. NW, Washington, DC 20005. Internet: http://www.hbi.org

▸ National Center for Construction Education and Research, P.O. Box 141104, Gainesville, FL 32614-1104. Internet: http://www.nccer.org

Engineering Technicians

(O*NET 17-3021.00, 17-3022.00, 17-3023.01, 17-3023.02, 17-3023.03, 17-3024.00, 17-3025.00, 17-3026.00, 17-3027.00, and 17-3029.99)

Significant Points

- Because the type and quality of training programs vary considerably, prospective students should carefully investigate training programs before enrolling.
- Electrical and electronic engineering technicians make up 34 percent of all engineering technicians.
- Employment of engineering technicians often is influenced by the same local and national economic conditions that affect engineers; as a result, job outlook varies with industry and specialization.
- Opportunities will be best for individuals with an associate degree or extensive job training in engineering technology.

Nature of the Work

Engineering technicians use the principles and theories of science, engineering, and mathematics to solve technical problems in research and development, manufacturing, sales, construction, inspection, and maintenance. Their work is more limited in scope and application-oriented than that of scientists and engineers. Many engineering technicians assist engineers and scientists, especially in research and development. Others work in quality control, inspecting products and processes, conducting tests, or collecting data. In manufacturing, they may assist in product design, development, or production.

Engineering technicians who work in research and development build or set up equipment; prepare and conduct experiments; collect data; calculate or record results; and help engineers or scientists in other ways, such as making prototype versions of newly designed equipment. They also assist in design work, often using computer-aided design and drafting (CADD) equipment.

Most engineering technicians specialize, learning skills and working in the same disciplines as engineers. Occupational titles, therefore, tend to reflect engineering specialties. Some branches of engineering technology for which there are accredited programs of study are not covered in detail in this book, such as chemical engineering technology (the development of new chemical products and processes) and bioengineering technology (the development and implementation of biomedical equipment).

Aerospace engineering and operations technicians construct, test, and maintain aircraft and space vehicles. They may calibrate test equipment and determine causes of equipment malfunctions. Using computer and communications systems, aerospace engineering and operations technicians often record and interpret test data.

Civil engineering technicians help civil engineers plan and build highways, buildings, bridges, dams, wastewater treatment systems, and other structures, as well as do related research. Some estimate construction costs and specify materials to be used, and some may even prepare drawings or perform land-surveying duties.

Others may set up and monitor instruments used to study traffic conditions. (Drafters are covered elsewhere in this book.)

Electrical and electronics engineering technicians help design, develop, test, and manufacture electrical and electronic equipment such as communication equipment; radar, industrial, and medical monitoring or control devices; navigational equipment; and computers. They may work in product evaluation and testing, using measuring and diagnostic devices to adjust, test, and repair equipment. (Workers whose jobs are limited to repairing electrical and electronic equipment, who often are referred to as electronics technicians, are included with electrical and electronics installers and repairers elsewhere in this book.)

Electromechanical engineering technicians combine fundamental principles of mechanical engineering technology with knowledge of electrical and electronic circuits to design, develop, test, and manufacture electrical and computer-controlled mechanical systems. Their work often overlaps that of both electrical and electronics engineering technicians and mechanical engineering technicians.

Environmental engineering technicians work closely with environmental engineers and scientists in developing methods and devices used in the prevention, control, or correction of environmental hazards. They inspect and maintain equipment related to air pollution and recycling. Some inspect water and wastewater treatment systems to ensure that pollution control requirements are met.

Industrial engineering technicians study the efficient use of personnel, materials, and machines in factories, stores, repair shops, and offices. They prepare layouts of machinery and equipment, plan the flow of work, make statistical studies, and analyze production costs.

Mechanical engineering technicians help engineers design, develop, test, and manufacture industrial machinery, consumer products, and other equipment. They may assist in product tests—for example, by setting up instrumentation for auto crash tests. They may make sketches and rough layouts, record and analyze data, make calculations and estimates, and report on their findings. When planning production, mechanical engineering technicians prepare layouts and drawings of the assembly process and of parts to be manufactured. They estimate labor costs, equipment life, and plant space. Some test and inspect machines and equipment or work with engineers to eliminate production problems.

Working Conditions

Most engineering technicians work at least 40 hours a week in laboratories, offices, or manufacturing or industrial plants or on construction sites. Some may be exposed to hazards from equipment, chemicals, or toxic materials.

Training, Other Qualifications, and Advancement

Although it may be possible to qualify for certain engineering technician jobs without formal training, most employers prefer to hire someone with at least a 2-year associate degree in engineering technology. Training is available at technical institutes, community colleges, extension divisions of colleges and universities, and public and private vocational-technical schools and in the Armed Forces. Persons with college courses in science, engineering, and mathematics may qualify for some positions but may need additional specialized training and experience. Although employers usually do not require engineering technicians to be certified, such certification may provide jobseekers a competitive advantage.

Prospective engineering technicians should take as many high school science and math courses as possible to prepare for postsecondary programs in engineering technology. Most 2-year associate degree programs accredited by the Technology Accreditation Commission of the Accreditation Board for Engineering and Technology (ABET) require, at a minimum, college algebra and trigonometry and one or two basic science courses. Depending on the specialty, more math or science may be required. About 230 colleges offer ABET-accredited programs in engineering technology.

The type of technical courses required also depends on the specialty. For example, prospective mechanical engineering technicians may take courses in fluid mechanics, thermodynamics, and mechanical design; electrical engineering technicians may need classes in electrical circuits, microprocessors, and digital electronics; and those preparing to work in environmental engineering technology need courses in environmental regulations and safe handling of hazardous materials.

Because many engineering technicians assist in design work, creativity is desirable. Because these workers often are part of a team of engineers and other technicians, good communication skills and the ability to work well with others also are important.

Engineering technicians usually begin by performing routine duties under the close supervision of an experienced technician, technologist, engineer, or scientist. As they gain experience, they are given more difficult assignments with only general supervision. Some engineering technicians eventually become supervisors.

Many publicly and privately operated schools provide technical training, but the type and quality of training vary considerably. Therefore, prospective students should be careful in selecting a program. They should ascertain prospective employers' preferences and ask schools to provide information about the kinds of jobs obtained by program graduates, about instructional facilities and equipment, and about faculty qualifications. Graduates of ABET-accredited programs usually are recognized as having achieved an acceptable level of competence in the mathematics, science, and technical courses required for this occupation.

Technical institutes offer intensive technical training through application and practice, but they provide less theory and general education than do community colleges. Many technical institutes offer 2-year associate degree programs and are similar to or part of a community college or state university system. Other technical institutes are run by private, often for-profit organizations, sometimes called proprietary schools. Their programs vary considerably in length and types of courses offered, although some are 2-year associate degree programs.

Community colleges offer curriculums that are similar to those in technical institutes but include more theory and liberal arts. There may be little or no difference between programs at technical

institutes and community colleges, as both offer associate degrees. After completing the 2-year program, some graduates get jobs as engineering technicians, whereas others continue their education at 4-year colleges. However, there is a difference between an associate degree in pre-engineering and one in engineering technology. Students who enroll in a 2-year pre-engineering program may find it very difficult to find work as an engineering technician if they decide not to enter a 4-year engineering program because pre-engineering programs usually focus less on hands-on applications and more on academic preparatory work. Conversely, graduates of 2-year engineering technology programs may not receive credit for some of the courses they have taken if they choose to transfer to a 4-year engineering program. Colleges with these 4-year programs usually do not offer engineering technician training, but college courses in science, engineering, and mathematics are useful for obtaining a job as an engineering technician. Many 4-year colleges offer bachelor's degrees in engineering technology, but graduates of these programs often are hired to work as technologists or applied engineers, not technicians.

Area vocational-technical schools, another source of technical training, include postsecondary public institutions that serve local students and emphasize training needed by local employers. Most require a high school diploma or its equivalent for admission.

Other training in technical areas may be obtained in the Armed Forces. Many military technical training programs are highly regarded by employers. However, skills acquired in military programs are often narrowly focused and may be of limited applicability in civilian industry, which often requires broader training. Therefore, some additional training may be needed, depending on the acquired skills and the kind of job.

The National Institute for Certification in Engineering Technologies has established a voluntary certification program for engineering technicians. Certification is available at various levels, each level combining a written examination in 1 of about 30 specialties with a certain amount of job-related experience, a supervisory evaluation, and a recommendation.

Employment

Engineering technicians held 532,000 jobs in 2004. About a third were electrical and electronics engineering technicians, as indicated by the following tabulation.

Electrical and electronic engineering technicians	182,000
Civil engineering technicians	94,000
Industrial engineering technicians	69,000
Mechanical engineering technicians	48,000
Environmental engineering technicians	20,000
Electro-mechanical technicians	19,000
Aerospace engineering and operations technicians	9,500
Engineering technicians, except drafters, all other	91,000

About 36 percent of all engineering technicians worked in manufacturing, mainly in the computer and electronic equipment, transportation equipment, and machinery manufacturing industries. Another

22 percent worked in professional, scientific, and technical service industries, mostly in engineering or business services companies that do engineering work on contract for government, manufacturing firms, or other organizations.

In 2004, the federal government employed 37,000 engineering technicians. State governments employed 39,000, and local governments employed 27,000.

Job Outlook

Opportunities will be best for individuals with an associate degree or extensive job training in engineering technology. As technology becomes more sophisticated, employers will continue to look for technicians who are skilled in new technology and require a minimum of additional job training. An increase in the number of jobs related to public health and safety should create job opportunities for engineering technicians with the appropriate training and certification.

Overall employment of engineering technicians is expected to increase about as fast as the average for all occupations through 2014. Competitive pressures will force companies to improve and update manufacturing facilities and product designs, resulting in more jobs for engineering technicians. In addition to growth, many job openings will stem from the need to replace technicians who retire or leave the labor force.

Growth of engineering technician employment in some design functions may be dampened by increasing globalization of the development process. To reduce costs and speed project completion, some companies may relocate part of their development operations to facilities overseas, impacting both engineers and the engineering technicians that support them—particularly in electronics and computer-related areas. However, much of the work of engineering technicians requires on-site presence, so demand for engineering technicians within the United States should continue to grow.

Because engineering technicians work closely with engineers, employment of engineering technicians is often influenced by the same local and national economic conditions that affect engineers. As a result, the employment outlook varies with industry and specialization. Growth in the largest specialty—electrical and electronics engineering technicians—is expected to be about as fast as the average, while employment of environmental engineering technicians is expected to grow faster than average to meet the environmental demands of an ever-growing population.

Earnings

Median annual earnings in May 2004 of engineering technicians by specialty are shown in the following tabulation.

Aerospace engineering and operations technicians	$52,500
Electrical and electronic engineering technicians	46,310
Industrial engineering technicians	43,590
Mechanical engineering technicians	43,400
Electro-mechanical technicians	41,440
Environmental engineering technicians	38,550
Civil engineering technicians	38,480

Median annual earnings of electrical and electronics engineering technicians were $46,310 in May 2004. The middle 50 percent earned between $36,290 and $55,750. The lowest 10 percent earned less than $29,000, and the highest 10 percent earned more than $67,900. Median annual earnings in the industries employing the largest numbers of electrical and electronics engineering technicians in May 2004 are shown here.

Federal government	$64,160
Wired telecommunications carriers	51,250
Architectural, engineering, and related services	44,800
Navigational, measuring, electromedical, and control instruments manufacturing	42,780
Semiconductor and other electronic component manufacturing	41,300

Median annual earnings of civil engineering technicians were $38,480 in May 2004. The middle 50 percent earned between $29,880 and $48,590. The lowest 10 percent earned less than $24,180, and the highest 10 percent earned more than $57,550. Median annual earnings in the industries employing the largest numbers of civil engineering technicians in May 2004 are shown here.

Local government	$43,700
Architectural, engineering, and related services	37,470
State government	35,970

In May 2004, the average annual salary for aerospace engineering and operations technicians in the aerospace products and parts manufacturing industry was $52,250, and the average annual salary for environmental engineering technicians in the architectural, engineering, and related services industry was $36,530. The average annual salary for industrial engineering technicians in the semiconductor and other electronic component manufacturing industry was $40,020. In the architectural, engineering, and related services industry, the average annual salary for mechanical engineering technicians was $43,190.

Related Occupations

Engineering technicians apply scientific and engineering principles usually acquired in postsecondary programs below the baccalaureate level. Similar occupations include science technicians; drafters; surveyors, cartographers, photogrammetrists, and surveying technicians; and broadcast and sound engineering technicians and radio operators.

Sources of Additional Information

For information about careers in engineering technology, contact

▸ JETS (Junior Engineering Technical Society)—Guidance, 1420 King St., Suite 405, Alexandria, VA 22314-2794. Internet: http://www.jets.org

Information on ABET-accredited engineering technology programs is available from

▸ Accreditation Board for Engineering and Technology, Inc., 111 Market Plc., Suite 1050, Baltimore, MD 21202-4012. Internet: http://www.abet.org

Information on certification of engineering technicians, as well as job and career information, is available from

▸ National Institute for Certification in Engineering Technologies, 1420 King St., Alexandria, VA 22314-2794. Internet: http://www.nicet.org

Farmers, Ranchers, and Agricultural Managers

(O*NET 11-9011.01, 11-9011.02, 11-9011.03, and 11-9012.00)

Significant Points

■ Modern farming requires knowledge of new developments in agriculture, as well as work experience acquired through growing up on a farm or through postsecondary education.

■ Overall employment is projected to decline because of increasing productivity and consolidation of farms.

■ Horticulture and organic farming will provide better employment opportunities.

■ Small-scale farming is a major growth area and offers the best opportunity for entering the occupation.

Nature of the Work

American farmers, ranchers, and agricultural managers direct the activities of one of the world's largest and most productive agricultural sectors. They produce enough food and fiber to meet the needs of the United States and for export.

Farmers and ranchers own and operate mainly family-owned farms. They also may lease land from a landowner and operate it as a working farm. The type of farm they operate determines their specific tasks. On crop farms—farms growing grain, cotton, other fibers, fruit, and vegetables—farmers are responsible for preparing, tilling, planting, fertilizing, cultivating, spraying, and harvesting. After the harvest, they make sure that the crops are properly packaged, stored, or marketed. Livestock, dairy, and poultry farmers must feed and care for the animals and keep barns, pens, coops, and other farm buildings clean and in good condition. They also plan and oversee breeding and marketing activities. Horticultural specialty farmers oversee the production of ornamental plants, nursery products—such as flowers, bulbs, shrubbery, and sod—and fruits and vegetables grown in greenhouses. Aquaculture farmers raise fish and shellfish in marine, brackish, or fresh water, usually in ponds, floating net pens, raceways, or recirculating systems. They stock, feed, protect, and otherwise manage aquatic life sold for consumption or used for recreational fishing.

Responsibilities of farmers and ranchers range from caring for livestock to operating machinery to maintaining equipment and facilities. The size of the farm or ranch often determines which of these tasks farmers and ranchers will handle themselves. Operators of small farms usually perform all tasks, physical and administrative. They keep records for management and tax purposes, service machinery, maintain buildings, and grow vegetables and raise animals. Operators of large farms, by contrast, have employees who help with the physical work that small-farm operators do themselves. Although employment on most farms is limited to the farmer and one or two family workers or hired employees, some large farms have 100 or more full-time and seasonal workers. Some of these employees are in nonfarm occupations, working as truck drivers, sales representatives, bookkeepers, and computer specialists.

Agricultural managers manage the day-to-day activities of one or more farms, ranches, nurseries, timber tracts, greenhouses, and other agricultural establishments for farmers, absentee landowners, or corporations. Their duties and responsibilities vary widely, but focus on the business aspects of running a farm. On small farms, they may oversee the entire operation; on larger farms, they may oversee a single activity, such as marketing. Agricultural managers usually do not perform production activities; instead, they hire and supervise farm and livestock workers, who perform most of the daily production tasks. In these cases, managers may establish output goals; determine financial constraints; monitor production and marketing; hire, assign, and supervise workers; determine crop transportation and storage requirements; and oversee maintenance of the property and equipment.

Farmers, ranchers, and agricultural managers make many managerial decisions. Farm output and income are strongly influenced by the weather, disease, fluctuations in prices of domestic and foreign farm products, and federal farm programs. In crop production operations, farmers and managers usually determine the best time to plant seed, apply fertilizer and chemicals, and harvest and market the crops. They use different strategies to protect themselves from unpredictable changes in the markets for agricultural products. Many farmers and managers carefully plan the combination of crops they grow so that if the price of one crop drops, they will have sufficient income from another crop to make up for the loss. While most farm output is sold directly to food-processing companies, some farmers—particularly operators of smaller farms—may choose to sell their goods directly through farmers' markets or may use coöperatives to reduce their financial risk and to gain a larger share of the retail dollar. For example, in community-supported agriculture (CSA), coöperatives sell shares of a harvest to consumers prior to the planting season, thus freeing the farmer from having to bear all the financial risks and ensuring the farmer a market for the produce of the coming season.

Farmers, ranchers, and agricultural managers also negotiate with banks and other credit lenders to get the best financing deals for their equipment, livestock, and seed. They also must keep abreast of constantly changing prices for their products and manage the risk of fluctuating prices. Those who plan ahead may be able to store their crops or keep their livestock to take advantage of higher prices later in the year. Those who participate in the risky futures market, where contracts on future production of agricultural goods are bought and sold, can minimize the risk of sudden price changes by buying futures contracts which guarantee that they will get at least a certain price for their agricultural goods when they are ready to sell.

Like other businesses, farming operations have become more complex in recent years, so many farmers use computers to keep financial and inventory records. They also use computer databases and spreadsheets to manage breeding, dairy, and other farm operations.

Working Conditions

The work of full-time farmers, ranchers, and agricultural managers is often strenuous; work hours are frequently long, and they rarely have days off during the planting, growing, and harvesting seasons. Nevertheless, for those who enter farming or ranching, the disadvantages are counterbalanced by the quality of life in a rural area, working outdoors, being self-employed, and making a living off the land. Farmers and farm managers on crop farms usually work from sunrise to sunset during the planting and harvesting seasons. The rest of the year, they plan next season's crops, market their output, and repair machinery.

On livestock-producing farms and ranches, work goes on throughout the year. Animals, unless they are grazing, must be fed and watered every day, and dairy cows must be milked two or three times a day. Many livestock and dairy farmers monitor and attend to the health of their herds, which may include assisting in the birthing of animals. Such farmers rarely get the chance to get away unless they hire an assistant or arrange for a temporary substitute.

Farmers who grow produce and perishables have different demands on their time. For example, organic farmers must maintain cover crops during the cold months, thus keeping them occupied with farming beyond the typical growing season.

Farmwork also can be hazardous. Tractors and other farm machinery can cause serious injury, and workers must be constantly alert on the job. The proper operation of equipment and handling of chemicals are necessary to avoid accidents, safeguard one's health, and protect the environment.

On very large farms, farmers spend substantial time meeting with farm managers or farm supervisors in charge of various activities. Professional farm managers overseeing several farms may divide their time between traveling to meet farmers or landowners and planning the farm operations in their offices. As farming practices and agricultural technology become more sophisticated, farmers and farm managers are spending more time in offices and at computers, where they electronically manage many aspects of their businesses. Some farmers also spend time at conferences exchanging information, particularly during the winter months.

Training, Other Qualifications, and Advancement

Growing up on a family farm and participating in agricultural programs for young people, such as the National FFA Organization or the 4-H youth educational programs, are important sources of training for those interested in pursuing agriculture as a career. However, modern farming requires increasingly complex scientific, business, and financial decisions, so postsecondary education in agriculture is important even for people who were raised on farms.

The completion of a 2-year degree, or better, a 4-year bachelor's degree program in a college of agriculture, is becoming increasingly important for farm managers and for farmers and ranchers who

expect to make a living at farming. A degree in business or farm management with a concentration in agriculture is important, but even after obtaining formal education, novices may need to spend time working under an experienced farmer to learn how to put into practice the skills learned through academic training. A small number of farms offer, on a formal basis, apprenticeships to help young people acquire such practical skills.

Students should select the college most appropriate to their specific interests and location. All state university systems have at least one land-grant college or university with a school of agriculture. Common programs of study include agronomy, dairy science, agricultural economics and business, horticulture, crop and fruit science, and animal science. For students interested in aquaculture, formal programs also are available and include coursework in fisheries biology, fish culture, hatchery management and maintenance, and hydrology. Whatever one's interest, the college curriculum should include courses in agricultural production, marketing, and economics.

Agricultural managers can enhance their professional status through voluntary certification as an Accredited Farm Manager (AFM) by the American Society of Farm Managers and Rural Appraisers. Accreditation requires several years of farm management experience, the appropriate academic background—a bachelor's degree or, preferably, a master's degree in a field of agricultural science—and the passing of courses and examinations relating to the business, financial, and legal aspects of farm and ranch management.

Farmers, ranchers, and agricultural managers need to keep abreast of continuing advances in agricultural methods both in the United States and abroad as well as monitor changes in governmental regulations that may affect methods or markets for particular crops. Besides print journals that inform the agricultural community, the spread of the Internet allows quick access to the latest developments in areas such as agricultural marketing; legal arrangements; and growing crops, vegetables, and livestock. Electronic mail, online journals, and newsletters from agricultural organizations also speed the exchange of information directly between farming associations and individual farmers.

Farmers, ranchers, and agricultural managers also must have enough technical knowledge of crops, growing conditions, and plant diseases to make decisions that ensure the successful operation of their farms. A rudimentary knowledge of veterinary science, as well as animal husbandry, is important for livestock and dairy farmers. Knowledge of the relationship between farm operations—for example, the use of pesticides—and environmental conditions is essential. Mechanical aptitude and the ability to work with tools of all kinds also are valuable skills for a small-farm operator, who often maintains and repairs machinery or farm structures.

Farmers, ranchers, and agricultural managers need the managerial skills necessary to organize and operate a business. A basic knowledge of accounting and bookkeeping is essential in keeping financial records, while knowledge of sources of credit is vital for buying seed, fertilizer, and other inputs necessary for planting. It also is necessary to be familiar with complex safety regulations and requirements of governmental agricultural support programs. Computer skills are becoming increasingly important, especially on large farms, where computers are widely used for recordkeeping and business analysis. For example, some farmers, ranchers, and agricultural managers use personal computers to access the Internet to get the latest information on prices of farm products and other agricultural news. In addition, skills in personnel management, communication, and conflict resolution are equally important in the operation of a farm or ranch business.

Employment

Farmers, ranchers, and agricultural managers held nearly 1.3 million jobs in 2004. About 83 percent were self-employed. Most farmers, ranchers, and agricultural managers oversee crop production activities, while others manage livestock and dairy production. Most farmers and ranchers operate small farms on a part-time basis.

The soil, topography of the land, and climate often determine the type of farming and ranching done in a particular area. California, Texas, Iowa, Nebraska, and Kansas are the leading agricultural states.

Job Outlook

Market pressures and low prices for many agricultural goods will cause more farms to go out of business over the 2004–2014 period. The complexity of modern farming and keen competition among farmers leave little room for the marginally successful farmer. Therefore, the long-term trend toward the consolidation of farms into fewer and larger ones is expected to continue over the 2004–2014 period and result in a continued decline in employment of self-employed farmers and ranchers and slower-than-average growth in employment of salaried agricultural managers. As land, machinery, seed, and chemicals become more expensive, only well-capitalized farmers and corporations will be able to acquire many of the farms that become available. The larger, more productive farms are better able to withstand the adverse effects of climate and price fluctuations upon farm output and income. Larger farms also may have advantages in obtaining government subsidies and payments as these payments are usually based on per-unit production.

In addition, the agriculture sector continues to produce more with fewer workers. Increasing productivity in the U.S. agriculture industry is expected to allow greater domestic consumption needs and export requirements to be met with fewer farmers, ranchers, and agricultural managers overall. The overwhelming majority of job openings for self-employed farmers and ranchers will result from the need to replace farmers who retire or leave the occupation for economic or other reasons.

Despite the expected continued consolidation of farmland and the projected decline in overall employment of farmers, ranchers, and agricultural managers, an increasing number of small-scale farmers have developed successful market niches that involve personalized, direct contact with their customers. Many are finding opportunities in organic food production, as more consumers demand food grown without pesticides or chemicals. Others use farmers' markets that cater directly to urban and suburban consumers, allowing the farmers to capture a greater share of consumers' food dollars. Some small-scale farmers belong to collectively owned marketing coöperatives that process and sell their product. Other farmers participate in community-supported agriculture coöperatives that allow consumers to directly buy a share of the farmer's harvest.

Aquaculture may continue to provide some new employment opportunities over the 2004–2014 period. New concerns about overfishing and the depletion of the stock of some wild fish species will likely lead to more restrictions on deep-sea fishing even as public demand for the consumption of seafood continues to grow. This demand has spurred the growth of aquaculture farms that raise selected aquatic species—such as shrimp, salmon, trout and catfish—in pens or ponds. Aquaculture's presence even in landlocked states has increased as farmers attempt to diversify and cater to the growing demand for fish by consumers. In addition, growing demand for horticulture products, such as flowers, ornamentals, trees, shrubs, and other nonedibles, is expected to produce better employment opportunities for greenhouse and nursery farmers and managers.

Earnings

Incomes of farmers and ranchers vary greatly from year to year because prices of farm products fluctuate with weather conditions and other factors influencing the quantity and quality of farm output and the demand for those products. A farm that shows a large profit one year may show a loss the following year. According to the U.S. Department of Agriculture, the average net cash farm business income for farm operator households in 2004 was $15,603. This figure, however, does not reflect that farmers often receive government subsidies or other payments that supplement their incomes and reduce some of the risk of farming. Additionally, most farmers—primarily operators of small farms—have income from off-farm business activities or careers, often greater than that of their farm income.

Full-time, salaried farm managers had median weekly earnings of $621 in 2004. The middle half earned between $464 and $890. The highest-paid 10 percent earned more than $1,264, and the lowest-paid 10 percent earned less than $350.

Farmers and self-employed farm managers make their own provisions for benefits. As members of farm organizations, they may derive benefits such as group discounts on health and life insurance premiums.

Related Occupations

Farmers, ranchers, and agricultural managers strive to improve the quality of agricultural products and the efficiency of farms. Others whose work is related to agricultural products include agricultural engineers, agricultural and food scientists, agricultural workers, and purchasing agents and buyers of farm products.

Sources of Additional Information

For general information about farming and agricultural occupations, contact either of the following organizations:

▸ Center for Rural Affairs, P.O. Box 406, Walthill, NE 68067. Internet: http://www.cfra.org

▸ National FFA Organization, The National FFA Center, Attention Career Information Requests, P.O. Box 68690, Indianapolis, IN 46268-0960. Internet: http://www.ffa.org

For information about certification as an accredited farm manager, contact

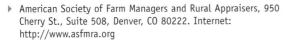

▸ American Society of Farm Managers and Rural Appraisers, 950 Cherry St., Suite 508, Denver, CO 80222. Internet: http://www.asfmra.org

For information on the USDA's program to help small farmers get started, contact

▸ Small Farm Program, U.S. Department of Agriculture, Coöperative State, Research, Education, and Extension Service, Stop 2220, Washington, DC 20250-2220. Internet: http://www.csrees.usda.gov/nea/ag_systems/part/smallfarms_part_directory.html/

For information on aquaculture, diversified agriculture, education, training, or community-supported agriculture, contact either of the following organizations:

▸ Alternative Farming System Information Center (AFSIC), National Agricultural Library USDA, 10301 Baltimore Ave., Room 132, Beltsville, MD 20705-2351. Internet: http://www.nal.usda.gov/afsic

▸ Appropriate Technology Transfer for Rural Areas (ATTRA), the National Sustainable Agriculture Information Service, P.O. Box 3657, Fayetteville, AR 72702. Internet: http://www.attra.ncat.org

File Clerks

(O*NET 43-4071.00)

Significant Points

■ About 3 out of 10 file clerks work part time.

■ A high school diploma or its equivalent is the most common educational requirement.

■ Employment is expected to decline through the year 2014.

Nature of the Work

The amount of information generated by organizations continues to grow rapidly. File clerks classify, store, retrieve, and update this information. In many small offices, they often have additional responsibilities, such as entering data, performing word processing, sorting mail, and operating copying or fax machines. File clerks are employed across the nation by organizations of all types.

File clerks, also called record, information, or record center clerks, examine incoming material and code it numerically, alphabetically, or by subject matter. They then store paper forms, letters, receipts, or reports or enter necessary information into other storage devices. Some clerks operate mechanized files that rotate to bring the needed records to them; others convert documents to film that is then stored on microforms, such as microfilm or microfiche. A growing number of file clerks use imaging systems that scan paper files or film and store the material on computers.

In order for records to be useful, they must be up to date and accurate. File clerks ensure that new information is added to files in a timely manner and may discard outdated file materials or transfer them to inactive storage. Clerks also check files at regular intervals to make sure that all items are correctly sequenced and placed. When records cannot be found, file clerks attempt to locate the missing material. As an organization's needs for information change, file clerks implement changes to the filing system.

When records are requested, file clerks locate them and give them to the person requesting them. A record may be a sheet of paper stored in a file cabinet or an image on microform. In the former case, the clerk retrieves the document manually and hands or forwards it to the requester. In the latter case, the clerk retrieves the microform and displays it on a microform reader. If necessary, file clerks make copies of records and distribute them. In addition, they keep track of materials removed from the files to ensure that borrowed files are returned.

Increasingly, file clerks are using computerized filing and retrieval systems that have a variety of storage devices, such as a mainframe computer, CD-ROM, or floppy disk. To retrieve a document in these systems, the clerk enters the document's identification code, obtains the location of the document, and gets the document for the patron. Accessing files in a computer database is much quicker than locating and physically retrieving paper files. Still, even when files are stored electronically, backup paper or electronic copies usually are also kept.

Working Conditions

File clerks usually work in areas that are clean, well lit, and relatively quiet. The work is not overly strenuous but may involve a lot of standing, walking, reaching, pulling, and bending, depending on the method used to retrieve files. Prolonged exposure to computer screens may lead to eyestrain for the many file clerks who work with computers.

Training, Other Qualifications, and Advancement

Most employers prefer applicants with a high school diploma or its equivalent or a mix of education and related experience. File clerks must be able to work with others, since part of the job may consist of helping fellow workers. These workers must be alert, accurate, and able to make quick decisions. Also, willingness to do routine and detailed work is important.

Most new employees are trained on the job under close supervision of more experienced employees. Proficiency with desktop computer software is becoming increasingly important as more files are now being stored electronically. These workers can advance to more senior clerical office positions such as receptionist or bookkeeping clerk.

Employment

File clerks held about 255,000 jobs in 2004. Although file clerk jobs are found in nearly every sector of the economy, more than 90 percent of these workers are employed in service-providing industries, including government. Health care establishments employed around 1 out of every 4 file clerks. About 3 out of every 10 file clerks worked part time in 2004.

Job Outlook

Employment of file clerks is expected to decline through the year 2014 largely due to productivity gains stemming from office automation and the consolidation of clerical jobs. Most files are stored digitally and can be retrieved electronically, reducing the demand for file clerks. Nonetheless, there will be some job opportunities for file clerks, as a large number of workers will be needed to replace workers who leave the occupation each year. Job turnover among file clerks reflects the lack of formal training requirements, limited advancement potential, and relatively low pay. Demand for file clerks stems from the need for these workers to record and retrieve information in organizations across the economy.

Jobseekers who have typing and other secretarial skills and who are familiar with a wide range of office machines, especially personal computers, should have the best job opportunities. File clerks should find opportunities for temporary or part-time work, especially during peak business periods.

Earnings

Median hourly earnings of file clerks in May 2004 were $10.11. The middle 50 percent earned between $8.22 and $12.59. The lowest 10 percent earned less than $6.97, and the highest 10 percent earned more than $15.72. Median hourly earnings in the industries employing the largest number of file clerks in May 2004 are shown in the following table.

Local government	$11.79
General medical and surgical hospitals	10.38
Legal services	10.32
Employment services	10.06
Offices of physicians	9.07

Related Occupations

File clerks classify and retrieve files. Other workers who perform similar duties include receptionists and information clerks and stock clerks and order fillers.

Sources of Additional Information

State employment service offices and agencies can provide information about job openings for file clerks.

Fire Fighting Occupations

(O*NET 33-1021.01, 33-1021.02, 33-2011.01, 33-2011.02, 33-2021.01, 33-2021.02, and 33-2022.00)

Significant Points

■ Fire fighting involves hazardous conditions and long, irregular hours.

■ About 9 out of 10 fire fighting workers are employed by municipal or county fire departments.

■ Applicants for municipal fire fighting jobs generally must pass written, physical, and medical examinations.

■ Although employment is expected to grow faster than the average, keen competition for jobs is expected because this occupation attracts many qualified candidates.

Nature of the Work

Every year, fires and other emergencies take thousands of lives and destroy property worth billions of dollars. Fire fighters help protect the public against these dangers by rapidly responding to a variety of emergencies. They are frequently the first emergency personnel at the scene of a traffic accident or medical emergency and may be called upon to put out a fire, treat injuries, or perform other vital functions.

During duty hours, fire fighters must be prepared to respond immediately to a fire or any other emergency that arises. Because fighting fires is dangerous and complex, it requires organization and teamwork. At every emergency scene, fire fighters perform specific duties assigned by a superior officer. At fires, they connect hose lines to hydrants, operate a pump to send water to high-pressure hoses, and position ladders to enable them to deliver water to the fire. They also rescue victims, provide emergency medical attention as needed, ventilate smoke-filled areas, and attempt to salvage the contents of buildings. Their duties may change several times while the company is in action. Sometimes they remain at the site of a disaster for days at a time, rescuing trapped survivors and assisting with medical treatment.

Fire fighters work in a variety of settings, including urban and suburban areas, airports, chemical plants, other industrial sites, and rural areas like grasslands and forests. They have also assumed a range of responsibilities, including emergency medical services. In fact, most calls to which fire fighters respond involve medical emergencies, and 65 percent of all fire departments provide emergency medical service. In addition, some fire fighters work in hazardous materials units that are trained for the control, prevention, and cleanup of materials; for example, these fire fighters respond to oil spills. Workers in urban and suburban areas, airports, and industrial sites typically use conventional fire fighting equipment and tactics, while forest fires and major hazardous materials spills call for different methods.

In national forests and parks, *forest fire inspectors and prevention specialists* spot fires from watchtowers and report their findings to headquarters by telephone or radio. Forest rangers patrol to ensure that travelers and campers comply with fire regulations. When fires break out, crews of fire fighters are brought in to suppress the blaze with heavy equipment, hand tools, and water hoses. Fighting forest fires, like fighting urban fires, is rigorous work. One of the most effective means of battling a blaze is creating fire lines—cutting down trees and digging out grass and all other combustible vegetation in the path of the fire—to deprive it of fuel. Elite fire fighters called smoke jumpers parachute from airplanes to reach otherwise inaccessible areas. This tactic, however, can be extremely hazardous because the crews have no way to escape if the wind shifts and causes the fire to burn toward them.

Between alarms, fire fighters clean and maintain equipment, conduct practice drills and fire inspections, and participate in physical fitness activities. They also prepare written reports on fire incidents and review fire science literature to keep abreast of technological developments and changing administrative practices and policies.

Most fire departments have a fire prevention division, usually headed by a fire marshal and staffed by *fire inspectors*. Workers in this division conduct inspections of structures to prevent fires and ensure compliance with fire codes. These fire fighters also work with developers and planners to check and approve plans for new buildings. Fire prevention personnel often speak on these subjects in schools and before public assemblies and civic organizations.

Some fire fighters become *fire investigators*, who determine the origin and causes of fires. They collect evidence, interview witnesses, and prepare reports on fires in cases where the cause may be arson or criminal negligence. They often are called upon to testify in court.

Working Conditions

Fire fighters spend much of their time at fire stations, which usually have features in common with a residential facility like a dormitory. When an alarm sounds, fire fighters respond rapidly, regardless of the weather or hour. Fire fighting involves the risk of death or injury from sudden cave-ins of floors, toppling walls, traffic accidents when responding to calls, and exposure to flames and smoke. Fire fighters also may come in contact with poisonous, flammable, or explosive gases and chemicals, as well as radioactive or other hazardous materials that may have immediate or long-term effects on their health. For these reasons, they must wear protective gear that can be very heavy and hot.

Work hours of fire fighters are longer and vary more widely than hours of most other workers. Many work more than 50 hours a week, and sometimes they may work even longer. In some agencies, fire fighters are on duty for 24 hours, then off for 48 hours, and receive an extra day off at intervals. In others, they work a day shift of 10 hours for 3 or 4 days, work a night shift of 14 hours for 3 or 4 nights, have 3 or 4 days off, and then repeat the cycle. In addition, fire fighters often work extra hours at fires and other emergencies and are regularly assigned to work on holidays. Fire lieutenants and fire captains often work the same hours as the fire fighters they supervise. Duty hours include time when fire fighters study, train, and perform fire prevention duties.

Training, Other Qualifications, and Advancement

Applicants for municipal fire fighting jobs generally must pass a written exam; tests of strength, physical stamina, coordination, and agility; and a medical examination that includes drug screening. Workers may be monitored on a random basis for drug use after accepting employment. Examinations are generally open to persons who are at least 18 years of age and have a high school education or the equivalent. Those who receive the highest scores in all phases of testing have the best chances for appointment. The completion of community college courses in fire science may improve an applicant's chances for appointment. In recent years, an increasing proportion of entrants to this occupation have had some postsecondary education.

As a rule, entry-level workers in large fire departments are trained for several weeks at the department's training center or academy. Through classroom instruction and practical training, the recruits study fire fighting techniques; fire prevention; hazardous materials control; local building codes; and emergency medical procedures, including first aid and cardiopulmonary resuscitation.

They also learn how to use axes, chain saws, fire extinguishers, ladders, and other fire fighting and rescue equipment. After successfully completing this training, the recruits are assigned to a fire company, where they undergo a period of probation.

Almost all departments require fire fighters to be certified as emergency medical technicians. While most fire departments require the lowest level of certification, EMT-Basic, larger departments in major metropolitan areas are increasingly requiring paramedic certification. Some departments include this training in the fire academy, while others prefer that recruits have EMT certification beforehand, but will give them up to 1 year to become certified on their own.

A number of fire departments have accredited apprenticeship programs lasting up to 4 years. These programs combine formal, technical instruction with on-the-job training under the supervision of experienced fire fighters. Technical instruction covers subjects such as fire fighting techniques and equipment, chemical hazards associated with various combustible building materials, emergency medical procedures, and fire prevention and safety.

In addition to participating in advanced training programs conducted by local fire departments, some fire fighters attend training sessions sponsored by the U.S. National Fire Academy. These training sessions cover topics such as executive development, anti-arson techniques, disaster preparedness, hazardous materials control, and public fire safety and education. Some states also have either voluntary or mandatory fire fighter training and certification programs. In addition, a number of colleges and universities offer courses leading to 2- or 4-year degrees in fire engineering or fire science. Many fire departments offer fire fighters incentives such as tuition reimbursement or higher pay for completing advanced training.

Among the personal qualities fire fighters need are mental alertness, self-discipline, courage, mechanical aptitude, endurance, strength, and a sense of public service. Initiative and good judgment also are extremely important because fire fighters make quick decisions in emergencies. Members of a crew live and work closely together under conditions of stress and danger for extended periods, so they must be dependable and able to get along well with others. Leadership qualities are necessary for officers, who must establish and maintain discipline and efficiency as well as direct the activities of fire fighters in their companies.

Most experienced fire fighters continue studying to improve their job performance and prepare for promotion examinations. To progress to higher-level positions, they acquire expertise in advanced fire fighting equipment and techniques, building construction, emergency medical technology, writing, public speaking, management and budgeting procedures, and public relations.

Opportunities for promotion depend upon the results of written examinations as well as job performance, interviews, and seniority. Increasingly, fire departments are using assessment centers, which simulate a variety of actual job performance tasks, to screen for the best candidates for promotion. The line of promotion usually is to engineer, lieutenant, captain, battalion chief, assistant chief, deputy chief, and, finally, chief. For promotion to positions higher than battalion chief, many fire departments now require a bachelor's degree, preferably in fire science, public administration, or a related field. An associate's degree is required for executive fire officer certification from the National Fire Academy.

Employment

Employment figures in this description include only paid career fire fighters—they do not cover volunteer fire fighters, who perform the same duties and may constitute the majority of fire fighters in a residential area. According to the U.S. Fire Administration, 70 percent of fire companies are staffed by volunteer fire fighters. In 2004, total employment in fire fighting occupations was about 353,000. Fire fighters held about 282,000 jobs, first-line supervisors/managers of fire fighting and prevention workers held about 56,000, and fire inspectors held about 15,000.

About 9 out of 10 fire fighting workers were employed by municipal or county fire departments. Some large cities have thousands of career fire fighters, while many small towns have only a few. Most of the remainder worked in fire departments on federal and state installations, including airports. Private fire fighting companies employ a small number of fire fighters and usually operate on a subscription basis.

In response to the expanding role of fire fighters, some municipalities have combined fire prevention, public fire education, safety, and emergency medical services into a single organization commonly referred to as a public safety organization. Some local and regional fire departments are being consolidated into countywide establishments in order to reduce administrative staffs, cut costs, and establish consistent training standards and work procedures.

Job Outlook

Prospective fire fighters are expected to face keen competition for available job openings. Many people are attracted to fire fighting because (1) it is challenging and provides the opportunity to perform an essential public service, (2) a high school education is usually sufficient for entry, and (3) a pension is guaranteed upon retirement after 25 years. Consequently, the number of qualified applicants in most areas exceeds the number of job openings, even though the written examination and physical requirements eliminate many applicants. This situation is expected to persist in coming years. Applicants with the best opportunities are those who are physically fit and score the highest on physical conditioning and mechanical aptitude exams. Those who have completed some fire fighter education at a community college and have EMT certification will have an additional advantage.

Employment of fire fighters is expected to grow faster than the average for all occupations through 2014. Most job growth will occur as volunteer fire fighting positions are converted to paid positions in growing suburban areas. In addition to job growth, openings are expected to result from the need to replace fire fighters who retire, stop working for other reasons, or transfer to other occupations.

Layoffs of fire fighters are uncommon. Fire protection is an essential service, and citizens are likely to exert considerable pressure on local officials to expand or at least preserve the level of fire protection. Even when budget cuts do occur, local fire departments usually trim expenses by postponing purchases of equipment or by not hiring new fire fighters rather than through staff reductions.

Earnings

Median hourly earnings of fire fighters were $18.43 in May 2004. The middle 50 percent earned between $13.65 and $24.14. The lowest 10 percent earned less than $9.71, and the highest 10 percent earned more than $29.21. Median hourly earnings were $18.78 in local government, $17.34 in the federal government, and $14.94 in state government.

Median annual earnings of first-line supervisors/managers of fire fighting and prevention workers were $58,920 in May 2004. The middle 50 percent earned between $46,880 and $72,600. The lowest 10 percent earned less than $36,800, and the highest 10 percent earned more than $90,860. First-line supervisors/managers of fire fighting and prevention workers employed in local government earned about $60,800 a year.

Median annual earnings of fire inspectors and investigators were $46,340 in May 2004. The middle 50 percent earned between $36,030 and $58,260 a year. The lowest 10 percent earned less than $28,420, and the highest 10 percent earned more than $71,490. Fire inspectors and investigators employed in local government earned about $48,020 a year.

According to the International City-County Management Association, average salaries in 2004 for sworn full-time positions were as follows:

	Minimum annual base salary	Maximum annual base salary
Fire chief	$68,701	$89,928
Deputy chief	63,899	79,803
Assistant fire chief	57,860	73,713
Battalion chief	58,338	73,487
Fire captain	49,108	59,374
Fire lieutenant	44,963	53,179
Fire prevention/code inspector	43,297	54,712
Engineer	41,294	52,461

Fire fighters who average more than a certain number of hours a week are required to be paid overtime. The hours threshold is determined by the department during the fire fighter's work period, which ranges from 7 to 28 days. Fire fighters often earn overtime for working extra shifts to maintain minimum staffing levels or for special emergencies.

Fire fighters receive benefits that usually include medical and liability insurance, vacation and sick leave, and some paid holidays. Almost all fire departments provide protective clothing (helmets, boots, and coats) and breathing apparatus, and many also provide dress uniforms. Fire fighters generally are covered by pension plans, often providing retirement at half pay after 25 years of service or if the individual is disabled in the line of duty.

Related Occupations

Like fire fighters, emergency medical technicians and paramedics and police and detectives respond to emergencies and save lives.

Sources of Additional Information

Information about a career as a fire fighter may be obtained from local fire departments and from either of the following organizations:

▸ International Association of Fire Fighters, 1750 New York Ave. NW, Washington, DC 20006. Internet: http://www.iaff.org

▸ U.S. Fire Administration, 16825 South Seton Ave., Emmitsburg, MD 21727. Internet: http://www.usfa.fema.gov

Information about professional qualifications and a list of colleges and universities offering 2- or 4-year degree programs in fire science or fire prevention may be obtained from

▸ National Fire Academy, 16825 South Seton Ave., Emmitsburg, MD 21727. Internet: http://www.usfa.fema.gov/nfa/index.htm

Food and Beverage Serving and Related Workers

(O*NET 35-3011.00, 35-3021.00, 35-3022.00, 35-3031.00, 35-3041.00, 35-9011.00, 35-9021.00, 35-9031.00, and 35-9099.99)

Significant Points

■ Most jobs are part time, so many opportunities exist for young people—about one-fourth of these workers are 16 to 19 years old, almost six times the proportion for all workers.

■ Job openings are expected to be abundant through 2014 because many of these workers transfer to other occupations or stop working, creating numerous openings.

■ Tips comprise a major portion of earnings, so keen competition is expected for jobs where potential earnings from tips are greatest—bartenders, waiters and waitresses, and other jobs in popular restaurants and fine dining establishments.

Nature of the Work

Food and beverage serving and related workers are the front line of customer service in restaurants, coffee shops, and other food service establishments. These workers greet customers, escort them to seats and hand them menus, take food and drink orders, and serve food and beverages. They also answer questions, explain menu items and specials, and keep tables and dining areas clean and set for new diners. Most work as part of a team, helping co-workers to improve workflow and customer service.

Waiters and waitresses, the largest group of these workers, take customers' orders, serve food and beverages, prepare itemized checks, and sometimes accept payment. Their specific duties vary considerably, depending on the establishment. In coffee shops serving routine, straightforward fare, such as salads, soups, and sandwiches, servers are expected to provide fast, efficient, and courteous service. In fine dining restaurants, where more complicated meals are prepared and often served over several courses, waiters and waitresses

provide more formal service, emphasizing personal, attentive treatment and a more leisurely pace. They may recommend certain dishes and identify ingredients or explain how various items on the menu are prepared. Some prepare salads, desserts, or other menu items tableside. Additionally, they may check the identification of patrons to ensure they meet the minimum age requirement for the purchase of alcohol and tobacco products.

Waiters and waitresses sometimes perform the duties of other food and beverage service workers. These tasks may include escorting guests to tables, serving customers seated at counters, clearing and setting up tables, or operating a cash register. However, full-service restaurants frequently hire other staff, such as hosts and hostesses, cashiers, or dining room attendants, to perform these duties.

Bartenders fill drink orders either taken directly from patrons at the bar or through waiters and waitresses who place drink orders for dining room customers. Bartenders check identification of customers seated at the bar to ensure they meet the minimum age requirement for the purchase of alcohol and tobacco products. They prepare mixed drinks, serve bottled or draught beer, and pour wine or other beverages. Bartenders must know a wide range of drink recipes and be able to mix drinks accurately, quickly, and without waste. Besides mixing and serving drinks, bartenders stock and prepare garnishes for drinks; maintain an adequate supply of ice, glasses, and other bar supplies; and keep the bar area clean for customers. They also may collect payment, operate the cash register, wash glassware and utensils, and serve food to customers seated at the bar. Bartenders usually are responsible for ordering and maintaining an inventory of liquor, mixes, and other bar supplies.

The majority of bartenders directly serve and interact with patrons. Bartenders should be friendly and enjoy talking with customers. Bartenders at service bars, on the other hand, have less contact with customers. They work in small bars often located off the kitchen in restaurants, hotels, and clubs where only waiters and waitresses place drink orders. Some establishments, especially larger, higher-volume ones, use equipment that automatically measures, pours, and mixes drinks at the push of a button. Bartenders who use this equipment, however, still must work quickly to handle a large volume of drink orders and be familiar with the ingredients for special drink requests. Much of a bartender's work still must be done by hand to fill each individual order.

Hosts and hostesses welcome guests and maintain reservation or waiting lists. They may direct patrons to coatrooms or restrooms or to a place to wait until their table is ready. Hosts and hostesses assign guests to tables suitable for the size of their group, escort patrons to their seats, and provide menus. They also schedule dining reservations, arrange parties, and organize any special services that are required. In some restaurants, they act as cashiers.

Dining room and cafeteria attendants and bartender helpers assist waiters, waitresses, and bartenders by cleaning tables, removing dirty dishes, and keeping serving areas stocked with supplies. Sometimes called backwaiters or runners, they bring meals out of the kitchen and assist waiters and waitresses by distributing dishes to individual diners. They also replenish the supply of clean linens, dishes, silverware, and glasses in the dining room and keep the bar stocked with glasses, liquor, ice, and drink garnishes. Dining room attendants set tables with clean tablecloths, napkins, silverware, glasses, and dishes and serve ice water, rolls, and butter. At the conclusion of meals, they remove dirty dishes and soiled linens from tables. Cafeteria attendants stock serving tables with food, trays, dishes, and silverware and may carry trays to dining tables for patrons. *Bartender helpers* keep bar equipment clean and wash glasses. *Dishwashers* clean dishes, cutlery, and kitchen utensils and equipment.

Counter attendants take orders and serve food in cafeterias, coffee shops, and carryout eateries. In cafeterias, they serve food displayed on steam tables, carve meat, dish out vegetables, ladle sauces and soups, and fill beverage glasses. In lunchrooms and coffee shops, counter attendants take orders from customers seated at the counter, transmit orders to the kitchen, and pick up and serve food. They also fill cups with coffee, soda, and other beverages and prepare fountain specialties, such as milkshakes and ice cream sundaes. Counter attendants also take carryout orders from diners and wrap or place items in containers. They clean counters, write itemized checks, and sometimes accept payment. Some counter attendants may prepare short-order items, such as sandwiches and salads.

Some food and beverage serving workers take orders from customers at counters or drive-through windows at fast-food restaurants. They assemble orders, hand them to customers, and accept payment. Many of these are *combined food preparation and serving workers* who also cook and package food, make coffee, and fill beverage cups using drink-dispensing machines.

Other workers serve food to patrons outside of a restaurant environment, such as in hotels, hospital rooms, or cars.

Working Conditions

Food and beverage service workers are on their feet most of the time and often carry heavy trays of food, dishes, and glassware. During busy dining periods, they are under pressure to serve customers quickly and efficiently. The work is relatively safe, but care must be taken to avoid slips, falls, and burns.

Part-time work is more common among food and beverage serving and related workers than among workers in almost any other occupation. In 2004, those on part-time schedules included half of all waiters and waitresses and 40 percent of all bartenders.

Food service and drinking establishments typically maintain long dining hours and offer flexible and varied work opportunities. Many food and beverage serving and related workers work evenings, weekends, and holidays. Many students and teenagers seek part-time or seasonal work as food and beverage serving and related workers as a first job to gain work experience or to earn spending money while in school. Around one-fourth of food and beverage serving and related workers were 16 to 19 years old—about six times the proportion for all workers.

Training, Other Qualifications, and Advancement

There are no specific educational requirements for food and beverage service jobs. Many employers prefer to hire high school graduates for waiter and waitress, bartender, and host and hostess positions, but completion of high school usually is not required for fast-food workers, counter attendants, dishwashers, and dining room attendants and bartender helpers. For many people a job as a food

and beverage service worker serves as a source of immediate income rather than a career. Many entrants to these jobs are in their late teens or early twenties and have a high school education or less. Usually, they have little or no work experience. Many are full-time students or homemakers. Food and beverage service jobs are a major source of part-time employment for high school and college students.

Restaurants rely on good food and quality customer service to retain loyal customers and succeed in a competitive industry. Food and beverage serving and related workers who exhibit excellent personal qualities—such as a neat, clean appearance; a well-spoken manner; an ability to work as a member of a team; and a pleasant way with patrons—will be highly sought after.

Waiters and waitresses need a good memory to avoid confusing customers' orders and to recall faces, names, and preferences of frequent patrons. These workers also should be comfortable using computers to place orders and generate customers' bills. Some may need to be quick at arithmetic so they can total bills manually. Knowledge of a foreign language is helpful to communicate with a diverse clientele and staff. Prior experience waiting on tables is preferred by restaurants and hotels that have rigid table service standards. Jobs at these establishments often offer higher wages and have greater income potential from tips, but they may also have stiffer employment requirements than other establishments, such as prior table service experience or higher education.

Usually, bartenders must be at least 21 years of age, but employers prefer to hire people who are 25 or older. Bartenders should be familiar with state and local laws concerning the sale of alcoholic beverages.

Most food and beverage serving and related workers pick up their skills on the job by observing and working with more-experienced workers. Some full-service restaurants also provide new dining room employees with some form of classroom-type training that alternates with periods of actual on-the-job work experience. These training programs communicate the operating philosophy of the restaurant, help establish a personal rapport with other staff, and instill a desire to work as a team. They also provide an opportunity to discuss customer service situations and the proper ways of handling unpleasant circumstances or unruly patrons with new employees. Additionally, managers, chefs, and servers may meet before each shift to discuss the menu and any new items or specials; review ingredients for any potential food allergies; and talk about any food safety, coordination between the kitchen and the dining room, and customer service issues from the previous day or shift.

Some employers, particularly those in fast-food restaurants, use self-instruction or online programs with audiovisual presentations and instructional booklets to teach new employees food preparation and service skills. Some public and private vocational schools, restaurant associations, and large restaurant chains provide classroom training in a generalized food service curriculum. All employees receive training on safe food handling procedures and sanitation practices.

Some bartenders acquire their skills by attending a bartending or vocational and technical school. These programs often include instruction on state and local laws and regulations, cocktail recipes, proper attire and conduct, and stocking a bar. Some of these schools help their graduates find jobs. Although few employers require any minimum level of educational attainment, some specialized training is usually needed in food handling and legal issues surrounding serving alcoholic beverages and tobacco. Employers are more likely to hire and promote based on people skills and personal qualities rather than education.

Due to the relatively small size of most food-serving establishments, opportunities for promotion are limited. After gaining experience, some dining room and cafeteria attendants and bartender helpers advance to waiter, waitress, or bartender jobs. For waiters, waitresses, and bartenders, advancement usually is limited to finding a job in a busier or more expensive restaurant or bar where prospects for tip earnings are better. Some bartenders, hosts and hostesses, and waiters and waitresses advance to supervisory jobs, such as dining room supervisor, maitre d'hotel, assistant manager, or restaurant general manager. A few bartenders open their own businesses. In larger restaurant chains, food and beverage service workers who excel at their work often are invited to enter the company's formal management training program. (For more information, see the description of food service managers elsewhere in this book.)

Employment

Food and beverage serving and related workers held 6.8 million jobs in 2004. The distribution of jobs among the various food and beverage serving workers was as follows:

Waiters and waitresses	2,252,000
Combined food preparation and serving workers, including fast food	2,150,000
Dishwashers	507,000
Bartenders	474,000
Counter attendants, cafeteria, food concession, and coffee shop	465,000
Dining room and cafeteria attendants and bartender helpers	401,000
Hosts and hostesses, restaurant, lounge, and coffee shop	328,000
Food servers, nonrestaurant	189,000
All other food preparation and serving related workers	64,000

The overwhelming majority of jobs for food and beverage serving and related workers were found in food services and drinking places, such as restaurants, coffee shops, and bars. Other jobs were found primarily in traveler accommodation (hotels); amusement, gambling, and recreation industries; educational services; grocery stores; nursing care facilities; civic and social organizations; and hospitals.

Jobs are located throughout the country but are typically plentiful in large cities and tourist areas. Vacation resorts offer seasonal employment, and some workers alternate between summer and winter resorts instead of remaining in one area the entire year.

Job Outlook

Job openings are expected to be abundant for food and beverage serving and related workers. Overall employment of these workers is expected to increase as fast as the average over the 2004–2014

period as population, personal incomes, and employment expand. While employment growth will create many new jobs, the overwhelming majority of openings will arise from the need to replace the high proportion of workers who leave the occupations each year. There is substantial movement into and out of these occupations because education and training requirements are minimal and the predominance of part-time jobs is attractive to people seeking a short-term source of income rather than a career. However, keen competition is expected for bartender, waiter and waitress, and other food and beverage service jobs in popular restaurants and fine dining establishments, where potential earnings from tips are greatest.

Projected employment growth between 2004 and 2014 varies somewhat by type of job; however, average employment growth is expected for almost all food and beverage serving and related occupations. Employment of combined food preparation and serving workers, which includes fast-food workers, is expected to increase as fast as the average in response to the continuing fast-paced lifestyle of many Americans and the addition of healthier foods at many fast-food restaurants. Average employment growth is expected for waiters and waitresses and hosts and hostesses because increases in the number of families and the more affluent 55-and-older population will result in more restaurants that offer table service and more varied menus. Employment of bartenders, dining room attendants, and dishwashers will grow more slowly than other food and beverage serving and related workers because diners increasingly are eating at more casual dining spots, such as coffee bars and sandwich shops, rather than at the full-service restaurants and drinking places that employ more of these workers.

Earnings

Food and beverage serving and related workers derive their earnings from a combination of hourly wages and customer tips. Earnings vary greatly, depending on the type of job and establishment. For example, fast-food workers and hosts and hostesses usually do not receive tips, so their wage rates may be higher than those of waiters and waitresses and bartenders in full-service restaurants, who typically earn more from tips than from wages. In some restaurants, workers contribute all or a portion of their tips to a tip pool, which is distributed among qualifying workers. Tip pools allow workers who don't usually receive tips directly from customers, such as dining room attendants, to feel a part of a team and to share in the rewards of good service.

In May 2004, median hourly earnings (including tips) of waiters and waitresses were $6.75. The middle 50 percent earned between $6.04 and $8.34. The lowest 10 percent earned less than $5.60, and the highest 10 percent earned more than $11.27 an hour. For most waiters and waitresses, higher earnings are primarily the result of receiving more in tips rather than higher hourly wages. Tips usually average between 10 and 20 percent of guests' checks; waiters and waitresses working in busy, expensive restaurants earn the most.

Bartenders had median hourly earnings (including tips) of $7.42 in May 2004. The middle 50 percent earned between $6.34 and $9.26. The lowest 10 percent earned less than $5.72, and the highest 10 percent earned more than $12.47 an hour. Like waiters and waitresses, bartenders employed in public bars may receive more than half of their earnings as tips. Service bartenders often are paid higher hourly wages to offset their lower tip earnings.

Median hourly earnings (including tips) of dining room and cafeteria attendants and bartender helpers were $7.10 in May 2004. The middle 50 percent earned between $6.24 and $8.25. The lowest 10 percent earned less than $5.68, and the highest 10 percent earned more than $9.88 an hour. Most received over half of their earnings as wages; the rest of their income was a share of the proceeds from tip pools.

Median hourly earnings of hosts and hostesses were $7.52 in May 2004. The middle 50 percent earned between $6.48 and $8.63. The lowest 10 percent earned less than $5.77, and the highest 10 percent earned more than $10.49 an hour. Wages comprised the majority of their earnings. In some cases, wages were supplemented by proceeds from tip pools.

Median hourly earnings of combined food preparation and serving workers, including fast food, were $7.06 in May 2004. The middle 50 percent earned between $6.18 and $8.25. The lowest 10 percent earned less than $5.65, and the highest 10 percent earned more than $9.85 an hour. Although some combined food preparation and serving workers receive a part of their earnings as tips, fast-food workers usually do not.

Median hourly earnings of counter attendants in cafeterias, food concessions, and coffee shops (including tips) were $7.53 in May 2004. The middle 50 percent earned between $6.50 and $8.59 an hour. The lowest 10 percent earned less than $5.80, and the highest 10 percent earned more than $10.38 an hour.

Median hourly earnings of dishwashers were $7.35 in May 2004. The middle 50 percent earned between $6.41 and $8.37. The lowest 10 percent earned less than $5.76, and the highest 10 percent earned more than $9.81 an hour.

Median hourly earnings of nonrestaurant food servers were $7.95 in May 2004. The middle 50 percent earned between $6.64 and $9.98. The lowest 10 percent earned less than $5.86, and the highest 10 percent earned more than $12.53 an hour.

Many beginning or inexperienced workers start earning the federal minimum wage of $5.15 an hour. However, a few states set minimum wages higher than the federal minimum. Also, various minimum wage exceptions apply under specific circumstances to disabled workers, full-time students, youth under age 20 in their first 90 days of employment, tipped employees, and student-learners. Tipped employees are those who customarily and regularly receive more than $30 a month in tips. The employer may consider tips as part of wages, but the employer must pay at least $2.13 an hour in direct wages. Employers also are permitted to deduct from wages the cost, or fair value, of any meals or lodging provided. Many employers, however, provide free meals and furnish uniforms. Food and beverage service workers who work full time often receive typical benefits, while part-time workers usually do not.

In some large restaurants and hotels, food and beverage serving and related workers belong to unions—principally the Hotel Employees and Restaurant Employees International Union and the Service Employees International Union.

Related Occupations

Other workers whose job involves serving customers and handling money include flight attendants, gaming services workers, and retail salespersons.

Sources of Additional Information

Information about job opportunities may be obtained from local employers and local offices of state employment services agencies.

A guide to careers in restaurants plus a list of 2- and 4-year colleges offering food service programs and related scholarship information is available from

▸ National Restaurant Association, 1200 17th St. NW, Washington, DC 20036-3097. Internet: http://www.restaurant.org

For general information on hospitality careers, contact

▸ International Council on Hotel, Restaurant, and Institutional Education, 2613 North Parham Rd., 2nd Floor, Richmond, VA 23294. Internet: http://www.chrie.org

Food Processing Occupations

(O*NET 51-3011.01, 51-3011.02, 51-3021.00, 51-3022.00, 51-3023.00, 51-3091.00, 51-3092.00, and 51-3093.00)

Significant Points

■ Most employees in manual food-processing jobs require little or no training prior to being hired.

■ As more jobs involving cutting and processing meat shift from retail stores to food-processing plants, job growth will be concentrated among lesser-skilled workers, who are employed primarily in manufacturing.

Nature of the Work

Food processing occupations include many different types of workers who process raw food products into the finished goods sold by grocers or wholesalers, restaurants, or institutional food services. These workers perform a variety of tasks and are responsible for producing many of the food products found in every household.

Butchers as well as meat, poultry, and fish cutters and trimmers are employed at different stages in the process by which animal carcasses are converted into manageable pieces of meat, known as boxed meat, that are suitable for sale to wholesalers and retailers. Meat, poultry, and fish cutters and trimmers commonly work in animal slaughtering and processing plants, while butchers and meatcutters usually are employed in retail establishments. As a result, the nature of these jobs varies significantly.

In animal slaughtering and processing plants, *slaughterers and meatpackers* slaughter cattle, hogs, goats, and sheep and cut the carcasses into large wholesale cuts, such as rounds, loins, ribs, and chucks, to facilitate the handling, distribution, and marketing of meat. In some of these plants, slaughterers and meatpackers also further process the large parts into cuts that are ready for retail use. These workers also produce hamburger meat and meat trimmings, which are used to prepare sausages, luncheon meats, and other fabricated meat products. Slaughterers and meatpackers usually work on assembly lines, with each individual responsible for only a few of the many cuts needed to process a carcass. Depending on the type of cut, these workers use knives, cleavers, meat saws, band saws, or other potentially dangerous equipment.

In grocery stores, wholesale establishments that supply meat to restaurants, and institutional food service facilities, *butchers and meatcutters* separate wholesale cuts of meat into retail cuts or individually sized servings. These workers cut meat into steaks and chops, shape and tie roasts, and grind beef for sale as chopped meat. Boneless cuts are prepared with the use of knives, slicers, or power cutters, while band saws are required to carve bone-in pieces of meat. Butchers and meatcutters in retail food stores also may weigh, wrap, and label the cuts of meat; arrange them in refrigerated cases for display; and prepare special cuts to fill unique orders by customers.

Poultry cutters and trimmers slaughter and cut up chickens, turkeys, and other types of poultry. Although the poultry processing industry is becoming increasingly automated, many jobs, such as trimming, packing, and deboning, are still done manually. As in the animal slaughtering and processing industry, most poultry cutters and trimmers perform routine cuts on poultry as it moves along production lines.

Unlike some of the other occupations just listed, *fish cutters and trimmers,* also called *fish cleaners*, are likely to be employed in both manufacturing and retail establishments. These workers primarily scale, cut, and dress fish by removing the head, scales, and other inedible portions and cutting the fish into steaks or fillets. In retail markets, these workers may also wait on customers and clean fish to order.

Meat, poultry, and fish cutters and trimmers also prepare ready-to-heat foods. This preparation often entails filleting meat or fish; cutting it into bite-sized pieces; preparing and adding vegetables; and applying sauces, marinades, or breading.

Bakers mix and bake ingredients in accordance with recipes to produce varying quantities of breads, pastries, and other baked goods. Bakers commonly are employed in grocery stores and specialty shops and produce small quantities of breads, pastries, and other baked goods for consumption on premises or for sale as specialty baked goods. In manufacturing, bakers produce goods in large quantities, using high-volume mixing machines, ovens, and other equipment. Goods produced in large quantities usually are available for sale through distributors, grocery stores, or manufacturers' outlets.

Others in food processing occupations include *food batchmakers,* who set up and operate equipment that mixes, blends, or cooks ingredients used in the manufacture of food products, according to formulas or recipes; *food cooking machine operators and tenders,* who operate or tend to cooking equipment such as steam-cooking vats, deep-fry cookers, pressure cookers, kettles, and boilers to prepare food products, such as meat, sugar, cheese, and grain; and *food and tobacco roasting, baking, and drying machine operators and tenders,* who use equipment to reduce the moisture content of food or tobacco products or to process food in preparation for canning. Some of the machines that are used include

hearth ovens, kiln driers, roasters, char kilns, steam ovens, and vacuum-drying equipment.

Working Conditions

Working conditions vary by type and size of establishment. In animal slaughtering and processing plants and large retail food establishments, butchers and meatcutters work in large meatcutting rooms equipped with power machines and conveyors. In small retail markets, the butcher or fish cleaner may work in a cramped space behind the meat or fish counter. To prevent viral and bacterial infections, work areas must be kept clean and sanitary.

Butchers and meatcutters, poultry and fish cutters and trimmers, and slaughterer and meatpackers often work in cold, damp rooms. The work areas are refrigerated to prevent meat from spoiling and are damp because meat cutting generates large amounts of blood, condensation, and fat. Cool, damp floors increase the likelihood of slips and falls. In addition, cool temperatures, long periods of standing, and repetitious physical tasks make the work tiring. As a result, butchers as well as meat, poultry, and fish cutters and trimmers are more susceptible to injury than are most other workers.

Injuries include cuts and occasional amputations, which occur when knives, cleavers, or power tools are used improperly. Also, repetitive slicing and lifting often lead to cumulative trauma injuries, such as carpal tunnel syndrome. To reduce the incidence of cumulative trauma injuries, some employers have reduced employee workloads, added prescribed rest periods, redesigned jobs and tools, and promoted increased awareness of early warning signs so that steps can be taken to prevent further injury. Nevertheless, workers in the occupation still face the serious threat of disabling injuries.

Most traditional bakers work in bakeries, cake shops, hot-bread shops, hotels, restaurants, and cafeterias and in the bakery departments of supermarkets. Bakers may work under hot and noisy conditions. Also, bakers typically work under strict order deadlines and critical time-sensitive baking requirements, both of which can induce stress. Bakers usually work in shifts and may work early mornings, evenings, weekends, and holidays. While many bakers often work as part of a team, they also may work alone when baking particular items. These workers may supervise assistants and teach apprentices and trainees. Bakers in retail establishments may be required to serve customers.

Other food processing workers—such as food batchmakers; food and tobacco roasting, baking, and drying machine operators and tenders; and food cooking machine operators and tenders—typically work in production areas that are specially designed for food preservation or processing. Food batchmakers, in particular, work in kitchen-type, assembly-line production facilities. Because this work involves food, work areas must meet governmental sanitary regulations. The ovens, as well as the motors of blenders, mixers, and other equipment, often make work areas very warm and noisy. There are some hazards, such as burns, created by the equipment that these workers use. Food batchmakers; food and tobacco roasting, baking, and drying machine operators; and food cooking machine operators and tenders spend a great deal of time on their feet and generally work a regular 40-hour week that may include evening and night shifts.

Training, Other Qualifications, and Advancement

Training varies widely among food processing occupations. However, most manual food processing workers require little or no training prior to being hired.

Most butchers as well as poultry and fish cutters and trimmers acquire their skills on the job through formal and informal training programs. The length of training varies significantly. Simple cutting operations require a few days to learn, while more complicated tasks, such as eviscerating slaughtered animals, generally require several months to learn. The training period for highly skilled butchers at the retail level may be 1 or 2 years.

Generally, on-the-job trainees begin by doing less difficult jobs, such as making simple cuts or removing bones. Under the guidance of experienced workers, trainees learn the proper use and care of tools and equipment and how to prepare various cuts of meat. After demonstrating skill with various meatcutting tools, trainees learn to divide carcasses into wholesale cuts and wholesale cuts into retail and individual portions. Trainees also may learn to roll and tie roasts, prepare sausage, and cure meat. Those employed in retail food establishments often are taught operations, such as inventory control, meat buying, and recordkeeping. In addition, growing concern about food-borne pathogens in meats has led employers to offer numerous safety seminars and extensive training in food safety to employees.

Skills that are important to meat, poultry, and fish cutters and trimmers include manual dexterity, good depth perception, color discrimination, and good hand-eye coordination. Physical strength often is needed to lift and move heavy pieces of meat. Butchers and fish cleaners who wait on customers should have a pleasant personality, a neat appearance, and the ability to communicate clearly. In some states, a health certificate is required for employment.

Bakers often start as apprentices or trainees. Apprentice bakers usually start in craft bakeries, while trainees usually begin in store bakeries, such as those in supermarkets. Bakers need to be skilled in baking, icing, and decorating. They also need to be able to follow instructions, have an eye for detail, and communicate well with others. Knowledge of bakery products and ingredients, as well as mechanical mixing and baking equipment, is important. Many apprentice bakers participate in correspondence study and may work towards a certificate in baking. Working as a baker's assistant or at other activities that involve handling food also is a useful tool for training. The complexity of the skills required for certification as a baker often is underestimated. Bakers need to know about applied chemistry; ingredients and nutrition; government health and sanitation regulations; business concepts; and production processes, including how to operate and maintain machinery. Modern food plants typically use high-speed automated equipment that often is operated by computers.

Food machine operators and tenders usually are trained on the job. They learn to run the different types of equipment by watching and helping other workers. Training can last anywhere from a month to a year, depending on the complexity of the tasks and the number of products involved. A degree in the appropriate area—dairy processing for those working in dairy product operations, for example—is helpful for advancement to a lead worker or a supervisory role. Most food batchmakers participate in on-the-job training, usually from about a month to a year. Some food batchmakers learn their trade through an approved apprenticeship program.

Food processing workers in retail or wholesale establishments may progress to supervisory jobs, such as department managers or team leaders in supermarkets. A few of these workers may become buyers for wholesalers or supermarket chains. Some food processing workers go on to open their own markets or bakeries. In processing plants, workers may advance to supervisory positions or become team leaders.

Employment

Food processing workers held 725,000 jobs in 2004. Employment among the various types of food processing occupations was distributed as follows:

Bakers	166,000
Meat, poultry, and fish cutters and trimmers	140,000
Slaughterers and meat packers	136,000
Butchers and meat cutters	134,000
Food batchmakers	87,000
Food cooking machine operators and tenders	43,000
Food and tobacco roasting, baking, and drying machine operators and tenders	18,000

Thirty-five percent of all food processing workers were employed in animal slaughtering and processing plants. Another 23 percent were employed at grocery stores. Most of the remainder worked in other food manufacturing industries. Butchers, meatcutters, and bakers are employed in almost every city and town in the nation, while most other food processing jobs are concentrated in communities with food-processing plants.

Job Outlook

Overall employment in the food processing occupations is projected to grow about as fast as the average for all occupations through 2014. Increasingly, cheaper meat imports from abroad will have a negative effect on domestic employment in many food processing occupations. As more jobs involving cutting and processing meat shift from retail stores to food-processing plants, job growth will be concentrated among lesser-skilled workers, who are employed primarily in manufacturing. Nevertheless, job opportunities should be available at all levels of the occupation due to the need to replace experienced workers who transfer to other occupations or leave the labor force.

As the nation's population grows, the demand for meat, poultry, and seafood should continue to increase. Successful marketing by the poultry industry is likely to increase demand for chicken and ready-to-heat products. Similarly, the development of prepared food products that are lower in fat and more nutritious promises to stimulate the consumption of red meat. The trend toward preparing meat in containers at the processing level also should contribute to demand for animal slaughterers and meatpackers.

Lesser-skilled meat, poultry, and fish cutters and trimmers—who work primarily in animal slaughtering and processing plants—should experience average employment growth. With the growing popularity of labor-intensive, ready-to-heat poultry products, demand for poultry workers should remain firm. Fish cutters also will be in demand as the task of preparing ready-to-heat fish goods gradually shifts from retail stores to processing plants. Also, advances in fish farming, or "aquaculture," should help meet the growing demand for fish and produce opportunities for fish cutters.

Employment of more highly skilled butchers and meatcutters, who work primarily in retail stores, is expected to grow more slowly than average. Automation and the consolidation of the animal slaughtering and processing industries are enabling employers to transfer employment from higher-paid butchers to lower-wage slaughterers and meatpackers in meatpacking plants. At present, most red meat arrives at grocery stores partially cut up, but a growing share of meat is being delivered prepackaged, with additional fat removed, to wholesalers and retailers. This trend is resulting in less work and, thus, fewer jobs for retail butchers.

While high-volume production equipment limits the demand for bakers in manufacturing, overall employment of bakers is expected to increase about as fast as average due to growing numbers of large wholesale bakers in stores, specialty shops, and traditional bakeries. In addition to the growing numbers of cookie, muffin, and cinnamon roll bakeries, the numbers of specialty bread and bagel shops have been growing, spurring demand for bread and pastry bakers.

Employment of food batchmakers, food cooking machine operators and tenders, and food and tobacco cooking and roasting machine operators and tenders is expected to grow more slowly than average. As more of this work is being done at the manufacturing level rather than at the retail level, potential employment gains will be offset by productivity gains from automated cooking and roasting equipment.

Earnings

Earnings vary by industry, skill, geographic region, and educational level. Median annual earnings of butchers and meatcutters were $25,890 in May 2004. The middle 50 percent earned between $19,780 and $34,260. The highest 10 percent earned more than $41,980 annually, while the lowest 10 percent earned less than $15,920. Butchers and meatcutters employed at the retail level typically earn more than those in manufacturing. Median annual earnings in the industries employing the largest numbers of butchers and meatcutters in May 2004 were as follows:

Other general merchandise stores	$31,900
Grocery stores	27,030
Specialty food stores	22,010
Animal slaughtering and processing	21,440

Meat, poultry, and fish cutters and trimmers typically earn less than butchers and meatcutters. In May 2004, median annual earnings for these lower-skilled workers were $18,900. The middle 50 percent earned between $16,240 and $22,360. The highest 10 percent earned more than $27,430, while the lowest 10 percent earned less than $14,410. Median annual earnings in the industries employing the largest numbers of meat, poultry, and fish cutters and trimmers in May 2004 are shown in the following tabulation:

Grocery and related product wholesalers	$20,790
Grocery stores	20,650
Animal slaughtering and processing	18,660
Seafood product preparation and packaging	18,040

Median annual earnings of bakers were $21,330 in May 2004. The middle 50 percent earned between $17,070 and $27,210. The highest 10 percent earned more than $34,410, and the lowest 10 percent earned less than $14,680. Median annual earnings in the industries employing the largest numbers of bakers in May 2004 are given in the following tabulation:

Other general merchandise stores	$23,390
Bakeries and tortilla manufacturing	22,170
Grocery stores	21,340
Full-service restaurants	19,980
Limited-service eating places	18,690

Median annual earnings of food batchmakers were $22,090 in May 2004. The middle 50 percent earned between $17,010 and $28,790. The highest 10 percent earned more than $35,540, and the lowest 10 percent earned less than $14,370. Median annual earnings in the industries employing the largest numbers of food batchmakers in May 2004 are presented in the following tabulation:

Dairy product manufacturing	$26,550
Other food manufacturing	23,970
Fruit and vegetable preserving and specialty food manufacturing	23,230
Sugar and confectionery product manufacturing	21,420
Bakeries and tortilla manufacturing	20,890

In May 2004, median annual earnings for slaughterers and meatpackers were $20,860. The middle 50 percent earned between $18,120 and $23,920. The highest 10 percent earned more than $27,910, and the lowest 10 percent earned less than $15,520. Median annual earnings in animal slaughtering and processing, the industry employing the largest number of slaughterers and meatpackers, were $20,900 in May 2004.

Median annual earnings for food cooking machine operators and tenders were $20,850 in May 2004. The middle 50 percent earned between $16,680 and $26,670. The highest 10 percent earned more than $33,780, and the lowest 10 percent earned less than $13,930. Median annual earnings in fruit and vegetable preserving and specialty food manufacturing, the industry employing the largest number of food cooking machine operators and tenders, were $24,370 in May 2004.

In May 2004, median annual earnings for food and tobacco roasting, baking, and drying machine operators and tenders were $23,840. The middle 50 percent earned between $18,600 and $30,590. The highest 10 percent earned more than $37,000, and the lowest 10 percent earned less than $15,000.

Food processing workers generally received typical benefits, including pension plans for union members or those employed by grocery stores. However, poultry workers rarely earned substantial benefits. In 2004, 21 percent of all food processing workers were union members or were covered by a union contract. Many food processing workers are members of the United Food and Commercial Workers International Union.

Related Occupations

Food processing workers must be skilled at both hand and machine work and must have some knowledge of processes and techniques that are involved in handling and preparing food. Other occupations that require similar skills and knowledge include chefs, cooks, and food preparation workers.

Sources of Additional Information

State employment service offices can provide information about job openings for food processing occupations.

Food Service Managers

(O*NET 11-9051.00)

Significant Points

■ Experience as food and beverage preparation and service workers is essential for promotion into managerial positions; however, applicants with a college degree in restaurant and institutional food service management should have the best job opportunities.

■ Many new food service manager jobs will arise in the food services and drinking places industry as the number of establishments increases along with the population.

■ Job opportunities for salaried food service managers should be better than for self-employed managers because more restaurant managers will be employed by regional or national restaurant chains to run their establishments.

Nature of the Work

Food service managers are responsible for the daily operations of restaurants and other establishments that prepare and serve meals and beverages to customers. Besides coordinating activities among various departments, such as kitchen, dining room, and banquet operations, food service managers ensure that customers are satisfied with their dining experience. In addition, they oversee the inventory and ordering of food, equipment, and supplies and arrange for the routine maintenance and upkeep of the restaurant, its equipment, and facilities. Managers generally are responsible for all of the administrative and human-resource functions of running the business, including recruiting new employees and monitoring employee performance and training.

In most full-service restaurants and institutional food service facilities, the management team consists of a *general manager*, one or more *assistant managers*, and an *executive chef*. The executive chef is responsible for all food preparation activities, including running kitchen operations, planning menus, and maintaining quality standards for food service. In limited-service eating places, such as sandwich shops, coffee bars, or fast-food establishments, managers, not executive chefs, are responsible for supervising routine food

preparation operations. Assistant managers in full-service facilities generally oversee service in the dining rooms and banquet areas. In larger restaurants and fast-food or other food service facilities that serve meals daily and maintain longer hours, individual assistant managers may supervise different shifts of workers. In smaller restaurants, formal titles may be less important, and one person may undertake the work of one or more food service positions. For example, the executive chef also may be the general manager or even sometimes an owner. (For additional information on these other workers, see material on chefs, cooks, and food preparation workers elsewhere in this book.)

One of the most important tasks of food service managers is assisting executive chefs as they select successful menu items. This task varies by establishment depending on the seasonality of menu items, the frequency with which restaurants change their menus, and the introduction of daily or weekly specials. Many restaurants rarely change their menus while others make frequent alterations. Managers or executive chefs select menu items, taking into account the likely number of customers and the past popularity of dishes. Other issues considered when planning a menu include whether there was any unserved food left over from prior meals that should not be wasted, the need for variety, and the seasonal availability of foods. Managers or executive chefs analyze the recipes of the dishes to determine food, labor, and overhead costs and to assign prices to various dishes. Menus must be developed far enough in advance that supplies can be ordered and received in time.

Managers or executive chefs estimate food needs, place orders with distributors, and schedule the delivery of fresh food and supplies. They plan for routine services or deliveries, such as linen services or the heavy cleaning of dining rooms or kitchen equipment, to occur during slow times or when the dining room is closed. Managers also arrange for equipment maintenance and repairs and coordinate a variety of services such as waste removal and pest control. Managers or executive chefs receive deliveries and check the contents against order records. They inspect the quality of fresh meats, poultry, fish, fruits, vegetables, and baked goods to ensure that expectations are met. They meet with representatives from restaurant supply companies and place orders to replenish stocks of tableware, linens, paper products, cleaning supplies, cooking utensils, and furniture and fixtures.

Managers must be good communicators. They need to speak well, often in several languages, with a diverse clientele and staff. They must motivate employees to work as a team to ensure that food and service meet appropriate standards. Managers also must ensure that written supply orders are clear and unambiguous.

Managers interview, hire, train, and, when necessary, fire employees. Retaining good employees is a major challenge facing food service managers. Managers recruit employees at career fairs, contact schools that offer academic programs in hospitality or culinary arts, and arrange for newspaper advertising to attract additional applicants. Managers oversee the training of new employees and explain the establishment's policies and practices. They schedule work hours, making sure that enough workers are present to cover each shift. If employees are unable to work, managers may have to call in alternates to cover for them or fill in themselves when needed. Some managers may help with cooking, clearing tables, or other tasks when the restaurant becomes extremely busy.

Food service managers ensure that diners are served properly and in a timely manner. They investigate and resolve customers' complaints about food quality or service. They monitor orders in the kitchen to determine where backups may occur, and they work with the chef to remedy any delays in service. Managers direct the cleaning of the dining areas and the washing of tableware, kitchen utensils, and equipment to comply with company and government sanitation standards. Managers also monitor the actions of their employees and patrons on a continual basis to ensure the personal safety of everyone. They make sure that health and safety standards and local liquor regulations are obeyed.

In addition to their regular duties, food service managers perform a variety of administrative assignments, such as keeping employee work records; preparing the payroll; and completing paperwork to comply with licensing laws and reporting requirements of tax, wage and hour, unemployment compensation, and Social Security laws. Some of this work may be delegated to an assistant manager or bookkeeper, or it may be contracted out, but most general managers retain responsibility for the accuracy of business records. Managers also maintain records of supply and equipment purchases and ensure that accounts with suppliers are paid.

Technology influences the jobs of food service managers in many ways, enhancing efficiency and productivity. Many restaurants use computers to track orders, inventory, and the seating of patrons. Point-of-service (POS) systems allow servers to key in a customer's order, either at the table, using a hand-held device, or from a computer terminal in the dining room, and send the order to the kitchen instantaneously so preparation can begin. The same system totals and prints checks, functions as a cash register, connects to credit card authorizers, and tracks sales. To minimize food costs and spoilage, many managers use inventory-tracking software to compare the record of sales from the POS with a record of the current inventory. Some establishments enter an inventory of standard ingredients and suppliers into their POS system. When supplies of particular ingredients run low, they can be ordered directly from the supplier using preprogrammed information. Computers also allow restaurant and food service managers to keep track of employee schedules and paychecks more efficiently.

Food service managers use the Internet to track industry news, find recipes, conduct market research, purchase supplies or equipment, recruit employees, and train staff. Internet access also makes service to customers more efficient. Many restaurants maintain Web sites that include menus and online promotions, provide information about the restaurant's location, and offer patrons the option to make a reservation.

Managers tally the cash and charge receipts received and balance them against the record of sales. They are responsible for depositing the day's receipts at the bank or securing them in a safe place. Finally, managers are responsible for locking up the establishment; checking that ovens, grills, and lights are off; and switching on alarm systems.

Working Conditions

Food service managers are among the first to arrive in the morning and the last to leave at night. Long hours—12 to 15 per day, 50 or more per week, and sometimes 7 days a week—are common.

Managers of institutional food service facilities, such as school, factory, or office cafeterias, work more regular hours because the operating hours of these establishments usually conform to the operating hours of the business or facility they serve. However, hours for many managers are unpredictable.

Managers should be calm, flexible, and able to work through emergencies, such as a fire or flood, in order to ensure everyone's safety. Managers also should be able to fill in for absent workers on short notice. Managers often experience the pressures of simultaneously coordinating a wide range of activities. When problems occur, it is the manager's responsibility to resolve them with minimal disruption to customers. The job can be hectic, and dealing with irate customers or uncooperative employees can be stressful.

Managers also may experience the typical minor injuries of other restaurant workers, such as muscle aches, cuts, or burns. They might endure physical discomfort from moving tables or chairs to accommodate large parties, receiving and storing daily supplies from vendors, or making minor repairs to furniture or equipment.

Training, Other Qualifications, and Advancement

Experience in the food services industry, whether as a full-time waiter or waitress or as a part-time or seasonal counter attendant, is essential training for a food services manager. Many food service management companies and national or regional restaurant chains recruit management trainees from 2- and 4-year college hospitality management programs that require internships and real-life experience to graduate. Some restaurant chains prefer to hire people with degrees in restaurant and institutional food service management, but they often hire graduates with degrees in other fields who have demonstrated experience, interest, and aptitude. Many restaurant and food service manager positions—particularly self-service and fast-food—are filled by promoting experienced food and beverage preparation and service workers. Waiters, waitresses, chefs, and fast-food workers demonstrating potential for handling increased responsibility sometimes advance to assistant manager or management trainee jobs. Executive chefs need extensive experience working as chefs, and general managers need prior restaurant experience, usually as assistant managers.

A bachelor's degree in restaurant and food service management provides particularly strong preparation for a career in this occupation. Almost 1,000 colleges and universities offer 4-year programs in restaurant and hospitality management or institutional food service management; a growing number of university programs offer graduate degrees in hospitality management or similar fields. For those not interested in pursuing a 4-year degree, community and junior colleges, technical institutes, and other institutions offer programs in the field leading to an associate degree or other formal certification. Both 2- and 4-year programs provide instruction in subjects such as nutrition, sanitation, and food planning and preparation, as well as accounting, business law and management, and computer science. Some programs combine classroom and laboratory study with internships providing on-the-job experience. In addition, many educational institutions offer culinary programs in food preparation. Such training can lead to a career as a cook or chef and provide a foundation for advancement to an executive chef position.

Many larger food service operations will provide, or offer to pay for, technical training, such as computer or business courses, so that employees can acquire the business skills necessary to read a spreadsheet or understand the concepts and practices of running a business. Generally, this requires a long-term commitment on the employee's part to both the employer and to the profession.

Most restaurant chains and food service management companies have rigorous training programs for management positions. Through a combination of classroom and on-the-job training, trainees receive instruction and gain work experience in all aspects of the operation of a restaurant or institutional food service facility. Areas include food preparation, nutrition, sanitation, security, company policies and procedures, personnel management, recordkeeping, and preparation of reports. Training on use of the restaurant's computer system is increasingly important as well. Usually, trainees receive their first permanent assignment as an assistant manager after 6 months or a year.

Most employers emphasize personal qualities when hiring managers. For example, self-discipline, initiative, and leadership ability are essential. Managers must be able to solve problems and concentrate on details. They need good communication skills to deal with customers and suppliers as well as to motivate and direct their staff. A neat and clean appearance is important because managers must convey self-confidence and show respect in dealing with the public. Because food service management can be physically demanding, good health and stamina are important.

The certified Foodservice Management Professional (FMP) designation is a measure of professional achievement for food service managers. Although not a requirement for employment or advancement in the occupation, voluntary certification provides recognition of professional competence, particularly for managers who acquired their skills largely on the job. The National Restaurant Association Educational Foundation awards the FMP designation to managers who achieve a qualifying score on a written examination, complete a series of courses that cover a range of food service management topics, and meet standards of work experience in the field.

Willingness to relocate often is essential for advancement to positions with greater responsibility. Managers typically advance to larger establishments or regional management positions within restaurant chains. Some eventually open their own food service establishments.

Employment

Food service managers held about 371,000 jobs in 2004. Most managers were salaried, but more than 40 percent were self-employed in independent restaurants or other small food service establishments. About 70 percent of all salaried jobs for food service managers were in full-service restaurants or limited-service eating places, such as fast-food restaurants and cafeterias. Other salaried jobs were in drinking places (alcoholic beverages) and in special food services—an industry that includes food service contractors who supply food services at institutional, governmental, commercial, or industrial locations. A small number of salaried jobs were in traveler accommodation (hotels); educational services; amusement, gambling, and recreation industries; nursing care facilities; and hospitals. Jobs are located throughout the country, with large cities and tourist areas providing more opportunities for full-service dining positions.

Job Outlook

Employment of food service managers is expected to grow about as fast as average for all occupations through 2014. In addition to job openings arising out of employment growth, the need to replace managers who transfer to other occupations or stop working will create many job opportunities. Although practical experience is an integral part of finding a food service management position, applicants with a degree in restaurant, hospitality, or institutional food service management will have an edge; those with higher-level degrees should have the best opportunities.

Projected employment growth varies by industry. Most new jobs will arise in full-service restaurants and limited-service eating places as the number of these establishments increase along with the population. Manager jobs in special food services, an industry that includes food service contractors, will increase as hotels, schools, health care facilities, and other businesses contract out their food services to firms in this industry. Food service manager jobs still are expected to increase in hotels, schools, and health care facilities, but growth will be slowed as contracting out becomes more common.

Job opportunities should be better for salaried managers than for self-employed managers. More new restaurants are affiliated with national or regional chains than are independently owned and operated. As this trend continues, fewer owners will manage restaurants themselves, and more restaurant managers will be employed by larger companies to run individual establishments.

Earnings

Median annual earnings of salaried food service managers were $39,610 in May 2004. The middle 50 percent earned between $31,010 and $51,460. The lowest 10 percent earned less than $24,500, and the highest 10 percent earned more than $68,860. Median annual earnings in the industries employing the largest numbers of food service managers in May 2004 were as follows:

Traveler accommodation	$43,660
Special food services	43,530
Full-service restaurants	41,490
Limited-service eating places	36,400
Elementary and secondary schools	36,290

In addition to receiving typical benefits, most salaried food service managers are provided free meals and the opportunity for additional training, depending on their length of service. Some food service managers, especially those in full-service restaurants, may earn bonuses depending on sales volume or revenue.

Related Occupations

Food service managers direct the activities of a hospitality-industry business and provide a service to customers. Other managers and supervisors in hospitality-oriented businesses include gaming managers, lodging managers, sales worker supervisors, and first-line supervisors or managers of food preparation and serving workers.

Sources of Additional Information

Information about a career as a food service manager, 2- and 4-year college programs in restaurant and food service management, and certification as a Foodservice Management Professional is available from

▸ National Restaurant Association Educational Foundation, 175 West Jackson Blvd., Suite 1500, Chicago, IL 60604-2702. Internet: http://www.nraef.org

General information on hospitality careers may be obtained from

▸ The International Council on Hotel, Restaurant, and Institutional Education, 2613 North Parham Rd., 2nd Floor, Richmond, VA 23294. Internet: http://www.chrie.org

Additional information about job opportunities in food service management may be obtained from local employers and from local offices of state employment services agencies.

Gaming Services Occupations

(O*NET 39-1011.00, 39-1012.00, 39-3011.00, 39-3012.00, 39-3019.99, and 39-3099.99)

Significant Points

■ Job opportunities are available nationwide and are no longer limited to Nevada and New Jersey.

■ Workers need a license issued by a regulatory agency, such as a state casino control board or commission; licensure requires proof of residency in the state in which gaming workers are employed.

■ Employment is projected to grow faster than average.

■ Job prospects are best for those with a degree or certification in gaming or a hospitality-related field, previous training or experience in casino gaming, and strong interpersonal and customer service skills.

Nature of the Work

Legalized gambling in the United States today includes casino gaming, state lotteries, pari-mutuel wagering on contests such as horse or dog racing, and charitable gaming. Gaming, the playing of games of chance, is a multibillion-dollar industry that is responsible for the creation of a number of unique service occupations.

The majority of all gaming services workers are employed in casinos. Their duties and titles may vary from one establishment to another. Despite differences in job title and task, however, workers perform many of the same basic functions in all casinos. Some positions are associated with oversight and direction—supervision, surveillance, and investigation—while others involve working with the games or patrons themselves, performing such activities as tending slot machines, handling money, writing and running tickets, and dealing cards or running games.

Like nearly every business establishment, casinos have workers who direct and oversee day-to-day operations. *Gaming supervisors* oversee the gaming operations and personnel in an assigned area. They circulate among the tables and observe the operations to ensure that all of the stations and games are covered for each shift. It is not uncommon for gaming supervisors to explain and interpret the operating rules of the house to patrons who may have difficulty understanding the rules. Gaming supervisors also may plan and organize activities to create a friendly atmosphere for the guests staying in their hotels or in casino hotels. Periodically, they address and adjust complaints about service.

Some gaming occupations demand specially acquired skills—dealing blackjack, for example—that are unique to casino work. Others require skills common to most businesses, such as the ability to conduct financial transactions. In both capacities, the workers in these jobs interact directly with patrons in attending to slot machines, making change, cashing or selling tokens and coins, writing and running for other games, and dealing cards at table games. Part of their responsibility is to make those interactions enjoyable.

Slot key persons coordinate and supervise the slot department and its workers. Their duties include verifying and handling payoff winnings to patrons, resetting slot machines after completing the payoff, and refilling machines with money. Slot key persons must be familiar with a variety of slot machines and be able to make minor repairs and adjustments to the machines as needed. If major repairs are required, slot key persons determine whether the slot machine should be removed from the floor. Working the floor as frontline personnel, they enforce safety rules and report hazards.

Gaming and sportsbook writers and runners assist in the operations of games such as bingo and keno in addition to taking bets on sporting events. They scan tickets presented by patrons and calculate and distribute winnings. Some writers and runners operate the equipment that randomly selects the numbers. Others may announce numbers selected; pick up tickets from patrons; collect bets; or receive, verify, and record patrons' cash wagers.

Gaming dealers operate table games such as craps, blackjack, and roulette. Standing or sitting behind the table, dealers provide dice, dispense cards to players, or run the equipment. Some dealers also monitor the patrons for infractions of casino rules. Gaming dealers must be skilled in customer service and in executing their game. Dealers determine winners, calculate and pay winning bets, and collect losing bets. Because of the fast-paced work environment, most gaming dealers are competent in at least two games, usually blackjack and craps.

Working Conditions

The atmosphere in casinos is generally filled with fun and often considered glamorous. However, casino work can also be physically demanding. Most occupations require that workers stand for long periods; some require the lifting of heavy items. The atmosphere in casinos exposes workers to certain hazards, such as cigarette, cigar, and pipe smoke. Noise from slot machines, gaming tables, and talking workers and patrons may be distracting to some, although workers wear protective headgear in areas where loud machinery is used to count money.

Most casinos are open 24 hours a day, seven days a week and offer three staggered shifts.

Training, Other Qualifications, and Advancement

There usually are no minimum educational requirements for entry-level gaming jobs, although most employers prefer at least a high school diploma or GED. Each casino establishes its own requirements for education, training, and experience. Some of the major casinos and slot manufacturers run their own training schools, and almost all provide some form of in-house training in addition to requiring certification. The type and quantity of classes needed may vary. Many institutions of higher learning give training toward certificates in gaming, as well as offering an associate, bachelor's, or master's degree in a hospitality-related field such as hospitality management, hospitality administration, or hotel management. Some schools offer training in games, gaming supervision, slot attendant and slot repair technician work, slot department management, and surveillance and security.

Gaming services workers are required to have a license issued by a regulatory agency, such as a state casino control board or commission. Applicants for a license must provide photo identification, offer proof of residency in the state in which they anticipate working, and pay a fee. Age requirements vary by state. The licensing application process also includes a background investigation.

In addition to possessing a license, gaming services workers need superior customer service skills. Casino gaming workers provide entertainment and hospitality to patrons, and the quality of their service contributes to an establishment's success or failure. Therefore, gaming workers need good communication skills, an outgoing personality, and the ability to maintain their composure even when dealing with angry or demanding patrons. Personal integrity also is important because workers handle large amounts of money.

Gaming services workers who manage money should have some experience handling cash or using calculators or computers. For such positions, most casinos administer a math test to assess an applicant's level of competency.

Most gaming supervisors have experience in other gaming occupations, typically as dealers, and have a broad knowledge of casino rules, regulations, procedures, and games. While an associate or bachelor's degree is beneficial, it is not a requirement for most positions. Gaming supervisors must have strong leadership, organizational, and communication skills. Excellent customer service and employee skills also are necessary.

Slot key persons do not need to meet formal educational requirements to enter the occupation, but completion of slot attendant or slot technician training is helpful. As with most other gaming workers, slot key persons receive on-the-job training during the first several weeks of employment.

Gaming and sportsbook writers and runners must have at least a high school diploma or GED. Most of these workers receive on-the-job training. Because gaming and sportsbook writers and runners work closely with patrons, they need excellent customer service skills.

Most gaming dealers acquire their skills by attending a dealer school or vocational and technical school. Most of these schools are found in Nevada and New Jersey. They teach the rules and procedures of the games as well as state and local laws and regulations.

Graduation from one of these schools does not guarantee a job at many casinos, however, as most casinos require prospective dealers to also audition for open positions. During the audition, personal qualities are assessed along with knowledge of the games. Experienced dealers, who often are able to attract new or return business, have the best job prospects. Dealers with more experience are placed at the "high-roller" tables.

Advancement opportunities in casino gaming depend less on workers' previous casino duties and titles than on their ability and eagerness to learn new jobs. For example, an entry-level gaming worker eventually might advance to become a dealer or card room manager or to assume some other supervisory position.

Employment

Gaming services occupations provided 177,000 jobs in 2004. Employment by occupational specialty was distributed as follows:

Gaming dealers	83,000
Gaming supervisors	38,000
Slot key persons	23,000
Gaming and sports book writers and runners	18,000
Gaming service workers, all other	15,000

Gaming services workers are found mainly in the traveler accommodation and gaming industries. Most are employed in commercial casinos, including land-based or riverboat casinos, in 11 states: Colorado, Illinois, Indiana, Iowa, Louisiana, Michigan, Mississippi, Missouri, Nevada, New Jersey, and South Dakota. The largest number works in casinos in Nevada, and the second-largest group works in similar establishments in Atlantic City, New Jersey. Mississippi, which boasts the greatest number of riverboat casinos in operation, employs the most workers in that venue. In addition, there are 28 states with Indian casinos. Legal lotteries are held in 40 states and the District of Columbia, and pari-mutuel wagering is legal in 40 states. Forty-seven states and the District of Columbia also allow charitable gaming. Other states have recently passed legislation to permit gambling, but no casinos have been opened as of yet.

For most workers, gaming licensure requires proof of residency in the state in which gaming workers are employed. But some gaming services workers do not limit themselves to one state or even one country, finding jobs on the small number of casinos located on luxury cruise liners that travel the world. These individuals live and work aboard the vessel.

Job Outlook

With demand for gaming showing no sign of waning, employment in gaming services occupations is projected to grow faster than the average for all occupations through 2014. Even during the recent downturn in the economy, revenues at casinos have risen. In addition, the increasing popularity and prevalence of Indian casinos, particularly in California, and pari-mutuel casinos will provide substantial job openings that were not available in the past. With many states benefiting from casino gambling in the form of tax revenue or agreements with Indian tribes, additional states are reconsidering their opposition to legalized gambling and will likely approve the construction of more casinos and other gaming establishments during the next decade. Some job growth will occur in established gaming areas in Nevada and Atlantic City, New Jersey, but most of the openings in these locations will come from job turnover.

The increase in gaming reflects growth in the population and in its disposable income, both of which are expected to continue. Higher expectations for customer service among gaming patrons also should result in more jobs for gaming services workers.

Job prospects in gaming services occupations will be best for those with previous casino gaming experience, a degree or technical or vocational training in gaming or a hospitality-related field, and strong interpersonal and customer service skills. As a direct result of increasing demand for additional table games in gaming establishments, the most rapid growth is expected among gaming dealers. However, there are generally more applicants than jobs for dealers, creating keen competition for jobs. In addition to job openings arising from employment growth, opportunities will result from the need to replace workers transferring to other occupations or leaving the labor force.

Earnings

Wage earnings for gaming services workers vary according to occupation, level of experience, training, location, and size of the gaming establishment. The following were median earnings for various gaming services occupations in May 2004:

Gaming supervisors	$40,840
Slot key persons	23,010
Gaming service workers, all other	20,820
Gaming and sports book writers and runners	18,390
Gaming dealers	14,340

Gaming dealers generally receive a large portion of their earnings from tokes, which are tips in the form of tokens received from players. Earnings from tokes can vary depending on the table games the dealer operates and the personal traits of the dealer.

Related Occupations

Many other occupations provide hospitality and customer service. Some examples of related occupations are security guards and gaming surveillance officers, sales worker supervisors, cashiers, gaming change persons and booth cashiers, retail salespersons, gaming cage workers, and tellers.

Sources of Additional Information

For additional information on careers in gaming, visit your public library and your state gaming regulatory agency or casino control commission.

Information on careers in gaming also is available from

▸ American Gaming Association, 555 13th St. NW, Suite 1010 East, Washington, DC 20004. Internet: http://www.americangaming.org

Grounds Maintenance Workers

(O*NET 37-1012.01, 37-1012.02, 37-3011.00, 37-3012.00, 37-3013.00, and 37-3019.99)

Significant Points

■ Opportunities should be very good, especially for workers willing to work seasonal or variable schedules, because of significant job turnover and increasing demand by landscaping services companies.

■ Many beginning jobs have low earnings and are physically demanding.

■ Most workers learn through short-term on-the-job training.

Nature of the Work

Attractively designed, healthy, and well-maintained lawns, gardens, and grounds create a positive first impression, establish a peaceful mood, and increase property values. Grounds maintenance workers perform the variety of tasks necessary to achieve a pleasant and functional outdoor environment. They also care for indoor gardens and plantings in commercial and public facilities, such as malls, hotels, and botanical gardens.

The duties of *landscaping workers* and *groundskeeping workers* are similar and often overlap. Landscaping workers physically install and maintain landscaped areas. They grade property; install lighting or sprinkler systems; and build walkways, terraces, patios, decks, and fountains. In addition to initially transporting and planting new vegetation, they transplant, mulch, fertilize, and water flowering plants, trees, and shrubs and mow and water lawns. A growing number of residential and commercial clients, such as managers of office buildings, shopping malls, multiunit residential buildings, and hotels and motels, favor full-service landscape maintenance. Landscaping workers perform a range of duties, including mowing, edging, trimming, fertilizing, dethatching, and mulching for such clients on a regular basis during the growing season.

Groundskeeping workers, also called *groundskeepers*, maintain a variety of facilities, including athletic fields, golf courses, cemeteries, university campuses, and parks. In addition to caring for sod, plants, and trees, they rake and mulch leaves, clear snow from walkways and parking lots, and use irrigation methods to adjust the amount of water consumption and prevent waste. They see to the proper upkeep and repair of sidewalks, parking lots, groundskeeping equipment, pools, fountains, fences, planters, and benches.

Groundskeeping workers who care for athletic fields keep natural and artificial turf in top condition, mark out boundaries, and paint turf with team logos and names before events. They must make sure that the underlying soil on fields with natural turf has the required composition to allow proper drainage and to support the grasses used on the field. Groundskeeping workers mow, water, fertilize, and aerate the fields regularly. They also vacuum and disinfect synthetic turf after its use in order to prevent the growth of harmful bacteria, and they remove the turf and replace the cushioning pad periodically.

Workers who maintain golf courses are called *greenskeepers*. Greenskeepers do many of the same things as other groundskeepers. In addition, greenskeepers periodically relocate the holes on putting greens to eliminate uneven wear of the turf and to add interest and challenge to the game. Greenskeepers also keep canopies, benches, ball washers, and tee markers repaired and freshly painted.

Some groundskeeping workers specialize in caring for cemeteries and memorial gardens. They dig graves to specified depths, generally using a backhoe. They mow grass regularly, apply fertilizers and other chemicals, prune shrubs and trees, plant flowers, and remove debris from graves.

Groundskeeping workers in parks and recreation facilities care for lawns, trees, and shrubs; maintain athletic fields and playgrounds; clean buildings; and keep parking lots, picnic areas, and other public spaces free of litter. They also may remove snow and ice from roads and walkways, erect and dismantle snow fences, and maintain swimming pools. These workers inspect buildings and equipment, make needed repairs, and keep everything freshly painted.

Landscaping and groundskeeping workers use hand tools such as shovels, rakes, pruning and regular saws, hedge and brush trimmers, and axes, as well as power lawn mowers, chain saws, snowblowers, and electric clippers. Some use equipment such as tractors and twin-axle vehicles. Landscaping and groundskeeping workers at parks, schools, cemeteries, and golf courses may use sod cutters to harvest sod that will be replanted elsewhere.

Pesticide handlers, sprayers, and applicators, vegetation, mix pesticides, herbicides, fungicides, or insecticides and apply them through sprays, dusts, or vapors into the soil or onto trees, shrubs, lawns, or botanical crops. Those working for chemical lawn service firms are more specialized, inspecting lawns for problems and applying fertilizers, herbicides, pesticides, and other chemicals to stimulate growth and prevent or control weeds, diseases, or insect infestation. Many practice integrated pest-management techniques.

Tree trimmers and pruners cut away dead or excess branches from trees or shrubs either to maintain rights-of-way for roads, sidewalks, or utilities or to improve the appearance, health, and value of trees. Some of these workers also specialize in pruning, trimming, and shaping ornamental trees and shrubs for private residences, golf courses, or other institutional grounds. Tree trimmers and pruners use handsaws, pruning hooks, shears, and clippers. When trimming near power lines, they usually use truck-mounted lifts and power pruners.

Supervisors of landscaping and groundskeeping workers perform various functions. They prepare cost estimates, schedule work for crews on the basis of weather conditions or the availability of equipment, perform spot checks to ensure the quality of the service, and suggest changes in work procedures. In addition, supervisors train workers in their tasks; keep employees' time records and record work performed; and even assist workers when deadlines are near. Supervisors who own their own business are also known as *landscape contractors*. They may also call themselves *landscape designers* if they create landscape design plans.

Supervisors of tree trimmers and pruners are often referred to as arborists. Arborists specialize in the care of individual trees and are trained and equipped to provide proper care. Some arborists plant trees, and most can recommend types of trees that are appropriate for a specific location, as the wrong tree in the wrong location could lead to future problems as a result of limited growing space, insects, diseases, or poor growth. Arborists are employed by cities to improve urban green space, utilities to maintain power distribution networks, and companies to care for residential and commercial properties, as well as many other settings.

Working Conditions

Many of the jobs for grounds maintenance workers are seasonal, meaning that they are in demand mainly in the spring, summer, and fall, when most planting, mowing, trimming, and cleanup are necessary. Most of the work is performed outdoors in all kinds of weather. It can be physically demanding and repetitive, involving much bending, lifting, and shoveling. Workers in landscaping and groundskeeping may be under pressure to get the job completed, especially when they are preparing for scheduled events such as athletic competitions.

Those who work with pesticides, fertilizers, and other chemicals, as well as dangerous equipment and tools such as power lawn mowers, chain saws, and power clippers, must exercise safety precautions. Workers who use motorized equipment must take care to protect themselves against hearing damage.

Training, Other Qualifications, and Advancement

There usually are no minimum educational requirements for entry-level positions in grounds maintenance, although a diploma is necessary for some jobs. In 2004, most workers had a high school education or less. Short-term on-the-job training generally is sufficient to teach new hires how to operate equipment such as mowers, trimmers, leaf blowers, and small tractors and to follow correct safety procedures. Entry-level workers must be able to follow directions and learn proper planting and maintenance procedures for their localities. They also must learn how to repair the equipment they're using. If driving is an essential part of a job, employers look for applicants with a good driving record and some experience driving a truck. Employers also look for responsible, self-motivated individuals because grounds maintenance workers often work with little supervision. Workers who deal directly with customers must get along well with people.

Laborers who demonstrate a willingness to work hard and quickly, have good communication skills, and take an interest in the business may advance to crew leader or other supervisory positions. Advancement or entry into positions such as grounds manager and landscape contractor usually requires some formal education beyond high school and several years of progressively more responsible experience.

Most states require certification for workers who apply pesticides. Certification requirements vary, but usually include passing a test on the proper and safe use and disposal of insecticides, herbicides, and fungicides. Some states require that landscape contractors be licensed.

The Professional Grounds Management Society (PGMS) offers certification to grounds managers who have a combination of 8 years of experience and formal education beyond high school and who pass an examination covering subjects such as equipment management, personnel management, environmental issues, turf care, ornamentals, and circulatory systems. The PGMS also offers certification to groundskeepers who have a high school diploma or equivalent, plus 2 years of experience in the grounds maintenance field.

The Professional Landcare Network (PLANET) offers the designations "Certified Landscape Professional" (Exterior and Interior) and "Certified Landscape Technician" (Exterior or Interior) to those who meet established education and experience standards and who pass a specific examination. The hands-on test for technicians covers areas such as the operation of maintenance equipment and the installation of plants by reading a plan. A written safety test also is administered. PLANET also offers the designations "Certified Turfgrass Professional" (CTP) and "Certified Ornamental Landscape Professional" (COLP), which require written exams.

Some workers with groundskeeping backgrounds may start their own businesses after several years of experience.

Employment

Grounds maintenance workers held about 1.5 million jobs in 2004. Employment was distributed as follows:

Landscaping and groundskeeping workers 1,177,000

First-line supervisors/managers of landscaping, lawn service, and groundskeeping workers..........184,000

Tree trimmers and pruners 55,000

Pesticide handlers, sprayers, and applicators, vegetation 30,000

Grounds maintenance workers, all other 21,000

About one-third of the workers in grounds maintenance were employed in companies providing landscaping services to buildings and dwellings. Others worked for property management and real-estate development firms, lawn and garden equipment and supply stores, and amusement and recreation facilities, such as golf courses and racetracks. Some were employed by local governments, installing and maintaining landscaping for parks, schools, hospitals, and other public facilities.

Almost 1 out of every 4 grounds maintenance workers was self-employed, providing landscape maintenance directly to customers on a contract basis. About 1 of every 7 worked part time; about 8 percent were of school age.

Job Outlook

Those interested in grounds maintenance occupations should find plentiful job opportunities in the future. Demand for their services is growing, and because wages for beginners are low and the work is physically demanding, many employers have difficulty attracting enough workers to fill all openings, creating very good job opportunities. In addition, high turnover will generate a large number of job openings, including at the supervisory and managerial level.

More workers also will be needed to keep up with increasing demand by lawn care and landscaping companies. Employment of grounds maintenance workers is expected to grow faster than the average for all occupations through the year 2014. Expected growth in the construction of all types of buildings, from office buildings to shopping malls and residential housing, plus more highways and parks, will increase demand for grounds maintenance workers. In addition, the upkeep and renovation of existing landscaping and grounds are continuing sources of demand for grounds maintenance workers. Owners of many buildings and facilities recognize the importance of "curb appeal" in attracting business and maintaining the value of the property and are expected to use grounds maintenance services more extensively to maintain and upgrade their properties. Grounds maintenance workers working for state and local governments, however, may face budget cuts, which may affect hiring.

Homeowners are a growing source of demand for grounds maintenance workers. Many two-income households lack the time to take care of their lawn, so they are increasingly hiring people to maintain it for them. They also know that a nice yard will increase the property's value. In addition, there is a growing interest by homeowners in their backyards, as well as a desire to make the yards more attractive for outdoor entertaining. With many newer homes having more and bigger windows overlooking the yard, it becomes more important to maintain and beautify the grounds. Also, as the population ages, more elderly homeowners will require lawn care services to help maintain their yards.

Job opportunities for tree trimmers and pruners should also increase as utility companies step up pruning of trees around electric lines to prevent power outages. Additionally, tree trimmers and pruners will be needed to help combat infestations caused by new species of insects from other countries. Ash trees in Michigan, for example, have been especially hurt by a pest from China.

Job opportunities for nonseasonal work are more numerous in regions with temperate climates, where landscaping and lawn services are required all year. However, opportunities may vary with local economic conditions.

Earnings

Median hourly earnings in May 2004 of grounds maintenance workers were as follows:

First-line supervisors/managers of landscaping, lawn service, and groundskeeping workers $16.99

Tree trimmers and pruners 12.57

Pesticide handlers, sprayers, and applicators, vegetation 12.30

Landscaping and groundskeeping workers..................9.82

Grounds maintenance workers, all other 9.57

Median hourly earnings in the industries employing the largest numbers of landscaping and groundskeeping workers in May 2004 were as follows:

Elementary and secondary schools $13.25

Local government 11.25

Services to buildings and dwellings 9.78

Other amusement and recreation industries................9.14

Employment services 8.64

Related Occupations

Grounds maintenance workers perform most of their work outdoors and have some knowledge of plants and soils. Others whose jobs may require that they work outdoors are agricultural workers; farmers, ranchers, and agricultural managers; forest, conservation, and logging workers; landscape architects; and biological scientists.

Sources of Additional Information

For career and certification information on tree trimmers and pruners, contact

▸ Tree Care Industry Association, 3 Perimeter Rd., Unit I, Manchester, NH 03103-3341. Internet: http://www.TreeCareIndustry.org

▸ International Society of Arboriculture, P.O. Box 3129, Champaign, IL 61826-3129.

For information on work as a landscaping and groundskeeping worker, contact either of the following organizations:

▸ Professional Landcare Network, 950 Herndon Parkway, Suite 450, Herndon, VA 20170-5528. Internet: http://www.landcarenetwork.org/

▸ Professional Grounds Management Association, 720 Light St., Baltimore, MD 21230-3850 Internet: http://www.pgms.org

For information on becoming a licensed pesticide applicator, contact your state's Department of Agriculture or Department of Environmental Protection or Conservation.

Heating, Air-Conditioning, and Refrigeration Mechanics and Installers

(O*NET 49-9021.01 and 49-9021.02)

Significant Points

■ Employment is projected to grow faster than average.

■ Job prospects are expected to be excellent, particularly for those with training from an accredited technical school or with formal apprenticeship training.

■ Obtaining certification through one of several organizations is increasingly recommended by employers and may increase advancement opportunities.

Nature of the Work

Heating and air-conditioning systems control the temperature, humidity, and the total air quality in residential, commercial, industrial, and other buildings. Refrigeration systems make it possible to store and transport food, medicine, and other perishable items. Heating, air-conditioning, and refrigeration mechanics and installers—also called technicians—install, maintain, and repair such systems. Because heating, ventilation, air-conditioning, and refrigeration systems often are referred to as HVACR systems, these workers also may be called HVACR technicians.

Heating, air-conditioning, and refrigeration systems consist of many mechanical, electrical, and electronic components, such as motors, compressors, pumps, fans, ducts, pipes, thermostats, and switches. In central forced-air heating systems, for example, a furnace heats air that is distributed throughout the building via a system of metal or fiberglass ducts. Technicians must be able to maintain, diagnose, and correct problems throughout the entire system. To do this, they adjust system controls to recommended settings and test the performance of the entire system, using special tools and test equipment.

Technicians often specialize in either installation or maintenance and repair, although they are trained to do both. They also may specialize in doing heating work or air-conditioning or refrigeration work. Some specialize in one type of equipment—for example, hydronics (water-based heating systems), solar panels, or commercial refrigeration. Technicians also try to sell service contracts to their clients. Service contracts provide for regular maintenance of the heating and cooling systems and they help to reduce the seasonal fluctuations of this type of work.

Technicians follow blueprints or other specifications to install oil, gas, electric, solid-fuel, and multiple-fuel heating systems and air-conditioning systems. After putting the equipment in place, they install fuel and water supply lines, air ducts and vents, pumps, and other components. They may connect electrical wiring and controls and check the unit for proper operation. To ensure the proper functioning of the system, furnace installers often use combustion test equipment, such as carbon dioxide testers, carbon monoxide testers, combustion analyzers, and oxygen testers.

After a furnace or air-conditioning unit has been installed, technicians often perform routine maintenance and repair work to keep the systems operating efficiently. They may adjust burners and blowers and check for leaks. If the system is not operating properly, they check the thermostat, burner nozzles, controls, or other parts to diagnose and then correct the problem.

During the summer, when the heating system is not being used, heating equipment technicians do maintenance work, such as replacing filters, ducts, and other parts of the system that may accumulate dust and impurities during the operating season. During the winter, air-conditioning mechanics inspect the systems and do required maintenance, such as overhauling compressors.

Refrigeration mechanics install, service, and repair industrial and commercial refrigerating systems and a variety of refrigeration equipment. They follow blueprints, design specifications, and manufacturers' instructions to install motors, compressors, condensing units, evaporators, piping, and other components. They connect this equipment to the ductwork, refrigerant lines, and electrical power source. After making the connections, they charge the system with refrigerant, check it for proper operation, and program control systems.

When air-conditioning and refrigeration technicians service equipment, they must use care to conserve, recover, and recycle chlorofluorocarbon (CFC), hydrochlorofluorocarbon (HCFC), hydrofluorocarbon (HFC), and other refrigerants used in air-conditioning and refrigeration systems. The release of these refrigerants can be harmful to the environment. Technicians conserve the refrigerant by making sure that there are no leaks in the system; they recover it by venting the refrigerant into proper cylinders; they recycle it for reuse with special filter-dryers; or they insure that the refrigerant is properly disposed.

Heating, air-conditioning, and refrigeration mechanics and installers are adept at using a variety of tools, including hammers, wrenches, metal snips, electric drills, pipe cutters and benders, measurement gauges, and acetylene torches, to work with refrigerant lines and air ducts. They use voltmeters, thermometers, pressure gauges, manometers, and other testing devices to check airflow, refrigerant pressure, electrical circuits, burners, and other components.

Other craftworkers sometimes install or repair cooling and heating systems. For example, on a large air-conditioning installation job, especially where workers are covered by union contracts, ductwork might be done by sheet metal workers and duct installers; electrical work by electricians; and installation of piping, condensers, and other components by pipelayers, plumbers, pipefitters, and steamfitters. Home appliance repairers usually service room air conditioners and household refrigerators.

Working Conditions

Heating, air-conditioning, and refrigeration mechanics and installers work in homes, retail establishments, hospitals, office buildings, and factories—anywhere there is climate-control equipment. They may be assigned to specific job sites at the beginning of each day or may be dispatched to a variety of locations if they are making service calls.

Technicians may work outside in cold or hot weather or in buildings that are uncomfortable because the air-conditioning or heating equipment is broken. In addition, technicians might have to work in awkward or cramped positions and sometimes are required to work in high places. Hazards include electrical shock, burns, muscle strains, and other injuries from handling heavy equipment. Appropriate safety equipment is necessary when handling refrigerants because contact can cause skin damage, frostbite, or blindness. Inhalation of refrigerants when working in confined spaces also is a possible hazard.

The majority of mechanics and installers work at least a 40-hour week. During peak seasons, they often work overtime or irregular hours. Maintenance workers, including those who provide maintenance services under contract, often work evening or weekend shifts and are on call. Most employers try to provide a full workweek year-round by scheduling both installation and maintenance work, and many manufacturers and contractors now provide or even require service contracts. In most shops that service both heating and air-conditioning equipment, employment is stable throughout the year.

Training, Other Qualifications, and Advancement

Because of the increasing sophistication of heating, air-conditioning, and refrigeration systems, employers prefer to hire those with technical school training or those who have completed an apprenticeship. Some mechanics and installers, however, still learn the trade informally on the job.

Many secondary and postsecondary technical and trade schools, junior and community colleges, and the U.S. Armed Forces offer 6-month to 2-year programs in heating, air-conditioning, and refrigeration. Students study theory, design, and equipment construction, as well as electronics. They also learn the basics of installation, maintenance, and repair. There are three accrediting agencies that have set academic standards for HVACR programs. These accrediting bodies are HVAC Excellence, the National Center for Construction Education and Research (NCCER), and the Partnership for Air Conditioning, Heating, and Refrigeration Accreditation (PHARA). After completing these programs, new technicians generally need between an additional 6 months and 2 years of field experience before they can be considered proficient.

Apprenticeship programs frequently are run by joint committees representing local chapters of the Air-Conditioning Contractors of America, the Mechanical Contractors Association of America, Plumbing-Heating-Cooling Contractors—National Association, and locals of the sheet metal workers' International Association or the United Association of Journeymen and Apprentices of the Plumbing and Pipefitting Industry of the United States and Canada. Other apprenticeship programs are sponsored by local chapters of the Associated Builders and Contractors and the National Association of Home Builders. Formal apprenticeship programs normally last 3 to 5 years and combine on-the-job training with classroom instruction. Classes include subjects such as the use and care of tools; safety practices; blueprint reading; and the theory and design of heating, ventilation, air-conditioning, and refrigeration systems. Applicants for these programs must have a high school diploma or equivalent. Math and reading skills are essential. After completing an apprenticeship program, technicians are considered skilled trades workers and capable of working alone. These programs are also a pathway to certification and, in some cases, college credits.

Those who acquire their skills on the job usually begin by assisting experienced technicians. They may begin by performing simple tasks such as carrying materials, insulating refrigerant lines, or cleaning furnaces. In time, they move on to more difficult tasks, such as cutting and soldering pipes and sheet metal and checking electrical and electronic circuits.

Courses in shop math, mechanical drawing, applied physics and chemistry, electronics, blueprint reading, and computer applications provide a good background for those interested in entering this occupation. Some knowledge of plumbing or electrical work also is helpful. A basic understanding of electronics is becoming more important because of the increasing use of this technology in equipment controls. Because technicians frequently deal directly with the public, they should be courteous and tactful, especially when dealing with an aggravated customer. They also should be in good physical condition because they sometimes have to lift and move heavy equipment.

All technicians who purchase or work with refrigerants must be certified in their proper handling. To become certified to purchase and handle refrigerants, technicians must pass a written examination specific to the type of work in which they specialize. The three possible areas of certification are Type I—servicing small appliances, Type II—high-pressure refrigerants, and Type III—low-pressure refrigerants. Exams are administered by organizations approved by the U.S. Environmental Protection Agency, such as trade schools, unions, contractor associations, or building groups.

Several organizations have begun to offer basic self-study, classroom, and Internet courses for individuals with limited experience. In addition to understanding how systems work, technicians also must learn about refrigerant products and the legislation and regulations that govern their use.

Throughout the learning process, job candidates may have to take a number of tests that measure their skills in the field. For those with less than 1 year of experience and taking classes, the industry has developed a series of exams to test basic competency in residential heating and cooling, light commercial heating and cooling, and commercial refrigeration. These are referred to as "entry-level" certification exams and are commonly conducted at both secondary and postsecondary technical and trade schools. For HVACR technicians who have at least one year of experience performing installations and 2 years of experience performing maintenance and repair, they can take a number of different tests to certify their competency in working with more specific types of equipment, such as oil-burning furnaces. The tests are offered through Refrigeration Service Engineers Society (RSES), HVAC Excellence, The Carbon Monoxide Safety Association (COSA), Air Conditioning and Refrigeration Safety Coalition, and North American Technician Excellence, Inc. (NATE), among others. Passing these tests and obtaining certification is increasingly recommended by employers and may increase advancement opportunities.

Advancement usually takes the form of higher wages. Some technicians, however, may advance to positions as supervisor or service manager. Others may move into areas such as sales and marketing. Still others may become building superintendents, cost estimators, or, with the necessary certification, teachers. Those with sufficient money and managerial skill can open their own contracting business.

Employment

Heating, air-conditioning, and refrigeration mechanics and installers held about 270,000 jobs in 2004; almost half worked for plumbing, heating, and air-conditioning contractors. The remainder was employed in a variety of industries throughout the country, reflecting a widespread dependence on climate-control systems. Some worked for fuel oil dealers, refrigeration and air-conditioning service and repair shops, schools, and stores that sell heating and air-conditioning systems. Local governments, the federal government, hospitals, office buildings, and other organizations that operate large air-conditioning, refrigeration, or heating systems employed others. About 15 percent of mechanics and installers were self-employed.

Job Outlook

Job prospects for heating, air-conditioning, and refrigeration mechanics and installers are expected to be excellent, particularly for those with training from an accredited technical school or with formal apprenticeship training and especially in the fastest-growing areas of the country. A growing number of retirements of highly skilled technicians is expected to generate many job openings. In addition, employment of heating, air-conditioning, and refrigeration mechanics and installers is projected to increase faster than the average for all occupations through the year 2014. As the population and stock of buildings grows, so does the demand for residential,

commercial, and industrial climate-control systems. The increased complexity of HVACR systems, increasing the possibility that equipment may malfunction, also will create opportunities for service technicians. Technicians who specialize in installation work may experience periods of unemployment when the level of new construction activity declines, but maintenance and repair work usually remains relatively stable. People and businesses depend on their climate-control systems and must keep them in good working order, regardless of economic conditions.

Concern for the environment has prompted the development of new energy-saving heating and air-conditioning systems. An emphasis on better energy management should lead to the replacement of older systems and the installation of newer, more efficient systems in existing homes and buildings. Also, demand for maintenance and service work should increase as businesses and homeowners strive to keep increasingly complex systems operating at peak efficiency. Regulations prohibiting the discharge and production of CFC and HCFC refrigerants should continue to result in the need to replace many existing air-conditioning systems or modify them to use new environmentally safe refrigerants. The pace of replacement in the commercial and industrial sectors will quicken if Congress or individual states cut the time needed to fully depreciate the cost of new HVACR systems, which is being considered.

A growing focus on improving indoor air quality, as well as the increasing use of refrigerated equipment by a growing number of stores and gasoline stations that sell food, also should contribute to the creation of more jobs for heating, air-conditioning, and refrigeration technicians.

Earnings

Median hourly earnings of heating, air-conditioning, and refrigeration mechanics and installers were $17.43 in May 2004. The middle 50 percent earned between $13.51 and $22.21 an hour. The lowest 10 percent earned less than $10.88, and the top 10 percent earned more than $27.11. Median hourly earnings in the industries employing the largest numbers of heating, air-conditioning, and refrigeration mechanics and installers in May 2004 were

Hardware and plumbing and heating equipment
and supplies merchant wholesalers $19.51

Direct selling establishments 17.81

Elementary and secondary schools 17.56

Commercial and industrial machinery and
equipment (except automotive and electronic)
repair and maintenance 17.52

Building equipment contractors..............................16.80

Apprentices usually begin at about 50 percent of the wage rate paid to experienced workers. As they gain experience and improve their skills, they receive periodic increases until they reach the wage rate of experienced workers.

Heating, air-conditioning, and refrigeration mechanics and installers enjoy a variety of employer-sponsored benefits. In addition to typical benefits such as health insurance and pension plans, some employers pay for work-related training and provide uniforms, company vans, and tools.

About 16 percent of heating, air-conditioning, and refrigeration mechanics and installers are members of a union. The unions to which the greatest numbers of mechanics and installers belong are the sheet metal workers International Association and the United Association of Journeymen and Apprentices of the Plumbing and Pipefitting Industry of the United States and Canada.

Related Occupations

Heating, air-conditioning, and refrigeration mechanics and installers work with sheet metal and piping and repair machinery such as electrical motors, compressors, and burners. Other workers who have similar skills include boilermakers; home appliance repairers; electricians; sheet metal workers; and pipelayers, plumbers, pipefitters, and steamfitters.

Sources of Additional Information

For more information about opportunities for training, certification, and employment in this trade, contact local vocational and technical schools; local heating, air-conditioning, and refrigeration contractors; a local of the unions or organizations previously mentioned; a local joint union-management apprenticeship committee; or the nearest office of the state employment service or apprenticeship agency.

For information on career opportunities, training, and technician certification, contact

▶ Air-Conditioning Contractors of America (ACCA), 2800 Shirlington Rd., Suite 300, Arlington, VA 22206. Internet: http://www.acca.org

▶ Refrigeration Service Engineers Society (RSES), 1666 Rand Rd., Des Plaines, IL 60016-3552. Internet: http://www.rses.org

▶ Plumbing-Heating-Cooling Contractors (PHCC), 180 S. Washington St., P.O. Box 6808, Falls Church, VA 22046. Internet: http://www.phccweb.org

▶ Sheet Metal and Air-Conditioning Contractors National Association, 4201 Lafayette Center Dr., Chantilly, VA 20151-1209. Internet: http://www.smacna.org

▶ HVAC Excellence, P.O. Box 491, Mt. Prospect, IL 60056. Internet: http://www.hvacexcellence.org

▶ North American Technician Excellence (NATE), 4100 North Fairfax Dr., Suite 210, Arlington, VA 22203. Internet: http://www.natex.org

▶ Air-Conditioning and Refrigeration Institute, 4100 North Fairfax Dr., Suite 200, Arlington, VA 22203. Internet: http://www.coolcareers.org or http://www.ari.org

▶ Carbon Monoxide Safety Association, P.O. Box 669, Eastlake, CO 80614. Internet: http://www.cosafety.org

▶ National Occupational Competency Testing Institute. Internet: http://www.nocti.org

▶ Associated Builders and Contractors, Workforce Development Department, 4250 North Fairfax Dr., 9th Floor, Arlington, VA 22203. Internet: http://www.trytools.org

▶ Home Builders Institute, National Association of Home Builders, 1201 15th St. NW, 6th Floor, Washington, DC 20005-2800. Internet: http://www.hbi.org

▶ Mechanical Contractors Association of America, 1385 Piccard Dr., Rockville, MD 20850-4329. Internet: http://www.mcaa.org

▶ National Center for Construction Education and Research, P.O. Box 141104, Gainesville, FL, 32601. Internet: http://www.nccer.org

Industrial Machinery Mechanics and Maintenance Workers

(O*NET 49-9041.00 and 49-9043.00)

Significant Points

■ Highly skilled mechanics usually learn their trade through a 4-year apprenticeship program, while lower-skilled maintenance workers receive short-term on-the-job training.

■ Employment is projected to grow more slowly than average, but applicants with broad skills in machine repair and maintenance should have favorable job prospects.

■ Unlike some manufacturing occupations, these workers usually are not affected by changes in production.

Nature of the Work

A wide range of employees is required to keep sophisticated industrial machinery running smoothly—from highly skilled industrial machinery mechanics to lower-skilled machinery maintenance workers who perform routine tasks. Their work is vital to the success of industrial facilities, not only because an idle machine will delay production, but also because a machine that is not properly repaired and maintained may damage the machine or the final product or injure an operator.

The most basic tasks in this process are performed by *machinery maintenance workers*. These employees are responsible for cleaning and lubricating machinery, performing basic diagnostic tests, checking performance, and testing damaged machine parts to determine whether major repairs are necessary. In carrying out these tasks, maintenance workers must follow machine specifications and adhere to maintenance schedules. Maintenance workers may perform minor repairs, but major repairs are generally left to machinery mechanics.

Industrial machinery mechanics, also called industrial machinery repairers or maintenance machinists, are highly skilled workers who maintain and repair machinery in a plant or factory. To do this effectively, they must be able to detect minor problems and correct them before they become major problems. Machinery mechanics use their understanding of the equipment, technical manuals, and careful observation to discover the cause. For example, after hearing a vibration from a machine, the mechanic must decide whether it is due to worn belts, weak motor bearings, or some other problem. Computerized diagnostic systems and vibration analysis techniques are aiding in determining the problem, but mechanics still need years of training and experience.

After diagnosing the problem, the industrial machinery mechanic disassembles the equipment to repair or replace the necessary parts. When repairing electronically controlled machinery, mechanics may work closely with electronic repairers or electricians who maintain the machine's electronic parts. (A description of electrical and electronic installers and repairers appears elsewhere in this book.)

Increasingly, mechanics need electronic and computer skills in order to repair sophisticated equipment on their own. Once a repair is made, mechanics perform tests to ensure that the machine is running smoothly.

Primary responsibilities of industrial machinery mechanics include repair, preventive maintenance, and installation of new machinery. For example, they adjust and calibrate automated manufacturing equipment, such as industrial robots. As plants retool and invest in new equipment, they increasingly rely on mechanics to properly situate and install the machinery. In many plants, this has traditionally been the job of millwrights, but mechanics are increasingly called upon to carry out this task.

Industrial machinery mechanics and machinery maintenance workers use a variety of tools to perform repairs and preventive maintenance. They may use a screwdriver and wrench to adjust a motor or use a hoist to lift a printing press off the ground. When replacements for broken or defective parts are not readily available, or when a machine must be quickly returned to production, mechanics may sketch a part to be fabricated by the plant's machine shop. Mechanics use catalogs to order replacement parts and often follow blueprints, technical manuals, and engineering specifications to maintain and fix equipment. By keeping complete and up-to-date records, mechanics try to anticipate trouble and service equipment before factory production is interrupted.

Working Conditions

In production facilities, these workers are subject to common shop injuries such as cuts, bruises, and strains. They also may work in awkward positions, including on top of ladders or in cramped conditions under large machinery, which exposes them to additional hazards. They often use protective equipment such as hardhats, safety glasses, steel-tipped shoes, hearing protectors, and belts.

Because factories and other facilities cannot afford to have industrial machinery out of service for long periods, mechanics may be called to the plant at night or on weekends for emergency repairs. Overtime is common among industrial machinery mechanics; about 30 percent work over 40 hours a week.

Training, Other Qualifications, and Advancement

Machinery maintenance workers typically receive short-term on-the-job training in order to perform routine tasks, such as setting up, cleaning, lubricating, and starting machinery. This training may be offered by experienced workers, professional trainers, or product representatives.

Industrial machinery mechanics, on the other hand, often learn their trade through 4-year apprenticeship programs that combine classroom instruction with on-the-job-training. These programs usually are sponsored by a local trade union. Other mechanics start as helpers and learn the skills of the trade informally or by taking courses offered by machinery manufacturers and community colleges.

Mechanics learn from experienced repairers how to operate, disassemble, repair, and assemble machinery. Classroom instruction focuses on subjects such as shop mathematics, blueprint reading, welding, electronics, and computer training.

Employers prefer to hire those who have completed high school or technical school and have taken courses in mechanical drawing, mathematics, blueprint reading, computers, and electronics. Mechanical aptitude and manual dexterity are important characteristics for workers in this trade. Good reading comprehension is also necessary to understand the technical manuals of a wide range of machines. And, in general, good physical conditioning and agility are necessary because repairers sometimes have to lift heavy objects or climb to reach equipment.

Opportunities for advancement vary by specialty. Machinery maintenance workers may gain additional skills to make more complex repairs to machinery or work as supervisors. Industrial machinery mechanics also may advance either by working with more complicated equipment or by becoming supervisors. The most highly skilled repairers can be promoted to master mechanic or can become millwrights.

Employment

Industrial machinery mechanics and maintenance workers held about 306,000 jobs in 2004. Of these, 220,000 were held by the more highly skilled industrial machinery mechanics, while machinery maintenance workers accounted for 86,000 jobs. Two out of three workers were employed in the manufacturing sector, in industries such as food processing, textile mills, chemicals, fabricated metal products, motor vehicles, and primary metals. Others worked for government agencies, public utilities, mining companies, and other establishments in which industrial machinery is used.

Job Outlook

Employment of industrial machinery mechanics and maintenance workers is projected to grow more slowly than the average for all occupations through 2014. Nevertheless, applicants with broad skills in machine repair and maintenance should have favorable job prospects. Many mechanics are expected to retire in coming years, and employers have reported difficulty in recruiting young workers with the necessary skills to be industrial machinery mechanics. Most job openings will stem from the need to replace workers who transfer to other occupations or who retire or leave the labor force for other reasons.

As more firms introduce automated production equipment, these workers will be needed to ensure that these machines are properly maintained and consistently in operation. However, many new machines are capable of self-diagnosis, increasing their reliability and somewhat reducing the need for repairers.

Industrial machinery mechanics and maintenance workers are not usually affected by changes in production. During slack periods, when some plant workers are laid off, mechanics often are retained to do major overhaul jobs and to keep expensive machinery in working order. Although these workers may face layoffs or a reduced workweek when economic conditions are particularly severe, they usually are less affected than other workers because machines have to be maintained regardless of production level.

Earnings

Median hourly earnings of industrial machinery mechanics were $18.78 in May 2004. The middle 50 percent earned between $15.09 and $22.95. The lowest 10 percent earned less than $12.14, and the highest 10 percent earned more than $27.59.

Machinery maintenance workers earned less than the higher-skilled industrial machinery mechanics. Median hourly earnings of machinery maintenance workers were $15.79 in May 2004. The middle 50 percent earned between $12.21 and $20.18. The lowest 10 percent earned less than $9.60, and the highest 10 percent earned more than $24.59.

Earnings vary by industry and geographic region. Median hourly earnings in the industries employing the largest numbers of industrial machinery mechanics in May 2004 were

Electric power generation, transmission, and distribution	$25.78
Motor vehicle parts manufacturing	21.79
Plastics product manufacturing	18.04
Machinery, equipment, and supplies merchant wholesalers	17.74
Commercial and industrial machinery and equipment (except automotive and electronic) repair and maintenance	16.93

About 25 percent of industrial machinery mechanics and maintenance workers are union members. Labor unions that represent these workers include the United Steelworkers of America; the United Auto Workers; the International Association of Machinists and Aerospace Workers; the United Brotherhood of Carpenters and Joiners of America; and the International Union of Electronic, Electrical, Salaried, Machine, and Furniture Workers-Communications Workers of America.

Related Occupations

Other occupations that involve repairing and maintaining machinery include aircraft and avionics equipment mechanics and service technicians; automotive service technicians and mechanics; diesel service technicians and mechanics; elevator installers and repairers; heating, air-conditioning, and refrigeration mechanics and installers; heavy vehicle and mobile equipment service technicians and mechanics; machinists; maintenance and repair workers, general; millwrights; and small engine mechanics.

Sources of Additional Information

Information about employment and apprenticeship opportunities may be obtained from local employers, from local offices of the state employment service, or from

▸ United Brotherhood of Carpenters and Joiners of America, 6801 Placid St., Las Vegas, NV 89119. Internet: http://www.carpenters.org

▸ National Tooling and Machining Association, 9300 Livingston Rd., Fort Washington, MD 20744. Internet: http://www.ntma.org

Inspectors, Testers, Sorters, Samplers, and Weighers

(O*NET 51-9061.01, 51-9061.02, 51-9061.03, 51-9061.04, and 51-9061.05)

Significant Points

■ Two in three are employed in manufacturing establishments.

■ While a high school diploma is sufficient for basic testing of products, complex precision-inspecting positions are filled by experienced assemblers, machine operators, or mechanics who already have a thorough knowledge of the products and production processes.

■ Employment is expected to decline, reflecting the growth of automated inspection and the redistribution of quality-control responsibilities from inspectors to other production workers.

Nature of the Work

Inspectors, testers, sorters, samplers, and weighers ensure that your food will not make you sick, that your car will run properly, and that your pants will not split the first time you wear them. These workers monitor or audit quality standards for virtually all manufactured products, including foods, textiles, clothing, glassware, motor vehicles, electronic components, computers, and structural steel. As product quality becomes increasingly important to the success of many manufacturing firms, daily duties of inspectors have changed. In some cases, the job titles of these workers also have been changed to *quality-control inspector* or a similar name, reflecting the growing importance of quality.

Regardless of title, all inspectors, testers, sorters, samplers, and weighers work to guarantee the quality of the goods their firms produce. Job duties, even within one company, vary by the type of products produced or the stage of production. Specific job duties also vary across the wide range of industries in which these workers are found. For example, materials inspectors may check products by sight, sound, feel, smell, or even taste to locate imperfections such as cuts, scratches, bubbles, missing pieces, misweaves, or crooked seams. These workers also may verify dimensions, color, weight, texture, strength, or other physical characteristics of objects. Mechanical inspectors generally verify that parts fit, move correctly, and are properly lubricated; check the pressure of gases and the level of liquids; test the flow of electricity; and do a test run to check for proper operation. Some jobs involve only a quick visual inspection; others require a longer, detailed one. Sorters may separate goods according to length, size, fabric type, or color, while samplers test or inspect a sample taken from a batch or production run for malfunctions or defects. Weighers weigh quantities of materials for use in production.

Inspectors, testers, sorters, samplers, and weighers are involved at every stage of the production process. Some inspectors examine materials received from a supplier before sending them to the production line. Others inspect components and assemblies or perform a final check on the finished product. Depending on their skill level, inspectors also may set up and test equipment, calibrate precision instruments, repair defective products, or record data.

Inspectors, testers, sorters, samplers, and weighers rely on a number of tools to perform their jobs. Although some still use handheld measurement devises such as micrometers, calipers, and alignment gauges, it is more common for them to operate electronic inspection equipment, such as coordinate measuring machines (CMMs). These machines use sensitive probes to measure a part's dimensional accuracy and allow the inspector to analyze the results using computer software. Inspectors testing electrical devices may use voltmeters, ammeters, and oscilloscopes to test insulation, current flow, and resistance. All the tools that inspectors use are maintained by calibration technicians, who ensure that they work properly and generate accurate readings.

Inspectors mark, tag, or note problems. They may reject defective items outright, send them for repair or correction, or fix minor problems themselves. If the product is acceptable, inspectors may screw a nameplate onto it, tag it, stamp it with a serial number, or certify it in some other way.

Inspectors, testers, sorters, samplers, and weighers record the results of their inspections, compute the percentage of defects and other statistical measures, and prepare inspection and test reports. Some electronic inspection equipment automatically provides test reports containing these inspection results. When defects are found, inspectors notify supervisors and help to analyze and correct the production problems.

The emphasis on finding the root cause of defects is a basic tenet of modern management and production philosophies. Industrial production managers work closely with the inspectors to reduce defects and improve quality. In the past, a certain level of defects was considered acceptable because variations would always occur. Current philosophies emphasize constant quality improvement through analysis and correction of the causes of defects. The nature of inspectors' work has changed from merely checking for defects to determining the cause of those defects.

Increased emphasis on quality control in manufacturing means that inspection is more fully integrated into the production process than in the past. Now, companies have integrated teams of inspection and production workers to jointly review and improve product quality. In addition, many companies now use self-monitoring production machines to ensure that the output is produced within quality standards. Self-monitoring machines can alert inspectors to production problems and automatically repair defects in some cases.

Some firms have completely automated inspection with the help of advanced vision inspection systems, using machinery installed at one or several points in the production process. Inspectors in these firms monitor the equipment, review output, and perform random product checks.

Testers repeatedly test existing products or prototypes under real-world conditions. For example, they may purposely abuse a machine by not changing its oil to see when failure occurs. They may devise automated machines to repeat a basic task thousands of times, such as opening and closing a car door. Through these tests, companies determine how long a product will last, what parts will break down first, and how to improve durability.

Working Conditions

Working conditions vary by industry and establishment size. As a result, some inspectors examine similar products for an entire shift, whereas others examine a variety of items. In manufacturing, it is common for most inspectors to remain at one workstation. Inspectors in some industries may be on their feet all day and may have to lift heavy objects, whereas in other industries, they sit during most of their shift and do little strenuous work. Workers in heavy manufacturing plants may be exposed to the noise and grime of machinery; in other plants, inspectors work in clean, air-conditioned environments suitable for carrying out controlled tests. Other inspectors rarely see the products they are inspecting and instead do the majority of their work examining electronic readouts in front of a computer.

Some inspectors work evenings, nights, or weekends. Shift assignments generally are made on the basis of seniority. Overtime may be required to meet production goals.

Training, Other Qualifications, and Advancement

Training requirements vary, based on the responsibilities of the inspector, tester, sorter, sampler, or weigher. For workers who perform simple "pass/fail" tests of products, a high school diploma generally is sufficient together with basic in-house training. Training for new inspectors may cover the use of special meters, gauges, computers, and other instruments; quality-control techniques; blueprint reading; safety; and reporting requirements. There are some postsecondary training programs in testing, but many employers prefer to train inspectors on the job.

Complex precision-inspecting positions are filled by experienced assemblers, machine operators, or mechanics who already have a thorough knowledge of the products and production processes. To advance to these positions, experienced workers may need training in statistical process control, new automation, or the company's quality assurance policies. As automated inspection equipment and electronic recording of results is common, computer skills are also important.

In general, inspectors, testers, sorters, samplers, and weighers need mechanical aptitude, math and communication skills, and good hand-eye coordination and vision. Advancement for these workers frequently takes the form of higher pay. They also may advance to inspector of more complex products, supervisor, or related positions such as purchaser of materials and equipment.

Employment

Inspectors, testers, sorters, samplers, and weighers held about 508,000 jobs in 2004. About 2 in 3 worked in manufacturing establishments that produced such products as motor vehicle parts, plastics products, semiconductor and other electronic components, and aerospace products and parts. Inspectors, testers, sorters, samplers, and weighers also were found in employment services; architectural, engineering, and related services; wholesale trade; and government agencies.

Job Outlook

Like that of many other occupations concentrated in manufacturing industries, employment of inspectors, testers, sorters, samplers, and weighers is expected to decline through the year 2014. The decline stems primarily from the growing use of automated inspection and the redistribution of some quality-control responsibilities from inspectors to production workers. Although numerous job openings will arise due to turnover in this large occupation, many of these jobs will be open only to experienced workers with advanced skills.

Employment of inspectors, testers, sorters, samplers, and weighers will be positively affected by the continuing focus on quality in American industry. The emphasis on improving quality and productivity has led manufacturers to invest in automated inspection equipment and to take a more systematic approach to quality inspection. Continued improvements in technologies, such as spectrophotometers and computer-assisted visual inspection systems, allow firms to effectively automate inspection tasks, increasing worker productivity and reducing the demand for inspectors. Inspectors will continue to operate these automated machines and monitor the defects they detect. Thus, while the increased emphasis on quality has increased the importance of inspection, the increased automation of inspection has limited the demand for inspectors.

Apart from automation, firms are integrating quality control into the production process. Many inspection duties are being redistributed from specialized inspectors to fabrication and assembly workers who monitor quality at every stage of the production process. In addition, the growing implementation of statistical process control is resulting in "smarter" inspection. Using this system, firms survey the sources and incidence of defects so that they can better focus their efforts on reducing production of defective products.

In some industries, however, automation is not a feasible alternative to manual inspection. Where key inspection elements are oriented toward size, such as length, width, or thickness, automation will become more important in the future. But where taste, smell, texture, appearance, fabric complexity, or product performance is important, inspection will continue to be done by workers. Employment of inspectors, testers, sorters, samplers, and weighers is expected to increase in the rapidly growing employment services industry as more manufacturers and industrial firms hire temporary inspectors to increase the flexibility of their staffing strategies.

Earnings

Median hourly earnings of inspectors, testers, sorters, samplers, and weighers were $13.66 in May 2004. The middle 50 percent earned between $10.43 and $18.23 an hour. The lowest 10 percent earned less than $8.30 an hour, and the highest 10 percent earned more than $24.45 an hour. Median hourly earnings in the industries employing the largest numbers of inspectors, testers, sorters, samplers, and weighers in May 2004 were

Motor vehicle parts manufacturing	$16.54
Architectural, engineering, and related services	15.59
Semiconductor and other electronic component manufacturing	12.94
Plastics product manufacturing	12.40
Employment services	10.08

Related Occupations

Other workers who conduct inspections include agricultural inspectors, construction and building inspectors, fire inspectors and investigators, occupational health and safety specialists and technicians, and transportation inspectors.

Sources of Additional Information

For general information about inspection and testing, contact

▸ American Society for Quality, 600 North Plankinton Ave., Milwaukee, WI 53203. Internet: http://www.asq.org

Interviewers

(O*NET 43-4061.01, 43-4061.02, 43-4111.00, and 43-4131.00)

Significant Points

■ A high school diploma or its equivalent is the most common educational requirement.

■ The number of interviewers, except eligibility and loan, is projected to grow faster than average; however, the number of loan interviewers and clerks and eligibility interviewers for government programs is projected to decline.

Nature of the Work

Interviewers obtain information from individuals and business representatives who are opening bank accounts, trying to obtain loans, seeking admission to medical facilities, participating in consumer surveys, applying to receive aid from government programs, or providing data for various other purposes. By mail, by telephone, or in person, these workers solicit and verify information, create files, and perform a number of other related tasks.

The specific duties and job titles of *interviewers, except eligibility and loan*, depend upon the type of employer. In doctors' offices and other health care facilities, for example, *interviewing clerks* also are known as *admitting interviewers* or *patient representatives*. These workers obtain all preliminary information required for a patient's record or for his or her admission to a hospital, such as the patient's name, address, age, medical history, present medications, previous hospitalizations, religion, persons to notify in case of emergency, attending physician, and party responsible for payment. In some cases, interviewing clerks may be required to verify that an individual is eligible for health benefits or to work out financing options for those who might need them.

Other duties of interviewers in health care include assigning patients to rooms and summoning escorts to take patients to their rooms; sometimes, interviewers may escort patients themselves. Using the facility's computer system, interviewers schedule laboratory work, X rays, and surgeries; prepare admission and discharge records; and route these medical records to appropriate departments. They also may bill patients, receive payments, and answer the telephone. In an outpatient or office setting, interviewers schedule appointments, keep track of cancellations, and provide general information about care. In addition, the role of the admissions staff, particularly in hospitals, is expanding to include a wide range of patient services, from assisting patients with financial and medical questions to helping family members find hotel rooms.

Interviewing clerks who conduct market research surveys and polls for research firms have somewhat different responsibilities. These interviewers ask a series of prepared questions, record the responses, and forward the results to management. They may ask individuals questions about their occupation and earnings, political preferences, buying habits, satisfaction with certain goods or services sold to them, or other aspects of their lives. Although most interviews are conducted over the telephone, some are conducted in focus groups or by randomly polling people in a public place. More recently, the Internet is being used to elicit people's opinions. Almost all interviewers use computers or similar devices to enter the responses to questions.

Eligibility interviewers, government programs, determine the eligibility of individuals applying to receive government assistance, such as welfare, unemployment benefits, Social Security benefits, and public housing. These interviewers gather the relevant personal and financial information on an applicant and, on the basis of the rules and regulations of the particular government program, grant, modify, deny, or terminate an individual's eligibility for the program in question. They also help to detect fraud committed by persons who try to obtain benefits that they are not eligible to receive.

Loan interviewers and clerks review individuals' credit history and obtain the information needed to determine the creditworthiness of applicants for loans and credit cards. These workers spend much of their day on the telephone, obtaining information from credit bureaus, employers, banks, credit institutions, and other sources to determine an applicant's credit history and ability to pay back a loan or charge.

Loan clerks, also called *loan processing clerks*, *loan closers*, or *loan service clerks*, assemble documents pertaining to a loan, process the paperwork associated with the loan, and ensure that all information is complete and verified. Mortgage loans are the primary type of loan handled by loan clerks, who also may have to order appraisals of the property, set up escrow accounts, and secure any additional information required to transfer the property.

The specific duties of loan clerks vary by specialty. Loan closers, for example, complete the loan process by gathering the proper documents for signature at the closing, including deeds of trust, property insurance papers, and title commitments. They set the time and place for the closing, make sure that all parties are present, and ensure that all conditions for settlement have been met. After the settlement, the loan closer records all of the documents involved and submits the final package to the owner of the loan. Loan service clerks maintain the payment records on a loan once it is issued. These clerical workers process the paperwork for payment of fees to insurance companies and tax authorities and also may record changes in clients' addresses and ownership of a loan. When necessary, they answer calls from customers with routine inquiries as well.

Loan interviewers have duties that are similar to those of loan clerks. They interview potential borrowers; help them fill out applications for loans; investigate the applicant's background and references; verify the information on the application; and forward any findings, reports, or documents to the company's appraisal department. Finally, interviewers inform the applicant as to whether the loan has been accepted or denied.

Working Conditions

Working conditions vary for different types of interviewers, but most of these workers work in areas that are clean, well lit, and relatively quiet. Most of these workers work a standard 35 to 40 hour week, but evening and weekend work may be required in some establishments. Some interviewers may conduct surveys on the street or in shopping malls, or they may even go door to door.

Training, Other Qualifications, and Advancement

Most employers prefer applicants with a high school diploma or its equivalent or a mix of education and related experience. Because interviewers deal with the public, they must have a pleasant personality, clear speaking voice, and professional appearance. Familiarity with computers and strong interpersonal skills are very important. Fluency in a foreign language also can be beneficial.

New employees are generally trained on the job, working under the close supervision of more experienced employees, although some firms offer formal training. Some loan interviewers also take courses in credit offered by banking and credit associations, public and private vocational schools, and colleges and universities.

Experienced interviewers may advance to positions with added responsibilities or supervisory duties. Many organizations elect to fill open positions by promoting qualified individuals from within the company. Interviewers who obtain additional skills or training will have the best opportunities. For certain managerial positions, a college degree may be required.

Employment

Interviewers held about 515,000 jobs in 2004. Approximately 199,000 were interviewers, except eligibility and loan; 218,000 were loan interviewers and clerks; and 98,000 were eligibility interviewers, government programs. About 2 out of every 5 interviewers, except eligibility and loan, worked in health care and social assistance industries, while most loan interviewers and clerks worked in financial institutions. Almost all eligibility interviewers, government programs, worked in state and local government. Around 1 out of every 4 interviewers, except eligibility and loan, worked part time.

Job Outlook

Employment of interviewers is expected to grow more slowly than the average for all occupations through 2014. However, the projected change in employment varies by specialty. Most job openings should arise from the need to replace the numerous interviewers who leave the occupation or the labor force each year. Prospects for filling these openings will be best for applicants with a broad range of job skills, such as good customer service, math, and telephone skills. In addition to openings for full-time jobs, opportunities also should be available for part-time and temporary jobs.

The number of interviewers, except eligibility and loan, is projected to grow faster than average, reflecting growth in the health care and social assistance sector. This sector will hire more admissions interviewers as health care facilities consolidate staff and expand the role of the admissions staff and as an aging and growing population requires more visits to health care practitioners. In addition, an increasing use of market research will create more jobs requiring interviewers to collect data. In the future, though, more market research is expected to be conducted over the Internet, thus reducing the need for telephone interviewers to make individual calls.

The number of loan interviewers and clerks is projected to decline due to advances in technology that are making these workers more productive. Despite a projected increase in the number of applications for loans, automation will increase productivity so that fewer workers will be required to process, check, and authorize applications than in the past. The effects of automation on employment will be moderated, however, by the many interpersonal aspects of the job. Mortgage loans, for example, require loan processors to personally verify financial data on the application, and loan closers are needed to assemble documents and prepare them for settlement. Employment, however, also will be adversely affected by changes in the financial services industry. For example, significant consolidation has occurred among mortgage loan servicing companies. As a result, fewer mortgage banking companies are involved in servicing loans, making the function more efficient and reducing the need for loan service clerks.

The job outlook for loan interviewers and clerks is sensitive to overall economic activity. A downturn in the economy or a rise in interest rates usually leads to a decline in the demand for loans, particularly mortgage loans, and can result in layoffs. Even in slow economic times, however, job openings will arise from the need to replace workers who leave the occupation for various reasons.

Like that of loan interviewers and clerks, employment of eligibility interviewers for government programs also is projected to decline due to advances in technology and the transformation of government aid programs over the last decade. Automation should have a significant effect on these workers because, as with credit and loan ratings, eligibility for government aid programs can be determined instantaneously by entering information into a computer. The job outlook for eligibility interviewers, however, also is sensitive to overall economic activity; a severe slowdown in the economy will cause more people to apply for government aid programs, increasing demand for eligibility interviewers.

Earnings

Median hourly earnings of eligibility interviewers, government programs, in May 2004 were $15.92. The middle 50 percent earned between $13.04 and $19.32. The lowest 10 percent earned less than $11.19, and the highest 10 percent earned more than $21.83. Median hourly earnings of eligibility interviewers, government programs, was $15.67 in state government and $16.43 in local government in May 2004.

Median hourly earnings of loan interviewers and clerks in May 2004 were $13.94. The middle 50 percent earned between $11.45 and $17.26. The lowest 10 percent earned less than $9.48, and the highest 10 percent earned more than $21.20. Median hourly earnings of loan interviewers and clerks in depository credit intermediation was $13.13 in May 2004, while median hourly earnings in nondepository credit intermediation was $14.48.

Median hourly earnings of interviewers, except eligibility and loan, in May 2004 were $11.38. The middle 50 percent earned between $9.19 and $13.93. The lowest 10 percent earned less than $7.57, and the highest 10 percent earned more than $16.98. Median hourly earnings in the industries employing the largest number of interviewers, except eligibility and loan, in May 2004 were as follows:

State government	$16.78
Colleges, universities, and professional schools	13.55
General medical and surgical hospitals	11.94
Scientific research and development services	10.71
Other professional, scientific, and technical Services	8.89

Related Occupations

Interviewers obtain information from individuals. Other workers who perform similar duties include procurement clerks, customer service representatives, and bill and account collectors.

Sources of Additional Information

State employment service offices can provide information about employment opportunities for interviewers.

For specific information on a career as a loan processor or loan closer, contact

▸ Mortgage Bankers Association of America, 1919 Pennsylvania Ave. NW, Washington, DC 20006. Internet: http://www.mbaa.org

Jewelers and Precious Stone and Metal Workers

(O*NET 51-9071.01, 51-9071.02, 51-9071.03, 51-9071.04, 51-9071.05, and 51-9071.06)

Significant Points

■ About 40 percent of all jewelers are self-employed.

■ Jewelers usually learn their trade in vocational or technical schools, through distance-learning centers, or on the job.

■ Prospects for new jewelers should be excellent; many employers have difficulty finding and retaining workers with the right skills to replace those who retire or who leave the occupation for other reasons.

Nature of the Work

Jewelers and precious stone and metal workers use a variety of common and specialized hand tools and equipment to design and manufacture new pieces of jewelry; cut, set, and polish gemstones; repair or adjust rings, necklaces, bracelets, earrings, and other jewelry; and appraise jewelry, precious metals, and gems. Jewelers usually specialize in one or more of these areas and may work for large jewelry manufacturing firms, for small retail jewelry shops, or as owners of their own businesses. Regardless of the type of work done or the work setting, jewelers require a high degree of skill, precision, and attention to detail.

Some jewelers design or make their own jewelry. Following their own designs or those created by designers or customers, they begin by shaping the metal or by carving wax to make a model for casting the metal. The individual parts then are soldered together, and the jeweler may mount a diamond or other gem or may engrave a design into the metal. Others do finishing work, such as setting stones, polishing, or engraving. Typical repair work includes enlarging or reducing ring sizes, resetting stones, and replacing broken clasps and mountings.

In larger manufacturing businesses, jewelers usually specialize in a single operation. *Mold and model makers* create models or tools for the jewelry that is to be produced. *Assemblers* solder or fuse jewelry and their parts; they also may set stones. *Engravers* etch designs into the metal with specialized tools, and *polishers* bring a finished luster to the final product.

Jewelers typically do the handiwork required to produce a piece of jewelry, while *gemologists* and laboratory graders analyze, describe, and certify the quality and characteristics of gemstones. Gemologists may work in gemological laboratories or as quality control experts for retailers, importers, or manufacturers. After using microscopes, computerized tools, and other grading instruments to examine gemstones or finished pieces of jewelry, they write reports certifying that the items are of a particular quality. Many jewelers also study gemology in order to become familiar with the physical properties of the gemstones with which they work.

Jewelry *appraisers* carefully examine jewelry to determine its value, after which they write appraisal documents. They determine the value of a piece by researching the jewelry market, using reference books, auction catalogs, price lists, and the Internet. They may work for jewelry stores, appraisal firms, auction houses, pawnbrokers, or insurance companies. Many gemologists also become appraisers.

In small retail stores or repair shops, jewelers and appraisers may be involved in all aspects of the work. Those who own or manage stores or shops also hire and train employees; order, market, and sell merchandise; and perform other managerial duties.

New technology is helping to produce jewelry of higher quality at a reduced cost and in a shorter amount of time. For example, lasers are often used for cutting and improving the quality of stones, for applying intricate engraving or design work, and for inscribing personal messages or identification on jewelry. Jewelers also use lasers to weld metals together in milliseconds with no seams or blemishes, improving the quality and appearance of jewelry.

Some manufacturing firms use computer-aided design and manufacturing (CAD/CAM) to facilitate product design and automate some steps in the moldmaking and modelmaking process. CAD allows jewelers to create a virtual-reality model of a piece of jewelry. Using CAD, jewelers can modify the design, change the stone, or try a different setting and see the changes on a computer screen before cutting a stone or performing other costly steps. Once they are satisfied with the model, CAM produces it in a waxlike or other material.

After the mold of the model is made, it is easier for manufacturing firms to produce numerous copies of a given piece of jewelry, which are then distributed to retail establishments across the country. Similar techniques may be used in the retail setting, allowing individual customers to review their jewelry designs with the jeweler and make modifications before committing themselves to the expense of a customized piece of jewelry.

Working Conditions

A jeweler's work involves a great deal of concentration and attention to detail. Working on precious stones and metals while trying to satisfy customers' and employers' demands for speed and quality can cause fatigue or stress. However, the use of more ergonomically correct jewelers' benches has eliminated most of the strain and discomfort caused by spending long periods bending over a workbench in one position.

Lasers require both careful handling to avoid injury and steady hands to direct precision tasks. In larger manufacturing plants and some smaller repair shops, chemicals, sharp or pointed tools, and jewelers' torches pose safety threats and may cause injury if proper care is not taken. Most dangerous chemicals, however, have been replaced with synthetic, less toxic products to meet safety requirements.

In repair shops, jewelers usually work alone with little supervision. In retail stores, they may talk with customers about repairs, perform custom design work, and even do some selling. Because many of their materials are valuable, jewelers must observe strict security procedures, including working behind locked doors that are opened only by a buzzer, working on the other side of barred windows, making use of burglar alarms, and, in larger jewelry establishments, working in the presence of armed guards.

Training, Other Qualifications, and Advancement

Jewelers usually learn their trade in vocational or technical schools, through distance-learning centers, or on the job. Colleges and art and design schools offer programs that can lead to the degree of bachelor of fine arts or master of fine arts in jewelry design. Formal training in the basic skills of the trade enhances one's employment and advancement opportunities. Many employers prefer jewelers with design, repair, and sales skills.

For those interested in working in a jewelry store or repair shop, vocational and technical training or courses offered by public and private colleges are the best sources of training. In these programs, which can vary in length from 6 months to 1 year, students learn the use and care of jewelers' tools and machines and basic jewelrymaking and jewelry-repairing skills, such as designing, casting, and setting and polishing stones. Technical school courses also cover topics such as blueprint reading, math, and shop theory. To enter some technical school programs and most college programs, a high school diploma or its equivalent is required. However, some schools specializing in jewelry training do not require graduation from high school. Computer-aided design is being used increasingly in the jewelry field, and students—especially those interested in design and manufacturing—may wish to obtain training in CAD; however, most employers will provide such training.

Various institutes offer courses and programs in gemology. Programs cover a wide range of topics, including the identification and grading of diamonds and gemstones.

Most employers feel that vocational school and technical school graduates need up to a year of additional supervised on-the-job training or apprenticeship in order to refine their repair skills and learn more about the operation of the store or shop. In addition, some employers encourage workers to improve their skills by enrolling in short-term technical school courses such as fabricating, jewelry design, jewelry manufacturing, wax carving, and gemology. Employers may pay all or part of the cost of this additional training.

In jewelry manufacturing plants, workers traditionally develop their skills through informal apprenticeships and on-the-job training. The apprenticeship or training period lasts up to 1 year, depending on the difficulty of the specialty. Training usually focuses on casting, setting stones, making models, or engraving. In recent years, a growing number of technical schools have begun to offer training designed for jewelers working in manufacturing. Employers in manufacturing may prefer graduates of these programs because they are familiar with the production process, requiring less on-the-job training.

The precise and delicate nature of jewelry work requires finger and hand dexterity, good hand-eye coordination, patience, and concentration. Artistic ability and fashion consciousness are major assets because jewelry must be stylish and attractive. Those who work in jewelry stores have frequent contact with customers and should be neat, personable, and knowledgeable about the merchandise. In addition, employers require workers of good character because jewelers work with valuable materials.

Advancement opportunities are limited and depend greatly on an individual's skill and initiative. In manufacturing, some jewelers advance to supervisory jobs, such as master jeweler or head jeweler, but for most, advancement takes the form of higher pay for doing the same job. Jewelers who work in jewelry stores or repair shops may become managers; some open their own businesses.

Those interested in starting their own business should first establish themselves and build a reputation for their work within the jewelry trade. Once they obtain sufficient credit from jewelry suppliers and wholesalers, they can acquire the necessary inventory. Also, because the jewelry business is highly competitive, jewelers who plan to open their own store should have sales experience, as well as knowledge of marketing and business management. Courses in these areas often are available from technical schools and community colleges.

Employment

Jewelers and precious stone and metal workers held about 42,000 jobs in 2004. About 40 percent of these workers were self-employed; many operated their own store or repair shop, and some specialized in designing and creating custom jewelry.

About 1 out of 5 jobs for jewelers and precious stone and metal workers were in other miscellaneous manufacturing, which includes jewelry and silverware manufacturing. Another 3 out of 10 jobs were in retail trade, primarily in jewelry, luggage, and leather goods

stores. A small number of jobs were with merchant wholesalers of miscellaneous durable goods and in repair shops providing repair and maintenance of personal and household goods. Although jewelry stores and repair shops were found in every city and in many small towns, most jobs were in larger metropolitan areas. In 2004, many jewelers employed in manufacturing worked in Rhode Island, New York, or California.

Job Outlook

Employment of jewelers and precious stone and metal workers is expected to decline slightly through 2014. Employment opportunities, however, should be excellent. New jewelers will be needed to replace those who retire or who leave the occupation for other reasons. When master jewelers retire, they take with them years of experience that require substantial time and financial resources to replace. Many employers have difficulty finding and retaining jewelers with the right skills and the necessary knowledge. Some technological advances have made jewelrymaking more efficient; however, many tasks cannot be fully automated. Jewelry work is a labor-intensive process that requires excellent handiwork.

The increasing numbers of affluent individuals, working women, double-income households, and fashion-conscious men are expected to keep jewelry sales strong. The population aged 45 and older, which accounts for a major portion of jewelry sales, also is on the rise.

Nontraditional jewelry marketers, such as discount stores, mail-order and catalogue companies, television shopping networks, and Internet retailers, have expanded the number of buying options and increased their sales volume. However, these establishments require fewer sales staff, limiting employment opportunities for jewelers and precious stone and metal workers who work mainly in sales. Because such establishments enjoy increases in sales, however, they will need highly skilled jewelers to make and repair the jewelry they sell.

Opportunities in jewelry stores and repair shops will be best for graduates from training programs for jewelers or gemologists. Despite an increase in sales by nontraditional jewelry marketers, traditional jewelers should not be affected greatly because they have the advantage of being able to build client relationships based on trust. Many clients prefer to work directly with a jeweler to ensure that the product is of the highest quality and meets their specifications. Many traditional jewelers expand their businesses as clients recommend their services to friends and relatives.

The jewelry industry can be cyclical. During economic downturns, demand for jewelry products and for jewelers tends to decrease. However, demand for repair workers should remain strong even during economic slowdowns because maintaining and repairing jewelry is an ongoing process. In fact, demand for jewelry repair may increase during recessions as people repair or restore existing pieces rather than purchase new ones. Also, many nontraditional vendors typically do not offer repair services.

Within manufacturing, increasing automation will adversely affect employment of low-skilled occupations, such as assemblers and polishers. Automation will have a lesser impact on more creative, highly skilled positions, such as moldmakers and modelmakers. Furthermore, small manufacturers, which typify the industry, will have an increasingly difficult time competing with the larger manufacturers when it comes to supplying large retailers.

Because of recent international trade agreements, exports are increasing modestly as manufacturers become more competitive in foreign markets. However, imports from foreign manufacturers are increasing more rapidly than exports due to these same agreements. Imports compete mainly with mass-produced jewelry. Therefore, employment in luxury and custom jewelry manufacturing is least susceptible to decline caused by import competition.

Earnings

Median annual earnings for jewelers and precious stone and metal workers were $27,400 in May 2004. The middle 50 percent earned between $20,510 and $37,280. The lowest 10 percent earned less than $16,040, and the highest 10 percent earned more than $49,020. In May 2004, median annual earnings in the industries employing the largest numbers of jewelers and precious stone and metal workers were $30,530 in jewelry, luggage, and leather goods stores and $23,590 in other miscellaneous manufacturing.

Most jewelers start out with a base salary, but once they become more proficient, they may begin charging by the number of pieces completed. Jewelers who work in retail stores may earn a commission for each piece of jewelry sold. Many jewelers also enjoy a variety of benefits, including reimbursement from their employers for work-related courses and discounts on jewelry purchases.

Related Occupations

Jewelers and precious stone and metal workers do precision handwork. Other skilled workers who do similar jobs include precision instrument and equipment repairers; welding, soldering, and brazing workers; and woodworkers. Some jewelers and precious stone and metal workers create their own jewelry designs. Other occupations that require visual arts abilities include artists and related workers and various designers—commercial and industrial, fashion, floral, graphic, and interior. Finally, some jewelers and precious stone and metal workers are involved in the buying and selling of stones, metals, or finished pieces of jewelry. Similar occupations include retail salespersons and sales representatives in wholesale trade.

Sources of Additional Information

Information on job opportunities and training programs for jewelers is available from

▶ Gemological Institute of America, 5345 Armada Dr., Carlsbad, CA 92008. Internet: http://www.gia.edu

For information on the jewelry industry and on schools offering jewelry-related programs and degrees by state, contact

▶ Manufacturing Jewelers and Suppliers of America, 45 Royal Little Dr., Providence, RI 02904.

To receive a list of accredited technical schools that have programs in gemology, contact

▶ Accrediting Commission of Career Schools and Colleges of Technology, 2101 Wilson Blvd., Suite 302, Arlington, VA 22201. Internet: http://www.accsct.org

For more information about careers in the jewelry industry, including different career paths, training options, and a list of schools, contact

▶ Jewelers of America, 52 Vanderbilt Ave., 19th Floor, New York, NY 10017. Internet: http://www.jewelers.org

Licensed Practical and Licensed Vocational Nurses

(O*NET 29-2061.00)

Significant Points

■ Training lasting about 1 year is available in about 1,200 state-approved programs, mostly in vocational or technical schools.

■ Applicants for jobs in hospitals may face competition as the number of hospital jobs for licensed practical nurses declines; however, rapid employment growth is projected in other health care industries, with the best job opportunities occurring in nursing care facilities and in home health care services.

■ Replacement needs will be a major source of job openings, as many workers leave the occupation permanently.

Nature of the Work

Licensed practical nurses (LPNs) or licensed vocational nurses (LVNs) care for the sick, injured, convalescent, and disabled under the direction of physicians and registered nurses. (The work of registered nurses is described elsewhere in this book.)

Most LPNs provide basic bedside care, taking vital signs such as temperature, blood pressure, pulse, and respiration. They also prepare and give injections and enemas, monitor catheters, apply dressings, treat bedsores, and give alcohol rubs and massages. LPNs monitor their patients and report adverse reactions to medications or treatments. They collect samples for testing, perform routine laboratory tests, feed patients, and record food and fluid intake and output. To help keep patients comfortable, LPNs assist with bathing, dressing, and personal hygiene. In states where the law allows, they may administer prescribed medicines or start intravenous fluids. Some LPNs help to deliver, care for, and feed infants. Experienced LPNs may supervise nursing assistants and aides.

In addition to providing routine bedside care, LPNs in nursing care facilities help to evaluate residents' needs, develop care plans, and supervise the care provided by nursing aides. In doctors' offices and clinics, they also may make appointments, keep records, and perform other clerical duties. LPNs who work in private homes may prepare meals and teach family members simple nursing tasks.

Working Conditions

Most licensed practical nurses in hospitals and nursing care facilities work a 40-hour week, but because patients need round-the-clock care, some work nights, weekends, and holidays. They often stand for long periods and help patients move in bed, stand, or walk.

LPNs may face hazards from caustic chemicals, radiation, and infectious diseases such as hepatitis. They are subject to back injuries when moving patients and shock from electrical equipment. They often must deal with the stress of heavy workloads. In addition, the patients they care for may be confused, irrational, agitated, or uncooperative.

Training, Other Qualifications, and Advancement

All states and the District of Columbia require LPNs to pass a licensing examination, known as the NCLEX-PN, after completing a state-approved practical nursing program. A high school diploma or its equivalent usually is required for entry, although some programs accept candidates without a diploma and some are designed as part of a high school curriculum.

In 2004, approximately 1,200 state-approved programs provided training in practical nursing. Most training programs are available from technical and vocational schools or from community and junior colleges. Other programs are available through high schools, hospitals, and colleges and universities.

Most practical nursing programs last about 1 year and include both classroom study and supervised clinical practice (patient care). Classroom study covers basic nursing concepts and patient care–related subjects, including anatomy, physiology, medical-surgical nursing, pediatrics, obstetrics, psychiatric nursing, the administration of drugs, nutrition, and first aid. Clinical practice usually is in a hospital, but sometimes includes other settings.

In some employment settings, such as nursing homes, LPNs can advance to become charge nurses who oversee the work of other LPNs and of nursing aides. Some LPNs also choose to become registered nurses through numerous LPN-to-RN training programs.

LPNs should have a caring, sympathetic nature. They should be emotionally stable because working with the sick and injured can be stressful. They also should have keen observational, decision-making, and communication skills. As part of a health care team, they must be able to follow orders and work under close supervision.

Employment

Licensed practical nurses held about 726,000 jobs in 2004. About 27 percent of LPNs worked in hospitals, 25 percent in nursing care facilities, and another 12 percent in offices of physicians. Others worked for home health care services; employment services; community care facilities for the elderly; public and private educational services; outpatient care centers; and federal, state, and local government agencies. About 1 in 5 worked part time.

Job Outlook

Employment of LPNs is expected to grow about as fast as average for all occupations through 2014 in response to the long-term care needs of an increasing elderly population and the general growth of health care services. Replacement needs will be a major source of job openings, as many workers leave the occupation permanently. Applicants for jobs in hospitals may face competition as the number of hospital jobs for LPNs declines; however, rapid employment growth is projected in other health care industries, with the best job opportunities occurring in nursing care facilities and in home health care services.

Employment of LPNs in hospitals is expected to continue to decline. Sophisticated procedures once performed only in hospitals are being performed in physicians' offices and in outpatient care centers such as ambulatory surgical and emergency medical centers, largely because of advances in technology. Consequently, employment of LPNs in most health care industries outside the traditional hospital setting is projected to grow faster than average.

Employment of LPNs is expected to grow much faster than average in home health care services. Home health care agencies also will offer the most new jobs for LPNs because of an increasing number of older persons with functional disabilities, consumer preference for care in the home, and technological advances that make it possible to bring increasingly complex treatments into the home.

Employment of LPNs in nursing care facilities is expected to grow about as fast as average because of the growing number of aged and disabled persons in need of long-term care. In addition, LPNs in nursing care facilities will be needed to care for the increasing number of patients who have been discharged from the hospital but who have not recovered enough to return home. However, changes in consumer preferences towards less restrictive and more cost-effective care from assisted living facilities and home health care agencies will limit employment growth.

Earnings

Median annual earnings of licensed practical nurses were $33,970 in May 2004. The middle 50 percent earned between $28,830 and $40,670. The lowest 10 percent earned less than $24,480, and the highest 10 percent earned more than $46,270. Median annual earnings in the industries employing the largest numbers of licensed practical nurses in May 2004 were

Employment services	$41,550
Nursing care facilities	35,460
Home health care services	35,180
General medical and surgical hospitals	32,570
Offices of physicians	30,400

Related Occupations

LPNs work closely with people while helping them. So do emergency medical technicians and paramedics; medical assistants; nursing, psychiatric, and home health aides; registered nurses; social and human service assistants; and surgical technologists.

Sources of Additional Information

For information about practical nursing, contact any of the following organizations:

▶ National Association for Practical Nurse Education and Service, Inc., P.O. Box 25647, Alexandria, VA 22313. Internet: http://www.napnes.org

▶ National League for Nursing, 61 Broadway, New York, NY 10006. Internet: http://www.nln.org

▸ National Federation of Licensed Practical Nurses, Inc., 605 Poole Dr., Garner, NC 27529. Internet: http://www.nflpn.org

Information on the NCLEX-PN licensing exam is available from

▸ National Council of State Boards of Nursing, 111 East Wacker Dr., Suite 2900, Chicago, IL 60611. Internet: http://www.ncsbn.org

A list of state-approved LPN programs is available from individual state boards of nursing.

Line Installers and Repairers

(O*NET 49-9051.00 and 49-9052.00)

Significant Points

■ Line installers and repairers work outdoors; conditions can be hazardous.

■ Employers prefer applicants with knowledge of electricity and electronics obtained through experience or classroom training.

■ Overall employment is projected to increase more slowly than average, although a growing number of retirements should create very good job opportunities, especially for electrical power-line installers and repairers.

■ Earnings are higher than in most other occupations that do not require postsecondary education.

Nature of the Work

Vast networks of wires and cables provide customers with electrical power and communications services. Networks of electrical power lines deliver electricity from generating plants to customers. Communications networks of telephone and cable television lines provide voice, video, and other communications services. These networks are constructed and maintained by *electrical powerline installers and repairers* and *telecommunications line installers and repairers.*

While the work performed by telecommunications and electrical powerline installers is quite similar, they are two distinct occupations. Working with power lines requires specialized knowledge of transformers, electrical power distribution systems, and substations. Working with telecommunications lines requires specialized knowledge of fiber optics and telecommunications switches and routers. While both powerline and telecommunications line installers have specialized knowledge, the procedures for installing both kinds of lines are quite similar.

All line installers, or line erectors, install new lines by constructing utility poles, towers, and underground trenches to carry the wires and cables. Line erectors use a variety of construction equipment, including digger derricks, trenchers, cable plows, and borers. Digger derricks are trucks equipped with augers and cranes; workers use augers to dig holes in the ground, and cranes are used to set utility poles in place. Trenchers and cable plows are used to cut openings in the earth for the laying of underground cables. Borers, which tunnel under the earth, are used to install tubes for the wire without opening a trench in the soil.

When construction is complete, line installers string cable along the poles, towers, tunnels, and trenches. While working on poles and towers, installers first use truck-mounted buckets to reach the top of the structure or physically climb the pole or tower. Next, they pull up cable from large reels mounted on trucks. The line is then set in place and pulled so that it has the correct amount of tension. Finally, line installers attach the cable to the structure, using hand and hydraulic tools. When working with electrical power lines, installers bolt or clamp insulators onto the poles before attaching the cable. Underground cable is laid directly in a trench, pulled through a tunnel, or strung through a conduit running through a trench.

Other installation duties include setting up service for customers and installing network equipment. To set up service, line installers string cable between the customers' premises and the lines running on poles or towers or in trenches. They install wiring to houses and check the connection for proper voltage readings. Line installers also may install a variety of equipment. Workers on telephone and cable television lines install amplifiers and repeaters that maintain the strength of communications transmissions. Workers on electrical power lines install and replace transformers, circuit breakers, switches, fuses, and other equipment to control and direct the electrical current.

In addition to installation, line installers and repairers also are responsible for maintenance of electrical, telecommunications, and cable television lines. Workers periodically travel in trucks, helicopters, and airplanes to visually inspect the wires and cables. Sensitive monitoring equipment can automatically detect malfunctions on the network, such as loss of current flow. When line repairers identify a problem, they travel to the location of the malfunction and repair or replace defective cables or equipment. Bad weather or natural disasters can cause extensive damage to networks. Line installers and repairers must respond quickly to these emergencies to restore critical utility and communications services. This can often involve working outdoors in adverse weather conditions.

Installation and repair work may require splicing, or joining together, separate pieces of cable. Each cable contains numerous individual wires; splicing the cables together requires that each wire in one piece of cable be joined to another wire in the matching piece. Line installers splice cables using small hand tools, epoxy, or mechanical equipment. At each splice, they place insulation over the conductor and seal the splice with moistureproof covering. At some companies, *cable splicing technicians* perform splices on larger lines.

Communications networks are transitioning to fiber-optic cables instead of conventional wire or metal cables. Fiber-optic cables are made of hair-thin strands of glass, which convey pulses of light. These cables carry much more information at higher speeds than conventional cables. The higher transmission capacity of fiber-optic cable has allowed communication networks to offer upgraded services, such as high-speed Internet access. Splicing fiber-optic cable requires specialized equipment that carefully slices, matches, and aligns individual glass fibers. The fibers are joined by either electrical fusion (welding) or a mechanical fixture and gel (glue). More newly constructed buildings are being wired with fiber-optic lines.

Working Conditions

Line installers and repairers must climb and maintain their balance while working on poles and towers. They lift equipment and work in a variety of positions, such as stooping or kneeling. Their work often requires that they drive utility vehicles, travel long distances, and work outdoors under a variety of weather conditions. Many line installers and repairers work a 40-hour week; however, emergencies may require overtime work. For example, when severe weather damages electrical and communications lines, line installers and repairers may work long and irregular hours to restore service.

Line installers and repairers encounter serious hazards on their jobs and must follow safety procedures to minimize potential danger. They wear safety equipment when entering utility holes and test for the presence of gas before going underground. Electric powerline workers have the more hazardous jobs. High-voltage power lines can cause electrocution, and line installers and repairers must consequently use electrically insulated protective devices and tools when working with live cables. Power lines are typically higher than telephone and cable television lines, increasing the risk of severe injury due to falls. To prevent these injuries, line installers and repairers must use fall-protection equipment when working on poles or towers.

Training, Other Qualifications, and Advancement

Employers of line installers and repairers usually require applicants to have at least a high school diploma. They also strongly prefer applicants with a technical knowledge of electricity or electronics or experience obtained through vocational/technical programs, community colleges, or the Armed Forces. Programs in telecommunications, electronics, or electricity are offered by many community or technical colleges. These programs often are operated with assistance from local employers and unions. Some schools, working with local companies, offer 1-year certificate programs that emphasize hands-on field work. More advanced 2-year associate degree programs provide students with a broader knowledge of telecommunications and electrical utilities technology through courses in electricity, electronics, fiber optics, and microwave transmission. Graduates of these programs often get preferential treatment in the hiring process.

Prospective employees also should possess a basic knowledge of algebra and trigonometry and have mechanical ability. Customer service and interpersonal skills also are important, especially for those dealing with customers. Because the work entails lifting heavy objects (many employers require applicants to be able to lift at least 50 pounds), climbing, and other physical activity, applicants should have stamina, strength, and coordination and must be unafraid of heights. The ability to distinguish colors is necessary because wires and cables may be color-coded. A good driving record is important because workers often hold commercial driver's licenses and operate company-owned vehicles.

Line installers and repairers receive most of their training on the job. Electrical line installers and repairers often must complete formal apprenticeships or other employer training programs. These programs, which can last up to 5 years, combine on-the-job training with formal classroom courses and are sometimes administered jointly by the employer and the union representing the workers. The unions include the International Brotherhood of Electrical Workers, the Communications Workers of America, and the Utility Workers

Union of America. Government safety regulations strictly define the training and education requirements for apprentice electrical line installers.

Line installers and repairers working for telephone and cable television companies receive several years of on-the-job training. They also may attend training or take online courses provided by equipment manufacturers, schools, unions, or industry training organizations. The Society of Cable Television Engineers (SCTE) provides certification programs for line installers and repairers. Applicants for certification must be employed in the cable television industry and attend training sessions at local SCTE chapters.

Entry-level line installers may be hired as ground workers; helpers; or tree trimmers, who clear branches from telephone and power lines. These workers may advance to positions stringing cable and performing service installations. With experience, they may advance to more sophisticated maintenance and repair positions responsible for increasingly larger portions of the network. Promotion to supervisory or training positions also is possible, but more advanced supervisory positions often require a college diploma.

Employment

Line installers and repairers held about 251,000 jobs in 2004. Approximately 147,000 were telecommunications line installers and repairers; the remainder were electrical powerline installers and repairers. Nearly all line installers and repairers worked for telecommunications; construction; or electric power generation, transmission, and distribution companies. Approximately 4,800 line installers and repairers were self-employed. Many of these were contractors employed by the telecommunications companies to handle customer service problems and installations.

Job Outlook

Overall employment of line installers and repairers is expected to grow more slowly than the average for all occupations through 2014. However, because many line installers and repairers are nearing retirement, job opportunities for new workers in this field should be very good, particularly for electrical powerline installers. Some companies are expanding their hiring in anticipation of increased retirements.

Employment of telecommunications line installers is projected to grow about as fast as the average for all occupations. Much of their work will involve replacing old wiring with fiber-optic cable and expanding their networks to provide customers with high-speed access to data, video, and graphics. Line installers and repairers will be needed to construct and maintain the networks. However, the increasing use of wireless systems, increasingly reliable lines, and improved speeds of data transmission over existing lines will limit employment growth. The number of households with wired telephone service is declining because of the increasing use of wireless telephones. Wireless networks do not require as many technicians to maintain and expand their systems, a characteristic that will reduce job growth. Satellite television providers are also providing strong competition. As wireless systems offer higher-speed Internet access, the number of households with wired phone or cable TV should decline further.

Very little employment growth is expected among electrical power-line installers and repairers. Despite consistently rising demand for electricity, industry deregulation is pushing companies to cut costs and maintenance, which tends to reduce employment. Most new jobs are expected to arise in the construction industry.

Earnings

Earnings for line installers and repairers are higher than those in most other occupations that do not require postsecondary education. Median hourly earnings for electrical powerline installers and repairers were $23.61 in May 2004. The middle 50 percent earned between $18.00 and $27.64. The lowest 10 percent earned less than $13.31, and the highest 10 percent earned more than $32.54. Median hourly earnings in the industries employing the largest numbers of electrical powerline installers and repairers in May 2004 are shown here:

Electric power generation, transmission, and
   distribution $24.96
Wired telecommunications carriers...........................24.15
Local government 22.25
Utility system construction...................................18.01
Building equipment contractors..............................15.77

Median hourly earnings for telecommunications line installers and repairers were $19.39 in May 2004. The middle 50 percent earned between $13.98 and $25.10. The lowest 10 percent earned less than $10.96, and the highest 10 percent earned more than $28.56. Median hourly earnings in the industries employing the largest numbers of telecommunications line installers and repairers in May 2004 are shown here:

Wired telecommunications carriers $24.80
Cable and other subscription programming 17.36
Cable and other program distribution......................16.58
Building equipment contractors...............................15.76
Utility system construction....................................14.53

Most line installers and repairers belong to unions, principally the Communications Workers of America, the International Brotherhood of Electrical Workers, and the Utility Workers Union of America. For these workers, union contracts set wage rates, wage increases, and the time needed to advance from one job level to the next.

Related Occupations

Other workers who install and repair electrical and electronic equipment include broadcast and sound engineering technicians and radio operators, electricians, and radio and telecommunications equipment installers and repairers.

Sources of Additional Information

For more details about employment opportunities, contact the telephone, cable television, or electrical power companies in your community. For general information and some educational resources on line installer and repairer jobs, write to

▶ Communications Workers of America, 501 3rd St. NW, Washington, DC 20001.

▶ International Brotherhood of Electrical Workers, Telecommunications Department, 1125 15th St. NW, Washington, DC 20005.

Machine Setters, Operators, and Tenders—Metal and Plastic

(O*NET 51-4021.00, 51-4022.00, 51-4023.00, 51-4031.01, 51-4031.02, 51-4031.03, 51-4031.04, 51-4032.00, 51-4033.01, 51-4033.02, 51-4034.00, 51-4035.00, 51-4051.00, 51-4052.00, 51-4061.00, 51-4062.00, 51-4071.00, 51-4072.01, 51-4072.02, 51-4072.03, 51-4072.04, 51-4072.05, 51-4081.01, 51-4081.02, 51-4191.01, 51-4191.02, 51-4191.03, 51-4192.00, 51-4193.01, 51-4193.02, 51-4193.03, 51-4193.04, 51-4194.00, and 51-4199.99)

Significant Points

■ Manufacturing industries employ 10 out of 11 workers.

■ A few weeks of on-the-job training is sufficient for most workers to learn basic machine operations, but a year or more is required to become a highly skilled operator or setter.

■ Employment in most machine setter, operator, and tender occupations will decline over the 2004–2014 period as a result of productivity improvements and competition for jobs from abroad.

Nature of the Work

Consider the parts of a toaster, such as the metal or plastic housing or the lever that lowers the toast. These parts, and many other metal and plastic products, are produced by machine setters, operators, and tenders—metal and plastic. In fact, machine tool operators in the metalworking and plastics industries play a major role in producing most of the consumer products on which we rely daily.

In general, these workers can be separated into two groups—those who set up machines for operation and those who tend the machines during production. Setup workers prepare the machines *prior* to production and may adjust the machinery during its operation. Operators and tenders primarily monitor the machinery *during* its operation, sometimes loading or unloading the machine or making minor adjustments to the controls. Many workers both set up and operate equipment. Because the setup process requires an understanding of the entire production process, setters usually have more training and are more highly skilled than those who simply operate or tend machinery. As new automation simplifies the setup process, however, less-skilled workers also are increasingly able to set up machines for operation.

Setters, operators, and tenders usually are identified by the type of machine with which they work. Some examples of specific titles are drilling- and boring-machine toolsetters, milling- and planing-machine tenders, and lathe- and turning-machine tool operators. Job duties usually vary with the size of the firm and the type of machine being operated. Although some workers specialize in one or two types of machinery, many are trained to set up or operate a variety of machines. Increasing automation allows machine setters to operate multiple machines simultaneously. In addition, newer production techniques, such as team-oriented "lean" manufacturing, require machine operators to rotate between different machines. Rotating assignments result in more varied work, but also require workers to have a wider range of skills.

Machine setters, operators, and tenders—metal set up and tend machines that cut and form all types of metal parts. Setup workers plan and set up the sequence of operations according to blueprints, layouts, or other instructions. Often this involves loading a computer program with instructions into the machine's computer controls. On all machines, including those with computer controls, setup workers respond to problems during operation by adjusting the speed, feed, and other variables; choosing the proper coolants and lubricants; and selecting the instruments or tools for each operation. Using micrometers, gauges, and other precision measuring instruments, they also may compare the completed work with the tolerance limits stated in the specifications.

Although there are many different types of metalworking machine tools that require specific knowledge and skills, most operators perform similar tasks. Whether tending grinding machines that remove excess material from the surface of machined products or presses that extrude metal through a die to form wire, operators usually perform simple, repetitive operations that can be learned quickly. Typically, these workers place metal stock in a machine on which the operating specifications have already been set. They may watch one or more machines and make minor adjustments according to their instructions. Regardless of the type of machine they operate, machine tenders usually depend on skilled setup workers for major adjustments when the machines are not functioning properly.

Machine setters, operators, and tenders—plastic set up and tend machines that transform plastic compounds—chemical-based products that can be produced in powder, pellet, or syrup form—into a wide variety of consumer goods such as toys, tubing, and auto parts. These products are manufactured by various methods, of which injection molding is the most common. The injection-molding machine heats and liquefies a plastic compound and forces it into a mold. After the part has cooled and hardened, the mold opens and the part is released. Many common kitchen products are produced with this method. To produce long parts such as pipes or window frames, an extruding machine usually is employed. These machines force a plastic compound through a die that contains an opening with the desired shape of the final product. Blow molding is another common plasticsworking technique. Blow-molding machines force hot air into a mold that contains a plastic tube. As the air moves into the mold, the tube is inflated to the shape of the mold, and a plastic container is formed. The familiar 2-liter soft-drink bottles are produced by this method.

Workers in three distinct specialties–setters, operators, and tenders—operate injection-molding machines. Most other types of plastic machines function in a similar manner. A typical injection-molding machine may have 25 different controls that can be adjusted. Setters or technicians set up the machines prior to their operation. These workers are responsible for repairing any major problem. Operators monitor the many gauges on injection-molding machines, adjusting different inputs, pressures, and speeds to main-

tain quality. Tenders remove the cooled plastic from the mold, loading the product into boxes.

Working Conditions

Most machine setters, operators, and tenders—metal and plastic work in areas that are clean, well lit, and well ventilated. Nevertheless, many operators require stamina because they are on their feet much of the day and may do moderately heavy lifting. Also, these workers operate powerful, high-speed machines that can be dangerous if strict safety rules are not observed. Most operators wear protective equipment, such as safety glasses and earplugs, to protect against flying particles of metal or plastic and against noise from the machines. However, many modern machines are enclosed, minimizing the exposure of workers to noise, dust, and lubricants used during machining. Other required safety equipment varies by work setting and machine. For example, those in the plastics industry who work near materials that emit dangerous fumes or dust must wear face masks or self-contained breathing apparatus.

Most workers in the occupation put in a 40-hour week, but overtime is common during periods of increased production. Because many metalworking and plastics working shops operate more than one shift daily, some operators work nights and weekends.

Training, Other Qualifications, and Advancement

Machine setters, operators, and tenders—metal and plastic learn their skills on the job. Trainees begin by observing and assisting experienced workers, sometimes in formal training programs. Under supervision, they may start as tenders, supplying materials, starting and stopping the machine, or removing finished products from it. Then they advance to the more difficult tasks performed by operators, such as adjusting feed speeds, changing cutting tools, or inspecting a finished product for defects. Eventually, they become responsible for their own machines.

The complexity of the equipment largely determines the time required to become an operator. Most operators learn the basic machine operations and functions in a few weeks, but they may need a year or more to become skilled operators or to advance to the more highly skilled job of setter. Although many operators learn on the job, some community colleges and other educational institutions offer courses and certifications in operating metal and plastics machines. In addition to providing on-the-job training, some employers send promising machine tenders to operator classes. Other employers prefer to hire workers who have completed, or currently are enrolled in, a training program.

Setters or technicians normally need a thorough knowledge of the machinery and of the products being manufactured because they often plan the sequence of work, make the first production run, and determine which adjustments need to be made. Strong analytical abilities are particularly important for this job. Some companies have formal training programs for operators and setters; often, the programs combine classroom instruction with on-the-job training.

Although no special education is required for many jobs in the occupation, employers prefer to hire applicants with good basic skills. Many require employees to have a high school education and to read, write, and speak English. Because machinery is becoming more complex and shop-floor organization is changing, employers increasingly look for persons with good communication and interpersonal skills. Mechanical aptitude, manual dexterity, and experience working with machinery also are helpful. Those interested in becoming machine setters, operators, and tenders can improve their employment opportunities by completing high school courses in shop and blueprint reading and by gaining a working knowledge of the properties of metals and plastics. A solid math background, including courses in algebra, geometry, trigonometry, and basic statistics, also is useful. With increasing automation, experience with computers also is helpful.

Job opportunities and advancement can be enhanced as well by becoming certified in a particular machining skill. The National Institute for Metalworking Skills has developed standards for machine setters, operators, and tenders—metal. After taking a course approved by the organization and passing a written exam and performance requirement, the worker is issued a credential that signifies competence in a specific machining operation. The Society of Plastics Industry, the national trade association representing plastics manufacturers, also certifies workers in that industry. To achieve machine-operator certification, 2 years of experience operating a plastics-processing machine is recommended, and one must pass a computer-based exam.

Advancement for operators usually takes the form of higher pay, although there are some limited opportunities for operators to advance to new positions as well. For example, they can become multiple-machine operators, setup operators, or trainees for the more highly skilled position of machinist, tool and die maker, or computer-control programmer or operator. (See the description of machinists elsewhere in this book.) Some setup workers may advance to supervisory positions.

Employment

Machine setters, operators, and tenders—metal and plastic held about 1.1 million jobs in 2004. Approximately 10 of 11 jobs were found in manufacturing, primarily in fabricated metal product manufacturing, plastics and rubber products manufacturing, primary metal manufacturing, machinery manufacturing, and motor vehicle parts manufacturing. The following tabulation shows the distribution of employment of machine setters, operators, and tenders—metal and plastic by detailed occupation.

Cutting, punching, and press machine setters,
   operators, and tenders, metal and plastic 251,000
Molding, coremaking, and casting machine setters,
   operators, and tenders, metal and plastic 157,000
Grinding, lapping, polishing, and buffing machine
   tool setters, operators, and tenders, metal
   and plastic 101,000
Multiple machine tool setters, operators, and
   tenders, metal and plastic 97,000
Extruding and drawing machine setters, operators,
   and tenders, metal and plastic 89,000
Lathe and turning machine tool setters, operators,
   and tenders, metal and plastic 71,000

Metal workers and plastic workers, all other 55,000
Drilling and boring machine tool setters,
   operators, and tenders, metal and plastic 42,000
Plating and coating machine setters, operators,
   and tenders, metal and plastic 40,000
Forging machine setters, operators, and tenders,
   metal and plastic 38,000
Rolling machine setters, operators, and tenders,
   metal and plastic 37,000
Milling and planing machine setters, operators,
   and tenders, metal and plastic 31,000
Heat treating equipment setters, operators,
   and tenders, metal and plastic 26,000
Tool grinders, filers, and sharpeners 21,000
Metal-refining furnace operators and tenders..........17,000
Foundry mold and coremakers 17,000
Pourers and casters, metal 14,000
Lay-out workers, metal and plastic........................11,000
Model makers, metal and plastic 8,100
Patternmakers, metal and plastic..........................6,000

Job Outlook

Overall employment in the various machine setter, operator, and tender occupations is expected to decline over the 2004–2014 period. In general, employment of these workers will be affected by technological advances, changing demand for the goods they produce, foreign competition, and the reorganization of production processes. Despite the overall employment decline, a large number of machine setter, operator, and tender jobs will become available due to an expected surge in retirements as some baby boomers become eligible for retirement by the end of the decade.

One of the most important factors influencing employment change in this occupation is the implementation of labor-saving machinery. In order to remain competitive by improving quality and lowering production costs, many firms are adopting new technologies, such as computer-controlled machine tools and robots. Computer-controlled equipment allows operators to tend a greater number of machines simultaneously and often makes setup easier, thereby reducing the amount of time setup workers spend on each machine. Robots are being used to load and unload parts from machines. The lower-skilled manual machine tool operators and tenders are more likely to be eliminated by these new technologies because the functions they perform are more easily automated.

The demand for machine setters, operators, and tenders—metal and plastic largely mirrors the demand for the parts they produce. The consumption of plastic products has grown as they have been substituted for metal goods in many consumer and manufactured products in recent years. The process is likely to continue and should result in stronger demand for machine operators in plastics than in metal.

Both the plastics and metal industries, however, face stiff foreign competition that is limiting the demand for domestically produced parts. One way in which larger U.S. producers have responded to this competition is by moving production operations to other countries where labor costs are lower. These moves are likely to continue and will further reduce employment opportunities for many machine operators, setters, and tenders—metal and plastic in the United States. Another way domestic manufacturers compete with low-wage foreign competition is by increasing their use of automated systems, which can make manufacturing establishments more competitive by improving their productivity. However, increased automation also limits employment growth.

Workers with a thorough background in machine operations, exposure to a variety of machines, and a good working knowledge of the properties of metals and plastics will be best able to adjust to the changing environment. In addition, new shop-floor arrangements will reward workers with good basic mathematics and reading skills, good communication skills, and the ability and willingness to learn new tasks. As workers adapt to team-oriented production methods, those who can operate multiple machines will have the best job opportunities.

Earnings

Earnings for machine operators can vary by size of the company, union or nonunion status, industry, and skill level and experience of the operator. Also, temporary employees, who are being hired in greater numbers, usually get paid less than company-employed workers. The median hourly earnings in May 2004 for a variety of machine setters, operators, and tenders—metal and plastic were

Model makers, metal and plastic $21.28

Patternmakers, metal and plastic...........................17.86

Metal workers and plastic workers, all other 16.15

Metal-refining furnace operators and tenders 15.74

Lay-out workers, metal and plastic 15.65

Lathe and turning machine tool setters, operators,
and tenders, metal and plastic 15.04

Milling and planing machine setters, operators,
and tenders, metal and plastic 14.91

Tool grinders, filers, and sharpeners.......................14.52

Rolling machine setters, operators, and tenders,
metal and plastic 14.33

Heat-treating equipment setters, operators, and
tenders, metal and plastic 14.26

Multiple machine tool setters, operators,
and tenders, metal and plastic 14.06

Pourers and casters, metal 13.92

Drilling and boring machine tool setters, operators,
and tenders, metal and plastic 13.69

Foundry mold and coremakers 13.37

Forging machine setters, operators, and tenders,
metal and plastic 13.22

Grinding, lapping, polishing, and buffing machine
tool setters, operators, and tenders, metal and
plastic...13.19

Extruding and drawing machine setters, operators,
and tenders, metal and plastic 13.18

Plating and coating machine setters, operators,
and tenders, metal and plastic 12.96

Cutting, punching, and press machine setters,
operators, and tenders, metal and plastic 12.45

Molding, coremaking, and casting machine setters,
operators, and tenders, metal and plastic 11.63

Related Occupations

Workers in occupations closely related to machine setters, operators, and tenders—metal and plastic include machinists; tool and die makers; assemblers and fabricators; computer control programmers and operators; and welding, soldering, and brazing workers. Often, machine operators are responsible for checking the quality of parts being produced, work similar to that of inspectors, testers, sorters, samplers, and weighers.

Sources of Additional Information

For general information about metal machine setters, operators, and tenders, contact

▸ National Tooling and Machining Association, 9300 Livingston Rd., Fort Washington, MD 20744. Internet: http://www.ntma.org

▸ Precision Metalforming Association Educational Foundation, 6363 Oak Tree Blvd., Independence, OH 44131. Internet: http://www.pmaef.org

▸ Precision Machine Products Association, 6700 West Snowville Rd., Brecksville, OH 44141-3292. Internet: http://www.pmpa.org

For information on schools and employers with training programs in plastics, contact

▸ Society of Plastics Industry, 1667 K St. NW, Suite 1000, Washington, DC 20006. Internet: http://www.plasticsindustry.org

Machinists

(O*NET 51-4041.00)

Significant Points

■ Machinists learn in apprenticeship programs, informally on the job, and in vocational schools or community or technical colleges.

■ Many entrants previously have worked as machine setters, operators, or tenders.

■ Job opportunities are expected to be good.

Nature of the Work

Machinists use machine tools, such as lathes, milling machines, and machining centers, to produce precision metal parts. Although they may produce large quantities of one part, precision machinists often produce small batches or one-of-a-kind items. They use their knowledge of the working properties of metals and their skill with machine tools to plan and carry out the operations needed to make machined products that meet precise specifications.

Before they machine a part, machinists must carefully plan and prepare the operation. These workers first review electronic or written blueprints or specifications for a job. Next, they calculate where to cut or bore into the workpiece (the piece of steel, aluminum, titanium, plastic, silicon, or any other material that is being shaped), how fast to feed the workpiece into the machine, and how much material to remove. They then select tools and materials for the job, plan the sequence of cutting and finishing operations, and mark the workpiece to show where cuts should be made.

After this layout work is completed, machinists perform the necessary machining operations. They position the workpiece on the machine tool—drill press, lathe, milling machine, or other type of machine—set the controls, and make the cuts. During the machining process, they must constantly monitor the feed rate and speed of the machine. Machinists also ensure that the workpiece is being properly lubricated and cooled, because the machining of metal products generates a significant amount of heat. The temperature of the workpiece is a key concern because most metals expand when heated; machinists must adjust the size of their cuts relative to the temperature. Some rare but increasingly popular metals, such as titanium, are machined at extremely high temperatures.

Machinists detect some problems by listening for specific sounds—for example, a dull cutting tool or excessive vibration. Dull cutting tools are removed and replaced. Cutting speeds are adjusted to compensate for harmonic vibrations, which can decrease the accuracy of cuts, particularly on newer high-speed spindles and lathes. After the work is completed, machinists use both simple and highly sophisticated measuring tools to check the accuracy of their work against blueprints.

Some machinists, often called production machinists, may produce large quantities of one part, especially parts requiring the use of complex operations and great precision. Many modern machine tools are computer numerically controlled (CNC). CNC machines, following a computer program, control the cutting tool speed, change dull tools, and perform all of the necessary cuts to create a part. Frequently, machinists work with computer control programmers to determine how the automated equipment will cut a part. The programmer may determine the path of the cut, while the machinist determines the type of cutting tool, the speed of the cutting tool, and the feed rate. Because most machinists train in CNC programming, they may write basic programs themselves and often set offsets (modify programs) in response to problems encountered during test runs. After the production process is designed, relatively simple and repetitive operations normally are performed by machine setters, operators, and tenders.

Some manufacturing techniques employ automated parts loaders, automatic tool changers, and computer controls, allowing machine tools to operate without anyone present. One production machinist, working 8 hours a day, might monitor equipment, replace worn cutting tools, check the accuracy of parts being produced, adjust offsets, and perform other tasks on several CNC machines that operate 24 hours a day (lights-out manufacturing). During lights-out manufacturing, a factory may need only a few machinists to monitor the entire factory.

Other machinists do maintenance work—repairing or making new parts for existing machinery. To repair a broken part, maintenance machinists may refer to blueprints and perform the same machining operations that were needed to create the original part.

Because the technology of machining is changing rapidly, machinists must learn to operate a wide range of machines. Along with operating machines that use metal cutting tools to shape workpieces, machinists operate machines that cut with lasers, water jets, or electrified wires. While some of the computer controls may be similar, machinists must understand the unique cutting properties of these different machines. As engineers create new types of machine tools and new materials to machine, machinists must constantly learn new machining properties and techniques.

Working Conditions

Today, most machine shops are relatively clean, well lit, and ventilated. Many computer-controlled machines are partially or totally enclosed, minimizing the exposure of workers to noise, debris, and the lubricants used to cool workpieces during machining. Nevertheless, working around machine tools presents certain dangers, and workers must follow safety precautions. Machinists wear protective equipment, such as safety glasses to shield against bits of flying metal and earplugs to dampen machinery noise. They also must exercise caution when handling hazardous coolants and lubricants, although many common water-based lubricants present little hazard. The job requires stamina, because machinists stand most of the day and, at times, may need to lift moderately heavy workpieces. Modern factories extensively employ autoloaders and overhead cranes, reducing heavy lifting.

Many machinists work a 40-hour week. Evening and weekend shifts are becoming more common as companies justify investments in more expensive machinery by extending hours of operation. However, this trend is somewhat offset by the increasing use of lights-out manufacturing and the use of machine operators for less desirable shifts. Overtime is common during peak production periods.

Training, Other Qualifications, and Advancement

Machinists train in apprenticeship programs, informally on the job, and in vocational schools or community or technical colleges. Experience with machine tools is helpful. In fact, many entrants previously have worked as machine setters, operators, or tenders. Persons interested in becoming machinists should be mechanically inclined, have good problem-solving abilities, be able to work independently, and be able to do highly accurate work (tolerances may reach 1/10,000th of an inch) that requires concentration and physical effort.

High school or vocational school courses in mathematics (especially trigonometry), blueprint reading, metalworking, and drafting are highly recommended. Apprenticeship programs consist of shop training and related classroom instruction lasting up to 4 years. In shop training, apprentices work almost full time and are supervised by an experienced machinist while learning to operate various machine tools. Classroom instruction includes math, physics, materials science, blueprint reading, mechanical drawing, and quality and safety practices. In addition, as machine shops have increased their use of computer-controlled equipment, training in the operation and programming of CNC machine tools has become essential. Apprenticeship classes are often taught in cooperation with local community or vocational colleges. A growing number of machinists learn the trade through 2-year associate degree programs at community or technical colleges. Graduates of these programs still need significant on-the-job experience before they are fully qualified.

To boost the skill level of machinists and to create a more uniform standard of competency, a number of training facilities and colleges are implementing curriculums that incorporate national skills standards developed by the National Institute of Metalworking Skills (NIMS). After completing such a curriculum and passing a performance requirement and written exam, trainees are granted a NIMS credential, which provides formal recognition of competency in a metalworking field. Completing a recognized certification program provides a machinist with better career opportunities.

As new automation is introduced, machinists normally receive additional training to update their skills. This training usually is provided by a representative of the equipment manufacturer or a local technical school. Some employers offer tuition reimbursement for job-related courses.

Machinists can advance in several ways. Experienced machinists may become CNC programmers, tool and die makers, or mold makers or be promoted to supervisory or administrative positions in their firms. A few open their own shops.

Employment

Machinists held about 370,000 jobs in 2004. Most machinists work in small machining shops or in manufacturing industries, such as machinery manufacturing and transportation equipment manufacturing (motor vehicle parts and aerospace products and parts). Maintenance machinists work in most industries that use production machinery.

Job Outlook

Despite relatively slow employment growth, job opportunities for machinists should continue to be good. Many young people with the necessary educational and personal qualifications needed to obtain machining skills often prefer to attend college or may not wish to enter production occupations. Therefore, the number of workers obtaining the skills and knowledge necessary to fill machinist jobs is expected to be less than the number of job openings arising each year from the need to replace experienced machinists who transfer to other occupations or retire and from job growth.

Employment of machinists is projected to grow more slowly than the average for all occupations over the 2004–2014 period because of rising productivity among these workers and strong foreign competition. Machinists will become more efficient as a result of the expanded use of and improvements in technologies such as CNC machine tools, autoloaders, and high-speed machining. This allows fewer machinists to accomplish the same amount of work previously performed by more workers. Technology is not expected to affect the employment of machinists as significantly as that of most other production occupations, however, because machinists monitor and maintain many automated systems. Due to modern production techniques, employers prefer workers, such as machinists, who have a wide range of skills and are capable of performing almost any task in a machine shop.

Employment levels in this occupation are influenced by economic cycles—as the demand for machined goods falls, machinists involved in production may be laid off or forced to work fewer hours. Employment of machinists involved in plant maintenance, however, often is more stable because proper maintenance and repair of costly equipment remain critical to manufacturing operations, even when production levels fall.

Earnings

Median hourly earnings of machinists were $16.33 in May 2004. The middle 50 percent earned between $12.84 and $20.33. The lowest 10 percent earned less than $10.08, while the top 10 percent earned more than $24.34. Median hourly earnings in the manufacturing industries employing the largest number of machinists in May 2004 were

Aerospace product and parts manufacturing	$17.78
Motor vehicle parts manufacturing	17.46
Metalworking machinery manufacturing	17.06
Machine shops; turned product; and screw, nut, and bolt manufacturing	15.87
Employment services	11.09

Apprentices earn much less than machinists, but earnings increase quickly as they improve their skills. Also, most employers pay for apprentices' training classes.

Related Occupations

Occupations most closely related to that of machinist are other machining occupations, which include tool and die makers; machine setters, operators, and tenders—metal and plastic; and computer control programmers and operators. Another occupation that requires precision and skill in working with metal is welding, soldering, and brazing workers.

Sources of Additional Information

For general information about machinists, contact

▶ Precision Machine Products Association, 6700 West Snowville Rd., Brecksville, OH 44141-3292. Internet: http://www.pmpa.org

For a list of training centers and apprenticeship programs, contact

▶ National Tooling and Machining Association, 9300 Livingston Rd., Fort Washington, MD 20744. Internet: http://www.ntma.org

For general occupational information and a list of training programs, contact

▶ Precision Metalforming Association Educational Foundation, 6363 Oak Tree Blvd., Independence, OH 44131-2500. Internet: http://www.pmaef.org

Maintenance and Repair Workers, General

(O*NET 49-9042.00)

Significant Points

- General maintenance and repair workers are employed in almost every industry.

- Many workers learn their skills informally on the job; others learn by working as helpers to other repairers or to construction workers such as carpenters, electricians, or machinery repairers.

- Job opportunities should be favorable, with many openings occurring as a result of turnover in this large occupation.

Nature of the Work

Most craft workers specialize in one kind of work, such as plumbing or carpentry. General maintenance and repair workers, however, have skills in many different crafts. They repair and maintain machines, mechanical equipment, and buildings and work on plumbing, electrical, and air-conditioning and heating systems. They build partitions; make plaster or drywall repairs; and fix or paint roofs, windows, doors, floors, woodwork, and other parts of building structures. They also maintain and repair specialized equipment and machinery found in cafeterias, laundries, hospitals, stores, offices, and factories. Typical duties include troubleshooting and fixing faulty electrical switches, repairing air-conditioning motors, and unclogging drains. New buildings sometimes have computer-controlled systems that allow maintenance workers to make adjustments in building settings and monitor for problems from a central location. For example, they can remotely control light sensors that turn off lights automatically after a set amount of time or identify a broken ventilation fan that needs to be replaced.

General maintenance and repair workers inspect and diagnose problems and determine the best way to correct them, frequently checking blueprints, repair manuals, and parts catalogs. They obtain supplies and repair parts from distributors or storerooms. Using common hand and power tools such as screwdrivers, saws, drills, wrenches, and hammers, as well as specialized equipment and electronic testing devices, these workers replace or fix worn or broken parts, where necessary, or make adjustments to correct malfunctioning equipment and machines.

General maintenance and repair workers also perform routine preventive maintenance and ensure that machines continue to run smoothly, building systems operate efficiently, and the physical condition of buildings does not deteriorate. Following a checklist, they may inspect drives, motors, and belts; check fluid levels; replace filters; and perform other maintenance actions. Maintenance and repair workers keep records of their work.

Employees in small establishments, where they are often the only maintenance worker, make all repairs, except for very large or difficult jobs. In larger establishments, their duties may be limited to the general maintenance of everything in a workshop or a particular area.

Working Conditions

General maintenance and repair workers often carry out several different tasks in a single day at any number of locations. They may work inside of a single building or in several different buildings. They may have to stand for long periods; lift heavy objects; and work in uncomfortably hot or cold environments, in awkward and cramped positions, or on ladders. They are subject to electrical shock, burns, falls, cuts, and bruises. Most general maintenance workers work a 40-hour week. Some work evening, night, or weekend shifts or are on call for emergency repairs.

Those employed in small establishments often operate with only limited supervision. Those working in larger establishments frequently are under the direct supervision of an experienced worker.

Training, Other Qualifications, and Advancement

Many general maintenance and repair workers learn their skills informally on the job. They start as helpers, watching and learning from skilled maintenance workers. Helpers begin by doing simple jobs, such as fixing leaky faucets and replacing light bulbs, and progress to more difficult tasks, such as overhauling machinery or building walls. Some learn their skills by working as helpers to other repair or construction workers, including carpenters, electricians, or machinery repairers.

Necessary skills also can be learned in high school shop classes and postsecondary trade or vocational schools. It generally takes from 1 to 4 years of on-the-job training or school, or a combination of both, to become fully qualified, depending on the skill level required. Because a growing number of new buildings rely on computers to control various of their systems, general maintenance and repair workers may need basic computer skills, such as how to log onto a central computer system and navigate through a series of menus. Usually, companies that install computer-controlled equipment provide on-site training for general maintenance and repair workers.

Graduation from high school is preferred for entry into this occupation. High school courses in mechanical drawing, electricity, woodworking, blueprint reading, science, mathematics, and computers are useful. Mechanical aptitude, the ability to use shop mathematics, and manual dexterity are important. Good health is necessary because the job involves much walking, standing, reaching, and heavy lifting. Difficult jobs require problem-solving ability, and many positions require the ability to work without direct supervision.

Many general maintenance and repair workers in large organizations advance to maintenance supervisor or become a craftworker such as an electrician, a heating and air-conditioning mechanic, or a plumber. Within small organizations, promotion opportunities are limited.

Employment

General maintenance and repair workers held 1.3 million jobs in 2004. They were employed in almost every industry. Around 1 in 5 worked in manufacturing industries, almost evenly distributed through all sectors, while about 1 in 6 worked for different government bodies. Others worked for wholesale and retail firms and for real estate firms that operate office and apartment buildings.

Job Outlook

Job opportunities should be favorable, especially for those with experience in maintenance or related fields. General maintenance and repair is a large occupation with significant turnover. Additionally, many job openings are expected to result from the retirement of many experienced maintenance workers over the next decade.

Employment of general maintenance and repair workers is expected to grow about as fast as the average for all occupations through 2014. Employment is related to the number of buildings—for example, office and apartment buildings, stores, schools, hospitals, hotels, and factories—and the amount of equipment needing maintenance and repair. However, as machinery becomes more advanced and requires less maintenance, the need for general maintenance and repair workers diminishes. Also, as more buildings are controlled by computers, buildings can be monitored more efficiently.

Earnings

Median hourly earnings of general maintenance and repair workers were $14.76 in May 2004. The middle 50 percent earned between $11.11 and $19.17. The lowest 10 percent earned less than $8.70, and the highest 10 percent earned more than $23.40. Median hourly earnings in the industries employing the largest numbers of general maintenance and repair workers in May 2004 are shown in the following tabulation:

Local government	$15.70
Elementary and secondary schools	14.93
Activities related to real estate	12.71
Lessors of real estate	11.96
Traveler accommodation	11.19

Some general maintenance and repair workers are members of unions, including the American Federation of State, County, and Municipal Employees and the United Auto Workers.

Related Occupations

Some duties of general maintenance and repair workers are similar to those of carpenters; pipelayers, plumbers, pipefitters, and steamfitters; electricians; and heating, air-conditioning, and refrigeration mechanics. Other duties are similar to those of coin, vending, and amusement machine servicers and repairers; electrical and electronics installers and repairers; electronic home entertainment equipment installers and repairers; and radio and telecommunications equipment installers and repairers.

Sources of Additional Information

Information about job opportunities may be obtained from local employers and local offices of the state employment service.

Material Moving Occupations

(O*NET 53-1021.00, 53-7011.00, 53-7021.00, 53-7031.00, 53-7032.01, 53-7032.02, 53-7033.00, 53-7041.00, 53-7051.00, 53-7061.00, 53-7062.01, 53-7062.02, 53-7062.03, 53-7063.00, 53-7064.00, 53-7071.01, 53-7071.02, 53-7072.00, 53-7073.00, 53-7081.00, 53-7111.00, 53-7121.00, and 53-7199.99)

Significant Points

- Job openings should be numerous because the occupation is very large and turnover is relatively high.
- Most jobs require little work experience or training.
- Pay is low, and the seasonal nature of the work may reduce earnings.

Nature of the Work

Material moving workers are categorized into two groups—operators and laborers. Operators use machinery to move construction materials, earth, petroleum products, and other heavy materials. Generally, they move materials over short distances—around construction sites, factories, or warehouses. Some move materials onto or off of trucks and ships. Operators control equipment by moving levers, wheels, and/or foot pedals; operating switches; or turning dials. They also may set up and inspect equipment, make adjustments, and perform minor maintenance or repairs. Laborers and hand material movers manually handle freight, stock, or other materials; clean vehicles, machinery, and other equipment; feed materials into or remove materials from machines or equipment; and pack or package products and materials.

Material moving occupations are classified by the type of equipment they operate or the goods they handle. Each piece of equipment requires different skills, as do different types of loads. (For information on *operating engineers; paving, surfacing, and tamping equipment operators; and pile-driver operators*, see the description of construction equipment operators elsewhere in this book.)

Industrial truck and tractor operators drive and control industrial trucks or tractors equipped to move materials around warehouses, storage yards, factories, or construction sites. A typical industrial truck, often called a forklift or lift truck, has a hydraulic lifting mechanism and forks for moving heavy and large objects. Industrial truck and tractor operators also may operate tractors that pull trailers loaded with materials, goods, or equipment within factories and warehouses or around outdoor storage areas.

Excavating and loading machine and dragline operators tend or operate machinery equipped with scoops, shovels, or buckets to dig and load sand, gravel, earth, or similar materials into trucks or onto conveyors. Construction and mining industries employ the majority of excavation and loading machine and dragline operators. *Dredge operators* excavate waterways, removing sand, gravel, rock, or other materials from harbors, lakes, rivers, and streams. Dredges are used primarily to maintain navigable channels but also are used to restore wetlands and other aquatic habitats; reclaim land; and create and maintain beaches.

Underground mining loading machine operators use underground loading machines to load coal, ore, or rock into shuttles and mine cars or onto conveyors. Loading equipment may include power shovels, hoisting engines equipped with cable-drawn scraper or scoop, and machines equipped with gathering arms and conveyors.

Crane and tower operators work mechanical boom and cable or tower and cable equipment to lift and move materials, machinery, and other heavy objects. Operators extend and retract horizontally mounted booms and lower and raise hooks attached to load lines. Most operators are guided by other workers using hand signals or a radio. Operators position loads from an onboard console or from a remote console at the site. While crane and tower operators are noticeable at office building and other construction sites, the biggest group works in primary metal, metal fabrication, and transportation equipment manufacturing industries that use heavy, bulky materials. *Hoist and winch operators* control movement of cables, cages, and platforms to move workers and materials for manufacturing, logging, and other industrial operations. They work in positions such as derrick operators and hydraulic boom operators. Many hoist and winch operators are found in manufacturing or construction industries.

Pump operators tend, control, and operate power-driven pumps and manifold systems that transfer gases, oil, or other materials to vessels or equipment. They maintain the equipment to regulate the flow of materials according to a schedule set up by petroleum engineers and production supervisors. *Gas compressor and gas pumping station operators* operate steam, gas, electric-motor-, or internal-combustion-engine-driven compressors. They transmit, compress, or recover gases, such as butane, nitrogen, hydrogen, and natural gas. *Wellhead pumpers* operate power pumps and auxiliary equipment to produce flows of oil or gas from extraction sites.

Tank car, truck, and ship loaders operate ship-loading and -unloading equipment, conveyors, hoists, and other specialized material-handling equipment such as railroad tank car–unloading equipment. They may gauge or sample shipping tanks and test them for leaks. *Conveyor operators and tenders* control and tend conveyor systems that move materials to or from stockpiles, processing stations, departments, or vehicles. *Shuttle car operators* run diesel or electric-powered shuttle cars in underground mines, transporting materials from the working face to mine cars or conveyors.

Laborers and hand freight, stock, and material movers manually move materials and perform other unskilled general labor. These workers move freight, stock, and other materials to and from storage and production areas, loading docks, delivery vehicles, ships, and containers. Their specific duties vary by industry and work setting. In factories, they may move raw materials or finished goods between loading docks, storage areas, and work areas, as well as sort materials and supplies and prepare them according to their work orders. Specialized workers within this group include baggage and cargo handlers, who work in transportation industries, and truck loaders and unloaders.

Hand packers and packagers manually pack, package, or wrap a variety of materials. They may inspect items for defects, label cartons, stamp information on products, keep records of items packed, and stack packages on loading docks. This group also includes order fillers, who pack materials for shipment, as well as grocery store courtesy clerks. In grocery stores, they may bag groceries, carry packages to customers' cars, and return shopping carts to designated areas.

Machine feeders and offbearers feed materials into or remove materials from automatic equipment or machines tended by other workers.

Cleaners of vehicles and equipment clean machinery, vehicles, storage tanks, pipelines, and similar equipment, using water and other cleaning agents, vacuums, hoses, brushes, cloths, and other cleaning equipment.

Refuse and recyclable material collectors gather refuse and recyclables from homes and businesses into their truck for transport to a dump, landfill, or recycling center. They lift and empty garbage cans or recycling bins by hand or operate a hydraulic lift truck that picks up and empties dumpsters. They work along scheduled routes.

Working Conditions

Material moving work tends to be repetitive and physically demanding. Workers may lift and carry heavy objects and stoop, kneel, crouch, or crawl in awkward positions. Some work at great heights and some work outdoors, regardless of weather and climate. Some jobs expose workers to fumes, odors, loud noises, harmful materials and chemicals, or dangerous machinery. To protect their eyes, respiratory systems, and hearing, these workers wear safety clothing, such as gloves, hardhats, and other safety devices. These jobs have become much less dangerous as safety equipment—such as overhead guards on lift trucks—has become common. Accidents usually can be avoided by observing proper operating procedures and safety practices.

Material movers generally work 8-hour shifts, though longer shifts also are not uncommon. In industries that work around the clock, material movers may work overnight shifts. Some do this because the establishment does not want to disturb customers during normal business hours. Refuse and recyclable material collectors often work shifts starting at 5 or 6 a.m. Some material movers work only during certain seasons, such as when the weather permits construction activity.

Training, Other Qualifications, and Advancement

Little work experience or training is required for most material moving occupations. Some employers prefer applicants with a high school diploma, but most simply require workers to be at least 18 years old and physically able to perform the work. For those jobs requiring physical exertion, employers may require that applicants pass a physical exam. Some employers also require drug testing or background checks before employment. Material movers often are younger than workers in other occupations, reflecting the limited training but significant physical requirements of many of these jobs.

Material movers generally learn skills informally, on the job, from more experienced workers or their supervisors. Workers who handle toxic chemicals or use industrial trucks or other dangerous equipment must receive specialized training in safety awareness and procedures. Many of the training requirements are standardized through the U.S. Occupational Safety and Health Administration. This training is usually provided by the employer. Employers also must certify that each operator has received the training and evaluate each operator at least once every 3 years. For other operators, such as crane operators and those working with specialized loads, there are some training and apprenticeship programs, such as that offered by the International Union of Industrial Engineers, as well as certifying institutions, such as the National Commission for the Certification of Crane Operators. Some employers may require crane operators to be certified. Twelve states have laws requiring crane operators to be licensed. Licensing requirements typically include a written as well as a skills test to demonstrate that the licensee can operate a crane safely.

Material moving equipment operators need a good sense of balance, the ability to judge distances, and eye-hand-foot coordination. For jobs that involve dealing with the public, such as grocery store courtesy clerks, workers should be pleasant and courteous. Most jobs require basic arithmetic skills and the ability to read procedural manuals, to understand orders, and other billing documents. Mechanical aptitude and training in automobile or diesel mechanics can be helpful because some operators may perform basic maintenance on their equipment. Experience operating mobile equipment—such as tractors on farms or heavy equipment in the Armed Forces—is an asset. As material moving equipment becomes more advanced, workers will need to be increasingly comfortable with technology.

In many of these occupations, experience may allow workers to qualify or become trainees for jobs such as construction trades workers; assemblers or other production workers; motor vehicle operators; or vehicle and mobile equipment mechanics, installers, and repairers. In many workplaces, new employees gain experience in a material moving position before being promoted to a better-paying and more highly skilled job. Some may eventually advance to become supervisors.

Employment

Material movers held 5.1 million jobs in 2004. They were distributed among the detailed occupations as follows:

Laborers and freight, stock, and material movers, hand	2,430,000
Packers and packagers, hand	877,000
Industrial truck and tractor operators	635,000
Cleaners of vehicles and equipment	347,000
First-line supervisors/managers of helpers, laborers, and material movers, hand	173,000
Refuse and recyclable material collectors	149,000
Machine feeders and offbearers	148,000
Excavating and loading machine and dragline operators	86,000
Conveyor operators and tenders	53,000
Crane and tower operators	44,000
Tank car, truck, and ship loaders	17,000
Wellhead pumpers	11,000
Pump operators, except wellhead pumpers	11,000
Hoist and winch operators	5,600
Gas compressor and gas pumping station operators	5,100
Loading machine operators, underground mining	4,300
Shuttle car operators	3,100
Dredge operators	2,500
All other material moving workers	58,000

About 29 percent of all material movers worked in the wholesale trade or retail trade industries. Another 22 percent worked in manufacturing, 14 percent in transportation and warehousing, 4 percent in construction and mining, and 15 percent in the employment services industry on a temporary or contract basis. For example, companies that need workers for only a few days, to move materials or to clean up a site, may contract with temporary help agencies specializing in providing suitable workers on a short-term basis. A small proportion of material movers were self-employed.

Material movers work in every part of the country. Some work in remote locations on large construction projects such as highways and dams, while others work in factories, warehouses, or mining operations.

Job Outlook

Job openings should be numerous because the occupation is very large and turnover is relatively high—characteristic of occupations requiring little prior or formal training. Many openings will arise from the need to replace workers who transfer to other occupations or those who retire or leave the labor force for other reasons.

Employment in material moving occupations is projected to increase more slowly than the average for all occupations through 2014. Improvements in equipment, such as automated storage and retrieval systems and conveyors, will continue to raise productivity and moderate the demand for material movers.

Employment growth will stem from an expanding economy, especially in industries involved with the production, distribution, and sales of goods. Employment also will grow in the warehousing and storage industry as more firms contract out their warehousing functions to this industry. For example, a frozen food manufacturer may reduce its costs by outsourcing these functions to a refrigerated warehousing firm, which can more efficiently deal with the specialized storage needs of frozen food. Job growth for material movers depends on the growth or decline of employing industries and the type of equipment the workers operate or the materials they handle. For example, jobs in mining are expected to decline due to continued productivity increases within that industry. Job growth generally will be slower in large establishments, as they increasingly turn to automation for their material moving needs.

Both construction and manufacturing are very sensitive to changes in economic conditions, so the number of job openings in these industries will fluctuate. Although increasing automation will eliminate some routine tasks, new jobs will be created by the need to operate and maintain new equipment.

Earnings

Median hourly earnings of material moving workers in May 2004 were relatively low, as indicated by the following tabulation:

First-line supervisors/managers of helpers,
  laborers, and material movers, hand....................$18.40

Crane and tower operators 17.99

Pump operators, except wellhead pumpers 17.04

Wellhead pumpers 16.31

Hoist and winch operators 16.19

Tank car, truck, and ship loaders 15.59

Excavating and loading machine and dragline
  operators..15.37

Material moving workers, all other..........................13.87

Industrial truck and tractor operators.....................12.78

Refuse and recyclable material collectors 12.38

Conveyor operators and tenders 12.23

Machine feeders and offbearers 10.68

Laborers and freight, stock, and material movers,
  hand..9.67

Cleaners of vehicles and equipment.........................8.41

Packers and packagers, hand 8.25

Wages vary according to experience and job responsibilities. Wages usually are higher in metropolitan areas. Seasonal peaks and lulls in workload can affect the number of hours scheduled and, therefore, earnings. Certified crane operators tend to have a slightly higher hourly rate than those who are not certified.

Related Occupations

Other workers who operate mechanical equipment include construction equipment operators; machine setters, operators, and tenders—metal and plastic; rail transportation workers; and truck drivers and driver/sales workers. Other entry-level workers who perform mostly physical work are agricultural workers; building cleaning workers; construction laborers; forest, conservation, and logging workers; and grounds maintenance workers.

Sources of Additional Information

For information about job opportunities and training programs, contact local state employment service offices, building or construction contractors, manufacturers, and wholesale and retail establishments.

Information on safety and training requirements is available from

▸ U.S. Department of Labor, Occupational Safety and Health Administration (OSHA), 200 Constitution Ave. NW, Washington, DC 20210. Internet: http://www.osha.gov

Information on industrial truck and tractor operators is available from

▸ Industrial Truck Association, 1750 K St. NW, Suite 460, Washington, DC 20006. Internet: http://www.indtrk.org

Information on training and apprenticeships for industrial truck operators is available from

▸ International Union of Industrial Engineers, 1125 17th St. NW, Washington, DC 20036. Internet: http://www.iuoe.org

Information on crane and derrick certification and licensure is available from

▸ National Commission for the Certification of Crane Operators, 2750 Prosperity Ave., Suite 505, Fairfax, VA 22031. Internet: http://www.nccco.org

Medical Assistants

(O*NET 31-9092.00)

Significant Points

■ About 6 out of 10 medical assistants work in offices of physicians.

■ Some medical assistants are trained on the job, but many complete 1- or 2-year programs in vocational-technical high schools, postsecondary vocational schools, and community and junior colleges.

■ Medical assistants is projected to be one of the fastest-growing occupations over the 2004–2014 period.

■ Job prospects should be best for medical assistants with formal training or experience, particularly those with certification.

Nature of the Work

Medical assistants perform administrative and clinical tasks to keep the offices of physicians, podiatrists, chiropractors, and other health practitioners running smoothly. They should not be confused with physician assistants, who examine, diagnose, and treat patients under the direct supervision of a physician.

The duties of medical assistants vary from office to office, depending on the location and size of the practice and the practitioner's specialty. In small practices, medical assistants usually are generalists, handling both administrative and clinical duties and reporting directly to an office manager, physician, or other health practitioner. Those in large practices tend to specialize in a particular area under the supervision of department administrators.

Medical assistants perform many administrative duties, including answering telephones, greeting patients, updating and filing patients' medical records, filling out insurance forms, handling correspondence, scheduling appointments, arranging for hospital admission and laboratory services, and handling billing and bookkeeping.

Clinical duties vary according to state law and include taking medical histories and recording vital signs, explaining treatment procedures to patients, preparing patients for examination, and assisting the physician during the examination. Medical assistants collect and prepare laboratory specimens or perform basic laboratory tests on the premises, dispose of contaminated supplies, and sterilize medical instruments. They instruct patients about medications and special diets, prepare and administer medications as directed by a physician, authorize drug refills as directed, telephone prescriptions to a pharmacy, draw blood, prepare patients for X rays, take electrocardiograms, remove sutures, and change dressings.

Medical assistants also may arrange examining room instruments and equipment, purchase and maintain supplies and equipment, and keep waiting and examining rooms neat and clean.

Ophthalmic medical assistants and *podiatric medical assistants* are examples of specialized assistants who have additional duties. Ophthalmic medical assistants help ophthalmologists provide eye care. They conduct diagnostic tests, measure and record vision, and test eye muscle function. They also show patients how to insert, remove, and care for contact lenses, and they apply eye dressings. Under the direction of the physician, ophthalmic medical assistants may administer eye medications. They also maintain optical and surgical instruments and may assist the ophthalmologist in surgery. Podiatric medical assistants make castings of feet, expose and develop X rays, and assist podiatrists in surgery.

Working Conditions

Medical assistants work in well-lighted, clean environments. They constantly interact with other people and may have to handle several responsibilities at once.

Most full-time medical assistants work a regular 40-hour week. Many work part time, evenings, or weekends.

Training, Other Qualifications, and Advancement

Most employers prefer graduates of formal programs in medical assisting. Such programs are offered in vocational-technical high schools, postsecondary vocational schools, and community and junior colleges. Postsecondary programs usually last either 1 year, resulting in a certificate or diploma, or 2 years, resulting in an associate degree. Courses cover anatomy, physiology, and medical terminology, as well as typing, transcription, recordkeeping, accounting, and insurance processing. Students learn laboratory techniques, clinical and diagnostic procedures, pharmaceutical principles, the administration of medications, and first aid. They study office practices, patient relations, medical law, and ethics. Accredited programs include an internship that provides practical experience in physicians' offices, hospitals, or other health care facilities.

Both the Commission on Accreditation of Allied Health Education Programs (CAAHEP) and the Accrediting Bureau of Health Education Schools (ABHES) accredit programs in medical assisting. In 2005, there were over 500 medical assisting programs accredited by CAAHEP and about 170 accredited by ABHES. The Committee on Accreditation for Ophthalmic Medical Personnel approved 17 programs in ophthalmic medical assisting and 2 programs in ophthalmic clinical assisting.

Formal training in medical assisting, while generally preferred, is not always required. Some medical assistants are trained on the job, although this practice is less common than in the past. Applicants usually need a high school diploma or the equivalent. Recommended high school courses include mathematics, health, biology, typing, bookkeeping, computers, and office skills. Volunteer experience in the health care field also is helpful.

Although medical assistants are not licensed, some states require them to take a test or a course before they can perform certain tasks, such as taking X rays or giving injections.

Employers prefer to hire experienced workers or certified applicants who have passed a national examination indicating that the medical assistant meets certain standards of competence. The American Association of Medical Assistants awards the Certified Medical Assistant credential; American Medical Technologists awards the Registered Medical Assistant credential; the American Society of Podiatric Medical Assistants awards the Podiatric Medical Assistant, Certified credential; and the Joint Commission on Allied Health Personnel in Ophthalmology awards credentials at three levels: Certified Ophthalmic Assistant, Certified Ophthalmic Technician, and Certified Ophthalmic Medical Technologist.

Medical assistants deal with the public; therefore, they must be neat and well groomed and have a courteous, pleasant manner. Medical assistants must be able to put patients at ease and explain physicians' instructions. They must respect the confidential nature of medical information. Clinical duties require a reasonable level of manual dexterity and visual acuity.

Medical assistants may be able to advance to office manager. They may qualify for a variety of administrative support occupations or may teach medical assisting. With additional education, some enter other health occupations, such as nursing and medical technology.

Employment

Medical assistants held about 387,000 jobs in 2004. About 6 out of 10 worked in offices of physicians; about 14 percent worked in public and private hospitals, including inpatient and outpatient facilities; and 11 percent worked in offices of other health practitioners, such as chiropractors, optometrists, and podiatrists. The rest worked mostly in outpatient care centers, public and private educational services, other ambulatory health care services, state and local government agencies, employment services, medical and diagnostic laboratories, and nursing care facilities.

Job Outlook

Employment of medical assistants is expected to grow much faster than the average for all occupations through the year 2014 as the health care industry expands because of technological advances in medicine and the growth and aging of the population. Increasing utilization of medical assistants in the rapidly growing health care industry will further stimulate job growth. In fact, medical assistants is projected to be one of the fastest-growing occupations over the 2004–2014 period.

Employment growth will be driven by the increase in the number of group practices, clinics, and other health care facilities that need a high proportion of support personnel, particularly the flexible medical assistant who can handle both administrative and clinical duties. Medical assistants work primarily in outpatient settings, a rapidly growing sector of the health care industry.

In view of the preference of many health care employers for trained personnel, job prospects should be best for medical assistants with formal training or experience, particularly for those with certification.

Earnings

The earnings of medical assistants vary, depending on their experience, skill level, and location. Median annual earnings of medical assistants were $24,610 in May 2004. The middle 50 percent earned between $20,650 and $28,930. The lowest 10 percent earned less than $18,010, and the highest 10 percent earned more than $34,650. Median annual earnings in the industries employing the largest numbers of medical assistants in May 2004 were

Colleges, universities, and professional schools $27,490

Outpatient care centers 25,360

General medical and surgical hospitals 25,160

Offices of physicians 24,930

Offices of other health practitioners......................21,930

Related Occupations

Workers in other medical support occupations include dental assistants, medical records and health information technicians, medical secretaries, occupational therapist assistants and aides, pharmacy aides, and physical therapist assistants and aides.

Sources of Additional Information

Information about career opportunities and the Certified Medical Assistant exam is available from

▸ American Association of Medical Assistants, 20 North Wacker Dr., Suite 1575, Chicago, IL 60606. Internet: http://www.aama-ntl.org

Information about career opportunities and the Registered Medical Assistant certification exam is available from

▸ American Medical Technologists, 710 Higgins Rd., Park Ridge, IL 60068-5765.

Information about career opportunities, training programs, and certification for ophthalmic medical personnel is available from

▸ Joint Commission on Allied Health Personnel in Ophthalmology, 2025 Woodlane Dr., St. Paul, MN 55125-2998. Internet: http://www.jcahpo.org/newsite/index.htm

Information about certification for podiatric assistants is available from

▸ American Society of Podiatric Medical Assistants, 2l24 South Austin Blvd., Cicero, IL 60804. Internet: http://www.aspma.org

For a list of educational programs in medical assisting accredited by the Commission on Accreditation of Allied Health Education Programs, contact

▸ Commission on Accreditation of Allied Health Education Programs, 1361 Park St., Clearwater, FL 33756. Internet: http://www.caahep.org

A list of ABHES-accredited educational programs in medical assisting is available from

▸ Accrediting Bureau of Health Education Schools, 7777 Leesburg Pike, Suite 314 N, Falls Church, VA 22043. Internet: http://www.abhes.org

Musicians, Singers, and Related Workers

(O*NET 27-2041.01, 27-2041.02, 27-2041.03, 27-2042.01, and 27-2042.02)

Significant Points

■ Part-time schedules and intermittent unemployment are common; many musicians supplement their income with earnings from other sources.

■ Aspiring musicians begin studying an instrument or training their voices at an early age.

■ Competition for jobs is keen; those who can play several instruments and perform a wide range of musical styles should enjoy the best job prospects.

Nature of the Work

Musicians, singers, and related workers play musical instruments; sing, compose or arrange music; or conduct groups in instrumental or vocal performances. They may perform solo or as part of a group. Musicians, singers, and related workers entertain live audiences in nightclubs, concert halls, and theaters featuring opera, musical theater, or dance. Many of these entertainers play for live audiences; others perform exclusively for recording or production studios. Regardless of the setting, musicians, singers, and related workers spend considerable time practicing alone and with their bands, orchestras, or other musical ensembles.

Musicians often gain their reputation or professional standing by exhibiting a high level of professionalism and proficiency in a particular kind of music or performance. However, those who learn several related instruments and who can perform equally well in several musical styles have better employment opportunities. Instrumental musicians, for example, may play in a symphony orchestra, rock group, or jazz combo one night; appear in another ensemble the next; and work in a studio band the following day. Some play a variety of string, brass, woodwind, or percussion instruments or electronic synthesizers.

Singers interpret music and text, using their knowledge of voice production, melody, and harmony. They sing character parts or perform in their own individual style. Singers are often classified according to their voice range—soprano, contralto, tenor, baritone, or bass—or by the type of music they sing, such as opera, rock, popular, folk, rap, or country and western.

Music directors conduct, direct, plan, and lead instrumental or vocal performances by musical groups, such as orchestras, choirs, and glee clubs. *Conductors* lead instrumental music groups, such as symphony orchestras, dance bands, show bands, and various popular ensembles. These leaders audition and select musicians, choose the music most appropriate for their talents and abilities, and direct rehearsals and performances. Choral directors lead choirs and glee clubs, sometimes working with a band or an orchestra conductor.

Directors audition and select singers and lead them at rehearsals and performances to achieve harmony, rhythm, tempo, shading, and other desired musical effects.

Composers create original music such as symphonies, operas, sonatas, radio and television jingles, film scores, and popular songs. They transcribe ideas into musical notation, using harmony, rhythm, melody, and tonal structure. Although most composers and songwriters practice their craft on instruments and transcribe the notes with pen and paper, some use computer software to compose and edit their music.

Arrangers transcribe and adapt musical compositions to a particular style for orchestras, bands, choral groups, or individuals. Components of music—including tempo, volume, and the mix of instruments needed—are arranged to express the composer's message. While some arrangers write directly into a musical composition, others use computer software to make changes.

Working Conditions

Musicians typically perform at night and on weekends. They spend much additional time practicing or in rehearsal. Full-time musicians with long-term employment contracts, such as those with symphony orchestras or television and film production companies, enjoy steady work and less travel. Nightclub, solo, or recital musicians frequently travel to perform in a variety of local settings and may tour nationally or internationally. Because many musicians find only part-time or intermittent work, experiencing unemployment between engagements, they often supplement their income with other types of jobs. The stress of constantly looking for work leads many musicians to accept permanent, full-time jobs in other occupations while working only part time as musicians.

Most instrumental musicians work closely with a variety of other people, including their colleagues, agents, employers, sponsors, and audiences. Although they usually work indoors, some perform outdoors for parades, concerts, and festivals. In some nightclubs and restaurants, smoke and odors may be present and lighting and ventilation may be poor.

Training, Other Qualifications, and Advancement

Aspiring musicians begin studying an instrument at an early age. They may gain valuable experience playing in a school or community band or an orchestra or with a group of friends. Singers usually start training when their voices mature. Participation in school musicals or choirs often provides good early training and experience.

Musicians need extensive and prolonged training and practice to acquire the necessary skills, knowledge, and ability to interpret music at a professional level. Like other artists, musicians and singers continually strive to stretch themselves—exploring different forms of music. Formal training may be obtained through private study with an accomplished musician, in a college or university music program, or in a music conservatory. For university or conservatory study, an audition generally is necessary. The National Association of Schools of Music accredits more than 600 college-level programs in music. Courses typically include music theory, music

interpretation, composition, conducting, and performance in a particular instrument or in voice. Music directors, composers, conductors, and arrangers need considerable related work experience or advanced training in these subjects.

Many colleges, universities, and music conservatories grant bachelor's or higher degrees in music. A master's or doctoral degree usually is required to teach advanced music courses in colleges and universities; a bachelor's degree may be sufficient to teach basic courses. A degree in music education qualifies graduates for a state certificate to teach music in public elementary or secondary schools. Musicians who do not meet public school music education requirements may teach in private schools and recreation associations or instruct individual students in private sessions.

Musicians must be knowledgeable about a broad range of musical styles but keenly aware of the form that interests them most. Having a broader range of interest, knowledge, and training can help expand employment opportunities and musical abilities. Voice training and private instrumental lessons, taken especially when the individual is young, also help develop technique and enhance one's performance.

Young persons considering careers in music should have musical talent, versatility, creativity, poise, and a good stage presence. Because quality performance requires constant study and practice, self-discipline is vital. To sustain a career as a musician or singer, performers must achieve a level of performing excellence and be counted on to be on their game whenever they perform. Moreover, musicians who play in concerts or in nightclubs and those who tour must have physical stamina to endure frequent travel and an irregular performance schedule. Because musicians and singers always must make their performances look effortless, preparation and practice are important. Musicians and singers also must be prepared to face the anxiety of intermittent employment and of rejection when auditioning for work.

Advancement for musicians usually means becoming better known, finding work more easily, and performing for higher earnings. Successful musicians often rely on agents or managers to find them performing engagements, negotiate contracts, and develop their careers.

Employment

Musicians, singers, and related workers held about 249,000 jobs in 2004. Around 40 percent worked part time; almost half were self-employed. Many found jobs in cities in which entertainment and recording activities are concentrated, such as New York, Los Angeles, Las Vegas, Chicago, and Nashville.

Musicians, singers, and related workers are employed in a variety of settings. Of those who earn a wage or salary, almost two-thirds were employed by religious organizations and almost one-fourth by performing arts companies such as professional orchestras, small chamber music groups, opera companies, musical theater companies, and ballet troupes. Musicians and singers also perform in nightclubs and restaurants and for weddings and other events. Well-known musicians and groups may perform in concerts, appear on radio and television broadcasts, and make recordings and music videos. The Armed Forces also offer careers in their bands and smaller musical groups.

Job Outlook

Competition for jobs for musicians, singers, and related workers is expected to be keen. The vast number of persons with the desire to perform will continue to greatly exceed the number of openings. Talent alone is no guarantee of success: Many people start out to become musicians or singers but leave the profession because they find the work difficult, the discipline demanding, and the long periods of intermittent unemployment unendurable.

Overall employment of musicians, singers, and related workers is expected to grow about as fast as the average for all occupations through 2014. Most new wage and salary jobs for musicians will arise in religious organizations. Slower-than-average growth is expected for self-employed musicians, who generally perform in nightclubs, concert tours, and other venues. Growth in demand for musicians will generate a number of job opportunities, and many openings also will arise from the need to replace those who leave the field each year because they are unable to make a living solely as musicians or for other reasons.

Earnings

Median hourly earnings of musicians and singers were $17.85 in May 2004. The middle 50 percent earned between $9.68 and $30.75. The lowest 10 percent earned less than $6.47, and the highest 10 percent earned more than $53.59. Median hourly earnings were $20.70 in performing arts companies and $12.17 in religious organizations. Annual earnings data for musicians and singers were not available because of the wide variation in the number of hours worked by musicians and singers and the short-term nature of many jobs, which may last for 1 day or 1 week; it is extremely rare for musicians and singers to have guaranteed employment that exceeds 3 to 6 months.

Median annual earnings of salaried music directors and composers were $34,570 in May 2004. The middle 50 percent earned between $24,040 and $51,770. The lowest 10 percent earned less than $15,960, and the highest 10 percent earned more than $75,380.

Yearly earnings typically reflect the number of gigs a freelance musician or singer played or the number of hours and weeks of salaried contract work, in addition to a performer's professional reputation and setting: Performers who can fill large concert halls, arenas, or outdoor stadiums generally command higher pay than those who perform in local clubs. Soloists or headliners usually receive higher earnings than band members or opening acts. The most successful musicians earn performance or recording fees that far exceed the median earnings.

According to the American Federation of Musicians, weekly minimum salaries in major orchestras ranged from about $700 to $2,080 during the 2004–2005 performing season. Each orchestra works out a separate contract with its local union, but individual musicians may negotiate higher salaries. Top orchestras have a season ranging from 24 to 52 weeks, with 18 orchestras reporting 52-week contracts. In regional orchestras, minimum salaries are often less because fewer performances are scheduled. Regional orchestra musicians often are paid for their services without any guarantee of future employment. Community orchestras often have even more limited levels of funding and offer salaries that are much lower for seasons of shorter duration.

Although musicians employed by some symphony orchestras work under master wage agreements, which guarantee a season's work up to 52 weeks, many other musicians face relatively long periods of unemployment between jobs. Even when employed, many musicians and singers work part time in unrelated occupations. Thus, their earnings usually are lower than earnings in many other occupations. Moreover, because they may not work steadily for one employer, some performers cannot qualify for unemployment compensation, and few have typical benefits such as sick leave or paid vacations. For these reasons, many musicians give private lessons or take jobs unrelated to music to supplement their earnings as performers.

Many musicians belong to a local of the American Federation of Musicians. Professional singers who perform live often belong to a branch of the American Guild of Musical Artists; those who record for the broadcast industries may belong to the American Federation of Television and Radio Artists.

Related Occupations

Musical instrument repairers and tuners (part of precision instrument and equipment repairers) require technical knowledge of musical instruments. Others whose work involves the performing arts include actors, producers, and directors; announcers; and dancers and choreographers.

Sources of Additional Information

For general information about music and music teacher education and a list of accredited college-level programs, contact

▸ National Association of Schools of Music, 11250 Roger Bacon Dr., Suite 21, Reston, VA 20190. Internet: http://nasm.arts-accredit.org

Nursing, Psychiatric, and Home Health Aides

(O*NET 31-1011.00, 31-1012.00, and 31-1013.00)

Significant Points

■ Home health aides is projected to be the fastest-growing occupation through 2014.

■ Numerous job openings and excellent job opportunities are expected.

■ Most jobs are in nursing and residential care facilities, hospitals, and home health care services.

■ Modest entry requirements, low pay, high physical and emotional demands, and lack of advancement opportunities characterize this occupation.

Nature of the Work

Nursing and psychiatric aides help care for physically or mentally ill, injured, disabled, or infirm individuals confined to hospitals, nursing care facilities, and mental health settings. Home health aides have duties that are similar, but they work in patients' homes or residential care facilities.

Nursing aides—also known as nursing assistants, certified nursing assistants, geriatric aides, unlicensed assistive personnel, orderlies, or hospital attendants—perform routine tasks under the supervision of nursing and medical staff. They answer patients' call lights; deliver messages; serve meals; make beds; and help patients to eat, dress, and bathe. Aides also may provide skin care to patients; take their temperature, pulse rate, respiration rate, and blood pressure; and help them to get into and out of bed and walk. They also may escort patients to operating and examining rooms, keep patients' rooms neat, set up equipment, store and move supplies, and assist with some procedures. Aides observe patients' physical, mental, and emotional conditions and report any change to the nursing or medical staff.

Nursing aides employed in nursing care facilities often are the principal caregivers, having far more contact with residents than do other members of the staff. Because some residents may stay in a nursing care facility for months or even years, aides develop ongoing relationships with them and interact with them in a positive, caring way.

Home health aides help elderly, convalescent, or disabled persons live in their own homes instead of in a health care facility. Under the direction of nursing or medical staff, they provide health-related services, such as administering oral medications. Like nursing aides, home health aides may check patients' pulse rate, temperature, and respiration rate; help with simple prescribed exercises; keep patients' rooms neat; and help patients to move from bed, bathe, dress, and groom. Occasionally, they change nonsterile dressings, give massages and alcohol rubs, or assist with braces and artificial limbs. Experienced home health aides also may assist with medical equipment such as ventilators, which help patients breathe.

Most home health aides work with elderly or disabled persons who need more extensive care than family or friends can provide. Some help discharged hospital patients who have relatively short-term needs.

In home health agencies, a registered nurse, physical therapist, or social worker usually assigns specific duties to and supervises home health aides, who keep records of the services they perform and record each patient's condition and progress. The aides report changes in a patient's condition to the supervisor or case manager.

Psychiatric aides, also known as mental health assistants or psychiatric nursing assistants, care for mentally impaired or emotionally disturbed individuals. They work under a team that may include psychiatrists, psychologists, psychiatric nurses, social workers, and therapists. In addition to helping patients to dress, bathe, groom themselves, and eat, psychiatric aides socialize with them and lead them in educational and recreational activities. Psychiatric aides may play games such as cards with the patients; watch television with them; or participate in group activities, such as sports or field trips. They observe patients and report any physical or behavioral signs that might be important for the professional staff to know. They accompany patients to and from examinations and treatment. Because they have such close contact with patients, psychiatric aides can have a great deal of influence on their patients' outlook and treatment.

Working Conditions

Most full-time aides work about 40 hours a week, but, because patients need care 24 hours a day, some aides work evenings, nights, weekends, and holidays. Many work part time. In 2004, 25 percent of aides worked part time compared with 16 percent of all workers. Aides spend many hours standing and walking, and they often face heavy workloads. Aides must guard against back injury because they may have to move patients into and out of bed or help them to stand or walk. Aides also may face hazards from minor infections and major diseases, such as hepatitis, but can avoid infections by following proper procedures.

Aides often have unpleasant duties, such as emptying bedpans and changing soiled bed linens. The patients they care for may be disoriented, irritable, or uncooperative. Psychiatric aides must be prepared to care for patients whose illness may cause violent behavior. While their work can be emotionally demanding, many aides gain satisfaction from assisting those in need.

Home health aides may go to the same patient's home for months or even years. However, most aides work with a number of different patients, each job lasting a few hours, days, or weeks. Home health aides often visit multiple patients on the same day.

Home health aides generally work alone, with periodic visits from their supervisor. They receive detailed instructions explaining when to visit patients and what services to perform. Aides are individually responsible for getting to patients' homes, and they may spend a good portion of the working day traveling from one patient to another. Because mechanical lifting devices available in institutional settings are seldom available in patients' homes, home health aides are particularly susceptible to injuries resulting from overexertion when they assist patients.

Training, Other Qualifications, and Advancement

In many cases, a high school diploma or equivalent is necessary for a job as a nursing or psychiatric aide. However, a high school diploma generally is not required for jobs as home health aides. Hospitals may require previous experience as a nursing aide or home health aide. Nursing care facilities often hire inexperienced workers, who must complete a minimum of 75 hours of mandatory training and pass a competency evaluation as part of a state-approved training program within 4 months of their employment. Aides who complete the program are known as certified nurse assistants (CNAs) and are placed on the state registry of nursing aides. Some states also require psychiatric aides to complete a formal training program. However, most psychiatric aides learn their skills on the job from experienced workers.

Nursing and psychiatric aide training is offered in high schools, vocational-technical centers, some nursing care facilities, and some community colleges. Courses cover body mechanics, nutrition, anatomy and physiology, infection control, communication skills, and resident rights. Personal care skills, such as how to help patients to bathe, eat, and groom themselves, also are taught.

Some employers provide classroom instruction for newly hired aides, while others rely exclusively on informal on-the-job instruction by a licensed nurse or an experienced aide. Such training may last from several days to a few months. Aides also may attend lectures, workshops, and in-service training.

The federal government has guidelines for home health aides whose employers receive reimbursement from Medicare. Federal law requires home health aides to pass a competency test covering a wide range of areas: communication; documentation of patient status and care provided; reading and recording of vital signs; basic infection-control procedures; basic bodily functions; maintenance of a healthy environment; emergency procedures; physical, emotional, and developmental characteristics of patients; personal hygiene and grooming; safe transfer techniques; normal range of motion and positioning; and basic nutrition.

A home health aide may receive training before taking the competency test. Federal law suggests at least 75 hours of classroom and practical training supervised by a registered nurse. Training and testing programs may be offered by the employing agency but must meet the standards of the Center for Medicare and Medicaid Services. State regulations for training programs vary.

The National Association for Home Care offers national certification for home health aides. The certification is a voluntary demonstration that the individual has met industry standards. Some states also require aides to be licensed.

Aides must be in good health. A physical examination, including state-regulated tests such as those for tuberculosis, may be required. A criminal background check also is usually required for employment.

Applicants should be tactful, patient, understanding, emotionally stable, and dependable and should have a desire to help people. They also should be able to work as part of a team; have good communication skills; and be willing to perform repetitive, routine tasks. Home health aides should be honest and discreet because they work in private homes. They also will need access to their own car or public transportation to reach patients' homes.

For some individuals, these occupations serve as entry-level jobs, as in the case of high school and college students who may work while also attending school. In addition, experience as an aide can help individuals decide whether to pursue a career in health care. Opportunities for advancement within these occupations are limited. Aides generally need additional formal training or education in order to enter other health occupations. The most common health care occupations for former aides are licensed practical nurse, registered nurse, and medical assistant.

Employment

Nursing, psychiatric, and home health aides held about 2.1 million jobs in 2004. Nursing aides held the most jobs—approximately 1.5 million. Home health aides held roughly 624,000 jobs, and psychiatric aides held about 59,000 jobs. Around 42 percent of nursing aides worked in nursing care facilities, and another 27 percent worked in hospitals. Most home health aides—about 34 percent—were employed by home health care services. Others were employed in nursing and residential care facilities and social assistance agencies. Around 54 percent of all psychiatric aides worked in hospitals, primarily in psychiatric and substance abuse hospitals, although some also worked in the psychiatric units of general medical and surgical hospitals. Others were employed in state government agencies;

residential mental retardation, mental health, and substance abuse facilities; outpatient care centers; and nursing care facilities.

Job Outlook

Numerous job openings for nursing, psychiatric, and home health aides will arise from a combination of fast employment growth and high replacement needs. High replacement needs in this large occupation reflect modest entry requirements, low pay, high physical and emotional demands, and lack of opportunities for advancement. For these same reasons, many people are unwilling to perform the kind of work required by the occupation, limiting the number of entrants. Many aides also leave the occupation to attend training programs for other health care occupations. Therefore, persons who are interested in, and suited for, this work should have excellent job opportunities.

Overall employment of nursing, psychiatric, and home health aides is projected to grow much faster than the average for all occupations through the year 2014, although individual occupational growth rates will vary. Home health aides is expected to be the fastest-growing occupation as a result of both growing demand for home services from an aging population and efforts to contain costs by moving patients out of hospitals and nursing care facilities as quickly as possible. Consumer preference for care in the home and improvements in medical technologies for in-home treatment also will contribute to much-faster-than-average employment growth for home health aides.

Nursing aide employment will not grow as fast as home health aide employment, largely because nursing aides are concentrated in slower-growing nursing care facilities and hospitals. Employment of nursing aides is expected to grow faster than the average for all occupations through 2014 in response to the long-term care needs of an increasing elderly population. Financial pressures on hospitals to discharge patients as soon as possible should boost admissions to nursing care facilities. As a result, job opportunities will be more numerous in nursing and residential care facilities than in hospitals. Modern medical technology also will drive demand for nursing aides because, as the technology saves and extends more lives, it increases the need for long-term care provided by aides.

Employment of psychiatric aides—the smallest of the three occupations—is expected to grow more slowly than the average for all occupations. Most psychiatric aides currently work in hospitals, but most job growth will be in residential mental health facilities and in home health care agencies. There is a long-term trend toward treating mental health patients outside of hospitals because it is more cost effective and allows patients to live more normal lives. Demand for psychiatric aides in residential facilities will rise in response to growth in the number of older persons—many of whom will require mental health services—but also as an increasing number of mentally disabled adults, who were formerly cared for by their elderly parents, seek care. Job growth also could be affected by changes in government funding of programs for the mentally ill.

Earnings

Median hourly earnings of nursing aides, orderlies, and attendants were $10.09 in May 2004. The middle 50 percent earned between $8.59 and $12.09 an hour. The lowest 10 percent earned less than

$7.31, and the highest 10 percent earned more than $14.02 an hour. Median hourly earnings in the industries employing the largest numbers of nursing aides, orderlies, and attendants in May 2004 were as follows:

Employment services	$11.29
Local government	11.10
General medical and surgical hospitals	10.44
Nursing care facilities	9.86
Community care facilities for the elderly	9.56

Nursing and psychiatric aides in hospitals generally receive at least 1 week of paid vacation after 1 year of service. Paid holidays and sick leave, hospital and medical benefits, extra pay for late-shift work, and pension plans also are available to many hospital employees and to some nursing care facility employees.

Median hourly earnings of home health aides were $8.81 in May 2004. The middle 50 percent earned between $7.52 and $10.38 an hour. The lowest 10 percent earned less than $6.52, and the highest 10 percent earned more than $12.32 an hour. Median hourly earnings in the industries employing the largest numbers of home health aides in May 2004 were as follows:

Nursing care facilities	$9.11
Residential mental retardation, mental health, and substance abuse facilities	8.97
Home health care services	8.57
Community care facilities for the elderly	8.57
Individual and family services	8.47

Home health aides receive slight pay increases with experience and added responsibility. Usually, they are paid only for the time worked in the home, not for travel time between jobs. Most employers hire only on-call hourly workers and provide no benefits.

Median hourly earnings of psychiatric aides were $11.19 in May 2004. The middle 50 percent earned between $9.09 and $14.09 an hour. The lowest 10 percent earned less than $7.63, and the highest 10 percent earned more than $16.74 an hour. Median hourly earnings in the industries employing the largest numbers of psychiatric aides in May 2004 were as follows:

General medical and surgical hospitals	$11.31
Psychiatric and substance abuse hospitals	11.06
Residential mental retardation, mental health, and substance abuse facilities	9.37

Related Occupations

Nursing, psychiatric, and home health aides help people who need routine care or treatment. So do childcare workers, licensed practical and licensed vocational nurses, medical assistants, occupational therapist assistants and aides, personal and home care aides, physical therapist assistants and aides, and registered nurses.

Sources of Additional Information

Information about employment opportunities may be obtained from local hospitals, nursing care facilities, home health care agencies, psychiatric facilities, state boards of nursing, and local offices of the state employment service.

Information on licensing requirements for nursing and home health aides and lists of state-approved nursing aide programs are available from state departments of public health, departments of occupational licensing, boards of nursing, and home care associations.

Office and Administrative Support Worker Supervisors and Managers

(O*NET 43-1011.01 and 43-1011.02)

Significant Points

■ Most jobs are filled by promoting office or administrative support workers from within the organization.

■ Office automation will cause employment in some office and administrative support occupations to grow slowly or even decline, resulting in slower-than-average growth among supervisors and managers.

■ Applicants are likely to encounter keen competition because their numbers should greatly exceed the number of job openings.

Nature of the Work

All organizations need timely and effective office and administrative support to operate efficiently. Office and administrative support supervisors and managers coordinate this support. These workers are employed in virtually every sector of the economy, working in positions as varied as teller supervisor, customer services manager, or shipping and receiving supervisor.

Although specific functions of office and administrative support supervisors and managers vary significantly, they share many common duties. For example, supervisors perform administrative tasks to ensure that their staffs can work efficiently. Equipment and machinery used in their departments must be in good working order. If the computer system goes down or a fax machine malfunctions, the supervisors must try to correct the problem or alert repair personnel. They also request new equipment or supplies for their department when necessary.

Planning the work and supervising the staff are key functions of this job. To do these effectively, the supervisor must know the strengths and weaknesses of each member of the staff, as well as the results required from and time allotted to each job. Supervisors must make allowances for unexpected staff absences and other disruptions by adjusting assignments or performing the work themselves if the situation requires it.

After allocating work assignments and issuing deadlines, office and administrative support supervisors and managers oversee the work to ensure that it is proceeding on schedule and meeting established quality standards. This may involve reviewing each person's work on a computer—as in the case of accounting clerks—or listening to how a worker deals with customers—as in the case of customer services representatives. When supervising long-term projects, the supervisor may meet regularly with staff members to discuss their progress.

Office and administrative support supervisors and managers also evaluate each worker's performance. If a worker has done a good job, the supervisor indicates that in the employee's personnel file and may recommend a promotion or other award. Alternatively, if a worker is performing inadequately, the supervisor discusses the problem with the employee to determine the cause and helps the worker to improve his or her performance. This might require sending the employee to a training course or arranging personal counseling. If the situation does not improve, the supervisor may recommend a transfer, demotion, or dismissal.

Office and administrative support supervisors and managers usually interview and evaluate prospective employees. When new workers arrive on the job, supervisors greet them and provide orientation to acquaint them with their organization and its operating routines. Some supervisors may be actively involved in recruiting new workers—for example, by making presentations at high schools and business colleges. They also may serve as the primary liaisons between their offices and the general public through direct contact and by preparing promotional information.

Supervisors help train new employees in organization and office procedures. They may teach new employees how to use the telephone system and operate office equipment. Because most administrative support work is computerized, they also must teach new employees to use the organization's computer system. When new office equipment or updated computer software is introduced, supervisors train experienced employees to use it efficiently or, if this is not possible, arrange for their employees to receive special outside training.

Office and administrative support supervisors and managers often act as liaisons between the administrative support staff and the professional, technical, and managerial staff. This may involve implementing new company policies or restructuring the workflow in their departments. They also must keep their superiors informed of their progress and any potential problems. Often, this communication takes the form of research projects and progress reports. Because supervisors and managers have access to information such as their department's performance records, they may compile and present these data for use in planning or designing new policies.

Office and administrative support supervisors and managers also may have to resolve interpersonal conflicts among the staff. In organizations covered by union contracts, supervisors must know the provisions of labor-management agreements and run their departments accordingly. They also may meet with union representatives to discuss work problems or grievances.

Working Conditions

Office and administrative support supervisors and managers are employed in a wide variety of work settings, but most work in clean and well-lit offices that usually are comfortable.

Most office and administrative support supervisors and managers work a standard 40-hour week. However, because some organizations operate around the clock, supervisors may have to work nights, weekends, and holidays. Sometimes, supervisors rotate among the three 8-hour shifts in a workday; in other cases, shifts are assigned on the basis of seniority.

Training, Other Qualifications, and Advancement

Most firms fill office and administrative support supervisory and managerial positions by promoting office or administrative support workers from within their organizations. To become eligible for promotion to a supervisory position, administrative support workers must prove they are capable of handling additional responsibilities. When evaluating candidates, supervisors look for strong teamwork, problem-solving, leadership, and communication skills, as well as determination, loyalty, poise, and confidence. They also look for more specific supervisory attributes, such as the ability to organize and coordinate work efficiently, to set priorities, and to motivate others. Increasingly, supervisors need a broad base of office skills coupled with personal flexibility to adapt to changes in organizational structure and move among departments when necessary.

In addition, supervisors must pay close attention to detail to identify and correct errors made by the staff they oversee. Good working knowledge of the organization's computer system also is an advantage. Many employers require postsecondary training—in some cases, an associate or even a bachelor's degree.

Administrative support workers with potential supervisory abilities may be given occasional supervisory assignments. To prepare for full-time supervisory duties, workers may attend in-house training or take courses in time management, project management, or interpersonal relations.

Some office and administrative support supervisor positions are filled with people from outside the organization. These positions may serve as entry-level training for potential higher-level managers. New college graduates may rotate through departments of an organization at this level to learn the work of the organization.

Employment

Office and administrative support supervisors and managers held 1.5 million jobs in 2004. Although jobs for office and administrative support supervisors and managers are found in practically every industry, the largest number are found in organizations with a large administrative support workforce, such as banks, wholesalers, government agencies, retail establishments, business service firms, health care facilities, schools, and insurance companies. Because of most organizations' need for continuity of supervision, few office and administrative support supervisors and managers work on a temporary or part-time basis.

Job Outlook

Like those seeking other supervisory and managerial occupations, applicants for jobs as office and administrative support worker supervisors and managers are likely to encounter keen competition because the number of applicants should greatly exceed the number of job openings. Employment is expected to grow more slowly than the average for all occupations through 2014. Besides the job openings arising from growth, a large number of openings will stem from the need to replace workers who transfer to other occupations or leave this large occupation for other reasons.

Employment of office and administrative support supervisors and managers is determined largely by the demand for administrative support workers. New technology should increase office and administrative support workers' productivity and allow a wider variety of tasks to be performed by people in professional positions. These trends will cause employment in some administrative support occupations to grow slowly or even decline. As a result, supervisors will direct smaller permanent staffs—supplemented by increased use of temporary administrative support staff—and perform more professional tasks. Office and administrative support managers will coordinate the increasing amount of administrative work and make sure that the technology is applied and running properly. However, organizational restructuring should continue to reduce employment in some managerial positions, distributing more responsibility to office and administrative support supervisors.

Earnings

Median annual earnings of office and administrative support supervisors and managers were $41,030 in May 2004; the middle 50 percent earned between $31,860 and $53,110. The lowest-paid 10 percent earned less than $25,190, while the highest-paid 10 percent earned more than $67,800. In May 2004, median annual earnings in the industries employing the largest numbers of office and administrative support supervisors and managers were

Insurance carriers	$49,610
Local government	42,100
State government	40,930
Offices of physicians	39,690
Depository credit intermediation	36,980

In addition to typical benefits, some office and administrative support supervisors and managers, particularly in the private sector, may receive additional compensation in the form of bonuses and stock options.

Related Occupations

Office and administrative support supervisors and managers must understand and sometimes perform the work of those whom they oversee, including bookkeeping, accounting, and auditing clerks; cashiers; communications equipment operators; customer service representatives; data entry and information processing workers; general office clerks; receptionists and information clerks; stock clerks and order fillers; order clerks; and tellers. Their supervisory and administrative duties are similar to those of other supervisors and managers.

Sources of Additional Information

For information related to a wide variety of management occupations, including educational programs and certified designations, contact

▸ National Management Association, 2210 Arbor Blvd., Dayton, OH 45439. Internet: http://www.nma1.org

▸ International Association of Administrative Professionals, 10502 NW Ambassador Dr., P.O. Box 20404, Kansas City, MO 64195-0404. Internet: http://www.iaap-hq.org

Office Clerks, General

(O*NET 43-9061.00)

Significant Points

■ Employment growth and high replacement needs in this large occupation will result in numerous job openings.

■ Prospects should be best for those with knowledge of basic computer applications and office machinery as well as good communication skills.

■ Part-time and temporary positions are common.

Nature of the Work

Rather than performing a single specialized task, general office clerks have responsibilities that often change daily with the needs of the specific job and the employer. Whereas some clerks spend their days filing or keyboarding, others enter data at a computer terminal. They also can be called on to operate photocopiers, fax machines, and other office equipment; prepare mailings; proofread documents; and answer telephones and deliver messages.

The specific duties assigned to a clerk vary significantly, depending on the type of office in which he or she works. An office clerk in a doctor's office, for example, would not perform the same tasks that a clerk in a large financial institution or in the office of an auto parts wholesaler would perform. Although both may sort checks, keep payroll records, take inventory, and access information, clerks also perform duties unique to their employer, such as organizing medications, making transparencies for a presentation, or filling orders received by fax machine.

Clerks' duties also vary by level of experience. Whereas inexperienced employees make photocopies, stuff envelopes, or record inquiries, experienced clerks usually are given additional responsibilities. For example, they may maintain financial or other records, set up spreadsheets, verify statistical reports for accuracy and completeness, handle and adjust customer complaints, work with vendors, make travel arrangements, take inventory of equipment and supplies, answer questions on departmental services and functions, or help prepare invoices or budgetary requests. Senior office clerks may be expected to monitor and direct the work of lower-level clerks.

Working Conditions

For the most part, general office clerks work in comfortable office settings. Those on full-time schedules usually work a standard 40-hour week; however, some work shifts or overtime during busy periods. About 16 percent of clerks work part time. Many clerks also work in temporary positions.

Training, Other Qualifications, and Advancement

Although most office clerk jobs are entry-level administrative support positions, employers may prefer or require previous office or business experience. Employers usually require a high school diploma or equivalent, and some require basic computer skills, including familiarity with word-processing software, as well as other general office skills.

Training for this occupation is available through business education programs offered in high schools, community and junior colleges, and postsecondary vocational schools. Courses in office practices, word processing, and other computer applications are particularly helpful.

Because general office clerks usually work with other office staff, they should be cooperative and able to work as part of a team. Employers prefer individuals who are able to perform a variety of tasks and satisfy the needs of the many departments within a company. In addition, applicants should have good communication skills, be detail-oriented, and be adaptable.

General office clerks who exhibit strong communication, interpersonal, and analytical skills may be promoted to supervisory positions. Others may move into different, more senior administrative jobs, such as receptionist, secretary, or administrative assistant. After gaining some work experience or specialized skills, many workers transfer to jobs with higher pay or greater advancement potential. Advancement to professional occupations within an organization normally requires additional formal education, such as a college degree.

Employment

General office clerks held about 3.1 million jobs in 2004. Most are employed in relatively small businesses. Although they work in every sector of the economy, about 46 percent worked in local government; health care and social assistance; administrative and support services; finance and insurance; or professional, scientific, and technical services industries.

Job Outlook

Employment growth and high replacement needs in this large occupation will result in numerous job openings for general office clerks. In addition to those for full-time jobs, many job openings are expected for part-time and temporary general office clerks. Prospects should be best for those who have knowledge of basic computer applications and office machinery—such as fax machines, telephone systems, and scanners—and good writing and communication skills. As general administrative support duties continue to be consolidated, employers will increasingly seek well-rounded individuals with highly developed communication skills and the ability to perform multiple tasks.

Employment of general office clerks is expected to grow more slowly than the average for all occupations through the year 2014. The employment outlook for these workers will be affected by the increasing use of technology, expanding office automation, and the consolidation of administrative support tasks. Automation has led to productivity gains, allowing a wide variety of duties to be performed by fewer office workers. However, automation also has led to a consolidation of administrative support staffs and a diversification of job responsibilities. This consolidation increases the demand for general office clerks because they perform a variety of administrative support tasks. It will become increasingly common within small businesses to find a single general office clerk in charge of all administrative support work.

Job opportunities may vary from year to year because the strength of the economy affects demand for general office clerks. Companies tend to employ more workers when the economy is strong. Industries least likely to be affected by economic fluctuations tend to be the most stable places for employment.

Earnings

Median annual earnings of general office clerks were $22,770 in May 2004; the middle 50 percent earned between $18,090 and $28,950 annually. The lowest 10 percent earned less than $14,530, and the highest 10 percent earned more than $35,810. Median annual salaries in the industries employing the largest numbers of general office clerks in May 2004 were

Local government	$25,880
State government	24,970
Elementary and secondary schools	23,500
Colleges, universities, and professional schools	23,160
Employment services	20,910

Related Occupations

The duties of general office clerks can include a combination of bookkeeping, keyboarding, office machine operation, and filing. Other office and administrative support workers who perform similar duties include bookkeeping, accounting, and auditing clerks; communications equipment operators; customer service representatives; data entry and information processing workers; order clerks; receptionists and information clerks; secretaries and administrative assistants; stock clerks and order fillers; and tellers. Non-clerical entry-level workers include cashiers; counter and rental clerks; and food and beverage serving and related workers.

Sources of Additional Information

State employment service offices and agencies can provide information about job openings for general office clerks.

For information related to administrative occupations, including educational programs and certified designations, contact

▸ International Association of Administrative Professionals, 10502 NW Ambassador Dr., P.O. Box 20404, Kansas City, MO 64195-0404. Internet: http://www.iaap-hq.org

Order Clerks

(O*NET 43-4151.00)

Significant Points

- Employment is expected to decline because of growth in online retailing and in business-to-business electronic commerce and the use of automated systems that make placing orders easy and convenient.
- A high school diploma or its equivalent is the most common educational requirement.

Nature of the Work

Order clerks receive and process orders for a variety of goods or services, such as spare parts for machines, consumer appliances, gas and electric power connections, film rentals, and articles of clothing. They sometimes are called order-entry clerks, sales representatives, order processors, or order takers.

Orders for materials, merchandise, or services can come from inside or from outside of an organization. In large companies with many worksites, such as automobile manufacturers, clerks order parts and equipment from the company's warehouses. Inside order clerks receive orders from other workers employed by the same company or from salespersons in the field.

Many other order clerks, however, receive orders from outside companies or individuals. Order clerks in wholesale businesses, for instance, receive orders from retail establishments for merchandise that the retailer, in turn, sells to the public. An increasing number of order clerks are working for catalog companies and online retailers, receiving orders from individual customers by telephone, fax, regular mail, or e-mail. Order clerks dealing primarily with the public sometimes are referred to as outside order clerks.

Computers provide order clerks with ready access to information such as stock numbers, prices, and inventory. The successful filling of an order frequently depends on having the right products in stock and being able to determine which products are most appropriate for the customer's needs. Some order clerks—especially those in industrial settings—must be able to give price estimates for entire jobs, not just single parts. Others must be able to take special orders, give expected arrival dates, prepare contracts, and handle complaints.

Many order clerks receive orders directly by telephone, entering the required information as the customer places the order. However, a rapidly increasing number of orders now are received through computer systems, the Internet, faxes, and e-mail. In some cases, these orders are sent directly from the customer's terminal to the order clerk's terminal. Orders received by regular mail are sometimes scanned into a database that is instantly accessible to clerks.

Clerks review orders for completeness and clarity. They may fill in missing information or contact the customer for the information. Clerks also contact customers if the customers need additional information, such as prices or shipping dates, or if delays in filling the order are anticipated. For orders received by regular mail, clerks extract checks or money orders, sort them, and send them for processing.

After an order has been verified and entered, the customer's final cost is calculated. The clerk then routes the order to the proper department—such as the warehouse—which actually sends out or delivers the item in question.

In organizations with sophisticated computer systems, inventory records are adjusted automatically as sales are made. In less-automated organizations, order clerks may adjust inventory records. Clerks also may notify other departments when inventories are low or when filling certain orders would deplete supplies.

Some order clerks must establish priorities in filling orders. For example, an order clerk in a blood bank may receive a request from a hospital for a certain type of blood. The clerk must first find out whether the request is routine or an emergency and then take appropriate action.

Working Conditions

Order clerks usually work a standard 40-hour workweek. Most order clerks work in areas that are clean, well lit, and relatively quiet. These workers sit for long periods of time in front of computer terminals, which may cause eyestrain and headaches. Order clerks in retail establishments typically work overtime during peak holiday seasons, when sales volume is high.

Training, Other Qualifications, and Advancement

Employers prefer applicants with a high school diploma or its equivalent or a mix of education and related experience. Most employers prefer workers who are computer literate and have a working knowledge of word-processing and spreadsheet software.

Most order clerks are trained on the job under the close supervision of more experienced employees. Proficiency with computer software is becoming increasingly important because most orders are being filed electronically. By taking on more duties, ambitious order clerks can receive higher pay or become eligible for advancement opportunities. Some use their experience as an order clerk to move into sales positions.

Employment

Order clerks held about 293,000 jobs in 2004. Over 50 percent of order clerks were employed in wholesale and retail trade establishments, and another 16 percent were employed in manufacturing firms. Other jobs for order clerks were in industries such as information, warehousing and storage, couriers, and business support services.

Job Outlook

Job openings for order clerks likely will be limited as improvements in technology and office automation continue to increase worker productivity. While overall employment of order clerks is expected to decline through the year 2014, numerous openings will occur each year to replace order clerks who transfer to other occupations or leave the labor force completely. Many of these openings will be for seasonal work, especially in catalog companies or online retailers catering to holiday gift buyers.

The growth in online retailing and in business-to-business electronic commerce, and the use of automated systems that make placing orders easy and convenient, will decrease demand for order clerks. The spread of electronic data interchange, which enables computers to communicate directly with each other, allows orders within establishments to be placed with little human intervention. In addition, internal systems allowing a firm's employees to place orders directly are becoming increasingly common. Outside orders placed over the Internet often are entered directly into the computer by the customer; thus, the order clerk is not involved at all in placing the order. Some companies also use automated phone menus that are accessible with a touch-tone phone to receive orders, and others use answering machines. Developments in voice recognition technology may further reduce the demand for order clerks.

Furthermore, increased automation will allow current order clerks to be more productive, with each clerk able to handle an increasingly higher volume of orders. Sophisticated inventory control and automatic billing systems permit companies to track inventory and accounts with much less help from order clerks than in the past.

Earnings

Median hourly earnings of order clerks in May 2004 were $12.07. The middle 50 percent earned between $9.45 and $15.53. The lowest 10 percent earned less than $7.75, and the highest 10 percent earned more than $19.34. Median hourly earnings in electronic shopping and mail-order houses were $9.83, while median earnings in machinery, equipment, and supplies merchant wholesalers were $14.05 in May 2004. In business support services, median hourly earnings were $9.71 in May 2004.

Related Occupations

Order clerks receive and process orders. Other workers who perform similar duties include stock clerks and order fillers as well as hotel, motel, and resort desk clerks.

Sources of Additional Information

State employment service offices and agencies can provide information about job openings for order clerks.

Painters and Paperhangers

(O*NET 47-2141.00 and 47-2142.00)

Significant Points

- Employment prospects should be excellent due to the expected job growth coupled with the large numbers of workers who retire or leave the occupation for other jobs.
- Most workers learn informally on the job as helpers, but training experts recommend completion of an apprenticeship program.
- Nearly one-half of all painters and paperhangers are self employed.

Nature of the Work

Paint and wall coverings make surfaces clean, attractive, and bright. In addition, paints and other sealers protect exterior surfaces from wear caused by exposure to the weather.

Painters apply paint, stain, varnish, and other finishes to buildings and other structures. They choose the right paint or finish for the surface to be covered, taking into account durability, ease of handling, method of application, and customers' wishes. Painters first prepare the surfaces to be covered so that the paint will adhere properly. This may require removing the old coat of paint by stripping, sanding, wire brushing, burning, or water and abrasive blasting. Painters also wash walls and trim to remove dirt and grease, fill nail holes and cracks, sandpaper rough spots, and brush off dust. On new surfaces, they apply a primer or sealer to prepare the surface for the finish coat. Painters also mix paints and match colors, relying on knowledge of paint composition and color harmony. In large paint shops or hardware stores, these functions are automated.

There are several ways to apply paint and similar coverings. Painters must be able to choose the right paint applicator for each job, depending on the surface to be covered, the characteristics of the finish, and other factors. Some jobs need only a good bristle brush with a soft, tapered edge; others require a dip or fountain pressure roller; still others can best be done using a paint sprayer. Many jobs need several types of applicators. The right tools for each job not only expedite the painter's work but also produce the most attractive surface.

When working on tall buildings, painters erect scaffolding, including "swing stages," scaffolds suspended by ropes or cables attached to roof hooks. When painting steeples and other conical structures, they use a bosun's chair, a swing-like device.

Paperhangers cover walls and ceilings with decorative wall coverings made of paper, vinyl, or fabric. They first prepare the surface to be covered by applying "sizing," which seals the surface and makes the covering adhere better. When redecorating, they may first remove the old covering by soaking, steaming, or applying solvents. When necessary, they patch holes and take care of other imperfections before hanging the new wall covering.

After the surface has been prepared, paperhangers must prepare the paste or other adhesive. Then, they measure the area to be covered, check the covering for flaws, cut the covering into strips of the proper size, and closely examine the pattern in order to match it when the strips are hung. Much of this process can now be handled by specialized equipment.

The next step is to brush or roll the adhesive onto the back of the covering, if needed, and to then place the strips on the wall or ceiling, making sure the pattern is matched, the strips are hung straight, and the edges are butted together to make tight, closed seams. Finally, paperhangers smooth the strips to remove bubbles and wrinkles, trim the top and bottom with a razor knife, and wipe off any excess adhesive.

Working Conditions

Most painters and paperhangers work 40 hours a week or less; about one-fourth have variable schedules or work part time. Painters and paperhangers must stand for long periods, often working from scaffolding and ladders. Their jobs also require a considerable amount of climbing and bending. These workers must have stamina because much of the work is done with their arms raised overhead. Painters often work outdoors but seldom in wet, cold, or inclement weather. Some painting jobs can leave a worker covered with paint.

Painters and paperhangers sometimes work with materials that are hazardous or toxic, such as when they are required to remove lead-based paints. In the most dangerous situations, painters work in a sealed self-contained suit to prevent inhalation of or contact with hazardous materials.

Training, Other Qualifications, and Advancement

Painting and paperhanging is learned mostly through on-the-job training and by working as a helper to an experienced painter. However, there are a number of formal and informal training programs that provide more thorough instruction and a better career foundation. In general, the more formal the training received, the more likely the individual will enter the profession at a higher level. Besides apprenticeships, some workers gain skills by attending technical schools that offer training prior to employment. These schools can take about a year to complete. Others receive training through local vocational high schools. Applicants should have good manual dexterity and color sense. There are limited opportunities for informal training for paperhangers because there are fewer paperhangers and helpers are usually not required.

If available, apprenticeships are usually the best way to enter the profession. They generally provide a mixture of classroom instruction and on-the-job training. Apprenticeships for painters and paperhangers consist of 2 to 4 years of on-the-job training, supplemented by 144 hours of related classroom instruction each year. Apprentices or helpers generally must be at least 18 years old and in good physical condition. A high school education or its equivalent, with courses in mathematics, usually is required to enter an apprenticeship program. Apprentices receive instruction in color harmony, use and care of tools and equipment, surface preparation, application techniques, paint mixing and matching, characteristics of different finishes, blueprint reading, wood finishing, and safety.

Whether a painter learns the trade through a formal apprenticeship or informally as a helper, on-the-job instruction covers similar skill areas. Under the direction of experienced workers, trainees carry supplies, erect scaffolds, and do simple painting and surface preparation tasks while they learn about paint and painting equipment. As they gain experience, trainees learn to prepare surfaces for painting and paperhanging, to mix paints, and to apply paint and wall coverings efficiently and neatly. Near the end of their training, they may learn decorating concepts, color coordination, and cost-estimating techniques. In addition to learning craft skills, painters must become familiar with safety and health regulations so that their work complies with the law.

Painters and paperhangers may advance to supervisory or estimating jobs with painting and decorating contractors. Many establish their own painting and decorating businesses. For those who would like to advance, it is increasingly important to be able to communicate in both English and Spanish in order to relay instructions and safety precautions to workers with limited English skills; Spanish-speaking workers make up a large part of the construction workforce in many areas. Painting contractors need good English skills in order to deal with clients and subcontractors.

Employment

Painters and paperhangers held about 486,000 jobs in 2004; most were painters. Around one-third of painters and paperhangers work for painting and wall covering contractors engaged in new construction, repair, restoration, or remodeling work. In addition, organizations that own or manage large buildings—such as apartment complexes—employ maintenance painters, as do some schools, hospitals, factories, and government agencies.

Self-employed independent painting contractors accounted for nearly one-half of all painters and paperhangers, significantly greater than the one in five of construction trades workers in general.

Job Outlook

Job prospects should be excellent because each year thousands of painters retire or leave for jobs in other occupations. There are no strict training requirements for entry into these jobs, so many people with limited skills work as painters or helpers for a short time and then move on to other types of work. Many fewer openings will arise for paperhangers because the number of these jobs is comparatively small.

In addition to the need to replace experienced workers who leave, new jobs will be created. Employment of painters is expected to grow as fast as the average for all occupations through the year 2014, reflecting increases in the level of new construction and in the stock of buildings and other structures that require maintenance and renovation. The relatively short life of exterior paints as well as changing color trends will stir demand for painters. Painting is labor-intensive and not susceptible to technological changes that might make workers more productive and slow employment growth. Paperhangers should see slower-than-average employment growth as easy application materials and reduced demand for paperhanging services limits growth.

Jobseekers considering these occupations should expect some periods of unemployment, especially until they gain experience. Many construction projects are of short duration, and construction activity is cyclical and seasonal in nature. Remodeling, restoration, and maintenance projects, however, often provide many jobs for painters and paperhangers even when new construction activity declines. The most versatile painters and skilled paperhangers generally are best able to keep working steadily during downturns in the economy.

Earnings

In May 2004, median hourly earnings of painters, construction and maintenance, were $14.55. The middle 50 percent earned between $11.59 and $19.04. The lowest 10 percent earned less than $9.47, and the highest 10 percent earned more than $25.11. Median hourly earnings in the industries employing the largest numbers of painters in May 2004 were as follows:

Local government $18.36

Residential building construction............................15.09

Nonresidential building construction 14.97

Building finishing contractors................................14.44

Employment services 11.31

In May 2004, median earnings for paperhangers were $15.73. The middle 50 percent earned between $12.23 and $20.71. The lowest 10 percent earned less than $9.57, and the highest 10 percent earned more than $26.58.

Earnings for painters may be reduced on occasion because of bad weather and the short-term nature of many construction jobs. Hourly wage rates for apprentices usually start at 40 to 50 percent of the rate for experienced workers and increase periodically.

Some painters and paperhangers are members of the International Brotherhood of Painters and Allied Trades. Some maintenance painters are members of other unions.

Related Occupations

Painters and paperhangers apply various coverings to decorate and protect wood, drywall, metal, and other surfaces. Other construction occupations in which workers do finishing work include carpenters; carpet, floor, and tile installers and finishers; drywall installers, ceiling tile installers, and tapers; painting and coating workers, except construction and maintenance; and plasterers and stucco masons.

Sources of Additional Information

For details about painting and paperhanging apprenticeships or work opportunities, contact local painting and decorating contractors, local trade organizations, a local of the International Union of Painters and Allied Trades, a local joint union-management apprenticeship committee, or an office of the state apprenticeship agency or employment service.

For information about the work of painters and paperhangers and training opportunities, contact

▶ International Union of Painters and Allied Trades, 1750 New York Ave. NW, Washington, DC 20006. Internet: http://www.iupat.org

▶ Associated Builders and Contractors, Workforce Development Department, 4250 North Fairfax Dr., 9th Floor, Arlington, VA 22203. Internet: http://www.trytools.org

▶ National Center for Construction Education and Research, P.O. Box 141104, Gainesville, FL 32614-1104. Internet: http://www.nccer.org

▶ Painting and Decorating Contractors of America, 11960 Westline Industrial Drive, Suite 201, St. Louis, MO 63146-3209. Internet: http://www.pdca.org

Painting and Coating Workers, Except Construction and Maintenance

(O*NET 51-9121.01, 51-9121.02, 51-9122.00, and 51-9123.00)

Significant Points

■ About 70 percent of jobs are in manufacturing establishments.

■ Most workers acquire their skills on the job; for most operators, training lasts from a few days to several months, but becoming skilled in all aspects of automotive painting usually requires 1 to 2 years.

■ Overall employment is projected to grow more slowly than average; transportation equipment painters are expected to grow about as fast as average, while coating, painting, and spraying machine setters, operators, and tenders are expected to decline.

Nature of the Work

Millions of items ranging from cars to candy are covered by paint, plastic, varnish, chocolate, or some other type of coating solution. Often, the protection provided by the paint or coating is essential to the product, as with the coating of insulating material covering wires and other electrical and electronic components. Also, many paints and coatings have dual purposes; for example, the paint finish on an automobile heightens the visual appearance of the vehicle while providing protection from corrosion.

Coating, painting, and spraying machine setters, operators, and tenders control the machinery that applies these paints and coatings to a wide range of manufactured products. Perhaps the most straightforward technique is simply dipping an item in a large vat of paint or other coating. This is the technique used by *dippers*, who immerse racks or baskets of articles in vats of paint, liquid plastic, or other solutions by means of a power hoist. Similarly, *tumbling barrel painters* deposit articles made of porous materials into a barrel of paint, varnish, or other coating; the barrel is then rotated to ensure thorough coverage.

Another familiar technique is spraying products with a solution of paint or some other coating. *Spray machine operators* use spray guns to coat metal, wood, ceramic, fabric, paper, and food products with paint and other coating solutions. Following a formula, operators fill the machine's tanks with a mixture of paints or chemicals, adding prescribed amounts of solution. Then they adjust nozzles on the guns to obtain the proper dispersion of the spray, and they hold or position the guns so as to direct the spray onto the article. Operators also check the flow and viscosity of the paint or solution and visually inspect the quality of the coating. When products are drying, these workers often must regulate the temperature and air circulation in drying ovens. Individuals who paint, coat, or decorate articles such as furniture, glass, pottery, toys, cakes, and books are known as *painting, coating, and decorating workers*.

Painting and coating workers use various types of machines to coat a range of products. Frequently, their job title reflects the specialized nature of the machine or of the coating being applied. For example, *enrobing machine operators* coat, or "enrobe," confectionery, bakery, and other food products with melted chocolate, cheese, oils, sugar, or other substances. *Paper-coating machine operators* spray "size" on rolls of paper to give it its gloss or finish. *Silvering applicators* spray silver, tin, and copper solutions on glass in the manufacture of mirrors.

In response to concerns about air pollution and worker safety, manufacturers increasingly are using new types of paints and coatings, instead of high-solvent paints, on their products. Water-based paints and powder coatings are two of the most common. These compounds do not emit as many volatile organic compounds into the air and can be applied to a variety of products. Powder coatings are sprayed much as are liquid paints and then are heated to melt and cure the coating.

The adoption of new types of paints often is accompanied by a conversion to more-automated painting equipment that the operator sets and monitors. When using these machines, operators position the automatic spray guns, set the nozzles, and synchronize the action of the guns with the speed of the conveyor carrying articles through the machine and drying ovens. The operator also may add solvents or water to the paint vessel, thereby preparing the paint for application. During the operation of the equipment, these workers tend painting machines, observe gauges on the control panel, and check articles for evidence of any variation from specifications. The operator then uses a spray gun to "touch up" spots where necessary.

Although the majority of painting and coating workers are employed in manufacturing, the best-known group refinishes old and damaged cars, trucks, and buses in automotive body repair and paint shops. *Transportation equipment painters*, or *automotive painters*, are among the most highly skilled manual spray operators because they perform intricate, detailed work and mix paints to match the original color, a task that is especially difficult if the color has faded.

To prepare a vehicle for painting, painters or their helpers use power sanders and sandpaper to remove the original paint or rust and then fill small dents and scratches with body filler. They also remove or mask parts they do not want to paint, such as chrome trim, headlights, windows, and mirrors. Automotive painters use a spray gun to apply several coats of paint. They apply enamel or water-based primers to vehicles with metal bodies and flexible primers to newer vehicles with plastic body parts. Controlling the spray gun by hand, they apply successive coats until the finish of the repaired sections of the vehicle matches that of the original, undamaged portions. To speed drying between coats, they may place the freshly painted vehicle under heat lamps or in a special infrared oven. After each coat of primer dries, they sand the surface to remove any irregularities and to improve the adhesion of the next coat. Final sanding of the primers may be done by hand with a fine grade of sandpaper. A sealer then is applied and allowed to dry, followed by the final topcoat.

Working Conditions

Painting and coating workers typically work indoors and may be exposed to dangerous fumes from paint and coating solutions.

Although painting usually is done in special ventilated booths, operators typically wear masks or respirators that cover their noses and mouths, even in such booths. In addition, federal legislation has led to a decrease in workers' exposure to hazardous chemicals by regulating emissions of volatile organic compounds and other hazardous air pollutants. This legislation also has led to the increasing use of more sophisticated paint booths and fresh-air systems that provide a safer work environment.

Operators have to stand for long periods, and when using a spray gun, they may have to bend, stoop, or crouch in uncomfortable positions to reach different parts of the article. Most operators work a normal 40-hour week, but self-employed automotive painters sometimes work more than 50 hours a week, depending on the number of vehicles customers want repainted.

Training, Other Qualifications, and Advancement

Most painting and coating workers acquire their skills on the job, usually by watching and helping other, more experienced workers. For most setters, operators, and tenders, as well as for painting, coating, and decorating workers, training lasts from a few days to several months. Coating, painting, and spraying machine setters, operators, and tenders who modify the operation of computer-controlled equipment while it is running may require additional training in computer operations and minor programming.

Similarly, most transportation equipment painters start as helpers and gain their skills informally on the job. Becoming skilled in all aspects of automotive painting usually requires 1 to 2 years of on-the-job training. Beginning helpers usually remove trim, clean and sand surfaces to be painted, mask surfaces they do not want painted, and polish finished work. As helpers gain experience, they progress to more complicated tasks, such as mixing paint to achieve a good match and using spray guns to apply primer coats or final coats to small areas.

Painters should have keen eyesight and a good sense of color. The completion of high school generally is not required, but is advantageous. Additional instruction is offered at many community colleges and vocational or technical schools. Such programs enhance one's employment prospects and can speed promotion to the next level.

Some employers sponsor training programs to help their workers become more productive. Training is available from manufacturers of chemicals, paints, or equipment or from other private sources and may include safety and quality tips, as well as impart knowledge of products, equipment, and general business practices. Some automotive painters are sent to technical schools to learn the intricacies of mixing and applying different types of paint.

Voluntary certification by the National Institute for Automotive Service Excellence (ASE) is recognized as the standard of achievement for automotive painters. For certification, painters must pass a written examination and have at least 2 years of experience in the field. High school, trade or vocational school, or community or junior college training in automotive refinishing that meets ASE standards may substitute for up to 1 year of experience. To retain their certification, painters must retake the examination at least every 5 years.

Experienced painting and coating workers with leadership ability may become team leaders or supervisors. Those who acquire practical experience, college, or other formal training may become sales or technical representatives for chemical or paint companies. Eventually, some automotive painters open their own shops.

Employment

Painting and coating workers held about 186,000 jobs in 2004. Lesser-skilled coating, painting, and spraying machine setters, operators, and tenders accounted for about 103,000 jobs, while more-skilled transportation equipment painters constituted about 53,000. Another 29,000 jobs were held by painting, coating, and decorating workers.

Approximately 70 percent of salaried jobs were found in manufacturing establishments, where the workers applied coatings to items such as fabricated metal products; motor vehicles and related equipment; industrial machines; household and office furniture; and plastic, wood, and paper products. Outside manufacturing, workers included automotive painters employed by independent automotive repair shops and workers employed by body repair and paint shops operated by retail motor vehicle dealers. About 6 percent of painting and coating workers were self-employed.

Job Outlook

Overall employment of painting and coating workers is expected to grow more slowly than the average for all occupations through the year 2014. Employment growth for highly skilled transportation painters and automotive refinishers is projected to be faster than for painting, coating, and decorating workers. In addition to jobs arising from growth, some jobs will become available each year as employers replace experienced operators who transfer to other occupations or leave the labor force.

Despite increasing demand for more manufactured goods, employment of coating, painting, and spraying machine setters, operators, and tenders is expected to decline as part of that demand will be met by products manufactured abroad. Employment will be further decreased by improvements in the automation of paint and coating applications that will raise worker productivity. For example, operators will be able to coat goods more rapidly as they use sophisticated industrial machinery that moves and aims spray guns more efficiently. Legislation has set limits on the emissions of ozone-forming volatile organic compounds and is expected to impede job growth among operators in manufacturing. As manufacturing firms switch to water-based and powder coatings to comply with the law, they will introduce more efficient automation.

Painting, coating, and decorating workers should grow more slowly than the average for all occupations. Increasing demand for hand-painted tiles and related specialty products will lead to growth among these workers. Although competition from imports should temper increases in employment, the specialized skills required by workers in this occupation should keep them from seeing as much of an impact of automation on employment.

Since the detailed work of refinishing automobiles in collision repair shops and motor vehicle dealerships does not lend itself to automation, painters employed in these establishments are projected to experience employment growth about as fast as the average for all occupations. As the demand for refinishing continues to grow, slower productivity growth among these workers will lead to employment increases that are more in line with the growing demand for their services.

The number of job openings for painting and coating workers in manufacturing industries may fluctuate from year to year due to cyclical changes in economic conditions. When demand for manufactured goods lessens, production may be suspended or reduced, and workers may be laid off or face a shortened workweek. Automotive painters, by contrast, can expect relatively steady work because automobiles damaged in accidents require repair and refinishing regardless of the state of the economy.

Earnings

Median hourly earnings of coating, painting, and spraying machine setters, operators, and tenders were $12.64 in May 2004. The middle 50 percent earned between $10.16 and $15.78 an hour. The lowest 10 percent earned less than $8.54, and the highest 10 percent earned more than $19.39 an hour.

Median hourly earnings of transportation equipment painters were $16.89 in May 2004. The middle 50 percent earned between $12.85 and $22.74 an hour. The lowest 10 percent earned less than $10.17, and the highest 10 percent earned more than $27.52 an hour. Median hourly earnings of transportation equipment painters were $16.84 in automotive repair and maintenance shops and $24.13 in motor vehicle manufacturing.

Median hourly earnings of painting, coating, and decorating workers were $10.95 in May 2004. The middle 50 percent earned between $8.76 and $13.94 an hour. The lowest 10 percent earned less than $7.44, and the highest 10 percent earned more than $18.23 an hour.

Many automotive painters employed by motor vehicle dealers and independent automotive repair shops receive a commission based on the labor cost charged to the customer. Under this method, earnings depend largely on the amount of work a painter does and how fast it is completed. Employers frequently guarantee commissioned painters a minimum weekly salary. Helpers and trainees usually receive an hourly rate until they become sufficiently skilled to work on commission. Trucking companies, bus lines, and other organizations that repair and refinish their own vehicles usually pay by the hour.

Many painting and coating machine operators belong to unions, including the International Brotherhood of Painters and Allied Trades, the Sheet Metal Workers International Association, and the International Brotherhood of Teamsters. Most union operators work for manufacturers and large motor vehicle dealers.

Related Occupations

Other occupations similar to painting and coating workers include painters and paperhangers; woodworkers; and machine setters, operators, and tenders—metal and plastic.

Sources of Additional Information

For more details about work opportunities, contact local manufacturers, automotive body repair shops, motor vehicle dealers, vocational schools, locals of unions representing painting and coating workers, or the local office of the state employment service. The state employment service also may be a source of information about training programs.

Information on how to become a certified automotive painter is available from

▸ National Institute for Automotive Service Excellence (ASE), 101 Blue Seal Dr. SE, Leesburg, VA 20175. Internet: http://www.asecert.org

Paralegals and Legal Assistants

(O*NET 23-2011.00)

Significant Points

■ About 7 out of 10 work for law firms; others work for corporate legal departments and government agencies.

■ Most entrants have an associate's degree in paralegal studies or a bachelor's degree coupled with a certificate in paralegal studies.

■ Employment is projected to grow much faster than average as employers try to reduce costs by hiring paralegals to perform tasks formerly carried out by lawyers.

■ Competition for jobs should continue; experienced, formally trained paralegals should have the best employment opportunities.

Nature of the Work

While lawyers assume ultimate responsibility for legal work, they often delegate many of their tasks to paralegals. In fact, *paralegals*—also called *legal assistants*—are continuing to assume a growing range of tasks in the nation's legal offices and perform many of the same tasks as lawyers. Nevertheless, they are still explicitly prohibited from carrying out duties that are considered to be the practice of law, such as setting legal fees, giving legal advice, and presenting cases in court.

One of a paralegal's most important tasks is helping lawyers prepare for closings, hearings, trials, and corporate meetings. Paralegals investigate the facts of cases and ensure that all relevant information is considered. They also identify appropriate laws, judicial decisions, legal articles, and other materials that are relevant to assigned cases. After they analyze and organize the information, paralegals may prepare written reports that attorneys use in determining how cases should be handled. Should attorneys decide to file lawsuits on behalf of clients, paralegals may help prepare the legal arguments, draft pleadings and motions to be filed with the court, obtain affidavits, and assist attorneys during trials. Paralegals also organize and track files of all important case documents and make them available and easily accessible to attorneys.

In addition to this preparatory work, paralegals perform a number of other vital functions. For example, they help draft contracts, mortgages, separation agreements, and instruments of trust. They also may assist in preparing tax returns and planning estates. Some paralegals coordinate the activities of other law office employees and maintain financial office records. Various additional tasks may differ, depending on the employer.

Paralegals are found in all types of organizations, but most are employed by law firms, corporate legal departments, and various government offices. In these organizations, they can work in many different areas of the law, including litigation, personal injury, corporate law, criminal law, employee benefits, intellectual property, labor law, bankruptcy, immigration, family law, and real estate. As the law has become more complex, paralegals have responded by becoming more specialized. Within specialties, functions often are broken down further so that paralegals may deal with a specific area. For example, paralegals specializing in labor law may concentrate exclusively on employee benefits.

The duties of paralegals also differ widely with the type of organization in which they are employed. Paralegals who work for corporations often assist attorneys with employee contracts, shareholder agreements, stock-option plans, and employee benefit plans. They also may help prepare and file annual financial reports, maintain corporate minutes, record resolutions, and prepare forms to secure loans for the corporation. Paralegals often monitor and review government regulations to ensure that the corporation is aware of new requirements and is operating within the law. Increasingly, experienced paralegals are assuming additional supervisory responsibilities such as overseeing team projects and serving as a communications link between the team and the corporation.

The duties of paralegals who work in the public sector usually vary within each agency. In general, paralegals analyze legal material for internal use, maintain reference files, conduct research for attorneys, and collect and analyze evidence for agency hearings. They may prepare informative or explanatory material on laws, agency regulations, and agency policy for general use by the agency and the public. Paralegals employed in community legal-service projects help the poor, the aged, and others who are in need of legal assistance. They file forms, conduct research, prepare documents, and, when authorized by law, may represent clients at administrative hearings.

Paralegals in small and medium-size law firms usually perform a variety of duties that require a general knowledge of the law. For example, they may research judicial decisions on improper police arrests or help prepare a mortgage contract. Paralegals employed by large law firms, government agencies, and corporations, however, are more likely to specialize in one aspect of the law.

Familiarity with computer use and technical knowledge have become essential to paralegal work. Computer software packages and the Internet are used to search legal literature stored in computer databases and on CD-ROM. In litigation involving many supporting documents, paralegals usually use computer databases to retrieve, organize, and index various materials. Imaging software allows paralegals to scan documents directly into a database, while billing programs help them to track hours billed to clients. Computer software packages also are used to perform tax computations and explore the consequences of various tax strategies for clients.

Working Conditions

Paralegals employed by corporations and government usually work a standard 40-hour week. Although most paralegals work year round, some are temporarily employed during busy times of the year and then are released when the workload diminishes. Paralegals who work for law firms sometimes work very long hours when they are under pressure to meet deadlines. Some law firms reward such loyalty with bonuses and additional time off.

These workers handle many routine assignments, particularly when they are inexperienced. As they gain experience, paralegals usually assume more varied tasks with additional responsibility. Paralegals do most of their work at desks in offices and law libraries. Occasionally, they travel to gather information and perform other duties.

Training, Other Qualifications, and Advancement

There are several ways to become a paralegal. The most common is through a community college paralegal program that leads to an associate's degree. The other common method of entry, mainly for those who already have a college degree, is through a program that leads to a certification in paralegal studies. A small number of schools also offer bachelor's and master's degrees in paralegal studies. Some employers train paralegals on the job, hiring college graduates with no legal experience or promoting experienced legal secretaries. Other entrants have experience in a technical field that is useful to law firms, such as a background in tax preparation for tax and estate practice or in criminal justice, nursing, or health administration for personal injury practice.

An estimated 1,000 colleges and universities, law schools, and proprietary schools offer formal paralegal training programs. Approximately 260 paralegal programs are approved by the American Bar Association (ABA). Although many programs do not require such approval, graduation from an ABA-approved program can enhance one's employment opportunities. The requirements for admission to these programs vary. Some require certain college courses or a bachelor's degree, others accept high school graduates or those with legal experience, and a few schools require standardized tests and personal interviews.

Paralegal programs include 2-year associate degree's programs, 4-year bachelor's degree programs, and certificate programs that can take only a few months to complete. Most certificate programs provide intensive and, in some cases, specialized paralegal training for individuals who already hold college degrees, while associate's and bachelor's degree programs usually combine paralegal training with courses in other academic subjects. The quality of paralegal training programs varies; the better programs usually include job placement services. Programs generally offer courses introducing students to the legal applications of computers, including how to perform legal research on the Internet. Many paralegal training programs also offer an internship in which students gain practical experience by working for several months in a private law firm, the office of a public defender or attorney general, a bank, a corporate legal department, a legal aid organization, or a government agency. Experience gained in internships is an asset when one is seeking a job after graduation. Prospective students should examine the experiences of recent graduates before enrolling in a paralegal program.

Although most employers do not require certification, earning a voluntary certificate from a professional society may offer advantages in the labor market. The National Association of Legal Assistants (NALA), for example, has established standards for certification requiring various combinations of education and experience. Paralegals who meet these standards are eligible to take a 2-day examination, given three times each year at several regional testing centers. Those who pass this examination may use the Certified Legal Assistant (CLA) designation. The NALA also offers an advanced paralegal certification for those who want to specialize in other areas of the law. In addition, the Paralegal Advanced Competency Exam, administered through the National Federation of Paralegal Associations, offers professional recognition to paralegals with a bachelor's degree and at least 2 years of experience. Those who pass this examination may use the Registered Paralegal (RP) designation.

Paralegals must be able to document and present their findings and opinions to their supervising attorney. They need to understand legal terminology and have good research and investigative skills. Familiarity with the operation and applications of computers in legal research and litigation support also is important. Paralegals should stay informed of new developments in the laws that affect their area of practice. Participation in continuing legal education seminars allows paralegals to maintain and expand their knowledge of the law.

Because paralegals frequently deal with the public, they should be courteous and uphold the ethical standards of the legal profession. The National Association of Legal Assistants, the National Federation of Paralegal Associations, and a few states have established ethical guidelines for paralegals to follow.

Paralegals usually are given more responsibilities and require less supervision as they gain work experience. Experienced paralegals who work in large law firms, corporate legal departments, or government agencies may supervise and delegate assignments to other paralegals and clerical staff. Advancement opportunities also include promotion to managerial and other law-related positions within the firm or corporate legal department. However, some paralegals find it easier to move to another law firm when seeking increased responsibility or advancement.

Employment

Paralegals and legal assistants held about 224,000 jobs in 2004. Private law firms employed 7 out of 10 paralegals and legal assistants; most of the remainder worked for corporate legal departments and various levels of government. Within the federal government, the U.S. Department of Justice is the largest employer, followed by the Social Security Administration and the U.S. Department of the Treasury. A small number of paralegals own their own businesses and work as freelance legal assistants, contracting their services to attorneys or corporate legal departments.

Job Outlook

Employment for paralegals and legal assistants is projected to grow much faster than average for all occupations through 2014. Employers are trying to reduce costs and increase the availability and efficiency of legal services by hiring paralegals to perform tasks formerly carried out by lawyers. Besides new jobs created by employment growth, additional job openings will arise as people leave the occupation. Despite projections of rapid employment growth, competition for jobs should continue as many people seek to go into this profession; however, experienced, formally trained paralegals should have the best employment opportunities.

Private law firms will continue to be the largest employers of paralegals, but a growing array of other organizations, such as corporate legal departments, insurance companies, real estate and title insurance firms, and banks hire paralegals. Corporations in particular are boosting their in-house legal departments to cut costs. Demand for paralegals also is expected to grow as an expanding population increasingly requires legal services, especially in areas such as intellectual property, health care, international law, elder issues, criminal law, and environmental law. Paralegals who specialize in areas such as real estate, bankruptcy, medical malpractice, and product liability should have ample employment opportunities. The growth of pre-paid legal plans also should contribute to the demand for legal services. Paralegal employment is expected to increase as organizations presently employing paralegals assign them a growing range of tasks and as paralegals are increasingly employed in small and medium-size establishments. A growing number of experienced paralegals are expected to establish their own businesses.

Job opportunities for paralegals will expand in the public sector as well. Community legal-service programs, which provide assistance to the poor, elderly, minorities, and middle-income families, will employ additional paralegals to minimize expenses and serve the most people. Federal, state, and local government agencies; consumer organizations; and the courts also should continue to hire paralegals in increasing numbers.

To a limited extent, paralegal jobs are affected by the business cycle. During recessions, demand declines for some discretionary legal services, such as planning estates, drafting wills, and handling real estate transactions. Corporations are less inclined to initiate certain types of litigation when falling sales and profits lead to fiscal belt tightening. As a result, full-time paralegals employed in offices adversely affected by a recession may be laid off or have their work hours reduced. However, during recessions, corporations and individuals are more likely to face other problems that require legal assistance, such as bankruptcies, foreclosures, and divorces. Paralegals, who provide many of the same legal services as lawyers at a lower cost, tend to fare relatively better in difficult economic conditions.

Earnings

Earnings of paralegals and legal assistants vary greatly. Salaries depend on education, training, experience, the type and size of employer, and the geographic location of the job. In general, paralegals who work for large law firms or in large metropolitan areas earn more than those who work for smaller firms or in less populated regions. In addition to earning a salary, many paralegals receive bonuses. In May 2004, full-time wage and salary paralegals and legal assistants had median annual earnings, including bonuses, of $39,130. The middle 50 percent earned between $31,040 and $49,950. The top 10 percent earned more than $61,390, while the bottom 10 percent earned less than $25,360. Median annual earnings in the industries employing the largest numbers of paralegals in May 2004 were as follows:

Federal government	$59,370
Local government	38,260
Legal services	37,870
State government	34,910

Related Occupations

Among the other occupations that call for a specialized understanding of the law and the legal system, but do not require the extensive training of a lawyer, are law clerks; title examiners, abstractors, and searchers; claims adjusters, appraisers, examiners, and investigators; and occupational health and safety specialists and technicians.

Sources of Additional Information

General information on a career as a paralegal can be obtained from

▸ Standing Committee on Paralegals, American Bar Association, 321 North Clark St., Chicago, IL 60610. Internet: http://www.abanet.org/legalservices/paralegals

For information on the Certified Legal Assistant exam, schools that offer training programs in a specific state, and standards and guidelines for paralegals, contact

▸ National Association of Legal Assistants, Inc., 1516 South Boston St., Suite 200, Tulsa, OK 74119. Internet: http://www.nala.org

Information on a career as a paralegal, schools that offer training programs, job postings for paralegals, the Paralegal Advanced Competency Exam, and local paralegal associations can be obtained from

▸ National Federation of Paralegal Associations, 2517 Eastlake Ave. East, Suite 200, Seattle, WA 98102. Internet: http://www.paralegals.org

Information on paralegal training programs, including the pamphlet *How to Choose a Paralegal Education Program*, may be obtained from

▸ American Association for Paralegal Education, 19 Mantua Rd., Mt. Royal, NJ 08061. Internet: http://www.aafpe.org

Information on obtaining positions as occupational health and safety specialists and technicians with the federal government is available from the Office of Personnel Management through USAJOBS, the federal government's official employment information system. This resource for locating and applying for job opportunities can be accessed through the Internet at http://www.usajobs.opm.gov or through an interactive voice response telephone system at (703) 724-1850 or TDD (978) 461-8404. These numbers are not toll free, and charges may result.

Payroll and Timekeeping Clerks

(O*NET 43-3051.00)

Significant Points

■ Payroll and timekeeping clerks are found in every industry.

■ Most employers prefer applicants with a high school diploma; computer skills are very desirable.

■ Those who have completed a certification program, indicating that they can handle more complex payroll issues, will have an advantage in the job market.

Nature of the Work

Payroll and timekeeping clerks perform a vital function: ensuring that employees are paid on time and that their paychecks are accurate. If inaccuracies occur, such as monetary errors or incorrect amounts of vacation time, these workers research and correct the records. In addition, they may perform various other clerical tasks. Automated timekeeping systems that allow employees to enter the number of hours they have worked directly into a computer have eliminated much of the data entry and review by time-keepers and have elevated the job of payroll clerk. In offices that have not automated this function, however, payroll and time-keeping clerks still perform many of the traditional job functions.

The fundamental task of *timekeeping clerks* is distributing and collecting timecards each pay period. These workers review employee work charts, timesheets, and timecards to ensure that information is properly recorded and that records have the signatures of authorizing officials. In companies that bill for the time spent by staff, such as law or accounting firms, timekeeping clerks make sure that the hours recorded are charged to the correct job so that clients can be properly billed. These clerks also review computer reports listing timecards that cannot be processed because of errors, and they contact the employee or the employee's supervisor to resolve the problem. In addition, timekeeping clerks are responsible for informing managers and other employees about procedural changes in payroll policies.

Payroll clerks, also called payroll technicians, screen timecards for calculating, coding, or other errors. They compute pay by subtracting allotments, including federal and state taxes and contributions to retirement, insurance, and savings plans, from gross earnings. Increasingly, computers are performing these calculations and alerting payroll clerks to problems or errors in the data. In small organizations or for new employees whose records are not yet entered into a computer system, clerks may perform the necessary calculations manually. In some small offices, clerks or other employees in the accounting department process payroll.

Payroll clerks record changes in employees' addresses; close out files when workers retire, resign, or transfer; and advise employees on income tax withholding and other mandatory deductions. They also issue and record adjustments to workers' pay because of previous errors or retroactive increases. Payroll clerks need to follow changes in tax and deduction laws so they are aware of the most recent revisions. Finally, they prepare and mail earnings and tax-withholding statements for employees' use in preparing income tax returns.

In small offices, payroll and timekeeping duties are likely to be included in the duties of a general office clerk, a secretary, or an accounting clerk. However, large organizations employ specialized payroll and timekeeping clerks to perform these functions. In offices that have automated timekeeping systems, payroll clerks perform more analysis of the data, examine trends, and work with computer systems. They also spend more time answering employees' questions and processing unique data.

Working Conditions

Payroll and timekeeping clerks usually work in clean, pleasant, and comfortable office settings. Clerks usually work a standard 35- to 40-hour week; however, longer hours might be necessary during busy periods. Payroll and timekeeping clerks also may face stress at times, particularly from the pressure to meet deadlines.

Training, Other Qualifications, and Advancement

Most employers prefer applicants with a high school diploma or GED. Computer skills are very desirable. Payroll and timekeeping clerks learn their skills through a combination of on-the-job experience and informal training. Training also can be attained through programs in high schools, business schools, and community colleges. New workers receive training in payroll, timekeeping, personnel issues, workplace practices, and company policies.

Payroll and timekeeping clerks must be able to interact and communicate with individuals at all levels of the organization. In addition, clerks should demonstrate poise, tactfulness, and diplomacy and have a high level of interpersonal skills in order to handle sensitive and confidential situations.

Most organizations specializing in payroll and timekeeping offer classes intended to enhance the marketable skills of their members. Some organizations offer certification programs; completion of a certification program indicates competence and can enhance one's advancement opportunities. For example, the American Payroll Association offers two levels of certification, the Fundamental Payroll Certification (FPC) and the Certified Payroll Professional (CPP). The FPC is open to all individuals who wish to demonstrate basic payroll competency. The more advanced CPP is available those who have been employed in the practice of payroll for at least 3 years and who have obtained the FPC within the last 18 months. Both require experience and a passing score on a comprehensive exam.

Employment

Payroll and timekeeping clerks held about 214,000 jobs in 2004. They can be found in every industry, but a growing number work for employment services companies as temporary employees or for accounting, tax preparation, bookkeeping, and payroll services firms, which increasingly are taking on the payroll function as a service to other companies. Approximately 18 percent of all payroll and timekeeping clerks worked part time in 2004.

Job Outlook

Employment of payroll and timekeeping clerks is expected to grow about as fast as the average for all occupations through 2014. In addition to job growth, numerous job openings will arise each year as payroll and timekeeping clerks leave the labor force or transfer to other occupations. Those who have completed a certification program, indicating that they can handle more complex payroll issues, will have an advantage in the job market.

As entering and recording payroll and timekeeping information becomes more simplified, the job itself is becoming more complex, with companies now offering a greater variety of pension, 401(k), and other investment plans to their employees. Also, the growing use of garnishment of wages for child support is adding to the complexity. These developments will fuel the demand for payroll and timekeeping clerks, who will be needed to record and monitor such information.

Firms increasingly are outsourcing the payroll function. As a result, the best employment opportunities are expected to be in companies that specialize in payroll, including companies in the employment services industry and the accounting, tax preparation, bookkeeping, and payroll services industry. Many of these companies are data-processing facilities, but accounting firms also are taking on the payroll function to supplement their accounting work.

The increasing use of computers will limit employment growth of payroll and timekeeping clerks. For example, automated time clocks, which calculate employee hours, allow large organizations to centralize their timekeeping duties in one location. At individual sites, employee hours increasingly are tracked by computer and verified by managers. This information is compiled and sent to a central office to be processed by payroll clerks. In addition, the growing use of direct deposit will reduce the need to draft paychecks, because these funds are transferred automatically each pay period. Also, more organizations are allowing employees to update their payroll records electronically. In smaller organizations, payroll and timekeeping duties are being assigned to secretaries, general office clerks, or accounting clerks. Furthermore, the greater complexity of the job, coupled with the automation of records that is simplifying data entry, is resulting in payroll professionals, not payroll and timekeeping clerks, doing more of the work.

Earnings

Salaries of payroll and timekeeping clerks may vary considerably. The region of the country, size of city, and type and size of establishment all influence salary levels. Also, the level of expertise required and the complexity and uniqueness of a clerk's responsibilities may affect earnings.

Median annual earnings of payroll and timekeeping clerks in May 2004 were $30,350. The middle 50 percent earned between $24,430 and $36,930. The lowest 10 percent earned less than $19,680, and the highest 10 percent earned more than $44,270. Median annual earnings in the industries employing the largest numbers of payroll and timekeeping clerks in May 2004 were

Management of companies and enterprises	$32,600
Elementary and secondary schools	32,390
Local government	31,620
Accounting, tax preparation, bookkeeping, and payroll services	29,040
Employment services	28,010

Some employers offer educational assistance to payroll and timekeeping clerks.

Related Occupations

Payroll and timekeeping clerks perform a vital financial function—ensuring that employees are paid on time and that their paychecks are accurate. In addition, they may perform various other office and administrative support duties. Other financial clerks include bill and account collectors; billing and posting clerks and machine operators; bookkeeping, accounting, and auditing clerks; gaming cage workers; procurement clerks; and tellers.

Sources of Additional Information

For general information about payroll and timekeeping clerks, contact

▸ American Payroll Association, 660 North Main Ave., Suite 100, Suite 660, San Antonio, TX 78205-1217. Internet: http://www.americanpayroll.org

▸ WorldatWork, 14040 N. Northsight Blvd., Scottsdale, AZ 85260. Internet: http://www.worldatwork.org

Information on employment opportunities for payroll and timekeeping clerks is available from local offices of the state employment service.

Personal and Home Care Aides

(O*NET 39-9021.00)

Significant Points

■ Job opportunities are expected to be excellent because of rapid growth in home health care and high replacement needs.

■ Skill requirements are low, as is the pay.

■ About 33 percent of personal and home care aides work part time; most aides work with a number of different clients, each job lasting a few hours, days, or weeks.

Nature of the Work

Personal and home care aides help elderly, disabled, ill, and mentally disabled persons live in their own homes or in residential care facilities instead of in health facilities. Most personal and home care aides work with elderly or physically or mentally disabled clients who need more extensive personal and home care than family or friends can provide. Some aides work with families in which a parent is incapacitated and small children need care. Others help discharged hospital patients who have relatively short-term needs. (*Home health aides*—who provide health-related services, rather than mainly housekeeping and routine personal care—are discussed in the description of nursing, psychiatric, and home health aides elsewhere in this book.)

Personal and home care aides—also called *homemakers, caregivers, companions*, and *personal attendants*—provide housekeeping and routine personal care services. They clean clients' houses, do laundry, and change bed linens. Aides may plan meals (including special diets), shop for food, and cook. Aides also may help clients get out of bed, bathe, dress, and groom. Some accompany clients to doctors' appointments or on other errands.

Personal and home care aides provide instruction and psychological support to their patients. They may advise families and patients on nutrition, cleanliness, and household tasks. Aides also may assist in toilet training a severely mentally handicapped child, or they may just listen to clients talk about their problems.

In home health care agencies, a registered nurse, physical therapist, or social worker assigns specific duties and supervises personal and home care aides. Aides keep records of services performed and of clients' condition and progress. They report changes in the client's condition to the supervisor or case manager. In carrying out their work, aides cooperate with health care professionals, including registered nurses, therapists, and other medical staff.

Working Conditions

The personal and home care aide's daily routine may vary. Aides may go to the same home every day for months or even years. However, most aides work with a number of different clients, each job lasting a few hours, days, or weeks. Aides often visit four or five clients on the same day.

Surroundings differ from case to case. Some homes are neat and pleasant, whereas others are untidy and depressing. Some clients are pleasant and cooperative; others are angry, abusive, depressed, or otherwise difficult.

Personal and home care aides generally work on their own, with periodic visits by their supervisor. They receive detailed instructions explaining when to visit clients and what services to perform for them. About one-third of aides work part time, and some work weekends or evenings to suit the needs of their clients.

Aides are individually responsible for getting to the client's home. They may spend a good portion of the working day traveling from one client to another. Because mechanical lifting devices that are available in institutional settings are seldom available in patients' homes, aides must be careful to avoid overexertion or injury when they assist clients.

Training, Other Qualifications, and Advancement

In some states, the only requirement for employment is on-the-job training, which generally is provided by most employers. Other states may require formal training, which is available from community colleges, vocational schools, elder care programs, and home health care agencies. The National Association for Home Care and Hospice (NAHC) offers national certification for personal and home

care aides. Certification is a voluntary demonstration that the individual has met industry standards. Certification requires the completion of a standard 75-hour course and written exam developed by NAHC. Home care aides seeking certification are evaluated on 17 different skills by a registered nurse.

Personal and home care aides should have a desire to help people and not mind hard work. They should be responsible, compassionate, emotionally stable, and cheerful. In addition, aides should be tactful, honest, and discreet because they work in private homes. Aides also must be in good health. A physical examination, including state-mandated tests such as those for tuberculosis, may be required. A criminal background check also may be required for employment. Additionally, personal and home care aides are responsible for their own transportation to reach patients' homes.

Advancement for personal and home care aides is limited. In some agencies, workers start out performing homemaker duties, such as cleaning. With experience and training, they may take on personal care duties. Some aides choose to receive additional training to become nursing and home health aides, licensed practical nurses, or registered nurses. Some experienced personal and home care aides may start their own home care agency.

Employment

Personal and home care aides held about 701,000 jobs in 2004. The majority of jobs were in home health care services; individual and family services; residential care facilities; and private households. Self-employed aides have no agency affiliation or supervision and accept clients, set fees, and arrange work schedules on their own.

Job Outlook

Excellent job opportunities are expected for this occupation because rapid employment growth and high replacement needs are projected to produce a large number of job openings.

Employment of personal and home care aides is projected to grow much faster than the average for all occupations through the year 2014. The number of elderly people, an age group characterized by mounting health problems and requiring some assistance with daily activities, is projected to rise substantially. In addition to the elderly, other patients, such as the mentally disabled, will increasingly rely on home care. This trend reflects several developments, including efforts to contain costs by moving patients out of hospitals and nursing care facilities as quickly as possible; the realization that treatment can be more effective in familiar rather than clinical surroundings; and the development and improvement of medical technologies for in-home treatment.

In addition to job openings created by the increase in demand for these workers, replacement needs are expected to lead to many openings. The relatively low skill requirements, low pay, and high emotional demands of the work result in high replacement needs. For these same reasons, many people are reluctant to seek jobs in the occupation. Therefore, persons who are interested in and suited for this work—particularly those with experience or training as personal care, home health, or nursing aides—should have excellent job prospects.

Earnings

Median hourly earnings of personal and home care aides were $8.12 in May 2004. The middle 50 percent earned between $6.83 and $9.70 an hour. The lowest 10 percent earned less than $5.93, and the highest 10 percent earned more than $10.87 an hour. Median hourly earnings in the industries employing the largest numbers of personal and home care aides in May 2004 were as follows:

Residential mental retardation, mental health, and substance abuse facilities	$9.09
Vocational rehabilitation services	8.76
Community care facilities for the elderly	8.49
Individual and family services	8.48
Home health care services	6.99

Most employers give slight pay increases with experience and added responsibility. Aides usually are paid only for the time they work in the home, not for travel time between jobs. Employers often hire on-call hourly workers and provide no benefits.

Related Occupations

Personal and home care aides combine the duties of caregivers and social service workers. Workers in related occupations that involve personal contact to help others include childcare workers; nursing, psychiatric, and home health aides; occupational therapist assistants and aides; physical therapist assistants and aides; and social and human service assistants.

Sources of Additional Information

Information about employment opportunities may be obtained from local hospitals, nursing care facilities, home health care agencies, psychiatric facilities, residential mental health facilities, social assistance agencies, and local offices of the state employment service.

Pharmacy Technicians

(O*NET 29-2052.00)

Significant Points

- Job opportunities are expected to be good for full-time and part-time work, especially for those with certification or previous work experience.

- Many technicians work evenings, weekends, and holidays.

- About 7 out of 10 of jobs are in retail pharmacies, grocery stores, department stores, or mass retailers.

Nature of the Work

Pharmacy technicians help licensed pharmacists provide medication and other health care products to patients. Technicians usually perform routine tasks to help prepare prescribed medication for patients, such as counting tablets and labeling bottles. Technicians refer any questions regarding prescriptions, drug information, or health matters to a pharmacist.

Pharmacy aides work closely with pharmacy technicians. They often are clerks or cashiers who primarily answer telephones, handle money, stock shelves, and perform other clerical duties. Pharmacy technicians usually perform more complex tasks than do pharmacy aides, although in some states their duties and job titles may overlap.

Pharmacy technicians who work in retail or mail-order pharmacies have varying responsibilities, depending on state rules and regulations. Technicians receive written prescriptions or requests for prescription refills from patients. They also may receive prescriptions sent electronically from the doctor's office. They must verify that the information on the prescription is complete and accurate. To prepare the prescription, technicians must retrieve, count, pour, weigh, measure, and sometimes mix the medication. Then, they prepare the prescription labels, select the type of prescription container, and affix the prescription and auxiliary labels to the container. Once the prescription is filled, technicians price and file the prescription, which must be checked by a pharmacist before it is given to the patient. Technicians may establish and maintain patient profiles, prepare insurance claim forms, and stock and take inventory of prescription and over-the-counter medications.

In hospitals, nursing homes, and assisted-living facilities, technicians have added responsibilities, including reading patients' charts and preparing and delivering the medicine to patients. Still, the pharmacist must check the order before it is delivered to the patient. The technician then copies the information about the prescribed medication onto the patient's profile. Technicians also may assemble a 24-hour supply of medicine for every patient. They package and label each dose separately. The packages are then placed in the medicine cabinets of patients until the supervising pharmacist checks them for accuracy. The packages are then given to the patients.

Working Conditions

Pharmacy technicians work in clean, organized, well-lighted, and well-ventilated areas. Most of their workday is spent on their feet. They may be required to lift heavy boxes or to use stepladders to retrieve supplies from high shelves.

Technicians work the same hours that pharmacists work. These may include evenings, nights, weekends, and holidays, particularly in facilities, such as hospitals and retail pharmacies, that are open 24 hours a day. As their seniority increases, technicians often acquire increased control over the hours they work. There are many opportunities for part-time work in both retail and hospital settings.

Training, Other Qualifications, and Advancement

Although most pharmacy technicians receive informal on-the-job training, employers favor those who have completed formal training and certification. However, there are currently few state and no federal requirements for formal training or certification of pharmacy technicians. Employers who have insufficient resources to give on-the-job training often seek formally educated pharmacy technicians. Formal education programs and certification emphasize the technician's interest in and dedication to the work. In addition to the military, some hospitals, proprietary schools, vocational or technical colleges, and community colleges offer formal education programs.

Formal pharmacy technician education programs require classroom and laboratory work in a variety of areas, including medical and pharmaceutical terminology, pharmaceutical calculations, pharmacy recordkeeping, pharmaceutical techniques, and pharmacy law and ethics. Technicians also are required to learn medication names, actions, uses, and doses. Many training programs include internships, in which students gain hands-on experience in actual pharmacies. Students receive a diploma, a certificate, or an associate's degree, depending on the program.

Prospective pharmacy technicians with experience working as an aide in a community pharmacy or volunteering in a hospital may have an advantage. Employers also prefer applicants with strong customer service and communication skills, as well as those with experience managing inventories, counting tablets, measuring dosages, and using computers. Technicians entering the field need strong mathematics, spelling, and reading skills. A background in chemistry, English, and health education also may be beneficial. Some technicians are hired without formal training, but under the condition that they obtain certification within a specified period to retain their employment.

The Pharmacy Technician Certification Board administers the National Pharmacy Technician Certification Examination. This exam is voluntary in most states and displays the competency of the individual to act as a pharmacy technician. However, more states and employers are requiring certification as reliance on pharmacy technicians grows. Eligible candidates must have a high school diploma or GED and no felony convictions, and those who pass the exam earn the title of Certified Pharmacy Technician (CPhT). The exam is offered several times per year at various locations nationally. Employers—often pharmacists—know that individuals who pass the exam have a standardized body of knowledge and skills. Many employers also will reimburse the costs of the exam as an incentive for certification.

Certified technicians must be recertified every 2 years. Technicians must complete 20 contact hours of pharmacy-related topics within the 2-year certification period to become eligible for recertification. Contact hours are awarded for on-the-job training, attending lectures, and college coursework. At least 1 contact hour must be in pharmacy law. Contact hours can be earned from several different sources, including pharmacy associations, pharmacy colleges, and pharmacy technician training programs. Up to 10 contact hours can be earned when the technician is employed under the direct supervision and instruction of a pharmacist.

Successful pharmacy technicians are alert, observant, organized, dedicated, and responsible. They should be willing and able to take directions. They must be precise; details are sometimes a matter of life and death. Although a pharmacist must check and approve all their work, they should be able to work independently without constant instruction from the pharmacist. Candidates interested in becoming pharmacy technicians cannot have prior records of drug or substance abuse.

Strong interpersonal and communication skills are needed because pharmacy technicians interact daily with patients, co-workers, and health care professionals. Teamwork is very important because technicians often are required to work with pharmacists, aides, and other technicians.

Employment

Pharmacy technicians held about 258,000 jobs in 2004. About 7 out of 10 jobs were in retail pharmacies, either independently owned or part of a drugstore chain, grocery store, department store, or mass retailer. About 2 out of 10 jobs were in hospitals and a small proportion was in mail-order and Internet pharmacies, clinics, pharmaceutical wholesalers, and the federal government.

Job Outlook

Good job opportunities are expected for full-time and part-time work, especially for technicians with formal training or previous experience. Job openings for pharmacy technicians will result from the expansion of retail pharmacies and other employment settings and from the need to replace workers who transfer to other occupations or leave the labor force.

Employment of pharmacy technicians is expected to grow much faster than the average for all occupations through 2014 because as the population grows and ages, demand for pharmaceuticals will increase dramatically. The increased number of middle-aged and elderly people—who use more prescription drugs than younger people—will spur demand for technicians in all practice settings. With advances in science, more medications are becoming available to treat a greater number of conditions.

In addition, cost-conscious insurers, pharmacies, and health systems will continue to expand the role of technicians. As a result, pharmacy technicians will assume responsibility for some of the more routine tasks previously performed by pharmacists. Pharmacy technicians also will need to learn and master new pharmacy technology as it emerges. For example, robotic machines are being increasingly used to dispense medicine into containers; technicians must oversee the machines, stock the bins, and label the containers. Thus, while automation is increasingly incorporated into the job, it will not necessarily reduce the need for technicians.

Almost all states have legislated the maximum number of technicians who can safely work under a pharmacist at one time. In some states, technicians have assumed more medication-dispensing duties as pharmacists have become more involved in patient care, resulting in more technicians per pharmacist. Changes in these laws could directly affect employment.

Earnings

Median hourly earnings of wage and salary pharmacy technicians in May 2004 were $11.37. The middle 50 percent earned between $9.40 and $13.85. The lowest 10 percent earned less than $7.96, and the highest 10 percent earned more than $16.61. Median hourly earnings in the industries employing the largest numbers of pharmacy technicians in May 2004 were

General medical and surgical hospitals $12.93

Grocery stores...11.77

Other general merchandise stores 11.11

Certified technicians may earn more. Shift differentials for working evenings or weekends also can increase earnings. Some technicians belong to unions representing hospital or grocery store workers.

Related Occupations

This occupation is most closely related to pharmacists and pharmacy aides. Workers in other medical support occupations include dental assistants, licensed practical and licensed vocational nurses, medical transcriptionists, medical records and health information technicians, occupational therapist assistants and aides, physical therapist assistants and aides, and surgical technologists.

Sources of Additional Information

For information on the Certified Pharmacy Technician designation, contact

▸ Pharmacy Technician Certification Board, 2215 Constitution Ave. NW, Washington DC 20037-2985. Internet: http://www.ptcb.org

For a list of accredited pharmacy technician training programs, contact

▸ American Society of Health-System Pharmacists, 7272 Wisconsin Ave., Bethesda, MD 20814. Internet: http://www.ashp.org

For pharmacy technician career information, contact

▸ National Pharmacy Technician Association, P.O. Box 683148, Houston, TX 77268. Internet: http://www.pharmacytechnician.org

(O*NET 27-4021.01 and 27-4021.02)

Significant Points

- Competition for jobs is expected to be keen because the work is attractive to many people.

- Technical expertise, a "good eye," imagination, and creativity are essential.

- More than half of all photographers are self-employed; the most successful are adept at operating a business and able to take advantage of opportunities provided by rapidly changing technologies.

Nature of the Work

Photographers produce and preserve images that paint a picture, tell a story, or record an event. To create commercial-quality photographs, photographers need both technical expertise and creativity. Producing a successful picture requires choosing and presenting a subject to achieve a particular effect and selecting the appropriate equipment. For example, photographers may enhance the subject's appearance with natural or artificial light, shoot the subject from an interesting angle, draw attention to a particular aspect of the subject by blurring the background, or use various lenses to produce desired levels of detail at various distances from the subject.

Today, most photographers use digital cameras instead of traditional silver-halide film cameras, although some photographers use both types, depending on their own preference and the nature of the assignment. Regardless of the camera they use, photographers also employ an array of other equipment—from lenses, filters, and tripods to flash attachments and specially constructed lighting equipment—to improve the quality of their work.

Digital cameras capture images electronically, allowing them to be edited on a computer. Images can be stored on portable memory devices such as compact discs (CDs) or on smaller "minipocket" storage devices such as flash cards, which are small memory cards used in digital cameras. Once the raw image has been transferred to a computer, photographers can use processing software to crop or modify the image and enhance it through color correction and other specialized effects. As soon as a photographer has finished editing the image, it can be sent anywhere in the world over the Internet.

Photographers also can create electronic portfolios of their work and display them on their own Web page, allowing them to reach prospective customers directly. Digital technology also allows the production of larger, more colorful, and more accurate prints or images for use in advertising, photographic art, and scientific research. Photographers who process their own digital images need to have computers, high-quality printers, and editing software, as well as the technical knowledge to use these tools effectively.

Photographers who use cameras with silver-halide film often send their film to laboratories for processing. Color film requires expensive equipment and exacting conditions for correct processing and printing. Other photographers develop and print their own photographs using their own fully equipped darkroom, especially if they use black-and-white film or seek to achieve special effects. Photographers who do their own film developing must invest in additional developing and printing equipment and acquire the technical skills to operate it.

Some photographers specialize in areas such as portrait, commercial and industrial, scientific, news, or fine arts photography. *Portrait photographers* take pictures of individuals or groups of people and often work in their own studios. Some specialize in weddings, religious ceremonies, or school photographs and may work on location. Portrait photographers who own and operate their own business have many responsibilities in addition to taking pictures. They must arrange for advertising, schedule appointments, set and adjust equipment, purchase supplies, keep records, bill customers, pay bills, and—if they have employees—hire, train, and direct their workers. Many also process their own images, design albums, and mount and frame the finished photographs.

Commercial and industrial photographers take pictures of various subjects, such as buildings, models, merchandise, artifacts, and landscapes. These photographs are used in a variety of media, including books, reports, advertisements, and catalogs. Industrial photographers often take pictures of equipment, machinery, products, workers, and company officials. The pictures are used for various purposes—for example, analysis of engineering projects; publicity; or records of equipment development or deployment, such as placement of an offshore oil rig. This photography frequently is done on location.

Scientific photographers take images of a variety of subjects to illustrate or record scientific or medical data or phenomena, using knowledge of scientific procedures. They typically possess additional knowledge in areas such as engineering, medicine, biology, or chemistry.

News photographers, also called *photojournalists*, photograph newsworthy people; places; and sporting, political, and community events for newspapers, journals, magazines, or television.

Fine arts photographers sell their photographs as fine artwork. In addition to technical proficiency, fine arts photographers need artistic talent and creativity.

Self-employed, or *freelance, photographers* usually specialize in one of the above fields. In addition to carrying out assignments under direct contract with clients, they may license the use of their photographs through stock-photo agencies or market their work directly to the public. Stock-photo agencies sell magazines and other customers the right to use photographs, and they pay the photographer a commission. These agencies require an application from the photographer and a sizable portfolio of pictures. Once accepted, photographers usually are required to submit a large number of new photographs each year.

Working Conditions

Working conditions for photographers vary considerably. Photographers employed in government and advertising studios usually work a 5-day, 40-hour week. On the other hand, news photographers often work long, irregular hours and must be available to work on short notice. Many photographers work part time or on variable schedules. Most photographers spend only a small portion of their work schedule actually taking photographs. Their most common activities are editing images on a computer—if they use a digital camera—and looking for new business—if they are self-employed.

Portrait photographers usually work in their own studios but also may travel to take photographs at the client's location, such as a school, a company office, or a private home. News and commercial photographers frequently travel locally, stay overnight on assignments, or travel to distant places for long periods.

Some photographers work in uncomfortable or even dangerous surroundings, especially news photographers covering accidents, natural disasters, civil unrest, or military conflicts. Many photographers must wait long hours in all kinds of weather for an event to take place and stand or walk for long periods while carrying heavy equipment. News photographers often work under strict deadlines.

Self-employment allows for greater autonomy, freedom of expression, and flexible scheduling. However, income can be uncertain and the continuous, time-consuming search for new clients can be stressful. Some self-employed photographers hire assistants who help seek out new business.

Training, Other Qualifications, and Advancement

Employers usually seek applicants with a "good eye," imagination, and creativity, as well as a good technical understanding of photography. Entry-level positions in photojournalism or in industrial or scientific photography generally require a college degree in photography or in a field related to the industry in which the photographer seeks employment. Freelance and portrait photographers need technical proficiency, gained through either a degree program, vocational training, or extensive photography experience.

Photography courses are offered by many universities, community and junior colleges, vocational-technical institutes, and private trade and technical schools. Basic courses in photography cover equipment, processes, and techniques. Bachelor's degree programs, especially those including business courses, provide a well-rounded education. Art schools offer useful training in design and composition.

Individuals interested in a career in photography should try to develop contacts in the field by subscribing to photographic newsletters and magazines; joining camera clubs; and seeking summer or part-time employment in camera stores, newspapers, or photo studios.

Photographers may start out as assistants to experienced photographers. Assistants acquire the technical knowledge needed to be a successful photographer and also learn other skills necessary to run a portrait or commercial photography business. Freelance photographers also should develop an individual style of photography to differentiate themselves from the competition. Some photographers enter the field by submitting an unsolicited portfolio of photographs to magazines and to art directors at advertising agencies; for freelance photographers, a good portfolio is critical.

Photographers need good eyesight, artistic ability, and good hand-eye coordination. They should be patient, accurate, and detail-oriented. Photographers should be able to work well with others, as they frequently deal with clients, graphic designers, and advertising and publishing specialists. Photographers need to know how to use computer software programs and applications that allow them to prepare and edit images, and those who market directly to clients should be familiar with using the Internet to display their work.

Portrait photographers need the ability to help people relax in front of the camera. Commercial and fine arts photographers must be imaginative and original. News photographers must not only be good with a camera, but also understand the story behind an event so that their pictures match the story. They must be decisive in recognizing a potentially good photograph and act quickly to capture it. Photographers who operate their own business, or freelance, need business skills as well as talent. These individuals must know how to prepare a business plan; submit bids; write contracts; keep financial records; market their work; hire models, if needed; get permission to shoot on locations that normally are not open to the public; obtain releases to use photographs of people; license and price photographs; and secure copyright protection for their work. To protect their rights and their work, self-employed photographers require basic knowledge of licensing and copyright laws, as well as knowledge of contracts and negotiation procedures.

After several years of experience, magazine and news photographers may advance to photography or picture editor positions. Some photographers teach at technical schools, film schools, or universities.

Employment

Photographers held about 129,000 jobs in 2004. More than half were self-employed, a much higher proportion than for most occupations. Some self-employed photographers have contracts with advertising agencies, magazine publishers, or other businesses to do individual projects for a set fee, while others operate portrait studios or provide photographs to stock-photo agencies.

Most salaried photographers work in portrait or commercial photography studios; most of the others work for newspapers, magazines, and advertising agencies. Photographers work in all areas of the country, but most are employed in metropolitan areas.

Job Outlook

Photographers can expect keen competition for job openings because the work is attractive to many people. The number of individuals interested in positions as commercial and news photographers usually is much greater than the number of openings. Those who succeed in landing a salaried job or attracting enough work to earn a living by freelancing are likely to be adept at operating a business and to be among the most creative, able to find and exploit the new opportunities available from rapidly changing technologies. Related work experience, job-related training, or some unique skill or talent—such as a background in computers or electronics—also are beneficial to prospective photographers.

Employment of photographers is expected to increase about as fast as the average for all occupations through 2014. Demand for portrait photographers should increase as the population grows. Growth of Internet versions of magazines, journals, and newspapers will require increasing numbers of commercial photographers to provide digital images. The Internet also should make it easier for freelancers to market directly to their customers, increasing opportunities for self-employment.

Job growth, however, will be constrained somewhat by the widespread use of digital photography and the falling price of digital equipment. Improvements in digital technology reduce barriers of entry into this profession and allow more individual consumers and businesses to produce, store, and access photographic images on their own. Declines in the newspaper industry also will reduce demand for photographers to provide still images for print. Salaried jobs in particular may be difficult to find as more companies contract with freelancers rather than hire their own photographers.

Earnings

Median annual earnings of salaried photographers were $26,080 in May 2004. The middle 50 percent earned between $18,380 and $37,370. The lowest 10 percent earned less than $15,000, and the highest 10 percent earned more than $54,180. Median annual earnings in the industries employing the largest numbers of salaried photographers were $32,800 for newspapers and periodicals and $23,100 for other professional, scientific, and technical services.

Salaried photographers—more of whom work full time—tend to earn more than those who are self-employed. Because most freelance and portrait photographers purchase their own equipment, they incur considerable expense acquiring and maintaining cameras and accessories. Unlike news and commercial photographers, few fine arts photographers are successful enough to support themselves solely through their art.

Related Occupations

Other occupations requiring artistic talent and creativity include architects, except landscape and naval; artists and related workers; commercial and industrial designers; fashion designers; graphic designers; and television, video, and motion picture camera operators and editors. Photojournalists are often required to cover news stories in much the same way as news analysts, reporters, and correspondents. The processing work that photographers do on computers is similar to the work of prepress technicians and workers and desktop publishers.

Sources of Additional Information

Career information on photography is available from

▸ Professional Photographers of America, Inc., 229 Peachtree St. NE, Suite 2200, Atlanta, GA 30303.

▸ National Press Photographers Association, Inc., 3200 Croasdaile Dr., Suite 306, Durham, NC 27705. Internet: http://www.nppa.org

▸ American Society of Media Photographers, Inc., 150 North Second St., Philadelphia, PA 19106. Internet: http://www.asmp.org

Pipelayers, Plumbers, Pipefitters, and Steamfitters

(O*NET 47-2151.00, 47-2152.01, 47-2152.02, and 47-2152.03)

Significant Points

■ Job opportunities should be excellent because not enough people are seeking training.

■ Pipelayers, plumbers, pipefitters, and steamfitters make up one of the largest and highest-paid construction occupations.

Nature of the Work

Most people are familiar with plumbers, who come to their home to unclog a drain or install an appliance. In addition to these activities, however, pipelayers, plumbers, pipefitters, and steamfitters install, maintain, and repair many different types of pipe systems. For example, some systems move water to a municipal water treatment plant and then to residential, commercial, and public buildings. Other systems dispose of waste, provide gas to stoves and furnaces, or provide for heating and cooling needs. Pipe systems in power plants carry the steam that powers huge turbines. Pipes also are used in manufacturing plants to move material through the production process. Specialized piping systems are very important in both pharmaceutical and computer-chip manufacturing.

Although pipelaying, plumbing, pipefitting, and steamfitting sometimes are considered a single trade, workers generally specialize in one of five areas. *Pipelayers* lay clay, concrete, plastic, or cast-iron pipe for drains, sewers, water mains, and oil or gas lines. Before laying the pipe, pipelayers prepare and grade the trenches, either manually or with machines. After laying the pipe, they weld, glue, cement or otherwise join the pieces together. *Plumbers* install and repair the water, waste disposal, drainage, and gas systems in homes and commercial and industrial buildings. Plumbers also install plumbing fixtures—bathtubs, showers, sinks, and toilets—and appliances such as dishwashers and water heaters. *Pipefitters* install and repair both high- and low-pressure pipe systems used in manufacturing, in the generation of electricity, and in the heating and cooling of buildings. They also install automatic controls that are increasingly being used to regulate these systems. Some pipefitters specialize in only one type of system. *Steamfitters* install pipe systems that move liquids or gases under high pressure. *Sprinklerfitters* install automatic fire sprinkler systems in buildings.

Pipelayers, plumbers, pipefitters, and steamfitters use many different materials and construction techniques, depending on the type of project. Residential water systems, for example, incorporate copper, steel, and plastic pipe that can be handled and installed by one or two plumbers. Municipal sewerage systems, on the other hand, are made of large cast-iron pipes; installation normally requires crews of pipefitters. Despite these differences, all pipelayers, plumbers, pipefitters, and steamfitters must be able to follow building plans or blueprints and instructions from supervisors, lay out the job, and work efficiently with the materials and tools of their trade. Computers and specialized software are used to create blueprints and plan layouts.

When construction plumbers install piping in a new house, for example, they work from blueprints or drawings that show the planned location of pipes, plumbing fixtures, and appliances. Recently, plumbers have become more involved in the design process. Their knowledge of codes and the operation of plumbing systems can cut costs. They first lay out the job to fit the piping into the structure of the house with the least waste of material. Then they measure and mark areas in which pipes will be installed and connected. Construction plumbers also check for obstructions such as electrical wiring and, if necessary, plan the pipe installation around the problem.

Sometimes, plumbers have to cut holes in walls, ceilings, and floors of a house. For some systems, they may hang steel supports from ceiling joists to hold the pipe in place. To assemble a system, plumbers—using saws, pipe cutters, and pipe-bending machines—cut and bend lengths of pipe. They connect lengths of pipe with fittings, using methods that depend on the type of pipe used. For plastic pipe, plumbers connect the sections and fittings with adhesives. For copper pipe, they slide a fitting over the end of the pipe and solder it in place with a torch.

After the piping is in place in the house, plumbers install the fixtures and appliances and connect the system to the outside water or sewer lines. Finally, using pressure gauges, they check the system to ensure that the plumbing works properly.

Working Conditions

Pipefitters and steamfitters most often work in industrial and power plants. Plumbers work in commercial and residential settings where water and septic systems need to be installed and maintained. Pipelayers work outdoors, sometime in remote areas, as they build the pipelines that connect sources of oil, gas, and chemicals with the users of these materials. Sprinklerfitters work mostly in multistory buildings that require the use of sprinkler systems.

Because pipelayers, plumbers, pipefitters, and steamfitters frequently must lift heavy pipes, stand for long periods, and sometimes work in uncomfortable or cramped positions, they need physical strength as well as stamina. They also may have to work outdoors in inclement weather. In addition, they are subject to possible falls from ladders, cuts from sharp tools, and burns from hot pipes or soldering equipment.

Pipelayers, plumbers, pipefitters, and steamfitters engaged in construction generally work a standard 40-hour week; those involved in maintaining pipe systems, including those who provide maintenance services under contract, may have to work evening or weekend shifts, as well as be on call. These maintenance workers may spend quite a bit of time traveling to and from worksites.

Training, Other Qualifications, and Advancement

Pipelayers, plumbers, pipefitters, and steamfitters enter into the profession in a variety of ways. Most residential and industrial plumbers get their training in career and technical schools and community colleges and from on-the-job training. Pipelayers, plumbers, pipefitters, and steamfitters who work mainly for commercial enterprises are usually trained through formal apprenticeship programs.

Apprenticeship programs generally provide the most comprehensive training available for these jobs. They are administered by either union locals and their affiliated companies or by nonunion contractor organizations. Organizations that sponsor apprenticeships include the United Association of Journeymen and Apprentices of the Plumbing and Pipefitting Industry of the United States and Canada; local employers of either the Mechanical Contractors Association of America, the National Association of Plumbing-Heating-Cooling Contractors, or the National Fire Sprinkler Association; the Associated Builders and Contractors; the National Association of Plumbing-Heating-Cooling Contractors; the American Fire Sprinkler Association; or the Home Builders Institute of the National Association of Home Builders.

Apprenticeships—both union and nonunion—consist of 4 or 5 years of on-the-job training in addition to at least 144 hours per year of related classroom instruction. Classroom subjects include drafting and blueprint reading, mathematics, applied physics and chemistry, safety, and local plumbing codes and regulations. On the job, apprentices first learn basic skills, such as identifying grades and types of pipe, using the tools of the trade, and safely unloading materials. As apprentices gain experience, they learn how to work with various types of pipe and how to install different piping systems and plumbing fixtures. Apprenticeship gives trainees a thorough knowledge of all aspects of the trade. Although most pipelayers, plumbers, pipefitters, and steamfitters are trained through apprenticeship, some still learn their skills informally on the job.

Applicants for union or nonunion apprentice jobs must be at least 18 years old and in good physical condition. Apprenticeship committees may require applicants to have a high school diploma or its equivalent. Armed Forces training in pipelaying, plumbing, and pipefitting is considered very good preparation. In fact, persons with this background may be given credit for previous experience when entering a civilian apprenticeship program. Secondary or postsecondary courses in shop, plumbing, general mathematics, drafting, blueprint reading, computers, and physics also are good preparation.

Although there are no uniform national licensing requirements, most communities require plumbers to be licensed. Licensing requirements vary from area to area, but most localities require workers to pass an examination that tests their knowledge of the trade and of local plumbing codes.

With additional training, some pipelayers, plumbers, pipefitters, and steamfitters become supervisors for mechanical and plumbing contractors. Others, especially plumbers, go into business for themselves, often starting as a self-employed plumber working from home. Some eventually become owners of businesses employing many workers and may spend most of their time as managers rather than as plumbers. Others move into closely related areas such as construction management or building inspection.

Employment

Pipelayers, plumbers, pipefitters, and steamfitters constitute one of the largest construction occupations, holding about 561,000 jobs in 2004. About 1 in 2 worked for plumbing, heating, and air-conditioning contractors engaged in new construction, repair, modernization, or maintenance work. Others did maintenance work for a variety of industrial, commercial, and government employers. For example, pipefitters were employed as maintenance personnel in the petroleum and chemical industries, in which manufacturing operations require the moving of liquids and gases through pipes. More than 1 in 10 pipelayers, plumbers, pipefitters, and steamfitters were self-employed. Almost 1 in 3 pipelayers, plumbers, pipefitters, and steamfitters belonged to a union.

Jobs for pipelayers, plumbers, pipefitters, and steamfitters are distributed across the country in about the same proportion as the general population.

Job Outlook

Job opportunities are expected to be excellent, as demand for skilled pipelayers, plumbers, pipefitters, and steamfitters is expected to outpace the supply of workers trained in this craft. Many employers report difficulty finding potential workers with the right qualifications. In addition, many people currently working in these trades are expected to retire over the next 10 years, which will create additional job openings.

Employment of pipelayers, plumbers, pipefitters, and steamfitters is expected to grow about as fast as the average for all occupations through the year 2014. Demand for plumbers will stem from new construction and building renovation. Bath remodeling, in particular, is expected to continue to grow and create more jobs for plumbers. In addition, repair and maintenance of existing residential systems will keep plumbers employed. Demand for pipefitters and steamfitters will be driven by maintenance activities for places having extensive systems of pipes, such as power plants, water and wastewater treatment plants, office buildings, and factories. Growth of pipelayer jobs will stem from the building of new water and

sewer lines and pipelines to new oil and gas fields. Demand for sprinklerfitters will increase due to changes to state and local rules for fire protection in homes and businesses.

Traditionally, many organizations with extensive pipe systems have employed their own plumbers or pipefitters to maintain equipment and keep systems running smoothly. But, to reduce labor costs, many of these firms no longer employ full-time, in-house plumbers or pipefitters. Instead, when they need a plumber, they rely on workers provided under service contracts by plumbing and pipefitting contractors.

Construction projects generally provide only temporary employment. When a project ends, some pipelayers, plumbers, pipefitters, and steamfitters may be unemployed until they can begin work on a new project, although most companies are trying to limit these periods of unemployment in order to retain workers. In addition, the jobs of pipelayers, plumbers, pipefitters, and steamfitters are generally less sensitive to changes in economic conditions than jobs in other construction trades. Even when construction activity declines, maintenance, rehabilitation, and replacement of existing piping systems, as well as the increasing installation of fire sprinkler systems, provide many jobs for pipelayers, plumbers, pipefitters, and steamfitters.

Earnings

Pipelayers, plumbers, pipefitters, and steamfitters are among the highest-paid construction occupations. In May 2004, median hourly earnings of pipelayers were $13.68. The middle 50 percent earned between $11.05 and $18.69. The lowest 10 percent earned less than $9.19, and the highest 10 percent earned more than $25.07. Also in May 2004, median hourly earnings of plumbers, pipefitters, and steamfitters were $19.85. The middle 50 percent earned between $15.01 and $26.67. The lowest 10 percent earned less than $11.62, and the highest 10 percent earned more than $33.72. Median hourly earnings in the industries employing the largest numbers of plumbers, pipefitters, and steamfitters in May 2004 were as follows:

Natural gas distribution	$23.86
Nonresidential building construction	21.55
Building equipment contractors	19.85
Utility system construction	18.29
Local government	16.30

Apprentices usually begin at about 50 percent of the wage rate paid to experienced pipelayers, plumbers, pipefitters, and steamfitters. Wages increase periodically as skills improve. After an initial waiting period, apprentices receive the same benefits as experienced pipelayers, plumbers, pipefitters, and steamfitters.

Many pipelayers, plumbers, pipefitters, and steamfitters are members of the United Association of Journeymen and Apprentices of the Plumbing and Pipefitting Industry of the United States and Canada.

Related Occupations

Other occupations in which workers install and repair mechanical systems in buildings are boilermakers; electricians; elevator installers and repairers; heating, air-conditioning, and refrigeration mechanics and installers; industrial machinery installation, repair, and maintenance workers; millwrights; sheet metal workers; and stationary engineers and boiler operators. Other related occupations include construction managers and construction and building inspectors.

Sources of Additional Information

For information about apprenticeships or work opportunities in pipelaying, plumbing, pipefitting, and steamfitting, contact local plumbing, heating, and air-conditioning contractors; a local or state chapter of the National Association of Plumbing, Heating, and Cooling Contractors; a local chapter of the Mechanical Contractors Association; a local chapter of the United Association of Journeymen and Apprentices of the Plumbing and Pipefitting Industry of the United States and Canada; or the nearest office of your state employment service or apprenticeship agency.

For information about apprenticeship opportunities for pipelayers, plumbers, pipefitters, and steamfitters, contact

> ▶ United Association of Journeymen and Apprentices of the Plumbing and Pipefitting Industry, 901 Massachusetts Ave. NW, Washington, DC 20001. Internet: http://www.ua.org

For more information about training programs for pipelayers, plumbers, pipefitters, and steamfitters, contact

> ▶ Associated Builders and Contractors, Workforce Development Department, 4250 North Fairfax Dr., 9th Floor, Arlington, VA 22203. Internet: http://www.trytools.org

> ▶ Home Builders Institute, National Association of Home Builders, 1201 15th St. NW, Washington, DC 20005. Internet: http://www.hbi.org

For general information about the work of pipelayers, plumbers, and pipefitters, contact

> ▶ Mechanical Contractors Association of America, 1385 Piccard Dr., Rockville, MD 20850. Internet: http://www.mcaa.org

> ▶ Plumbing-Heating-Cooling Contractors—National Association, 180 S. Washington St., Falls Church, VA 22040. Internet: http://www.phccweb.org

> ▶ National Center for Construction Education and Research, P.O. Box 141104, Gainesville, FL 32614-1104. Internet: http://www.nccer.org

For general information about the work of sprinklerfitters, contact

> ▶ American Fire Sprinkler Association, Inc., 9696 Skillman St., Suite 300, Dallas, TX 75243-8264. Internet: http://www.firesprinkler.org

> ▶ National Fire Sprinkler Association, P.O. Box 1000, Patterson, NY 12563. Internet: http://www.nfsa.org

Police and Detectives

(O*NET 33-1012.00, 33-3021.01, 33-3021.02, 33-3021.03, 33-3021.04, 33-3021.05, 33-3031.00, 33-3051.01, 33-3051.02, 33-3051.03, and 33-3052.00)

Significant Points

■ Police and detective work can be dangerous and stressful.

■ Competition should remain keen for higher-paying jobs with state and federal agencies and police departments in affluent areas; opportunities will be better in local and special police

departments that offer relatively low salaries or in urban communities where the crime rate is relatively high.

■ Applicants with college training in police science or military police experience should have the best opportunities.

Nature of the Work

People depend on police officers and detectives to protect their lives and property. Law enforcement officers, some of whom are state or federal special agents or inspectors, perform these duties in a variety of ways, depending on the size and type of their organization. In most jurisdictions, they are expected to exercise authority when necessary, whether on or off duty.

Uniformed police officers have general law enforcement duties, including maintaining regular patrols and responding to calls for service. They may direct traffic at the scene of an accident, investigate a burglary, or give first aid to an accident victim. In large police departments, officers usually are assigned to a specific type of duty. Many urban police agencies are involved in community policing—a practice in which an officer builds relationships with the citizens of local neighborhoods and mobilizes the public to help fight crime.

Police agencies are usually organized into geographic districts, with uniformed officers assigned to patrol a specific area, such as part of the business district or outlying residential neighborhoods. Officers may work alone, but in large agencies, they often patrol with a partner. While on patrol, officers attempt to become thoroughly familiar with their patrol area and remain alert for anything unusual. Suspicious circumstances and hazards to public safety are investigated or noted, and officers are dispatched to individual calls for assistance within their district. During their shift, they may identify, pursue, and arrest suspected criminals; resolve problems within the community; and enforce traffic laws.

Public college and university police forces, public school district police, and agencies serving transportation systems and facilities are examples of special police agencies. These agencies have special geographic jurisdictions and enforcement responsibilities in the United States. Most sworn personnel in special agencies are uniformed officers; a smaller number are investigators.

Some police officers specialize in such diverse fields as chemical and microscopic analysis, training and firearms instruction, or handwriting and fingerprint identification. Others work with special units, such as horseback, bicycle, motorcycle, or harbor patrol; canine corps; special weapons and tactics (SWAT); or emergency response teams. A few local and special law enforcement officers primarily perform jail-related duties or work in courts. Regardless of job duties or location, police officers and detectives at all levels must write reports and maintain meticulous records that will be needed if they testify in court.

Sheriffs and deputy sheriffs enforce the law on the county level. Sheriffs are usually elected to their posts and perform duties similar to those of a local or county police chief. Sheriffs' departments tend to be relatively small, most having fewer than 50 sworn officers. Deputy sheriffs have law enforcement duties similar to those of officers in urban police departments. Police and sheriffs' deputies who provide security in city and county courts are sometimes called bailiffs. (For information on other officers who work in jails and prisons, see the description of correctional officers elsewhere in this book.)

State police officers (sometimes called *state troopers* or *highway patrol officers*) arrest criminals statewide and patrol highways to enforce motor vehicle laws and regulations. State police officers are best known for issuing traffic citations to motorists. At the scene of accidents, they may direct traffic, give first aid, and call for emergency equipment. They also write reports used to determine the cause of the accident. State police officers are frequently called upon to render assistance to other law enforcement agencies, especially those in rural areas or small towns.

State law enforcement agencies operate in every state except Hawaii. Most full-time sworn personnel are uniformed officers who regularly patrol and respond to calls for service. Others work as investigators, perform court-related duties, or carry out administrative or other assignments.

Detectives are plainclothes investigators who gather facts and collect evidence for criminal cases. Some are assigned to interagency task forces to combat specific types of crime. They conduct interviews, examine records, observe the activities of suspects, and participate in raids or arrests. Detectives and state and federal agents and inspectors usually specialize in investigating one of a wide variety of violations, such as homicide or fraud. They are assigned cases on a rotating basis and work on them until an arrest and conviction occurs or until the case is dropped.

Fish and game wardens enforce fishing, hunting, and boating laws. They patrol hunting and fishing areas, conduct search and rescue operations, investigate complaints and accidents, and aid in prosecuting court cases.

The federal government maintains a high profile in many areas of law enforcement. *Federal Bureau of Investigation (FBI) agents* are the government's principal investigators, and they are responsible for investigating violations of more than 200 categories of federal law and conducting sensitive national security investigations. Agents may conduct surveillance, monitor court-authorized wiretaps, examine business records, investigate white-collar crime, or participate in sensitive undercover assignments. The FBI investigates organized crime, public corruption, financial crime, fraud against the government, bribery, copyright infringement, civil rights violations, bank robbery, extortion, kidnapping, air piracy, terrorism, espionage, interstate criminal activity, drug trafficking, and other violations of federal statutes.

U.S. Drug Enforcement Administration (DEA) agents enforce laws and regulations relating to illegal drugs. Not only is the DEA the lead agency for domestic enforcement of federal drug laws, it also has sole responsibility for coordinating and pursuing U.S. drug investigations abroad. Agents may conduct complex criminal investigations, carry out surveillance of criminals, and infiltrate illicit drug organizations using undercover techniques.

U.S. marshals and deputy marshals protect the federal courts and ensure the effective operation of the judicial system. They provide protection for the federal judiciary, transport federal prisoners, protect federal witnesses, and manage assets seized from criminal enterprises. They enjoy the widest jurisdiction of any federal law enforcement agency and are involved to some degree in nearly all federal law enforcement efforts. In addition, U.S. marshals pursue and arrest federal fugitives.

Bureau of Alcohol, Tobacco, Firearms, and Explosives agents regulate and investigate violations of federal firearms and explosives laws as well as federal alcohol and tobacco tax regulations.

The U.S. Department of State *Bureau of Diplomatic Security special agents* are engaged in the battle against terrorism. Overseas, they advise ambassadors on all security matters and manage a complex range of security programs designed to protect personnel, facilities, and information. In the United States, they investigate passport and visa fraud, conduct personnel security investigations, issue security clearances, and protect the Secretary of State and a number of foreign dignitaries. They also train foreign civilian police and administer a counter-terrorism reward program.

The *Department of Homeland Security* employs numerous law enforcement officers under several different agencies, including *Customs and Border Protection, Immigration and Customs Enforcement,* and the *U.S. Secret Service. U.S. Border Patrol agents* protect more than 8,000 miles of international land and water boundaries. Their missions are to detect and prevent the smuggling and unlawful entry of undocumented foreign nationals into the United States; to apprehend those persons violating the immigration laws; and to interdict contraband, such as narcotics.

Immigration inspectors interview and examine people seeking entrance to the United States and its territories. They inspect passports to determine whether people are legally eligible to enter the United States. Immigration inspectors also prepare reports, maintain records, and process applications and petitions for immigration or temporary residence in the United States.

Customs inspectors enforce laws governing imports and exports by inspecting cargo, baggage, and articles worn or carried by people, vessels, vehicles, trains, and aircraft entering or leaving the United States. These inspectors examine, count, weigh, gauge, measure, and sample commercial and noncommercial cargoes entering and leaving the United States. Customs inspectors seize prohibited or smuggled articles; intercept contraband; and apprehend, search, detain, and arrest violators of U.S. laws. *Customs agents* investigate violations, such as narcotics smuggling, money laundering, child pornography, and customs fraud, and they enforce the Arms Export Control Act. During domestic and foreign investigations, they develop and use informants; conduct physical and electronic surveillance; and examine records from importers and exporters, banks, couriers, and manufacturers. They conduct interviews, serve on joint task forces with other agencies, and get and execute search warrants.

Federal Air Marshals provide air security by fighting attacks targeting U.S. airports, passengers, and crews. They disguise themselves as ordinary passengers and board flights of U.S. air carriers to locations worldwide.

U.S. Secret Service special agents protect the President, Vice President, and their immediate families; Presidential candidates; former Presidents; and foreign dignitaries visiting the United States. Secret Service agents also investigate counterfeiting, forgery of government checks or bonds, and fraudulent use of credit cards.

Other federal agencies employ police and special agents with sworn arrest powers and the authority to carry firearms. These agencies include the Postal Service, the Bureau of Indian Affairs Office of Law Enforcement, the Forest Service, and the National Park Service.

Working Conditions

Police and detective work can be very dangerous and stressful. In addition to the obvious dangers of confrontations with criminals, police officers and detectives need to be constantly alert and ready to deal appropriately with a number of other threatening situations. Many law enforcement officers witness death and suffering resulting from accidents and criminal behavior. A career in law enforcement may take a toll on their private lives.

Uniformed officers, detectives, agents, and inspectors are usually scheduled to work 40-hour weeks, but paid overtime is common. Shift work is necessary because protection must be provided around the clock. Junior officers frequently work weekends, holidays, and nights. Police officers and detectives are required to work at any time their services are needed and may work long hours during investigations. In most jurisdictions, whether on or off duty, officers are expected to be armed and to exercise their authority whenever necessary.

The jobs of some federal agents such as U.S. Secret Service and DEA special agents require extensive travel, often on very short notice. They may relocate a number of times over the course of their careers. Some special agents in agencies such as the U.S. Border Patrol work outdoors in rugged terrain for long periods and in all kinds of weather.

Training, Other Qualifications, and Advancement

Civil service regulations govern the appointment of police and detectives in most states, large municipalities, and special police agencies, as well as in many smaller jurisdictions. Candidates must be U.S. citizens, usually must be at least 20 years of age, and must meet rigorous physical and personal qualifications. In the federal government, candidates must be at least 21 years of age but less than 37 years of age at the time of appointment. Physical examinations for entrance into law enforcement often include tests of vision, hearing, strength, and agility. Eligibility for appointment usually depends on performance in competitive written examinations and previous education and experience. In larger departments, where the majority of law enforcement jobs are found, applicants usually must have at least a high school education, and some departments require a year or two of college coursework. Federal and state agencies typically require a college degree. Candidates should enjoy working with people and meeting the public.

Because personal characteristics such as honesty, sound judgment, integrity, and a sense of responsibility are especially important in law enforcement, candidates are interviewed by senior officers, and their character traits and backgrounds are investigated. In some agencies, candidates are interviewed by a psychiatrist or a psychologist or given a personality test. Most applicants are subjected to lie detector examinations or drug testing. Some agencies subject sworn personnel to random drug testing as a condition of continuing employment.

Before their first assignments, officers usually go through a period of training. In state and large local departments, recruits get training in their agency's police academy, often for 12 to 14 weeks. In small agencies, recruits often attend a regional or state academy. Training includes classroom instruction in constitutional law and civil rights, state laws and local ordinances, and accident investigation. Recruits also receive training and supervised experience in patrol, traffic control, use of firearms, self-defense, first aid, and emergency response. Police departments in some large cities hire high school graduates who are still in their teens as police cadets or trainees. They do clerical work and attend classes, usually for 1 to 2 years, at which point they reach the minimum age requirement and may be appointed to the regular force.

Police officers usually become eligible for promotion after a probationary period ranging from 6 months to 3 years. In a large department, promotion may enable an officer to become a detective or to specialize in one type of police work, such as working with juveniles. Promotions to corporal, sergeant, lieutenant, and captain usually are made according to a candidate's position on a promotion list as determined by scores on a written examination and on-the-job performance.

Most states require at least two years of college study to qualify as a fish and game warden. Applicants must pass written and physical examinations and vision, hearing, psychological, and drug tests similar to those taken by other law enforcement officers. Once hired, officers attend a training academy lasting from 3 to 12 months, sometimes followed by further training in the field.

To be considered for appointment as an FBI agent, an applicant must be a graduate of an accredited law school or a college graduate with one of the following: a major in accounting, electrical engineering, or information technology; fluency in a foreign language; or three years of related full-time work experience. All new agents undergo 18 weeks of training at the FBI Academy on the U.S. Marine Corps base in Quantico, Virginia.

Applicants for special agent jobs with the U.S. Secret Service and the Bureau of Alcohol, Tobacco, and Firearms must have a bachelor's degree, a minimum of three years' related work experience, or a combination of education and experience. Prospective special agents undergo 11 weeks of initial criminal investigation training at the Federal Law Enforcement Training Center in Glynco, Georgia, and another 17 weeks of specialized training with their particular agencies.

Applicants for special agent jobs with the DEA must have a college degree with at least a 2.95 grade point average or specialized skills or work experience, such as foreign language fluency, technical skills, law enforcement experience, or accounting experience. DEA special agents undergo 14 weeks of specialized training at the FBI Academy in Quantico, Virginia.

U.S. Border Patrol agents must be U.S. citizens, be younger than 37 years of age at the time of appointment, possess a valid driver's license, and pass a three-part examination on reasoning and language skills. A bachelor's degree or previous work experience that demonstrates the ability to handle stressful situations, make decisions, and take charge is required for a position as a Border Patrol agent. Applicants may qualify through a combination of education and work experience.

Postal inspectors must have a bachelor's degree and 1 year of related work experience. It is desirable that they have one of several professional certifications, such as that of certified public accountant. They also must pass a background investigation, meet certain health requirements, undergo a drug screening test, possess a valid state driver's license, and be a U.S. citizen between 21 and 36 years of age when hired.

Law enforcement agencies are encouraging applicants to take postsecondary school training in law enforcement-related subjects. Many entry-level applicants for police jobs have completed some formal postsecondary education, and a significant number are college graduates. Many junior colleges, colleges, and universities offer programs in law enforcement or administration of justice. Other courses helpful in preparing for a career in law enforcement include accounting, finance, electrical engineering, computer science, and foreign languages. Physical education and sports are helpful in developing the competitiveness, stamina, and agility needed for many law enforcement positions. Knowledge of a foreign language is an asset in many federal agencies and urban departments.

Continuing training helps police officers, detectives, and special agents improve their job performance. Through police department academies, regional centers for public safety employees established by the states, and federal agency training centers, instructors provide annual training in self-defense tactics, firearms, use-of-force policies, sensitivity and communications skills, crowd-control techniques, relevant legal developments, and advances in law enforcement equipment. Many agencies pay all or part of the tuition for officers to work toward degrees in criminal justice, police science, administration of justice, or public administration and pay higher salaries to those who earn such a degree.

Employment

Police and detectives held about 842,000 jobs in 2004. About 80 percent were employed by local governments. State police agencies employed about 12 percent, and various federal agencies employed about 6 percent. A small proportion worked for educational services, rail transportation, and contract investigation and security services.

According to the U.S. Bureau of Justice Statistics, police and detectives employed by local governments primarily worked in cities with more than 25,000 inhabitants. Some cities have very large police forces, while thousands of small communities employ fewer than 25 officers each.

Job Outlook

The opportunity for public service through law enforcement work is attractive to many because the job is challenging and involves much personal responsibility. Furthermore, law enforcement officers in many agencies may retire with a pension after 25 or 30 years of service, allowing them to pursue a second career while still in their 40s or 50s. Because of relatively attractive salaries and benefits, the number of qualified candidates exceeds the number of job openings in federal law enforcement agencies and in most state police departments, resulting in increased hiring standards and selectivity by employers. Competition should remain keen for higher-paying jobs with state and federal agencies and police departments in more affluent areas. Opportunities will be better in local and special police

departments, especially in departments that offer relatively low salaries or in urban communities where the crime rate is relatively high. Applicants with college training in police science, military police experience, or both should have the best opportunities.

Employment of police and detectives is expected to grow about as fast as the average for all occupations through 2014. A more security-conscious society and concern about drug-related crimes should contribute to the increasing demand for police services. However, employment growth will be hindered by reductions in federal hiring grants to local police departments and by expectations of low crime rates by the general public.

The level of government spending determines the level of employment for police and detectives. The number of job opportunities, therefore, can vary from year to year and from place to place. Layoffs, on the other hand, are rare because retirements enable most staffing cuts to be handled through attrition. Trained law enforcement officers who lose their jobs because of budget cuts usually have little difficulty finding jobs with other agencies. The need to replace workers who retire, transfer to other occupations, or stop working for other reasons will be the source of many job openings.

Earnings

Police and sheriff's patrol officers had median annual earnings of $45,210 in May 2004. The middle 50 percent earned between $34,410 and $56,360. The lowest 10 percent earned less than $26,910, and the highest 10 percent earned more than $68,880. Median annual earnings were $44,750 in federal government, $48,980 in state government, and $45,010 in local government.

In May 2004, median annual earnings of police and detective supervisors were $64,430. The middle 50 percent earned between $49,370 and $80,510. The lowest 10 percent earned less than $36,690, and the highest 10 percent earned more than $96,950. Median annual earnings were $86,030 in federal government, $62,300 in state government, and $63,590 in local government.

In May 2004, median annual earnings of detectives and criminal investigators were $53,990. The middle 50 percent earned between $40,690 and $72,280. The lowest 10 percent earned less than $32,180, and the highest 10 percent earned more than $86,010. Median annual earnings were $75,700 in federal government, $46,670 in state government, and $49,650 in local government.

Federal law provides special salary rates to federal employees who serve in law enforcement. Additionally, federal special agents and inspectors receive law enforcement availability pay (LEAP)—equal to 25 percent of the agent's grade and step—awarded because of the large amount of overtime that these agents are expected to work. For example, in 2005, FBI agents entered federal service as GS-10 employees on the pay scale at a base salary of $42,548, yet they earned about $53,185 a year with availability pay. They could advance to the GS-13 grade level in field nonsupervisory assignments at a base salary of $64,478, which was worth $80,597 with availability pay. FBI supervisory, management, and executive positions in grades GS-14 and GS-15 paid a base salary of about $76,193 and $89,625 a year, respectively, which amounted to $95,241 or $112,031 per year including availability pay. Salaries were slightly higher in selected areas where the prevailing local pay level was higher. Because federal agents may be eligible for a special law enforcement benefits package, applicants should ask their recruiter for more information.

According to the International City-County Management Association's annual Police and Fire Personnel, Salaries, and Expenditures Survey, average salaries for sworn full-time positions in 2004 were as follows:

	Minimum annual base salary	Maximum annual base salary
Police chief	$72,924	$92,983
Deputy chief	61,110	76,994
Police captain	60,908	75,497
Police lieutenant	56,115	67,580
Police sergeant	49,895	59,454
Police corporal	41,793	51,661

Total earnings for local, state, and special police and detectives frequently exceed the stated salary because of payments for overtime, which can be significant. In addition to the common benefits—paid vacation, sick leave, and medical and life insurance—most police and sheriffs' departments provide officers with special allowances for uniforms. Because police officers usually are covered by liberal pension plans, many retire at half pay after 25 or 30 years of service.

Related Occupations

Police and detectives maintain law and order, collect evidence and information, and conduct investigations and surveillance. Workers in related occupations include correctional officers, private detectives and investigators, and security guards and gaming surveillance officers.

Sources of Additional Information

Information about entrance requirements may be obtained from federal, state, and local law enforcement agencies.

For general information about sheriffs and to learn more about the National Sheriffs' Association scholarship, contact

▸ National Sheriffs' Association, 1450 Duke St., Alexandria, VA 22314. Internet: http://www.sheriffs.org

Information about qualifications for employment as a FBI Special Agent is available from the nearest state FBI office. The address and phone number are listed in the local telephone directory. Internet: http://www.fbi.gov

Information on career opportunities, qualifications, and training for U.S. Secret Service Special Agents is available from the Secret Service Personnel Division at (202) 406-5800, (888) 813-8777, or (888) 813-USSS. Internet: http://www.treas.gov/usss

Information about qualifications for employment as a DEA Special Agent is available from the nearest DEA office, or call (800) DEA-4288. Internet: http://www.usdoj.gov/dea

Information about career opportunities, qualifications, and training to become a deputy marshal is available from

▸ U.S. Marshals Service, Human Resources Division—Law Enforcement Recruiting, Washington, DC 20530-1000. Internet: http://www.usmarshals.gov

For information on operations and career opportunities in the U.S. Bureau of Alcohol, Tobacco, Firearms, and Explosives operations, contact

▸ U.S. Bureau of Alcohol, Tobacco, Firearms, and Explosives Personnel Division, 650 Massachusetts Ave. NW, Room 4100, Washington, DC 20226. Internet: http://www.atf.treas.gov

Information about careers in U.S. Customs and Border Protection is available from

▸ U.S. Customs and Border Protection, 1300 Pennsylvania Ave. NW, Washington, DC 20229. Internet: http://www.cbp.gov

Information about law enforcement agencies within the Department of Homeland Security is available from

▸ U.S. Department of Homeland Security, Washington, DC 20528. Internet: http://www.dhs.gov

Postal Service Workers

(O*NET 43-5051.00, 43-5052.00, and 43-5053.00)

Significant Points

- Employment of Postal Service workers is expected to decline because of the increasing use of automation and electronic communication, such as the Internet.

- Keen competition is expected because the number of qualified applicants should continue to exceed the number of job openings.

- Qualification is based on an examination.

- Applicants customarily wait 1 to 2 years or more after passing the examination before being hired.

Nature of the Work

Each week, the U.S. Postal Service delivers billions of pieces of mail, including letters, bills, advertisements, and packages. To do this in an efficient and timely manner, the Postal Service employs about 619,000 individuals. Most Postal Service workers are clerks; mail carriers; or mail sorters, processors, and processing machine operators. Postal clerks wait on customers at post offices, whereas mail sorters, processors, and processing machine operators sort incoming and outgoing mail at post offices and mail processing centers. Mail carriers deliver mail to urban and rural residences and businesses throughout the United States.

Postal Service clerks, also known as *window clerks*, sell stamps, money orders, postal stationery, and mailing envelopes and boxes. They also weigh packages to determine postage and check that packages are in satisfactory condition for mailing. These clerks register, certify, and insure mail and answer questions about postage rates, post office boxes, mailing restrictions, and other postal matters. Window clerks also help customers file claims for damaged packages.

Postal Service mail sorters, processors, and processing machine operators prepare incoming and outgoing mail for distribution. These workers are commonly referred to as mail handlers, distribution clerks, mail processors, or mail processing clerks. They load and unload postal trucks and move mail around a mail processing center with forklifts, small electric tractors, or hand-pushed carts. They also load and operate mail processing, sorting, and canceling machinery.

Postal Service mail carriers deliver mail once it has been processed and sorted. Although carriers are classified by their type of route—either city or rural—duties of city and rural carriers are similar. Most travel established routes, delivering and collecting mail. Mail carriers start work at the post office early in the morning, when they arrange the mail in delivery sequence. Automated equipment has reduced the time that carriers need to sort the mail, allowing them to spend more time delivering it.

Mail carriers cover their routes on foot, by vehicle, or a combination of both. On foot, they carry a heavy load of mail in a satchel or push it on a cart. In most urban and rural areas, they use a car or small truck. Although the Postal Service provides vehicles to city carriers, most rural carriers must use their own automobiles. Deliveries are made house-to-house, to roadside mailboxes, and to large buildings such as offices or apartments, which generally have all of their tenants' mailboxes in one location.

Besides delivering and collecting mail, carriers collect money for postage-due and COD (cash-on-delivery) fees and obtain signed receipts for registered, certified, and insured mail. If a customer is not home, the carrier leaves a notice that tells where special mail is being held. After completing their routes, carriers return to the post office with mail gathered from street collection boxes, homes, and businesses and turn in the mail, receipts, and money collected during the day.

Some city carriers may have specialized duties such as delivering only parcels or picking up mail from mail collection boxes. In contrast to city carriers, rural carriers provide a wider range of postal services in addition to delivering and picking up mail. For example, rural carriers may sell stamps and money orders and register, certify, and insure parcels and letters. All carriers, however, must be able to answer customers' questions about postal regulations and services and provide change-of-address cards and other postal forms when requested.

Working Conditions

Window clerks usually work in the public portion of clean, well-ventilated, and well-lit buildings. They have a variety of duties and frequent contact with the public, but they rarely work at night. However, they may have to deal with upset customers, stand for long periods, and be held accountable for an assigned stock of stamps and funds. Depending on the size of the post office in which they work, they also may be required to sort mail.

Despite the use of automated equipment, the work of mail sorters, processors, and processing machine operators can be physically demanding. Workers may have to move heavy sacks of mail around a mail processing center. These workers usually are on their feet, reaching for sacks and trays of mail or placing packages and bundles into sacks and trays. Processing mail can be tiring and boring. Many sorters, processors, and machine operators work at night or on weekends because most large post offices process mail around the clock and the largest volume of mail is sorted during the evening and night

shifts. Workers can experience stress as they process mail under tight production deadlines and quotas.

Most carriers begin work early in the morning—those with routes in a business district can start as early as 4 a.m. Overtime hours are frequently required for urban carriers. A carrier's schedule has its advantages, however. Carriers who begin work early in the morning are through by early afternoon and spend most of the day on their own, relatively free from direct supervision. Carriers spend most of their time outdoors, delivering mail in all kinds of weather. Even those who drive often must walk periodically when making deliveries and must lift heavy sacks of parcel post items when loading their vehicles. In addition, carriers must be cautious of potential hazards on their routes. Wet and icy roads and sidewalks can be treacherous, and each year dogs attack numerous carriers.

Training, Other Qualifications, and Advancement

Postal Service workers must be at least 18 years old. They must be U.S. citizens or have been granted permanent resident-alien status in the United States, and males must have registered with the Selective Service upon reaching age 18. Applicants should have a basic competency of English. Qualification is based on a written examination that measures speed and accuracy at checking names and numbers and the ability to memorize mail distribution procedures. Applicants must pass a physical examination and drug test and may be asked to show that they can lift and handle mail sacks weighing 70 pounds. Applicants for mail carrier positions must have a driver's license and a good driving record and must receive a passing grade on a road test.

Jobseekers should contact the post office or mail processing center where they wish to work to determine when an exam will be given. Applicants' names are listed in order of their examination scores. Five points are added to the score of an honorably discharged veteran and 10 points are added to the score of a veteran who was wounded in combat or is disabled. When a vacancy occurs, the appointing officer chooses one of the top three applicants; the rest of the names remain on the list to be considered for future openings until their eligibility expires—usually 2 years after the examination date.

Relatively few people become postal clerks or mail carriers on their first job because of keen competition and the customary waiting period of 1 to 2 years or more after passing the examination. It is not surprising, therefore, that most entrants transfer from other occupations.

New Postal Service workers are trained on the job by experienced workers. Many post offices offer classroom instruction on safety and defensive driving. Workers receive additional instruction when new equipment or procedures are introduced. In these cases, workers usually are trained by another postal employee or a training specialist.

Postal clerks and mail carriers should be courteous and tactful when dealing with the public, especially when answering questions or receiving complaints. A good memory and the ability to read rapidly and accurately are important. Good interpersonal skills also are vital, because mail distribution clerks work closely with other postal workers, frequently under the tension and strain of meeting dispatch or transportation deadlines and quotas.

Postal Service workers often begin on a part-time, flexible basis and become regular or full time in order of seniority as vacancies occur. Full-time workers may bid for preferred assignments, such as the day shift or a high-level nonsupervisory position. Carriers can look forward to obtaining preferred routes as their seniority increases. Postal Service workers can advance to supervisory positions on a competitive basis.

Employment

The U.S. Postal Service employed 75,000 clerks; 335,000 mail carriers; and 209,000 mail sorters, processors, and processing machine operators in 2004. Most of them worked full time. Most postal clerks provided window service at post office branches. Many mail sorters, processors, and processing machine operators sorted mail at major metropolitan post offices; others worked at mail processing centers. The majority of mail carriers worked in cities and suburbs, while the rest worked in rural areas.

Postal Service workers are classified as casual, part-time flexible, part-time regular, or full time. Casuals are hired for 90 days at a time to help process and deliver mail during peak mailing or vacation periods. Part-time flexible workers do not have a regular work schedule or weekly guarantee of hours but are called as the need arises. Part-time regulars have a set work schedule of fewer than 40 hours per week, often replacing regular full-time workers on their scheduled day off. Full-time postal employees work a 40-hour week over a 5-day period.

Job Outlook

Employment of Postal Service workers is expected to decline through 2014. Still, many jobs will become available because of the need to replace those who retire or leave the occupation. Those seeking jobs as Postal Service workers can expect to encounter keen competition. The number of applicants should continue to exceed the number of job openings because of the occupation's low entry requirements and attractive wages and benefits.

A small decline in employment is expected among window clerks over the 2004–2014 projection period. Efforts by the Postal Service to provide better service may somewhat increase the demand for window clerks, but the demand for such clerks will be offset by the use of electronic communication, such as the Internet, and private delivery companies. Employment of mail sorters, processors, and processing machine operators is expected to decline because of the increasing use of automated materials handling equipment and optical character readers, barcode sorters, and other automated sorting equipment.

A small decline in employment among mail carriers is expected through 2014. Competition from alternative delivery systems and the increasing use of electronic communication are expected to influence the demand for mail carriers. In addition, the Postal Service is moving toward more centralized mail delivery, such as the use of cluster boxes, to cut down on the number of door-to-door deliveries. The best employment opportunities for mail carriers are expected to be in less urbanized areas as the number of addresses to which mail must be delivered continues to grow, especially in fast-growing rural areas. However, increased use of the "delivery point sequencing" system, which allows machines to sort mail directly by the order of delivery, should reduce the amount of time that carriers spend sorting their mail, allowing them more time to handle longer routes.

The role of the Postal Service as a government-approved monopoly continues to be a topic of debate. Any legislative changes that would privatize or deregulate the Postal Service might affect employment of all its workers. Employment and schedules in the Postal Service fluctuate with the demand for its services. When mail volume is high, full-time employees work overtime, part-time workers get additional hours, and casual workers may be hired. When mail volume is low, overtime is curtailed, part-timers work fewer hours, and casual workers are discharged.

Earnings

Median annual earnings of Postal Service mail carriers were $44,450 in May 2004. The middle 50 percent earned between $37,590 and $50,580. The lowest 10 percent had earnings of less than $31,980, while the top 10 percent earned more than $54,240. Rural mail carriers are reimbursed for mileage put on their own vehicles while delivering mail.

Median annual earnings of Postal Service clerks were $40,950 in 2004. The middle 50 percent earned between $37,880 and $44,030. The lowest 10 percent had earnings of less than $36,040, while the top 10 percent earned more than $50,510.

Median annual earnings of Postal Service mail sorters, processors, and processing machine operators were $39,430 in 2004. The middle 50 percent earned between $36,240 and $42,620. The lowest 10 percent had earnings of less than $24,290, while the top 10 percent earned more than $44,540.

Postal Service workers enjoy a variety of employer-provided benefits similar to those enjoyed by federal government workers. The American Postal Workers Union, the National Association of Letter Carriers, the National Postal Mail Handlers Union, and the National Rural Letter Carriers Association together represent most of these workers.

Related Occupations

Other occupations with duties similar to those of Postal Service clerks include cashiers; counter and rental clerks; file clerks; and shipping, receiving, and traffic clerks. Others with duties related to those of Postal Service mail carriers include couriers and messengers and truck drivers and driver/sales workers. Occupations whose duties are related to those of Postal Service mail sorters, processors, and processing machine operators include inspectors, testers, sorters, samplers, and weighers and material moving occupations.

Sources of Additional Information

Local post offices and state employment service offices can supply details about entrance examinations and specific employment opportunities for Postal Service workers.

Prepress Technicians and Workers

(O*NET 51-5021.00, 51-5022.01, 51-5022.02, 51-5022.03,
51-5022.04, 51-5022.05, 51-5022.06, 51-5022.07, 51-5022.08,
51-5022.09, 51-5022.10, 51-5022.11, 51-5022.12, and 51-5022.13)

Significant Points

- Most prepress technician jobs now require formal postsecondary graphic communications training in the various types of computer software used in digital imaging.

- Employment is projected to decline as the increased use of computers in typesetting and page layout requires fewer prepress technicians.

Nature of the Work

The printing process has three stages—prepress, press, and binding or postpress. In small print shops, *job printers* are usually responsible for all three stages. They check proofs for errors and print clarity and correct mistakes, print the job, and attach each copy's pages together. In most printing firms, however, each of the stages is the responsibility of a specialized group of workers. *Prepress technicians and workers* are responsible for the first stage, preparing the material for printing presses. They perform a variety of tasks involved with transforming text and pictures into finished pages and making printing plates of the pages.

Advances in computer software and printing technology continue to change prepress work. Most customers today are able to provide printers with pages of material that look like the desired finished product they want printed and bound in volume. Using a process called "desktop publishing," customers are increasingly using their own computers to do much of the typesetting and page layout work formerly done by designers on artboards. Much of this work is now done by desktop publishers or graphic designers with knowledge of publishing software. It is increasingly common for prepress technicians or other printing workers to receive files from the customer on a computer disk or submitted electronically via e-mail or file transfer protocol, known as FTP, that contains typeset material already laid out in pages.

Prepress work is now done with the use of digital imaging technology by prepress technicians known as "preflight technicians" or production coordinators. Using this technology, these technicians take the electronic files received from customers, check it for completeness, and format it into pages using electronic page layout systems. Even though the pages may already be laid out, they still may have to be formatted to fit the dimensions of the paper stock to be used. When color printing is required, the technicians use digital color page-makeup systems to electronically produce an image of the printed pages and then use off-press color proofing systems to print a copy, or "proof," of the pages as they will appear when printed. The technician then has the proofs delivered or mailed to the customer for a final check. Once the customer gives the "OK to print," technicians use laser "imagesetters" to expose digital images of the pages directly onto thin aluminum printing plates.

Platemakers for a long time used a photographic process to make printing plates. The flat, a layout sheet onto which a negative has been attached, was placed on top of a thin metal plate coated with a light-sensitive resin. Exposure to ultraviolet light activated the chemical in parts of the plate not protected by the film's dark areas. The plate was then developed in a solution that removes the unexposed nonimage area, exposing bare metal. The chemical on areas of the plate exposed to the light hardened and became water repellent. The hardened parts of the plate form the text and images to be printed. Now, the printing industry has largely moved to technology known as "direct-to-plate," by which the prepress technicians send the data directly to a plating system, bypassing the need for stripping film onto a flat.

During the printing process, the plate is first covered with a thin coat of water. The water adheres only to the bare metal nonimage areas and is repelled by the hardened areas that were exposed to light. Next, the plate comes in contact with a rubber roller covered with oil-based ink. Because oil and water do not mix, the ink is repelled by the water-coated area and sticks to the hardened areas. The ink covering the hardened text is transferred to paper.

Working Conditions

Prepress technicians and workers usually work in clean, air-conditioned areas with little noise. Some workers may develop eyestrain from working in front of a video display terminal or musculoskeletal problems such as backaches. Those platemakers who still work with toxic chemicals face the hazard of skin irritations. Workers are often subject to stress and the pressures of short deadlines and tight work schedules.

Prepress employees usually work an 8-hour day. Some workers—particularly those employed by newspapers—work night shifts, weekends, and holidays.

Training, Other Qualifications, and Advancement

Digital imaging technology has largely replaced cold type print technology. Instead of painstakingly taping pieces of photographic negatives to flats, today's prepress technicians use computer software skills to electronically modify and lay out the material; in some cases, the first time the material appears on paper is when the final product rolls off the printing press. Traditionally, prepress technicians and workers started as helpers and were trained on the job, with some jobs requiring years of experience performing the detailed handwork to become skillful enough to perform even difficult tasks quickly. Today, persons seeking to enter prepress technician jobs require formal postsecondary graphic communications training in the various types of computer software used in digital imaging.

Postsecondary graphic communications programs are available from a variety of sources. For beginners, 2-year associate degree programs offered by community and junior colleges and technical schools and some 4-year bachelor's degree programs in graphic design colleges teach the latest prepress skills and allow students to practice applying them. However, bachelor's programs usually are intended for students who may eventually move into management positions in printing or design jobs. Community and junior colleges, 4-year colleges and universities, vocational-technical institutes, industry-sponsored update and retraining programs, and private trade and technical schools all also offer prepress-related courses for workers who do not wish to enroll in a degree program. Many workers with experience in other printing jobs take a few college graphic communications courses to upgrade their skills and qualify for prepress jobs. Prepress training designed to train skilled workers already employed in the printing industry also is offered through unions in the printing industry. Many employers view individuals with a combination of experience in the printing industry and formal training in the new digital technology as the best candidates for prepress jobs. The experience of these applicants in printing press operator or other jobs provides them with an understanding of how printing plants operate, familiarizes them with basic prepress functions, and demonstrates their reliability and interest in advancing in the industry.

Employers prefer workers with good communication skills, both oral and written, for prepress jobs. Prepress technicians and workers should be able to deal courteously with people because, when prepress problems arise, they sometimes have to contact the customer to resolve them. Also, in small shops, they may take customer orders. Persons interested in working for firms using advanced printing technology need to know the basics of electronics and computers. Mathematical skills also are essential for operating many of the software packages used to run modern, computerized prepress equipment. At times, prepress personnel may have to perform computations in order to estimate job costs.

Prepress technicians and workers need good manual dexterity, and they must be able to pay attention to detail and work independently. Good eyesight, including visual acuity, depth perception, field of view, color vision, and the ability to focus quickly, is also a needed asset. Artistic ability is often a plus. Employers also seek persons who possess an even temperament and an ability to adapt, important qualities for workers who often must meet deadlines and learn how to use new software or operate new equipment.

Employment

Prepress technicians and workers overall held about 141,000 jobs in 2004. Of these, approximately 63,000 were employed as job printers; the remainder was employed as prepress technicians and other prepress workers. Most prepress jobs are found in the printing industry, while newspaper publishing employs the second-largest number of prepress technicians and workers.

The printing and publishing industries are two of the most geographically dispersed in the United States, and prepress jobs are found throughout the country. However, jobs are concentrated in large metropolitan areas such as Chicago, Los Angeles–Long Beach, New York City, Minneapolis–St. Paul, Philadelphia, Boston, and Washington, DC.

Job Outlook

Overall employment of prepress technicians and workers is expected to decline through 2014. Demand for printed material

should continue to grow, spurred by rising levels of personal income, increasing school enrollments, higher levels of educational attainment, and expanding markets. But the use of computers and publishing software—often by the clients of the printing company—will result in rising productivity of prepress technicians.

Computer software now allows office workers to specify text typeface and style and to format pages at a desktop computer terminal, shifting many prepress functions away from the traditional printing plants into advertising and public relations agencies, graphic design firms, and large corporations. Many companies are turning to in-house desktop publishing as page layout and graphic design capabilities of computer software have improved and become less expensive and more user-friendly. Some firms are finding it less costly to prepare their own newsletters and other reports than to send them out to trade shops. At newspapers, writers and editors also are doing more composition using publishing software. Rapid growth in the use of desktop publishing software already has eliminated most prepress typesetting and composition technician jobs associated with the older technologies, such as cold type. However, opportunities will be favorable for prepress technicians with strong computer skills, such as preflight technicians, who are employed to check materials prepared by clients and adapt it for printing.

In order to compete in the desktop publishing environment, commercial printing companies are adding desktop publishing and electronic prepress work to the list of services they provide. Electronic prepress technicians, digital proofers, platemakers, and graphic designers are using new equipment and ever-changing software to design and lay out publications and complete their printing more quickly. The increasing range of services offered by printing companies using new digital technologies mean that opportunities in prepress work will be best for those with computer backgrounds who have completed postsecondary programs in printing technology or graphic communications. Workers with this background will be better able to adapt to the continuing evolution of publishing and printing technology.

Earnings

Median hourly earnings of prepress technicians and workers were $15.30 in May 2004. The middle 50 percent earned between $11.69 and $20.01 an hour. The lowest 10 percent earned less than $9.06, and the highest 10 percent earned more than $24.82 an hour.

For job printers, median hourly earnings were $15.41 in May 2004. The middle 50 percent earned between $12.00 and $20.04 an hour. The lowest 10 percent earned less than $9.57, while the highest 10 percent earned more than $24.05 an hour.

Median hourly earnings in commercial printing, the industry employing the largest number of prepress technicians and workers, were $15.91 in May 2004, while the figure for these workers in the newspaper, periodical, and book publishing industry was $14.22 an hour. For job printers, median hourly earnings in commercial printing in May 2004 were $15.67, while in the newspaper, periodical, and book publishing industry, median hourly earnings were $15.63.

Wage rates for prepress technicians and workers vary according to occupation, level of experience, training, location, size of firm, and union membership status.

Related Occupations

Prepress technicians and workers use artistic skills in their work. These skills also are essential for artists and related workers, graphic designers, and desktop publishers. Moreover, many of the skills used in Web site design also are employed in prepress technology.

In addition to typesetters, other workers who operate machines equipped with keyboards include data entry and information processing workers. Prepress technicians' work also is tied in closely with that of printing machine operators, including job printers.

Sources of Additional Information

Details about training programs may be obtained from local employers such as newspapers and printing shops or from local offices of the state employment service.

For information on careers and training in printing and the graphic arts, write to

▸ Graphic Arts Education and Research Foundation, 1899 Preston White Dr., Reston, VA 20191-5468. Internet: http://www.makeyourmark.org

▸ Graphic Communications Conference of the International Brotherhood of Teamsters, 1900 L St. NW, Washington, DC 20036-5007. Internet: http://www.gciu.org

▸ Printing Industries of America/Graphic Arts Technical Foundation, 200 Deer Run Rd., Sewickley, PA 15143-2324.

Printing Machine Operators

(O*NET 51-5023.01, 51-5023.02, 51-5023.03, 51-5023.04, 51-5023.05, 51-5023.06, 51-5023.07, 51-5023.08, and 51-5023.09)

Significant Points

■ Most printing machine operators are trained on the job.

■ Those skilled in digital printing operations will have the best job opportunities as more printing firms convert to this printing process because of the rising demand for customized print jobs.

■ The expected retirements of skilled press operators will create openings for workers with the proper training.

Nature of the Work

Printing machine operators, also known as press operators, prepare, operate, and maintain the printing presses in a pressroom. Duties of printing machine operators vary according to the type of press they operate—offset lithography, gravure, flexography, screen printing, letterpress, and digital. Offset lithography, which transfers an inked impression from a rubber-covered cylinder to paper or other material, is the dominant printing process. With gravure, the recesses on an etched plate or cylinder are inked and pressed to paper. Flexography is a form of rotary printing in which ink is applied to a surface by a flexible rubber printing plate with a raised image area. Use of flexography should increase over the next decade, but letterpress, in which an inked, raised surface is pressed against paper, remains in existence only as specialty printing. In addition to the major printing processes, plateless or nonimpact processes are coming into general use. Plateless processes—including digital, electrostatic, and ink-jet printing—are used for copying, duplicating, and document and specialty printing, usually by quick and in-house printing shops, and increasingly by commercial printers for short-run jobs and variable-data printing.

To prepare presses for printing, machine operators install and adjust the printing plate, adjust pressure, ink the presses, load paper, and adjust the press to the paper size. Press operators ensure that paper and ink meet specifications and adjust margins and the flow of ink to the inking rollers accordingly. They then feed paper through the press cylinders and adjust feed and tension controls. However, new technology becoming available skips these steps and sends the files directly to the press.

While printing presses are running, press operators monitor their operation and keep the paper feeders well stocked. They make adjustments to correct uneven ink distribution, speed, and temperatures in the drying chamber, if the press has one. If paper jams or tears and the press stops, which can happen with some offset presses, operators quickly correct the problem to minimize downtime. Similarly, operators working with other high-speed presses constantly look for problems, making quick corrections to avoid expensive losses of paper and ink. Throughout the run, operators must regularly pull sheets to check for any printing imperfections, though much of this checking for quality is now being done by computers.

In most shops, press operators also perform preventive maintenance. They oil and clean the presses and make minor repairs.

Machine operators' jobs differ from one shop to another because of differences in the kinds and sizes of presses. Small commercial shops are operated by one person and tend to have relatively small presses, which print only one or two colors at a time. Operators who work with large presses have assistants and helpers. Large newspaper, magazine, and book printers use giant "in-line web" presses that require a crew of several press operators and press assistants. These presses are fed paper in big rolls up to 50 inches or more in width. Presses print the paper on both sides; trim, assemble, score, and fold the pages; and count the finished sections as they come off the press.

Most plants have or will soon have installed printing presses with computers and sophisticated instruments to control press operations, making it possible to set up for jobs in less time. Computers allow press operators to perform many of their tasks electronically. With this equipment, press operators monitor the printing process on a control panel or computer monitor, which allows them to adjust the press electronically.

Working Conditions

Operating a press can be physically and mentally demanding and sometimes tedious. Printing machine operators are on their feet most of the time. Often, operators work under pressure to meet deadlines. Most printing presses are capable of high printing speeds, and adjustments must be made quickly to avoid waste. Pressrooms are noisy, and workers in certain areas wear ear protectors. Working with press machinery can be hazardous, but accidents can be avoided when press operators follow safe work practices. The threat of accidents has decreased with newer computerized presses because operators make most adjustments from a control panel.

Many press operators, particularly those who work for newspapers, work weekends, nights, and holidays. They also may work overtime to meet deadlines.

Training, Other Qualifications, and Advancement

Although completion of a formal apprenticeship or a postsecondary program in printing equipment operation continues to be the best way to learn the trade, most printing machine operators are trained on the job while they work as assistants or helpers to experienced operators. Beginning press operators load, unload, and clean presses. With time and training, they may move up to become fully qualified press operators on the type of equipment on which they trained. Some operators gain experience on many kinds of printing presses during the course of their career.

Apprenticeships for press operators, once the dominant method for preparing for this occupation, are becoming less prevalent. When they are offered by the employer, they usually include on-the-job instruction and some related classroom training or correspondence school courses. Apprenticeships used to be for a fixed period of time, but now completion is based on ability to demonstrate competencies.

In contrast, formal postsecondary programs in printing equipment operation offered by technical and trade schools, community colleges, and universities are growing in importance. Some postsecondary school programs require 2 years of study and award an associate degree. Postsecondary courses in printing are increasingly important because they provide the theoretical and technical knowledge needed to operate advanced equipment.

Persons who wish to become printing machine operators need mechanical aptitude to make press adjustments and repairs. Oral and writing skills also are required. Operators should possess the mathematical skills necessary to compute percentages, weights, and measures and to calculate the amount of ink and paper needed to do a job. Because of technical developments in the printing industry, courses in chemistry, electronics, color theory, and physics are helpful.

Technological changes have had a tremendous effect on the skills needed by printing machine operators. New presses now require operators to possess basic computer skills. Even experienced operators periodically receive retraining and skill updating. For example, printing plants that change from sheet-fed offset presses to digital presses have to retrain the entire press crew because skill requirements for the two types of presses are different.

Printing machine operators may advance in pay and responsibility by working on a more complex printing press. Through experience and demonstrated ability, for example, a one-color sheet-fed press operator may become a four-color sheet-fed press operator. Others may advance to pressroom supervisor and become responsible for an entire press crew. Press operators can also draw on their knowledge of press operations to become cost estimators, providing estimates of printing jobs to potential customers.

Employment

Printing machine operators held about 191,000 jobs in 2004. Nearly half of all operator jobs were in the printing industry. Paper manufacturers and newspaper publishers were also large employers. Additional jobs were in the "in-plant" section of organizations and businesses that do their own printing—such as banks, insurance companies, government agencies, and universities.

The printing and newspaper publishing industries are two of the most geographically dispersed in the United States, and press operators can find jobs throughout the country. However, jobs are concentrated in large printing centers such as Chicago, Los Angeles–Long Beach, New York, Minneapolis–St. Paul, Philadelphia, Boston, and Washington, DC.

Job Outlook

Employment of printing machine operators is expected to grow more slowly than average through 2014 as the output of printed materials is expected to keep going up, but increasing automation of the printing industry and the outsourcing of production to foreign countries will moderate the increase. Looming retirements of printing machine operators and the need for workers trained on increasingly computerized printing equipment will also create many job openings over the next decade, particularly for those persons who qualify for formal apprenticeship training or who complete postsecondary training programs in printing.

Demand for books and magazines will increase as school enrollments rise and information proliferates. Additional growth will also come from the increasing ability of the printing industry to profitably print shorter runs—smaller quantities—which should widen the market for printed materials as production costs decline. However, small printing jobs will increasingly be run on sophisticated high-speed digital printing equipment that requires a more complex set of operator skills, such as database management.

Demand for commercial printing also will continue to be driven by increased expenditures for print advertising materials. New market research techniques are leading advertisers to increase spending on messages targeted to specific audiences and should continue to require the printing of a wide variety of catalogs, direct mail enclosures, newspaper inserts, and other kinds of print advertising. Newspaper printing also will continue to provide jobs.

Employment will not grow in line with output, however, because increased use of new computerized printing equipment will require fewer operators. This will especially be true with the increasing automation of the large printing presses used in the newspaper industry. In addition, more companies are having their work printed out of the country when time sensitivity of the material is not an issue. Also, new business practices within the publishing industry, such as printing-on-demand and electronic publishing, will cut into the production of printed materials. Printing-on-demand refers to the printing of materials as they are requested by customers, in contrast to printing thousands of copies of a publication prior to purchase, many of which are subsequently discarded.

Earnings

Median hourly earnings of printing machine operators were $14.38 in May 2004. The middle 50 percent earned between $10.73 and $18.83 an hour. The lowest 10 percent earned less than $8.54, and the highest 10 percent earned more than $23.06 an hour. Median hourly earnings in the industries employing the largest numbers of printing machine operators in May 2004 were

Newspaper, periodical, book, and directory publishers	$16.46
Converted paper product manufacturing	15.72
Printing and related support activities	15.16
Plastics product manufacturing	13.76
Advertising and related services	12.68

The basic wage rate for a printing machine operator depends on the geographic area in which the work is located and on the type of press being run: Pay varies by the complexity of the press and its size. Workers covered by union contracts usually have higher earnings in the newspaper industry.

Related Occupations

Other workers who set up and operate production machinery include machine setters, operators, and tenders—metal and plastic; and bookbinders and bindery workers.

Sources of Additional Information

Details about apprenticeships and other training opportunities may be obtained from local employers, such as newspapers and printing shops, local offices of the Graphic Communications Conference of the International Brotherhood of Teamsters, local affiliates of Printing Industries of America/Graphic Arts Technical Foundation, or local offices of the state employment service.

For general information about press operators, write to

▸ Graphic Communications Conference of the International Brotherhood of Teamsters, 1900 L St. NW, Washington, DC 20036-5007. Internet: http://www.gciu.org

For information on careers and training in printing and the graphic arts, write to

▸ NPES The Association for Suppliers of Printing Publishing, and Converting Technologies, 1899 Preston White Dr., Reston, VA 20191-4367. Internet: http://www.npes.org/education/index.html

▸ Printing Industry of America/Graphic Arts Technical Foundation, 200 Deer Run Rd., Sewickley, PA 15143.

▸ Graphic Arts Education and Research Foundation, 1899 Preston White Dr., Reston, VA 20191-5468. Internet: http://www.makeyourmark.org

Production, Planning, and Expediting Clerks

(O*NET 43-5061.00)

Significant Points

■ Many production, planning, and expediting jobs are at the entry level and do not require more than a high school diploma.

■ Manufacturing firms and wholesale and retail trade establishments are the primary employers.

■ Production, planning, and expediting clerks work closely with supervisors who must approve production and work schedules.

Nature of the Work

Production, planning, and expediting clerks coordinate and expedite the flow of information, work, and materials within or among offices. Most of their work is done according to production, work, or shipment schedules that are devised by supervisors who determine work progress and completion dates. Production, planning, and expediting clerks compile reports on the progress of work and on production problems. They also may schedule workers, estimate costs, schedule the shipment of parts, keep an inventory of materials, inspect and assemble materials, and write special orders for services and merchandise. In addition, they may route and deliver parts to ensure that production quotas are met and that merchandise is delivered on the date promised.

Production and planning clerks compile records and reports on various aspects of production, such as materials and parts used, products produced, machine and instrument readings, and frequency of defects. These workers prepare work tickets or other production guides and distribute them to other workers. Production and planning clerks coordinate, schedule, monitor, and chart production and its progress, either manually or with electronic equipment. They also gather information from customers' orders or other specifications and use the information to prepare a detailed production sheet that serves as a guide in assembling or manufacturing the product.

Expediting clerks contact vendors and shippers to ensure that merchandise, supplies, and equipment are forwarded on the specified shipping dates. They communicate with transportation companies to prevent delays in transit, and they may arrange for the distribution of materials upon their arrival. They may even visit work areas of vendors and shippers to check the status of orders. Expediting clerks locate and distribute materials to specified production areas. They may inspect products for quality and quantity to ensure their adherence to specifications. They also keep a chronological list of due dates and may move work that does not meet the production schedule to the top of the list.

Working Conditions

Production, planning, and expediting clerks work closely with supervisors who must approve production and work schedules. The typical workweek is Monday through Friday.

Training, Other Qualifications, and Advancement

Many production, planning, and expediting jobs are at the entry level and do not require more than a high school diploma. Employers, however, prefer to hire those familiar with computers and other electronic office and business equipment. Applicants who have taken business courses or have specific job-related experience may be preferred. Because communication with other people is an integral part of some jobs in the occupation, good oral and written communication skills are essential. Typing, filing, recordkeeping, and other clerical skills also are important.

Production, planning, and expediting clerks usually learn the job by doing routine tasks under close supervision. They learn how to count and mark stock, and then they start keeping records and taking inventory. Strength; stamina; good eyesight; and an ability to work at repetitive tasks, sometimes under pressure, are important characteristics. Production, planning, and expediting clerks must learn both how their company operates and the company's priorities before they can begin to write production and work schedules efficiently.

Advancement opportunities for production, planning, and expediting clerks vary with the place of employment.

Employment

In 2004, production, planning, and expediting clerks held 292,000 jobs. Jobs in manufacturing made up 42 percent. Another 14 percent were in wholesale and retail trade establishments.

Job Outlook

As increasing pressure is put on firms to manufacture and deliver their goods more quickly and efficiently, the need for production, planning, and expediting clerks will grow, although the expected decline in overall employment in manufacturing will result in slower-than-average employment growth for production, planning, and expediting clerks through 2014. The work of production, planning, and expediting clerks is less likely to be automated than the work of many other administrative support occupations. In addition to openings due to employment growth, job openings will arise from the need to replace production, planning, and expediting clerks who leave the labor force or transfer to other occupations.

Earnings

Median annual earnings of production, planning, and expediting clerks in May 2004 were $36,340. The middle 50 percent earned between $27,690 and $45,880. The lowest 10 percent earned less than $21,690, and the highest 10 percent earned more than $55,850.

These workers usually receive the same benefits as most other workers. If uniforms are required, employers generally provide them or offer an allowance to purchase them.

Related Occupations

Other workers who coordinate the flow of information to assist the production process include cargo and freight agents; shipping, receiving, and traffic clerks; stock clerks and order fillers; and weighers, measurers, checkers, and samplers, recordkeeping.

Sources of Additional Information

Information about job opportunities may be obtained from local employers and from local offices of the state employment service.

Purchasing Managers, Buyers, and Purchasing Agents

(O*NET 11-3061.00, 13-1021.00, 13-1022.00, and 13-1023.00)

Significant Points

■ Forty-three percent are employed in wholesale trade or manufacturing establishments.

■ Some firms promote qualified employees to these positions, while other employers recruit college graduates; regardless of academic preparation, new employees need 1 to 5 years to learn the specifics of their employer's business.

■ Overall employment growth is expected to be slower than average.

■ Opportunities should be best for those with a college degree.

Nature of the Work

Purchasing managers, buyers, and purchasing agents make up a key component of a firm's supply chain. They buy the goods and services the company or institution needs either to resell to customers or for the establishment's own use. *Wholesale and retail buyers* purchase goods for resale, such as clothing or electronics, and *purchasing agents* buy goods and services for use by their own company or organization such as raw materials for manufacturing or office supplies. *Purchasing agents and buyers of farm products* purchase goods such as grain, Christmas trees, and tobacco for further processing or resale. Purchasing professionals consider price, quality, availability, reliability, and technical support when choosing suppliers and merchandise. They try to get the best deal for their company, meaning the highest-quality goods and services at the lowest possible cost to their companies. In order to accomplish these tasks successfully, purchasing managers, buyers, and purchasing agents study sales records and inventory levels of current stock, identify foreign and domestic suppliers, and keep abreast of changes affecting both the supply of, and demand for, needed products and materials.

In large industrial organizations, a distinction often is drawn between the work of a buyer or purchasing agent and that of a *purchasing manager*. Purchasing agents commonly focus on routine purchasing tasks, often specializing in a commodity or group of related commodities, such as steel, lumber, cotton, grains, fabricated metal products, or petroleum products. Purchasing agents usually track market conditions, price trends, and futures markets. Purchasing managers usually handle the more complex or critical purchases and may supervise a group of purchasing agents handling other goods and services. Whether a person is titled purchasing manager,

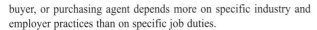

buyer, or purchasing agent depends more on specific industry and employer practices than on specific job duties.

Purchasing specialists employed by government agencies or manufacturing firms usually are called *purchasing directors, managers,* or *agents* or *contract specialists.* These workers acquire materials, parts, machines, supplies, services, and other inputs to the production of a final product. Some purchasing managers specialize in negotiating and supervising supply contracts and are called contract or supply managers. Purchasing agents and managers obtain items ranging from raw materials, fabricated parts, machinery, and office supplies to construction services and airline tickets. Often, purchasing specialists in government place solicitations for services and accept bids and offers through the Internet. Government purchasing agents and managers must follow strict laws and regulations in their work in order to avoid any appearance of impropriety. To be effective, purchasing specialists must have a working technical knowledge of the goods or services to be purchased.

Purchasing specialists who buy finished goods for resale are employed by wholesale and retail establishments, where they commonly are known as *buyers* or *merchandise managers.* Wholesale and retail buyers are an integral part of a complex system of distribution and merchandising that caters to the vast array of consumer needs and desires. Wholesale buyers purchase goods directly from manufacturers or from other wholesale firms for resale to retail firms, commercial establishments, institutions, and other organizations. In retail firms, buyers purchase goods from wholesale firms or directly from manufacturers for resale to the public. Buyers largely determine which products their establishment will sell. Therefore, it is essential that they have the ability to predict what will appeal to consumers. They must constantly stay informed of the latest trends because failure to do so could jeopardize profits and the reputation of their company. They keep track of inventories and sales levels through computer software that is linked to the store's cash registers. Buyers also follow ads in newspapers and other media to check competitors' sales activities, and they watch general economic conditions to anticipate consumer buying patterns. Buyers working for large and medium-sized firms usually specialize in acquiring one or two lines of merchandise, whereas buyers working for small stores may purchase the establishment's complete inventory.

The use of private-label merchandise and the consolidation of buying departments have increased the responsibilities of retail buyers. Private-label merchandise, produced for a particular retailer, requires buyers to work closely with vendors to develop and obtain the desired product. The downsizing and consolidation of buying departments increases the demands placed on buyers because, although the amount of work remains unchanged, there are fewer people to accomplish it. The result is an increase in the workloads and levels of responsibility for all.

Many merchandise managers assist in the planning and implementation of sales promotion programs. Working with merchandise executives, they determine the nature of the sale and purchase items accordingly. Merchandise managers may work with advertising personnel to create an ad campaign. For example, they may determine in which media the advertisement will be placed—newspapers, direct mail, television, or some combination of all three. In addition, merchandise managers often visit the selling floor to ensure that goods are properly displayed. Buyers stay in constant contact with store and department managers to find out what products are selling well and which items the customers are demanding to be added to the product line. Often, assistant buyers are responsible for placing orders and checking shipments.

Evaluating suppliers is one of the most critical functions of a purchasing manager, buyer, or purchasing agent. Many firms now run on a lean manufacturing schedule and use just-in-time inventories, so any delays in the supply chain can shut down production and cost the firm its customers and reputation. Purchasing professionals use many resources to find out all they can about potential suppliers. The Internet has become an effective tool in searching catalogs, trade journals, and industry and company publications and directories. Purchasing professionals will attend meetings, trade shows, and conferences to learn of new industry trends and make contacts with suppliers. Purchasing managers, agents, and buyers will usually interview prospective suppliers and visit their plants and distribution centers to asses their capabilities. It is important to make certain that the supplier is capable of delivering the desired goods or services on time and in the correct quantities without sacrificing quality. Once all of the necessary information on suppliers is gathered, orders are placed and contracts are awarded to those suppliers who meet the purchaser's needs. Most of the transaction process is now automated using electronic purchasing systems that link the supplier and firms together through the Internet.

Purchasing professionals can gain instant access to the specifications for thousands of commodities, inventory records, and their customers' purchase records to avoid overpaying for goods and to avoid shortages of popular goods or surpluses of goods that do not sell as well. These systems permit faster selection, customization, and ordering of products, and they allow buyers to concentrate on the qualitative and analytical aspects of the job. Long-term contracts are an important strategy of purchasing professionals because they allow purchasers to consolidate their supply bases around fewer suppliers. In today's global economy, purchasing managers, buyers, and purchasing agents should expect to deal with foreign suppliers, which may require travel to other countries, and to be familiar with other cultures and languages.

Changing business practices have altered the traditional roles of purchasing or supply management specialists in many industries. For example, manufacturing companies increasingly involve workers in this occupation at most stages of product development because of their ability to forecast a part's or material's cost, availability, and suitability for its intended purpose. Furthermore, potential problems with the supply of materials may be avoided by consulting the purchasing department in the early stages of product design.

Purchasing specialists often work closely with other employees in their own organization when deciding on purchases, an arrangement sometimes called team buying. For example, before submitting an order, they may discuss the design of custom-made products with company design engineers, talk about problems involving the quality of purchased goods with quality assurance engineers and production supervisors, or mention shipment problems to managers in the receiving department.

Working Conditions

Most purchasing managers, buyers, and purchasing agents work in comfortable offices. They frequently work more than the standard 40-hour week because of special sales, conferences, or production deadlines. Evening and weekend work also is common before holiday and back-to-school seasons for those working in retail trade. Consequently, many retail firms discourage the use of vacation time during peak periods.

Buyers and merchandise managers often work under great pressure. Because wholesale and retail stores are so competitive, buyers need physical stamina to keep up with the fast-paced nature of their work.

Many purchasing managers, buyers, and purchasing agents travel at least several days a month. Purchasers for worldwide manufacturing companies and large retailers, as well as buyers of high fashion, may travel outside the United States.

Training, Other Qualifications, and Advancement

Qualified persons may begin as trainees, purchasing clerks, expediters, junior buyers, or assistant buyers. Retail and wholesale firms prefer to hire applicants who have a college degree and who are familiar with the merchandise they sell and with wholesaling and retailing practices. Some retail firms promote qualified employees to assistant buyer positions; others recruit and train college graduates as assistant buyers. Most employers use a combination of methods.

Educational requirements tend to vary with the size of the organization. Large stores and distributors prefer applicants who have completed a bachelor's degree program with a business emphasis. Many manufacturing firms put yet a greater emphasis on formal training, preferring applicants with a bachelor's or master's degree in engineering, business, economics, or one of the applied sciences. A master's degree is essential for advancement to many top-level purchasing manager jobs.

Regardless of academic preparation, new employees must learn the specifics of their employers' business. Training periods vary in length, with most lasting 1 to 5 years. In wholesale and retail establishments, most trainees begin by selling merchandise, supervising sales workers, checking invoices on material received, and keeping track of stock. As they progress, retail trainees are given increased buying-related responsibilities.

In manufacturing, new purchasing employees often are enrolled in company training programs and spend a considerable amount of time learning about their firm's operations and purchasing practices. They work with experienced purchasers to learn about commodities, prices, suppliers, and markets. In addition, they may be assigned to the production planning department to learn about the material requirements system and the inventory system the company uses to keep production and replenishment functions working smoothly.

Purchasing managers, buyers, and purchasing agents must know how to use both word processing and spreadsheet software, as well as the Internet. Other important qualities include the ability to analyze technical data in suppliers' proposals; good communication, negotiation, and mathematical skills; knowledge of supply-chain management; and the ability to perform financial analyses.

Persons who wish to become wholesale or retail buyers should be good at planning and decisionmaking and have an interest in merchandising. Anticipating consumer preferences and ensuring that goods are in stock when they are needed requires resourcefulness, good judgment, and self-confidence. Buyers must be able to make decisions quickly and to take risks. Marketing skills and the ability to identify products that will sell also are very important. Employers often look for leadership ability, too, because buyers spend a large portion of their time supervising assistant buyers and dealing with manufacturers' representatives and store executives.

Experienced buyers may advance by moving to a department that manages a larger volume or by becoming a merchandise manager. Others may go to work in sales for a manufacturer or wholesaler.

An experienced purchasing agent or buyer may become an assistant purchasing manager in charge of a group of purchasing professionals before advancing to purchasing manager, supply manager, or director of materials management. At the top levels, duties may overlap with other management functions, such as production, planning, logistics, and marketing.

Regardless of industry, continuing education is essential for advancement. Many purchasers participate in seminars offered by professional societies and take college courses in supply management. Professional certification is becoming increasingly important, especially for those just entering the occupation.

In private industry, recognized marks of experience and professional competence are the Accredited Purchasing Practitioner (APP) and Certified Purchasing Manager (CPM) designations, conferred by the Institute for Supply Management, and the Certified Purchasing Professional (CPP) and Certified Professional Purchasing Manager (CPPM) designations, conferred by the American Purchasing Society. In federal, state, and local government, the indications of professional competence are Certified Professional Public Buyer (CPPB) and Certified Public Purchasing Officer (CPPO), conferred by the National Institute of Governmental Purchasing. Most of these certifications are awarded only after work-related experience and education requirements are met and written or oral exams are successfully completed.

Employment

Purchasing managers, buyers, and purchasing agents held about 520,000 jobs in 2004. Forty-three percent worked in the wholesale trade and manufacturing industries, and another twelve percent worked in retail trade. The remainder worked mostly in service establishments, such as hospitals, or different levels of government. A small number were self-employed.

The following tabulation shows the distribution of employment by occupational specialty:

Purchasing agents, except wholesale, retail, and farm products	273,000
Wholesale and retail buyers, except farm products	156,000
Purchasing managers	75,000
Purchasing agents and buyers, farm products	16,000

Job Outlook

Overall employment of purchasing managers, buyers, and purchasing agents is expected to grow slower than the average for all occupations through the year 2014. Offsetting some declines for purchasing workers in the manufacturing sector will be increases in the services sector. Companies in the services sector, which have typically made purchases on an ad hoc basis, are beginning to realize that centralized purchasing offices may be more efficient. Also, many purchasing agents are now charged with procuring services that were traditionally done in-house in the past, such as computer and IT (information technology) support, in addition to traditionally contracted services such as advertising. Demand for purchasing workers will be limited by improving software, which has eliminated much of the paperwork involved in ordering and procuring supplies, and also by the growing number of purchases being made electronically through the internet and electronic data interchange (EDI). Despite slower-than-average growth, some job openings will result from the need to replace workers who transfer to other occupations or leave the labor force.

Employment of purchasing managers is expected to grow more slowly than average. The use of the Internet to conduct electronic commerce has made information easier to obtain, thus increasing the productivity of purchasing managers. The Internet also allows both large and small companies to bid on contracts. Exclusive supply contracts and long-term contracting have allowed companies to negotiate with fewer suppliers less frequently.

Employment of wholesale and retail buyers, except farm products, also is projected to grow more slowly than average. In the retail industry, mergers and acquisitions have caused buying departments to consolidate. In addition, larger retail stores are eliminating local buying departments and centralizing them at their headquarters.

Employment of purchasing agents, except wholesale, retail, and farm products, is expected to increase more slowly than average, limited by the increased globalization of the U.S. economy. As more materials and supplies come from abroad, firms have begun to outsource more of their purchasing duties to foreign purchasing agents who are located closer to the foreign suppliers of goods and materials they will need. This trend is expected to continue, but it will likely be limited to routine transactions, with complex and critical purchases still being handled in-house.

Finally, employment of purchasing agents and buyers, farm products, also is projected to increase more slowly than average as overall growth in agricultural industries decreases and retailers in the grocery-related industries consolidate.

Persons who have a bachelor's degree in business should have the best chance of obtaining a buyer position in wholesale or retail trade or within government. A bachelor's degree, combined with industry experience and knowledge of a technical field, will be an advantage for those interested in working for a manufacturing or industrial company. Government agencies and larger companies usually require a master's degree in business or public administration for top-level purchasing positions.

Earnings

Median annual earnings of purchasing managers were $72,450 in May 2004. The middle 50 percent earned between $54,150 and $94,970 a year. The lowest 10 percent earned less than $41,300, and the highest 10 percent earned more than $121,600 a year.

Median annual earnings for purchasing agents and buyers, farm products, were $43,720 in May 2004. The middle 50 percent earned between $33,100 and $59,420 a year. The lowest 10 percent earned less than $25,260, and the highest 10 percent earned more than $82,330 a year.

Median annual earnings for wholesale and retail buyers, except farm products, were $42,230 in May 2004. The middle 50 percent earned between $31,550 and $57,010 a year. The lowest 10 percent earned less than $24,380, and the highest 10 percent earned more than $79,340 a year. Median annual earnings in the industries employing the largest numbers of wholesale and retail buyers, except farm products, in May 2004 were

Management of companies and enterprises	$49,770
Grocery and related product wholesalers	43,910
Wholesale electronic markets and agents and brokers	43,860
Building material and supplies dealers	35,850
Grocery stores	32,790

Median annual earnings for purchasing agents, except wholesale, retail, and farm products, were $47,680 in May 2004. The middle 50 percent earned between $36,760 and $62,600 a year. The lowest 10 percent earned less than $29,640, and the highest 10 percent earned more than $79,710 a year. Median annual earnings in the industries employing the largest numbers of purchasing agents, except wholesale, retail, and farm products, in May 2004 were

Federal executive branch and United States Postal Service	$63,940
Aerospace product and parts manufacturing	55,820
Management of companies and enterprises	53,750
Local government	44,730
General medical and surgical hospitals	37,090

Purchasing managers, buyers, and purchasing agents receive the same benefits package as other workers, including vacations, sick leave, life and health insurance, and pension plans. In addition to receiving standard benefits, retail buyers often earn cash bonuses based on their performance and may receive discounts on merchandise bought from their employer.

Related Occupations

Workers in other occupations who need a knowledge of marketing and the ability to assess consumer demand include those in advertising, marketing, promotions, public relations, and sales managers; food service managers; insurance sales agents; lodging managers; sales engineers; and sales representatives, wholesale and manufacturing.

Sources of Additional Information

Further information about education, training, employment, and certification for purchasing careers is available from

▶ American Purchasing Society, North Island Center, Suite 203, 8 East Galena Blvd., Aurora, IL 60506.

▶ Institute for Supply Management, P.O. Box 22160, Tempe, AZ 85285-2160. Internet: http://www.ism.ws

▶ National Institute of Governmental Purchasing, Inc., 151 Spring St., Suite 300, Herndon, VA 20170-5223. Internet: http://www.nigp.org

Radio and Telecommunications Equipment Installers and Repairers

(O*NET 49-2021.00, 49-2022.01, 49-2022.02, 49-2022.03, 49-2022.04, and 49-2022.05)

Significant Points

■ Employment is projected to decline.

■ Job opportunities will vary by specialty; for example, good opportunities should be available for central office and PBX installers and repairers experienced in current technology, while station installers and repairers can expect keen competition.

■ Applicants with computer skills and postsecondary electronics training should have the best opportunities.

■ Weekend and holiday hours are common; repairers may be on call around the clock in case of emergencies.

Nature of the Work

Telephones and radios depend on a variety of equipment to transmit communications signals. From electronic switches that route telephone signals to their destinations to radio transmitters and receivers that relay signals from wireless phones, the workers who set up and maintain this sophisticated equipment are called radio and telecommunications equipment installers and repairers. These workers no longer just work on equipment that transmits voice signals, but also transmissions such as data, graphics, and video.

Central office installers set up switches, cables, and other equipment in central offices. These locations are the hubs of a telecommunications network—they contain the switches and routers that direct packets of information to their destinations. Although most telephone lines connecting houses to central offices and switching stations are still copper, the lines connecting these central hubs are fiber optic. Fiber-optic lines have led to a revolution in switching equipment. The greatly increased transmission capacity of each line has allowed a few fiber-optic lines to replace many copper lines. Packet switching equipment is evolving rapidly, ever increasing the amount of information that a single fiber-optic line can carry. These switches and routers have the ability to transmit, process, amplify,

and direct a massive amount of information. Installing and maintaining this equipment requires a high level of technical knowledge.

The increasing reliability of telephone switches and routers has simplified maintenance. New self-monitoring telephone switches alert repairers to malfunctions. Some switches allow repairers to diagnose and correct problems from remote locations. When faced with a malfunction, the repairer may refer to manufacturers' manuals that provide maintenance instructions.

When problems with telecommunications equipment arise, telecommunications equipment repairers diagnose the source of the problem by testing each of the different parts of the equipment, which requires an understanding of how the software and hardware interact. Repairers often use spectrum and/or network analyzers to locate the problem. A network analyzer sends a signal through the equipment to detect any distortion in the signal. The nature of the signal distortion often directs the repairer to the source of the problem. To fix the equipment, repairers may use small hand tools, including pliers and screwdrivers, to remove and replace defective components such as circuit boards or wiring. Newer equipment is easier to repair because whole boards and parts are designed to be quickly removed and replaced. Repairers also may install updated software or programs that maintain existing software.

Cable television companies employ technicians to install and maintain their distribution centers, called head ends. Their work is similar to central office installers.

PBX installers and repairers set up private branch exchange (PBX) switchboards, which relay incoming, outgoing, and interoffice calls within a single location or organization. To install switches and switchboards, installers first connect the equipment to power lines and communications cables and install frames and supports. They test the connections to ensure that adequate power is available and that the communication links function. They also install equipment such as power systems, alarms, and telephone sets. New switches and switchboards are computerized; workers install software or program the equipment to provide specific features. For example, as a cost-cutting feature, an installer may program a PBX switchboard to route calls over different lines at different times of the day. However, other workers, such as computer support specialists, generally handle complex programming. (The work of computer support specialists is outlined in this book's description of computer support specialists and systems administrators.) Finally, the installer performs tests to verify that the newly installed equipment functions properly. If a problem arises, PBX repairers determine whether it is located within the PBX system or originates in the telephone lines maintained by the local phone company.

Due to rapidly developing technologies, PBX installers must adapt and learn new technologies. Instead of installing PBX systems, companies are choosing to install voice-over Internet protocol (VoIP) systems. VoIP systems operate like a PBX system, but they use a company's computer wiring to run Internet access, network applications, and telephone communications. Specialized phones have their own Internet protocol (IP) addresses. The phones can be plugged into any port in the system and still use the same number.

Station installers and repairers, telephone—commonly known as *telephone installers and repairers* or *telecommunications service technicians*—install and repair telephone wiring and equipment on customers' premises. They install telephone or digital subscriber line (DSL) service by connecting customers' telephone wires to outside service lines. These lines run on telephone poles or in underground conduits. The installer may climb poles or ladders to make the connections. Once the connection is made, the line is tested. When a maintenance problem occurs, repairers test the customers' lines to determine if the problem is located in the customers' premises or in the outside service lines. When onsite procedures fail to resolve installation or maintenance problems, repairers may request support from their technical service center. Line installers and repairers install the wires and cables that connect customers with central offices.

Radio mechanics install and maintain radio transmitting and receiving equipment. This includes stationary equipment mounted on transmission towers and mobile equipment, such as radio communications systems in service and emergency vehicles. Radio mechanics do not work on cellular communications towers and equipment. Newer radio equipment is self-monitoring and may alert mechanics to potential malfunctions. When malfunctions occur, these mechanics examine equipment for damaged components and loose or broken wires. They use electrical measuring instruments to monitor signal strength, transmission capacity, interference, and signal delay, as well as hand tools to replace defective components and parts and to adjust equipment so that it performs within required specifications.

Working Conditions

Radio and telecommunications equipment installers and repairers generally work in clean, well-lighted, air-conditioned surroundings, such as a telephone company's central office, a customer's location, or an electronic repair shop or service center. Telephone installers and repairers work on rooftops, ladders, and telephone poles. Telephone, PBX, and VoIP installers must travel to a customer's location. Radio mechanics may maintain equipment located on the tops of transmissions towers. While working outdoors, these workers are subject to a variety of weather conditions.

Nearly all radio and telecommunications equipment installers and repairers work full time. Many work regular business hours to meet the demand for repair services during the workday. Schedules are more irregular at companies that need repair services 24 hours a day or where installation and maintenance must take place after business hours. At these locations, mechanics work a variety of shifts, including weekend and holiday hours. Repairers may be on call around the clock, in case of emergencies, and may have to work overtime.

The work of most repairers involves lifting, reaching, stooping, crouching, and crawling. Adherence to safety precautions is important in order to guard against work hazards. These hazards include falls, minor burns, electrical shock, and contact with hazardous materials.

Training, Other Qualifications, and Advancement

Most employers seek applicants with postsecondary training in electronics and a familiarity with computers. Training sources include 2-year and 4-year college programs in electronics or communications, trade schools, and equipment and software manufacturers. Military experience with communications equipment is valued by many employers. Some equipment repairers begin working in telecommunications companies as line installers or telephone installers before moving up to the job of central office installer and other more complex work.

Newly hired repairers usually receive some training from their employers. This may include formal classroom training in electronics, communications systems, or software and informal hands-on training assisting an experienced repairer. Large companies may send repairers to outside training sessions to keep them informed about new equipment and service procedures. As networks have become more sophisticated—often including equipment from a variety of companies—the knowledge needed for installation and maintenance also has increased.

Telecommunications equipment companies provide much of the training on specific equipment. With the rapid advances in switches, routers, and other equipment, repairers need to continually take courses and work to obtain manufacturers' certifications on the latest technology.

Repairers must be able to distinguish colors, because wires are color-coded, and they must be able to hear distinctions in the various tones on a telephone system. For positions that require climbing poles and towers, workers must be in good physical shape. Repairers who handle assignments alone at a customer's site must be able to work without close supervision. For workers who frequently contact customers, a pleasant personality, neat appearance, and good communications skills also are important.

Experienced repairers with advanced training may become specialists or troubleshooters who help other repairers diagnose difficult problems or may work with engineers in designing equipment and developing maintenance procedures. Because of their familiarity with equipment, repairers are particularly well qualified to become manufacturers' sales workers. Workers with leadership ability also may become maintenance supervisors or service managers. Some experienced workers open their own repair services or shops or become wholesalers or retailers of electronic equipment.

Employment

Radio and telecommunications equipment installers and repairers held about 222,000 jobs in 2004. About 215,000 were telecommunications equipment installers and repairers, except line installers, mostly working in the telecommunications industry, and the rest were radio mechanics. Radio mechanics worked in electronic and precision equipment repair and maintenance, telecommunications, electronics and appliance stores, and many other industries.

Job Outlook

Employment of radio and telecommunications equipment installers and repairers is expected to decline through 2014. Although the need for installation work will remain as companies seek to upgrade their telecommunications networks, there will be a declining need for maintenance work—performed by telecommunications equipment installers and repairers, except line installers—because of increasingly reliable self-monitoring and self-diagnosing equipment and because installation of higher-capacity equipment will reduce the amount of equipment needed. The replacement of two-way radio systems with wireless systems, especially in service vehicles, will eliminate the need in many companies for onsite radio mechanics. The increased reliability of wireless equipment and the use of self-monitoring systems also will continue to lessen the need for radio mechanics. Applicants with computer skills and postsecondary electronics training should have the best opportunities for radio and telecommunications equipment installer and repairer jobs.

Job opportunities will vary by specialty. For example, good opportunities should be available for central office and PBX installers and repairers experienced in current technology as the growing popularity of VoIP, expanded multimedia offerings such as video on demand, and other telecommunications services continue to place additional demand on telecommunications networks. These new services require high data transfer rates, which can be achieved only by installing new optical switching and routing equipment. Extending high-speed communications from central offices to customers also will require the installation of more advanced switching and routing equipment. Whereas increased reliability and automation of switching equipment will limit opportunities, these effects will be somewhat offset by the demand for installation and upgrading of switching equipment.

Station installers and repairers can expect keen competition. Prewired buildings and the increasing reliability of telephone equipment will reduce the need for installation and maintenance of customers' telephones. Upgrading internal lines in businesses and the wiring of new homes and businesses with fiber-optic lines should offset some of these losses. As cellular telephones have increased in popularity, the number of pay phones is declining, which also will adversely affect employment of station installers and repairers, as pay phone installation and maintenance is one of their major functions.

Earnings

In May 2004, median hourly earnings of telecommunications equipment installers and repairers, except line installers were $23.96. The middle 50 percent earned between $19.46 and $27.07. The bottom 10 percent earned less than $14.65, whereas the top 10 percent earned more than $30.85. The median hourly earnings of these workers in the wired telecommunications carriers (telephone) industry were $24.92 in May 2004.

Median hourly earnings of radio mechanics in May 2004 were $17.65. The middle 50 percent earned between $13.59 and $21.90. The bottom 10 percent earned less than $10.42, whereas the top 10 percent earned more than $27.62.

Related Occupations

Related occupations that involve work with electronic equipment include broadcast and sound engineering technicians and radio operators; computer, automated teller, and office machine repairers; electronic home entertainment equipment installers and repairers; and electrical and electronics installers and repairers. Line installers and repairers also set up and install telecommunications equipment. Engineering technicians also may repair electronic equipment as part of their duties.

Sources of Additional Information

For information on career and training opportunities, contact

▸ International Brotherhood of Electrical Workers, Telecommunications Department, 1125 15th St. NW, Room 807, Washington, DC 20005.

▸ Communications Workers of America, 501 3rd St. NW, Washington, DC 20001.

For information on training and professional certifications for those already employed by cable telecommunications firms, contact

▸ Society of Cable Telecommunications Engineers, Certification Department, 140 Phillips Rd., Exton, PA 19341-1318. Internet: http://www.scte.org

Radiologic Technologists and Technicians

(O*NET 29-2034.01 and 29-2034.02)

Significant Points

■ Job opportunities are expected to be favorable; some employers report difficulty hiring sufficient numbers of radiologic technologists and technicians.

■ Formal training programs in radiography range in length from 1 to 4 years and lead to a certificate, an associate degree, or a bachelor's degree.

■ Although hospitals will remain the primary employer, a greater number of new jobs will be found in physicians' offices and diagnostic imaging centers.

Nature of the Work

Radiologic technologists and technicians take X rays and administer nonradioactive materials into patients' bloodstreams for diagnostic purposes. Some specialize in diagnostic imaging technologies, such as computerized tomography (CT) and magnetic resonance imaging (MRI).

In addition to radiologic technologists and technicians, others who conduct diagnostic imaging procedures include cardiovascular technologists and technicians and nuclear medicine technologists.

Radiologic technologists and technicians, also referred to as *radiographers*, produce X-ray films (radiographs) of parts of the human body for use in diagnosing medical problems. They prepare patients for radiologic examinations by explaining the procedure, removing articles such as jewelry, through which X rays cannot pass, and positioning patients so that the parts of the body can be appropriately radiographed. To prevent unnecessary exposure to radiation, these workers surround the exposed area with radiation protection devices, such as lead shields, or limit the size of the X-ray beam. Radiographers position radiographic equipment at the correct angle and height over the appropriate area of a patient's body. Using instruments similar to a measuring tape, they may measure the thickness of the section to be radiographed and set controls on the X-ray machine to produce radiographs of the appropriate density, detail, and contrast. They place the X-ray film under the part of the patient's body to be examined and make the exposure. They then remove the film and develop it.

Experienced radiographers may perform more complex imaging procedures. For fluoroscopies, radiographers prepare a solution of contrast medium for the patient to drink, allowing the radiologist (a physician who interprets radiographs) to see soft tissues in the body. Some radiographers, called *CT technologists,* operate CT scanners to produce cross-sectional images of patients. Radiographers who operate machines that use strong magnets and radio waves, rather than radiation, to create an image are called *MRI technologists.*

Radiologic technologists and technicians must follow physicians' orders precisely and conform to regulations concerning the use of radiation to protect themselves, their patients, and their co-workers from unnecessary exposure.

In addition to preparing patients and operating equipment, radiologic technologists and technicians keep patient records and adjust and maintain equipment. They also may prepare work schedules, evaluate purchases of equipment, or manage a radiology department.

Working Conditions

Most full-time radiologic technologists and technicians work about 40 hours a week. They may, however, have evening, weekend, or on-call hours. Opportunities for part-time and shift work also are available.

Physical stamina is important, because technologists and technicians are on their feet for long periods and may lift or turn disabled patients. Technologists and technicians work at diagnostic machines, but also may perform some procedures at patients' bedsides. Some travel to patients in large vans equipped with sophisticated diagnostic equipment.

Although radiation hazards exist in this occupation, they are minimized by the use of lead aprons, gloves, and other shielding devices, as well as by instruments monitoring exposure to radiation. Technologists and technicians wear badges measuring radiation levels in the radiation area, and detailed records are kept on their cumulative lifetime dose.

Training, Other Qualifications, and Advancement

Preparation for this profession is offered in hospitals, colleges and universities, vocational-technical institutes, and the U.S. Armed Forces. Hospitals, which employ most radiologic technologists and technicians, prefer to hire those with formal training.

Formal training programs in radiography range in length from 1 to 4 years and lead to a certificate, an associate degree, or a bachelor's degree. Two-year associate degree programs are most prevalent.

Some 1-year certificate programs are available for experienced radiographers or individuals from other health occupations, such as medical technologists and registered nurses, who want to change fields or specialize in CT or MRI. A bachelor's or master's degree in one of the radiologic technologies is desirable for supervisory, administrative, or teaching positions.

The Joint Review Committee on Education in Radiologic Technology accredits most formal training programs for the field. The committee accredited 606 radiography programs in 2005. Radiography programs require, at a minimum, a high school diploma or the equivalent. High school courses in mathematics, physics, chemistry, and biology are helpful. The programs provide both classroom and clinical instruction in anatomy and physiology, patient care procedures, radiation physics, radiation protection, principles of imaging, medical terminology, positioning of patients, medical ethics, radiobiology, and pathology.

Federal legislation protects the public from the hazards of unnecessary exposure to medical and dental radiation by ensuring that operators of radiologic equipment are properly trained. Under this legislation, the federal government sets voluntary standards that the states may use for accrediting training programs and certifying individuals who engage in medical or dental radiography.

In 2005, 38 states certified radiologic technologists and technicians. Certification, which is voluntary, is offered by the American Registry of Radiologic Technologists. To be eligible for certification, technologists generally must graduate from an accredited program and pass an examination. Many employers prefer to hire certified radiographers. To be recertified, radiographers must complete 24 hours of continuing education every two years.

Radiologic technologists and technicians should be sensitive to patients' physical and psychological needs. They must pay attention to detail, follow instructions, and work as part of a team. In addition, operating complicated equipment requires mechanical ability and manual dexterity.

With experience and additional training, staff technologists may become specialists, performing CT scanning, angiography, and magnetic resonance imaging. Experienced technologists also may be promoted to supervisor, chief radiologic technologist, and, ultimately, department administrator or director. Depending on the institution, courses or a master's degree in business or health administration may be necessary for the director's position. Some technologists progress by leaving the occupation to become instructors or directors in radiologic technology programs; others take jobs as sales representatives or instructors with equipment manufacturers.

Employment

Radiologic technologists and technicians held about 182,000 jobs in 2004. More than half of all jobs were in hospitals. Most of the rest were in offices of physicians; medical and diagnostic laboratories, including diagnostic imaging centers; and outpatient care centers.

Job Outlook

Job opportunities are expected to be favorable. Some employers report difficulty hiring sufficient numbers of radiologic technologists and technicians. Imbalances between the demand for, and supply of, radiologic technologists and technicians should spur efforts to attract and retain qualified workers, such as improved compensation and working conditions. Radiologic technologists who also are experienced in more complex diagnostic imaging procedures, such as CT and MRI, will have better employment opportunities, brought about as employers seek to control costs by using multiskilled employees.

Employment of radiologic technologists and technicians is expected to grow faster than the average for all occupations through 2014 as the population grows and ages, increasing the demand for diagnostic imaging. Although health care providers are enthusiastic about the clinical benefits of new technologies, the extent to which they are adopted depends largely on cost and reimbursement considerations. For example, digital imaging technology can improve the quality of the images and the efficiency of the procedure, but remains expensive. Some promising new technologies may not come into widespread use because they are too expensive and third-party payers may not be willing to pay for their use.

Hospitals will remain the principal employer of radiologic technologists and technicians. However, a greater number of new jobs will be found in offices of physicians and diagnostic imaging centers. Health facilities such as these are expected to grow rapidly through 2014 due to the strong shift toward outpatient care encouraged by third-party payers and made possible by technological advances that permit more procedures to be performed outside the hospital. Some job openings also will arise from the need to replace technologists and technicians who leave the occupation.

Earnings

Median annual earnings of radiologic technologists and technicians were $43,350 in May 2004. The middle 50 percent earned between $36,170 and $52,430. The lowest 10 percent earned less than $30,020, and the highest 10 percent earned more than $60,210. Median annual earnings in the industries employing the largest numbers of radiologic technologists and technicians in May 2004 were

Medical and diagnostic laboratories $46,620

General medical and surgical hospitals 43,960

Offices of physicians 40,290

Related Occupations

Radiologic technologists and technicians operate sophisticated equipment to help physicians, dentists, and other health practitioners diagnose and treat patients. Workers in related occupations include cardiovascular technologists and technicians, clinical laboratory technologists and technicians, diagnostic medical sonographers, nuclear medicine technologists, radiation therapists, and respiratory therapists.

Sources of Additional Information

For career information, send a stamped, self-addressed business-size envelope with your request to

▸ American Society of Radiologic Technologists, 15000 Central Ave. SE, Albuquerque, NM 87123-3917. Internet: http://www.asrt.org

For the current list of accredited education programs in radiography, write to

▸ Joint Review Committee on Education in Radiologic Technology, 20 N. Wacker Dr., Suite 2850, Chicago, IL 60606-3182. Internet: http://www.jrcert.org

For information on certification, contact

▸ American Registry of Radiologic Technologists, 1255 Northland Dr., St. Paul, MN 55120-1155. Internet: http://www.arrt.org

Real Estate Brokers and Sales Agents

(O*NET 41-9021.00 and 41-9022.00)

Significant Points

■ Real estate brokers and sales agents often work evenings and weekends and usually are on call to suit the needs of clients.

■ A license is required in every state and the District of Columbia.

■ Although gaining a job may be relatively easy, beginning workers may face competition from well-established, more experienced agents and brokers in obtaining listings and in closing an adequate number of sales.

■ Employment is sensitive to swings in the economy, especially interest rates; during periods of declining economic activity and increasing interest rates, the volume of sales and the resulting demand for sales workers fall.

Nature of the Work

One of the most complex and significant financial events in peoples' lives is the purchase or sale of a home or investment property. Because of this complexity and significance, people typically seek the help of real estate brokers and sales agents when buying or selling real estate.

Real estate brokers and sales agents have a thorough knowledge of the real estate market in their communities. They know which neighborhoods will best fit clients' needs and budgets. They are familiar with local zoning and tax laws and know where to obtain financing. Agents and brokers also act as intermediaries in price negotiations between buyers and sellers.

Real estate agents usually are independent sales workers who provide their services to a licensed real estate broker on a contract basis. In return, the broker pays the agent a portion of the commission earned from the agent's sale of the property. Brokers are independent businesspeople who sell real estate owned by others; they also may rent or manage properties for a fee. When selling real estate, brokers arrange for title searches and for meetings between buyers and sellers during which the details of the transactions are agreed upon and the new owners take possession of the property. A broker may help to arrange favorable financing from a lender for the prospective buyer; often, this makes the difference between success and failure in closing a sale. In some cases, brokers and agents assume primary responsibility for closing sales; in others, lawyers or lenders do. Brokers supervise agents who may have many of the same job duties. Brokers also supervise their own offices, advertise properties, and handle other business matters. Some combine other types of work, such as selling insurance or practicing law, with their real estate business.

Besides making sales, agents and brokers must have properties to sell. Consequently, they spend a significant amount of time obtaining listings—agreements by owners to place properties for sale with the firm. When listing a property for sale, agents and brokers compare the listed property with similar properties that recently sold in order to determine a competitive market price for the property. Once the property is sold, both the agent who sold it and the agent who obtained the listing receive a portion of the commission. Thus, agents who sell a property that they themselves have listed can increase their commission.

Most real estate brokers and sales agents sell residential property. A small number—usually employed in large or specialized firms—sell commercial, industrial, agricultural, or other types of real estate. Every specialty requires knowledge of that particular type of property and clientele. Selling or leasing business property requires an understanding of leasing practices, business trends, and the location of the property. Agents who sell or lease industrial properties must know about the region's transportation, utilities, and labor supply. Whatever the type of property, the agent or broker must know how to meet the client's particular requirements.

Before showing residential properties to potential buyers, agents meet with them to get a feeling for the type of home the buyers would like. In this prequalifying phase, the agent determines how much the buyers can afford to spend. In addition, the agent and the buyer usually sign a loyalty contract that states that the agent will be the only one to show houses to buyers. An agent or broker then generates lists of properties for sale, their location and description, and available sources of financing. In some cases, agents and brokers use computers to give buyers a virtual tour of properties in which they are interested. With a computer, buyers can view interior and exterior images or floor plans without leaving the real estate office.

Agents may meet several times with prospective buyers to discuss and visit available properties. Agents identify and emphasize the most pertinent selling points. To a young family looking for a house, they may emphasize the convenient floor plan, the area's low crime rate, and the proximity to schools and shopping centers. To a potential investor, they may point out the tax advantages of owning a rental property and the ease of finding a renter. If bargaining over price becomes necessary, agents must follow their client's instructions carefully and may have to present counteroffers in order to get the best possible price.

Once both parties have signed the contract, the real estate broker or agent must make sure that all special terms of the contract are met before the closing date. For example, the agent must make sure that the mandated and agreed-upon inspections, including that of the home and termite and radon inspections, take place. Also, if the seller agrees to any repairs, the broker or agent must see that they are made. Increasingly, brokers and agents are handling environmental problems as well by making sure that the properties they sell meet environmental regulations. For example, they may be responsible for dealing with lead paint on the walls. While loan officers, attorneys, or other persons handle many details, the agent must ensure that they are carried out.

Working Conditions

Advances in telecommunications and the ability to retrieve data about properties over the Internet allow many real estate brokers and sales agents to work out of their homes instead of real estate offices. Even with this convenience, much of the time of these workers is spent away from their desks—showing properties to customers, analyzing properties for sale, meeting with prospective clients, or researching the state of the market.

Agents and brokers often work more than a standard 40-hour week. They usually work evenings and weekends and are always on call to suit the needs of clients. Although the hours are long and frequently irregular, most agents and brokers have the freedom to determine their own schedule. Consequently, they can arrange their work so that they can have time off when they want it. Business usually is slower during the winter season.

Training, Other Qualifications, and Advancement

In every state and the District of Columbia, real estate brokers and sales agents must be licensed. Prospective agents must be high school graduates, be at least 18 years old, and pass a written test. The examination—more comprehensive for brokers than for agents—includes questions on basic real estate transactions and laws affecting the sale of property. Most states require candidates for the general sales license to complete between 30 and 90 hours of classroom instruction. Those seeking a broker's license need between 60 and 90 hours of formal training and a specific amount of experience selling real estate, usually 1 to 3 years. Some states waive the experience requirements for the broker's license for applicants who have a bachelor's degree in real estate.

State licenses typically must be renewed every 1 or 2 years; usually, no examination needs to be taken. However, many states require continuing education for license renewals. Prospective agents and brokers should contact the real estate licensing commission of the state in which they wish to work in order to verify the exact licensing requirements.

As real estate transactions have become more legally complex, many firms have turned to college graduates to fill positions. A large number of agents and brokers have some college training. College courses in real estate, finance, business administration, statistics, economics, law, and English are helpful. For those who intend to start their own company, business courses such as marketing and accounting are as significant as courses in real estate or finance.

Personality traits are equally as important as one's academic background. Brokers look for applicants who possess a pleasant personality, are honest, and present a neat appearance. Maturity, good judgment, trustworthiness, and enthusiasm for the job are required in order to encourage prospective customers in this highly competitive field. Agents should be well organized; be detail oriented; and have a good memory for names, faces, and business particulars.

Those interested in jobs as real estate agents often begin in their own communities. Their knowledge of local neighborhoods is a clear advantage. Under the direction of an experienced agent, beginners learn the practical aspects of the job, including the use of computers to locate or list available properties and identify sources of financing.

Many firms offer formal training programs for both beginners and experienced agents. Larger firms usually offer more extensive programs than smaller firms. More than a thousand universities, colleges, and junior colleges offer courses in real estate. At some, a student can earn an associate's or bachelor's degree with a major in real estate; several offer advanced degrees. Many local real estate associations that are members of the National Association of Realtors sponsor courses covering the fundamentals and legal aspects of the field. Advanced courses in mortgage financing, property development and management, and other subjects also are available.

Advancement opportunities for agents may take the form of higher rates of commission. As agents gain knowledge and expertise, they become more efficient in closing a greater number of transactions and increase their earnings. In many large firms, experienced agents can advance to sales manager or general manager. Persons who have received their broker's license may open their own offices. Others with experience and training in estimating property value may become real estate appraisers, and people familiar with operating and maintaining rental properties may become property managers. Experienced agents and brokers with a thorough knowledge of business conditions and property values in their localities may enter mortgage financing or real estate investment counseling.

Employment

In 2004, real estate brokers and sales agents held about 460,000 jobs; real estate sales agents held approximately 24 percent of these jobs. Many worked part time, combining their real estate activities with other careers. About 6 out of 10 real estate agents and brokers were self-employed. Real estate is sold in all areas, but employment is concentrated in large urban areas and in rapidly growing communities.

Most real estate firms are relatively small; indeed, some are one-person businesses. By contrast, some large real estate firms have several hundred agents operating out of numerous branch offices. Many brokers have franchise agreements with national or regional real estate organizations. Under this type of arrangement, the broker pays a fee in exchange for the privilege of using the more widely known name of the parent organization. Although franchised brokers often receive help in training sales staff and running their offices, they bear the ultimate responsibility for the success or failure of their firms.

Real estate brokers and sales agents are older, on average, than most other workers. Historically, many homemakers and retired persons were attracted to real estate sales by the flexible and part-time work schedules characteristic of the field. These individuals could enter, leave, and later return to the occupation, depending on the strength of the real estate market, their family responsibilities, or other personal circumstances. Recently, however, the attractiveness of part-time real estate work has declined as increasingly complex legal and technological requirements are raising startup costs associated with becoming an agent.

Job Outlook

Employment of real estate brokers and sales agents is expected to grow about as fast as the average for all occupations through the year 2014 because of the increasing housing needs of a growing population, as well as the perception that real estate is a good investment. Relatively low interest rates should continue to stimulate sales of real estate, resulting in the need for more agents and brokers. In addition, a large number of job openings will arise each year from the need to replace workers who transfer to other occupations or leave the labor force. However, job growth will be somewhat limited by the increasing use of technology, which is improving the productivity of agents and brokers. For example, prospective customers often can perform their own searches for properties that meet their criteria by accessing real estate information on the Internet. The increasing use of technology is likely to be more detrimental to part-time or temporary real estate agents than to full-time agents because part-time agents generally are not able to compete with full-time agents who have invested in new technology. Changing legal requirements, such as disclosure laws, also may dissuade some who are not serious about practicing full time from continuing to work part time.

This occupation is relatively easy to enter and is attractive because of its flexible working conditions; the high interest in, and familiarity with, local real estate markets that entrants often have; and the potential for high earnings. Therefore, although gaining a job as a real estate agent or broker may be relatively easy, beginning agents and brokers may face competition from their well-established, more experienced counterparts in obtaining listings and in closing an adequate number of sales. Well-trained, ambitious people who enjoy selling—particularly those with extensive social and business connections in their communities—should have the best chance for success.

Employment of real estate brokers and sales agents often is sensitive to swings in the economy, especially interest rates. During periods of declining economic activity and increasing interest rates, the volume of sales and the resulting demand for sales workers falls. As a result, the earnings of agents and brokers decline, and many work fewer hours or leave the occupation altogether.

Earnings

The median annual earnings of salaried real estate sales agents, including commissions, were $35,670 in May 2004. The middle 50 percent earned between $23,500 and $58,110 a year. The lowest 10 percent earned less than $17,600, and the highest 10 percent earned more than $92,770. Median annual earnings in the industries employing the largest number of real estate sales agents in May 2004 were as follows:

Residential building construction $54,770
Offices of real estate agents and brokers...............37,970
Activities related to real estate 32,460
Lessors of real estate 25,840

Median annual earnings of salaried real estate brokers, including commission, were $58,720 in May 2004. The middle 50 percent earned between $33,480 and $99,820 a year. Median annual earning of real estate brokers were $61,550 in offices of real estate agents and brokers and $44,920 in activities related to real estate.

Commissions on sales are the main source of earnings of real estate agents and brokers. The rate of commission varies according to whatever the agent and broker agree on, the type of property, and its value. The percentage paid on the sale of farm and commercial properties or unimproved land is typically higher than the percentage paid for selling a home.

Commissions may be divided among several agents and brokers. When the property is sold, the broker or agent who obtained the listing usually shares the commission with the broker or agent who made the sale and with the firm that employs each of them. Although an agent's share varies greatly from one firm to another, often it is about half of the total amount received by the firm. Agents who both list and sell a property maximize their commission.

Income usually increases as an agent gains experience, but individual motivation, economic conditions, and the type and location of the property also affect earnings. Sales workers who are active in community organizations and in local real estate associations can broaden their contacts and increase their earnings. A beginner's earnings often are irregular because a few weeks or even months may go by without a sale. Although some brokers allow an agent to draw against future earnings from a special account, the practice is not common with new employees. The beginner, therefore, should have enough money to live for about 6 months or until commissions increase.

Related Occupations

Selling expensive items such as homes requires maturity, tact, and a sense of responsibility. Other sales workers who find these character traits important in their work include insurance sales agents; retail salespersons; sales representatives, wholesale and manufacturing; and securities, commodities, and financial services sales agents. Although not involving sales, the work of property, real estate, and community association managers, as well as appraisers and assessors of real estate, requires an understanding of real estate.

Sources of Additional Information

Information on licensing requirements for real estate brokers and sales agents is available from most local real estate organizations or from the state real estate commission or board.

More information about opportunities in real estate is available on the Internet site of the following organization:

▸ National Association of Realtors. Internet: http://www.realtor.org

Receptionists and Information Clerks

(O*NET 43-4171.00)

Significant Points

■ Good interpersonal skills are critical.

■ A high school diploma or its equivalent is the most common educational requirement.

■ Employment is expected to grow faster than average.

Nature of the Work

Receptionists and information clerks are charged with a responsibility that may have a lasting impact on the success of an organization: making a good first impression. These workers often are the first representatives of an organization that a visitor may encounter, so good interpersonal skills—being courteous, professional, and helpful—are critical. Receptionists answer telephones, route and screen calls, greet visitors, respond to inquiries from the public, and provide information about the organization. Some receptionists are responsible for the coordination of all mail into and out of the office. In addition, receptionists contribute to the security of an organization by helping to monitor the access of visitors— a function that has become increasingly important since the terrorist attacks of September 11, 2001, heightened security concerns.

Whereas some tasks are common to most receptionists and information clerks, the specific responsibilities of receptionists vary with the type of establishment in which they work. For example, receptionists in hospitals and in doctors' offices may gather patients' personal and financial information and direct them to the proper waiting rooms. In corporate headquarters, receptionists may greet visitors and manage the scheduling of the board room or common conference area. In beauty or hair salons, by contrast, receptionists arrange appointments, direct customers to the hairstylist, and may serve as cashiers. In factories, large corporations, and government offices, they may provide identification cards and arrange for escorts to take visitors to the proper office. Those working for bus and train companies respond to inquiries about departures, arrivals, stops, and other related matters.

Increasingly, receptionists use multiline telephone systems, personal computers, and fax machines. Despite the widespread use of automated answering systems or voice mail, many receptionists still take messages and inform other employees of visitors' arrivals or cancellation of an appointment. When they are not busy with callers, most receptionists are expected to perform a variety of office duties, including opening and sorting mail, collecting and distributing parcels, transmitting and delivering facsimiles, updating appointment calendars, preparing travel vouchers, and performing basic bookkeeping, word processing, and filing.

Working Conditions

Receptionists who greet customers and visitors usually work in areas that are highly visible and designed and furnished to make a good impression. Most work stations are clean, well lighted, and relatively quiet. The work performed by some receptionists and information clerks may be tiring, repetitious, and stressful as many receptionists spend all day answering continuously ringing telephones and sometimes encounter difficult or irate callers. The work environment, however, may be very friendly and motivating for individuals who enjoy greeting customers face to face and making them feel comfortable.

Training, Other Qualifications, and Advancement

Although hiring requirements for receptionists and information clerks vary by industry, a high school diploma or its equivalent is the most common educational requirement. Good interpersonal skills and being technologically proficient also are important to employers.

Receptionists and information clerks generally receive on-the-job training. However, employers often look for applicants who already possess certain skills, such as prior computer experience or answering telephones. Some employers also may prefer some formal office education or training. On the job, they learn how to operate the telephone system and computers. They also learn the proper procedures for greeting visitors and for distributing mail, faxes, and parcels.

Advancement for receptionists generally comes about either by transferring to a more responsible occupation or by being promoted to a supervisory position. Receptionists with especially strong computer skills may advance to a better-paying job as a secretary or an administrative assistant.

Employment

Receptionists and information clerks held about 1.1 million jobs in 2004. More than 90 percent worked in service-providing industries. Among service-providing industries, health care and social assistance industries—including doctors' and dentists' offices, hospitals, nursing homes, urgent-care centers, surgical centers, and clinics—employed about one-third of all receptionists and information clerks. Manufacturing, wholesale and retail trade, government, and real estate industries also employed large numbers of receptionists and information clerks. More than 3 of every 10 receptionists and information clerks worked part time.

Job Outlook

Employment of receptionists and information clerks is expected to grow faster than the average for all occupations through 2014. This increase will result from rapid growth in service-providing industries—including physicians' offices, law firms, temporary help agencies, and consulting firms—where most are employed. In addition, turnover in this large occupation will create numerous openings as receptionists and information clerks transfer to other occupations or leave the labor force altogether. Opportunities should be best for persons with a wide range of clerical and technical skills, particularly those with related work experience.

Technology will have conflicting effects on the demand for receptionists and information clerks. The increasing use of voice mail and other telephone automation reduces the need for receptionists by allowing one receptionist to perform work that formerly required several. However, the increasing use of other technology has caused a consolidation of clerical responsibilities and growing demand for workers with diverse clerical and technical skills. Because receptionists and information clerks may perform a wide variety of clerical tasks, they should continue to be in demand. Further, they perform many tasks that are interpersonal in nature and are not easily automated, ensuring continued demand for their services in a variety of establishments.

Earnings

Median hourly earnings of receptionists and information clerks in May 2004 were $10.50. The middle 50 percent earned between $8.62 and $12.88. The lowest 10 percent earned less than $7.21, and the highest 10 percent earned more than $15.53. Median hourly earnings in the industries employing the largest number of receptionists and information clerks in May 2004 are shown in the following table.

Offices of dentists	$12.37
General medical and surgical hospitals	11.07
Offices of physicians	10.92
Employment services	10.28
Personal care services	8.16

In 2005, the federal government typically paid salaries ranging from $22,937 to $27,818 a year to beginning receptionists with a high school diploma or 6 months of experience. The average annual salary for all receptionists employed by the federal government was about $29,185 in 2005.

Related Occupations

Receptionists deal with the public and often direct people to others who can assist them. Other workers who perform similar duties include dispatchers, secretaries and administrative assistants, and customer service representatives.

Sources of Additional Information

State employment offices can provide information on job openings for receptionists.

Registered Nurses

(O*NET 29-1111.00)

Significant Points

■ Registered nurses constitute the largest health care occupation, with 2.4 million jobs.

■ About 3 out of 5 jobs are in hospitals.

■ The three major educational paths to registered nursing are a bachelor's degree, an associate degree, and a diploma from an approved nursing program.

■ Registered nurses are projected to create the second-largest number of new jobs among all occupations; job opportunities in most specialties and employment settings are expected to be excellent, with some employers reporting difficulty in attracting and retaining enough RNs.

Nature of the Work

Registered nurses (RNs), regardless of specialty or work setting, perform basic duties that include treating patients, educating patients and the public about various medical conditions, and providing advice and emotional support to patients' family members.

RNs record patients' medical histories and symptoms, help to perform diagnostic tests and analyze results, operate medical machinery, administer treatment and medications, and help with patient follow-up and rehabilitation.

RNs teach patients and their families how to manage their illness or injury, including post-treatment home care needs, diet and exercise programs, and self-administration of medication and physical therapy. Some RNs also are trained to provide grief counseling to family members of critically ill patients. RNs work to promote general health by educating the public on various warning signs and symptoms of disease and where to go for help. RNs also might run general health screening or immunization clinics, blood drives, and public seminars on various conditions.

RNs can specialize in one or more patient care specialties. The most common specialties can be divided into roughly four categories—by work setting or type of treatment; disease, ailment, or condition; organ or body system type; or population. RNs may combine specialties from more than one area—for example, pediatric oncology or cardiac emergency—depending on personal interest and employer needs.

RNs may specialize by work setting or by type of care provided. For example, *ambulatory care nurses* treat patients with a variety of illnesses and injuries on an outpatient basis, either in physicians' offices or in clinics. Some ambulatory care nurses are involved in telehealth, providing care and advice through electronic communications media such as videoconferencing or the Internet. *Critical care nurses* work in critical or intensive care hospital units and provide care to patients with cardiovascular, respiratory, or pulmonary failure. *Emergency,* or *trauma, nurses* work in hospital emergency departments and treat patients with life-threatening conditions caused by accidents, heart attacks, and strokes. Some emergency nurses are flight nurses, who provide medical care to patients who must be flown by helicopter to the nearest medical facility. *Holistic nurses* provide care such as acupuncture, massage therapy and aromatherapy, and biofeedback, which are meant to treat patients' mental and spiritual health in addition to their physical health. *Home health care nurses* provide at-home care for patients who are recovering from surgery, accidents, and childbirth. *Hospice and palliative care nurses* provide care for, and help ease the pain of, terminally ill patients outside of hospitals. *Infusion nurses* administer medications, fluids, and blood to patients through injections into patients' veins. *Long-term care nurses* provide medical services on a recurring basis to patients with chronic physical or mental disorders. *Medical-surgical nurses* provide basic medical care to a variety of patients in all health settings. *Occupational health nurses* provide treatment for job-related injuries and illnesses and help employers to detect workplace hazards and implement health and safety standards. *Perianesthesia nurses* provide preoperative and postoperative care to patients undergoing anesthesia during surgery. *Perioperative nurses* assist surgeons by selecting and handling instruments, controlling bleeding, and suturing incisions. Some of these nurses also can specialize in plastic and reconstructive surgery. *Psychiatric nurses* treat patients with personality and mood disorders. *Radiologic nurses* provide care to patients undergoing diagnostic radiation procedures such as ultrasounds and magnetic resonance imaging. *Rehabilitation nurses* care for patients with temporary and perma-

nent disabilities. *Transplant nurses* care for both transplant recipients and living donors and monitor signs of organ rejection.

RNs specializing in a particular disease, ailment, or condition are employed in virtually all work settings, including physicians' offices, outpatient treatment facilities, home health care agencies, and hospitals. For instance, *addictions nurses* treat patients seeking help with alcohol, drug, and tobacco addictions. *Developmental disabilities nurses* provide care for patients with physical, mental, or behavioral disabilities; care may include help with feeding, controlling bodily functions, and sitting or standing independently. *Diabetes management nurses* help diabetics to manage their disease by teaching them proper nutrition and showing them how to test blood sugar levels and administer insulin injections. *Genetics nurses* provide early detection screenings and treatment of patients with genetic disorders, including cystic fibrosis and Huntington's disease. *HIV/AIDS nurses* care for patients diagnosed with HIV and AIDS. *Oncology nurses* care for patients with various types of cancer and may administer radiation and chemotherapies. Finally, *wound, ostomy, and continence nurses* treat patients with wounds caused by traumatic injury, ulcers, or arterial disease; provide postoperative care for patients with openings that allow for alternative methods of bodily waste elimination; and treat patients with urinary and fecal incontinence.

RNs specializing in treatment of a particular organ or body system usually are employed in specialty physicians' offices or outpatient care facilities, although some are employed in hospital specialty or critical care units. For example, *cardiac and vascular nurses* treat patients with coronary heart disease and those who have had heart surgery, providing services such as postoperative rehabilitation. *Dermatology nurses* treat patients with disorders of the skin, such as skin cancer and psoriasis. *Gastroenterology nurses* treat patients with digestive and intestinal disorders, including ulcers, acid reflux disease, and abdominal bleeding. Some nurses in this field also specialize in endoscopic procedures, which look inside the gastrointestinal tract using a tube equipped with a light and a camera that can capture images of diseased tissue. *Gynecology nurses* provide care to women with disorders of the reproductive system, including endometriosis, cancer, and sexually transmitted diseases. *Nephrology nurses* care for patients with kidney disease caused by diabetes, hypertension, or substance abuse. *Neuroscience nurses* care for patients with dysfunctions of the nervous system, including brain and spinal cord injuries and seizures. *Ophthalmic nurses* provide care to patients with disorders of the eyes, including blindness and glaucoma, and to patients undergoing eye surgery. *Orthopedic nurses* care for patients with muscular and skeletal problems, including arthritis, bone fractures, and muscular dystrophy. *Otorhinolaryngology nurses* care for patients with ear, nose, and throat disorders, such as cleft palates, allergies, and sinus disorders. *Respiratory nurses* provide care to patients with respiratory disorders such as asthma, tuberculosis, and cystic fibrosis. *Urology nurses* care for patients with disorders of the kidneys, urinary tract, and male reproductive organs, including infections, kidney and bladder stones, and cancers.

Finally, RNs may specialize by providing preventive and acute care in all health care settings to various segments of the population, including newborns (neonatology), children and adolescents (pediatrics), adults, and the elderly (gerontology or geriatrics). RNs also may provide basic health care to patients outside of health care settings in such venues as correctional facilities, schools, summer camps, and the military. Some RNs travel around the United States and abroad providing care to patients in areas with shortages of medical professionals.

Most RNs work as staff nurses, providing critical health care services along with physicians, surgeons, and other health care practitioners. However, some RNs choose to become advanced practice nurses, who often are considered primary health care practitioners and work independently or in collaboration with physicians. For example, *clinical nurse specialists* provide direct patient care and expert consultations in one of many of the nursing specialties listed above. *Nurse anesthetists* administer anesthesia, monitor patient's vital signs during surgery, and provide post-anesthesia care. *Nurse-midwives* provide primary care to women, including gynecological exams, family planning advice, prenatal care, assistance in labor and delivery, and neonatal care. *Nurse practitioners* provide basic preventive health care to patients and increasingly serve as primary and specialty care providers in mainly medically underserved areas. The most common areas of specialty for nurse practitioners are family practice, adult practice, women's health, pediatrics, acute care, and gerontology; however, there are many other specialties. In most states, advanced practice nurses can prescribe medications.

Some nurses have jobs that require little or no direct patient contact. Most of these positions still require an active RN license. *Case managers* ensure that all of the medical needs of patients with severe injuries and illnesses are met, including the type, location, and duration of treatment. *Forensics nurses* combine nursing with law enforcement by treating and investigating victims of sexual assault, child abuse, or accidental death. *Infection control nurses* identify, track, and control infectious outbreaks in health care facilities; develop methods of outbreak prevention and biological terrorism responses; and staff immunization clinics. *Legal nurse consultants* assist lawyers in medical cases by interviewing patients and witnesses, organizing medical records, determining damages and costs, locating evidence, and educating lawyers about medical issues. *Nurse administrators* supervise nursing staff, establish work schedules and budgets, and maintain medical supply inventories. *Nurse educators* teach student nurses and also provide continuing education for RNs. *Nurse informaticists* collect, store, and analyze nursing data in order to improve efficiency, reduce risk, and improve patient care. RNs also may work as health care consultants, public policy advisors, pharmaceutical and medical supply researchers and salespersons, and medical writers and editors.

Working Conditions

Most RNs work in well-lighted, comfortable health care facilities. Home health and public health nurses travel to patients' homes, schools, community centers, and other sites. RNs may spend considerable time walking and standing. Patients in hospitals and nursing care facilities require 24-hour care; consequently, nurses in these institutions may work nights, weekends, and holidays. RNs also may be on call—available to work on short notice. Nurses who work in office settings are more likely to work regular business hours. About 23 percent of RNs worked part time in 2004, and 7 percent held more than one job.

Nursing has its hazards, especially in hospitals, nursing care facilities, and clinics, where nurses may care for individuals with infectious diseases. RNs must observe rigid, standardized guidelines to guard against disease and other dangers, such as those posed by radiation, accidental needle sticks, chemicals used to sterilize instruments, and anesthetics. In addition, they are vulnerable to back injury when moving patients, shocks from electrical equipment, and hazards posed by compressed gases. RNs who work with critically ill patients also may suffer emotional strain from observing patient suffering and from close personal contact with patients' families.

Training, Other Qualifications, and Advancement

In all states and the District of Columbia, students must graduate from an approved nursing program and pass a national licensing examination, known as the NCLEX-RN, in order to obtain a nursing license. Nurses may be licensed in more than one state, either by examination or by the endorsement of a license issued by another state. Currently 18 states participate in the Nurse Licensure Compact Agreement, which allows nurses to practice in member states without recertifying. All states require periodic renewal of licenses, which may involve continuing education.

There are three major educational paths to registered nursing: A bachelor's of science degree in nursing (BSN), an associate degree in nursing (ADN), and a diploma. BSN programs, offered by colleges and universities, take about 4 years to complete. In 2004, 674 nursing programs offered degrees at the bachelor's level. ADN programs, offered by community and junior colleges, take about 2 to 3 years to complete. About 846 RN programs in 2004 granted associate degrees. Diploma programs, administered in hospitals, last about 3 years. Only 69 programs offered diplomas in 2004. Generally, licensed graduates of any of the three types of educational programs qualify for entry-level positions as staff nurses.

Many RNs with an ADN or diploma later enter bachelor's programs to prepare for a broader scope of nursing practice. Often, they can find a staff nurse position and then take advantage of tuition reimbursement benefits to work toward a BSN by completing an RN-to-BSN program. In 2004, there were 600 RN-to-BSN programs in the United States. Accelerated master's degree programs in nursing also are available. These programs combine 1 year of an accelerated BSN program with 2 years of graduate study. In 2004, there were 137 RN-to-MSN programs.

Accelerated BSN programs also are available for individuals who have a bachelor's or higher degree in another field and who are interested in moving into nursing. In 2004, more than 165 of these programs were available. Accelerated BSN programs last 12 to 18 months and provide the fastest route to a BSN for individuals who already hold a degree.

Individuals considering nursing should carefully weigh the advantages and disadvantages of enrolling in a BSN program, because if they do, their advancement opportunities usually are broader. In fact, some career paths are open only to nurses with a bachelor's or master's degree. A bachelor's degree often is necessary for administrative positions and is a prerequisite for admission to graduate nursing programs in research, consulting, and teaching and all four advanced practice nursing specialties—clinical nurse specialists, nurse anesthetists, nurse-midwives, and nurse practitioners. Individuals who complete a bachelor's receive more training in areas such as communication, leadership, and critical thinking, all of which are becoming more important as nursing care becomes more complex. Additionally, bachelor's degree programs offer more clinical experience in nonhospital settings. In 2004, 417 nursing schools offered master's degrees, 93 offered doctoral degrees, and 46 offered accelerated BSN-to-doctoral programs.

All four advanced practice nursing specialties require at least a master's degree. Most programs last about 2 years and require a BSN degree, and some programs require at least 1 to 2 years of clinical experience as an RN for admission. In 2004, there were 329 master's and post-master's programs offered for nurse practitioners, 218 master's and post-master's programs for clinical nurse specialists, 92 programs for nurse anesthetists, and 45 programs for nurse-midwives. Upon completion of a program, most advanced practice nurses become nationally certified in their area of specialty. In some states, certification in a specialty is required in order to practice that specialty.

All nursing education programs include classroom instruction and supervised clinical experience in hospitals and other health care facilities. Students take courses in anatomy, physiology, microbiology, chemistry, nutrition, psychology and other behavioral sciences, and nursing. Coursework also includes the liberal arts for ADN and BSN students.

Supervised clinical experience is provided in hospital departments such as pediatrics, psychiatry, maternity, and surgery. A growing number of programs include clinical experience in nursing care facilities, public health departments, home health agencies, and ambulatory clinics.

Nurses should be caring, sympathetic, responsible, and detail oriented. They must be able to direct or supervise others, correctly assess patients' conditions, and determine when consultation is required. They need emotional stability to cope with human suffering, emergencies, and other stresses.

Some RNs start their careers as licensed practical nurses or nursing aides and then go back to school to receive their RN degree. Most RNs begin as staff nurses, and with experience and good performance often are promoted to more responsible positions. In management, nurses can advance to assistant head nurse or head nurse and, from there, to assistant director, director, and vice president. Increasingly, management-level nursing positions require a graduate or an advanced degree in nursing or health services administration. They also require leadership, negotiation skills, and good judgment.

Some nurses move into the business side of health care. Their nursing expertise and experience on a health care team equip them to manage ambulatory, acute, home-based, and chronic care. Employers—including hospitals, insurance companies, pharmaceutical manufacturers, and managed care organizations, among others—need RNs for health planning and development, marketing, consulting, policy development, and quality assurance. Other nurses work as college and university faculty or conduct research.

Foreign-educated nurses wishing to work in the United States must obtain a work visa. Applicants are required to undergo a review of their education and licensing credentials and pass a nursing certification and English proficiency exam, both conducted by the Commission on Graduates of Foreign Nursing Schools. (The commission is an immigration-neutral, nonprofit organization that is recognized internationally as an authority on credentials evaluation in the health care field.) Applicants from Australia, Canada (except Quebec), Ireland, New Zealand, and the United Kingdom are exempt from the language proficiency exam. In addition to these national requirements, most states have their own requirements.

Employment

As the largest health care occupation, registered nurses held about 2.4 million jobs in 2004. About 3 out of 5 jobs were in hospitals, in inpatient and outpatient departments. Others worked in offices of physicians, nursing care facilities, home health care services, employment services, government agencies, and outpatient care centers. The remainder worked mostly in social assistance agencies and educational services, public and private. About 1 in 4 RNs worked part time.

Job Outlook

Job opportunities for RNs in all specialties are expected to be excellent. Employment of registered nurses is expected to grow much faster than average for all occupations through 2014, and, because the occupation is very large, many new jobs will result. In fact, registered nurses are projected to create the second-largest number of new jobs among all occupations. Thousands of job openings also will result from the need to replace experienced nurses who leave the occupation, especially as the median age of the registered nurse population continues to rise.

Much-faster-than-average growth will be driven by technological advances in patient care, which permit a greater number of medical problems to be treated, and by an increasing emphasis on preventive care. In addition, the number of older people, who are much more likely than younger people to need nursing care, is projected to grow rapidly.

Employers in some parts of the country and in certain employment settings are reporting difficulty in attracting and retaining an adequate number of RNs, primarily because of an aging RN workforce and a lack of younger workers to fill positions. Enrollments in nursing programs at all levels have increased more rapidly in the past couple of years as students seek jobs with stable employment. However, many qualified applicants are being turned away because of a shortage of nursing faculty to teach classes. The need for nursing faculty will only increase as a large number of instructors nears retirement. Many employers also are relying on foreign-educated nurses to fill open positions.

Even though employment opportunities for all nursing specialties are expected to be excellent, they can vary by employment setting. For example, employment is expected to grow more slowly in hospitals—which comprise health care's largest industry—than in most other health care industries. While the intensity of nursing care is likely to increase, requiring more nurses per patient, the number of inpatients (those who remain in the hospital for more than 24 hours) is not likely to grow by much. Patients are being discharged earlier, and more procedures are being done on an outpatient basis, both inside and outside hospitals. Rapid growth is expected in hospital outpatient facilities, such as those providing same-day surgery, rehabilitation, and chemotherapy.

Despite the slower employment growth in hospitals, job opportunities should still be excellent because of the relatively high turnover of hospital nurses. RNs working in hospitals frequently work overtime and night and weekend shifts and also treat seriously ill and injured patients, all of which can contribute to stress and burnout. Hospital departments in which these working conditions occur most frequently—critical care units, emergency departments, and operating rooms—generally will have more job openings than other departments.

To attract and retain qualified nurses, hospitals may offer signing bonuses, family-friendly work schedules, or subsidized training. A growing number of hospitals also are experimenting with online bidding to fill open shifts, in which nurses can volunteer to fill open shifts at premium wages. This can decrease the amount of mandatory overtime that nurses are required to work.

More and more sophisticated procedures, once performed only in hospitals, are being performed in physicians' offices and in outpatient care centers, such as freestanding ambulatory surgical and emergency centers. Accordingly, employment is expected to grow much faster than average in these places as health care in general expands. However, RNs may face greater competition for these positions because they generally offer regular working hours and more comfortable working environments.

Employment in nursing care facilities is expected to grow faster than average because of increases in the number of elderly, many of whom require long-term care. In addition, the financial pressure on hospitals to discharge patients as soon as possible should produce more admissions to nursing care facilities. Job growth also is expected in units that provide specialized long-term rehabilitation for stroke and head injury patients, as well as units that treat Alzheimer's victims.

Employment in home health care is expected to increase rapidly in response to the growing number of older persons with functional disabilities, consumer preference for care in the home, and technological advances that make it possible to bring increasingly complex treatments into the home. The type of care demanded will require nurses who are able to perform complex procedures.

Generally, RNs with at least a bachelor's degree will have better job prospects than those without a bachelor's. In addition, all four advanced practice specialties—clinical nurse specialists, nurse practitioners, midwives, and anesthetists—will be in high demand, particularly in medically underserved areas such as inner cities and rural areas. Relative to physicians, these RNs increasingly serve as lower-cost primary care providers.

Earnings

Median annual earnings of registered nurses were $52,330 in May 2004. The middle 50 percent earned between $43,370 and $63,360. The lowest 10 percent earned less than $37,300, and the highest 10 percent earned more than $74,760. Median annual earnings in the industries employing the largest numbers of registered nurses in May 2004 were as follows:

Employment services	$63,170
General medical and surgical hospitals	53,450
Home health care services	48,990
Offices of physicians	48,250
Nursing care facilities	48,220

Many employers offer flexible work schedules, child care, educational benefits, and bonuses.

Related Occupations

Workers in other health care occupations with responsibilities and duties related to those of registered nurses are cardiovascular technologists and technicians; diagnostic medical sonographers; dietitians and nutritionists; emergency medical technicians and paramedics; licensed practical and licensed vocational nurses; massage therapists; medical and health services managers; nursing, psychiatric, and home health aides; occupational therapists; physical therapists; physician assistants; physicians and surgeons; radiologic technologists and technicians; respiratory therapists; and surgical technologists.

Sources of Additional Information

For information on a career as a registered nurse and nursing education, contact

▸ National League for Nursing, 61 Broadway, New York, NY 10006. Internet: http://www.nln.org

For information on nursing career options; financial aid; and listings of BSN, graduate, and accelerated nursing programs, contact

▸ American Association of Colleges of Nursing, 1 Dupont Circle NW, Suite 530, Washington, DC 20036. Internet: http://www.aacn.nche.edu

For additional information on registered nurses, including credentialing, contact

▸ American Nurses Association, 8515 Georgia Ave., Suite 400, Silver Spring, MD 20910. Internet: http://nursingworld.org

For information on the NCLEX-RN exam and a list of individual states' boards of nursing, contact

▸ National Council of State Boards of Nursing, 111 E. Wacker Dr., Suite 2900, Chicago, IL 60611. Internet: http://www.ncsbn.org

For information on obtaining U.S. certification and work visas for foreign-educated nurses, contact

▸ Commission on Graduates of Foreign Nursing Schools, 3600 Market St., Suite 400, Philadelphia, PA 19104. Internet: http://www.cgfns.org

For a list of accredited clinical nurse specialist programs, contact

▸ National Association of Clinical Nurse Specialists, 2090 Linglestown Rd., Suite 107, Harrisburg, PA 17110. Internet: http://www.nacns.org/cnsdirectory.shtml

For information on nurse anesthetists, including a list of accredited programs, contact

▸ American Association of Nurse Anesthetists, 222 Prospect Ave., Park Ridge, IL 60068.

For information on nurse-midwives, including a list of accredited programs, contact

▸ American College of Nurse-Midwives, 8403 Colesville Rd., Suite 1550, Silver Spring, MD 20910. Internet: http://www.midwife.org

For information on nurse practitioners, including a list of accredited programs, contact

▸ American Academy of Nurse Practitioners, P.O. Box 12846, Austin, TX 78711. Internet: http://www.aanp.org

Reservation and Transportation Ticket Agents and Travel Clerks

(O*NET 43-4181.01 and 43-4181.02)

Significant Points

■ Most jobs are found in large metropolitan airports, downtown ticket offices, large reservation centers, and train or bus stations.

■ A high school diploma or its equivalent is the most common educational requirement.

■ Employment is expected to grow more slowly than average because of the significant impact of technology on worker productivity.

■ Applicants for jobs are likely to encounter considerable competition; those who have previous experience in the travel industry, in sales, or in customer service should have the best chances.

Nature of the Work

Each year, millions of Americans travel by plane, train, ship, bus, and automobile. Many of these travelers rely on the services of reservation and transportation ticket agents and travel clerks, who perform functions as varied as selling tickets, confirming reservations, checking baggage, and providing tourists with useful travel information.

Most *reservation agents* work for large hotel chains or airlines, helping people to plan trips and make reservations. They usually work in large reservation centers, answering telephone or e-mail inquiries and offering suggestions and information about travel arrangements, such as routes, schedules, rates, and types of accommodation. Reservation agents quote fares and room rates, provide travel information, and make and confirm transportation and hotel reservations. Most agents use proprietary networks to obtain, as quickly as possible, information needed to make, change, or cancel reservations for customers.

Transportation ticket agents are sometimes known as passenger service agents, passenger booking clerks, reservation clerks, airport service agents, ticket clerks, or ticket sellers. They work in airports, train stations, and bus stations, selling tickets, assigning seats to passengers, and checking baggage. In addition, they may answer inquiries and give directions, examine passports and visas, or check in pets. They may be required to assist customers who have trouble operating self-service ticket printing machines, which also are

known as kiosks. Other ticket agents, more commonly known as *gate* or *station agents*, work in airport terminals, assisting passengers boarding airplanes. These workers direct passengers to the correct boarding area; check tickets and seat assignments; make boarding announcements; and provide special assistance to young, elderly, or disabled passengers when they board or disembark.

Most *travel clerks* are employed by membership organizations, such as automobile clubs. These workers, sometimes called *member services counselors* or *travel counselors*, plan trips; calculate mileage; and offer travel suggestions, such as the best route from the point of origin to the destination, to club members. Travel clerks also may prepare an itinerary indicating points of interest, restaurants, overnight accommodations, and availability of emergency services during a trip. In some cases, they make rental car, hotel, and restaurant reservations for club members.

Passenger rate clerks generally work for bus companies. They sell tickets for regular bus routes and arrange nonscheduled or chartered trips. They plan travel routes, compute rates, and keep customers informed of appropriate details. They also may arrange travel accommodations.

Working Conditions

Most reservation and transportation ticket agents and travel clerks work in areas that are clean and well lit. This is especially true for agents who greet customers and visitors in person. Reservation and ticket agents may spend much of their day talking on the telephone; however, they commonly work away from the public, often in large centralized reservation or phone centers. Because a large number of agents or clerks may share the same workspace, it may be crowded and noisy.

Although most reservation and transportation ticket agents and travel clerks work a standard 40-hour week, about 2 out of 10 work part time. Some high school and college students are employed part time in this occupation, working after school or during vacations. Some agents work evenings, late nights, weekends, and holidays. In general, employees with the most seniority tend to be assigned the more desirable shifts.

The work performed by reservation and transportation ticket agents and travel clerks may be repetitive and stressful. They often work under stringent time constraints or must meet quotas on the number of calls answered or reservations made. Difficult or angry customers also can create stressful situations, as agents usually bear the brunt of customers' dissatisfaction. Agents may work on their feet for a large portion of their shift and may have to lift heavy baggage. In addition, prolonged exposure to a computer monitor, which is common in this occupation, may lead to eyestrain.

Training, Other Qualifications, and Advancement

A high school diploma or its equivalent is the most common educational requirement for reservation and transportation ticket agent and travel clerk jobs. Some employers, however, prefer applicants who have completed college coursework in management or business. Experience with computers, including good typing skills, also is usually required. Some jobs require applicants to be over 18 years of age and posses a valid driver's license. Agents who handle passenger luggage must be able to lift heavy objects.

Most airline reservation and ticket agents learn their skills through formal company training programs that can last several weeks. Here, they learn company and industry policies as well as ticketing procedures. Trainees also learn to use the airline's computer system to obtain information on schedules, fares, and the availability of seats; to make reservations for passengers; and to plan passenger itineraries. In addition, they must become familiar with airport and airline code designations, regulations, and safety procedures. After completing classroom instruction, new agents work under the direct guidance of a supervisor or experienced agent. During this time, the supervisors may, for example, monitor telephone conversations to improve the quality of customer service so that agents learn to provide customer service in a courteous manner while limiting the time spent on each call.

In contrast to those who work for airlines, reservation and transportation ticket agents and travel clerks who work for automobile clubs, bus lines, and railroads are trained on the job through short in-house classes that last several days.

Many reservation and transportation ticket agents and travel clerks deal directly with the public, so a professional appearance and a pleasant personality are important. A clear speaking voice and fluency in the English language also are essential because these employees frequently use the telephone or public-address systems. In addition, fluency in a foreign language is becoming increasingly helpful for those seeking reservation and ticket agent jobs.

Reservation and transportation ticket agents and travel clerks may advance by being transferred to a position with more responsibilities or by being promoted to a supervisory position. Many travel companies fill supervisory and managerial positions by promoting individuals within their organization, so those who acquire additional skills, experience, and training improve their opportunities for advancement. Some companies require that candidates for supervisory positions have an associate degree in a business-related field, such as management, business administration, or marketing. Within the airline industry, a ticket agent may advance to lead worker on the shift.

Employment

Reservation and transportation ticket agents and travel clerks held about 163,000 jobs in 2004. About 6 out of 10 are employed by airlines. Others work for automobile clubs, hotels and other lodging places, railroad companies, bus lines, and other companies that provide transportation services.

Although agents and clerks are found throughout the country, most work in large metropolitan airports, downtown ticket offices, large reservation centers, and train or bus stations. The remainder work in small regional airports or in small communities served only by intercity bus or railroad lines.

Job Outlook

Applicants for reservation and transportation ticket agent jobs are likely to encounter considerable competition because the supply of qualified applicants will exceed the expected number of job openings. Entry requirements for these jobs are minimal, and many

people seeking to get into the airline industry or another travel-related business often start out in such positions. The jobs provide excellent travel benefits, and many people view airline and other travel-related jobs as glamorous. Applicants who have previous experience in the travel industry, in sales, or in customer service should have the best chances.

Employment of reservation and transportation ticket agents and travel clerks is expected to grow more slowly than the average for all occupations through 2014. Although a growing population will demand additional travel services, employment of these workers will grow more slowly than this demand because of the significant impact of technology on worker productivity. Automated reservations and ticketing, as well as "ticketless" travel, for example, are reducing the need for some workers. Most train stations and airports now have self-service ticket printing machines, called kiosks, which enable passengers to make reservations, purchase tickets, and check in for train rides and flights themselves. Many passengers also are able to check flight times and fares, make reservations, purchase tickets, and check in for flights on the Internet. Nevertheless, not all travel-related passenger services can be fully automated, primarily for safety and security reasons. As a result, job openings will continue to become available as the occupation grows and as workers transfer to other occupations, retire, or leave the labor force altogether.

Employment of reservation and transportation ticket agents and travel clerks is sensitive to cyclical swings in the economy. During recessions, discretionary passenger travel and transportation service companies are less likely to hire new workers and may even resort to layoffs.

Earnings

Median annual earnings of reservation and transportation ticket agents and travel clerks in May 2004 were $27,750. The middle 50 percent earned between $21,430 and $39,410. The lowest 10 percent earned less than $17,720, and the highest 10 percent earned more than $45,100. Many employers offer discounts on travel services to their employees. In May 2004, median annual earnings in the industries employing the larges number of agents were

Scheduled air transportation	$31,750
Travel arrangement and reservation services	22,370
Traveler accommodation	22,050

Related Occupations

Other occupations that provide travel-related services include hotel, motel, and resort desk clerks; travel agents; and flight attendants. Other occupations that make sales and provide information to customers include counter and rental clerks, order clerks, customer service representatives, and receptionists and information clerks.

Sources of Additional Information

For information about job opportunities as reservation and transportation ticket agents and travel clerks, write to the personnel manager of individual transportation companies. Addresses of airlines are available from

‣ Air Transport Association of America, 1301 Pennsylvania Ave. NW, Suite 1100, Washington, DC 20004-1707.

Retail Salespersons

(O*NET 41-2031.00)

Significant Points

■ Good employment opportunities are expected because of the need to replace the large number of workers who leave the occupation each year.

■ Most salespersons work evenings and weekends, particularly during sales and other peak retail periods.

■ Employers look for people who enjoy working with others and who have tact, patience, an interest in sales work, a neat appearance, and the ability to communicate clearly.

Nature of the Work

Whether selling shoes, computer equipment, or automobiles, retail salespersons assist customers in finding what they are looking for and try to interest them in buying the merchandise. They describe a product's features, demonstrate its use, or show various models and colors. For some sales jobs, particularly those involving expensive and complex items, retail salespersons need special knowledge or skills. For example, salespersons who sell automobiles must be able to explain the features of various models, the manufacturers' specifications, the types of options and financing available, and the warranty.

Consumers spend millions of dollars every day on merchandise and often form their impression of a store by evaluating its sales force. Therefore, retailers stress the importance of providing courteous and efficient service to remain competitive. For example, when a customer wants an item that is not on the sales floor, the salesperson may check the stockroom, place a special order, or call another store to locate the item.

In addition to selling, most retail salespersons—especially those who work in department and apparel stores—make out sales checks; receive cash, checks, debit, and charge payments; bag or package purchases; and give change and receipts. Depending on the hours they work, retail salespersons may have to open or close cash registers. This work may include counting the money in the register; separating charge slips, coupons, and exchange vouchers; and making deposits at the cash office. Salespersons often are held responsible for the contents of their registers, and repeated shortages are cause for dismissal in many organizations. (Cashiers, who have similar duties, are discussed elsewhere in this book.)

Salespersons also may handle returns and exchanges of merchandise, wrap gifts, and keep their work areas neat. In addition, they may help stock shelves or racks, arrange for mailing or delivery of purchases, mark price tags, take inventory, and prepare displays.

Frequently, salespersons must be aware of special sales and promotions. They also must recognize security risks and thefts and know how to handle or prevent such situations.

Working Conditions

Most salespersons in retail trade work in clean, comfortable, well-lighted stores. However, they often stand for long periods and may need supervisory approval to leave the sales floor. They also may work outdoors if they sell items such as cars, plants, or lumber yard materials.

The Monday-through-Friday, 9-to-5 workweek is the exception rather than the rule in retail trade. Most salespersons work evenings and weekends, particularly during sales and other peak retail periods. The end-of-year holiday season is the busiest time for most retailers. As a result, many employers restrict the use of vacation time to some period other than Thanksgiving through the beginning of January.

The job can be rewarding for those who enjoy working with people. Patience and courtesy are required, especially when the work is repetitious and the customers are demanding.

Training, Other Qualifications, and Advancement

There usually are no formal education requirements for this type of work, although a high school diploma or the equivalent is preferred. Employers look for people who enjoy working with others and who have the tact and patience to deal with difficult customers. Among other desirable characteristics are an interest in sales work, a neat appearance, and the ability to communicate clearly and effectively. The ability to speak more than one language may be helpful for employment in communities where people from various cultures tend to live and shop. Before hiring a salesperson, some employers may conduct a background check, especially for a job selling high-priced items.

In most small stores, an experienced employee or the proprietor instructs newly hired sales personnel in making out sales checks and operating cash registers. In large stores, training programs are more formal and are usually conducted over several days. Topics generally discussed are customer service, security, the store's policies and procedures, and how to work a cash register. Depending on the type of product they are selling, employees may be given additional specialized training by manufacturers' representatives. For example, those working in cosmetics receive instruction on the types of products the store has available and for whom the cosmetics would be most beneficial. Likewise, salespersons employed by motor vehicle dealers may be required to participate in training programs designed to provide information on the technical details of standard and optional equipment available on new vehicle models. Since providing the best possible service to customers is a high priority for many employers, employees often are given periodic training to update and refine their skills.

As salespersons gain experience and seniority, they usually move to positions of greater responsibility and may be given their choice of departments in which to work. This often means moving to areas with potentially higher earnings and commissions. The highest earnings potential usually lies in selling "big-ticket" items—such as cars, jewelry, furniture, and electronic equipment—although doing so often requires extensive knowledge of the product and an extraordinary talent for persuasion.

Opportunities for advancement vary in small stores. In some establishments, advancement is limited because one person—often the owner—does most of the managerial work. In others, some salespersons are promoted to assistant managers. Large retail businesses usually prefer to hire college graduates as management trainees, making a college education increasingly important. However, motivated and capable employees without college degrees still may advance to administrative or supervisory positions in large establishments.

Retail selling experience may be an asset when one is applying for sales positions with larger retailers or in other industries, such as financial services, wholesale trade, or manufacturing.

Employment

Retail salespersons held about 4.3 million wage and salary jobs in 2004. They worked in stores ranging from small specialty shops employing a few workers to giant department stores with hundreds of salespersons. In addition, some were self-employed representatives of direct-sales companies and mail-order houses. The largest employers of retail salespersons are department stores, clothing and clothing accessories stores, building material and garden equipment and supplies dealers, other general merchandise stores, and motor vehicle and parts dealers.

This occupation offers many opportunities for part-time work and is especially appealing to students, retirees, and others seeking to supplement their income. However, most of those selling big-ticket items work full time and have substantial experience.

Because retail stores are found in every city and town, employment is distributed geographically in much the same way as the population.

Job Outlook

As in the past, employment opportunities for retail salespersons are expected to be good because of the need to replace the large number of workers who transfer to other occupations or leave the labor force each year. In addition, many new jobs will be created for retail salespersons as businesses seek to expand operations and enhance customer service. Employment is expected to grow about as fast as the average for all occupations through the year 2014, reflecting rising retail sales stemming from a growing population. Opportunities for part-time work should be abundant, and demand will be strong for temporary workers during peak selling periods, such as the end-of-year holiday season. The availability of part-time and temporary work attracts many people seeking to supplement their income.

During economic downturns, sales volumes and the resulting demand for sales workers usually decline. Purchases of costly items, such as cars, appliances, and furniture, tend to be postponed during difficult economic times. In areas of high unemployment, sales of many types of goods decline. However, because turnover among retail salespersons is high, employers often can adjust employment levels simply by not replacing all those who leave.

Despite the growing popularity of electronic commerce, Internet sales have not decreased the need for retail salespersons. Retail stores commonly use an online presence to complement their in-store sales; there are very few Internet-only apparel and specialty stores. Retail salespersons will remain important in assuring customers that they will receive specialized service and in improving customer satisfaction, something Internet services cannot do. Therefore, the impact of electronic commerce on employment of retail salespersons is expected to be minimal.

Earnings

The starting wage for many retail sales positions is the federal minimum wage, which was $5.15 an hour in 2004. In areas where employers have difficulty attracting and retaining workers, wages tend to be higher than the legislated minimum.

Median hourly earnings of retail salespersons, including commissions, were $8.98 in May 2004. The middle 50 percent earned between $7.46 and $12.22 an hour. The lowest 10 percent earned less than $6.38, and the highest 10 percent earned more than $17.85 an hour. Median hourly earnings in the industries employing the largest numbers of retail salespersons in May 2004 were as follows:

Automobile dealers	$18.61
Building material and supplies dealers	10.85
Department stores	8.47
Other general merchandise stores	8.36
Clothing stores	8.17

Compensation systems vary by type of establishment and merchandise sold. Salespersons receive hourly wages, commissions, or a combination thereof. Under a commission system, salespersons receive a percentage of the sales they make. This system offers sales workers the opportunity to increase their earnings considerably, but they may find that their earnings strongly depend on their ability to sell their product and on the ups and downs of the economy. Employers may use incentive programs such as awards, banquets, bonuses, and profit-sharing plans to promote teamwork among the sales staff.

Benefits may be limited in smaller stores, but benefits in large establishments usually are comparable to those offered by other employers. In addition, nearly all salespersons are able to buy their store's merchandise at a discount, with the savings depending on the type of merchandise.

Related Occupations

Salespersons use sales techniques, coupled with their knowledge of merchandise, to assist customers and encourage purchases. Workers in other occupations who use these same skills include sales representatives, wholesale and manufacturing; securities, commodities, and financial services sales agents; counter and rental clerks; real estate brokers and sales agents; purchasing managers, buyers, and purchasing agents; insurance sales agents; sales engineers; and cashiers.

Sources of Additional Information

Information on careers in retail sales may be obtained from the personnel offices of local stores or from state merchants' associations.

General information about retailing is available from

▸ National Retail Federation, 325 7th St. NW, Suite 1100, Washington, DC 20004.

Information about retail sales employment opportunities is available from

▸ Retail, Wholesale, and Department Store Union, 30 East 29th St., 4th Floor, New York, NY 10016.

Information about training for a career in automobile sales is available from

▸ National Automobile Dealers Association, Public Relations Department, 8400 Westpark Dr., McLean, VA 22102-3591. Internet: http://www.nada.org

Sales Representatives, Wholesale and Manufacturing

(O*NET 41-4011.01, 41-4011.02, 41-4011.03, 41-4011.04, 41-4011.05, 41-4011.06, and 41-4012.00)

Significant Points

■ Employment opportunities will be best for those with a college degree, the appropriate knowledge or technical expertise, and the personal traits necessary for successful selling. Job prospects for wholesale sales representatives will be better than those for manufacturing sales representatives, particularly in small firms.

■ Earnings of sales representatives usually are based on a combination of salary and commissions.

Nature of the Work

Sales representatives are an important part of manufacturers' and wholesalers' success. Regardless of the type of product they sell, their primary duties are to interest wholesale and retail buyers and purchasing agents in their merchandise and to address clients' questions and concerns. Sales representatives represent one or several manufacturers or wholesale distributors by selling one product or a complementary line of products. Sales representatives demonstrate their products and advise clients on how using these products can reduce costs and increase sales. They market their company's products to manufacturers, wholesale and retail establishments, construction contractors, government agencies, and other institutions. (Retail salespersons, who sell directly to consumers, are discussed elsewhere in this book.)

Depending on where they work, sales representatives have different job titles. Those employed directly by a manufacturer or wholesaler often are called *sales representatives. Manufacturers' agents* or *manufacturers' representatives* are self-employed sales workers or independent firms who contract their services to all types of manufacturing companies. Many of these titles, however, are used interchangeably.

Sales representatives spend much of their time traveling to and visiting with prospective buyers and current clients. During a sales call, they discuss the client's needs and suggest how their merchandise or services can meet those needs. They may show samples or catalogs that describe items their company stocks and inform customers about prices, availability, and ways in which their products can save money and boost productivity. Because a vast number of manufacturers and wholesalers sell similar products, sales representatives must emphasize any unique qualities of their products and services. Manufacturers' agents or manufacturers' representatives might sell several complementary products made by different manufacturers and, thus, take a broad approach to their customers' business. Sales representatives may help install new equipment and train employees in its use. They also take orders and resolve any problems with or complaints about the merchandise.

Obtaining new accounts is an important part of the job. Sales representatives follow leads from other clients, track advertisements in trade journals, participate in trade shows and conferences, and may visit potential clients unannounced. In addition, they may spend time meeting with and entertaining prospective clients during evenings and weekends.

In a process that can take several months, sales representatives present their product to a customer and negotiate the sale. Aided by a laptop computer connected to the Internet, or other telecommunications device, they can make a persuasive audiovisual sales pitch and often can answer technical and nontechnical questions immediately.

Frequently, sales representatives who lack technical expertise work as a team with a technical expert. In this arrangement, the technical expert—sometimes a sales engineer—attends the sales presentation to explain the product and answer questions or concerns. The sales representative makes the preliminary contact with customers, introduces the company's product, and closes the sale. The representative is then able to spend more time maintaining and soliciting accounts and less time acquiring technical knowledge. After the sale, representatives may make follow-up visits to ensure that the equipment is functioning properly and may even help train customers' employees to operate and maintain new equipment. Those selling consumer goods often suggest how and where merchandise should be displayed. Working with retailers, they may help arrange promotional programs, store displays, and advertising.

Sales representatives have several duties beyond selling products. They analyze sales statistics; prepare reports; and handle administrative duties, such as filing expense account reports, scheduling appointments, and making travel plans. They read about new and existing products and monitor the sales, prices, and products of their competitors.

Manufacturers' agents who operate a sales agency also must manage their business. This requires organizational and general business skills as well as knowledge of accounting, marketing, and administration.

Working Conditions

Some sales representatives have large territories and travel considerably. Because a sales region may cover several states, representatives may be away from home for several days or weeks at a time. Others work near their home base and travel mostly by car. Because of the nature of the work and the amount of travel, sales representatives may work more than 40 hours per week.

Although the hours are long and often irregular, most sales representatives have the freedom to determine their own schedule. Sales representatives often are on their feet for long periods and may carry heavy sample products, necessitating some physical stamina.

Dealing with different types of people can be stimulating but demanding. Sales representatives often face competition from representatives of other companies. Companies usually set goals or quotas that representatives are expected to meet. Because their earnings depend on commissions, manufacturers' agents are also under the added pressure to maintain and expand their clientele.

Training, Other Qualifications, and Advancement

The background needed for sales jobs varies by product line and market. Many employers hire individuals with previous sales experience who lack a college degree, but they increasingly prefer or require a bachelor's degree because job requirements have become more technical and analytical. Nevertheless, for some consumer products, factors such as sales ability, personality, and familiarity with brands are more important than educational background. On the other hand, firms selling complex, technical products may require a technical degree in addition to some sales experience. Many sales representatives attend seminars in sales techniques or take courses in marketing, economics, communication, or even a foreign language to provide the extra edge needed to make sales. In general, companies are looking for the best and brightest individuals who have the personality and desire to sell. Sales representatives need to be familiar with computer technology, as computers are increasingly used in the workplace to place and track orders and to monitor inventory levels.

Many companies have formal training programs for beginning sales representatives lasting up to 2 years. However, most businesses are accelerating these programs to reduce costs and expedite the returns from training. In some programs, trainees rotate among jobs in plants and offices to learn all phases of production, installation, and distribution of the product. In others, trainees take formal classroom instruction at the plant, followed by on-the-job training under the supervision of a field sales manager.

New workers may get training by accompanying experienced workers on their sales calls. As they gain familiarity with the firm's products and clients, the new workers are given increasing responsibility until they are eventually assigned their own territory. As businesses experience greater competition, increased pressure is placed upon sales representatives to produce sales.

Sales representatives stay abreast of new products and the changing needs of their customers in a variety of ways. They attend trade shows at which new products and technologies are showcased. They also attend conferences and conventions to meet other sales representatives and clients and discuss new product developments. In addition, the entire sales force may participate in company-sponsored meetings to review sales performance, product development, sales goals, and profitability.

There are many certifications designed to raise standards and develop the skills of sales representatives, wholesale and manufacturing. A few examples are the Certified Professional Manufacturers' Representative, the Certified Sales Professional, and the Certified National Pharmaceutical Representative. Certification may involve completion of formal training and passing an examination.

Those who want to become sales representatives should be goal-oriented, persuasive, and able to work well both independently and as part of a team. A pleasant personality and appearance, the ability to communicate well with people, and problem-solving skills are highly valued. Patience and perseverance also are key to completing a sale, which can take several months.

Frequently, promotion takes the form of an assignment to a larger account or territory where commissions are likely to be greater. Experienced sales representatives may move into jobs as sales trainers, who instruct new employees on selling techniques and on company policies and procedures. Those who have good sales records and leadership ability may advance to higher-level positions such as sales supervisor, district manager, or vice president of sales. In addition to advancement opportunities within a firm, some manufacturers' agents go into business for themselves. Others find opportunities in purchasing, advertising, or marketing research.

Employment

Manufacturers' and wholesale sales representatives held about 1.9 million jobs in 2004. About half of all salaried representatives worked in wholesale trade. Others were employed in manufacturing, retail trade, information, and construction. Because of the diversity of products and services sold, employment opportunities are available in every part of the country in a wide range of industries.

In addition to those working directly for a firm, many sales representatives are self-employed manufacturers' agents. They often form small sales firms and work for a straight commission based on the value of their own sales. Usually, however, manufacturers' agents gain experience and recognition with a manufacturer or wholesaler before becoming self-employed.

Job Outlook

Employment of sales representatives, wholesale and manufacturing, is expected to grow about as fast as the average for all occupations through the year 2014, primarily because of continued growth in the variety and number of goods to be sold. Also, many job openings will result from the need to replace workers who transfer to other occupations or leave the labor force.

Prospective customers require sales workers to demonstrate or illustrate the particulars of a good or service. Computer technology makes sales representatives more effective and productive, for example, by allowing them to provide accurate and current information to customers during sales presentations.

Job prospects for sales representatives, wholesale and manufacturing, will be best for persons with the appropriate knowledge or technical expertise as well as the personal traits necessary for successful selling. Opportunities will be better for wholesale sales representatives than for manufacturing sales representatives because manufacturers are expected to continue contracting out sales duties to independent agents rather than using in-house or direct selling personnel. Agents are paid only if they sell, a practice that reduces the overhead cost to their clients. Also, by using an agent who usually contracts his or her services to more than one company, companies can share costs with the other companies involved with that agent. As their customers and manufacturers continue to merge with other companies, independent agents and other wholesale trade firms will, in response, also merge with each other to better serve their clients. Although the demand for independent sales agents will increase over the 2004–2014 projection period, the supply is expected to remain stable, or possibly decline, because of the difficulties associated with self-employment. This factor could lead to many opportunities for sales representatives to start their own independent sales agencies.

Those interested in this occupation should keep in mind that direct selling opportunities in manufacturing are likely to be best for products for which there is strong demand. Furthermore, jobs will be most plentiful in small wholesale and manufacturing firms because a growing number of these companies will rely on agents to market their products as a way to control their costs and expand their customer base.

Employment opportunities and earnings may fluctuate from year to year because sales are affected by changing economic conditions, legislative issues, and consumer preferences.

Earnings

Compensation methods vary significantly by the type of firm and the product sold. Most employers use a combination of salary and commissions or salary plus bonus. Commissions usually are based on the amount of sales, whereas bonuses may depend on individual performance, on the performance of all sales workers in the group or district, or on the company's performance.

Median annual earnings of sales representatives, wholesale and manufacturing, technical and scientific products, were $58,580, including commissions, in May 2004. The middle 50 percent earned between $41,660 and $84,480 a year. The lowest 10 percent earned less than $30,270, and the highest 10 percent earned more than $114,540 a year. Median annual earnings in the industries employing the largest numbers of sales representatives, technical and scientific products, in May 2004 were as follows:

Computer systems design and related services $70,220

Wholesale electronic markets and agents and
brokers 65,990

Drugs and druggists' sundries merchant
wholesalers 60,130

Professional and commercial equipment and
supplies merchant wholesalers 59,080

Electrical and electronic goods merchant
wholesalers 52,870

Median annual earnings of sales representatives, wholesale and manufacturing, except technical and scientific products, were $45,400, including commission, in May 2004. The middle 50 percent earned between $32,640 and $65,260 a year. The lowest 10 percent earned less than $24,070, and the highest 10 percent earned more than $92,740 a year. Median annual earnings in the industries employing the largest numbers of sales representatives, except technical and scientific products, in May 2004 were as follows:

Wholesale electronic markets and agents
and brokers $50,680

Machinery, equipment, and supplies merchant
wholesalers 46,030

Professional and commercial equipment and
supplies merchant wholesalers 45,320

Grocery and related product wholesalers 44,210

Miscellaneous nondurable goods merchant
wholesalers 40,240

In addition to their earnings, sales representatives usually are reimbursed for expenses such as transportation costs, meals, hotels, and entertaining customers. They often receive benefits such as health and life insurance, pension plan, vacation and sick leave, personal use of a company car, and frequent flyer mileage. Some companies offer incentives such as free vacation trips or gifts for outstanding sales workers.

Unlike those working directly for a manufacturer or wholesaler, manufacturers' agents are paid strictly on commission and usually are not reimbursed for expenses. Depending on the type of product or products they are selling, their experience in the field, and the number of clients they have, they can earn significantly more or less than those working in direct sales.

Related Occupations

Sales representatives, wholesale and manufacturing, must have sales ability and knowledge of the products they sell. Other occupations that require similar skills include advertising, marketing, promotions, public relations, and sales managers; insurance sales agents; purchasing managers, buyers, and purchasing agents; real estate brokers and sales agents; retail salespersons; sales engineers; and securities, commodities, and financial services sales agents.

Sources of Additional Information

Information on careers for manufacturers' representatives and agents is available from

▶ Manufacturers' Agents National Association, One Spectrum Pointe, Suite 150, Lake Forest, CA 92630. Internet: http://www.manaonline.org

▶ Manufacturers' Representatives Educational Research Foundation, P.O. Box 247, Geneva, IL 60134. Internet: http://www.mrerf.org

Sales Worker Supervisors

(O*NET 41-1011.00 and 41-1012.00)

Significant Points

■ Overall employment is projected to grow more slowly than average; the number of self-employed sales worker supervisors is expected to decline.

■ Applicants with retail experience should have the best job opportunities.

- In many retail establishments, managers are promoted from within the company; a postsecondary degree may speed a sales worker supervisor's advancement into management.

- Long, irregular hours, including evenings and weekends, are common.

Nature of the Work

Sales worker supervisors oversee the work of sales and related workers, such as retail salespersons; cashiers; customer service representatives; stock clerks and order fillers; sales engineers; and sales representatives, wholesale and manufacturing. Sales worker supervisors are responsible for interviewing, hiring, and training employees, as well as for preparing work schedules and assigning workers to specific duties. Many of these workers hold job titles such as *sales manager* or *department manager*. Under the occupational classification system used in the *Occupational Outlook Handbook*, however, workers with the title *manager* who mainly supervise nonsupervisory workers are called *supervisors* rather than *managers*, even though many of these workers often perform numerous managerial functions. (Related occupations discussed elsewhere in this book are retail salespersons; cashiers; customer service representatives; stock clerks and order fillers; and sales representatives, wholesale and manufacturing.)

In retail establishments, sales worker supervisors ensure that customers receive satisfactory service and quality goods. They also answer customers' inquiries; deal with complaints; and sometimes handle purchasing, budgeting, and accounting. Their responsibilities vary with the size and type of establishment. As the size of retail stores and the types of goods and services increase, supervisors tend to specialize in one department or one aspect of merchandising. (Managers in eating and drinking places are discussed elsewhere in this book in the description of food service managers.)

Sales worker supervisors in large retail establishments, often referred to as department managers, provide day-to-day oversight of individual departments, such as shoes, cosmetics, or housewares in large department stores; produce and meat in grocery stores; and sales in automotive dealerships. These workers establish and implement policies, goals, objectives, and procedures for their specific departments; coordinate activities with other department heads; and strive for smooth operations within their departments. They supervise employees who price and ticket goods and place them on display; clean and organize shelves, displays, and inventories in stockrooms; and inspect merchandise to ensure that nothing is outdated. Sales worker supervisors also review inventory and sales records, develop merchandising techniques, and coordinate sales promotions. In addition, they may greet and assist customers and promote sales and good public relations.

Sales worker supervisors in nonretail establishments supervise and coordinate the activities of sales workers who sell industrial products, automobiles, or services such as advertising or Internet services. They may prepare budgets, make personnel decisions, devise sales-incentive programs, assign sales territories, and approve sales contracts.

In small or independent companies and retail stores, sales worker supervisors not only directly supervise sales associates, but also are responsible for the operation of the entire company or store. Some are self-employed business or store owners.

Working Conditions

Most sales worker supervisors have offices. In retail trade, their offices are within the stores, usually close to the areas they oversee. Although they spend some time in the office completing merchandise orders or arranging work schedules, a large portion of their workday is spent on the sales floor, supervising employees or selling.

Work hours of supervisors vary greatly among establishments because work schedules usually depend on customers' needs. Supervisors generally work at least 40 hours a week. Long, irregular hours are common, particularly during sales, holidays, and busy shopping hours and at times when inventory is taken. Supervisors are expected to work evenings and weekends but usually are compensated with a day off during the week. Hours can change weekly, and managers sometimes must report to work on short notice, especially when employees are absent. Independent owners often can set their own schedules, but hours must be convenient to customers.

Training, Other Qualifications, and Advancement

Sales worker supervisors usually acquire knowledge of management principles and practices—an essential requirement for a supervisory or managerial position in retail trade—through work experience. Many supervisors begin their careers on the sales floor as salespersons, cashiers, or customer service representatives. In these positions, they learn merchandising, customer service, and the basic policies and procedures of the company.

The educational backgrounds of sales worker supervisors vary widely. Regardless of the education they receive, recommended courses include accounting, marketing, management, and sales, as well as psychology, sociology, and communication. Supervisors also must be computer literate because almost all cash registers, inventory control systems, and sales quotes and contracts are computerized.

Supervisors who have postsecondary education often hold associate or bachelor's degrees in liberal arts, social sciences, business, or management. To gain experience, many college students participate in internship programs that usually are developed jointly by individual schools and firms.

The type and amount of training available to supervisors vary from company to company. Many national retail chains and companies have formal training programs for management trainees that include both classroom and on-site training. Training time may be as brief as 1 week but may also last more than 1 year in organizations that require trainees to gain experience during all sales seasons.

Ordinarily, classroom training includes topics such as interviewing and customer service skills, employee and inventory management, and scheduling. Management trainees may work in one specific department while training on the job, or they may rotate through several departments to gain a well-rounded knowledge of the company's operation. Training programs for retail franchises are generally extensive, covering all functions of the company's operation, including budgeting, marketing, management, finance, purchasing, product preparation, human resource management, and compensation. College graduates usually can enter management training programs directly.

Sales worker supervisors must get along with all types of people. They need initiative, self-discipline, good judgment, and decisiveness. Patience and a conciliatory temperament are necessary when dealing with demanding customers. Sales worker supervisors also must be able to motivate, organize, and direct the work of subordinates and communicate clearly and persuasively with customers and other supervisors.

Individuals who display leadership and team-building skills, self-confidence, motivation, and decisiveness become candidates for promotion to assistant manager or manager. A postsecondary degree may speed a sales worker supervisor's advancement into management because employers view it as a sign of motivation and maturity—qualities deemed important for promotion to more responsible positions. In many retail establishments, managers are promoted from within the company. In small retail establishments, where the number of positions is limited, advancement to a higher management position may come slowly. Large establishments often have extensive career ladder programs and may offer supervisors the opportunity to transfer to another store in the chain or to the central office if an opening occurs. Although promotions may occur more quickly in large establishments, some managers may need to relocate every several years in order to advance. Supervisors also can become advertising, marketing, promotions, public relations, and sales managers (workers who coordinate marketing plans, monitor sales, and propose advertisements and promotions) or purchasing managers, buyers, and purchasing agents (workers who purchase goods and supplies for their organization or for resale).

Some supervisors who have worked in their industry for a long time open their own stores or sales firms. However, retail trade and sales occupations are highly competitive, and although many independent owners succeed, some fail to cover expenses and eventually go out of business. To prosper, owners usually need good business sense and strong customer service and public relations skills.

Employment

Sales worker supervisors held about 2.2 million jobs in 2004. Approximately 36 percent were self-employed, most of whom were store owners. About 43 percent were wage and salary sales worker supervisors employed in the retail sector; some of the largest employers were grocery stores, department stores, motor vehicle and parts dealers, and clothing and clothing accessory stores. The remaining sales worker supervisors worked in nonretail establishments.

Job Outlook

Candidates who have retail experience—as a retail salesperson, cashier, or customer service representative, for example—will have the best opportunities for jobs as sales worker supervisors. As in other fields, competition is expected for supervisory jobs,

particularly those with the most attractive earnings and working conditions.

Employment of sales worker supervisors is expected to grow more slowly than the average for all occupations through the year 2014. Growth in the occupation will be restrained somewhat as retail companies hire more sales staff and increase the responsibilities of sales worker supervisors. Many job openings will occur as experienced supervisors move into higher levels of management, transfer to other occupations, or leave the labor force. However, as with other supervisory and managerial occupations, job turnover is relatively low.

The Internet and electronic commerce are creating new opportunities to reach and communicate with potential customers. Some firms are hiring Internet sales managers, who are in charge of maintaining an Internet site and answering inquiries relating to the product, to prices, and to the terms of delivery—a trend that will increase demand for these supervisors. Overall, Internet sales and electronic commerce may reduce the number of additional sales workers needed, thus reducing the number of additional supervisors required. However, the impact of electronic commerce on employment of sales worker supervisors should be minimal.

Projected employment growth of sales worker supervisors will mirror, in part, the patterns of employment growth in the industries in which they work. For example, faster-than-average employment growth is expected in many of the rapidly growing service-providing industries. In contrast, the number of self-employed sales worker supervisors is expected to decline as independent retailers face increasing competition from national chains.

Unlike mid-level and top-level managers, retail store managers generally will not be affected by the restructuring and consolidation taking place at the corporate headquarters of many retail chains.

Earnings

Salaries of sales worker supervisors vary substantially, depending on the level of responsibility the individual has; the person's length of service; and the type, size, and location of the firm.

In May 2004, median annual earnings of salaried supervisors of retail sales workers, including commissions, were $32,720. The middle 50 percent earned between $25,120 and $43,110 a year. The lowest 10 percent earned less than $20,110, and the highest 10 percent earned more than $58,400 a year. Median annual earnings in the industries employing the largest numbers of salaried supervisors of retail sales workers in May 2004 were as follows:

Building material and supplies dealers	$34,210
Grocery stores	31,360
Clothing stores	30,660
Other general merchandise stores	30,150
Gasoline stations	27,510

In May 2004, median annual earnings of salaried supervisors of nonretail sales workers, including commissions, were $59,300. The middle 50 percent earned between $43,350 and $87,580 a year. The lowest 10 percent earned less than $30,830, and the highest 10 percent earned more than $127,870 a year. Median annual earnings in the industries employing the largest numbers of salaried supervisors of nonretail sales workers in May 2004 were as follows:

Wholesale electronic markets and agents and
brokers $79,480

Professional and commercial equipment and
supplies merchant wholesalers 72,320

Machinery, equipment, and supplies merchant
wholesalers 61,150

Grocery and related product wholesalers 59,130

Postal Service 52,490

Compensation systems vary by type of establishment and by merchandise sold. Many supervisors receive a commission or a combination of salary and commission. Under a commission system, supervisors receive a percentage of department or store sales. Thus, supervisors have the opportunity to increase their earnings considerably, but their earnings depend on their ability to sell their product and the condition of the economy. Those who sell large amounts of merchandise or exceed sales goals often receive bonuses or other awards.

Related Occupations

Sales worker supervisors serve customers, supervise workers, and direct and coordinate the operations of an establishment. Others with similar responsibilities include financial managers, food service managers, lodging managers, and medical and health services managers.

Sources of Additional Information

Information on employment opportunities for sales worker supervisors may be obtained from the employment offices of various retail establishments or from state employment service offices.

General information on management careers in retail establishments is available from

▶ National Retail Federation, 325 7th St. NW, Suite 1100, Washington, DC 20004.

Information on management careers in grocery stores and on schools offering related programs is available from

▶ International Food Service Distributors Association, 201 Park Washington Ct., Falls Church, VA 22046-4521. Internet: http://www.ifdaonline.org

Information about management careers and training programs in the motor vehicle dealers industry is available from

▶ National Automobile Dealers Association, Public Relations Dept., 8400 Westpark Dr., McLean, VA 22102-3591. Internet: http://www.nada.org

Information about management careers in convenience stores is available from

▶ National Association of Convenience Stores, 1600 Duke St., Alexandria, VA 22314-3436.

Science Technicians

(O*NET 19-4011.01, 19-4011.02, 19-4021.00, 19-4031.00, 19-4041.01, 19-4041.02, 19-4051.01, 19-4051.02, 19-4091.00, 19-4092.00, and 19-4093.00)

Significant Points

- Science technicians in production jobs can be employed on day, evening, or night shifts; some other technicians work outdoors, sometimes in remote locations.

- Many employers prefer applicants who have at least 2 years of specialized training or an associate's degree.

- Projected job growth varies among occupational specialties; for example, forensic science technicians will grow much faster than average, while chemical technicians will grow more slowly than average.

- Job opportunities are expected to be best for graduates of applied science technology programs.

Nature of the Work

Science technicians use the principles and theories of science and mathematics to solve problems in research and development and to help invent and improve products and processes. However, their jobs are more practically oriented than those of scientists. Technicians set up, operate, and maintain laboratory instruments; monitor experiments; make observations; calculate and record results; and often develop conclusions. They must keep detailed logs of all of their work-related activities. Those who perform production work monitor manufacturing processes and may be involved in ensuring quality by testing products for proper proportions of ingredients, for purity, or for strength and durability.

As laboratory instrumentation and procedures have become more complex, the role of science technicians in research and development has expanded. In addition to performing routine tasks, many technicians now develop and adapt laboratory procedures to achieve the best results, interpret data, and devise solutions to problems under the direction of scientists. Moreover, technicians must master the laboratory equipment so that they can adjust settings when necessary and recognize when equipment is malfunctioning.

The increasing use of robotics to perform many routine tasks has freed technicians to operate more sophisticated laboratory equipment. Science technicians make extensive use of computers, computer-interfaced equipment, robotics, and high-technology industrial applications such as biological engineering.

Most science technicians specialize, learning skills and working in the same disciplines in which scientists work. Occupational titles, therefore, tend to follow the same structure as those for scientists. *Agricultural technicians* work with agricultural scientists in food, fiber, and animal research, production, and processing. Some conduct tests and experiments to improve the yield and quality of crops or to increase the resistance of plants and animals to disease, insects, or other hazards. Other agricultural technicians breed animals for the purpose of investigating nutrition. *Food science technicians* assist food scientists and technologists in research and development, production technology, and quality control. For example, food science technicians may conduct tests on food additives and preservatives to ensure compliance with Food and Drug Administration regulations regarding color, texture, and nutrients. These technicians analyze, record, and compile test results; order supplies to maintain laboratory inventory; and clean and sterilize laboratory equipment.

Biological technicians work with biologists studying living organisms. Many assist scientists who conduct medical research—helping to find a cure for cancer or AIDS, for example. Those who work in pharmaceutical companies help develop and manufacture medicinal and pharmaceutical preparations. Those working in the field of microbiology generally work as laboratory assistants, studying living organisms and infectious agents. Biological technicians also analyze organic substances, such as blood, food, and drugs, and some examine evidence in a forensic science laboratory. Biological technicians working in biotechnology laboratories use the knowledge and techniques gained from basic research by scientists, including gene splicing and recombinant DNA, and apply them in product development.

Chemical technicians work with chemists and chemical engineers, developing and using chemicals and related products and equipment. Generally, there are two types of chemical technicians: research and development technicians, who work in experimental laboratories, and process control technicians, who work in manufacturing or other industrial plants. Many research and development chemical technicians conduct a variety of laboratory procedures, from routine process control to complex research projects. For example, they may collect and analyze samples of air and water to monitor pollution levels, or they may produce compounds through complex organic synthesis. Most process technicians work in manufacturing, testing packaging for design, integrity of materials, and environmental acceptability. Often, process technicians who work in plants also focus on quality assurance, monitoring product quality or production processes and developing new production techniques. A few work in shipping to provide technical support and expertise for these functions.

Environmental science and protection technicians perform laboratory and field tests to monitor environmental resources and determine the contaminants and sources of pollution in the environment. They may collect samples for testing or be involved in abating, controlling, or remediating sources of environmental pollution. Some are responsible for waste management operations, control and management of hazardous materials inventory, or general activities involving regulatory compliance. Many environmental science technicians employed at private consulting firms work directly under the supervision of an environmental scientist.

Forensic science technicians investigate crimes by collecting and analyzing physical evidence. Often, they specialize in areas such as DNA analysis or firearm examination, performing tests on weapons or on substances such as fiber, glass, hair, tissue, and body fluids to determine their significance to the investigation. Proper collection and storage methods are important to protect the evidence. Forensic science technicians also prepare reports to document their findings and the laboratory techniques used, and they may provide information and expert opinion to investigators. When criminal cases come to trial, forensic science technicians often give testimony, as expert witnesses, on specific laboratory findings by identifying and classifying substances, materials, and other evidence collected at the scene of a crime. Some forensic science technicians work closely with other experts or technicians. For example, a forensic science technician may consult either a medical expert about the exact time and cause of a death or a technician who specializes in DNA typing in hopes of matching a DNA type to a suspect.

Forest and conservation technicians compile data on the size, content, and condition of forest land tracts. These workers usually work in a forest under the supervision of a forester, conducting specific tasks such as measuring timber, supervising harvesting operations, assisting in roadbuilding operations, and locating property lines and features. They also may gather basic information, such as data on species and populations of trees, disease and insect damage, tree seedling mortality, and conditions that may pose a fire hazard. In addition, forest and conservation technicians train and lead forest and conservation workers in seasonal activities, such as planting tree seedlings, putting out forest fires, and maintaining recreational facilities. Increasing numbers of forest and conservation technicians work in urban forestry—the study of individual trees in cities—and other nontraditional specialties, rather than in forests or rural areas.

Geological and petroleum technicians measure and record physical and geologic conditions in oil or gas wells, using advanced instruments lowered into the wells or analyzing the mud from the wells. In oil and gas exploration, these technicians collect and examine geological data or use scanning electron microscopes to test geological samples to determine their petroleum content and their mineral and element composition. Some petroleum technicians, called *scouts*, collect information about oil and gas well-drilling operations, geological and geophysical prospecting, and land or lease contracts.

Nuclear technicians operate nuclear test and research equipment, monitor radiation, and assist nuclear engineers and physicists in research. Some also operate remote control equipment to manipulate radioactive materials or materials to be exposed to radioactivity.

Other science technicians collect weather information or assist oceanographers.

Working Conditions

Science technicians work under a wide variety of conditions. Most work indoors, usually in laboratories, and have regular hours. Some occasionally work irregular hours to monitor experiments that cannot be completed during regular working hours. Production technicians often work in 8-hour shifts around the clock. Others, such as agricultural, forest and conservation, geological and petroleum, and environmental science and protection technicians, perform much of their work outdoors, sometimes in remote locations.

Some science technicians may be exposed to hazards from equipment, chemicals, or toxic materials. Chemical technicians sometimes work with toxic chemicals or radioactive isotopes, nuclear technicians may be exposed to radiation, and biological technicians sometimes work with disease-causing organisms or radioactive agents. Forensic science technicians often are exposed to human body fluids and firearms. However, these working conditions pose little risk if proper safety procedures are followed. For forensic science technicians, collecting evidence from crime scenes can be distressing and unpleasant.

Training, Other Qualifications, and Advancement

There are several ways to qualify for a job as a science technician. Many employers prefer applicants who have at least 2 years of specialized training or an associate's degree in applied science or science-related technology. Because employers' preferences vary, however, some science technicians have a bachelor's degree in chemistry, biology, or forensic science or have taken several science and math courses at 4-year colleges.

Many technical and community colleges offer associate's degrees in a specific technology or a more general education in science and mathematics. A number of 2-year associate's degree programs are designed to provide easy transfer to a 4-year college or university. Technical institutes usually offer technician training, but provide less theory and general education than do technical or community colleges. The length of programs at technical institutes varies, although 1-year certificate programs and 2-year associate's degree programs are common.

Approximately 20 colleges or universities offer a bachelor's degree program in forensic science; about another 20 schools offer a bachelor-of-science degree in chemistry, biochemistry, or genetic engineering with an emphasis on forensic science or criminology; and a few additional schools offer a bachelor-of-science degree with an emphasis in a specialty area, such as criminology, pathology, jurisprudence, investigation, odontology, toxicology, or forensic accounting. In contrast to some other science technician positions that require only a 2-year degree, forensic science positions usually require a 4-year degree to work in the field. Knowledge and understanding of legal procedures also can be helpful. Prospective forestry and conservation technicians can choose from more than 20 associate's degree programs in forest technology accredited by the Society of American Foresters.

Most chemical process technicians have a 2-year degree, usually an associate's degree in process technology, although in some cases a high school diploma is sufficient. These workers usually receive additional on-the-job training. Entry-level workers whose college training encompasses extensive hands-on experience with a variety of diagnostic laboratory equipment generally require less on-the-job training. Those with a high school diploma typically begin work as trainees under the direct supervision of a more experienced process technician. Many with only a high school diploma eventually earn a 2-year degree in process technology, often paid for by their employer.

Some schools offer cooperative-education or internship programs, allowing students the opportunity to work at a local company or some other workplace while attending classes during alternate terms. Participation in such programs can significantly enhance a student's employment prospects.

Persons interested in careers as science technicians should take as many high school science and math courses as possible. Science courses taken beyond high school, in an associate's or bachelor's degree program, should be laboratory oriented, with an emphasis on bench skills. A solid background in applied basic chemistry, physics, and math is vital. Because computers often are used in research and development laboratories, technicians should have strong computer skills, especially in computer modeling. Communication skills also are important: Technicians often are required to report their findings both orally and in writing. In addition, technicians should be able to work well with others, because teamwork is common. Organizational ability, an eye for detail, and skill in interpreting scientific results are important as well. A high mechanical aptitude, attention to detail, and analytical thinking are all important characteristics of science technicians.

Prospective science technicians can acquire good career preparation through 2-year formal training programs that combine the teaching of scientific principles and theory with practical hands-on application in a laboratory setting with up-to-date equipment. Graduates of 4-year bachelor's degree programs in science who have considerable experience in laboratory-based courses, have completed internships, or have held summer jobs in laboratories also are well qualified for science technician positions and are preferred by some employers. However, those with a bachelor's degree who accept technician jobs generally cannot find employment that uses their more advanced academic education.

Technicians usually begin work as trainees in routine positions under the direct supervision of a scientist or a more experienced technician. Job candidates whose training or educational background encompasses extensive hands-on experience with a variety of laboratory equipment, including computers and related equipment, usually require a short period of on-the-job training. As they gain experience, technicians take on more responsibility and carry out assignments under only general supervision, and some eventually become supervisors. However, technicians employed at universities often have their fortunes tied to those of particular professors; when those professors retire or leave, these technicians face uncertain employment prospects.

Employment

Science technicians held about 324,000 jobs in 2004. As indicated by the following tabulation, chemical and biological technicians accounted for 39 percent of all jobs:

Biological technicians	64,000
Chemical technicians	62,000
Forest and conservation technicians	33,000
Environmental science and protection technicians, including health	31,000
Agricultural and food science technicians	23,000
Geological and petroleum technicians	11,000
Forensic science technicians	9,800
Nuclear technicians	7,300

Chemical technicians held jobs in a wide range of manufacturing and service-providing industries. Thirty-five percent worked in chemical manufacturing and another 26 percent worked in professional, scientific, or technical services firms. About 27 percent of biological technicians also worked in professional, scientific, or technical services firms; most other biological technicians worked in pharmaceutical and medicine manufacturing or for federal, state, or local governments. Significant numbers of environmental science and protection technicians also worked for state and local governments and professional, scientific, and technical services firms. About 75 percent of forest and conservation technicians held jobs in the federal government; another 13 percent worked for state governments. Around 18 percent of agricultural and food science technicians worked for food-processing companies; most of the rest worked for scientific research and development services firms and state governments. Approximately 23 percent of all geological and petroleum technicians worked for oil and gas extraction companies, and forensic science technicians worked primarily for state and local governments.

Job Outlook

Job opportunities are expected to be best for graduates of applied science technology programs who are well trained on equipment used in industrial and government laboratories and production facilities. As the instrumentation and techniques used in industrial research, development, and production become increasingly more complex, employers are seeking individuals with highly developed technical and communication skills.

Overall employment of science technicians is expected to increase about as fast as the average for all occupations through the year 2014. The continued growth of scientific and medical research—particularly research related to biotechnology—as well as the development and production of technical products should stimulate demand for science technicians in many industries. The increase in the number of biological technicians will be about as fast as average, as the growing number of agricultural and medicinal products developed with the use of biotechnology techniques will boost demand for these workers. Also, stronger competition among pharmaceutical companies and an aging population are expected to contribute to the need for innovative and improved drugs, further spurring demand for biological technicians. The fastest employment growth of biological technicians should occur in the pharmaceutical and medicine manufacturing industry and educational services.

Job growth for chemical technicians is projected to be slower than average. The chemical manufacturing industry, the major employer of chemical technicians, is anticipated to experience a decline in overall employment as companies downsize and turn to outside contractors to provide specialized services. Job opportunities are expected to be more plentiful in pharmaceutical and medicine manufacturing as the public continues to demand newer and better pharmaceuticals. To meet this demand, pharmaceutical manufacturing firms are expected to continue to devote money to research and development, either through in-house teams or, increasingly, by contracting to professional, scientific, and technical services firms, spurring employment growth of chemical technicians in that industry. An increasing focus on quality assurance will require a greater number of process technicians, further stimulating demand for these workers.

Employment of environmental science and protection technicians should grow about as fast as the average; these workers will be needed to help regulate waste products; to collect air, water, and soil samples for measuring levels of pollutants; to monitor compliance with environmental regulations; and to clean up contaminated sites.

Limited demand for forest and conservation technicians within the federal government will lead to slower-than-average growth in this occupation, due to general downsizing and continued reductions in timber management on federal lands. Opportunities at state and local governments within specialties such as urban forestry and geographic information systems (GIS)—a locator system that uses satellites—may, however, provide some new jobs. In addition, an increased emphasis on specific conservation issues, such as environmental protection, preservation of water resources, and control of exotic and invasive pests, may provide some employment opportunities. Few opportunities will be available in the private sector.

Employment of agricultural and food science technicians is projected to grow about as fast as the average. Best opportunities will be in specific segments of the food-processing industry and in agricultural biotechnology, specifically in scientific research and development services. Research—particularly biotechnological research—will be necessary as it becomes increasingly important to balance greater agricultural output with protection and preservation of soil, water, and the ecosystem. In particular, research will be needed to combat insects and diseases as they further adapt to pesticides and as soil fertility and water quality continue to need improvement. State and local government also should provide many opportunities due to projected increases in employment and as the need to replace retiring workers is expected to accelerate.

Jobs for forensic science technicians are expected to increase much faster than average. Crime scene technicians who work for state public safety departments should experience favorable employment prospects. Jobseekers with a 4-year degree in a forensic science will enjoy much better opportunities than those with only a 2-year degree.

Slower-than-average employment growth is expected for geological and petroleum technicians because employment in the oil and gas extraction and mining industries, among the largest employers of geological and petroleum technicians, is expected to decline. Due to a lack of qualified candidates, however, prospective jobseekers should experience little competition for positions, especially in energy-related fields. Job opportunities also will be favorable in professional, scientific, and technical services firms because geological and petroleum technicians will be needed to assist environmental scientists and geoscientists as they provide consultation services for companies regarding environmental policy and federal government mandates, such as those requiring lower sulfur emissions.

Along with opportunities created by growth, many job openings should arise from the need to replace technicians who retire or leave the labor force for other reasons. During periods of economic recession, science technicians may be laid off.

Earnings

Median hourly earnings of science technicians in May 2004 were as follows:

Nuclear technicians $28.46

Forensic science technicians 21.16

Geological and petroleum technicians 19.35

Chemical technicians 18.35

Environmental science and protection technicians,
including health 16.99

Biological technicians 15.97

Agricultural and food science technicians 14.29

Forest and conservation technicians......................13.14

In 2005, the average annual salary in nonsupervisory, supervisory, and managerial positions in the federal government was $38,443 for biological science technicians, $50,264 for physical science technicians, $62,854 for geodetic technicians, $48,238 for hydrologic technicians, and $58,725 for meteorological technicians.

Related Occupations

Other technicians who apply scientific principles at a level usually acquired in 2-year associate's degree programs include engineering technicians, broadcast and sound engineering technicians and radio operators, drafters, and health technologists and technicians, especially clinical laboratory technologists and technicians, diagnostic medical sonographers, and radiologic technologists and technicians.

Sources of Additional Information

For information about a career as a chemical technician, contact

▸ American Chemical Society, Education Division, Career Publications, 1155 16th St. NW, Washington, DC 20036. Internet: http://www.acs.org

For career information and a list of undergraduate, graduate, and doctoral programs in forensic sciences, contact

▸ American Academy of Forensic Sciences, P.O. Box 669, Colorado Springs, CO, 80901. Internet: http://www.aafs.org

For general information on forestry technicians and a list of schools offering education in forestry, send a self-addressed, stamped business envelope to

▸ Society of American Foresters, 5400 Grosvenor Ln., Bethesda, MD 20814. Internet: http://www.safnet.org

Secretaries and Administrative Assistants

(O*NET 43-6011.00, 43-6012.00, 43-6013.00, and 43-6014.00)

Significant Points

■ Numerous job openings will result from the need to replace workers who leave this very large occupation each year.

■ Opportunities should be best for applicants with extensive knowledge of software applications.

■ Increasing office automation and organizational restructuring will lead to slower-than-average growth in overall employment of secretaries and administrative assistants, but average growth is projected for legal and medical secretaries.

Nature of the Work

As the reliance on technology continues to expand in offices, the role of the office professional has greatly evolved. Office automation and organizational restructuring have led secretaries and administrative assistants to assume responsibilities once reserved for managerial and professional staff. Many secretaries and administrative assistants now provide training and orientation for new staff, conduct research on the Internet, and operate and troubleshoot new office technologies. In spite of these changes, however, the core responsibilities for secretaries and administrative assistants have remained much the same: performing and coordinating an office's administrative activities and storing, retrieving, and integrating information for dissemination to staff and clients.

Secretaries and administrative assistants are responsible for a variety of administrative and clerical duties necessary to run an organization efficiently. They serve as information and communication managers for an office; plan and schedule meetings and appointments; organize and maintain paper and electronic files; manage projects; conduct research; and disseminate information by using the telephone, mail services, Web sites, and e-mail. They also may handle travel and guest arrangements.

Secretaries and administrative assistants are aided in these tasks by a variety of office equipment, such as fax machines, photocopiers, scanners, and videoconferencing and telephone systems. In addition, secretaries and administrative assistants often use computers to do tasks previously handled by managers and professionals: create spreadsheets; compose correspondence; manage databases; and create presentations, reports, and documents using desktop publishing software and digital graphics. They also may negotiate with vendors, maintain and examine leased equipment, purchase supplies, manage areas such as stockrooms or corporate libraries, and retrieve data from various sources. At the same time, managers and professionals have assumed many tasks traditionally assigned to secretaries and administrative assistants, such as keyboarding and answering the telephone. Because secretaries and administrative assistants often are not responsible for dictation and word processing, they have time to support more members of the executive staff. In a number of organizations, secretaries and administrative assistants work in teams to work flexibly and share their expertise.

Specific job duties vary with experience and titles. *Executive secretaries and administrative assistants*, for example, may perform fewer clerical tasks than do secretaries. In addition to arranging conference calls and scheduling meetings, they may handle more complex responsibilities such as conducting research, preparing statistical reports, training employees, and hiring and supervising other clerical staff.

Some secretaries and administrative assistants, such as legal and medical secretaries, perform highly specialized work requiring knowledge of technical terminology and procedures. For instance, *legal secretaries* prepare correspondence and legal papers such as summonses, complaints, motions, responses, and subpoenas under the supervision of an attorney or a paralegal. They also may review legal journals and assist with legal research—for example, by verifying quotes and citations in legal briefs. *Medical secretaries* transcribe dictation, prepare correspondence, and assist physicians or medical scientists with reports, speeches, articles, and conference proceedings. They also record simple medical histories, arrange for patients to be hospitalized, and order supplies. Most medical secretaries need to be familiar with insurance rules, billing practices, and hospital or laboratory procedures. Other technical secretaries who assist engineers or scientists may prepare correspondence, maintain their organization's technical library, and gather and edit materials for scientific papers.

Working Conditions

Secretaries and administrative assistants usually work in schools, hospitals, corporate settings, government agencies, or legal and medical offices. Their jobs often involve sitting for long periods. If they spend a lot of time keyboarding, particularly at a computer monitor, they may encounter problems of eyestrain, stress, and repetitive motion ailments such as carpal tunnel syndrome.

Office work can lend itself to alternative or flexible working arrangements, such as part-time work or telecommuting—especially if the job requires extensive computer use. About 19 percent of secretaries work part time, and many others work in temporary positions. A few participate in job-sharing arrangements, in which two people divide responsibility for a single job. The majority of secretaries and administrative assistants, however, are full-time employees who work a standard 40-hour week.

Training, Other Qualifications, and Advancement

High school graduates who have basic office skills may qualify for entry-level secretarial positions. However, employers increasingly require extensive knowledge of software applications, such as word processing, spreadsheets, and database management.

Secretaries and administrative assistants should be proficient in keyboarding and good at spelling, punctuation, grammar, and oral communication. Employers also look for good customer service and interpersonal skills because secretaries and administrative assistants must be tactful in their dealings with people. Discretion, good judgment, organizational or management ability, initiative, and the ability to work independently are especially important for higher-level administrative positions.

As office automation continues to evolve, retraining and continuing education will remain integral parts of secretarial jobs. Changes in the office environment have increased the demand for secretaries and administrative assistants who are adaptable and versatile.

Secretaries and administrative assistants may have to attend classes or participate in online education to learn how to operate new office technologies, such as information storage systems, scanners, the Internet, or new or updated software packages. They also may assist in selecting and maintaining office equipment.

Secretaries and administrative assistants acquire skills in various ways. Training ranges from high school vocational education programs that teach office skills and keyboarding to 1- and 2-year programs in office administration offered by business schools, vocational-technical institutes, and community colleges. Many temporary placement agencies also provide formal training in computer and office skills. However, many skills tend to be acquired through on-the-job instruction by other employees or by equipment and software vendors. Specialized training programs are available for students planning to become medical or legal secretaries or administrative technology specialists. Bachelor's degrees and professional certifications are becoming increasingly important as business continues to become more global.

Testing and certification for proficiency in entry-level office skills is available through organizations such as the International Association of Administrative Professionals; National Association of Legal Secretaries (NALS), Inc.; and Legal Secretaries International, Inc. As secretaries and administrative assistants gain experience, they can earn several different designations. Prominent designations include the Certified Professional Secretary (CPS) and the Certified Administrative Professional (CAP), which can be earned by meeting certain experience or educational requirements and passing an examination. Similarly, those with 1 year of experience in the legal field, or who have concluded an approved training course and who want to be certified as a legal support professional, can acquire the Accredited Legal Secretary (ALS) designation through a testing process administered by NALS. NALS offers two additional designations: Professional Legal Secretary (PLS), considered an advanced certification for legal support professionals, and a designation for proficiency as a paralegal. Legal Secretaries International confers the Certified Legal Secretary Specialist (CLSS) designation in areas such as intellectual property, criminal law, civil litigation, probate, and business law to those who have 5 years of legal experience and pass an examination. In some instances, certain requirements may be waived.

Secretaries and administrative assistants generally advance by being promoted to other administrative positions with more responsibilities. Qualified administrative assistants who broaden their knowledge of a company's operations and enhance their skills may be promoted to senior or executive secretary or administrative assistant, clerical supervisor, or office manager. Secretaries with word processing or data entry experience can advance to jobs as word processing or data entry trainers, supervisors, or managers within their own firms or in a secretarial, word processing, or data entry service bureau. Secretarial and administrative support experience also can lead to jobs such as instructor or sales representative with manufacturers of software or computer equipment. With additional training, many legal secretaries become paralegals.

Employment

Secretaries and administrative assistants held about 4.1 million jobs in 2004, ranking among the largest occupations in the U.S. economy. The following tabulation shows the distribution of employment by secretarial specialty:

Secretaries, except legal, medical, and executive	1,934,000
Executive secretaries and administrative assistants	1,547,000
Medical secretaries	373,000
Legal secretaries	272,000

Secretaries and administrative assistants are employed in organizations of every type. Around 9 out of 10 secretaries and administrative assistants are employed in service-providing industries, ranging from education and health care to government and retail trade. Most of the rest work for firms engaged in manufacturing or construction.

Job Outlook

Overall employment of secretaries and administrative assistants is expected to grow more slowly than the average for all occupations over the 2004–2014 period. In addition to those resulting from growth, numerous job openings will result from the need to replace workers who transfer to other occupations or leave this very large occupation for other reasons each year. Opportunities should be best for applicants with extensive knowledge of software applications, particularly experienced secretaries and administrative assistants.

Projected employment of secretaries and administrative assistants varies by occupational specialty. Employment growth in the health care and social assistance and legal services industries should lead to average growth for medical and legal secretaries. Employment of executive secretaries and administrative assistants is projected to grow about as fast as the average for all occupations. Growing industries—such as administrative and support services; health care and social assistance; educational services (private); and professional, scientific, and technical services—will continue to generate most new job opportunities. A decline in employment is expected for secretaries, except legal, medical, or executive; they account for about 47 percent of all secretaries and administrative assistants.

Increasing office automation and organizational restructuring will continue to make secretaries and administrative assistants more productive in coming years. Computers, e-mail, scanners, and voice message systems will allow secretaries and administrative assistants to accomplish more in the same amount of time. The use of automated equipment also is changing the distribution of work in many offices. In some cases, such traditional secretarial duties as keyboarding, filing, photocopying, and bookkeeping are being assigned to workers in other units or departments. Professionals and managers increasingly do their own word processing and data entry and handle much of their own correspondence rather than submit the work to secretaries and other support staff. Also, in some law and medical offices, paralegals and medical assistants are assuming some tasks formerly done by secretaries. As other workers assume more of these duties, there is a trend in many offices for professionals and managers to replace the traditional arrangement of one secretary per manager with secretaries and administrative assistants who support the work of systems, departments, or units. This approach often means that secretaries and administrative assistants assume added responsibilities and are seen as valuable members of a team, but it also contributes to the projected decline in the overall number of secretarial and administrative assistant positions.

Developments in office technology are certain to continue, and they will bring about further changes in the work of secretaries and administrative assistants. However, many secretarial and administrative duties are of a personal, interactive nature and, therefore, are not easily automated. Responsibilities such as planning conferences, working with clients, and instructing staff require tact and communication skills. Because technology cannot substitute for these personal skills, secretaries and administrative assistants will continue to play a key role in most organizations.

Earnings

Median annual earnings of executive secretaries and administrative assistants were $34,970 in May 2004. The middle 50 percent earned between $28,500 and $43,430. The lowest 10 percent earned less than $23,810, and the highest 10 percent earned more than $53,460. Median annual earnings in the industries employing the largest numbers of executive secretaries and administrative assistants in May 2004 were

Management of companies and enterprises	$38,950
Local government	36,940
Colleges, universities, and professional schools	34,280
Employment services	31,620
State government	30,750

Median annual earnings of legal secretaries were $36,720 in May 2004. The middle 50 percent earned between $29,070 and $46,390. The lowest 10 percent earned less than $23,270, and the highest 10 percent earned more than $56,590. Medical secretaries earned a median annual salary of $26,540 in May 2004. The middle 50 percent earned between $21,980 and $32,690. The lowest 10 percent earned less than $19,140, and the highest 10 percent earned more than $39,140. Median annual earnings of secretaries, except legal, medical, and executive, were $26,110 in May 2004.

Salaries vary a great deal, however, reflecting differences in skill, experience, and level of responsibility. Certification in this field usually is rewarded by a higher salary.

Related Occupations

Workers in a number of other occupations type, record information, and process paperwork. Among them are bookkeeping, accounting, and auditing clerks; receptionists and information clerks; communications equipment operators; court reporters; human resources assistants, except payroll and timekeeping; computer operators; data entry and information processing workers; paralegals and legal assistants; medical assistants; and medical records and health information technicians. A growing number of secretaries and administrative assistants share in managerial and human resource responsibilities. Occupations requiring these skills include office and administrative support supervisors and managers; computer and information systems managers; administrative services managers; and human resources, training, and labor relations managers and specialists.

Sources of Additional Information

State employment offices provide information about job openings for secretaries and administrative assistants.

For information on the latest trends in the profession, career development advice, and the CPS or CAP designations, contact

▸ International Association of Administrative Professionals, 10502 NW Ambassador Dr., P.O. Box 20404, Kansas City, MO 64195-0404. Internet: http://www.iaap-hq.org

Information on the CLSS designation can be obtained from

▸ Legal Secretaries International Inc. Internet: http://www.legalsecretaries.org

Information on the ALS, PLS, and paralegal certifications are available from

▸ National Association of Legal Secretaries, Inc., 314 East Third St., Suite 210, Tulsa, OK 74120. Internet: http://www.nals.org

Security Guards and Gaming Surveillance Officers

(O*NET 33-9031.00 and 33-9032.00)

Significant Points

■ Opportunities for most jobs should be favorable, but competition is expected for higher-paying positions at facilities requiring longer periods of training and a high level of security, such as nuclear power plants and weapons installations.

■ Because of limited formal training requirements and flexible hours, this occupation attracts many individuals seeking a second or part-time job.

■ Some positions, such as those of armored car guards, are hazardous.

Nature of the Work

Guards, who are also called *security officers*, patrol and inspect property to protect against fire, theft, vandalism, terrorism, and illegal activity. These workers protect their employer's investment, enforce laws on the property, and deter criminal activity and other problems. They use radio and telephone communications to call for assistance from police, fire, or emergency medical services as the situation dictates. Security guards write comprehensive reports outlining their observations and activities during their assigned shift. They also may interview witnesses or victims, prepare case reports, and testify in court.

Although all security guards perform many of the same duties, their specific duties vary with whether the guard works in a "static" security position or on a mobile patrol. Guards assigned to static security positions usually serve the client at one location for a specified length of time. These guards must become closely acquainted with the property and people associated with it and must often monitor alarms and closed-circuit TV cameras. In contrast, guards assigned to mobile patrol duty drive or walk from location to location and conduct security checks within an assigned geographical zone. They may detain or arrest criminal violators, answer service calls concerning criminal activity or problems, and issue traffic violation warnings.

The security guard's job responsibilities also vary with the size, type, and location of the employer. In department stores, guards protect people, records, merchandise, money, and equipment. They often work with undercover store detectives to prevent theft by customers or employees, and they help apprehend shoplifting suspects prior to the arrival of the police. Some shopping centers and theaters have officers who patrol their parking lots to deter car thefts and robberies. In office buildings, banks, and hospitals, guards maintain order and protect the institutions' property, staff, and customers. At air, sea, and rail terminals and other transportation facilities, guards protect people, freight, property, and equipment. Using metal detectors and high-tech equipment, they may screen passengers and visitors for weapons and explosives, ensure that nothing is stolen while a vehicle is being loaded or unloaded, and watch for fires and criminals.

Guards who work in public buildings such as museums or art galleries protect paintings and exhibits by inspecting people and packages entering and leaving the building. In factories, laboratories, government buildings, data-processing centers, and military bases, security officers protect information, products, computer codes, and defense secrets and check the credentials of people and vehicles entering and leaving the premises. Guards working at universities, parks, and sports stadiums perform crowd control, supervise parking and seating, and direct traffic. Security guards stationed at the entrance to bars and places of adult entertainment, such as nightclubs, prevent access by minors, collect cover charges at the door, maintain order among customers, and protect property and patrons.

Armored car guards protect money and valuables during transit. In addition, they protect individuals responsible for making commercial bank deposits from theft or bodily injury. When the armored car arrives at the door of a business, an armed guard enters, signs for the money, and returns to the truck with the valuables in hand. Carrying money between the truck and the business can be extremely hazardous; because of this risk, armored car guards usually wear bulletproof vests.

All security officers must show good judgment and common sense, follow directions and directives from supervisors, testify accurately in court, and follow company policy and guidelines. Guards should have a professional appearance and attitude and be able to interact with the public. They also must be able to take charge and direct others in emergencies or other dangerous incidents. In a large organization, the security manager often is in charge of a trained guard force divided into shifts; in a small organization, a single worker may be responsible for all security.

Gaming surveillance officers, also known as *surveillance agents,* and *gaming investigators* act as security agents for casino managers and patrons. Using primarily audio and video equipment in an observation room, they observe casino operations for irregular activities, such as cheating or theft, by either employees or patrons. They keep recordings that are sometimes used as evidence against alleged criminals in police investigations. Some casinos use a catwalk over one-way mirrors located above the casino floor to augment electronic surveillance equipment. Surveillance agents occasionally leave the surveillance room and walk the casino floor.

Working Conditions

Most security guards and gaming surveillance officers spend considerable time on their feet, either assigned to a specific post or patrolling buildings and grounds. Guards may be stationed at a guard desk inside a building to monitor electronic security and surveillance devices or to check the credentials of persons entering or leaving the premises. They also may be stationed at a guardhouse outside the entrance to a gated facility or community and may use a portable radio or cellular telephone that allows them to be in constant contact with a central station. The work usually is routine, but guards must be constantly alert for threats to themselves and the property they are protecting. Guards who work during the day may have a great deal of contact with other employees and members of the public. Gaming surveillance often takes place behind a bank of monitors controlling several cameras in a casino and thus can cause eyestrain.

Guards usually work at least 8-hour shifts for 40 hours per week and often are on call in case an emergency arises. Some employers have three shifts, and guards rotate to divide daytime, weekend, and holiday work equally. Guards usually eat on the job instead of taking a regular break away from the site. In 2004, 16 percent of guards worked part time, and many individuals held a second job as a guard to supplement their primary earnings.

Training, Other Qualifications, and Advancement

Most states require that guards be licensed. To be licensed as a guard, individuals must usually be at least 18 years old; pass a background check; and complete classroom training in such subjects as property rights, emergency procedures, and detention of suspected criminals. Drug testing often is required and may be random and ongoing.

Many employers of unarmed guards do not have any specific educational requirements. For armed guards, employers usually prefer individuals who are high school graduates or who hold an equivalent certification. Many jobs require a driver's license. For positions as armed guards, employers often seek people who have had responsible experience in other occupations.

Guards who carry weapons must be licensed by the appropriate government authority, and some receive further certification as special police officers, allowing them to make limited types of arrests while on duty. Armed guard positions have more stringent background checks and entry requirements than those of unarmed guards because of greater insurance liability risks. Compared with unarmed security guards, armed guards and special police typically enjoy higher earnings and benefits, greater job security, and more potential for advancement. Usually, they also are given more training and responsibility.

Rigorous hiring and screening programs consisting of background, criminal record, and fingerprint checks are becoming the norm in the occupation. Applicants are expected to have good character references, no serious police record, and good health. They should be mentally alert, emotionally stable, and physically fit to cope with emergencies. Guards who have frequent contact with the public should communicate well.

The amount of training guards receive varies. Training requirements are higher for armed guards because their employers are legally responsible for any use of force. Armed guards receive formal training in areas such as weapons retention and laws covering the use of force.

Many employers give newly hired guards instruction before they start the job and provide on-the-job training. An increasing number of states are making ongoing training a legal requirement for retention of certification. Guards may receive training in protection, public relations, report writing, crisis deterrence, and first aid, as well as specialized training relevant to their particular assignment.

The American Society for Industrial Security International has written voluntary training guidelines that are intended to provide regulating bodies consistent minimum standards for the quality of security services. These guidelines recommend that security guards receive at least 48 hours of training within the first 100 days of employment. The guidelines also suggest that security guards be required to pass a written or performance examination covering topics such as sharing information with law enforcement, crime prevention, handling evidence, the use of force, court testimony, report writing, interpersonal and communication skills, and emergency response procedures. In addition, they recommend annual training and additional firearms training for armed officers.

Guards who are employed at establishments placing a heavy emphasis on security usually receive extensive formal training. For example, guards at nuclear power plants undergo several months of training before being placed on duty—and even then, they perform their tasks only under close supervision. They are taught to use firearms, administer first aid, operate alarm systems and electronic security equipment, and spot and deal with security problems. Guards who are authorized to carry firearms may be periodically tested in their use.

Because many people do not stay long in this occupation, opportunities for advancement are good for those who are career security officers. Most large organizations use a military type of ranking that offers the possibility of advancement in both position and salary. Some guards may advance to supervisor or security manager positions. Guards with management skills may open their own contract security guard agencies. Pay rates vary substantially with the security level of the establishment, so there is also the opportunity to move to higher-paying jobs with increased experience and training.

In addition to possessing the keen observation skills required to perform their jobs, gaming surveillance officers and gaming investigators must have excellent verbal and writing abilities to document violations or suspicious behavior. They also need to be physically fit and have quick reflexes because they sometimes must detain individuals until local law enforcement officials arrive.

Gaming surveillance officers and investigators usually need some training beyond high school, but not a bachelor's degree; previous security experience is a plus. Several educational institutes offer certification programs. Training classes usually are conducted in a casino-like atmosphere and use surveillance camera equipment. Employers prefer either individuals with significant knowledge of casino operations through work experience or those with experience conducting investigations, such as former law enforcement officers.

Employment

Security guards and gaming surveillance officers held over 1.0 million jobs in 2004. Over half of all jobs for security guards were in investigation and security services, including guard and armored car services. These organizations provide security on a contract basis, assigning their guards to buildings and other sites as needed. Most

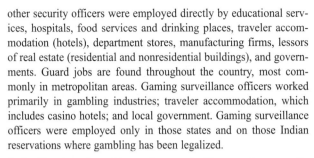

other security officers were employed directly by educational services, hospitals, food services and drinking places, traveler accommodation (hotels), department stores, manufacturing firms, lessors of real estate (residential and nonresidential buildings), and governments. Guard jobs are found throughout the country, most commonly in metropolitan areas. Gaming surveillance officers worked primarily in gambling industries; traveler accommodation, which includes casino hotels; and local government. Gaming surveillance officers were employed only in those states and on those Indian reservations where gambling has been legalized.

A significant number of law enforcement officers work as security guards when they are off duty in order to supplement their incomes. Often working in uniform and with the official cars assigned to them, they add a high-profile security presence to the establishment with which they have contracted. At construction sites and apartment complexes, for example, their presence often deters crime. (Police and detectives are discussed elsewhere in this book.)

Job Outlook

Opportunities for security guards and gaming surveillance officers should be favorable. Numerous job openings will stem from employment growth attributable to the demand for increased security and from the need to replace those who leave this large occupation each year. In addition to full-time job opportunities, the limited training requirements and flexible hours attract many persons seeking part-time or second jobs. However, competition is expected for higher-paying positions that require longer periods of training; these positions usually are found at facilities that require a high level of security, such as nuclear power plants or weapons installations.

Employment of security guards and gaming surveillance officers is expected to grow as fast as the average for all occupations through 2014 as concern about crime, vandalism, and terrorism continues to increase the need for security. Demand for guards also will grow as private security firms increasingly perform duties—such as providing security at public events and in residential neighborhoods—that were formerly handled by police officers. Casinos will continue to hire more surveillance officers as more states legalize gambling and as the number of casinos increases in states where gambling is already legal. In addition, casino security forces will employ more technically trained personnel as technology becomes increasingly important in thwarting casino cheating and theft.

Earnings

Median annual earnings of security guards were $20,320 in May 2004. The middle 50 percent earned between $16,640 and $25,510. The lowest 10 percent earned less than $14,390, and the highest 10 percent earned more than $33,270. Median annual earnings in the industries employing the largest numbers of security guards in May 2004 were as follows:

Elementary and secondary schools	$25,030
General medical and surgical hospitals	24,750
Local government	23,690
Traveler accommodation	21,710
Investigation and security services	19,030

Gaming surveillance officers and gaming investigators had median annual earnings of $25,840 in May 2004. The middle 50 percent earned between $20,430 and $33,790. The lowest 10 percent earned less than $17,710, and the highest 10 percent earned more than $42,420.

Related Occupations

Guards protect property, maintain security, and enforce regulations and standards of conduct in the establishments at which they work. Related security and protective service occupations include correctional officers, police and detectives, and private detectives and investigators.

Sources of Additional Information

Further information about work opportunities for guards is available from local security and guard firms and state employment service offices. Information about licensing requirements for guards may be obtained from the state licensing commission or the state police department. In states where local jurisdictions establish licensing requirements, contact a local government authority such as the sheriff, county executive, or city manager.

Shipping, Receiving, and Traffic Clerks

(O*NET 43-5071.00)

Significant Points

- Many shipping, receiving, and traffic clerk positions are at the entry level and do not require more than a high school diploma.
- Slower-than-average employment growth is expected as a result of increasing automation and the growing use of computers to store and retrieve shipping and receiving records.

Nature of the Work

Shipping, receiving, and traffic clerks keep records of all goods shipped and received. Their duties depend on the size of the establishment they work for and the level of automation used. Larger companies typically are better able to finance the purchase of computers and other equipment to handle some or all of a clerk's responsibilities. In smaller companies, a clerk maintains records, prepares shipments, and accepts deliveries. In both environments, shipping, receiving, and traffic clerks may lift cartons of various sizes.

Shipping clerks keep records of all outgoing shipments. They prepare shipping documents and mailing labels and make sure that orders have been filled correctly. Also, they record items taken from inventory and note when orders were filled. Sometimes they fill the order themselves, obtaining merchandise from the stockroom, noting when inventories run low, and wrapping or packing the goods in shipping containers. They also address and label packages, look up and compute freight or postal rates, and record the weight and cost of each shipment. In addition, shipping clerks may prepare invoices and furnish information about shipments to other parts of the company, such as the accounting department. Once a shipment is checked and ready to go, shipping clerks may move the goods from the plant—sometimes by forklift—to the shipping dock and direct their loading.

Receiving clerks perform tasks similar to those of shipping clerks. They determine whether orders have been filled correctly by verifying incoming shipments against the original order and the accompanying bill of lading or invoice. They make a record of the shipment and the condition of its contents. In many firms, receiving clerks either use hand-held scanners to record barcodes on incoming products or manually enter the information into a computer. These data then can be transferred to the appropriate departments. The shipment is checked for any discrepancies in quantity, price, and discounts. Receiving clerks may route or move shipments to the proper department, warehouse section, or stockroom. They also may arrange for adjustments with shippers whenever merchandise is lost or damaged. Receiving clerks in small businesses may perform some duties similar to those of stock clerks. In larger establishments, receiving clerks may control all receiving platform operations, such as scheduling of trucks, recording of shipments, and handling of damaged goods.

Traffic clerks maintain records on the destination, weight, and charges on all incoming and outgoing freight. They verify rate charges by comparing the classification of materials with rate charts. In many companies, this work may be automated. Information either is scanned or is entered by hand into a computer for use by the accounting department or other departments within the company. Traffic clerks also keep a file of claims for overcharges and for damage to goods in transit.

Working Conditions

Most jobs for shipping, receiving, and traffic clerks involve frequent standing, bending, walking, and stretching. Some lifting and carrying of smaller items also may be involved. Although automated devices have lessened the physical demands of this occupation, their use remains somewhat limited. The work still can be strenuous, even though mechanical material-handling equipment is employed to move heavy items.

The typical workweek is Monday through Friday; however, evening and weekend hours are common in some jobs and may be required in other jobs when large shipments are involved.

Training, Other Qualifications, and Advancement

Many shipping, receiving, and traffic clerk positions are at the entry level and do not require more than a high school diploma. Employers, however, prefer to hire those familiar with computers and other electronic office and business equipment.

Shipping, receiving, and traffic clerks usually learn the job by doing routine tasks under close supervision. They first learn how to count and mark stock, and then they start keeping records and taking inventory. Strength, stamina, good eyesight, and an ability to work at repetitive tasks, sometimes under pressure, are important characteristics.

Shipping, receiving, and traffic clerks who handle jewelry, liquor, or drugs may be bonded.

Shipping, receiving, and traffic clerks check items to be shipped and attach labels to them, making sure that the addresses are correct. Training in the use of automated equipment usually is done informally, on the job. As these occupations become more automated, however, workers in them may need longer periods of training to master the use of the equipment. Advancement opportunities for shipping, receiving, and traffic clerks vary with the place of employment. Shipping, receiving, and traffic clerks are promoted to head clerk, and those with a broad understanding of shipping and receiving may enter a related field, such as industrial traffic management.

Employment

Shipping, receiving, and traffic clerks held about 751,000 jobs in 2004. Almost three out of four were employed in manufacturing or by wholesale and retail establishments. Although jobs for shipping, receiving, and traffic clerks are found throughout the country, most clerks work in urban areas, where shipping depots in factories and wholesale establishments usually are located. (For information on workers who perform duties similar to those of shipping, receiving, and traffic clerks and who are employed by the U.S. Postal Service, see the statement on Postal Service workers elsewhere in this book.)

Job Outlook

Employment of shipping, receiving, and traffic clerks is expected to grow more slowly than the average for all occupations through 2014. Job growth will continue to be limited by automation as all but the smallest firms move to reduce labor costs by using computers to store and retrieve shipping and receiving records.

Methods of handling materials have changed significantly in recent years. Large warehouses are increasingly becoming automated, with equipment such as computerized conveyor systems, robots, computer-directed trucks, and automatic data storage and retrieval systems. Automation, coupled with the growing use of hand-held scanners and personal computers in shipping and receiving departments, has increased the productivity of shipping, receiving, and traffic clerks.

Despite technology, job openings will continue to arise because of increasing economic and trade activity and because certain tasks cannot be automated. For example, someone needs to check shipments before they go out and when they arrive to ensure that everything is in order. In addition, openings will occur because of the need to replace shipping, receiving, and traffic clerks who leave the occupation. Because this is an entry-level occupation, many vacancies are created by a worker's normal career progression.

Earnings

Median annual earnings of shipping, receiving, and traffic clerks in May 2004 were $24,400. The middle 50 percent earned between $19,600 and $30,720. The lowest 10 percent earned less than $16,290, and the highest 10 percent earned more than $37,610.

These workers usually receive the same benefits as most other workers. If uniforms are required, employers generally provide them or offer an allowance to purchase them.

Related Occupations

Shipping, receiving, and traffic clerks record, check, and often store materials that a company receives. They also process and pack goods for shipment. Other workers who perform similar duties are stock clerks and order fillers; production, planning, and expediting clerks; cargo and freight agents; and Postal Service workers.

Sources of Additional Information

Information about job opportunities may be obtained from local employers and local offices of the state employment service.

Social and Human Service Assistants

(O*NET 21-1093.00)

Significant Points

- While a bachelor's degree usually is not required, employers increasingly seek individuals with relevant work experience or education beyond high school.

- Employment is projected to grow much faster than average.

- Job opportunities should be excellent, particularly for applicants with appropriate postsecondary education, but pay is low.

Nature of the Work

Social and human service assistant is a generic term for people with a wide array of job titles, including human service worker, case management aide, social work assistant, community support worker, mental health aide, community outreach worker, life skill counselor, or gerontology aide. They usually work under the direction of workers from a variety of fields, such as nursing, psychiatry, psychology, rehabilitative or physical therapy, or social work. The amount of responsibility and supervision they are given varies a great deal. Some have little direct supervision; others work under close direction.

Social and human service assistants provide direct and indirect client services to ensure that individuals in their care reach their maximum level of functioning. They assess clients' needs, establish their eligibility for benefits and services such as food stamps, Medicaid, or welfare, and help to obtain them. They also arrange for transportation and escorts, if necessary, and provide emotional support. Social and human service assistants monitor and keep case records on clients and report progress to supervisors and case managers.

Social and human service assistants play a variety of roles in a community. They may organize and lead group activities, assist clients in need of counseling or crisis intervention, or administer a food bank or emergency fuel program. In halfway houses, group homes, and government-supported housing programs, they assist adults who need supervision with personal hygiene and daily living skills. They review clients' records, ensure that they take correct doses of medication, talk with family members, and confer with medical personnel and other caregivers to gain better insight into clients' backgrounds and needs. Social and human service assistants also provide emotional support and help clients become involved in their own well-being, in community recreation programs, and in other activities.

In psychiatric hospitals, rehabilitation programs, and outpatient clinics, social and human service assistants work with professional care providers, such as psychiatrists, psychologists, and social workers, to help clients master everyday living skills, communicate more effectively, and get along better with others. They support the client's participation in a treatment plan, such as individual or group counseling or occupational therapy.

Working Conditions

Working conditions of social and human service assistants vary. Some work in offices, clinics, and hospitals, while others work in group homes, shelters, sheltered workshops, and day programs. Many work under close supervision, while others work much of the time on their own, such as those who spend their time in the field visiting clients. Sometimes visiting clients can be dangerous even though most agencies do everything they can to ensure their workers' safety. Most work a 40-hour week, although some work in the evening and on weekends.

The work, while satisfying, can be emotionally draining. Understaffing and relatively low pay may add to the pressure. Turnover is reported to be high, especially among workers without academic preparation for this field.

Training, Other Qualifications, and Advancement

While a bachelor's degree usually is not required for entry into this occupation, employers increasingly seek individuals with relevant work experience or education beyond high school. Certificates or associate degrees in subjects such as social work, human services, gerontology, or one of the social or behavioral sciences meet most employers' requirements. Some jobs may require a bachelor's or master's degree in human services or a related field such as counseling, rehabilitation, or social work.

Human services degree programs have a core curriculum that trains students to observe patients and record information, conduct patient interviews, implement treatment plans, employ problem-solving techniques, handle crisis intervention matters, and use proper case management and referral procedures. General education courses in liberal arts, sciences, and the humanities also are part of the curriculum. Most programs offer the opportunity to take specialized courses related to addictions, gerontology, child protection, and other areas. Many degree programs require completion of a supervised internship.

Educational attainment often influences the kind of work employees may be assigned and the degree of responsibility that may be entrusted to them. For example, workers with no more than a high school education are likely to receive extensive on-the-job training to work in direct-care services, while employees with a college degree might be assigned to do supportive counseling, coordinate program activities, or manage a group home. Social and human service assistants with proven leadership ability, either from previous experience or as a volunteer in the field, often have greater autonomy in their work. Regardless of the academic or work background of employees, most employers provide some form of inservice training, such as seminars and workshops, to their employees.

There may be additional hiring requirements in group homes. For example, employers may require employees to have a valid driver's license or to submit to a criminal background investigation.

Employers try to select applicants who have a strong desire to help others and have effective communication skills, a strong sense of responsibility, and the ability to manage time effectively. Many human services jobs involve direct contact with people who are vulnerable to exploitation or mistreatment; therefore, patience, understanding, and a strong desire to help others are highly valued characteristics.

Formal education almost always is necessary for advancement. In general, advancement requires a bachelor's or master's degree in human services, counseling, rehabilitation, social work, or a related field. Typically, advancement brings case management, supervision, and administration roles.

Employment

Social and human service assistants held about 352,000 jobs in 2004. More than half worked in the health care and social assistance industries. One in three were employed by state and local governments, primarily in public welfare agencies and facilities for mentally disabled and developmentally challenged individuals.

Job Outlook

Job opportunities for social and human service assistants are expected to be excellent, particularly for applicants with appropriate postsecondary education. The number of social and human service assistants is projected to grow much faster than the average for all occupations between 2004 and 2014—ranking the occupation among the most rapidly growing. Many additional job opportunities will arise from the need to replace workers who advance into new positions, retire, or leave the workforce for other reasons. There will be more competition for jobs in urban areas than in rural areas, but qualified applicants should have little difficulty finding employment. Faced with rapid growth in the demand for social and human services, many employers increasingly rely on social and human service assistants to undertake greater responsibility for delivering services to clients.

Opportunities are expected to be good in private social service agencies, which provide such services as adult day care and meal delivery programs. Employment in private agencies will grow as state and local governments continue to contract out services to the private sector in an effort to cut costs. Demand for social services will expand with the growing elderly population, who are more likely to need these services. In addition, more social and human service assistants will be needed to provide services to pregnant teenagers,

the homeless, the mentally disabled and developmentally challenged, and substance abusers. Some private agencies have been employing more social and human service assistants in place of social workers, who are more educated and, thus, more highly paid.

Job training programs also are expected to require additional social and human service assistants. As social welfare policies shift focus from benefit-based programs to work-based initiatives, there will be more demand for people to teach job skills to the people who are new to, or returning to, the workforce.

Residential care establishments should face increased pressures to respond to the needs of the mentally and physically disabled. Many of these patients have been deinstitutionalized and lack the knowledge or the ability to care for themselves. Also, more community-based programs and supportive independent-living sites are expected to be established to house and assist the homeless and the mentally and physically disabled. As substance abusers are increasingly being sent to treatment programs instead of prison, employment of social and human service assistants in substance abuse treatment programs also will grow.

The number of jobs for social and human service assistants in local governments will grow, but not as fast as employment for social and human service assistants in other industries. Employment in the public sector may fluctuate with the level of funding provided by state and local governments. Also, some state and local governments are contracting out selected social services to private agencies in order to save money.

Earnings

Median annual earnings of social and human service assistants were $24,270 in May 2004. The middle 50 percent earned between $19,220 and $30,900. The top 10 percent earned more than $39,620, while the lowest 10 percent earned less than $15,480.

Median annual earnings in the industries employing the largest numbers of social and human service assistants in May 2004 were

State government	$29,270
Local government	28,230
Individual and family services	23,400
Vocational rehabilitation services	21,770
Residential mental retardation, mental health, and substance abuse facilities	20,410

Related Occupations

Workers in other occupations that require skills similar to those of social and human service assistants include social workers; counselors; childcare workers; occupational therapist assistants and aides; physical therapist assistants and aides; and nursing, psychiatric, and home health aides.

Sources of Additional Information

Information on academic programs in human services may be found in most directories of 2-year and 4-year colleges, available at libraries or career counseling centers.

For information on programs and careers in human services, contact

▶ National Organization for Human Services, 5601 Brodie Lane, Suite 620-215, Austin, TX 78745. Internet: http://www.nohse.org

▶ Council for Standards in Human Services Education, Harrisburg Area Community College, Human Services Program, One HACC Dr., Harrisburg, PA 17110-2999. Internet: http://www.cshse.org

Information on job openings may be available from state employment service offices or directly from city, county, or state departments of health, mental health and mental retardation, and human resources.

Stock Clerks and Order Fillers

(O*NET 43-5081.01, 43-5081.02, 43-5081.03, and 43-5081.04)

Significant Points

■ Employers prefer to hire stock clerks and order fillers who are familiar with computers and other electronic office and business equipment.

■ Employment is projected to decline due to the use of automation in factories, warehouses, and stores.

Nature of the Work

Stock clerks and order fillers receive, unpack, check, store, and track merchandise or materials. They keep records of items entering or leaving the stockroom and inspect damaged or spoiled goods. They sort, organize, and mark items with identifying codes, such as price, stock, or inventory control codes, so that inventories can be located quickly and easily. They also may be required to lift cartons of various sizes. In larger establishments, where they may be responsible for only one task, they may be called *stock-control clerks, merchandise distributors*, or *property custodians*. In smaller firms, they also may perform tasks usually handled by shipping and receiving clerks. (A separate description of shipping, receiving, and traffic clerks appears elsewhere in this book.)

In many firms, stock clerks and order fillers use hand-held scanners connected to computers to keep inventories up to date. In retail stores, stock clerks bring merchandise to the sales floor and stock shelves and racks. In stockrooms and warehouses, stock clerks store materials in bins, on floors, or on shelves. Instead of putting the merchandise on the sales floor or on shelves, order fillers take customers' orders and either hold the merchandise until the customers can pick it up or send it to them.

Working Conditions

Working conditions vary considerably by employment setting. Most jobs for stock clerks and order fillers involve frequent standing, bending, walking, and stretching. Some lifting and carrying of smaller items also may be involved. Although automated devices have lessened the physical demands of this occupation, their use remains somewhat limited. Even though mechanical material-handling equipment is employed to move heavy items, the work still can be strenuous.

The typical workweek is Monday through Friday; however, evening and weekend hours are common and may be required when large shipments are involved or when inventory is taken.

Training, Other Qualifications, and Advancement

Many stock clerk and order filler positions are at the entry level and do not require more than a high school diploma. Employers, however, prefer to hire those familiar with computers and other electronic office and business equipment. Typing, filing, recordkeeping, and other clerical skills also are important.

Stock clerks and order fillers usually learn the job by doing routine tasks under close supervision. They learn how to count and mark stock, and then they start keeping records and taking inventory. Strength; stamina; good eyesight; and an ability to work at repetitive tasks, sometimes under pressure, are important characteristics. Stock clerks whose sole responsibility is to bring merchandise to the sales floor to stock shelves and racks need little training. Stock clerks and order fillers who handle jewelry, liquor, or drugs may be bonded.

Training in the use of automated equipment usually is done informally on the job. As this occupation becomes more automated, however, workers may need longer periods of training to master the use of the equipment.

Advancement opportunities for stock clerks and order fillers vary with the place of employment. With additional training, some stock clerks and order fillers advance to jobs as warehouse manager or purchasing agent.

Employment

Stock clerks and order fillers held about 1.6 million jobs in 2004. More than three out of four work in wholesale and retail trade. The greatest numbers are found in grocery stores, followed by department stores. Jobs for stock clerks are found in all parts of the country, but most work in large urban areas that have many large suburban shopping centers, warehouses, and factories.

Job Outlook

Employment of stock clerks and order fillers is projected to decline through 2014 as a result of the use of automation in factories, warehouses, and stores. Because the occupation is very large and many jobs are entry level, however, numerous job openings will occur each year to replace those who transfer to other jobs or leave the labor force.

The growing use of computers for inventory control and the installation of new, automated equipment are expected to inhibit growth in demand for stock clerks and order fillers, especially in manufacturing and wholesale trade industries, where operations are most easily automated. In addition to using computerized inventory control systems, firms in these industries are relying more on sophisticated conveyor belts and automatic high stackers to store and retrieve goods. Also, expanded use of battery-powered, driverless, automatically guided vehicles can be expected.

Employment of stock clerks and order fillers who work in grocery, general merchandise, department, apparel, and accessories stores is expected to be somewhat less affected by automation because much of their work is done manually and is difficult to automate. In addition, the increasing role of large retail outlets and warehouses, as well as catalog, mail, telephone, and Internet shopping services, should bolster employment of stock clerks and order fillers in these sectors of retail trade.

Earnings

Median annual earnings of stock clerks and order fillers in May 2004 were $20,100. The middle 50 percent earned between $16,250 and $25,910. The lowest 10 percent earned less than $13,970, and the highest 10 percent earned more than $33,420.

These workers usually receive the same benefits as most other workers. If uniforms are required, employers generally provide them or offer an allowance to purchase them.

Related Occupations

Workers who also handle, move, organize, store, and keep records of materials include shipping, receiving, and traffic clerks; production, planning, and expediting clerks; cargo and freight agents; and procurement clerks.

Sources of Additional Information

State employment service offices can provide information about job openings for stock clerks and order fillers.

Teacher Assistants

(O*NET 25-9041.00)

Significant Points

■ About 4 in 10 teacher assistants work part time.

■ Educational requirements range from a high school diploma to some college training.

■ Workers with experience in helping special education students, or who can speak a foreign language, will be especially in demand.

Nature of the Work

Teacher assistants provide instructional and clerical support for classroom teachers, allowing teachers more time for lesson planning and teaching. Teacher assistants tutor and assist children in learning class material using the teacher's lesson plans, providing students with individualized attention. Teacher assistants also supervise students in the cafeteria, schoolyard, and hallways or on field trips. They record grades, set up equipment, and help prepare materials for instruction. Teacher assistants also are called teacher aides or instructional aides. Some assistants refer to themselves as paraeducators or paraprofessionals.

Some teacher assistants perform exclusively noninstructional or clerical tasks, such as monitoring nonacademic settings. Playground and lunchroom attendants are examples of such assistants. Most teacher assistants, however, perform a combination of instructional and clerical duties. They generally provide instructional reinforcement to children under the direction and guidance of teachers. They work with students individually or in small groups—listening while students read, reviewing or reinforcing class lessons, or helping them find information for reports. At the secondary school level, teacher assistants often specialize in a certain subject, such as math or science. Teacher assistants often take charge of special projects and prepare equipment or exhibits, such as for a science demonstration. Some assistants work in computer laboratories, helping students using computers and educational software programs.

In addition to instructing, assisting, and supervising students, teacher assistants grade tests and papers, check homework, keep health and attendance records, do typing and filing, and duplicate materials. They also stock supplies, operate audiovisual equipment, and keep classroom equipment in order.

Many teacher assistants work extensively with special education students. As schools become more inclusive, integrating special education students into general education classrooms, teacher assistants in both general education and special education classrooms increasingly assist students with disabilities. Teacher assistants attend to a disabled student's physical needs, including feeding, teaching good grooming habits, or assisting students riding the school bus. They also provide personal attention to students with other special needs, such as those who speak English as a second language or those who need remedial education. Teacher assistants help assess a student's progress by observing performance and recording relevant data.

While the majority of teacher assistants work in primary and secondary educational settings, others work in preschools and other child care centers. Often one or two assistants will work with a lead teacher in order to better provide the individual attention that young children require. In addition to assisting in educational instruction, they also supervise the children at play and assist in feeding and other basic care activities.

Teacher assistants also work with infants and toddlers who have developmental delays or other disabilities. Under the guidance of a teacher or therapist, teacher assistants perform exercises or play games to help the child develop physically and behaviorally. Some teacher assistants work with young adults to help them obtain a job or to apply for community services for the disabled.

Working Conditions

Approximately 4 in 10 teacher assistants work part time. However, even among full-time workers, about 16 percent work less than 40 hours per week. Most assistants who provide educational instruction work the traditional 9- to 10-month school year. Teacher assistants work in a variety of settings—including preschools, child care centers, and religious and community centers, where they work with young adults—but most work in classrooms in elementary, middle, and secondary schools. They also work outdoors supervising recess when weather allows, and they spend much of their time standing, walking, or kneeling.

Seeing students develop and gain appreciation of the joy of learning can be very rewarding. However, working closely with students can be both physically and emotionally tiring. Teacher assistants who work with special education students often perform more strenuous tasks, including lifting, as they help students with their daily routine. Those who perform clerical work may tire of administrative duties such as copying materials or typing.

Training, Other Qualifications, and Advancement

Educational requirements for teacher assistants vary by state or school district and range from a high school diploma to some college training, although employers increasingly prefer applicants with some college training. Teacher assistants with instructional responsibilities usually require more training than do those who do not perform teaching tasks. Federal regulations require teacher assistants with instructional responsibilities in Title I schools—those with a large proportion of students from low-income households—to meet one of three requirements: hold a 2-year or higher degree, have a minimum of 2 years of college, or pass a rigorous state or local assessment. Many schools also require previous experience in working with children and a valid driver's license. Some schools may require the applicant to pass a background check.

A number of 2-year and community colleges offer associate degree or certificate programs that prepare graduates to work as teacher assistants. However, most teacher assistants receive on-the-job training. Those who tutor and review lessons with students must have a thorough understanding of class materials and instructional methods and should be familiar with the organization and operation of a school. Teacher assistants also must know how to operate audiovisual equipment, keep records, and prepare instructional materials, as well as have adequate computer skills.

Teacher assistants should enjoy working with children from a wide range of cultural backgrounds and be able to handle classroom situations with fairness and patience. Teacher assistants also must demonstrate initiative and a willingness to follow a teacher's directions. They must have good writing skills and be able to communicate effectively with students and teachers. Teacher assistants who speak a second language, especially Spanish, are in great demand for communicating with growing numbers of students and parents whose primary language is not English.

Advancement for teacher assistants—usually in the form of higher earnings or increased responsibility—comes primarily with experience or additional education. Some school districts provide time away from the job or tuition reimbursement so that teacher assistants can earn their bachelor's degrees and pursue licensed teaching positions. In return for tuition reimbursement, assistants are often required to teach a certain length of time for the school district.

Employment

Teacher assistants held almost 1.3 million jobs in 2004. Nearly 3 in 4 worked for state and local government education institutions, mostly at the preschool and elementary school level. Private schools, child care centers, and religious organizations employed most of the rest.

Job Outlook

Employment of teacher assistants is expected to grow about as fast as the average for all occupations through 2014. In addition to job openings stemming from employment growth, numerous openings will arise as assistants leave their jobs and must be replaced. Many assistant jobs require limited formal education and offer relatively low pay, so each year many transfer to other occupations or leave the labor force to assume family responsibilities, to return to school, or for other reasons.

School enrollments are projected to increase only slowly over the next decade, but special education students and students for whom English is not their first language—the student populations for which teacher assistants are most needed—are expected to grow faster and increase as a share of the total school-age population. Legislation that requires students with disabilities and non-native English speakers to receive an education "equal" to that of other students, will continue to generate jobs for teacher assistants to accommodate these students' special needs. Children with special needs require much personal attention, and special education teachers, as well as general education teachers with special education students, rely heavily on teacher assistants.

The greater focus on quality and accountability that has been placed on education in recent years also is likely to lead to an increased demand for teacher assistants. Growing numbers of teacher assistants may be needed to help teachers prepare students for standardized testing and to provide extra assistance to students who perform poorly on standardized tests. This growth may be moderated, however, as schools are encouraged to allocate resources to hiring more full teachers for instructional purposes. An increasing number of after-school programs and summer programs also will create new opportunities for teacher assistants.

Opportunities for teacher assistant jobs are expected to be best for persons with at least 2 years of formal education after high school. Persons who can speak a foreign language should be in particular demand in school systems with large numbers of students whose families do not speak English at home. Demand is expected to vary by region of the country. Areas in which the population and school enrollments are expected to grow faster, such as many communities in the South and West, should have rapid growth in the demand for teacher assistants.

Earnings

Median annual earnings of teacher assistants in May 2004 were $19,410. The middle 50 percent earned between $15,410 and $24,320. The lowest 10 percent earned less than $13,010, and the highest 10 percent earned more than $29,220.

Full-time workers usually receive health coverage and other benefits. Teacher assistants who work part time ordinarily do not receive benefits.

In 2004, about 3 out of 10 teacher assistants belonged to unions—mainly the American Federation of Teachers and the National Education Association—which bargain with school systems over wages, hours, and the terms and conditions of employment.

Related Occupations

Teacher assistants who instruct children have duties similar to those of preschool, kindergarten, elementary, middle, and secondary school teachers, as well as special education teachers. However, teacher assistants do not have the same level of responsibility or training. The support activities of teacher assistants and their educational backgrounds are similar to those of childcare workers, library technicians, and library assistants. Teacher assistants who work with children with disabilities perform many of the same functions as occupational therapy assistants and aides.

Sources of Additional Information

For information on teacher assistants, including training and certification, contact

▸ American Federation of Teachers, Paraprofessional and School Related Personnel Division, 555 New Jersey Ave. NW, Washington, DC 20001.

▸ National Education Association, Educational Support Personnel Division, 1201 16th St. NW, Washington, DC 20036.

For information on a career as a teacher assistant, contact

▸ National Resource Center for Paraprofessionals, 6526 Old Main Hill, Utah State University, Logan, UT 84322. Internet: http://www.nrcpara.org

Human resource departments of school systems, school administrators, and state departments of education also can provide details about employment opportunities and required qualifications for teacher assistant jobs.

Teachers—Self-Enrichment Education

(O*NET 25-3021.00)

Significant Points

■ Part-time jobs, a lack of benefits, and self-employed workers are relatively common among self-enrichment teachers.

■ Teachers should have knowledge and enthusiasm for their subject, but little formal training is required.

■ Demand for self-enrichment courses is expected to rise as more people embrace lifelong learning and as growth continues in the numbers of retirees, who have more free time to take classes.

Nature of the Work

Self-enrichment teachers provide instruction in a wide variety of subjects that students take for personal enrichment or self-improvement. Some teach a series of classes that provide students with useful life skills, such as cooking, personal finance, and time management classes. Others provide group instruction intended solely for recreation, such as photography, pottery, and painting courses. Many others provide one-on-one instruction in a variety of subjects, including dance, singing, or playing a musical instrument. The instruction self-enrichment teachers provide seldom leads to a particular degree and attendance is voluntary, but dedicated, talented students sometimes go on to careers in the arts. Teachers who conduct courses on academic subjects in a non-academic setting, such as literature, foreign language, and history courses, are also included in this occupation.

Self-enrichment teachers provide instruction on a wide range of subjects, so they may have styles and methods of instruction that differ greatly. Most self-enrichment classes are relatively informal and not demanding of instructors. Some classes, such as pottery or sewing, may be largely hands-on, with the instructor demonstrating methods or techniques for the class, observing students as they attempt to do it themselves, and pointing out mistakes to students and offering suggestions to improve techniques. Other classes, such as those involving financial planning or religion and spirituality, may be more similar to a lecture in nature or rely more heavily on group discussions. Self-enrichment teachers may also teach classes offered through religious institutions, such as marriage preparation or classes in religion for children.

Many of the classes that self-enrichment educators teach are shorter in duration than classes taken for academic credit; some finish in 1 or 2 days to several weeks. These brief classes tend to be introductory in nature and generally focus on only one topic—for example, a cooking class that teaches students how to make bread. Some self-enrichment classes introduce children and youths to activities such as piano or drama and may be designed to last anywhere from 1 week to several months.

Many self-enrichment teachers provide one-on-one lessons to students. The instructor may only work with the student for an hour or two a week, but direct the student what they should practice in the interim until their next lesson. Many instructors work with the same students on a weekly basis for years and derive satisfaction from observing them mature and gain expertise. The most talented students may go on to paid careers as craft artists, painters, sculptors, dancers, singers, or musicians.

All self-enrichment teachers must prepare lessons beforehand and stay current in their fields. Many self-enrichment teachers are self-employed and provide instruction as a business. As such, they must collect any fees or tuition and keep records of students whose accounts are prepaid or in arrears. Although not a requirement for most types of classes, teachers may use computers and other modern technologies in their instruction or to maintain business records.

Working Conditions

Few self-enrichment education teachers are full-time salaried workers. Most either work part time or are self-employed. Some have several part-time teaching assignments, but it is most common for teachers to have a full-time job in another occupation, often related to the subject that they teach, in addition to their part-time teaching job. Although jobs in this occupation are primarily part time and pay is low, most teachers enjoy their work because it gives them the opportunity to share a subject they enjoy with others.

Many classes for adults are held in the evenings and on weekends in order to accommodate students who have a job or family responsibilities. Similarly, self-enrichment classes for children are usually held after school, on weekends, or during school vacations.

Students in self-enrichment programs attend by choice, so they tend to be highly motivated and eager to learn. Students also often bring unique experiences of their own to classes, which can make teaching these students rewarding and satisfying. Self-enrichment teachers must have a great deal of patience, however, particularly when working with young children.

Training, Other Qualifications, and Advancement

The main qualification for self-enrichment teachers is expertise in their subject area, but requirements may vary greatly with both the type of class taught and the place of employment. In some cases, a portfolio of one's work may be required. For example, to secure a job teaching a photography course, an applicant would need to show examples of previous work. Some self-enrichment teachers are trained educators or other professionals who teach enrichment classes in their spare time. In many self-enrichment fields, however, instructors are simply experienced in the field and want to share that experience with others.

In some disciplines, such as art or music, specific teacher training programs are available. Prospective dance teachers, for example, may complete programs that prepare them to instruct any number of types of dance—from ballroom dancing to ballet. In addition to knowledge of their subject, self-enrichment teachers should have good speaking skills and a talent for making the subject interesting. Patience and the ability to explain and instruct students at a basic level are important as well, particularly when one is working with children.

Opportunities for advancement in this profession are limited. Some part-time teachers are able to move into full-time teaching positions or program administrator positions, such as coordinator or director, when such vacancies occur. Experienced teachers may mentor new instructors.

Employment

Teachers of self-enrichment education held about 253,000 jobs in 2004. About 3 in 10 were self-employed. The largest numbers of teachers were employed by public and private educational institutions, religious organizations, and providers of social assistance and amusement and recreation services.

Job Outlook

Employment of self-enrichment education teachers is expected to grow faster than the average for all occupations through 2014. A large number of job openings is expected, due to both the growth of the occupation as well as to many existing teachers retiring or leaving their jobs for other reasons. New opportunities arise constantly in this occupation because many self-enrichment education jobs are short-term and are often held as a second job.

The need for self-enrichment teachers is expected to grow as more people embrace lifelong learning and as course offerings expand. Self-enrichment education will also grow as a result of demographic changes. Retirees are one of the larger groups of participants in self-enrichment education because they have more time for classes, and as the baby boomers begin to retire, demand for self-enrichment

education should grow. At the same time, the children of the baby boomers will be entering the age range of another large group of participants, young adults–who often are single and participate for the social as well as the educational experience.

Teachers who are knowledgeable in subjects that are not easily researched on the Internet and those that benefit from hands-on experiences, such as cooking, crafts, and the arts, will be in greater demand. Classes on self-improvement, personal finance, and computer and Internet-related subjects are also expected to be popular.

Earnings

Median hourly earnings of self-enrichment teachers were $14.85 in May 2004. The middle 50 percent earned between $10.39 and $20.80. The lowest 10 percent earned less than $7.90, and the highest 10 percent earned more than $28.85. Self-enrichment teachers are generally paid by the hour or for each class that they teach.

Part-time instructors are usually paid for each class that they teach and receive few benefits. Full-time teachers are generally paid a salary and may receive health insurance and other benefits.

Related Occupations

The work of self-enrichment teachers is closely related to that of other types of teachers, especially preschool, kindergarten, elementary school, middle school, and secondary school teachers. Self-enrichment teachers also teach a wide variety of subjects that may be related to the work done by those in many other occupations, such as dancers and choreographers; artists and related workers; musicians, singers, and related workers; recreation workers; and athletes, coaches, umpires, and related workers.

Sources of Additional Information

For information on employment of self-enrichment teachers, contact schools or local companies that offer self-enrichment programs.

Tellers

(O*NET 43-3071.00)

Significant Points

■ Most jobs require only a high school diploma; tellers should enjoy public contact, must feel comfortable handling large amounts of money, and should be discreet and trustworthy.

■ About 3 out of 10 tellers work part time.

■ Most job openings will arise from replacement needs because turnover is high.

■ Although the job outlook for tellers has improved recently, employment is projected to grow more slowly than average.

Nature of the Work

The teller is the person most people associate with a bank. Tellers make up approximately one-fourth of bank employees and conduct most of a bank's routine transactions. Among the responsibilities of tellers are cashing checks, accepting deposits and loan payments, and processing withdrawals. They also may sell savings bonds, accept payment for customers' utility bills and charge cards, process necessary paperwork for certificates of deposit, and sell travelers' checks. Some tellers specialize in handling foreign currencies or commercial or business accounts.

Being a teller requires a great deal of attention to detail. Before cashing a check, a teller must verify the date, the name of the bank, the identity of the person who is to receive payment, and the legality of the document. A teller also must make sure that the written and numerical amounts agree and that the account has sufficient funds to cover the check. The teller then must carefully count cash to avoid errors. Sometimes a customer withdraws money in the form of a cashier's check, which the teller prepares and verifies. When accepting a deposit, tellers must check the accuracy of the deposit slip before processing the transaction.

Prior to starting their shifts, tellers receive and count an amount of working cash for their drawers. A supervisor—usually the head teller—verifies this amount. Tellers use this cash for payments during the day and are responsible for its safe and accurate handling. Before leaving, tellers count their cash on hand, list the currency-received tickets on a balance sheet, make sure that the accounts balance, and sort checks and deposit slips. Over the course of a workday, tellers also may process numerous mail transactions. Some tellers replenish their cash drawers and corroborate deposits and payments to automated teller machines (ATMs).

In most banks, head tellers are responsible for the teller line. They set work schedules, ensure that the proper procedures are adhered to, and act as a mentor to less experienced tellers. In addition, head tellers may perform the typical duties of a teller, as needed, and may deal with the more difficult customer problems. They may access the vault, ensure that the correct cash balance is in the vault, and oversee large cash transactions. Technology continues to play a large role in the job duties of all tellers. In most banks, for example, tellers use computer terminals to record deposits and withdrawals. These terminals often give tellers quick access to detailed information on customer accounts. Tellers can use this information to tailor the bank's services to fit a customer's needs or to recommend an appropriate bank product or service.

As banks begin to offer more and increasingly complex financial services, tellers are being trained to identify sales opportunities. This task requires them to learn about the various financial products and services the bank offers so that they can briefly explain them to customers and refer interested customers to appropriate specialized sales personnel. In addition, tellers in many banks are being cross-trained to perform some of the functions of customer service representatives. (Customer service representatives are discussed separately in this book.)

Working Conditions

Tellers work in an office environment. They may experience eye and muscle strain, backaches, headaches, and repetitive motion injuries as a result of using computers on a daily basis. Tellers may have to sit for extended periods while reviewing detailed data.

Many tellers work regular business hours and a standard 40-hour week. A substantial number work just part time. Full-time and part-time tellers may work some evenings and weekends.

Training, Other Qualifications, and Advancement

Most tellers are required to have at least a high school diploma. Some have some college training or even a bachelor's degree in business, accounting, or liberal arts. Although a degree is rarely required, graduates may accept teller positions to get into a particular company or to enter the banking field with the hope of eventually being promoted to professional or managerial positions.

Experience working in an office environment or in customer service, and particularly cash-handling experience, can be important for tellers. Regardless of experience, employers prefer workers who have good communication skills and who are computer-literate; knowledge of word-processing and spreadsheet software also is valuable.

Once hired, tellers usually receive on-the-job training. Under the guidance of a supervisor or other senior worker, new employees learn company procedures. Some formal classroom training also may be necessary, such as training in specific computer software.

Tellers should enjoy contact with the public. They must have a strong aptitude for numbers and feel comfortable handling large amounts of money. They should be discreet and trustworthy, because they frequently come in contact with confidential material. Tellers also must be careful, orderly, and detail-oriented in order to avoid making errors and to recognize errors made by others.

Tellers can prepare for better jobs by taking courses offered throughout the country by banking and financial institutes, colleges and universities, and private training institutions.

Tellers usually advance by taking on more duties in the same occupation or by being promoted to head teller or to another supervisory job. Many banks and other employers fill supervisory and managerial positions by promoting individuals from within their organizations, so outstanding tellers who acquire additional skills, experience, and training improve their advancement opportunities.

Employment

Tellers held about 558,000 jobs in 2004. The overwhelming majority worked in commercial banks, savings institutions, or credit unions. The remainder worked in a variety of other finance and other industries. About 3 out of 10 worked part time.

Job Outlook

Employment prospects for tellers have improved recently. Employment is projected to grow, but more slowly than the average for all occupations through 2014. Banks are looking at their branch offices as places to attract customers for the increasing number and variety of financial products the banks sell. As recently as a few years ago, banks were closing branch offices and discouraging the use of tellers in an effort to cut costs, but in a turnaround, banks are now opening branch offices in more locations. They also are keeping them open longer during the day and on weekends, a practice that is expected to increase opportunities for tellers, particularly those who work part time. Most job openings will arise from replacement needs because turnover is high—a characteristic typical of large occupations that normally require little formal education and offer relatively low pay. Tellers who have excellent customer service skills, are knowledgeable about a variety of financial services, and can sell those services will be in greater demand in the future.

Despite the improved outlook, automation and technology will continue to reduce the need for tellers who perform only routine transactions. For example, ATMs and the increased use of direct deposit of paychecks and benefit checks have reduced the need for bank customers to interact with tellers for routine transactions. In addition, electronic banking is spreading rapidly throughout the banking industry. This type of banking, conducted over the telephone or the Internet, also will reduce the number of tellers over the long run.

Employment of tellers also is being affected by the increasing use of 24-hour telephone centers by many large banks. These centers allow a customer to interact with a bank representative at a distant location, either by telephone or by video terminal. Such centers usually are staffed by customer service representatives, who can handle a wider variety of transactions than tellers can, including applications for loans and credit cards.

Earnings

Salaries of tellers may vary with their experience and with the region of the country, size of city, and type and size of establishment. Median annual earnings of tellers were $21,120 in May 2004. The middle 50 percent earned between $18,320 and $23,900 a year. The lowest 10 percent earned less than $15,850, and the highest 10 percent earned more than $28,100 a year.

As in other occupations, part-time tellers may not enjoy the same benefits—such as vacations, health and life insurance, and pensions—as full-time workers.

Related Occupations

Tellers enter data into a computer, handle cash, and keep track of financial transactions. Other clerks who perform similar duties include bill and account collectors; billing and posting clerks and machine operators; bookkeeping, accounting, and auditing clerks; gaming cage workers; brokerage clerks; and credit authorizers, checkers, and clerks.

Sources of Additional Information

Information on employment opportunities for tellers is available from banks and other employers and local offices of the state employment service and from

▸ Bank Administration Institute, 1 North Franklin St., Chicago, IL 60606.

Textile, Apparel, and Furnishings Occupations

(O*NET 51-6011.01, 51-6011.02, 51-6011.03, 51-6021.01, 51-6021.02, 51-6021.03, 51-6031.01, 51-6031.02, 51-6041.00, 51-6042.00, 51-6051.00, 51-6052.01, 51-6052.02, 51-6061.00, 51-6062.00, 51-6063.00, 51-6064.00, 51-6091.00, 51-6092.00, 51-6093.00, and 51-6099.99)

Significant Points

■ Most workers learn through on-the-job training.

■ This group ranks among the most rapidly declining occupations because of increases in imports, offshore assembly, productivity gains from automation, and new fabrics that do not need as much processing.

■ Earnings of most workers are low.

Nature of the Work

Textile, apparel, and furnishings workers produce fibers, cloth, and upholstery and fashion them into a wide range of products that we use in our daily lives. Jobs range from those that involve computers to those in which the worker operates large industrial machinery and smaller power equipment to those that require substantial handwork.

Textile machine setters, operators, and tenders. Textile machine setters, operators, and tenders run machines that make textile products from fibers. Textiles are the basis of towels, bed linens, hosiery and socks, and nearly all clothing, but they also are a key ingredient in products ranging from roofing to tires. The first step in manufacturing textiles is preparing the natural or synthetic fibers. *Extruding and forming machine operators, synthetic and glass fibers,* set up and operate machines that extrude or force liquid synthetic material such as rayon, fiberglass, or liquid polymers through small holes and draw out filaments. Other operators put natural fibers such as cotton, wool, flax, or hemp through carding and combing machines that clean and align them into short lengths collectively called "sliver." In making sliver, operators may combine different types of natural fibers and synthetic filaments to give the product a desired texture, durability, or other characteristics. *Textile winding, twisting, and drawing-out machine operators* take the sliver and draw out, twist, and wind it to produce yarn, taking care to repair any breaks.

Textile bleaching and dyeing machine operators control machines that wash, bleach, or dye either yarn or finished fabrics and other products. *Textile knitting and weaving machine operators* put the yarn on machines that weave, knit, loop, or tuft it into a product. Woven fabrics are used to make apparel and other goods, whereas some knitted products (such as hosiery) and tufted products (such as carpeting) emerge in near-finished form. Different types of machines are used for these processes, but operators perform similar tasks, repairing breaks in the yarn and monitoring the yarn supply while tending many machines at once. *Textile cutting machine operators* trim the fabric into various widths and lengths, depending on its intended use.

Apparel workers. Apparel workers cut fabric and other materials and sew it into clothing and related products. Workers in a variety of occupations fall under the heading of apparel workers. *Tailors, dressmakers, and sewers* make custom clothing and alter and repair garments for individuals. However, workers in most apparel occupations are found in manufacturing, performing specialized tasks in the production of large numbers of garments that are shipped to retail establishments for sale.

Fabric and apparel patternmakers convert a clothing designer's original model of a garment into a pattern of separate parts that can be laid out on a length of fabric. After discussing the item with the designer, these skilled workers usually use a computer to outline the parts and draw in details to indicate the positions of pleats, buttonholes, and other features. (In the past, patternmakers laid out the parts on paper, using pencils and drafting instruments such as rulers.) Patternmakers then alter the size of the pieces in the pattern to produce garments of various sizes, and they may mark the fabric to show the best layout of pattern pieces to minimize waste of material.

Once an item's pattern has been made and marked, mass production of the garment begins. Cutters and trimmers take the patterns and cut out material, paying close attention to their work because mistakes are costly. Following the outline of the pattern, they place multiple layers of material on the cutting table and use an electric knife or other tools to cut out the various pieces of the garment; delicate materials may be cut by hand. In some companies, computer-controlled machines do the cutting.

Sewing machine operators join the parts of a garment together; reinforce seams, and attach buttons, hooks, zippers; and accessories to produce clothing. After the product is sewn, other workers remove lint and loose threads and inspect and package the garments.

Shoe and leather workers. Shoe and leather workers are employed either in manufacturing or in personal services. In shoe manufacturing, *shoe machine operators and tenders* operate a variety of specialized machines that perform cutting, joining, and finishing functions. In personal services, *shoe and leather workers and repairers* perform a variety of repairs and custom leatherwork for the general public. They construct, decorate, or repair shoes, belts, purses, saddles, luggage, and other leather products. They also may repair some products made of canvas or plastic. When making custom shoes or modifying existing footwear for people with foot problems or special needs, shoe and leather workers and repairers cut pieces of leather, shape them over a form shaped like a foot, and sew them together. They then attach soles and heels, using sewing machines or cement and nails. They also dye and polish the items, utilizing a buffing wheel for a smooth surface and lustrous shine. When making luggage, they fasten leather to a frame and attach handles and other hardware. They also cut and secure linings inside the frames and sew or stamp designs onto the exterior of the luggage. In addition to performing all of the preceding steps, saddlemakers often apply leather dyes and liquid topcoats to produce a glossy finish on a saddle. They also may decorate the surface of the saddle by hand-stitching or by stamping the leather with decorative patterns and designs. Shoe and leather

workers and repairers who own their own shops keep records and supervise other workers.

Upholsterers. *Upholsterers* make, fix, and restore furniture that is covered with fabric. Using hammers and tack pullers, upholsterers who restore furniture remove old fabric and stuffing to get down to the springs and wooden frame. Then they reglue loose sections of the frame and refinish exposed wood. The springs sit on a cloth mat, called webbing, that is attached to the frame. Upholsterers replace torn webbing, examine the springs, and replace broken or bent ones.

Upholsterers who make new furniture start with a bare wooden frame. First, they install webbing, tacking it to one side of the frame, stretching it tight, and tacking it to the other side. Then, they tie each spring to the webbing and to its neighboring springs. Next, they cover the springs with filler, such as foam, a polyester batt, or similar fibrous batting material, to form a smooth, rounded surface. Then they measure and cut fabric for the arms, backs, seats, sides, and other surfaces, leaving as little waste as possible. Finally, sewing the fabric pieces together and attaching them to the frame with tacks, staples, or glue, they affix any ornaments, such as fringes, buttons, or rivets. Sometimes, upholsterers provide pickup and delivery of the furniture they work on. They also help customers select new coverings by providing samples of fabrics and pictures of finished pieces.

Laundry and drycleaning workers. *Laundry and drycleaning workers* clean cloth garments, linens, draperies, blankets, and other articles. They also may clean leather, suede, furs, and rugs. When necessary, they treat spots and stains on articles before laundering or drycleaning. They tend machines during cleaning and ensure that items are not lost or misplaced with those of another customer. *Pressers, textile, garment, and related materials,* shape and remove wrinkles from items after steam-pressing them or ironing them by hand. Workers then assemble each customer's items, box or bag them, and prepare an itemized bill for the customer.

Working Conditions

Most people in textile, apparel, and furnishings occupations work a standard 5-day, 35- to 40-hour week. Working on evenings and weekends is common for shoe and leather workers; laundry and drycleaning workers; and tailors, dressmakers, and sewers employed in retail stores. Many textile and fiber mills often use rotating schedules of shifts so that employees do not continuously work nights or days. But these rotating shifts sometimes cause workers to have sleep disorders and stress-related problems.

Although much of the work in apparel manufacturing still is based on a piecework system that allows for little interpersonal contact, some apparel firms are placing more emphasis on teamwork and cooperation. Under this new system, individuals work closely with one another, and each team or module often governs itself, increasing the overall responsibility of each operator.

Working conditions vary by establishment and by occupation. In manufacturing, machinery in textile mills often is noisy, as are areas in which sewing and pressing are performed in apparel factories; patternmaking and spreading areas tend to be much quieter. Many older factories are cluttered, hot, and poorly lit and ventilated, but more modern facilities usually have more workspace and are well lit

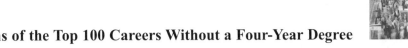

and ventilated. Textile machinery operators use protective glasses and masks that cover their noses and mouths to protect against airborne materials. Many machines operate at high speeds, and textile machinery workers must be careful not to wear clothing or jewelry that could get caught in moving parts. In addition, extruding and forming machine operators wear protective shoes and clothing when working with certain chemical compounds.

Work in apparel production can be physically demanding. Some workers sit for long periods, and others spend many hours on their feet, leaning over tables and operating machinery. Operators must be attentive while running sewing machines, pressers, automated cutters, and the like. A few workers wear protective devices such as gloves. In some instances, new machinery and production techniques have decreased the physical demands on workers. For example, newer pressing machines are controlled by foot pedals or by computer and do not require much strength to operate.

Laundries and drycleaning establishments often are hot and noisy; those in retail stores, however, tend to be less noisy and more comfortable. Areas in which shoe and leather workers make or repair shoes and other leather items can be noisy, and odors from leather dyes and stains frequently are present. Workers need to pay close attention when working with machines to avoid punctures, lacerations, and abrasions.

Upholstery work is not dangerous, but upholsterers usually wear protective gloves and clothing when using sharp tools and lifting and handling furniture or springs. During most of the workday, upholsterers stand and may do a lot of bending and heavy lifting. They also may work in awkward positions for short periods.

Training, Other Qualifications, and Advancement

Most employers prefer to hire high school graduates for jobs in textile, apparel, and furnishings occupations. Entrants with postsecondary vocational training or previous work experience in apparel production usually have a better chance of getting a job and advancing to a supervisory position. Regardless of the setting, workers usually begin by performing simple tasks.

In manufacturing, textile and apparel workers need good hand-eye coordination, manual dexterity, physical stamina, and the ability to perform repetitive tasks for long periods. Machine operators usually are trained on the job by more experienced employees or by machinery manufacturers' representatives. As they gain experience, these workers are assigned more difficult operations. Further advancement is limited, however. Some production workers may become first-line supervisors, but most can advance only to more skilled operator jobs. As machinery in the industry continues to become more complex, knowledge of the basics of computers and electronics will increasingly be an asset. In addition, the trends toward cross-training of operators and working in teams will increase the time needed to become fully trained on all machines and require interpersonal skills to work effectively with others.

Retailers prefer to hire custom tailors, dressmakers, and sewers with previous experience in apparel production, design, or alteration. Knowledge of fabrics, design, and construction is very important. Custom tailors sometimes learn these skills through courses in high school or a community college. Some experienced custom tailors open their own tailoring shop. Custom tailoring is a highly competitive field, however, and training in small-business operations can mean the difference between success and failure. Although laundries and drycleaners prefer entrants with previous work experience, they routinely hire inexperienced workers.

Precision shoe and leather workers and repairers generally learn their skills on the job. Manual dexterity and the mechanical aptitude to work with hand tools and machines are important in shoe repair and leatherworking. Shoe and leather workers who produce custom goods should have artistic ability as well. Beginners start as helpers for experienced workers, but, in manufacturing, they may attend more formal in-house training programs. Beginners gradually take on more tasks until they are fully qualified workers, a process that takes about 2 years in an apprenticeship program or as a helper in a shop. In a vocational training program, it can take 6 months to a year. Learning to make saddles takes longer. Shoe repairers need to keep their skills up to date to work with the rapidly changing footwear styles and materials. Some do this by attending trade shows; others attend specialized training seminars and workshops in custom shoemaking, shoe repair, and other leatherwork sponsored by associations. Some in the shoemaking and leatherworking occupations begin as workers or repairers and advance to salaried supervisory and managerial positions. Some open their own shop, but knowledge of business practices and management and a pleasant manner when dealing with customers are needed to stay in business.

Most upholsterers learn their skills on the job, but a few do so through apprenticeships. Inexperienced persons also may take training in basic upholstery in vocational schools and some community colleges. Upholsterers should have manual dexterity, good coordination, and the strength needed to lift heavy furniture. An eye for detail, a flair for color, and the ability to use fabrics creatively also are helpful. The length of training may vary from 6 weeks to 3 years. Upholsterers who work on custom-made pieces may train for 8 to 10 years. The primary forms of advancement for upholsterers are opening their own shop or moving into management. The upholstery business is highly competitive, so operating a shop successfully is difficult. In large shops and factories, experienced or highly skilled upholsterers may become supervisors or samplemakers.

Employment

Textile, apparel, and furnishings workers held 929,000 jobs in 2004. Employment in the detailed occupations that make up this group was distributed as follows:

Sewing machine operators	256,000
Laundry and dry-cleaning workers	235,000
Tailors, dressmakers, and sewers	85,000
Pressers, textile, garment, and related materials	82,000
Upholsterers	53,000
Textile winding, twisting, and drawing-out machine setters, operators, and tenders	53,000
Textile knitting and weaving machine setters, operators, and tenders	46,000
Textile cutting machine setters, operators, and tenders	28,000

All other textile, apparel, and furnishings
workers 23,000

Extruding and forming machine setters, operators,
and tenders, synthetic and glass fibers................23,000

Textile bleaching and dyeing machine operators
and tenders 21,000

Shoe and leather workers and repairers..................10,000

Fabric and apparel patternmakers 9,200

Shoe machine operators and tenders 4,600

Manufacturing jobs are concentrated in California, North Carolina, Georgia, New York, Texas, and South Carolina. Jobs in reupholstery, shoe repair and custom leatherwork, and laundry and drycleaning establishments are found in cities and towns throughout the nation. Overall, about 11 percent of all workers in textile, apparel, and furnishings occupations were self-employed; however, 54 percent of tailors, dressmakers, and sewers and 27 percent of upholsterers were self-employed.

Job Outlook

Employment of textile, apparel, and furnishings workers is expected to decline through 2014. Apparel workers have been among the most rapidly declining occupational groups in the economy, and increasing imports, the use of offshore assembly, and greater productivity through new automation will contribute to additional job losses. Also, many new textiles require less production and processing. Employment in specialty apparel and textiles, where it may be necessary for production facilities to be close to their market, might not decrease as much as in other areas of apparel and textile production. Because of the large size of this occupation, however, job openings arise each year from the need to replace workers who transfer to other occupations, retire, or leave the occupation for other reasons.

Employment in the domestic textile and apparel industries has declined in recent years as foreign producers have gained a greater share of the U.S. market. Domestic production of apparel and textiles will continue to move abroad, and imports to the U.S. market will increase. Declines in U.S. apparel production will cause reductions in domestic textile production because the apparel industry is the largest consumer of American-made textiles. Fierce competition in the market for apparel will keep domestic apparel and textile firms under intense pressure to cut costs and produce more with fewer workers.

Although the textile industry already is highly automated, it will continue to seek to increase worker productivity through the introduction of labor-saving machinery and the invention of new fibers and fabrics that reduce production costs. Despite advances in technology, the apparel industry has had difficulty employing automated equipment extensively due to the "soft" properties of textile products. The industry produces a wide variety of apparel items that change frequently with changes in style and season. Technological developments such as computer-aided marking and grading, computer-controlled cutters, semiautomatic sewing and pressing machines, and automated material-handling systems have increased output while reducing the need for some workers in larger firms. However, assembly continues to be the most labor-intensive step in the production of apparel, and increasing numbers of sewing machine operator jobs are expected to be lost to low-wage workers abroad. Still, improvements in productivity will allow many of the presewing functions of design, patternmaking, marking, and cutting to continue be done domestically, and employment of workers who perform these functions will not be as adversely affected.

Outside of the manufacturing sector, tailors, dressmakers, and sewers—the most skilled apparel workers—also are expected to experience declining employment. Demand for their services will continue to lessen because it is often cheaper to buy new apparel than to have clothes altered or repaired.

Employment of shoe and leather workers is expected to decline through 2014 as a result of growing imports of less expensive shoes and leather goods and increasing productivity of U.S. manufacturers. Also, buying new shoes often is cheaper than repairing worn or damaged ones. However, declines are expected to be offset somewhat as the population continues to age and more people need custom shoes for health reasons.

Employment of upholsterers is expected to decline through 2014 as new furniture and automotive seats use more durable coverings and as manufacturing firms continue to become more automated and efficient. Demand for the reupholstery of furniture also is expected to decline as the increasing manufacture of new, relatively inexpensive upholstered furniture causes many consumers simply to replace old, worn furniture. However, demand will continue to be steady for upholsterers who restore very valuable furniture. Most reupholstery work is labor intensive and not easily automated.

Earnings

Earnings of textile, apparel, and furnishings workers vary by occupation. Because many production workers in apparel manufacturing are paid according to the number of acceptable pieces they produce, their total earnings depend on skill, speed, and accuracy. Workers covered by union contracts tend to have higher earnings. Median hourly earnings by occupation in May 2004 were as follows:

Fabric and apparel patternmakers.........................$13.85

Extruding and forming machine setters, operators,
and tenders, synthetic and glass fibers 13.37

Upholsterers..12.35

Textile knitting and weaving machine setters,
operators, and tenders.......................................11.48

Textile winding, twisting, and drawing-out machine
setters, operators, and tenders 10.87

Tailors, dressmakers, and custom sewers 10.79

Textile bleaching and dyeing machine operators
and tenders 10.56

All other textile, apparel, and furnishings workers 10.34

Textile cutting machine setters, operators, and
tenders 9.80

Shoe machine operators and tenders 9.44

Shoe and leather workers and repairers 9.29

Sewers, hand 9.13

Sewing machine operators 8.61

Pressers, textile, garment, and related materials 8.33

Laundry and dry-cleaning workers 8.28

Benefits also vary. A few large employers, for example, include childcare in their benefits package. Apparel workers in retail trade also may receive a discount on their purchases from the company for which they work. In addition, some of the larger manufacturers operate company stores from which employees can purchase apparel products at significant discounts. Some small firms, however, offer only limited benefits.

Related Occupations

Textile, apparel, and furnishings workers apply their knowledge of textiles and leathers to fashion products with use of hand tools and machinery. Others who produce products using hand tools, machines, and their knowledge of the materials with which they work include assemblers and fabricators; medical, dental, and ophthalmic laboratory technicians; food-processing workers; jewelers and precious stone and metal workers; and woodworkers.

Sources of Additional Information

Information about job opportunities in textile, apparel, and furnishings occupations is available from local employers and local offices of state employment services.

Truck Drivers and Driver/Sales Workers

(O*NET 53-3031.00, 53-3032.01, 53-3032.02, and 53-3033.00)

Significant Points

■ Job opportunities should be favorable.

■ Competition is expected for jobs offering the highest earnings or most favorable work schedules.

■ A commercial driver's license is required to operate most larger trucks.

Nature of the Work

Truck drivers are a constant presence on the nation's highways and interstates. They deliver everything from automobiles to canned food. Firms of all kinds rely on trucks to pick up and deliver goods because no other form of transportation can deliver goods door-to-door. Even if some goods travel most of the way by ship, train, or airplane, almost everything is carried by trucks at some point in its journey.

Before leaving the terminal or warehouse, truck drivers check the fuel level and oil in their trucks. They also inspect the trucks to make sure that the brakes, windshield wipers, and lights are working and that a fire extinguisher, flares, and other safety equipment are aboard and in working order. Drivers make sure their cargo is secure and adjust the mirrors so that both sides of the truck are visible from the driver's seat. Drivers report equipment that is inoperable, missing, or loaded improperly to the dispatcher.

Once under way, drivers must be alert in order to prevent accidents. Drivers can see farther down the road because large trucks seat them higher off the ground than other vehicles. This allows them to see the road ahead and select lanes that are moving more smoothly as well as giving them warning of any dangerous road conditions ahead of them.

The duration of runs vary according to the types of cargo and the destinations. Local drivers may provide daily service for a specific route or region, while other drivers make longer intercity and interstate deliveries. Interstate and intercity cargo tends to vary from job to job more than local cargo. A driver's responsibilities and assignments change according to the type of loads transported and their vehicle's size.

New technologies are changing the way truck drivers work, especially long-distance truck drivers. Satellites and the Global Positioning System link many trucks with their company's headquarters. Troubleshooting information, directions, weather reports, and other important communications can be instantly relayed to the truck. Drivers can easily communicate with the dispatcher to discuss delivery schedules and courses of action in the event of mechanical problems. The satellite link also allows the dispatcher to track the truck's location, fuel consumption, and engine performance. Some drivers also work with computerized inventory tracking equipment. It is important for the producer, warehouse, and customer to know their product's location at all times so they can maintain a high quality of service.

Heavy truck and tractor-trailer drivers operate trucks or vans with a capacity of at least 26,000 pounds Gross Vehicle Weight (GVW). They transport goods including cars, livestock, and other materials in liquid, loose, or packaged form. Many routes are from city to city and cover long distances. Some companies use two drivers on very long runs—one drives while the other sleeps in a berth behind the cab. These "sleeper" runs can last for days or even weeks. Trucks on sleeper runs typically stop only for fuel, food, loading, and unloading.

Some heavy truck and tractor-trailer drivers who have regular runs transport freight to the same city on a regular basis. Other drivers perform ad hoc runs because shippers request varying service to different cities every day.

The U.S. Department of Transportation requires that drivers keep a log of their activities, the condition of the truck, and the circumstances of any accidents.

Long-distance heavy truck and tractor-trailer drivers spend most of their working time behind the wheel, but also may have to load or unload their cargo. This is especially common when drivers haul specialty cargo, because they may be the only ones at the destination familiar with procedures or certified to handle the materials. Autotransport drivers, for example, position cars on the trailers at the manufacturing plant and remove them at the dealerships. When picking up or delivering furniture, drivers of long-distance moving vans hire local workers to help them load or unload.

Light or delivery services truck drivers operate vans and trucks weighing less than 26,000 pounds GVW. They pick up or deliver merchandise and packages within a specific area. This may include short "turnarounds" to deliver a shipment to a nearby city, pick up another loaded truck or van, and drive it back to their home base the same day. These services may require use of electronic delivery tracking systems to track the whereabouts of the merchandise or packages. Light or delivery services truck drivers usually load or unload the merchandise at the customer's place of business. They may have helpers if there are many deliveries to make during the day or if the load requires heavy moving. Typically, before the driver arrives for work, material handlers load the trucks and arrange items for ease of delivery. Customers must sign receipts for goods and pay drivers the balance due on the merchandise if there is a cash-on-delivery arrangement. At the end of the day, drivers turn in receipts, payments, records of deliveries made, and any reports on mechanical problems with their trucks.

Some local truck drivers have sales and customer service responsibilities. The primary responsibility of *driver/sales workers*, or *route drivers*, is to deliver and sell their firm's products over established routes or within an established territory. They sell goods such as food products, including restaurant takeout items, or pick up and deliver items such as laundry. Their response to customer complaints and requests can make the difference between a large order and a lost customer. Route drivers may also take orders and collect payments.

The duties of driver/sales workers vary according to their industry, the policies of their employer, and the emphasis placed on their sales responsibility. Most have wholesale routes that deliver to businesses and stores rather than to homes. For example, wholesale bakery driver/sales workers deliver and arrange bread, cakes, rolls, and other baked goods on display racks in grocery stores. They estimate how many of each item to stock by paying close attention to what is selling. They may recommend changes in a store's order or encourage the manager to stock new bakery products. Laundries that rent linens, towels, work clothes, and other items employ driver/sales workers to visit businesses regularly to replace soiled laundry. Their duties also may include soliciting new customers along their sales route.

After completing their route, driver/sales workers place orders for their next deliveries based on product sales and customer requests.

Working Conditions

Truck driving has become less physically demanding because most trucks now have more comfortable seats; better ventilation; and improved, ergonomically designed cabs. Although these changes make the work environment less taxing, driving for many hours at a stretch, loading and unloading cargo, and making many deliveries can be tiring. Local truck drivers, unlike long-distance drivers, usually return home in the evening. Some self-employed long-distance truck drivers who own and operate their trucks spend most of the year away from home.

Design improvements in newer trucks have reduced stress and increased the efficiency of long-distance drivers. Many newer trucks are equipped with refrigerators, televisions, and bunks.

The U.S. Department of Transportation governs work hours and other working conditions of truck drivers engaged in interstate commerce. A long-distance driver may drive for 11 hours and work for up to 14 hours—including driving and non-driving duties—after having 10 hours off-duty. A driver may not drive after having worked for 60 hours in the past 7 days or 70 hours in the past 8 days unless they have taken at least 34 consecutive hours off-duty. Most drivers are required to document their time in a logbook. Many drivers, particularly on long runs, work close to the maximum time permitted because they typically are compensated according to the number of miles or hours they drive. Drivers on long runs face boredom, loneliness, and fatigue. Drivers often travel during nights, holidays, and weekends to avoid traffic delays.

Local truck drivers frequently work 50 or more hours a week. Drivers who handle food for chain grocery stores, produce markets, or bakeries typically work long hours—starting late at night or early in the morning. Although most drivers have regular routes, some have different routes each day. Many local truck drivers, particularly driver/sales workers, load and unload their own trucks. This requires considerable lifting, carrying, and walking each day.

Training, Other Qualifications, and Advancement

State and federal regulations govern the qualifications and standards for truck drivers. All drivers must comply with federal regulations and any state regulations that are in excess of those federal requirements. Truck drivers must have a driver's license issued by the state in which they live, and most employers require a clean driving record. Drivers of trucks designed to carry 26,000 pounds or more—including most tractor-trailers, as well as bigger straight trucks—must obtain a commercial driver's license (CDL) from the state in which they live. All truck drivers who operate trucks transporting hazardous materials must obtain a CDL, regardless of truck size. In order to receive the hazardous materials endorsement, a driver must be fingerprinted and submit to a criminal background check by the Transportation Security Administration. Federal regulations governing CDL administration allow for states to exempt farmers, emergency medical technicians, fire fighters, some military drivers, and snow and ice removers from the need for a CDL at the state's discretion. In many states, a regular driver's license is sufficient for driving light trucks and vans.

To qualify for a CDL, an applicant must have a clean driving record, pass a written test on rules and regulations, and then demonstrate that they can operate a commercial truck safely. A national database permanently records all driving violations committed by those with a CDL. A state will check these records and deny a CDL to those who already have a license suspended or revoked in another state. Licensed drivers must accompany trainees until they get their own CDL. A person may not hold more than one license at a time and must surrender any other licenses when a CDL is issued. Information on how to apply for a CDL may be obtained from state motor vehicle administrations.

Many states allow those who are as young as 18 years old to drive trucks within their borders. To drive a commercial vehicle between states, one must be 21 years of age, according to the U.S. Department of Transportation (U.S. DOT), which establishes minimum qualifications for truck drivers engaging in interstate commerce. Federal Motor Carrier Safety Regulations—published by U.S. DOT—require drivers to be at least 21 years old and to pass a physical examination once every 2 years. The main physical requirements include good hearing, at least 20/40 vision with glasses or corrective lenses, and a 70-degree field of vision in each eye.

Drivers may not be colorblind. Drivers must be able to hear a forced whisper in one ear at not less than 5 feet, with a hearing aid if needed. Drivers must have normal use of arms and legs and normal blood pressure. Drivers may not use any controlled substances, unless prescribed by a licensed physician. Persons with epilepsy or diabetes controlled by insulin are not permitted to be interstate truck drivers. Federal regulations also require employers to test their drivers for alcohol and drug use as a condition of employment and require periodic random tests of the drivers while they are on duty. A driver must not have been convicted of a felony involving the use of a motor vehicle; a crime involving drugs; driving under the influence of drugs or alcohol; refusing to submit to an alcohol test required by a state or its implied consent laws or regulations; leaving the scene of a crime; or causing a fatality through negligent operation of a motor vehicle. All drivers must be able to read and speak English well enough to read road signs, prepare reports, and communicate with law enforcement officers and the public.

Many trucking operations have higher standards than those described here. Many firms require that drivers be at least 22 years old, be able to lift heavy objects, and have driven trucks for 3 to 5 years. Many prefer to hire high school graduates and require annual physical examinations. Companies have an economic incentive to hire less risky drivers, as good drivers use less fuel and cost less to insure.

Taking driver-training courses is a desirable method of preparing for truck driving jobs and for obtaining a CDL. High school courses in driver training and automotive mechanics also may be helpful. Many private and public vocational-technical schools offer tractor-trailer driver training programs. Students learn to maneuver large vehicles on crowded streets and in highway traffic. They also learn to inspect trucks and freight for compliance with regulations. Some programs provide only a limited amount of actual driving experience. Completion of a program does not guarantee a job. Those interested in attending a driving school should check with local trucking companies to make sure the school's training is acceptable. Some states require prospective drivers to complete a training course in basic truck driving before being issued their CDL. The Professional Truck Driver Institute (PTDI), a nonprofit organization established by the trucking industry, manufacturers, and others, certifies driver training courses at truck driver training schools that meet industry standards and Federal Highway Administration guidelines for training tractor-trailer drivers.

Drivers must get along well with people because they often deal directly with customers. Employers seek driver/sales workers who speak well and have self-confidence, initiative, tact, and a neat appearance. Employers also look for responsible, self-motivated individuals who are able to work well with little supervision.

Training given to new drivers by employers is usually informal and may consist of only a few hours of instruction from an experienced driver, sometimes on the new employee's own time. New drivers may also ride with and observe experienced drivers before getting their own assignments. Drivers receive additional training to drive special types of trucks or handle hazardous materials. Some companies give 1 to 2 days of classroom instruction covering general duties, the operation and loading of a truck, company policies, and the preparation of delivery forms and company records. Driver/sales workers also receive training on the various types of products their

company carries so that they can effectively answer questions about the products and more easily market them to their customers.

Although most new truck drivers are assigned to regular driving jobs immediately, some start as extra drivers—substituting for regular drivers who are ill or on vacation. Extra drivers receive a regular assignment when an opening occurs.

New drivers sometimes start on panel trucks or other small straight trucks. As they gain experience and show competent driving skills, they may advance to larger, heavier trucks and finally to tractor-trailers.

The advancement of truck drivers generally is limited to driving runs that provide increased earnings, preferred schedules, or working conditions. Local truck drivers may advance to driving heavy or specialized trucks or transfer to long-distance truck driving. Working for companies that also employ long-distance drivers is the best way to advance to these positions. Few truck drivers become dispatchers or managers.

Some long-distance truck drivers purchase trucks and go into business for themselves. Although some of these owner-operators are successful, others fail to cover expenses and go out of business. Owner-operators should have good business sense as well as truck driving experience. Courses in accounting, business, and business mathematics are helpful. Knowledge of truck mechanics can enable owner-operators to perform their own routine maintenance and minor repairs.

Employment

Truck drivers and driver/sales workers held about 3.2 million jobs in 2004. Of these workers, 451,000 were driver/sales workers and 2.8 million were truck drivers. Most truck drivers find employment in large metropolitan areas or along major interstate roadways where trucking, retail, and wholesale companies tend to have their distribution outlets. Some drivers work in rural areas, providing specialized services such as delivering newspapers to customers.

The truck transportation industry employed 25 percent of all truck drivers and driver/sales workers in the United States. Another 25 percent worked for companies engaged in wholesale or retail trade. The remaining truck drivers and driver/sales workers were distributed across many industries, including construction and manufacturing.

Around 9 percent of all truck drivers and driver/sales workers were self-employed. Of these, a significant number were owner-operators who either served a variety of businesses independently or leased their services and trucks to a trucking company.

Job Outlook

Job opportunities should be favorable for truck drivers. In addition to growth in demand for truck drivers, numerous job openings will occur as experienced drivers leave this large occupation to transfer to other fields of work, retire, or leave the labor force for other reasons. Jobs vary greatly in terms of earnings, weekly work hours, the number of nights spent on the road, and quality of equipment. There may be competition for the jobs with the highest earnings and most favorable work schedules.

Overall employment of truck drivers and driver/sales workers is expected to increase about as fast as the average for all occupations through the year 2014, due to growth in the economy and in the amount of freight carried by truck. Competing forms of freight transportation—rail, air, and ship transportation—still require trucks to move the goods between ports, depots, airports, warehouses, retailers, and final consumers who are not connected to these other modes of transportation. Demand for long-distance drivers will remain strong because they can transport perishable and time-sensitive goods more effectively than alternate modes of transportation. Job opportunities for truck drivers with local carriers will be more competitive than those with long-distance carriers because of the more desirable working conditions of local carriers.

Job opportunities may vary from year to year as the output of the economy dictates the amount of freight to be moved. Companies tend to hire more drivers when the economy is strong and their services are in high demand. When the economy slows, employers hire fewer drivers or may lay off some drivers. Independent owner-operators are particularly vulnerable to slowdowns. Industries least likely to be affected by economic fluctuation, such as grocery stores, tend to be the most stable employers of truck drivers and driver/sales workers.

Earnings

Median hourly earnings of heavy truck and tractor-trailer drivers were $16.11 in May 2004. The middle 50 percent earned between $12.67 and $20.09 an hour. The lowest 10 percent earned less than $10.18, and the highest 10 percent earned more than $24.07 an hour. Median hourly earnings in the industries employing the largest numbers of heavy truck and tractor-trailer drivers in May 2004 were

General freight trucking $17.56
Grocery and related product wholesalers 17.32
Specialized freight trucking 15.61
Employment services 14.82
Cement and concrete product manufacturing 14.47

Median hourly earnings of light or delivery services truck drivers were $11.80 in May 2004. The middle 50 percent earned between $8.96 and $16.00 an hour. The lowest 10 percent earned less than $7.20, and the highest 10 percent earned more than $20.83 an hour. Median hourly earnings in the industries employing the largest numbers of light or delivery services truck drivers in May 2004 were

Couriers $17.94
General freight trucking 14.79
Grocery and related product wholesalers 12.44
Building material and supplies dealers 10.85
Automotive parts, accessories, and tire stores............8.07

Median hourly earnings of driver/sales workers, including commissions, were $9.66 in May 2004. The middle 50 percent earned between $6.94 and $14.59 an hour. The lowest 10 percent earned less than $5.96, and the highest 10 percent earned more than $19.81 an hour. Median hourly earnings in the industries employing the largest numbers of driver/sales workers in May 2004 were

Drycleaning and laundry services $14.67
Direct selling establishments 13.55

Grocery and related product wholesalers 12.36
Limited-service eating places 6.77
Full-service restaurants 6.59

Local truck drivers tend to be paid by the hour, with extra pay for working overtime. Employers pay long-distance drivers primarily by the mile. The per-mile rate can vary greatly from employer to employer and may even depend on the type of cargo they are hauling. Some long-distance drivers are paid a percent of each load's revenue. Typically, earnings increase with mileage driven, seniority, and the size and type of truck driven. Most driver/sales workers receive commissions based on their sales in addition to their hourly wages.

Most self-employed truck drivers are primarily engaged in long-distance hauling. Many truck drivers are members of the International Brotherhood of Teamsters. Some truck drivers employed by companies outside the trucking industry are members of unions representing the plant workers of the companies for which they work.

Related Occupations

Other driving occupations include ambulance drivers and attendants, except emergency medical technicians; bus drivers; and taxi drivers and chauffeurs. Another occupation involving sales duties is sales representatives, wholesale and manufacturing.

Sources of Additional Information

Information on truck driver employment opportunities is available from local trucking companies and local offices of the state employment service.

Information on career opportunities in truck driving may be obtained from

▸ American Trucking Associations, Inc., 2200 Mill Rd., Alexandria, VA 22314. Internet: http://www.trucking.org

A list of certified tractor-trailer driver training courses may be obtained from

▸ Professional Truck Driver Institute, 2200 Mill Rd., Alexandria, VA 22314. Internet: http://www.ptdi.org

Information on union truck driving can be obtained from

▸ The International Brotherhood of Teamsters, 25 Louisiana Ave. NW, Washington, DC 20001.

Welding, Soldering, and Brazing Workers

(O*NET 51-4121.01, 51-4121.02, 51-4121.03, 51-4121.04, 51-4121.05, 51-4122.01, 51-4122.02, 51-4122.03, and 51-4122.04)

Significant Points

■ More than 6 out of 10 jobs are found in manufacturing industries.

■ Training ranges from a few weeks of school or on-the-job training for low-skilled positions to several years of combined school and on-the-job training for highly skilled jobs.

- Employment is projected to grow more slowly than average.
- Job prospects should be excellent as employers report difficulty finding enough qualified people.

Nature of the Work

Welding is the most common way of permanently joining metal parts. In this process, heat is applied to metal pieces, melting and fusing them to form a permanent bond. Because of its strength, welding is used in shipbuilding, automobile manufacturing and repair, aerospace applications, and thousands of other manufacturing activities. Welding also is used to join beams when constructing buildings, bridges, and other structures and to join pipes in pipelines, power plants, and refineries.

Welders use many types of welding equipment set up in a variety of positions, such as flat, vertical, horizontal, and overhead. They may perform manual welding, in which the work is entirely controlled by the welder, or semiautomatic welding, in which the welder uses machinery, such as a wire feeder, to perform welding tasks.

There are about 100 different types of welding. Arc welding is the most common type. Standard arc welding involves two large metal alligator clips that carry a strong electrical current. One clip is attached to any part of the workpiece being welded. The second clip is connected to a thin welding rod. When the rod touches the workpiece, a powerful electrical circuit is created. The massive heat created by the electrical current causes both the workpiece and the steel core of the rod to melt together, cooling quickly to form a solid bond. During welding, the flux that surrounds the rod's core vaporizes, forming an inert gas that serves to protect the weld from atmospheric elements that might weaken it. Welding speed is important. Variations in speed can change the amount of flux applied, weakening the weld or weakening the surrounding metal by increasing heat exposure.

Two common but advanced types of arc welding are Tungsten Inert Gas (TIG) and Metal Inert Gas (MIG) welding. TIG welding often is used with stainless steel or aluminum. While TIG uses welding rods, MIG uses a spool of continuously fed wire, which allows the welder to join longer stretches of metal without stopping to replace the rod. In TIG welding, the welder holds the welding rod in one hand and an electric torch in the other hand. The torch is used to simultaneously melt the rod and the workpiece. In MIG welding, the welder holds the wire feeder, which functions like the alligator clip in arc welding. Instead of using gas flux surrounding the rod, TIG and MIG protect the initial weld from the environment by blowing inert gas onto the weld.

Like arc welding, soldering and brazing use molten metal to join two pieces of metal. However, the metal added during the process has a melting point lower than that of the workpiece, so only the added metal is melted, not the workpiece. Soldering uses metals with a melting point below 800 degrees Fahrenheit; brazing uses metals with a higher melting point. Because soldering and brazing do not melt the workpiece, these processes normally do not create the distortions or weaknesses in the workpiece that can occur with welding. Soldering commonly is used to join electrical, electronic, and other small metal parts. Brazing produces a stronger joint than does soldering and often is used to join metals other than steel, such as brass. Brazing can also be used to apply coatings to parts to reduce wear and protect against corrosion.

Skilled welding, soldering, and brazing workers generally plan work from drawings or specifications or use their knowledge of fluxes and base metals to analyze the parts to be joined. These workers then select and set up welding equipment, execute the planned welds, and examine welds to ensure that they meet standards or specifications. They are even examining the weld while they're welding. By observing problems with the weld, they compensate by adjusting the speed, voltage, amperage, or feed of the rod. Highly skilled welders often are trained to work with a wide variety of materials in addition to steel, such as titanium, aluminum, or plastics. Some welders have more limited duties, however. They perform routine jobs that already have been planned and laid out and do not require extensive knowledge of welding techniques.

Automated welding is used in an increasing number of production processes. In these instances, a machine or robot performs the welding tasks while monitored by a welding machine operator. Welding, soldering, and brazing machine setters, operators, and tenders follow specified layouts, work orders, or blueprints. Operators must load parts correctly and constantly monitor the machine to ensure that it produces the desired bond.

The work of arc, plasma, and oxy-gas cutters is closely related to that of welders. However, instead of joining metals, cutters use the heat from an electric arc, a stream of ionized gas (plasma), or burning gases to cut and trim metal objects to specific dimensions. Cutters also dismantle large objects, such as ships, railroad cars, automobiles, buildings, or aircraft. Some operate and monitor cutting machines similar to those used by welding machine operators. Plasma cutting has been increasing in popularity because, unlike other methods, it can cut a wide variety of metals, including stainless steel, aluminum, and titanium.

Working Conditions

Welding, soldering, and brazing workers often are exposed to a number of hazards, including the intense light created by the arc, poisonous fumes, and very hot materials. They wear safety shoes, goggles, hoods with protective lenses, and other devices designed to prevent burns and eye injuries and to protect them from falling objects. They normally work in well-ventilated areas to limit their exposure to fumes. Automated welding, soldering, and brazing machine operators are not exposed to as many dangers, however, and a face shield or goggles usually provide adequate protection for these workers.

Welders and cutters may work outdoors, often in inclement weather, or indoors, sometimes in a confined area designed to contain sparks and glare. Outdoors, they may work on a scaffold or platform high off the ground. In addition, they may be required to lift heavy objects and work in a variety of awkward positions while bending, stooping, or standing to perform work overhead.

Although about 52 percent of welders, solderers, and brazers work a 40-hour week, overtime is common, and some welders work up to 70 hours per week. Welders also may work in shifts as long as 12 hours. Some welders, solderers, brazers, and machine operators work in factories that operate around the clock, necessitating shift work.

Training, Other Qualifications, and Advancement

Training for welding, soldering, and brazing workers can range from a few weeks of school or on-the-job training for low-skilled positions to several years of combined school and on-the-job training for highly skilled jobs. Formal training is available in high schools; vocational schools; and postsecondary institutions, such as vocational-technical institutes, community colleges, and private welding schools. The Armed Forces operate welding schools as well. While some employers provide basic training, they prefer to hire workers with experience or more formal training. Courses in blueprint reading, shop mathematics, mechanical drawing, physics, chemistry, and metallurgy are helpful. An understanding of electricity also is very helpful and knowledge of computers is gaining importance, especially for welding, soldering, and brazing machine operators, who are becoming more responsible for the programming of computer-controlled machines, including robots.

Some welders become certified, a process whereby the employer sends a worker to an institution, such as an independent testing lab, equipment manufacturer, or technical school, to weld a test specimen according to specific codes and standards required by the employer. Testing procedures are based on the standards and codes set by industry associations with which the employer may be affiliated. If the welding inspector at the examining institution determines that the worker has performed according to the employer's guidelines, the inspector will then certify that the welder being tested is able to work with a particular welding procedure.

Welding, soldering, and brazing workers need good eyesight, hand-eye coordination, and manual dexterity. They should be able to concentrate on detailed work for long periods and be able to bend, stoop, and work in awkward positions. In addition, welders increasingly need to be willing to receive training and perform tasks in other production jobs.

Welders can advance to more-skilled welding jobs with additional training and experience. For example, they may become welding technicians, supervisors, inspectors, or instructors. Some experienced welders open their own repair shops.

Employment

Welding, soldering, and brazing workers held about 429,000 jobs in 2004. Of these jobs, more than 6 of every 10 were found in manufacturing. Jobs were concentrated in fabricated metal product manufacturing, transportation equipment manufacturing (motor vehicle body and parts and ship and boat building), machinery manufacturing (agriculture, construction, and mining machinery), architectural and structural metals manufacturing, and construction. Most jobs for welding, soldering, and brazing machine setters, operators, and tenders were found in the same manufacturing industries as skilled welding, soldering, and brazing workers.

Job Outlook

Employment of welding, soldering, and brazing workers is expected to grow more slowly than the average for all occupations over the 2004–2014 period. Despite this, job prospects should be excellent as employers report difficulty finding enough qualified people. In addition, many openings are expected to arise as a large number of workers retire over the next decade.

The major factor affecting employment of welders is the health of the industries in which they work. The manufacturing sector, which employs the most welding, soldering, and brazing workers, is expected to continue to decline as more manufacturing moves overseas. Because almost every manufacturing industry uses welding at some stage of manufacturing or in the repair and maintenance of equipment, this overall decline will affect the demand for welders, although some industries will fare better than others. The construction industry is expected to have solid growth over the next decade and an increasing demand for welders. Government funding for shipbuilding as well as for infrastructure repairs and improvements are expected to generate additional welding jobs.

Pressures to improve productivity and hold down labor costs are leading many companies to invest more in automation, especially computer-controlled and robotically controlled welding machinery. This will reduce the demand for some welders, solderers, and brazers because many repetitive jobs are being automated. The growing use of automation, however, should increase demand for welding, soldering, and brazing machine setters, operators, and tenders. Welders working on construction projects or in equipment repair will not be affected by technology change to the same extent because their jobs are often unique and not as easily automated.

Despite slower-than-average job growth, technology is creating more uses for welding in the workplace and expanding employment opportunities. For example, new ways are being developed to bond dissimilar materials and nonmetallic materials, such as plastics, composites, and new alloys. Also, laser beam and electron beam welding, new fluxes, and other new technologies and techniques are improving the results of welding, making it useful in a wider assortment of applications. Improvements in technology have also boosted welding productivity, making welding more competitive with other methods of joining materials.

Earnings

Median hourly earnings of welders, cutters, solderers, and brazers were $14.72 in May 2004. The middle 50 percent earned between $11.90 and $18.05. The lowest 10 percent had earnings of less than $9.79, while the top 10 percent earned more than $22.20. The range of earnings of welders reflects the wide range of skill levels. Median hourly earnings in the industries employing the largest numbers of welders, cutters, solderers, and brazers in May 2004 were

Motor vehicle parts manufacturing $16.47

Agriculture, construction, and mining machinery
    manufacturing 14.12

Architectural and structural metals manufacturing 13.98

Commercial and industrial machinery and
    equipment (except automotive and electronic)
    repair and maintenance 13.45

Motor vehicle body and trailer manufacturing 13.45

Median hourly earnings of welding, soldering, and brazing machine setters, operators, and tenders were $14.32 in May 2004. The middle 50 percent earned between $11.73 and $17.78. The lowest 10 percent had earnings of less than $9.63, while the top 10 percent earned more than $23.54. Median hourly earnings in motor vehicle parts manufacturing, the industry employing the largest numbers of welding machine operators in May 2004, were $15.43.

Many welders belong to unions. Among these are the International Association of Machinists and Aerospace Workers; the International Brotherhood of Boilermakers, Iron Ship Builders, Blacksmiths, Forgers, and Helpers; the International Union, United Automobile, Aerospace, and Agricultural Implement Workers of America; the United Association of Journeymen and Apprentices of the Plumbing, Pipefitting, Sprinkler Fitting Industry of the United States and Canada; and the United Electrical, Radio, and Machine Workers of America.

Related Occupations

Welding, soldering, and brazing workers are skilled metal workers. Other metal workers include machinists; machine setters, operators, and tenders—metal and plastic; computer control programmers and operators; tool and die makers; sheet metal workers; and boilermakers. Assemblers and fabricators of electrical and electronic equipment often assemble parts using soldering.

Sources of Additional Information

For information on training opportunities and jobs for welding, soldering, and brazing workers, contact local employers, the local office of the state employment service, or schools providing welding, soldering, or brazing training.

Information on careers and educational opportunities in welding is available from

▶ American Welding Society, 550 NW Lejeune Rd., Miami, FL 33126. Internet: http://www.aws.org

Woodworkers

(O*NET 51-7011.00, 51-7021.00, 51-7031.00, 51-7032.00, 51-7041.01, 51-7041.02, 51-7042.01, 51-7042.02, 51-7099.99)

Significant Points

- Most woodworkers are trained on the job; basic machine operations may be learned in a few months, but becoming a skilled woodworker often requires 2 or more years.

- Overall employment is expected to decline.

- Job prospects will be best for highly skilled woodworkers who produce customized output, which is less susceptible to automation and import competition, and for those who know how to operate computerized numerical control (CNC) machines.

- Employment is highly sensitive to economic cycles; during economic downturns, workers are subject to layoffs or reductions in hours.

Nature of the Work

Despite the development of sophisticated plastics and other materials, the demand for wood products continues unabated. Helping to meet this demand are woodworkers. Woodworkers are found in industries that produce wood, such as sawmills and plywood mills; in industries that use wood to produce furniture, kitchen cabinets, musical instruments, and other fabricated wood products; and in small shops that make architectural woodwork, furniture, and many other specialty items.

All woodworkers are employed at some stage of the process through which logs of wood are transformed into finished products. Some of these workers produce the structural elements of buildings; others mill hardwood and softwood lumber; still others assemble finished wood products. They operate machines that cut, shape, assemble, and finish raw wood to make the doors, windows, cabinets, trusses, plywood, flooring, paneling, molding, and trim that are components of most homes. Others may fashion home accessories, such as beds, sofas, tables, dressers, and chairs. In addition to these household goods, woodworkers also make sporting goods, including baseball bats and oars, as well as musical instruments, toys, caskets, tool handles, and thousands of other wooden items.

Production woodworkers set up, operate, and tend woodworking machines such as power saws, planers, sanders, lathes, jointers, and routers that cut and shape components from lumber, plywood, and other wood products. In sawmills, *sawing machine operators and tenders* set up, operate, or tend wood-sawing machines that cut logs into planks, timbers, or boards. In plants manufacturing wood products, woodworkers first determine the best method of shaping and assembling parts, working from blueprints, supervisors' instructions, or shop drawings that woodworkers themselves produce. Before cutting, they often must measure and mark the materials. They verify dimensions and may trim parts, using hand tools such as planes, chisels, wood files, or sanders, to ensure a tight fit. *Woodworking machine operators and tenders* set up, operate, or tend specific woodworking machines, such as drill presses, lathes, shapers, routers, sanders, planers, and wood-nailing machines. Lower-skilled operators may merely press a switch on a woodworking machine and monitor the automatic operation, whereas more highly skilled operators set up equipment, cut and shape wooden parts, and verify dimensions using a template, caliper, or rule.

The next step in the manufacturing process is the production of sub-assemblies using fasteners and adhesives. Next, the pieces are brought together to form a complete unit. The product is then finish-sanded; stained; and, if necessary, coated with a sealer, such as lacquer or varnish. Woodworkers may perform this work in teams or be assisted by a helper.

Woodworkers have been greatly affected by the introduction of computer-controlled machinery. This technology has raised worker productivity by allowing one operator to simultaneously tend a greater number of machines. An operator can program a CNC machine to perform a sequence of operations automatically, resulting in greater precision and reliability. The integration of computers with equipment has improved production speed and capability, simplified setup and maintenance requirements, and increased the demand for workers with computer skills.

While this costly equipment has had a great effect on workers in the largest, most efficient firms, precision or custom woodworkers—who generally work in smaller firms—have continued to employ the same production techniques they have used for many years. Workers such as *cabinetmakers and bench carpenters, modelmakers and patternmakers,* and *furniture finishers* work on a customized basis, often building one-of-a-kind items. These highly skilled precision woodworkers usually perform a complete cycle of tasks—cutting, shaping, and preparing surfaces and assembling prepared parts of complex wood components into a finished wood product. For this reason, these workers normally need substantial training and an ability to work from detailed instructions and specifications. In addition, they often are required to exercise independent judgment when undertaking an assignment.

Working Conditions

Working conditions vary by industry and specific job duties. In logging and sawmills, for example, working conditions are physically demanding because of the handling of heavy, bulky material. Workers in these industries also may encounter excessive noise, dust, and other air pollutants. However, the use of earplugs and respirators may partially alleviate these problems. Also, rigid adherence to safety precautions minimizes risk of injury from contact with rough wood stock, sharp tools, and power equipment. The risk of injury also is lowered by the installation of computer-controlled equipment, which reduces the physical labor and hands-on contact with machinery.

In furniture and kitchen cabinet manufacturing, employees who operate machinery often must wear ear and eye protection. They also must follow operating safety instructions and use safety shields or guards to prevent accidents. Those who work in the finishing area must be provided with an appropriate dust or vapor mask or a complete protective safety suit or must work in a finishing environment that removes all vapors and dust particles from the atmosphere. Prolonged standing, lifting, and fitting of heavy objects are common characteristics of the job.

Training, Other Qualifications, and Advancement

Most woodworkers are trained on the job, picking up skills informally from experienced workers. Most woodworkers learn basic machine operations and job tasks in a few months, but becoming a skilled woodworker often requires 2 or more years.

Woodworkers increasingly acquire skills through vocational education. Some may learn by working as carpenters on construction jobs. Others may attend colleges or universities that offer training in areas including wood technology, furniture manufacturing, wood engineering, and production management. These programs prepare students for positions in production, supervision, engineering, and management and are increasingly important as woodworking technology becomes more advanced.

Beginners usually observe and help experienced machine operators. They may supply material to, or remove fabricated products from, machines. Trainees also do simple machine operating jobs while closely supervised by experienced workers, but as beginners gain experience, they perform more complex jobs with less supervision. Some may learn to read blueprints, set up machines, and plan the sequence of the work. Employers seek applicants with a high school diploma or the equivalent because of the growing sophistication of machinery and the constant need for retraining. People seeking woodworking jobs can enhance their employment and advancement prospects by completing high school and receiving training in mathematics, science, and computer applications. Other important qualities for entrants in this occupation include mechanical ability, manual dexterity, and the ability to pay attention to detail.

Advancement opportunities often are limited and depend on education and training, seniority, and a worker's skills and initiative. Sometimes experienced woodworkers become inspectors or supervisors responsible for the work of a group of woodworkers. Production workers often can advance into these positions by assuming additional responsibilities and by attending workshops, seminars, or college programs. Those who are highly skilled may set up their own woodworking shops.

Employment

Woodworkers held about 364,000 jobs in 2004. Self-employed woodworkers, mostly cabinetmakers and furniture finishers, accounted for 14 percent of these jobs. Employment among detailed woodworking occupations was distributed as follows:

Cabinetmakers and bench carpenters	148,000
Woodworking machine setters, operators, and tenders, except sawing	92,000
Sawing machine setters, operators, and tenders, wood	58,000
Furniture finishers	34,000
Model makers, wood	3,200
Patternmakers, wood	2,500
All other woodworkers	26,000

Almost 3 out of 4 woodworkers were employed in manufacturing industries. One-third of woodworkers were found in establishments fabricating household and office furniture and fixtures, and 30 percent worked in wood product manufacturing, producing a variety of raw, intermediate, and finished woodstock. Wholesale and retail lumber dealers, furniture stores, reupholstery and furniture repair shops, and construction firms also employ woodworkers.

Woodworking jobs are found throughout the country. However, lumber and wood products-related production jobs are concentrated in the South and Northwest, close to the supply of wood, whereas furnituremakers are more prevalent in the Southeast. Custom shops can be found everywhere, but generally are concentrated in or near highly populated areas.

Job Outlook

Overall employment of woodworkers is expected to decline through 2014, although job growth and opportunities will vary by specialty. In general, opportunities for more highly skilled woodworkers will be better than for woodworkers in specialties susceptible to productivity improvements and competition from imported wood products.

Despite the expected overall decline in employment of woodworkers, many job opportunities still will arise each year because of the need to replace experienced woodworkers who transfer to other occupations or leave the labor force. Firms will need woodworkers with technical skills to operate their increasingly advanced computerized machinery. The number of new workers entering these occupations is expected to be low because, as school systems face tighter budgets, the first programs to be cut often are vocational-technical programs, including those that train woodworkers. Also, interest in pursuing these jobs will continue to decline as workers question the stability of manufacturing occupations. For these reasons, competition should be mild, and opportunities should be best for woodworkers who, through vocational education or experience, develop highly specialized woodworking skills or knowledge of CNC machine tool operation.

Employment of sawing and woodworking machine setters, operators, and tenders is expected to decline through 2014. Jobs in the United States will continue to be lost as imports grow. To remain competitive with these imports, some domestic firms are expected to continue to move their production processes to foreign countries, further reducing employment. Others are using advanced technology, such as robots and CNC machinery, to reduce the number of workers needed in production. These forces will prevent employment from rising with the demand for wood products, particularly in the mills and manufacturing plants where many processes can be automated. Among woodworking machine operators, job prospects will be best for those skilled in CNC machine tool operation.

Employment of furniture finishers is expected to decline. Since furniture is largely mass-produced, it is highly susceptible to import competition; the percentage of furniture sold in the United States that is produced abroad has steadily increased over the past 10 years, a trend that is expected to continue.

Employment of bench carpenters, cabinetmakers, modelmakers, patternmakers, and other specialized woodworking occupations will grow more slowly than the average. Demand for these workers will stem from increases in population, personal income, and business expenditures in addition to the continuing need for repair and renovation of residential and commercial properties. Therefore, opportunities should be available for those who specialize in items such as moldings, cabinets, stairs, and windows. Firms that focus on custom woodwork will be best able to compete against imports without transferring jobs offshore, so opportunities should be very good in specialized woodworking sectors, such as architectural woodworking. Modelmakers and patternmakers who know how to create and execute designs on a computer may have the best opportunities.

Employment in all woodworking specialties is highly sensitive to economic cycles. During economic downturns, workers are subject to layoffs or reductions in hours.

Earnings

Median hourly earnings of cabinetmakers and bench carpenters were $12.16 in May 2004. The middle 50 percent earned between $9.69 and $15.51. The lowest 10 percent earned less than $8.00, and the highest 10 percent earned more than $19.28. Median hourly earnings in the industries employing the largest numbers of cabinetmakers and bench carpenters in May 2004 are shown here:

Office furniture (including fixtures)
manufacturing $13.42
Household and institutional furniture and
kitchen cabinet manufacturing 11.83
Other wood product manufacturing 11.82

Median hourly earnings of sawing machine setters, operators, and tenders, wood, were $10.91 in May 2004. The middle 50 percent earned between $8.95 and $13.34. The lowest 10 percent earned less than $7.46, and the highest 10 percent earned more than $16.20. Median hourly earnings in the industries employing the largest numbers of sawing machine setters, operators, and tenders, wood, in May 2004, are shown here:

Sawmills and wood preservation $11.82
Veneer, plywood, and engineered wood product
manufacturing 11.49
Household and institutional furniture and kitchen
cabinet manufacturing......................................10.65
Other wood product manufacturing 10.49

Median hourly earnings of woodworking machine setters, operators, and tenders, except sawing, were $10.93 in May 2004. The middle 50 percent earned between $8.93 and $13.40. The lowest 10 percent earned less than $7.55, and the highest 10 percent earned more than $16.33. Median hourly earnings in the industries employing the largest numbers of woodworking machine setters, operators, and tenders, except sawing, in May 2004, are shown here:

Office furniture (including fixtures) manufacturing ..$11.66
Veneer, plywood, and engineered wood product
manufacturing 11.19
Household and institutional furniture and kitchen
cabinet manufacturing......................................11.00
Sawmills and wood preservation 10.83
Other wood product manufacturing 10.47

In May 2004, median hourly earnings were $11.35 for furniture finishers and $10.16 for all other woodworkers.

Some woodworkers, such as those in logging or sawmills who are engaged in processing primary wood and building materials, are members of the International Association of Machinists. Others belong to the United Brotherhood of carpenters and Joiners of America.

Related Occupations

Carpenters also work with wood. In addition, many woodworkers follow blueprints and drawings and use machines to shape and form raw wood into a final product. Workers who perform similar functions working with other materials include sheet metal workers, structural and reinforcing iron and metal workers, computer-control programmers and operators, machinists, and tool and die makers.

Sources of Additional Information

For information about woodworking occupations, contact local furniture manufacturers, sawmills and planing mills, cabinetmaking or millwork firms, lumber dealers, a local of one of the unions mentioned earlier, or the nearest office of the state employment service.

Writers and Editors

(O*NET 27-3041.00, 27-3042.00, 27-3043.01, 27-3043.02, 27-3043.03, and 27-3043.04)

Significant Points

- Most jobs in this occupation require a college degree in communications, journalism, or English, although a degree in a technical subject may be useful for technical-writing positions.

- The outlook for most writing and editing jobs is expected to be competitive because many people are attracted to the occupation.

- Online publications and services are growing in number and sophistication, spurring the demand for writers and editors, especially those with Web experience.

Nature of the Work

Communicating through the written word, writers and editors generally fall into one of three categories. *Writers and authors* develop original fiction and nonfiction for books, magazines, trade journals, online publications, company newsletters, radio and television broadcasts, motion pictures, and advertisements. *Editors* examine proposals and select material for publication or broadcast. They review and revise a writer's work for publication or dissemination. *Technical writers* develop technical materials, such as equipment manuals, appendixes, or operating and maintenance instructions. They also may assist in layout work.

Most writers and editors have at least a basic familiarity with technology, regularly using personal computers, desktop or electronic publishing systems, scanners, and other electronic communications equipment. Many writers prepare material directly for the Internet. For example, they may write for electronic newspapers or magazines, create short fiction or poetry, or produce technical documentation that is available only online. Also, they may write text for Web sites. These writers should be knowledgeable about graphic design, page layout, and multimedia software. In addition, they should be familiar with interactive technologies of the Web so that they can blend text, graphics, and sound together.

Writers—especially of nonfiction—are expected to establish their credibility with editors and readers through strong research and the use of appropriate sources and citations. Sustaining high ethical standards and meeting publication deadlines are essential.

Creative writers, poets, and lyricists, including novelists, playwrights, and screenwriters, create original works—such as prose, poems, plays, and song lyrics—for publication or performance. Some works may be commissioned by a sponsor; others may be written for hire (on the basis of the completion of a draft or an outline).

Nonfiction writers either propose a topic or are assigned one, often by an editor or publisher. They gather information about the topic through personal observation, library and Internet research, and interviews. Writers then select the material they want to use, organize it, and use the written word to express ideas and convey information. Writers also revise or rewrite sections, searching for the best organization or the right phrasing. *Copy writers* prepare advertising copy for use by publication or broadcast media or to promote the sale of goods and services. *Newsletter writers* produce information for distribution to association memberships, corporate employees, organizational clients, or the public.

Freelance writers sell their work to publishers, publication enterprises, manufacturing firms, public relations departments, or advertising agencies. Sometimes they contract with publishers to write a book or an article. Others may be hired to complete specific assignments, such as writing about a new product or technique.

Bloggers write for the Internet. Most bloggers write personal reflections on a subject of close personal or professional interest. Some blogs take the form of a personal diary; others read like reports from the field—first-hand, subjective accounts of an event or an activity. Most blogs are written for recreational reasons with little expectation of earning a fee; however, some blogs promote a business or support a cause and may generate interest or income through other activities.

Editors review, rewrite, and edit the work of writers. They may also do original writing. An editor's responsibilities vary with the employer and type and level of editorial position held. Editorial duties may include planning the content of books, technical journals, trade magazines, and other general-interest publications. Editors also decide what material will appeal to readers, review and edit drafts of books and articles, offer comments to improve the work, and suggest possible titles. In addition, they may oversee the production of the publications. In the book-publishing industry, an editor's primary responsibility is to review proposals for books and decide whether to buy the publication rights from the author.

Major newspapers and newsmagazines usually employ several types of editors. The *executive editor* oversees *assistant editors,* who have responsibility for particular subjects, such as local news, international news, feature stories, or sports. Executive editors generally have the final say about what stories are published and how they are covered. The *managing editor* usually is responsible for the daily operation of the news department. *Assignment editors* determine which reporters will cover a given story. *Copy editors* mostly review and edit a reporter's copy for accuracy, content, grammar, and style.

In smaller organizations, such as small daily or weekly newspapers or the membership or publications departments of nonprofit or similar organizations, a single editor may do everything or share responsibility with only a few other people. Executive and managing editors typically hire writers, reporters, and other employees. They also plan budgets and negotiate contracts with freelance writers, sometimes called "stringers" in the news industry. In broadcasting companies, *program directors* have similar responsibilities.

Editors and program directors often have assistants, many of whom hold entry-level jobs. These assistants, such as copy editors and *production assistants,* review copy for errors in grammar, punctuation, and spelling and check the copy for readability, style, and agreement with editorial policy. They suggest revisions, such as changing words and rearranging sentences, to improve clarity or accuracy. They also carry out research for writers and verify facts, dates, and statistics. Production assistants arrange page layouts of articles, photographs, and advertising; compose headlines; and prepare copy for printing. *Publication assistants* who work for publishing houses may read and evaluate manuscripts submitted by freelance writers, proofread printers' galleys, and answer letters about published material. Production assistants on small newspapers or in radio stations compile articles available from wire services or the Internet, answer phones, and make photocopies.

Technical writers put technical information into easily understandable language. They prepare operating and maintenance manuals, catalogs, parts lists, assembly instructions, sales promotion materials, and project proposals. Many technical writers work with engineers on technical subject matters to prepare written interpretations of engineering and design specifications and other information for a general readership. Technical writers also may serve as part of a team conducting usability studies to help improve the design of a product that still is in the prototype stage. They plan and edit technical materials and oversee the preparation of illustrations, photographs, diagrams, and charts.

Science and medical writers prepare a range of formal documents presenting detailed information on the physical or medical sciences. They convey research findings for scientific or medical professions and organize information for advertising or public relations needs. Many writers work with researchers on technical subjects to prepare written interpretations of data and other information for a general readership.

Working Conditions

Some writers and editors work in comfortable, private offices; others work in noisy rooms filled with the sound of keyboards and computer printers, as well as the voices of other writers tracking down information over the telephone. The search for information sometimes requires that writers travel to diverse workplaces, such as factories, offices, or laboratories, but many find their material through telephone interviews, the library, and the Internet.

Advances in electronic communications have changed the work environment for many writers. Laptop computers and wireless communications technologies allow growing numbers of writers to work from home and even on the road. The ability to e-mail, transmit, and download stories, research, or editorial review materials using the Internet allows writers and editors greater flexibility in where and how they complete assignments.

Some writers keep regular office hours, either to maintain contact with sources and editors or to establish a writing routine, but most writers set their own hours. Many writers, especially freelance writers, are paid per assignment; therefore, they work any number of hours necessary to meet a deadline. As a result, writers must be willing to work evenings, nights, or weekends to produce a piece acceptable to an editor or client by the publication deadline. Those who prepare morning or weekend publications and broadcasts also may regularly work nights and weekends.

While many freelance writers enjoy running their own businesses and the advantages of working flexible hours, most routinely face the pressures of juggling multiple projects with competing demands and the continual need to find new work in order to earn a living. Deadline pressures and long, erratic work hours—often part of the daily routine in these jobs—may cause stress, fatigue, or burnout; use of computers for extended periods may cause some individuals to experience back pain, eyestrain, or fatigue.

Training, Other Qualifications, and Advancement

A college degree generally is required for a position as a writer or editor. Although some employers look for a broad liberal arts background, most prefer to hire people with degrees in communications, journalism, or English. For those who specialize in a particular area, such as fashion, business, or law, additional background in the chosen field is expected. Knowledge of a second language is helpful for some positions.

Increasingly, technical writing requires a degree in, or some knowledge about, a specialized field—for example, engineering, business, or one of the sciences. In many cases, people with good writing skills can acquire specialized knowledge on the job. Some transfer from jobs as technicians, scientists, or engineers. Others begin as research assistants or as trainees in a technical information department, develop technical communication skills, and then assume writing duties.

Writers and editors must be able to express ideas clearly and logically and should love to write. Creativity, curiosity, a broad range of knowledge, self-motivation, and perseverance also are valuable. Writers and editors must demonstrate good judgment and a strong sense of ethics in deciding what material to publish. Editors also need tact and the ability to guide and encourage others in their work.

For some jobs, the ability to concentrate amid confusion and to work under pressure is essential. Familiarity with electronic publishing, graphics, and video production equipment increasingly is needed. Use of electronic and wireless communications equipment to send e-mail, transmit work, and review copy often is necessary. Online newspapers and magazines require knowledge of computer software used to combine online text with graphics, audio, video, and animation.

High school and college newspapers, literary magazines, community newspapers, and radio and television stations all provide valuable, but sometimes unpaid, practical writing experience. Many magazines, newspapers, and broadcast stations have internships for students. Interns write short pieces, conduct research and interviews, and learn about the publishing or broadcasting business.

In small firms, beginning writers and editors hired as assistants may actually begin writing or editing material right away. Opportunities for advancement can be limited, however. Many writers look for work on a short-term, project-by-project basis. Many small or not-for-profit organizations either do not have enough regular work or cannot afford to employ writers on a full-time basis. However, they routinely contract out work to freelance writers.

In larger businesses, jobs usually are more formally structured. Beginners generally do research, fact checking, or copy editing. Advancement to full-scale writing or editing assignments may occur more slowly for newer writers and editors in larger organizations than for employees of smaller companies. Advancement often is more predictable, though, coming with the assignment of more important articles.

Advancement for freelancers often means working on larger, more complex projects for more money. Building a reputation and establishing a track record for meeting deadlines also makes it easier to get future assignments, as does instituting long-term freelance relationships with the same publications.

The growing popularity of blogs could allow some writers to get their work read; a few well-written blogs may garner some recognition for the author and may lead to a few paid pieces in other print or electronic publications. However, most bloggers do not earn much money writing their blogs.

Employment

Writers and editors held about 320,000 jobs in 2004. More than one-third were self-employed. Writers and authors held about 142,000 jobs; editors, about 127,000 jobs; and technical writers, about 50,000 jobs. About one-half of the salaried jobs for writers and editors were in the information sector, which includes newspaper, periodical, book, and directory publishers; radio and television broadcasting; software publishers; motion picture and sound-recording industries; Internet service providers, Web search portals, and data-processing services; and Internet publishing and broadcasting. Substantial numbers also worked in advertising and related services, computer systems design and related services, and public and private educational services. Other salaried writers and editors worked in computer and electronic product manufacturing; government agencies; religious organizations; and business, professional, labor, political, and similar organizations.

Jobs with major book publishers, magazines, broadcasting companies, advertising agencies, and public relations firms are concentrated in New York, Chicago, Los Angeles, Boston, Philadelphia, and San Francisco; however, many writers work elsewhere and travel regularly to meet with personnel at the headquarters. Jobs with newspapers, business and professional journals, and technical and trade magazines are more widely dispersed throughout the country.

Thousands of other individuals work as freelance writers, earning some income from their articles, books, and, less commonly, television and movie scripts. Most support themselves with income derived from other sources.

Job Outlook

Employment of writers and editors is expected to grow about as fast as the average for all occupations through the year 2014. The outlook for most writing and editing jobs is expected to be competitive because many people with writing or journalism training are attracted to the occupation.

Employment of salaried writers and editors for newspapers, periodicals, book publishers, and nonprofit organizations is expected to increase as demand grows for these publications. Magazines and other periodicals increasingly are developing market niches, appealing to readers with special interests. Businesses and organizations are developing newsletters and Web sites, and more companies are experimenting with publishing materials directly on the Internet. Online publications and services are growing in number and sophistication, spurring the demand for writers and editors, especially those with Web experience. Advertising and public relations agencies, which also are growing, should be another source of new jobs.

Opportunities should be best for technical writers and those with training in a specialized field. Demand for technical writers and writers with expertise in areas such as law, medicine, or economics is expected to increase because of the continuing expansion of scientific and technical information and the need to communicate it to others. Legal, scientific, and technological developments and discoveries generate demand for people to interpret technical information for a more general audience. Rapid growth and change in the high-technology and electronics industries result in a greater need for people to write users' guides, instruction manuals, and training materials. This work requires people who not only are technically skilled as writers, but also are familiar with the subject area.

In addition to job openings created by employment growth, some openings will arise as experienced workers retire, transfer to other occupations, or leave the labor force. Replacement needs are relatively high in this occupation; many freelancers leave because they cannot earn enough money.

Earnings

Median annual earnings for salaried writers and authors were $44,350 in May 2004. The middle 50 percent earned between $31,720 and $62,930. The lowest 10 percent earned less than $23,330, and the highest 10 percent earned more than $91,260. Median annual earnings were $54,410 in advertising and related services and $37,010 in newspaper, periodical, book, and directory publishers.

Median annual earnings for salaried editors were $43,890 in May 2004. The middle 50 percent earned between $33,130 and $58,850. The lowest 10 percent earned less than $25,780, and the highest 10 percent earned more than $80,020. Median annual earnings of those working for newspaper, periodical, book, and directory publishers were $43,620.

Median annual earnings for salaried technical writers were $53,490 in May 2004. The middle 50 percent earned between $41,440 and $68,980. The lowest 10 percent earned less than $32,490, and the highest 10 percent earned more than $86,780. Median annual earnings in computer systems design and related services were $54,710.

According to the Society for Technical Communication, the median annual salary for entry-level technical writers was $42,500 in 2004. The median annual salary for midlevel nonsupervisory technical writers was $51,500, and for senior nonsupervisory technical writers, $66,000.

Related Occupations

Writers and editors communicate ideas and information. Other communications occupations include announcers; interpreters and translators; news analysts, reporters, and correspondents; and public relations specialists.

Sources of Additional Information

For information on careers in technical writing, contact

▶ Society for Technical Communication, Inc., 901 N. Stuart St., Suite 904, Arlington, VA 22203. Internet: http://www.stc.org

QUICK JOB SEARCH

Seven Steps to Getting a Good Job in Less Time

The Complete Text of a Results-Oriented Minibook

Millions of job seekers have found better jobs faster using the techniques in the *Quick Job Search*. So can you! The *Quick Job Search* covers the essential steps proven to cut job search time in half and is used widely by job search programs throughout North America. Topics include how to identify your key skills, define your ideal job, write a great resume quickly, use the most effective job search methods, get more interviews, and much more.

If you completed "Using the Job-Match Grid to Choose a Career" earlier in this book, the activities in this section will complement those efforts by helping you to define other skills you possess, focus your resume, and get a job quickly.

While it is a section in this book, the *Quick Job Search* is available from JIST Publishing as a separate booklet and in an expanded form as *Seven-Step Job Search*.

Quick Job Search Is Short, But It May Be All You Need

While *Quick Job Search* is short, it covers the basics on how to explore career options and conduct an effective job search. While these topics can seem complex, I have found some simple truths about looking for a job:

- If you are going to work, you might as well look for what you really want to do and are good at.

- If you are looking for a job, you might as well use techniques that will reduce the time it takes to find one—and that help you get a better job than you might otherwise.

That's what I emphasize in *Quick Job Search*.

Trust Me—Do the Worksheets. I know you will resist completing the worksheets. But trust me. They are worth your time. Doing them will give you a better sense of what you are good at, what you want to do, and how to go about getting it. You will also most likely get more interviews and present yourself better. Is this worth giving up a night of TV? Yes, I think so.

Once you finish this minibook and its activities, you will have spent more time planning your career than most people do. And you will know more than the average job seeker about finding a job.

Why Such a Short Book? I've taught job seeking skills for many years, and I've written longer and more detailed books than this one. Yet I have often been asked to tell someone, in a few minutes or hours, the most important things they should do in their career planning or job search. Instructors and counselors also ask the same question because they have only a short time to spend with folks they're trying to help. I've given this a lot of thought, and the seven topics in this book are the ones I think are most important to know.

This minibook is short enough to scan in a morning and conduct a more effective job search that afternoon. Granted, doing all the activities would take more time, but they will prepare you far better than scanning the book. Of course, you can learn more about all the topics it covers, but this minibook, *Quick Job Search,* may be all you need.

You can't just read about getting a job. The best way to get a job is to go out and get interviews! And the best way to get interviews is to make a job out of getting a job.

After many years of experience, I have identified just seven basic things you need to do that make a big difference in your job search. Each will be covered and expanded on in this minibook.

1. Identify your key skills.

2. Define your ideal job.

3. Learn the two most effective job search methods.

4. Create a superior resume and a portfolio.

5. Organize your time to get two interviews a day.

6. Dramatically improve your interviewing skills.

7. Follow up on all leads.

So, without further delay, let's get started!

 STEP 1: Identify Your Key Skills and Develop a "Skills Language" to Describe Yourself

One survey of employers found that about 90 percent of the people they interviewed might have the required job skills, but they could not describe those skills and thereby prove that they could do the job they sought. They could not answer the basic question "Why should I hire you?"

Knowing and describing your skills is essential to doing well in interviews. This same knowledge is important to help you decide what type of job you will enjoy and do well. For these reasons, I consider identifying your skills a necessary part of a successful career plan or job search.

The Three Types of Skills

Most people think of their skills as job-related skills, such as using a computer. But we all have other types of skills that are important for success on a job—and that are important to employers. The following triangle arranges skills in three groups, and I think that this is a very useful way to consider skills.

Let's look at these three types of skills—self-management, transferable, and job-related—and identify those that are most important to you.

Quip

We all have thousands of skills. Consider the many skills required to do even a simple thing like ride a bike or bake a cake. But, of all the skills you have, employers want to know those key skills you have for the job they need done. You must clearly identify these key skills and then emphasize them in interviews.

Self-Management Skills

To begin identifying your skills, answer the question in the box that follows.

YOUR GOOD WORKER TRAITS

Write down three things about yourself that you think make you a good worker. Think about what an employer might like about you or the way you work.

1. _____

2. _____

3. _____

You just wrote down the most important things for an employer to know about you! They describe your basic personality and your ability to adapt to new environments. They are some of the most important skills to emphasize in interviews, yet most job seekers don't realize their importance—and don't mention them.

Review the Self-Management Skills Checklist that follows and put a check mark beside any skills you have. The key self-management skills listed first cover abilities that employers find particularly important. If one or more of the key self-management skills apply to you, mentioning them in interviews can help you greatly.

SELF-MANAGEMENT SKILLS CHECKLIST

Following are the key self-management skills that employers value highly. Place a check by those you already have.

❑ Have good attendance   ❑ Arrive on time

❑ Get work done on time   ❑ Get along with co-workers

❑ Am honest   ❑ Follow instructions

❑ Get along with supervisor   ❑ Am hard working/productive

(continued)

(continued)

Place a check by other self-management skills you have.

❑ Ambitious	❑ Discreet	❑ Helpful
❑ Mature	❑ Physically strong	❑ Sincere
❑ Assertive	❑ Eager	❑ Humble
❑ Methodical	❑ Practical	❑ Spontaneous
❑ Capable	❑ Efficient	❑ Humorous
❑ Modest	❑ Problem-solving	❑ Steady
❑ Cheerful	❑ Energetic	❑ Imaginative
❑ Motivated	❑ Proud of work	❑ Tactful
❑ Competent	❑ Enthusiastic	❑ Independent
❑ Natural	❑ Quick to learn	❑ Team player
❑ Conscientious	❑ Expressive	❑ Industrious
❑ Open-minded	❑ Reliable	❑ Tenacious
❑ Creative	❑ Flexible	❑ Informal
❑ Optimistic	❑ Resourceful	❑ Thrifty
❑ Culturally tolerant	❑ Formal	❑ Intelligent
❑ Original	❑ Responsible	❑ Trustworthy
❑ Decisive	❑ Friendly	❑ Intuitive
❑ Patient	❑ Results-oriented	❑ Versatile
❑ Dependable	❑ Good-natured	❑ Loyal
❑ Persistent	❑ Self-confident	❑ Well-organized

List the other self-management skills you have that have not been mentioned but you think are important to include.

_____

_____

_____

After you finish checking the list, circle the five skills you feel are most important and write them in the box that follows.

YOUR TOP FIVE SELF-MANAGEMENT SKILLS

1. _____

2. _____

3. _____

4. _____

5. _____

 When thinking about their skills, some people find it helpful to complete the Essential Job Search Data Worksheet that starts on page 324. It organizes skills and accomplishments from previous jobs and other life experiences. Take a look at it and decide whether to complete it now or later.

Transferable Skills

We all have skills that can transfer from one job or career to another. For example, the ability to organize events could be used in a variety of jobs and may be essential for success in certain occupations. Your mission is to find a job that requires the skills you have and enjoy using.

It's not bragging if it's true. Using your new skills language may be uncomfortable at first, but employers need to learn about your skills. So practice saying positive things about the skills you have for the job. If you don't, who will?

TRANSFERABLE SKILLS CHECKLIST

Following are the key transferable skills that employers value highly. Place a check by those you already have. You may have used them in a previous job or in some non-work setting.

- ❑ Managing money/budgets
- ❑ Speaking in public
- ❑ Managing people
- ❑ Organizing/managing projects
- ❑ Meeting deadlines

- ❑ Using computers
- ❑ Meeting the public
- ❑ Writing well
- ❑ Negotiating

Place a check by the skills you have for working with data.

- ❑ Analyzing data
- ❑ Counting/taking inventory
- ❑ Auditing/checking for accuracy
- ❑ Investigating
- ❑ Budgeting
- ❑ Keeping financial records
- ❑ Calculating/computing

- ❑ Observing/inspecting
- ❑ Classifying data
- ❑ Paying attention to details
- ❑ Comparing/evaluating
- ❑ Researching/locating information
- ❑ Compiling/recording facts
- ❑ Synthesizing

Place a check by the skills you have for working with people.

- ❑ Administering
- ❑ Counseling people
- ❑ Being diplomatic
- ❑ Demonstrating

- ❑ Being kind
- ❑ Having insight
- ❑ Being outgoing
- ❑ Helping others

- ❑ Being patient
- ❑ Instructing others
- ❑ Being pleasant
- ❑ Interviewing people

(continued)

(continued)

- ❏ Being sensitive
- ❏ Listening
- ❏ Being sociable
- ❏ Persuading

- ❏ Being tactful
- ❏ Supervising
- ❏ Being tough
- ❏ Tolerating

- ❏ Caring for others
- ❏ Trusting
- ❏ Coaching
- ❏ Understanding
- ❏ Confronting others

Place a check by your skills in working with words and ideas.

- ❏ Being articulate
- ❏ Creating new ideas
- ❏ Being ingenious
- ❏ Designing
- ❏ Being inventive
- ❏ Editing

- ❏ Being logical
- ❏ Remembering information
- ❏ Communicating verbally
- ❏ Speaking publicly
- ❏ Corresponding with others
- ❏ Writing clearly

Place a check by the leadership skills you have.

- ❏ Being competitive
- ❏ Mediating problems
- ❏ Delegating
- ❏ Motivating people
- ❏ Directing others
- ❏ Motivating yourself
- ❏ Getting results
- ❏ Negotiating agreements

- ❏ Having self-confidence
- ❏ Planning events
- ❏ Influencing others
- ❏ Running meetings
- ❏ Making decisions
- ❏ Solving problems
- ❏ Making explanations
- ❏ Taking risks

Place a check by your creative or artistic skills.

- ❏ Appreciating music
- ❏ Expressing yourself
- ❏ Being artistic
- ❏ Performing/acting

- ❏ Dancing
- ❏ Playing instruments
- ❏ Drawing
- ❏ Presenting artistic ideas

Place a check by your skills for working with things.

- ❏ Assembling things
- ❏ Driving or operating vehicles
- ❏ Building things

- ❏ Operating tools/machines
- ❏ Constructing or repairing things

Add the other transferable skills you have that have not been mentioned but you think are important to include.

_____

_____

_____

When you are finished, circle the five transferable skills you feel are most important for you to use in your next job and list them below.

YOUR TOP FIVE TRANSFERABLE SKILLS

1. _____

2. _____

3. _____

4. _____

5. _____

Job-Related Skills

Job content or job-related skills are those you need to do a particular occupation. A carpenter, for example, needs to know how to use various tools. Before you select job-related skills to emphasize, you must first have a clear idea of the jobs you want. So let's put off developing your job-related skills list until you have defined the job you want—the topic that is covered next.

STEP 2: Define Your Ideal Job

Too many people look for a job without clearly knowing what they are looking for. Before you go out seeking a job, I suggest that you first define exactly what you want—not *just a job* but *the job*.

Most people think that a job objective is the same as a job title, but it isn't. You need to consider other elements of what makes a job satisfying for you. Then, later, you can decide what that job is called and what industry it might be in. You can compromise on what you consider your ideal job later if you need to.

EIGHT FACTORS TO CONSIDER IN DEFINING YOUR IDEAL JOB

As you try to define your ideal job, consider the following eight important questions. When you know what you want, your task then becomes finding a position that is as close to your ideal job as possible.

1. **What skills do you want to use?** From the skills lists in Step 1, select the top five skills that you enjoy using and most want to use in your next job.

   a._____

   b._____

   c._____

   d._____

   e._____

(continued)

(continued)

2. **What type of special knowledge do you have?** Perhaps you know how to fix radios, keep accounting records, or cook food. Write down the things you know from schooling, training, hobbies, family experiences, and other sources. One or more of these knowledge areas could make you a very special applicant in the right setting._____

_____

_____

3. **With what types of people do you prefer to work?** Do you like to work with competitive people, or do you prefer hardworking folks, creative personalities, relaxed people, or some other types?_____

_____

_____

4. **What type of work environment do you prefer?** Do you want to work inside, outside, in a quiet place, in a busy place, or in a clean or messy place; or do you want to have a window with a nice view? List the types of environments you prefer._____

_____

_____

5. **Where do you want your next job to be located—in what city or region?** If you are open to living and working anywhere, what would your ideal community be like? Near a bus line? Close to a childcare center?_____

_____

_____

6. **What benefits or income do you hope to have in your next job?** Many people will take less money or fewer benefits if they like a job in other ways—or if they need a job quickly to survive. Think about the minimum you would take as well as what you would eventually like to earn. Your next job will probably pay somewhere in between._____

_____

_____

7. **How much and what types of responsibility are you willing to accept?** Usually, the more money you want to make, the more responsibility you must accept. Do you want to work by yourself, be part of a group, or be in charge? If you want to be in charge, how many people are you willing to supervise?

_____

_____

_____

8. **What values are important or have meaning to you?** Do you have important values you would prefer to include in considering the work you do? For example, some people want to work to help others, clean up the environment, build structures, make machines work, gain power or prestige, or care for animals or plants. Think about what is important to you and how you might include this in your next job._____

_____

_____

_____

Is It Possible to Find Your Ideal Job?

Can you find a job that meets all the criteria you just defined? Perhaps. Some people do. The harder you look, the more likely you are to find it. But you will likely need to compromise, so it is useful to know what is *most* important to include in your next job. Go back over your responses to the eight factors and mark a few of those that you would most like to have or include in your ideal job.

FACTORS I WANT IN MY IDEAL JOB

Write a brief description of your ideal job. Don't worry about a job title, or whether you have the experience, or other practical matters yet._____

_____

_____

_____

How Can You Explore Specific Job Titles and Industries?

You might find your ideal job in an occupation you haven't considered yet. And, even if you are sure of the occupation you want, it may be in an industry that is unfamiliar to you. This combination of occupation and industry forms the basis for your job search, and you should consider a variety of options.

The jobs you could do

The industries where these jobs exist

Your ideal job exists in the overlap of those jobs that interest you most *and* in those industries that best meet your needs and interests!

There are thousands of job titles, and many jobs are highly specialized, employing just a few people. While one of these more specialized jobs may be just what you want, most work falls within more general job titles that employ large numbers of people.

REVIEW THE TOP JOBS IN THE WORKFORCE

The list of job titles that follows was based on a list developed by the U.S. Department of Labor. It contains approximately 270 major jobs that employ about 90 percent of the U.S. workforce.

The job titles are organized within 16 major groupings called interest areas, presented in bold type. These groupings will help you quickly identify fields most likely to interest you. Job titles are presented in regular type within these groupings.

Begin with the interest areas that appeal to you most, and underline any job title that interests you. (Don't worry for now about whether you have the experience or credentials to do these jobs.) Then quickly review the remaining interest areas, underlining any job titles there that interest you. Note that some job titles are listed more than once because they fit into more than one interest area. When you have gone through all 16 interest areas, go back and circle the 5 to 10 job titles that interest you most. These are the ones you will want to research in more detail.

1. **Agriculture and Natural Resources:** Agricultural and Food Scientists; Agricultural Workers; Biological Scientists; Conservation Scientists and Foresters; Engineers; Farmers, Ranchers, and Agricultural Managers; Fishers and Fishing Vessel Operators; Forest, Conservation, and Logging Workers; Grounds Maintenance Workers; Material Moving Occupations; Pest Control Workers; Purchasing Managers, Buyers, and Purchasing Agents; Science Technicians.

2. **Architecture and Construction:** Architects, except Landscape and Naval; Boilermakers; Brickmasons, Blockmasons, and Stonemasons; Carpenters; Carpet, Floor, and Tile Installers and Finishers; Cement Masons, Concrete Finishers, Segmental Pavers, and Terrazzo Workers; Construction and Building Inspectors; Construction Equipment Operators; Construction Laborers; Construction Managers; Drafters; Drywall Installers, Ceiling Tile Installers, and Tapers; Electrical and Electronics Installers and Repairers; Electricians; Elevator Installers and Repairers; Glaziers; Hazardous Materials Removal Workers; Heating, Air-Conditioning, and Refrigeration Mechanics and Installers; Home Appliance Repairers; Insulation Workers; Landscape Architects; Line Installers and Repairers; Maintenance and Repair Workers, General; Material Moving Occupations; Painters and Paperhangers; Pipelayers, Plumbers, Pipefitters, and Steamfitters; Plasterers and Stucco Masons; Radio and Telecommunications Equipment Installers and Repairers; Roofers; Sheet Metal Workers; Structural and Reinforcing Iron and Metal Workers; Surveyors, Cartographers, Photogrammetrists, and Surveying Technicians.

3. **Arts and Communication:** Actors, Producers, and Directors; Advertising, Marketing, Promotions, Public Relations, and Sales Managers; Air Traffic Controllers; Announcers; Artists and Related Workers; Barbers, Cosmetologists, and Other Personal Appearance Workers; Broadcast and Sound Engineering Technicians and Radio Operators; Commercial and Industrial Designers; Communications Equipment Operators; Dancers and Choreographers; Dispatchers; Fashion Designers; Floral Designers; Graphic Designers; Interior Designers; Interpreters and Translators; Musicians, Singers, and Related Workers; News Analysts, Reporters, and Correspondents; Photographers; Photographic Process Workers and Processing Machine Operators; Precision Instrument and Equipment Repairers; Public Relations Specialists; Television, Video, and Motion Picture Camera Operators and Editors; Writers and Editors.

4. **Business and Administration:** Accountants and Auditors; Administrative Services Managers; Billing and Posting Clerks and Machine Operators; Bookkeeping, Accounting, and Auditing Clerks; Brokerage Clerks; Budget Analysts; Building Cleaning Workers; Communications Equipment Operators; Data Entry and Information Processing Workers; Engineering Technicians; File Clerks; Human Resources Assistants, except Payroll and Timekeeping; Human Resources, Training, and Labor Relations Managers

and Specialists; Management Analysts; Meeting and Convention Planners; Meter Readers, Utilities; Office and Administrative Support Worker Supervisors and Managers; Office Clerks, General; Operations Research Analysts; Payroll and Timekeeping Clerks; Postal Service Workers; Procurement Clerks; Production, Planning, and Expediting Clerks; Secretaries and Administrative Assistants; Shipping, Receiving, and Traffic Clerks; Stock Clerks and Order Fillers; Top Executives; Weighers, Measurers, Checkers, and Samplers, Recordkeeping.

5. **Education and Training:** Archivists, Curators, and Museum Technicians; Counselors; Education Administrators; Fitness Workers; Instructional Coordinators; Librarians; Library Assistants, Clerical; Library Technicians; Teacher Assistants; Teachers—Adult Literacy and Remedial Education; Teachers—Postsecondary; Teachers—Preschool, Kindergarten, Elementary, Middle, and Secondary; Teachers—Self-Enrichment Education; Teachers—Special Education.

6. **Finance and Insurance:** Advertising Sales Agents; Appraisers and Assessors of Real Estate; Bill and Account Collectors; Claims Adjusters, Appraisers, Examiners, and Investigators; Cost Estimators; Credit Authorizers, Checkers, and Clerks; Financial Analysts and Personal Financial Advisors; Financial Managers; Insurance Sales Agents; Insurance Underwriters; Interviewers; Loan Officers; Market and Survey Researchers; Securities, Commodities, and Financial Services Sales Agents; Tellers.

7. **Government and Public Administration:** Agricultural Workers; Court Reporters; Fire Fighting Occupations; Inspectors, Testers, Sorters, Samplers, and Weighers; Occupational Health and Safety Specialists and Technicians; Police and Detectives; Science Technicians; Tax Examiners, Collectors, and Revenue Agents; Top Executives; Urban and Regional Planners.

8. **Health Science:** Agricultural Workers; Animal Care and Service Workers; Athletic Trainers; Audiologists; Cardiovascular Technologists and Technicians; Chiropractors; Clinical Laboratory Technologists and Technicians; Dental Assistants; Dental Hygienists; Dentists; Diagnostic Medical Sonographers; Dietitians and Nutritionists; Licensed Practical and Licensed Vocational Nurses; Massage Therapists; Medical and Health Services Managers; Medical Assistants; Medical Records and Health Information Technicians; Medical Transcriptionists; Nuclear Medicine Technologists; Nursing, Psychiatric, and Home Health Aides; Occupational Therapist Assistants and Aides; Occupational Therapists; Opticians, Dispensing; Optometrists; Pharmacists; Pharmacy Aides; Pharmacy Technicians; Physical Therapist Assistants and Aides; Physical Therapists; Physician Assistants; Physicians and Surgeons; Podiatrists; Radiation Therapists; Radiologic Technologists and Technicians; Recreational Therapists; Registered Nurses; Respiratory Therapists; Science Technicians; Speech-Language Pathologists; Surgical Technologists; Veterinarians; Veterinary Technologists and Technicians.

9. **Hospitality, Tourism, and Recreation:** Athletes, Coaches, Umpires, and Related Workers; Barbers, Cosmetologists, and Other Personal Appearance Workers; Building Cleaning Workers; Chefs, Cooks, and Food Preparation Workers; Flight Attendants; Food and Beverage Serving and Related Workers; Food Processing Occupations; Food Service Managers; Gaming Services Occupations; Hotel, Motel, and Resort Desk Clerks; Lodging Managers; Recreation Workers; Reservation and Transportation Ticket Agents and Travel Clerks; Travel Agents.

10. **Human Service:** Child Care Workers; Counselors; Interviewers; Personal and Home Care Aides; Probation Officers and Correctional Treatment Specialists; Psychologists; Social and Human Service Assistants; Social Workers.

(continued)

(continued)

11. **Information Technology:** Coin, Vending, and Amusement Machine Servicers and Repairers; Computer and Information Systems Managers; Computer Operators; Computer Programmers; Computer Scientists and Database Administrators; Computer Software Engineers; Computer Support Specialists and Systems Administrators; Computer Systems Analysts; Computer, Automated Teller, and Office Machine Repairers.

12. **Law and Public Safety:** Correctional Officers; Emergency Medical Technicians and Paramedics; Fire Fighting Occupations; Job Opportunities in the Armed Forces; Judges, Magistrates, and Other Judicial Workers; Lawyers; Paralegals and Legal Assistants; Police and Detectives; Private Detectives and Investigators; Science Technicians; Security Guards and Gaming Surveillance Officers.

13. **Manufacturing:** Agricultural Workers; Aircraft and Avionics Equipment Mechanics and Service Technicians; Assemblers and Fabricators; Automotive Body and Related Repairers; Automotive Service Technicians and Mechanics; Bookbinders and Bindery Workers; Computer Control Programmers and Operators; Desktop Publishers; Diesel Service Technicians and Mechanics; Electrical and Electronics Installers and Repairers; Electronic Home Entertainment Equipment Installers and Repairers; Food Processing Occupations; Heavy Vehicle and Mobile Equipment Service Technicians and Mechanics; Home Appliance Repairers; Industrial Machinery Mechanics and Maintenance Workers; Industrial Production Managers; Inspectors, Testers, Sorters, Samplers, and Weighers; Jewelers and Precious Stone and Metal Workers; Machine Setters, Operators, and Tenders—Metal and Plastic; Machinists; Material Moving Occupations; Medical, Dental, and Ophthalmic Laboratory Technicians; Millwrights; Painting and Coating Workers, except Construction and Maintenance; Photographic Process Workers and Processing Machine Operators; Power Plant Operators, Distributors, and Dispatchers; Precision Instrument and Equipment Repairers; Prepress Technicians and Workers; Printing Machine Operators; Radio and Telecommunications Equipment Installers and Repairers; Semiconductor Processors; Small Engine Mechanics; Stationary Engineers and Boiler Operators; Textile, Apparel, and Furnishings Occupations; Tool and Die Makers; Water and Liquid Waste Treatment Plant and System Operators; Water Transportation Occupations; Welding, Soldering, and Brazing Workers; Woodworkers.

14. **Retail and Wholesale Sales and Service:** Advertising, Marketing, Promotions, Public Relations, and Sales Managers; Cashiers; Counter and Rental Clerks; Customer Service Representatives; Demonstrators, Product Promoters, and Models; Funeral Directors; Order Clerks; Property, Real Estate, and Community Association Managers; Purchasing Managers, Buyers, and Purchasing Agents; Real Estate Brokers and Sales Agents; Receptionists and Information Clerks; Retail Salespersons; Sales Engineers; Sales Representatives, Wholesale and Manufacturing; Sales Worker Supervisors.

15. **Scientific Research, Engineering, and Mathematics:** Actuaries; Atmospheric Scientists; Biological Scientists; Chemists and Materials Scientists; Drafters; Economists; Engineering and Natural Sciences Managers; Engineering Technicians; Engineers; Environmental Scientists and Hydrologists; Geoscientists; Mathematicians; Medical Scientists; Photographers; Physicists and Astronomers; Psychologists; Science Technicians; Social Scientists, Other; Statisticians; Surveyors, Cartographers, Photogrammetrists, and Surveying Technicians.

16. **Transportation, Distribution, and Logistics:** Aircraft Pilots and Flight Engineers; Bus Drivers; Cargo and Freight Agents; Couriers and Messengers; Material Moving Occupations; Postal Service Workers; Rail Transportation Occupations; Taxi Drivers and Chauffeurs; Truck Drivers and Driver/Sales Workers; Water Transportation Occupations.

You can find thorough descriptions for 100 of the job titles in the preceding list in this book.

You can find thorough descriptions for the job titles in the preceding list in the Occupational Outlook Handbook, *published by the U.S. Department of Labor. Its descriptions include information on earnings, training and education needed to hold specific jobs, working conditions, advancement opportunities, projected growth, and sources for additional information. Most libraries have this book.*

You also can find descriptions of these jobs on the Internet. Go to www.bls.gov/oco/.

The New Guide for Occupational Exploration, *Fourth Edition, also provides more information on the interest areas used in this list. This book is published by JIST Works and describes about 1,000 major jobs, arranged within groupings of related jobs.*

Finally, "A Short List of Additional Resources" at the end of this minibook gives you resources for more job information.

CONSIDER MAJOR INDUSTRIES

What industry you work in is often as important as the career field. For example, some industries pay much better than others, and others may simply be more interesting to you. A book titled *40 Best Fields for Your Career* contains very helpful reviews for each of the major industries mentioned in the following list. Many libraries and bookstores carry this book, as well as the U.S. Department of Labor's *Career Guide to Industries,* or you can find the information on the Internet at www.CareerOINK.com or at www.bls.gov/oco/cg/.

Underline industries that interest you, and then learn more about the opportunities they present. Jobs in most careers are available in a variety of industries, so consider what industries fit you best and focus your job search in these.

Agriculture and natural resources: Agriculture, forestry, and fishing; mining; oil and gas extraction.

Manufacturing, construction, and utilities: Aerospace product and parts manufacturing; chemical manufacturing, except drugs; computer and electronic product manufacturing; construction; food manufacturing; machinery manufacturing; motor vehicle and parts manufacturing; pharmaceutical and medicine manufacturing; printing; steel manufacturing; textile, textile products, and apparel manufacturing; utilities.

Trade: Automobile dealers, clothing, accessories, and general merchandise stores; grocery stores; wholesale trade.

Transportation: Air transportation; truck transportation and warehousing.

Information: Broadcasting; Internet service providers, Web search portals, and data processing services; motion picture and video industries; publishing, except software; software publishing; telecommunications.

Financial activities: Banking; insurance; securities, commodities, and other investments.

Professional and business services: Advertising and public relations; computer systems design and related services; employment services; management, scientific, and technical consulting services; scientific research and development services.

Education, health care, and social services: Child daycare services; educational services; health care; social assistance, except child care.

(continued)

(continued)

> **Leisure and hospitality:** Art, entertainment, and recreation; food services and drinking places; hotels and other accommodations.
>
> **Government and advocacy, grantmaking, and civic organizations:** Advocacy, grantmaking, and civic organizations; federal government; state and local government, except education and health care.

THE TOP JOBS AND INDUSTRIES THAT INTEREST YOU

Go back over the lists of job titles and industries. For numbers 1 and 2 below, list the jobs that interest you most. Then select the industries that interest you most, and list them below in number 3. These are the jobs and industries you should research most carefully. Your ideal job is likely to be found in some combination of these jobs and industries, or in more specialized but related jobs and industries.

1. The five job titles that interest you most

   a._____

   b._____

   c._____

   d._____

   e._____

2. The five next most interesting job titles

   a._____

   b._____

   c._____

   d._____

   e._____

3. The industries that interest you most

   a._____

   b._____

   c._____

   d._____

   e._____

Is Self-Employment or Starting a Business an Option?

More than one in 10 workers are self-employed or own their own businesses. If these options interest you, consider them as well. Talk to people in similar roles to gather information and look for books and Web sites that provide information on options that are similar to those that interest you. A book titled *Best Jobs for the 21st*

Century (JIST Works) includes lists and descriptions of jobs with high percentages of self-employed. Also, the Small Business Administration's Web site at www.sba.gov is a good source of basic information on related topics.

SELF-EMPLOYMENT AREAS OF INTEREST

In the following space, write your current interest in self-employment or starting a business in an area related to your general job objective.

_____

_____

_____

Can You Identify Your Job-Related Skills Now That You've Defined Your Ideal Job?

Earlier, I suggested that you should first define the job you want and then identify key job-related skills you have that support your ability to do that job. These are the job-related skills to emphasize in interviews.

So, now that you have determined your ideal job, you can pinpoint the job-related skills it requires. If you haven't done so, complete the Essential Job Search Data Worksheet on pages 324–328. Completing it will give you specific skills and accomplishments to highlight.

Yes, completing that worksheet requires time, but doing so will help you clearly define key skills to emphasize in interviews—when what you say matters so much. People who complete that worksheet will do better in their interviews than those who don't. After you complete the Essential Job Search Data Worksheet, you are ready to list your top five job-related skills.

>
> **It's a hassle, but...** Completing the Essential Job Search Data Worksheet that starts on page 324 will help you define what you are good at—and remember examples of when you did things well. This information will help you define your ideal job and will be of great value in interviews. Look at the worksheet now, and promise to do it later today.

YOUR TOP FIVE JOB-RELATED SKILLS

List the top five job-related skills you think are most important. Include the job-related skills you have that you would most like to use in your next job.

1. _____

2. _____

3. _____

4. _____

5. _____

STEP 3: Use the Most Effective Methods to Find a Job in Less Time

Employer surveys have found that most employers don't advertise their job openings. They most often hire people they already know, people who find out about the jobs through word of mouth, or people who happen to be in the right place at the right time. Although luck plays a part in finding job openings, you can use the tips in this step to increase your luck.

Let's look at the job search methods that people use. The U.S. Department of Labor conducts a regular survey of unemployed people actively looking for work. Following are the results of their most recent findings.

Percentage of Unemployed People Who Use Various Job Search Methods

- Contacted employer directly: 62.7%
- Sent out resumes/filled out applications: 54.5%
- Contacted public employment agency: 19.9%
- Placed or answered help wanted ads: 16.4%

- Contacted friends or relatives: 18%
- Contacted private employment agency: 7.7%
- Used other active search methods: 11.8%

Source: U.S. Department of Labor, Current Population Survey

> **Note:** *This step covers a number of job search methods. Most of the material is presented as information, with a few interactive activities. While each topic is short and reasonably interesting, taking a break now and then will help you absorb it all.*

The survey shows that most people use more than one job search technique. For example, one person might read want ads, fill out applications, and ask friends for job leads. Others might send out resumes, contact everyone they know through previous jobs, and sign up at employment agencies.

But the survey covered only seven job search methods and asked only whether the job seeker did or did not use each method. The survey did not cover Internet job searches, nor did it ask whether a method actually worked in getting job offers.

Unfortunately, there hasn't been much conclusive recent research on the effectiveness of various job search methods. Most of what we know is based on older research and the observations of people who work directly with job seekers, such as professional resume writers and career counselors. I'll share what we do know about the effectiveness of job search methods in the content that follows.

Quip

Your job search objective. Almost everyone finds a job eventually, so your objective should be to find a good job in less time. The job search methods I emphasize in this minibook will help you do just that.

Get the Most Out of Less Effective Job Search Methods

The truth is that every job search method works for someone. But experience and research show that some methods are more effective than others are. Your task in the job search is to spend more of your time using more effective methods—and increase the effectiveness of all the methods you use.

So let's start by looking at some traditional job search methods and how you can increase their effectiveness. Only about one-third of all job seekers get their jobs using one of these methods, but you should still consider using them to some extent in your search. Later in the step, you'll read about the most effective methods, the ones you should devote the most time to in your search.

Newspaper and Internet Help Wanted Ads

Most jobs are never advertised, and only about 16 percent of all people get their jobs through the want ads. Everyone who reads the paper knows about these openings, so competition is fierce for the few advertised jobs.

The Internet also lists many job openings. But, as happens with newspaper ads, enormous numbers of people view these postings. Many job seekers make direct contact with employers via a company's Web site. Some people do get jobs through the bigger sites, so go ahead and apply. Just be sure to spend most of your time using more effective methods.

Filling Out Applications

Most employers require job seekers to complete an application form. Applications are designed to collect negative information, and employers use applications to screen people out. If, for example, your training or work history is not the best, you will often never get an interview, even if you can do the job.

Completing applications is a more effective approach for young and entry-level job seekers. The reason is that there is a shortage of workers for the relatively low-paying jobs typically sought by less-experienced job seekers. As a result, when trying to fill those positions, employers are more willing to accept a lack of experience or fewer job skills. Even so, you will get better results by filling out the application, if asked to do so, and then requesting an interview with the person in charge.

When you complete an application, make it neat and error-free, and do not include anything that could get you screened out. If necessary, leave a problem section blank. You can always explain situations in an interview.

Employment Agencies

There are three types of employment agencies. One is operated by the government and is free. The others, private employment agencies and temp agencies, are run as for-profit businesses and charge a fee to either you or an employer. Following are the advantages and disadvantages to using each.

The government employment service and One-Stop centers. Each state and province has a network of local offices to pay unemployment compensation, provide job leads, and offer other services—at no charge to you or to employers. The service's name varies by region. It may be called Job Service, Department of Labor, Unemployment Office, Workforce Development, or another name. Many of these offices are now also online, and some even require their users to sign up with a login and password to search for job leads and use other services on the Internet.

The Employment and Training Administration Web site at www.doleta.gov/uses gives you information on the programs provided by the government employment service, plus links to other useful sites. Canada's government employment Web site is at www.jobbank.gc.ca.

The government employment service lists only 5 to 10 percent of the available openings nationally, and only about 6 percent of all job seekers get their jobs there. Even so, visit your local office early in your job search. Find out whether you qualify for unemployment compensation and learn more about its services. Look into it— the price is right.

Private employment agencies. Private employment agencies are businesses that charge a fee either to you or to the employer who hires you. Fees can be from less than one month's pay to 15 percent or more of your annual salary. You will often see these agencies' ads in the help wanted section of the newspaper. Many have Web sites.

Be careful about using fee-based employment agencies. Recent research indicates that more people use and benefit from fee-based agencies than in the past. However, relatively few people who register with private agencies get a job through them.

If you use a private employment agency, ask for interviews with the employers who agree to pay the agency's fee. Do not sign an exclusive agreement or be pressured into accepting a job. Also, continue to actively look for your own leads. You can find these agencies in the phone book's yellow pages, and many state- or province-government Web sites offer lists of the private employment agencies in their states.

Temporary agencies. Temporary agencies offer jobs that last from several days to many months. They charge the employer an hourly fee, and then pay you a bit less and keep the difference. You pay no direct fee to the agency. Many private employment agencies now provide temporary jobs as well.

Temp agencies have grown rapidly for good reason. They provide employers with short-term help, and employers often use them to find people they might want to hire later. If the employers are dissatisfied, they can just ask the agency for different temp workers.

Temp agencies can help you survive between jobs and get experience in different work settings. Temp jobs provide a very good option while you look for long-term work, and you might get a job offer while working in a temp job. Holding a temporary job might even lead to a regular job with the same or a similar employer.

School and Other Employment Services

Only a small percentage of job seekers use school and other special employment services, probably because few job seekers have the service available to them. If you are a student or graduate, find out about any employment services at your school. Some schools provide free career counseling, resume-writing help, referrals to job openings, career interest tests, reference materials, Web sites listing job openings, and other services. Special career programs work with veterans, people with disabilities, welfare recipients, union members, professional groups, and many others. So check out these services and consider using them.

Mailing Versus Posting Resumes on the Internet

Many job search experts used to suggest that sending out lots of resumes was a great technique. That advice probably helped sell their resume books, but mailing resumes to people you do not know was never an effective approach. It very rarely works. A recent survey of 1,500 successful job seekers showed that only 2 percent found their positions through sending an unsolicited resume. The same is true for the Internet.

Although mailing your resume to strangers doesn't make much sense, posting it on the Internet might because

- It doesn't take much time.

- Many employers have the potential of finding your resume.

- You can post your resume on niche sites that attract only employers in your field.

- Your Internet resume is easily updated, allowing you to post your current accomplishments.

- You can easily link your resume to projects and Web sites that highlight your accomplishments.

Job searching on the Internet has its limitations, just like other methods. I'll cover resumes in more detail later and provide tips on using the Internet throughout this minibook.

Use the Two Job Search Methods That Work Best

The fact is that most jobs are not advertised, so how do *you* find them? The same way that about two-thirds of all job seekers do: networking with people you know (which I call making warm contacts) and directly contacting employers (which I call making cold contacts). Both of these methods are based on the job search rule you should know above all:

The Most Important Job Search Rule: Don't wait until the job opens before contacting the employer!

Employers fill most jobs with people they meet before a job is formally open. The trick is to meet people who can hire you before a job is formally available. Instead of asking whether the employer has any jobs open, I suggest that you say, *"I realize you may not have any openings now, but I would still like to talk to you about the possibility of future openings."*

Most Effective Job Search Method 1: Develop a Network of Contacts in Five Easy Stages

Studies find that 60 percent of all people located their jobs through a lead provided by a friend, a relative, or an acquaintance. That makes the people you know your number one source of job leads—more effective than all the traditional methods combined! Developing and using your contacts is called *networking,* and here's how it works:

1. **Make lists of people you know.** Make a thorough list of anyone you are friendly with. Then make a separate list of all your relatives. These two lists alone often add up to 25 to 100 people or more. Next, think of other groups of people that you have something in common with, such as former co-workers or classmates, members of your social or sports groups, members of your professional association, former employers, neighbors, and other groups. You might not know many of these people personally or well, but most will help you if you ask them.

2. **Contact each person in your list in a systematic way.** Obviously, some people will be more helpful than others, but any one of them might help you find a job lead.

3. **Present yourself well.** Begin with your friends and relatives. Call and tell them you are looking for a job and need their help. Be as clear as possible about the type of employment you want and the skills and qualifications you have. Look at the sample JIST Card and phone script later in this step for good presentation ideas.

4. **Ask your contacts for leads.** It is possible that your contacts will know of a job opening that interests you. If so, get the details and get right on it! More likely, however, they will not, so you should ask each person the Three Magic Networking Questions.

> **Quip**
>
> **Most jobs are never advertised because employers don't need to advertise or don't want to.** Employers trust people referred to them by someone they know far more than they trust strangers. And most jobs are filled by referrals and people that the employer knows, eliminating the need to advertise. So, your job search must involve more than looking at ads.

The Three Magic Networking Questions

- **Do you know of any openings for a person with my skills?**

  If the answer is "No" (which it usually is), then ask...

- **Do you know of someone else who might know of such an opening? If your contact does, get that name and ask for another one.**

  If he or she doesn't, ask...

(continued)

(continued)

- **Do you know of anyone who might know of someone else who might know of a job opening?**

  Another good way to ask this is "Do you know someone who knows lots of people?" If all else fails, this will usually get you a name.

5. **Contact these referrals and ask them the same questions.** From each person you contact, try to get two names of other people you might contact. Doing this consistently can extend your network of acquaintances by hundreds of people. Eventually, one of these people will hire you or refer you to someone who will!

If you are persistent in following these five steps, networking might be the only job search method you need. It works.

Dialing for dollars. The phone can get you more interviews per hour than any other job search tool. But it won't work unless you use it actively.

Most Effective Job Search Method 2: Contact Employers Directly

It takes more courage, but making direct contact with employers is a very effective job search technique. I call these cold contacts because people you don't know in advance will need to warm up to your inquiries. Two basic techniques for making cold contacts follow.

Use the yellow pages to find potential employers. Begin by looking at the index in the front of your phone book's yellow pages. For each entry, ask yourself, *"Would an organization of this kind need a person with my skills?"* If you answer *"Yes,"* then that organization or business type is a possible target. You can also rate "Yes" entries based on your interest, writing a "1" next to those that seem very interesting, a "2" next to those that you are not sure of, and a "3" next to those that aren't interesting at all.

Next, select a type of organization that got a "Yes" response and turn to that section of the yellow pages. Call each organization listed there and ask to speak to the person who is most likely to hire or supervise you—typically the manager of the business or a department head—not the personnel or human resources manager. A sample telephone script is included later in this section to give you ideas about what to say.

You can easily adapt this approach for use on the Internet by using sites such as www.yellowpages.com to get contacts anywhere in the world, or you can find phone and e-mail contacts on an employer's own Web site.

Drop in without an appointment. Another effective cold contact method is to just walk into a business or organization that interests you and ask to speak to the person in charge. Although dropping in is particularly effective in small businesses, it also works surprisingly well in larger ones. Remember to ask for an interview even if there are no openings now. If your timing is inconvenient, ask for a better time to come back for an interview.

The phone book's yellow pages provide the most complete, up-to-date listing of potential job search targets you can get. It organizes them into categories that are very useful for job seekers. Just find a category that interests you, evaluate each listing, and then contact employers that interest you. All it takes is a 30-second phone call. Ask to speak with the hiring authority.

Most Jobs Are with Small Employers

Businesses and organizations with fewer than 250 employees employ about 72 percent of all U.S. workers. Small organizations are also the source for around 75 percent of the new jobs created each year. They are simply too important to overlook in your job search! Many of them don't have personnel departments, which makes direct contacts even easier and more effective.

Create a Powerful Job Search Tool—the JIST Card®

Look at the sample cards that follow—they are JIST Cards, and they get results. Computer printed or even neatly written on a 3-by-5–inch card, JIST Cards include the essential information employers want to know.

A JIST Card Is a Mini Resume

JIST Cards have been used by thousands of job search programs and millions of people. Employers like their direct and timesaving format, and they have been proven as an effective tool to get job leads. Attach one to your resume. Give them to friends, relatives, and other contacts and ask them to pass them along to others who might know of an opening. Enclose them in thank-you notes after interviews. Leave one with employers as a business card. However you get them in circulation, you may be surprised at how well they work.

You can easily create JIST Cards on a computer and print them on card stock you can buy at any office supply store. Or have a few hundred printed cheaply by a local quick print shop. While they are often done as 3-by-5 cards, they can be printed in any size or format.

Sandy Nolan

Position: General Office/Clerical

Cell phone: (512) 232-9213

Email: snolan@aol.com

More than two years of work experience plus one year of training in office practices. Type 55 wpm, trained in word processing, post general ledger, have good interpersonal skills, and get along with most people. Can meet deadlines and handle pressure well.

Willing to work any hours.

Organized, honest, reliable, and hardworking.

Richard Straightarrow   Home: (602) 253-9678
                                            Message: (602) 257-6643
                                            E-mail: RSS@email.com

Objective: Electronics installation, maintenance, and sales

Four years of work experience plus a two-year A.S. degree in Electronics Engineering Technology. Managed a $360,000/year business while going to school full time, with grades in the top 25%. Familiar with all major electronic diagnostic and repair equipment. Hands-on experience with medical, consumer, communication, and industrial electronics equipment and applications. Good problem-solving and communication skills. Customer service oriented.

Willing to do what it takes to get the job done.

Self motivated, dependable, learn quickly.

A JIST Card Can Lead to an Effective Phone Script

The phone is an essential job search tool that can get you more interviews per hour than any other job search tool. But the technique won't work unless you use it actively throughout your search. After you have created your JIST Card, you can use it as the basis for a phone script to make warm or cold calls. Revise your JIST Card

Overcome phone phobia! Making cold calls takes guts, but most people can get one or more interviews an hour using cold calls. Start by calling people you know and people they refer you to. Then try calls to businesses that don't sound very interesting. As you get better, call more desirable targets.

content so that it sounds natural when spoken, and then edit it until you can read it out loud in about 30 seconds. The sample phone script that follows is based on the content of a JIST Card. Use it to help you modify your own JIST Card into a phone script.

"Hello. My name is Pam Nykanen. I am interested in a position in hotel management. I have four years' experience in sales, catering, and accounting with a 300-room hotel. I also have an associate degree in hotel management, plus one year of experience with the Brady Culinary Institute. During my employment, I helped double revenues from meetings and conferences and increased bar revenues by 46 percent. I have good problem-solving skills and am good with people. I am also well-organized, hardworking, and detail-oriented. When may I come in for an interview?"

With your script in hand, make some practice calls to warm or cold contacts. If making cold calls, contact the person most likely to supervise you. Then present your script just as you practiced it—without stopping.

Although the sample script assumes that you are calling someone you don't know, you can change it to address warm contacts and referrals. Making cold calls takes courage but works very well for many who are willing to do it.

Use the Internet in Your Job Search

The Internet has limitations as a job search tool. While many have used it to get job leads, it has not worked well for far more. Too many assume they can simply add their resume to resume databases, and employers will line up to hire them. Just like the older approach of sending out lots of resumes, good things sometimes happen, but not often.

I recommend two points that apply to all job search methods, including using the Internet:

- It is unwise to rely on just one or two methods in conducting your job search.

- It is essential that you use an active rather than a passive approach in your job search.

Use More Than One Job Search Method

I encourage you to use the Internet in your job search, but I suggest that you use it along with other techniques. Use the same sorts of job search techniques online as you do offline, including contacting employers directly and building up a network of personal contacts that can help you with your search.

Tips to Increase Your Effectiveness in Internet Job Searches

The following tips can increase the effectiveness of using the Internet in your job search:

- **Be as specific as possible in the job you seek.** This is important in using any job search method, and it's even more important in using the Internet in your job search. The Internet is enormous, so it is essential to be as focused as possible in your search. Narrow your job title or titles to be as specific as possible. Limit your search to specific industries or areas of specialization. Locate and use specialized job banks in your area of interest.

- **Have reasonable expectations.** Success on the Internet is more likely if you understand its limitations and strengths. For example, employers trying to find someone with skills in high demand, such as nurses, are more likely to use the Internet to recruit job candidates.

- **Limit your geographic options.** If you don't want to move or would move only to certain areas, state this preference on your resume and restrict your search to those areas. Many Internet sites allow you to view or search for only those jobs that meet your location criteria.

- **Create an electronic resume.** With few exceptions, resumes submitted on the Internet end up as simple text files with no graphic elements. Employers search databases of many resumes for those that include key words or meet other searchable criteria. So create a simple text resume for Internet use and include words that are likely to be used by employers searching for someone with your abilities. (See Step 4 for more on creating an electronic resume.)

- **Get your resume into the major resume databases.** Most Internet employment sites let you add your resume for free and then charge employers to advertise openings or to search for candidates. Although adding your resume to these databases is not likely to result in job offers, doing so allows you to use your stored resume to easily apply for positions that are posted at these sites. These easy-to-use sites often provide all sorts of useful information for job seekers.

- **Make direct contacts.** Visit the Web sites of organizations that interest you and learn more about them. Many post openings, allow you to apply online, offer information on benefits and work environment, or even provide access to staff who can answer your questions. Even if they don't, you can always search the site or e-mail a request for the name of the person in charge of the work that interests you and then communicate with that person directly.

- **Network.** You can network online, too, finding names and e-mail addresses of potential employer contacts or of other people who might know someone with job openings. Look at and participate in interest groups, professional association sites, alumni sites, chat rooms, e-mail discussion lists, and employer sites—these are just some of the many creative ways to network and interact with people via the Internet.

Check Out Career-Specific Sites First

Thousands of Internet sites provide lists of job openings and information on careers or education. Many have links to other sites that they recommend. Service providers such as America Online (www.aol.com) and the Microsoft Network (www.msn.com) have partnered with sites such as Careerbuilder.com to include career information and job listings plus links to other sites. Also check out www.jist.com and www.CareerOINK.com. Two additional career-related sites are Riley Guide at www.rileyguide.com and Monster.com at www.monster.com.

 STEP 4: Write a Simple Resume Now and a Better One Later

Sending out resumes and waiting for responses is not an effective job-seeking technique. But, many employers *will* ask you for a resume, and it can be a useful tool in your job search. I suggest that you begin with a simple resume you can complete quickly. I've seen too many people spend weeks working on a resume when they could have been out getting interviews instead. If you want a better resume, you can work on it on weekends and evenings. So let's begin with the basics.

Tips for Creating a Superior Resume

The following tips make sense for any resume format:

- **Write it yourself.** It's okay to look at other resumes for ideas, but write yours yourself. Doing so will force you to organize your thoughts and background.
- **Make it error-free.** One spelling or grammar error will create a negative impressionist (see what I mean?). Get someone else to review your final draft for any errors. Then review it again because these rascals have a way of slipping in.
- **Make it look good.** Poor copy quality, cheap paper, bad type quality, or anything else that creates a poor appearance will turn off employers to even the best resume content. Get professional help with design and printing if necessary. Many professional resume writers and even print shops offer writing and desktop design services if you need help.
- **Be brief, be relevant.** Many good resumes fit on one page, and few justify more than two. Include only the most important points. Use short sentences and action words. If it doesn't relate to and support the job objective, cut it!
- **Be honest.** Don't overstate your qualifications. If you end up getting a job you can't handle, who does it help? And a lie can result in your being fired later.
- **Be positive.** Emphasize your accomplishments and results. A resume is no place to be too humble or to display your faults.
- **Be specific.** Instead of saying, "I am good with people," say, "I supervised four people in the warehouse and increased productivity by 30 percent." Use numbers whenever possible, such as the number of people served, percentage of sales increase, or amount of dollars saved.

You should also know that everyone feels that he or she is a resume expert. Whatever you do, someone will tell you that it's wrong. Remember that a resume is simply a job search tool.

You should never delay or slow down your job search because your resume is not good enough. The best approach is to create a simple and acceptable resume as quickly as possible and then use it. As time permits, create a better one if you feel you must.

Avoid the resume pile. Resume experts often suggest that a dynamite resume will jump out of the pile. This is old-fashioned advice. It assumes that you are applying to large organizations and for advertised jobs. Today most jobs are with small employers and are not advertised. To avoid joining that stack of resumes in the first place, look for job openings that others overlook.

Writing Chronological Resumes

Most resumes use a chronological format where the most recent experience is listed first, followed by each previous job. This arrangement works fine for someone with work experience in several similar jobs, but not as well for those with limited experience or for career changers.

Look at the two resumes for Judith Jones that follow. Both use the chronological approach.

The first resume would work fine for most job search needs. It could be completed in about an hour.

Notice that the second one includes some improvements. The first resume is good, but most employers would like the additional positive information in the improved resume.

Basic Chronological Resume Example

Judith J. Jones

115 South Hawthorne Avenue
Chicago, Illinois 66204
(312) 653-9217 (home)
email: jj@earthlink.net

Leaves lots of options open by not using one job title.

Everything supports her job objective.

JOB OBJECTIVE

Desire a position in the office management, accounting, or administrative assistant area. Prefer a position requiring responsibility and a variety of tasks.

EDUCATION AND TRAINING

Acme Business College, Lincoln, Illinois
Graduate of a one-year business program.

John Adams High School, South Bend, Indiana
Diploma, business education.

U.S. Army
Financial procedures, accounting functions.

Other: Continuing-education classes and workshops in business communication, computer spreadsheet and database programs, scheduling systems, and customer relations.

Emphasis on all related education is important because it helps overcome her lack of "work" experience.

EXPERIENCE

Uses her education in this section to add credentials.

2003–present—Claims Processor, Blue Spear Insurance Co., Willmette, Illinois. Handle customer medical claims, develop management reports based on spreadsheets I created, exceed productivity goals.

2002–2003—Returned to school to upgrade my business and computer skills. Took courses in advanced accounting, spreadsheet and database programs, office management, human relations, and new office techniques.

1999–2002—E4, U.S. Army. Assigned to various stations as a specialist in financial operations. Promoted prior to honorable discharge.

1998–1999—Sandy's Boutique, Wilmette, Illinois. Responsible for counter sales, display design, cash register, and other tasks.

1996–1998—Held part-time and summer jobs throughout high school.

PERSONAL

I am reliable, hardworking, and good with people.

I give some tips you can use when you write your simple chronological resume. Use the preceding resume as your guide.

Improved Chronological Resume Example

Judith J. Jones

115 South Hawthorne Avenue
Chicago, Illinois 66204

jj@earthlink.net
(312) 653-9217

Adds lots of details to reinforce skills throughout.

Provides more details here.

JOB OBJECTIVE

Seeking a position requiring excellent business management expertise in an office environment. Position should require a variety of skills, including office management, word processing, and spreadsheet and database application use.

EDUCATION AND TRAINING

Acme Business College, Lincoln, IL
Completed one-year program in Professional Office Management. Achieved GPA in top 30% of class. Courses included word processing, accounting theory and systems, advanced spreadsheet and database applications, graphics design, time management, and supervision.

John Adams High School, South Bend, IN
Graduated with emphasis on business courses. Earned excellent grades in all business topics and won top award for word-processing speed and accuracy.

Other: Continuing-education programs at own expense, including business communications, customer relations, computer applications, and sales techniques.

EXPERIENCE

Uses numbers to reinforce results.

2003–present—**Claims Processor, Blue Spear Insurance Company**, Wilmette, IL. Process 50 complex medical insurance claims per day, almost 20% above department average. Created a spreadsheet report process that decreased department labor costs by more than $30,000 a year. Received two merit raises for performance.

2002–2003—**Returned to business school to gain advanced office skills.**

1999–2002—**Finance Specialist (E4), U.S. Army.** Systematically processed more than 200 invoices per day from commercial vendors. Trained and supervised eight employees. Devised internal system allowing 15% increase in invoices processed with a decrease in personnel. Managed department with a budget equivalent of more than $350,000 a year. Honorable discharge.

1998–1999—**Sales Associate promoted to Assistant Manager, Sandy's Boutique**, Wilmette, IL. Made direct sales and supervised four employees. Managed daily cash balances and deposits, made purchasing and inventory decisions, and handled all management functions during owner's absence. Sales increased 26% and profits doubled during tenure.

1996–1998—**Held various part-time and summer jobs through high school while maintaining GPA 3.0/4.0.** Earned enough to pay all personal expenses, including car insurance. Learned to deal with customers, meet deadlines, work hard, and handle multiple priorities.

STRENGTHS AND SKILLS

Reliable, with strong work ethic. Excellent interpersonal, written, and oral communication and math skills. Accept supervision well, effectively supervise others, and work well as a team member. General ledger, accounts payable, and accounts receivable expertise. Proficient in Microsoft Word, Excel, and Outlook; WordPerfect.

Tips for Writing a Simple Chronological Resume

Follow these tips as you write a basic chronological resume:

- **Name.** Use your formal name (not a nickname).
- **Address and contact information.** Avoid abbreviations in your address and include your ZIP code. If you may move, use a friend's address or include a forwarding address. Most employers will not write to you, so provide reliable phone numbers and other contact options. Always include your area code in your phone number because you never know where your resume might travel. Make sure that you have an answering machine or voice mail, and record a professional-sounding message. Include alternative ways to reach you, such as a cell phone and e-mail address.
- **Job objective.** You should almost always have one, even if it is general. Notice how Judith Jones keeps her options open with her broad job objective in her basic resume on page 309. Writing "secretary" or "clerical" might limit her from being considered for other jobs.
- **Education and training.** Include any training or education you've had that supports your job objective. If you did not finish a formal degree or program, list what you did complete and emphasize accomplishments. If your experience is not strong, add details here such as related courses and extracurricular activities. In the two examples, Judith Jones puts her business schooling in both the education and experience sections. Doing this fills a job gap and allows her to present her training as equal to work experience.
- **Previous experience.** Include the basics such as employer name, job title, dates employed, and responsibilities—but emphasize specific skills, results, accomplishments, superior performance, and so on.
- **Personal data.** Do not include irrelevant details such as height, weight, and marital status or a photo. Current laws do not allow an employer to base hiring decisions on these points. Providing this information can cause some employers to toss your resume. You can include information about hobbies or leisure activities in a special section that directly supports your job objective. The first sample includes a Personal section in which Judith lists some of her strengths, which are often not included in a resume.
- **References.** Make sure that each reference will make nice comments about you and ask each to write a letter of recommendation that you can give to employers. You do not need to list your references on your resume. List them on a separate page and give it to employers who ask. If your references are particularly good, however, you can mention this somewhere—the last section is often a good place.

When you have a simple, errorless, and eye-pleasing resume, get on with your job search. There is no reason to delay! If you want to create a better resume in your spare time (evenings or weekends), use the name and contact information you currently have and improve the other sections of the resume.

Tips for an Improved Chronological Resume

Use these tips to improve your simple resume:

- **Job objective.** A poorly written job objective can limit the jobs an employer might consider you for. Think of the skills you have and the types of jobs you want to do; describe them in general terms. Instead of using a narrow job title such as "restaurant manager," you might write "manage a small to mid-sized business."
- **Education and training.** New graduates should emphasize their recent training and education more than those with a few years of related work experience would. A more detailed education and training section might include specific courses you took, and activities or accomplishments that support your job objective or reinforce your key skills. Include other details that reflect how hard you work, such as working your way through school or handling family responsibilities.
- **Skills and accomplishments.** Include those that support your ability to do well in the job you seek now. Even small details count. Maybe your attendance was perfect, you met a tight deadline, or you did the work of others during vacations. Be specific and include numbers—even if you have to estimate them. Judith's improved chronological resume example features more accomplishments and skills. Notice the impact of the numbers to reinforce results.
- **Job titles.** Past job titles may not accurately reflect what you did. For example, your job title may have been "cashier," but you also opened the store, trained new staff, and covered for the boss on vacations. Perhaps "head cashier and assistant manager" would be more accurate. Check with your previous employer if you are not sure.

(continued)

(continued)

- **Promotions.** If you were promoted or got good evaluations, say so—"cashier, promoted to assistant manager," for example. You can list a promotion to a more responsible job as a separate job if doing so results in a stronger resume.
- **Gaps in employment and other problem areas.** Employee turnover is expensive, so few employers want to hire people who won't stay or who won't work out. Gaps in employment, jobs held for short periods, or a lack of direction in the jobs you've held are all concerns for employers. So consider your situation and try to give an explanation of a problem area. Here are a few examples:

  2007—Continued my education at...   2006 to present—Self-employed as barn painter and...

  2007—Traveled extensively throughout...   2006—Took year off to have first child

  Use entire years to avoid displaying employment gaps you can't explain easily. If you had a few months of unemployment at the beginning of 2006 and then began a job in mid-2006, for example, you can list the job as "2006 to 2007."

Writing Skills and Combination Resumes

Skip the negatives. Remember that a resume can get you screened out, but it is up to you to get the interview and the job. Cut out anything negative in your resume!

The skills resume emphasizes your most important skills, supported by specific examples of how you have used them. This type of resume allows you to use any part of your life history to support your ability to do the job you want.

While skills resumes can be very effective, creating them requires more work. And some employers don't like them because they can hide a job seeker's faults (such as job gaps, lack of formal education, or little related work experience) better than can a chronological resume. Still, a skills resume may make sense for you.

Look over the sample resumes that follow for ideas. Notice that one resume includes elements of a skills *and* a chronological resume. This so-called combination resume makes sense if your previous job history or education and training are positive.

More Resume Examples

A resume is not the most effective tool for getting interviews. A better approach is to make direct contact with those who hire or supervise people with your skills and ask them for an interview, even if no openings exist now. Then send a resume.

Find resume layout and presentation ideas in the four samples that follow.

The chronological resume sample on page 313 focuses on accomplishments through the use of numbers. While Jon's resume does not say so, it is obvious that he works hard and that he gets results.

The skills resume on page 314 is for a recent high school graduate whose only work experience was at a school office!

The combination resume on page 315 emphasizes Grant's relevant education and transferable skills because he has little work experience in the field.

The electronic resume on page 316 is appropriate for scanning or e-mail submission. It has a plain format that is easily read by scanners. It also has lots of key words that increase its chances of being selected when an employer searches a database.

Use the information from your completed Essential Job Search Data Worksheet to write your resume.

The Chronological Resume to Emphasize Results

This simple chronological resume has few but carefully chosen words. It has an effective summary at the beginning, and every word supports his job objective.

Jon Feder

2140 Beach Road
Pompano Beach, Florida 20000

Phone: (222) 333-4444
E-mail: jfeder@com.com

Objective: Management position in a major hotel *He emphasizes results!*

Summary of Experience: Three years of experience in sales, catering banquet services, and guest relations in a 75-room hotel. Doubled sales revenues from conferences and meetings. Increased dining room and bar revenues by 40%. Won prestigious national and local awards for increased productivity and services.

Experience: Beachcomber Hotel, Pompano Beach, Florida
Assistant Manager
20XX to Present

Notice his use of numbers to increase the impact of the statements.

- Oversee a staff of 24, including dining room and bar, housekeeping, and public relations operations.
- Introduced new menus and increased dining room revenues by 40%. Awarded *Saveur* magazine's prestigious first place Hotel Cuisine award as a result of my selection of chefs.
- Attracted 58% more bar patrons by implementing Friday night Jazz at the Beach.

Beachcombers' Suites, Hollywood Beach, Florida
Sales and Public Relations
20XX to 20XX

Bullets here and above improve readability and emphasize key points.

- Doubled venues per month from weddings, conferences, and meetings.
- Chosen Chamber of Commerce Newcomer of the Year 20XX for the increase in business within the community.

Education: Associate Degree in Hotel Management from Sullivan Technical Institute
Certificate in Travel Management from Phoenix University

While Jon had only a few years of related work experience, he used this resume to help him land a very responsible job in a large resort hotel.

The Skills Resume for Those with Limited Work Experience

In this skills resume, each skill directly supports the job objective of this recent high school graduate with very limited work experience.

Catalina A. Garcia

2340 N. Delaware Street · Denver, Colorado 81613
Home: (413) 643-2173 (Leave Message)
Cell phone: (413) 345-2189
E-mail: cagarcia@net.net

Position Desired

Office assistant in a fast-paced business

Support for her key skills comes from her activities: school, clubs, and volunteer work.

Skills and Abilities

Note her key skills.

Communications   Excellent written and verbal presentation skills. Use proper grammar and have a good speaking voice.

Interpersonal   Able to get along well with all types of people. Accept supervision. Received positive evaluation from previous supervisors.

Flexible   Willing to try new things and am interested in improving efficiency on assigned tasks.

Notice the emphasis on adaptive skills.

Attention to Detail   Maintained confidential student records accurately and efficiently. Uploaded 500 student records in one day without errors.

Hard Working   Worked 30 hours per week throughout high school and maintained above-average grades.

She makes good use of numbers.

This statement is very strong.

Student Contact   Cordially dealt with as many as 150 students a day in Dean's office.

Dependable   Never absent or tardy in four years.

Awards   English Department Student of the Year, April 20XX
20XX Outstanding Student Newspaper, Newspaper Association of America

Education

Denver North High School. Took advanced English and communication classes. Member of student newspaper staff and FCCLA for four years. Graduated in top 30% of class.

Other

Girls' basketball team for four years. This taught me discipline, teamwork, how to follow instructions, and hard work. I am ambitious, outgoing, reliable, and willing to work.

Catalina's resume makes it clear that she is talented and hard working.

The Combination Resume for Those Changing Careers

Grant just finished computer programming school and has no work experience in the field. After listing the topics covered in the course, he summarized his employment experience, specifying that he earned promotions quickly. This would be attractive to any employer.

Grant Thomas

717 Carlin Court • Mendelein, IL 60000 • (555) 555-3333
E-mail: gthomas@com.com

Profile

- Outstanding student and tutor
- Winner of international computer software design competition three years
- Capable of being self-directed and independent, but also a team player
- Effective communicator, both orally and written
- Creative problem solver

Education and Training

M.S. in Software Engineering, Massachusetts Institute of Technology, Cambridge, MA
B.S. in Computer Engineering, California State University, Fullerton, CA
A rigorous education that focuses on topics such as

He includes important information that specifies topics he studied.

- Structure and interpretation of computer programs
- Circuits and electronics
- Signals and systems
- Computation structures
- Microelectronic devices and circuits
- Computer system engineering
- Computer language engineering
- Mathematics for computer science
- Analog electronics laboratory
- Digital systems laboratory

The work experiences support the job objective.

Highlights of Experience and Abilities

- Develop, create, and modify general computer applications software.
- Analyze user needs and develop software solutions.
- Confer with system analysts, computer programmers, and others.
- Modify existing software to correct errors.
- Coordinate software system installation and monitor equipment functioning to ensure specifications are met.
- Supervise work of programmers and technicians.
- Train customers and employees to use new and modified software.

Employment History

Software Specialist, First Rate Computers, Mendelein, IL 20XX – Present
- Technician and Customer and Employee Trainer throughout high school
- Promoted to software specialist and worked as a full-time telecommuting employee while completing the B.S. and M.S. degrees

References available on request

The Electronic Resume

William Brown
409 S. Maish Road
Phoenix, AZ 50000

Because this electronic format is to be scanned or e-mailed, it has no bold, bullets, or italics.

Phone message: (300) 444-5567

E-mail: wbrown@email.com

OBJECTIVE

The many key words ensure that the employers' computer searches will select this resume.

Store management career track in car audio store

===
SUMMARY OF SKILLS

Strategic planning, time management, team building,
leadership, problem solving, quality customer service,
conflict resolution, increasing productivity, confident,
outgoing, high performing, aggressive sales

===
EXPERIENCE   *Note the results statements and numbers used below.*

Total of three years in sales

* SHIFT SUPERVISOR, Tech World, Audio Department, Phoenix,
AZ, April 20XX to present: Promoted to Shift Supervisor of
nine salespeople in three months. Responsible for strategic
planning, time management, team building, leadership,
problem solving, quality customer service, conflict
resolution, and increasing productivity. Highest-selling
team for three years.

* AUDIO SALESPERSON, Tech World, Audio Department, Phoenix,
AZ, January 20XX to April 20XX: Arranged display, organized
stockroom, sales to customers, and tracked inventory.
Highest-selling staff member for three months.

===
EDUCATION AND TRAINING

Phoenix High School, top 40% of class

Additional training: Team Building, Franklin Time Management
seminar, Team Building seminar

===
OTHER

* Installed audio systems in 10 cars: family, friends, and
my own.

* Member of United States Autosound Association (USAA)

Use a Career Portfolio to Support Your Resume

Your resume is impressive, but there is another way that you can show prospective employers evidence of who you are and what you can do—a career portfolio.

What Is a Career Portfolio?

Unlike a resume, a career portfolio is a collection of documents that can include a variety of items. Here are some items you may want to place in your portfolio:

- Resume
- School transcripts
- Summary of skills
- Credentials, such as diplomas and certificates of recognition
- Reference letters from school officials and instructors, former employers, or co-workers
- List of accomplishments: Describe hobbies and interests that are not directly related to your job objective and are not included on your resume.
- Examples of your work: Depending on your situation, you can include samples of your art, photographs of a project, audiotapes, videotapes, images of Web pages you developed, and other media that can provide examples of your work.

Place each item on a separate page when you assemble your career portfolio.

Create a Digital Portfolio

A digital portfolio, also known as an electronic portfolio, contains all the information from your career portfolio in an electronic format. This material is then copied onto a CD-ROM or published on a Web site. With a digital portfolio, you can present your skills to a greater number of people than you can your paper career portfolio.

YOUR CAREER PORTFOLIO

On the following lines, list the items you want to include in your career portfolio. Think specifically of those items that show your skills, education, and personal accomplishments.

_____

_____

_____

_____

_____

_____

_____

_____

_____

_____

STEP 5: Redefine What Counts as an Interview, and Then Get Two a Day

The average job seeker gets about five interviews a month—fewer than two a week. Yet many job seekers use the methods in this *Quick Job Search* to get two interviews a day. Getting two interviews a day equals 10 a week and 40 a month. That's 800 percent more interviews than the average job seeker gets. Who do you think will get a job offer quicker?

However, getting two interviews a day is nearly impossible unless you redefine what counts as an interview. If you define an interview in a different way, getting two a day is quite possible.

The New Definition of an Interview: Any face-to-face contact with someone who has the authority to hire or supervise a person with your skills—even if no opening exists at the time you talk with them.

If you use this new definition, it becomes *much* easier to get interviews. You can now interview with all sorts of potential employers, not just those who have job openings now. While most other job seekers look for advertised or actual openings, you can get interviews before a job opens up or before it is advertised and widely known. You will be considered for jobs that may soon be created but that others will not know about. And, of course, you can also interview for existing openings just as everyone else does.

Spending as much time as possible on your job search and setting a job search schedule are important parts of this Step.

Make Your Search a Full-Time Job

Job seekers average fewer than 15 hours a week looking for work. On average, unemployment lasts three or more months, with some people out of work far longer (for example, older workers and higher earners). My many years of experience researching job seeking indicate that the more time you spend on your job search each week, the less time you will likely remain unemployed.

Of course, using the more effective job search methods presented in this minibook also helps. Many job search programs that teach job seekers my basic approach of using more effective methods and spending more time looking have proven that these seekers often find a job in half the average time. More importantly, many job seekers also find better jobs using these methods.

So, if you are unemployed and looking for a full-time job, you should plan to look on a full-time basis. It just makes sense to do so, although many do not, or they start out well but quickly get discouraged. Most job seekers simply don't have a structured plan—they have no idea what they are going to do next Thursday. The plan that follows will show you how to structure your job search like a job.

Decide How Much Time You Will Spend Looking for Work Each Week and Day

First and most importantly, decide how many hours you are willing to spend each week on your job search. You should spend a minimum of 25 hours a week on hard-core job search activities with no goofing around. The following worksheet walks you through a simple but effective process to set a job search schedule for each week.

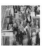

> ### PLAN YOUR JOB SEARCH WEEK
>
> 1. How many hours are you willing to spend each week looking for a job?_____
>
> 2. Which days of the week will you spend looking for a job?_____
>
> 3. How many hours will you look each day?_____
>
> 4. At what times will you begin and end your job search on each of these days?_____
>
> _____

Create a Specific Daily Job Search Schedule

Having a specific daily schedule is essential because most job seekers find it hard to stay productive each day. The sample daily schedule that follows is the result of years of research into what schedule gets the best results. I tested many schedules in job search programs I ran, and this particular schedule worked best.

Consider using a schedule like this sample daily schedule. Why? Because it works.

A Sample Daily Schedule That Works

Time	Activity
7–8 a.m.	Get up, shower, dress, eat breakfast
8–8:15 a.m.	Organize work space, review schedule for today's interviews and promised follow-ups, check e-mail, update schedule as needed
8:15–9 a.m.	Review old leads for follow-up needed today; develop new leads from want ads, yellow pages, the Internet, warm contact lists, and other sources; complete daily contact list
9–10 a.m.	Make phone calls and set up interviews
10–10:15 a.m.	Take a break
10:15–11 a.m.	Make more phone calls, set up more interviews
11 a.m.–Noon	Send follow-up notes and do other office activities as needed
Noon–1 p.m.	Lunch break, relax
1–3 p.m.	Go on interviews, make cold contacts in the field
Evening	Read job search books, make calls to warm contacts not reachable during the day, work on a better resume, spend time with friends and family, exercise, relax

If you are not accustomed to using a daily schedule book or electronic planner, promise yourself to get a good one tomorrow. Choose one that allows for each day's plan on an hourly basis, plus daily to-do lists. Record your daily schedule in advance, and then add interviews as they come. Get used to carrying your planner with you and use it!

You can find a variety of computer programs or pocket-sized electronic schedulers to help organize your job search. If you don't use electronic tools, a simple schedule book and other paper systems will work just fine.

STEP 6: Dramatically Improve Your Interviewing Skills

Interviews are where the job search action is. You have to get them; then you have to do well in them. According to surveys of employers, most job seekers do not effectively present the skills they have to do the job. Even worse, most job seekers can't answer one or more problem questions.

This lack of performance in interviews is one reason why employers will often hire a job seeker who does well in the interview over someone with better credentials. The good news is that you can do simple things to dramatically improve your interviewing skills. This section will emphasize interviewing tips and techniques that make the most difference.

Your First Impression May Be the Only One You Make

Some research suggests that if the interviewer forms a negative impression in the first five minutes of an interview, your chances of getting a job offer approach zero. I know from experience that many job seekers can create a lasting negative impression within seconds.

Tips for Interviewing

Because a positive first impression is so important, I share these suggestions to help you get off to a good start:

- **Make a good impression before you arrive.** Your resume, e-mails, applications, and other written correspondence create an impression before the interview, so make them professional and error-free.

- **Do some homework on the organization before you go.** You can often get information on a business and on industry trends from the Internet or a library.

- **Dress and groom the same way the interviewer is likely to be dressed—but cleaner!** Employer surveys find that almost half of all people's dress or grooming creates an initial negative impression. So this is a big problem. If necessary, get advice on your interviewing outfits from someone who dresses well. Pay close attention to your grooming, too—little things do count.

- **Be early.** Leave in plenty of time to be a few minutes early to an interview.

- **Be friendly and respectful with the receptionist.** Doing otherwise will often get back to the interviewer and result in a quick rejection.

- **Follow the interviewer's lead in the first few minutes.** It's often informal small talk but very important for that person to see how you interact. This is a good time to make a positive comment on the organization or even something you see in the office.

- **Understand that a traditional interview is not a friendly exchange.** In a traditional interview situation, there is a job opening, and you will be one of several applicants for it. In this setting, the employer's task is to eliminate all applicants but one. The interviewer's questions are designed to elicit information that can be used to screen you out. And your objective is to avoid getting screened out. It's hardly an open and honest interaction, is it?

  Setting up interviews before an opening exists eliminates the stress of a traditional interview. In pre-interviews, employers are not trying to screen you out, and you are not trying to keep them from finding out stuff about you. Having said that, knowing how to answer questions that might be asked in a traditional interview is good preparation for any interview you face.

- **Be prepared to answer the tough interview questions.** Your answers to a few key problem questions may determine whether you get a job offer. There are simply too many possible interview questions to cover one by one. Instead, 10 basic questions cover variations of most other interview questions. So, if you can learn to answer the Top 10 Problem Interview Questions well, you will know how to answer most others.

- **Be prepared for the most important interview question of all.** "Why should I hire you?" is the most important question of all to answer well. Do you have a convincing argument why someone should hire you over someone else? If you don't, you probably won't get that job you really want. So think carefully about why someone should hire you and practice your response. Then make sure you communicate this in the interview, even if the interviewer never asks the question in a clear way.

Top 10 Problem Interview Questions

1. Why should I hire you?
2. Why don't you tell me about yourself?
3. What are your major strengths?
4. What are your major weaknesses?
5. What sort of pay do you expect to receive?
6. How does your previous experience relate to the jobs we have here?
7. What are your plans for the future?
8. What will your former employer (or references) say about you?
9. Why are you looking for this type of position, and why here?
10. Why don't you tell me about your personal situation?

Follow the Three-Step Process for Answering Interview Questions

I've developed a three-step process for answering interview questions. I know this might seem too simple, but the three-step process is easy to remember and can help you create a good answer to most interview questions. The technique has worked for thousands of people, so consider trying it.

1. **Understand what is really being asked.**

   Most questions are designed to find out about your self-management skills and personality, but interviewers are rarely this blunt. The employer's *real* question is often one or more of the following:

   - Can I depend on you?

   - Are you easy to get along with?

   - Are you a good worker?

   - Do you have the experience and training to do the job if we hire you?

   - Are you likely to stay on the job for a reasonable period of time and be productive?

   Ultimately, if you don't convince the employer that you will stay and be a good worker, it won't matter if you have the best credentials—he or she won't hire you.

2. **Answer the question briefly in a nondamaging way.** Present the facts of your particular work experience as advantages, not disadvantages. Many interview questions encourage you to provide negative information. One classic question I included in my list of Top 10 Problem Interview Questions was "What are your major weaknesses?" This is obviously a trick question, and many people are just not prepared for it.

   A good response is to mention something that is not very damaging, such as *"I have been told that I am a perfectionist, sometimes not delegating as effectively as I might."*

   But your answer is not complete until you continue with the next step.

3. **Answer the real question by presenting your related skills.** Base your answer on the key skills you have that support the job, and give examples to support these skills. For example, an employer might say to a recent graduate, *"We were looking for someone with more experience in this field. Why should we consider you?"* Here is one possible answer:

"I'm sure there are people who have more experience, but I do have more than six years of work experience, including three years of advanced training and hands-on experience using the latest methods and techniques. Because my training is recent, I am open to new ideas and am used to working hard and learning quickly."

In the previous example (about your need to delegate), a good skills statement might be

"I've been working on this problem and have learned to let my staff do more, making sure that they have good training and supervision. I've found that their performance improves, and it frees me up to do other things."

Whatever your situation, learn to answer questions that present you well. It's essential to communicate your skills during an interview, and the three-step process can help you answer problem questions and dramatically improve your responses. It works!

How to Earn a Thousand Dollars a Minute

What do you do when the employer asks, "How much money would it take to get you to join our company?"

Tips on Negotiating Pay

Remember these few essential tips when it comes time to negotiate your pay:

- **The Number 1 Salary Negotiation Rule: The person who names a specific amount first loses.**
- **The only time to negotiate is after you have been offered the job.** Employers want to know how much you want to be paid so that they can eliminate you from consideration. They figure if you want too much, you won't be happy with their job and won't stay. And if you will take too little, they may think you don't have enough experience. So never discuss your salary expectations until an employer offers you the job.
- **If pressed, speak in terms of wide pay ranges.** If you are pushed to reveal your pay expectations early in an interview, ask the interviewer what the normal pay range is for this job. Interviewers will often tell you, and you can say that you would consider offers in this range.

  If you are forced to be more specific, speak in terms of a wide pay range. If you figure that the company will likely pay from $20,000 to $25,000 a year, for example, say that you would consider "any fair offer in the low to mid-twenties." This statement covers the employer's range and goes a bit higher. If all else fails, tell the interviewer that you would consider any reasonable offer.

  For this tip to work, you must know in advance what the job is likely to pay. You can get this information by asking people who do similar work, or from a variety of books and Internet sources of career information.
- **If you want the job, you should say so.** This is no time to be playing games.
- **Don't say "no" too quickly.** Never, ever turn down a job offer during an interview! Instead, thank the interviewer for the offer and ask to consider the offer overnight. You can turn it down tomorrow, saying how much you appreciate the offer and asking to be considered for other jobs that pay better or whatever. And it is okay to ask for additional pay or other concessions. But if you simply can't accept the offer, say why and ask the interviewer to keep you in mind for future opportunities. You just never know.

STEP 7: Follow Up on all Job Leads

It's a fact: People who follow up with potential employers and with others in their network get jobs more quickly than those who do not.

Thank-You Notes Make a Difference

Although thank-you notes can be e-mailed, most people appreciate and are more impressed by a mailed note. Here are some tips about mailed thank-you notes that you can easily adapt to e-mail use:

- You can handwrite or type thank-you notes on quality paper and matching envelopes.

- Keep the notes simple, neat, and error-free.

- Make sure to include a few copies of your JIST Card in the envelope.

Here is an example of a simple thank-you note.

April 5, XXXX

Mr. Kijek,

Thanks so much for your willingness to see me next Wednesday at 9 a.m. I know that I am one of many who are interested in working with your organization. I appreciate the opportunity to meet you and learn more about the position.

I've enclosed a JIST Card that presents the basics of my skills for this job and will bring my resume to the interview. Please call me if you have any questions at all.

Sincerely,

Bruce Vernon

Use Job Lead Cards to Follow Up

If you use contact management software, use it to schedule follow-up activities. But the simple paper system I describe here can work very well or can be adapted for setting up your contact management software.

- Use a simple 3-by-5–inch card to record essential information about each person in your network.

- Buy a 3-by-5–inch card file box and tabs for each day of the month.

- File the cards under the date you want to contact the person.

- Follow through by contacting the person on that date.

I've found that staying in touch with a good contact every other week can pay off big. Here's a sample card to give you ideas about creating your own.

ORGANIZATION: _Mutual Health Insurance_

CONTACT PERSON: _Anna Tomey_   PHONE: _317-355-0216_

SOURCE OF LEAD: _Aunt Ruth_

NOTES: _4/10 Called. Anna on vacation. Call back 4/15. 4/15 Interview set_
4/20 at 1:30. 4/20 Anna showed me around. They use the same computers
we used in school! (Friendly people.) Sent thank-you note and JIST
Card, call back 5/1. 5/1 Second interview 5/8 at 9 a.m.!

In Closing

This is a short book, but it may be all you need to get a better job in less time. I hope this will be true for you, and I wish you well in your search. Remember this: You won't get a job offer because someone knocks on your door and offers one. Job seeking does involve luck, but you are more likely to have good luck if you are out getting interviews.

I'll close this minibook with a few final tips:

- **Approach your job search as if it were a job itself.** Create and stick to a daily schedule, and spend at least 25 hours a week looking.

- **Follow up on each lead you generate and ask each contact for referrals.**

- **Set out each day to schedule at least two interviews.** Remember the new definition of an interview—an interview includes talking to potential employers who don't have an opening now.

- **Send out lots of thank-you notes and JIST Cards.**

- **When you want the job, tell the employer that you want it and why you should be hired over everyone else.**

Don't get discouraged. There are lots of jobs out there, and someone needs an employee with your skills—your job is to find that someone.

I wish you luck in your job search and in your life.

ESSENTIAL JOB SEARCH DATA WORKSHEET

Take some time to complete this worksheet carefully. It will help you write your resume and answer interview questions. You can also photocopy it and take it with you to help complete applications and as a reference throughout your job search. Use an erasable pen or pencil to allow for corrections. Whenever possible, emphasize skills and accomplishments that support your ability to do the job you want. Use extra sheets as needed.

Your name_____

Date completed_____

Job objective_____

Key Accomplishments

List three accomplishments that best prove your ability to do the kind of job you want.

 1. _____

 2. _____

 3. _____

Education and Training

Name of high school(s) and specific years attended_____

Subjects related to job objective_____

_____

Related extracurricular activities/hobbies/leisure activities_____

_____

Accomplishments/things you did well_____

_____

Specific things you can do as a result_____

_____

Schools you attended after high school, specific years attended, and degrees/certificates earned_____

_____

Courses related to job objective_____

_____

Related extracurricular activities/hobbies/leisure activities_____

_____

Accomplishments/things you did well_____

_____

Specific things you can do as a result_____

_____

Other Training

Include formal or informal learning, workshops, military training, skills you learned on the job or from hobbies—anything that will help support your job objective. Include specific dates, certificates earned, or other details as needed._____

_____

(continued)

(continued)

Work and Volunteer History

List your most recent job first, followed by each previous job. Military experience, unpaid or volunteer work, and work in a family business should be included here, too. If needed, use additional sheets to cover *all* significant paid or unpaid work experiences. Emphasize details that will help support your new job objective. Include numbers to support what you did: the number of people served over one or more years, number of transactions processed, percentage of sales increased, total inventory value you were responsible for, payroll of the staff you supervised, total budget responsible for, and so on. Emphasize results you achieved, using numbers to support them whenever possible. Mentioning these things on your resume and in an interview will help you get the job you want.

Job 1

Dates employed_____

Name of organization_____

Supervisor's name and job title_____

Address_____

Phone number/e-mail address/Web site_____

What did you accomplish and do well?_____

_____

Things you learned; skills you developed or used_____

_____

Raises, promotions, positive evaluations, awards_____

_____

Computer software, hardware, and other equipment you used_____

_____

Other details that might support your job objective_____

_____

Job 2

Dates employed_____

Name of organization_____

Supervisor's name and job title_____

Address_____

Phone number/e-mail address/Web site_____

What did you accomplish and do well?_____

_____

Things you learned; skills you developed or used_____

_____

Raises, promotions, positive evaluations, awards_____

_____

Computer software, hardware, and other equipment you used_____

_____

Other details that might support your job objective_____

_____

Job 3

Dates employed_____

Name of organization_____

Supervisor's name and job title_____

Address_____

Phone number/e-mail address/Web site_____

What did you accomplish and do well?_____

_____

Things you learned; skills you developed or used_____

_____

Raises, promotions, positive evaluations, awards_____

_____

Computer software, hardware, and other equipment you used_____

_____

Other details that might support your job objective_____

_____

References

Think of people who know your work well and will be positive about your work and character. Past supervisors are best. Contact them and tell them what type of job you want and your qualifications, and ask what they will say about you if contacted by a potential employer. Some employers will not provide references by phone, so ask them for a letter of reference in advance. If a past employer may say negative things, negotiate what they will say or get written references from others you worked with there.

Reference name_____

Position or title_____

Relationship to you_____

Contact information (complete address, phone number, e-mail address)____

(continued)

(continued)

Reference name_____

Position or title_____

Relationship to you_____

Contact information (complete address, phone number, e-mail address)_____

_____

Reference name_____

Position or title_____

Relationship to you_____

Contact information (complete address, phone number, e-mail address)_____

_____

A Short List of Additional Resources

Thousands of books and countless Internet sites provide information on career subjects. Space limitations do not permit me to describe the many good resources available, so I list here some of the most useful ones. Because this is my list, I've included books I've written or that JIST publishes. You should be able to find these and many other resources at libraries, bookstores, and Web bookselling sites.

Resume and Cover Letter Books

My books. *The Quick Resume & Cover Letter Book* is one of the top-selling resume books at various large bookstore chains. It is very simple to follow, is inexpensive, has good design, and has good sample resumes written by professional resume writers. For more in-depth but still quick help, check out my two books in the *Help in a Hurry* series: *Same-Day Resume* (with advice on creating a simple resume in an hour and a better one later) and *15-Minute Cover Letter,* co-authored with Louise Kursmark (offering sample cover letters and tips for writing them fast and effectively).

Other books published by JIST. The following titles include many sample resumes written by professional resume writers, as well as good advice: *Amazing Resumes* by Jim Bright and Joanne Earl; *Cover Letter Magic* by Wendy S. Enelow and Louise M. Kursmark; the entire *Expert Resumes* series by Enelow and Kursmark; *Federal Resume Guidebook* by Kathryn Kraemer Troutman; *Gallery of Best Resumes, Gallery of Best Cover Letters,* and other books by David F. Noble; and *Résumé Magic* by Susan Britton Whitcomb.

Job Search and Interviewing Books

My books. You may want to check out my two books in the *Help in a Hurry* series: *Seven-Step Job Search* (even more tips and step-by-step guidance to cut your job search time in half) and *Next-Day Job Interview* (quick tips for preparing for a job interview at the last minute). *The Very Quick Job Search* is a thorough book with detailed advice and a "quick" section of key tips you can finish in a few hours. *Getting the Job You Really Want* includes many in-the-book activities and good career decision-making and job search advice.

Other books published by JIST. Titles include *Inside Secrets of Finding a Teaching Job* by Warner, Bryan, and Warner; *Insider's Guide to Finding a Job* by Wendy S. Enelow and Shelly Goldman; *Job Search Handbook for People with Disabilities* by Daniel J. Ryan; *Job Search Magic* and *Interview Magic* by Susan Britton Whitcomb; *Ultimate Job Search* by Richard H. Beatty; and *Over-40 Job Search Guide* by Gail Geary.

Books with Information on Jobs

The primary reference books. The *Occupational Outlook Handbook* is the source of job titles listed in this book. Published by the U.S. Department of Labor and updated every other year, the *OOH* covers about 90 percent of the workforce. The *O*NET Dictionary of Occupational Titles* book has descriptions for more than 1,000 jobs based on the O*NET (Occupational Information Network) database developed by the Department of Labor. The *Enhanced Occupational Outlook Handbook* includes the *OOH* descriptions plus more than 7,000 additional descriptions of related jobs from the O*NET and other sources. The *New Guide for Occupational Exploration* allows you to explore major jobs based on your interests.

Other books published by JIST. Here are a few good books that include job descriptions and helpful details on career options: *Overnight Career Choice, Best Jobs for the 21st Century, 50 Best Jobs for Your Personality, 40 Best Fields for Your Career, 200 Best Jobs for College Graduates,* and *300 Best Jobs Without a Four-Year Degree.*

Internet Resources

There are too many Web sites to list, but here are a few places you can start. A book by Anne Wolfinger titled *Best Career and Education Web Sites* gives unbiased reviews of the most helpful sites and ideas on how to use them. *Job Seeker's Online Goldmine,* by Janet Wall, lists the extensive free online job search tools from government and other sources. This book's job descriptions also include Internet addresses for related organizations. And www.jist.com lists recommended sites for career, education, and related topics, along with comments on each. Be aware that some Web sites provide poor advice, so ask your librarian, instructor, or counselor for suggestions on those best for your needs.

Other Resources

Libraries. Most libraries have the books mentioned here, as well as many other resources. Many also provide Internet access so that you can research online information. Ask the librarian for help finding what you need.

People. People who hold the jobs that interest you are one of the best career information sources. Ask them what they like and don't like about their work, how they got started, and the education or training needed. Most people are helpful and will give advice you can't get any other way.

Career Counseling. A good vocational counselor can help you explore career options. Take advantage of this service if it is available to you! Also consider a career-planning course or program, which will encourage you to be more thorough in your thinking.

Sample Resumes for Some of the Top Jobs for People Without a Four-Year Degree

If you read the previous information, you know that I believe you should not depend on a resume alone in your job search. Even so, you will most likely need one, and you should have a good one.

Unlike some career authors, I do not preach that there is only one right way to do a resume. I encourage you to be an individual and to do what you think will work well for you. But I also know that some resumes are clearly better than others. The following pages contain some resumes that you can use as examples when preparing your own resume.

Each resume was written by a professional resume writer who is a member of one or more professional associations. These writers are highly qualified and hold various credentials. Most will provide help (for a fee) and welcome your contacting them (although this is not a personal endorsement).

The resumes appear in books published by JIST Works, including the following:

- *Best Resumes for College Students and New Grads* by Louise M. Kursmark

- *Expert Resumes for Health Care Careers* by Wendy S. Enelow and Louise M. Kursmark

- *Gallery of Best Resumes for People Without a Four-Year Degree* by David F. Noble

Contact Information for Resume Contributors

The following professional resume writers contributed resumes to this section. Their names are listed in alphabetical order. Each entry indicates which resume that person contributed.

Beverly and Mitch Baskin
Baskin Business & Career Services
6 Alberta Drive
Marlboro, NJ 07746
Other offices: 120 Wood Ave.
South, Iselin, NJ 08830; Forrestal
Village, Princeton, NJ 08540
Toll-free phone: (800) 300-4079
Fax: (732) 972-8846
E-mail: bbcs@att.net
Web site: www.baskincareer.com
Member: NRWA, NCDA, NECA,
MACCA, AMHCA
Certifications: Ed.S, MA, MMS,
LPC, NCCC, CPRW, MCC, PE,
NAJST
Resume on page 340

Janet L. Beckstrom
Word Crafter
1717 Montclair Ave.
Flint, MI 48503-2074
Toll-free phone: (800) 351-9818
Fax: (810) 232-9257
E-mail: wordcrafter@voyager.net
Member: CMI, PARW/CC
Certifications: CPRW
Resume on page 335

Carolyn S. Braden
Braden Resume Solutions
108 La Plaza Drive
Hendersonville, TN 37075
Phone: (615) 822-3317
Fax: (615) 826-9611
E-mail: bradenresume@comcast.net
Member: CMI, PARW/CC
Certifications: CPRW
Resume on pages 331–332

Jean Cummings
A Resume For Today
123 Minot Road
Concord, MA 01742
Phone (978) 317-9266
Toll-free phone: (800) 324-1699
Fax: (978) 964-0529
E-mail: jc@aResumeForToday.com
Web site:
www.aResumeForToday.com
Member: CMI, PARW/CC
Certifications: MAT, CPRW, CEIP
Resume on pages 341–342

Debbie Ellis
Phoenix Career Group
Toll-free phone: (800) 876-5506
Fax: (859) 236-3900
E-mail: debbie@
phoenixcareergroup.com
Web site:
www.phoenixcareergroup.com
Certifications: CPRW, MRW
Resume on page 338

Louise Garver
Career Directions, LLC
115 Elm Street, Ste. 203
Enfield, CT 06082
Phone: (860) 623-9476
Toll-free phone: (888) 222-3731
Fax: (860) 623-9473
E-mail: careerpro@cox.net
Web site: www.resumeimpact.com
Certifications: MA, CEIP, CMP,
CPRW, JCTC, MCDP
Resume on page 336

Jane Roqueplot
JaneCo's Sensible Solutions
194 N. Oakland Ave.
Sharon, PA 16146
Phone: (724) 342-0100
Toll-free phone: (888) 526-3267
Fax: (724) 346-5263
E-mail: jane@janecos.com
Web site: www.janecos.com
Member: CMI, NRWA, PRWRA,
PARW/CC, AJST, NCDA
Certifications: CPBA, CWDP,
CECC
Resume on page 333

Janice Shepherd
Write On Career Keys
Bellingham, WA 98226-4260
Phone: (360) 738-7958
Fax: (360) 738-1189
E-mail:
Janis@writeoncareerkeys.com
Web site:
www.writeoncareerkeys.com
Member: CMI, PARW/CC
Certifications: CPRW, JCTC,
CEIP
Resumes on pages 334 and 339

Tammy J. Smith
Professional Image Design, LLC
7030 Marshall Road
Olivet, MI 49076
Phone: (269) 209-3539
Toll-free phone: (877) 588-7459
Toll-free fax: (877) 588-7459
E-mail: ProResumeWriter@aol.com
Member: NRWA
Resume on page 337

Aircraft and Avionics Equipment Mechanics and Service Technicians

THOMAS A. NABORS
476 Murray Lane • Goodlettsville, TN 00000 • Home (555) 000-0000

AIRCRAFT MAINTENANCE & TECHNOLOGY

FAA-LICENSED A&P MECHANIC with more than 18 years of experience in the maintenance, repair, troubleshooting, and inspection of civilian and military aircraft. Familiar with all Federal Aviation Regulations (FARs). Qualified by experience, education, and training to assume new leadership and supervisory challenges. Expertise includes the following:

<u>Civilian Aircraft</u>:	Saab 340 (A, B, B+ models) – Saab 2000 – British Aerospace Bae-146 100/200 and JS 3100/3200 – Canadair CRJ – Embraer 120/135/145 – ATR-42/72 – DeHavilland Dash-8 – Shorts 360
<u>Military Aircraft</u>:	B-52 (G, H models) – C-130
<u>Airframe Structures</u>:	Sheet Metal – Composite – Painting
<u>Systems</u>:	Electrical Hydraulic – Landing Gear – Instrument – Flight Controls – Pneumatic – Heating/Pressurization – Fuel – Oxygen – Fire Extinguishing
<u>Powerplant</u>:	Turbine Engine – Fuel-Metering Systems – Ignition Systems – Propeller and Governing Systems

PROFESSIONAL EXPERIENCE

READYSTEP AIRTECH (a full-service, FAA Class 4 certified repair station) – Nashville, TN 1997–Present

Lead Aircraft Maintenance Technician (2001–Present)
- Promoted to manage and schedule work assignments of four Technicians and supervise training and performance. Make certain that Technicians use correct technical data.
- Ensure that planes are inspected according to schedule and are ready by delivery date. Order parts for various aircraft models.
- Follow FARs and airlines' procedures on standard maintenance and custom-requested items.

Aircraft Inspector (2000–2001)
- Evaluated the quality of maintenance and repair work performed by Technicians. Inspected and followed up on completed work and advised supervisor of any problem areas.

Aircraft Maintenance Technician (1997–2000)
- Performed maintenance, troubleshooting, and repair of aircraft systems.

U.S. AIR FORCE – Stationed at various AFBs throughout the country 1986–1997

Advanced through a series of increasingly responsible assignments based on knowledge of aircraft maintenance and repair, technical abilities, and overall performance. Received numerous medals for meritorious service and outstanding achievement throughout military career, including Commendation Medal, Achievement Medal, Outstanding Unit Award, and National Defense Service Medal. Served four years in support of Operation Desert Shield/Desert Storm. Held Secret Security Clearance.

Aircraft Maintenance Supervisor/Crew Chief – Ellsworth AFB, SD (1992–1997)
- Achieved impeccable quality assurance and safety records and was cited for superior after-flight inspections.

Continued . . .

(continued)

(continued)

THOMAS A. NABORS   Page 2

PROFESSIONAL EXPERIENCE (continued)

Aircraft Maintenance Supervisor—Wurtsmith AFB, MI (1991–1992)
- Selected for special maintenance position servicing B-52 aircraft for first-strike "real-world" missions in the Persian Gulf during Desert Storm. Inspected and troubleshot all types of problems under time-critical schedules. Twelve planes launched and 17 recovered in 48 hours; 24 ready aircraft launched in only five days.

Aircraft Maintenance Assistant Crew Chief—Fairchild AFB, WA (1987–1991)
- Trained and mentored mechanics servicing B-52H airplanes.
- Member of a team that achieved unprecedented aircraft sortie rates and systems reliability; received consistent 100% pass rates on safety practice evaluations.

Aircraft Maintenance Team Technician—Fairchild AFB, WA (1986–1987)
- Completed on-the-job training program ahead of peers with a final "closed book" test score of 90% in all areas (significantly above unit average).

EDUCATION & PROFESSIONAL DEVELOPMENT

FAA AIRFRAME & POWERPLANT LICENSE, 1994
License #000000000

AIRCRAFT MAINTENANCE TECHNOLOGY
Community College of the Air Force—Maxwell AFB, AL
Successfully completed 110 hours toward A.A.S. degree.

Supervisory Training:
Management & Human Resources Development / Total Quality Concepts, 1993
Introduction to Supervision & Training Management Courses, 1989

Technical Training:
Fam Classes in Saab 340 and ATR 72
Canadair CRJ Training
Weight and Balance & Hazardous Materials Handling Training, 1994
B-52H Engine Operations Certification Training
Aircraft Maintenance (B-52G/H) Crew Chief & Follow-On Training Courses
Aircraft Maintenance Career Development Course (with Honors), 1987
Aircraft Maintenance Technical Training School (160 hours), 1987

Computer Skills:
Sperry Remote Computer Terminal for Maintenance Data Collection
Microsoft Office (Word), Windows 3.1/95/98/Me/2000/XP
Internet navigation and research, e-mail, faxing, scanning

ADDITIONAL INFORMATION

Member of Tennessee Air National Guard (1998–Present)
Maintain and repair C-130H aircraft.

Willing to travel worldwide. Hold current U.S. passport.

Chefs, Cooks, and Food Preparation Workers

DONALD ARCHER
412 Old Castle Avenue • Sharon, Pennsylvania 16146 • 724-543-4671

"Compliments to the chef! This is the best prime rib I've ever eaten." — Ralph B
Monte Cello's, Sharon, PA

"Superb steak . . . cooked to perfection . . . excellent seasonings. My thanks to the chef." — Actress
Debbie Reynolds
Radisson Hotel, Sharon, PA

Knowledgeable in:
➢ Food Preparation
➢ Menu Creation
➢ Inventory
➢ Ordering Supplies and Food
➢ Event Planning
➢ Serving 1–2,500
➢ Nutrition
➢ Sanitation
➢ Security
➢ Policies & Procedures
➢ Personnel Management
➢ Staff Training
➢ Record Keeping
➢ Preparation of Reports

EDUCATION

Culinary Arts
International Culinary Academy—Pittsburgh, Pennsylvania

Winner Institute of Arts & Sciences—Transfer, Pennsylvania

Food Competitions and Food Shows

Liberal Arts
Criminal Justice/ Pre-Law Course Work
Kent State University— Champion, Ohio

EXECUTIVE CHEF / PERSONAL CHEF / CATERING

- Select menu items with an eye toward quality, variety, availability of seasonal foods, popularity of past dishes and likely number of customers. Collaborate with owner(s) to plan menus to attract specific clientele.

- Estimate food consumption. Select and appropriately price menu items to cost-effectively use food and other supplies.

- Oversee food preparation and cooking, examining quality and portion sizes to ensure dishes are prepared and garnished correctly and in a timely manner.

- Proficient knowledge of computer programs, especially to create menus; analyze recipes to determine food, labor and overhead costs; and calculate prices for various dishes.

- Hardworking, self-motivated individual with proven record of responsibility. Equally effective working independently as well as in a team effort. Work well with a wide range of people at all levels; comfortable leading, collaborating or training.

- Able to view situations/issues in a positive way and propose solutions to streamline operations. Organized and detail-oriented. Identify and resolve challenges using available resources.

- Effective communicator. Monitor actions of employees to ensure health and safety standards are maintained. Represent an organization in a professional manner and appearance.

- Receptive to relocation.

EXPERIENCE

EXECUTIVE CHEF, Monte Cello's—*Sharon, Pennsylvania*
SOUS CHEF, Mr. D's Food Fair—*Brookfield, Ohio*
KITCHEN MANAGER, Sidetrack Inn—*Warren, Ohio*
STORE MANAGER, Pit Stop Pizza—*Cortland, Ohio*
GRILL AND SAUTÉ CHEF, Radisson Hotel—*Sharon, Pennsylvania*
PREP CHEF, Avalon Inn—*Howland, Ohio*
ASSISTANT MANAGER, Moovies, Inc.—*Cortland, Ohio*
PERSONAL SECURITY TECHNICIAN, Independent Contractor—
various locations

MILITARY

Military Police, 1984–1987, Honorable Discharge
United States Marine Corp.

Computer Support Specialists and Systems Administrators

Shultz Griggs
Computer Professional

1234 Valentine Street
Towers, WA 71234
Mobile Phone: (777) 777-7000
Fax: (777) 777-7001
email: Schultzie@email.com

Established reputation for expertise within the computer industry—more than 22 years of experience. Personable, conscientious, resourceful. Strong aptitude for learning. Willing to relocate.

EXPERTISE

- Set up, configure, enhance, upgrade, and support computers, computer systems, and peripherals—including server clusters and networks.

- Develop custom software for clients; resolve software compatibility issues.

- Develop programs that interface with computer-controlled test equipment.

- EXPERT in use, installation, configuration, troubleshooting, and problem-solving of the following:

Software

Operating systems: Windows NT 4.0, Windows XP, Windows 2000 Pro, Windows 95/98, and Windows 3.1; exposure to UNIX (various) and Linux

Protocols: TCP/IP, NetBIOS, and NetBEUI

Applications: MS Word 2002, MS Excel 2002, MS Access, MS Outlook, Photoshop, Macromedia Dreamweaver, MS Frontpage, Adobe Pagemaker, MS Visual C++ 6.0, MS Visual Basic 6.0, MS J++, and Borland JBuilder

Languages: C++, C, BASIC, HTML, Java, JavaScript, XML, and Assembly Language

Hardware

Desktop computers and small to midsize servers

HP servers, workstations, and RAID products; Adaptec SCSI and Fiber Channel Controllers; 3COM hubs, switches, and network cards; and SMC hubs and network cards

IDE, SCSI, and Fiber Channel hard disk drives and tape backup products from various manufacturers. Exposure to SAN and NAS storage devices.

EXPERIENCE

Computer Professional, Computer Service, Towers, WA   1991–present

Evaluated, tested, and recommended networking, storage, and server hardware to clients; provided problem resolution for MIS departments. Developed testing methods to ensure reliability and compatibility; performed testing of computer, storage, and networking products. Configured new computer, network, and storage hardware for clients. Installed and configured operating systems and drivers for workstations and servers. Configured server clusters, network software, RAID arrays, and other storage options. Aided clients with operating system and application upgrade rollouts. Undertook small to medium-size customer software development projects.

- *Major clients included* Texaco, Alcoa Aluminum, County Community College, City of Towers, and State University.

Lead Programmer, Rioters Insurance Group, Wooden, WA   1982–1991

Managed the development, installation, and support of software applications used by banks and automobile dealers. Provided technical support by phone for software. Installed and configured networking hardware and software on site. Resolved software problems on site.

- *Exemplary accomplishments:* Developed applications in C and BASIC to perform loan calculations and to print forms and contracts; developed algorithms to calculate various types of loans; developed basic email system for loan approval.

CERTIFICATIONS / EDUCATION

CompTIA A+ in progress; Network+ in progress; Microsoft MCSE in progress

State University, B.S. Program, Major in Technology and Mathematics
Community College, A.S. Program, Electronics and Technology

Dental Assistants

Juanita P. Morales

3482 McCandlish Road
Grand Blanc, MI 48439
810-555-2396 • jpmsmiles@home.net

Profile

❖ Certification and training as **Dental Hygienist.**

❖ Experience as chair-side **Dental Assistant** in general and periodontal practices.

❖ Ability to earn **trust** and develop **rapport** with patients.

❖ Strong patient **assessment** and **education** skills.

❖ Training and experience in using **Prophy Jet** and **ultrasonic scalers.**

Dental Experience

CARO PERIODONTAL ASSOCIATES • Caro, MI	2005–Present
FAMILY DENTAL • Clarkston, MI	2001–2005
DR. ROGER ANDERSON • Rochester, MI	2000–2001
MACKIN ROAD DENTAL CLINIC • Lapeer, MI	1996–2000

Education

MOTT COMMUNITY COLLEGE • Flint, MI
Certificate in Dental Hygiene   2005
— Graduated in Top 10% of class
— Passed state and national exams
— Past President, MCC Dental Students Association

Selected Classes & Training

❖ "Infection Control in a Changing World"

❖ "Advanced Techniques in Root Planing and Instrument Sharpening"

❖ "AIDS: Oral Signs, Symptoms, and Treatments"

❖ "Periodontal Diseases in Children and Adolescents"

❖ "Periodontal Screening Record"

❖ "Strategies for Teamwork and Communication Skills"

Community Involvement

❖ International Institute — Event Assistant

❖ Spanish-Speaking Information Center — Volunteer Tutor

❖ Big Brothers/Big Sisters of Greater Flint — Big Sister

References available on request

Inspectors, Testers, Sorters, Samplers, and Weighers

Denise Sylvestor
467 Appleton Street
Dayton, OH 00000
(555) 555-5555

Summary

More than 13 years of experience in electronic assembly, quality-control inspection, shipping and receiving and production. Experience in leading and training other employees to perform productively.

Proficient in sub and final assembly, testing and inspection of electronic components, including printed circuit boards, wiring and other products.

Skilled in operating a variety of hand tools and machinery; able to assemble and handle simple to complex operations.

A team-oriented, dedicated, punctual employee recognized for the ability to learn quickly and produce quality work.

Computer skills include Microsoft Word for Windows.

Experience

Electronic Assembly/Machining

- Assemble and build printed circuit boards and automotive parts (exhaust and intake for Chrysler cars) from blueprints/schematics, using soldering iron, gauges and various other hand tools.
- Operate exhaust machine and make any necessary minor repairs/adjustments to Bradley Allen computer to maintain top production levels and minimize downtime.

Quality Control Inspection/Shipping & Receiving

- Inspect more than 340 boxes of electronic parts each day to ensure compliance with company standards, using chemicals and electric equipment.
- Record incoming and outgoing shipments as well as prepare items for shipment; verify information against bills of lading, invoices, orders and other records.

Team Leadership

- Selected by management in recognition of dependability and excellent performance as lead person on Cybex production line, overseeing team of 16 assemblers.
- Provide ongoing guidance, training and leadership to assembly team, maintaining top levels of productivity.

Employment History

Full-Time Caregiver, Dayton, OH (2002 to present)

AUTOMOTIVE CORPORATION, Dayton, OH (1994 to 2002)
Quality Control Inspector
Electronic Assembler
Machinist

WIRE COMPANY, Dayton, OH (1990 to 1994)
Automotive/Electronic Assembler

NEW VISIONS, Dayton, OH (1989 to 1990)
Electronic Assembler

Education

A.S. in Electronics Technology
Dayton Community College, Dayton, OH

Medical Assistants

Jennifer Black

(555) 555-5555

email@address.com
1234 West Street
Hometown, NY 01234

MEDICAL ASSISTANT

Triage	Injections	Patient Scheduling
Medical Terminology	Phlebotomy	Chart Updating
Patient Intake	Vital Signs	ICD and CPT Coding
Dosage Calculations	Infection Control	Insurance Claims
Sterilization Procedures	Urinalysis	Accounts Payable / Receivable
Blood Smears and Blood Tests	Hematocrit	Collections
Lab Equipment Operation	EKG	Data Entry

EXPERIENCE

Patient Care
- Cared for in-home patients with complex, multisymptom illnesses for three years
- Eased patient discomfort by conducting accurate assessment and drawing techniques
- Fostered healthy environment for diabetic patient through meal preparation, medication dispensing, and glucose-level monitoring

Administrative
- Improved cash flow by recovering uncollectible accounts in excess of $1,000,000
- Increased accuracy of patient files by designing and implementing new patient update sheet
- Exceeded daily quotas and minimized overhead expenses with effective scheduling and management of part-time employees

Computer Skills
- Microsoft Windows, Word, Excel, and Works
- Corel WordPerfect
- Medical software including Medical Manager and Great Plains

EDUCATION

College of Medical Careers, San Diego, CA
Medical Assistant Certificate, 1996
Valedictorian

High School, Anytown, PA
Diploma—Science Emphasis, 1992

RELATED EMPLOYMENT HISTORY

Billing Specialist, Bookkeeper, Medical Assistant (various—Indiana and Somerset, PA)	1996–1997
Medical Assistant (Internal Medical Office—San Diego, CA)	1996
Long-term/Acute Care Provider (self-employed)	1992–1995

Paralegals and Legal Assistants

Lydia C. Hendricks

65 Thorn Hill Court
Greenville, South Carolina 29607
Mobile (828) 516-4548 • Residence (828) 236-9925 • Email lydiac@earthlink.net

---

PARALEGAL / LEGAL SECRETARY

Dedicated to providing superior, uninterrupted administrative support to legal and non-legal staff.

Confident, articulate, and results-oriented legal-support professional offering a strong foundation of education and experience. Creative and enthusiastic with proven record of success in prioritizing and processing heavy workflow without supervision. Superior organization and communication skills; committed to personal and professional growth. Looking to join an established team that rewards hard work and personal achievement with stability and the opportunity for increased responsibility.

IMMEDIATE VALUES OFFERED

- Highly proficient in word processing, data entry, and Dictaphone transcription using Microsoft application software; noticed for maintaining consistently superior levels of accuracy.
- Organized, efficient, and thorough; maintain flexibility in changing work assignments.
- Perform well under stress, taking pressure off superiors and peers.
- Proficient in the planning and execution of projects in time-critical environments.
- Dependable and successful problem-resolution and time-management solutions.
- Creative and cooperative, working equally well individually or as part of a team.
- Outstanding record of performance, reliability, confidentiality, and ethical business standards.
- Computer skills include Microsoft Word 97/2000 and Windows 95/98, and WordPerfect; familiarity with Microsoft Excel, PowerPoint, and Access. Typing rate approximately 80 WPM.

LEGAL EXPERIENCE

Criminal / Civil	Powers of Attorney	Complaints
Domestic Relations	Divorce	Exhibits / Witness Lists
Affidavits	Adoption	QDRO
Subpoenas	Probate	Personal Injury
Motions	Wills	Client Interviewing
Orders	Estates	Real Estate
Research	Worker's Compensation	Mortgages / Deeds

SUMMER INTERNSHIP EXPERIENCE

Paralegal, **Tranter & Tranter, Attorneys and Counselors At Law** Greenville, SC 2004
(Temporary Replacement) Legal Secretary, **Elmer George, Attorney At Law** Spartanburg, SC 2003–04

EDUCATION AND SPECIAL CERTIFICATIONS

Associate of Science Degree, Paralegal Studies — Sullivan College, Greenville, SC
Magna Cum Laude Distinction
Dean's List
Degree Awarded 6/2005

Attended South Carolina Business College, 19 credit hours accumulated, Legal Writing
Attended Hutchinson Community College, 24 credit hours accumulated, Criminal Justice

Commissioned Notary Public, South Carolina State-at-Large — Status, current

Pharmacy Technicians

Priscilla K. Balding

3333 Tree Lane
Spokane, WA 99214
(509) 727-7347

Pharmacy — Medical Billing — Medical Office Administration

PROFILE

Team-spirited professional, patient and resourceful. Positive attitude, creative thinker/problem solver—effective in streamlining operations, improving productivity, and reducing costs.

Able to handle multiple responsibilities, set priorities, clearly communicate ideas to others, and respond positively to demanding situations. Recognized for speed, accuracy, quality of work, and outstanding customer service.

QUALIFICATIONS

- Insurance Billing—online and hand-billing experience for all insurances including Medicare and Medicaid—detailed working knowledge of insurance plans, overrides, and billing codes.
- 11 years' pharmacy experience—drug formulary, ingredients, compounding, analyzing prescriptions/inventory management/recordkeeping.
- Outstanding customer service—recipient of numerous "Mystery Shopper" Customer Service Awards.

Added Value:

- 10+ years' experience in hospitality industry—catering, staff management, event planning.

CAREER SUMMARY

Pharmacy Technician Level A, Rite-Aid, Spokane, WA, 1995–Present
Completed training program to become PTLA while working as cashier.

Main source of flow for prescriptions—analyze prescriptions; type prescriptions; count, compound, and dispense drugs. Order drugs and supplies. Provide extensive, caring, and informed Customer Service—established loyal customer base.

Access insurance company computers—set up prescriptions, calculate supply and quantity—utilize knowledge of limitations of different insurance plans. Maintain customer records and profiles on nationally linked proprietary computer system.

Assistant Manager, Wellington Yacht Club, Spokane, WA, 1989–1992
Answered to Board of Directors and General Manager of Catering and Fine Dining establishment.

Supervised up to 30 employees in all aspects of food and beverage area of Club. Assisted chef with menu planning and food-cost control. Instrumental in bringing about modernization of service styles. Initiated systems to improve efficiency and food service.

Food and Beverage/Catering Manager, Holiday Inn, Spokane, WA, 1988–1995 *(now Best Western Lakeway)*

Oversaw staff of 60+ people—purchasing, scheduling, event planning, budgeting. Assisted chef with menu planning. Involved with entire remodel and re-imaging of hotel and lounge—participated in selecting and training staff, initiating new procedures, implementing new computer system.

PROFESSIONAL DEVELOPMENT

Washington State Pharmacy Technician License—current
Pharmacy Training, Rite-Aid
Coursework in Accounting/General Business, City Community College

Purchasing Managers, Buyers, and Purchasing Agents

Nora T. Collins

56 MacArthur Road • Somerset, NJ 08873 • 732.958.4791 • noracol7@prodigy.net

SENIOR BUYER

Procurement ~ Materials Management ~ Sourcing ~ Inventory

Performance-driven, dynamic professional with demonstrated abilities in procurement, out-sourcing, and negotiating for manufacturing or wholesale distribution environments.

An independent self-starter with a solid history of utilizing out-of-the-box approaches, adapting to new business environments, and negotiating win-win agreements.

Competencies

- Purchasing/Buying
- Stock Control/Leveling
- Customer Relations
- Organizational/Project Management
- Material Distribution/Supply Chain
- Inventory Control/Management
- Resource/Materials Management
- Contract Negotiations/Vendor Relations

Professional Experience

American Bouquet Company, Inc. (1984–Present)
Purchasing Manager

Performed all buying functions for the New Jersey, Florida, and South America manufacturing facilities. Promoted numerous times over a 20-year career with the company.

Continually acknowledged for dramatically improving the firm's profitability with each assignment.

Handle disposition of defective merchandise and determine inventory levels in the warehouse while analyzing new order trends and then conducting precise inventories.

With a solid knowledge of hard-goods pricing, designed and created several new products and product lines that were significant revenue earners for the company.

Coordinated vendor operations with factory and shipping schedules and developed "Just in Time" procedures.

Improved quality and consistency of incoming merchandise by taking a tough stance with vendors.

Final authority for approving all vendor invoices for payment.

- Reduced a $1 million inventory by 50% with improved delivery scheduling.
- Reduced costs and price levels by selecting innovative vendors and changing the inventory system to augment production.
- Pioneered a company import program to purchase hard goods, reducing manufacturing costs substantially.

Real Estate Brokers and Sales Agents

JOSEPH K. THORNSTEIN

400 Rindge Avenue
Worcester, MA 55555

thornstein42@earthlink.net

Office: (555) 555-5555
Mobile: (555) 555-5555

REAL ESTATE DEVELOPMENT CONSULTANT

Strong record of completing more than 35 development projects, from the development review, licensing, and permitting process through to final approvals. Recruited to manage the most high-profile, controversial, and environmentally sensitive projects.

- Exceptional ability to build agreement with town boards and community groups and to guide projects through complex regulatory and litigation processes on time and on budget.

- Broad and deep expertise in the industry. Able to quickly develop a feel for the community and assess whether a project is likely to be a "go," saving time and money and improving the company's bottom line.

- Excellent reputation within the New England real estate development industry. Extensive network of positive relationships with town officers, planning boards, and state and federal agencies.

- Politically and interpersonally savvy with expert conflict-management, communication, and presentation skills. Adept at breaking down barriers and turning opposing stakeholders into allies.

Development Projects

- Skilled Nursing & Alzheimer's Facilities	- Single-Family Homes
- Medical Office Buildings	- Condominiums & Apartment Complexes
- Corporate Office Centers	- Assisted Living Facilities
- Industrial Facilities	- Multiuse Facilities

Real Estate Development Skill Set

- Development review, permitting, & licensing	- Hire & manage development consultants
- Liaison with federal, state, & local agencies	- Make presentations to town planning boards & community groups
- Negotiate option / purchase agreements	
- Perform due diligence	- Conduct real-estate & construction-loan closings
- Develop & administer budgets	- Siting & land acquisition

PROFESSIONAL EXPERIENCE

WORCESTER PROPERTIES, Worcester, MA   2001–Present
Real Estate Development Consultant

Representative Project

- **Southbridge Corporate Center,** Southbridge, MA
  A $110 million project to develop an 82-acre stone quarry into a high-end corporate office building.

  Full development review, licensing, and permitting accountability from day one to final approvals.

  Challenge: Lay the groundwork for developing a controversial project in a strongly anti-development town. Solve zoning and jurisdictional problems concerning wastewater treatment. Work against a December 2001 deadline to avoid the company's having to negotiate a costly new land option.

  Actions: Successfully drove the project through a land court, an appeals court, and the State Supreme Court. Hired corporate consultants who could communicate well with town planning boards and community groups. Represented the project at 120 public hearings and neighborhood-group meetings. Negotiated with selectmen. Built relationships with local board members. Cleared a major roadblock— resulting from a decision by a neighboring town not to accept other towns' waste—by developing a plan for a $1.2 million on-site treatment plant. Completed entire MEPA, DEP, MHD, and ACOE processes.

  Results: Won all final permits and approvals for the development of "the most-litigated land parcel in the Commonwealth of Massachusetts going back 45 years."

(continued)

JOSEPH K. THORNSTEIN

BERTRAND COMPANIES, Worcester, MA   1992–2001
Second-largest nursing home developer in the U.S.
Development Officer for Massachusetts

Accountable for project development from inception to final approvals. Projects included nursing home facilities, medical office buildings, high-end single-family homes, and corporate office centers. Performed due diligence; hired and managed development team of architects, engineers, and other specialists; and made presentations.

Representative Project

- **Southbridge Nursing Home,** Southbridge, MA

    Challenge: Site is a $15 million facility in a suburban town. Overcome strong neighborhood and community opposition by developing negotiated solutions. Determine optimal use for the 40% of the existing structure not required by the architectural plans.

    Actions: Hired the development team. Researched possible sites. Met with town officials and planning boards. Established a "good neighbor" relationship by allowing $1-a-time use of the auditorium. Made a strategic decision to install a CORF (comprehensive outpatient rehabilitation facility) and medical offices in the 32,000 sq. ft. of space not required by the nursing home. Neutralized strong opposition from the planning board and neighbors by negotiating creative solutions such as lowering the height of light poles, moving the parking lot, and building buffers.

    Results: Achieved buy-in from all necessary groups and gained project approval within a tight nine-month time frame and within the development process budget.

SANDERSON ASSOCIATES, INC., Manchester, NH   1986–1992
Vice President

Charged with developing the NH and MA markets for the company's real estate acquisition / development business. Staffed a 10-person acquisition department. Managed the development review process.

- Instrumental in growing sales from $2 million to $115 million in four years.
- Established new divisions in NJ, CT, ME, FL, and DC/VA.

Representative Project

- **Residential / Multifamily Condominium Housing,** Salem, NH

    Challenge: Overcome strong community opposition to the proposed 204-unit housing development. Address concerns about the tax increases and quality-of-life impacts resulting from a large influx of new residents using the roads and requiring costly town services (schools, police, fire).

    Actions: Actively listened to citizen concerns and then performed in-depth research on actual impacts. Hired a finance specialist to determine costs and benefits. Made a convincing case in a public presentation that the project would result in a financial net gain.

    Results: Successfully achieved all approvals within nine months.

EDUCATION

MOUNT MONADNOCK COMMUNITY COLLEGE, Princeton, MA
A.A. Degree in Mathematics

Important Trends in Jobs and Industries

In putting this section together, my objective was to give you a quick review of major labor market trends. To accomplish this, I included three excellent articles that originally appeared in U.S. Department of Labor publications.

The first article is "Tomorrow's Jobs." It provides a superb—and short—review of the major trends that will affect your career in the years to come. Read it for ideas on selecting a career path for the long term.

The second article is "Employment Trends in Major Industries." While you may not have thought much about it, the industry you work in is just as important as your occupational choice. This great article will help you learn about major trends affecting various industries.

The third article, "Job Outlook for People Who Don't Have a Bachelor's Degree," discusses the large number of job openings for people without a four-year degree. It also covers high-paying jobs that do not require a four-year degree. The article can help you focus on promising careers in many industries.

Tomorrow's Jobs

Making informed career decisions requires reliable information about opportunities in the future. Opportunities result from the relationships between the population, the labor force, and the demand for goods and services.

Population ultimately limits the size of the labor force—individuals working or looking for work—which constrains how much can be produced. Demand for various goods and services determines employment in the industries providing them. Occupational employment opportunities, in turn, result from demand for skills needed within specific industries. Opportunities for medical assistants and other healthcare occupations, for example, have surged in response to rapid growth in demand for health services.

Examining the past and projecting changes in these relationships is the foundation of the U.S. Department of Labor's Occupational Outlook Program. "Tomorrow's Jobs" presents highlights of Bureau of Labor Statistics projections of the labor force and occupational and industry employment that can help guide your career plans.

Population

Population trends affect employment opportunities in a number of ways. Changes in population influence the demand for goods and services. For example, a growing and aging population has increased the demand for health services. Equally important, population changes produce corresponding changes in the size and demographic composition of the labor force.

The U.S. civilian noninstitutional population is expected to increase by 23.9 million over the 2004–2014 period, at a slower rate of growth than during both the 1994–2004 and 1984–1994 periods (Chart 1). Continued growth will mean more consumers of goods and services, spurring demand for workers in a wide range of occupations and industries. The effects of population growth on various occupations will differ. The differences are partially accounted for by the age distribution of the future population.

The youth population, aged 16 to 24, will grow 2.9 percent over the 2004–2014 period. As the baby boomers

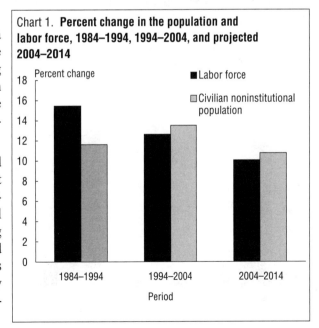

Chart 1. **Percent change in the population and labor force, 1984–1994, 1994–2004, and projected 2004–2014**

continue to age, the group aged 55 to 64 will increase by 36 percent or 10.4 million persons, more than any other group. The group aged 35 to 44 will decrease in size, reflecting the birth dearth following the baby boom generation.

Minorities and immigrants will constitute a larger share of the U.S. population in 2014. The number of Hispanics is projected to continue to grow much faster than those of all other racial and ethnic groups.

Labor Force

Population is the single most important factor in determining the size and composition of the labor force—that is, people who are either working or looking for work. The civilian labor force is projected to increase by 14.7 million, or 10 percent, to 162.1 million over the 2004–2014 period.

The U.S. workforce will become more diverse by 2014. White, non-Hispanic persons will continue to make up a decreasing share of the labor force, falling from 70 percent in 2004 to 65.6 percent in 2014 (Chart 2). However, despite relatively slow growth, white, non-Hispanics will remain the largest group in the labor force in 2014. Asians are projected to account for an increasing share of the labor force by 2014, growing from 4.3 to 5.1 percent. Hispanics are projected to be the fastest growing of the four labor force groups, growing by 33.7 percent. By 2014, Hispanics will continue to constitute a larger proportion of the labor force than will blacks, whose share will grow from 11.3 percent to 12.0 percent.

The numbers of men and women in the labor force will grow, but the number of women will grow at a faster rate than the number of men. The male labor force is projected to grow by 9.1 percent from 2004 to 2014, compared with 10.9 percent for women. As a result, men's share of the labor force is expected to decrease from 53.6 to 53.2 percent, while women's share is expected to increase from 46.4 to 46.8 percent.

The youth labor force, aged 16 to 24, is expected to slightly decrease its share of the labor force to 13.7 percent by 2014. The primary working age group, between 25 and 54 years old, is projected to decline from 69.3 percent of the labor force in 2004 to 65.2 percent by 2014. Workers 55 and older, on the other hand, are projected to increase from 15.6 percent to 21.2 percent of the labor force between 2004 and 2014, due to the aging of the baby-boom generation (Chart 3).

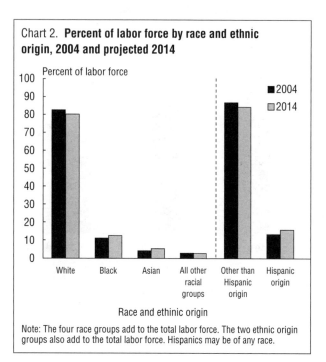

Chart 2. **Percent of labor force by race and ethnic origin, 2004 and projected 2014**

Note: The four race groups add to the total labor force. The two ethnic origin groups also add to the total labor force. Hispanics may be of any race.

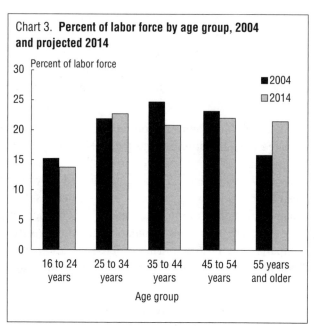

Chart 3. **Percent of labor force by age group, 2004 and projected 2014**

Employment

Total employment is expected to increase from 145.6 million in 2004 to 164.5 million in 2014, or by 13 percent. The 18.9 million jobs that will be added by 2014 will not be evenly distributed across major industrial and occupational groups. Changes in consumer demand, technology, and many other factors will contribute to the continually changing employment structure in the U.S. economy.

The following two sections examine projected employment change from both industrial and occupational perspectives. The industrial profile is discussed in terms of primary wage and salary employment. Primary employment excludes secondary jobs for those who hold multiple jobs. The exception is employment in agriculture, which includes self-employed and unpaid family workers in addition to wage and salary workers.

The occupational profile is viewed in terms of total employment—including primary and secondary jobs for wage and salary, self-employed, and unpaid family workers. Of the nearly 146 million jobs in the U.S. economy in 2004, wage and salary workers accounted for 133.5 million; self-employed workers accounted for 12.1 million; and unpaid family workers accounted for about 141,000. Secondary employment accounted for 1.7 million jobs. Self-employed workers held 9 out of 10 secondary jobs; wage and salary workers held most of the remainder.

Industry

Service-providing industries. The long-term shift from goods-producing to service-providing employment is expected to continue. Service-providing industries are expected to account for approximately 18.7 million of the 18.9 million new wage and salary jobs generated over the 2004–2014 period (Chart 4).

Education and health services. This industry supersector is projected to grow faster, 30.6 percent, and add more jobs than any other industry supersector. About 3 out of every 10 new jobs created in the U.S. economy will be in either the healthcare and social assistance or private educational services sectors.

Healthcare and social assistance—including private hospitals, nursing and residential care facilities, and individual and family services—will grow by 30.3 percent and add 4.3 million new jobs. Employment growth will be driven by increasing demand for healthcare and social assistance because of an aging population and longer life expectancies. Also, as more women enter the labor force, demand for childcare services is expected to grow. Private educational services will grow by 32.5 percent and add 898,000 new jobs through 2014. Rising student enrollments at all levels of education will create demand for educational services.

Professional and business services. This industry supersector, which includes some of the fastest-growing industries in the U.S. economy, will grow by 27.8 percent and add more than 4.5 million new jobs.

Employment in administrative and support and waste management and remediation services will grow by 31 percent and add 2.5 million new jobs to the economy by 2014. The fastest-growing industry in this sector will be employment services, which will grow by 45.5 percent and will contribute almost two-thirds of all new jobs in

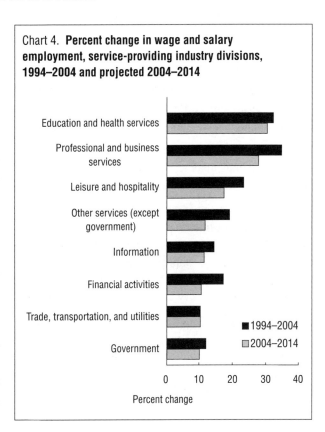

Chart 4. **Percent change in wage and salary employment, service-providing industry divisions, 1994–2004 and projected 2004–2014**

administrative and support and waste management and remediation services. Employment services ranks among the fastest-growing industries in the nation and is expected to be among those that provide the most new jobs.

Employment in professional, scientific, and technical services will grow by 28.4 percent and add 1.9 million new jobs by 2014. Employment in computer systems design and related services will grow by 39.5 percent and add almost one-fourth of all new jobs in professional, scientific, and technical services. Employment growth will be driven by the increasing reliance of businesses on information technology and the continuing importance of maintaining system and network security. Management, scientific, and technical consulting services also will grow very rapidly, by 60.5 percent, spurred by the increased use of new technology and computer software and the growing complexity of business.

Management of companies and enterprises will grow by 10.6 percent and add 182,000 new jobs.

Information. Employment in the information supersector is expected to increase by 11.6 percent, adding 364,000 jobs by 2014. Information contains some of the fast-growing computer-related industries such as software publishers; Internet publishing and broadcasting; and Internet service providers, Web search portals, and data processing services. Employment in these industries is expected to grow by 67.6 percent, 43.5 percent, and 27.8 percent, respectively. The information supersector also includes telecommunications; broadcasting; and newspaper, periodical, book, and directory publishers. Increased demand for residential and business land-line and wireless services, cable service, high-speed Internet connections, and software will fuel job growth among these industries.

Leisure and hospitality. Overall employment will grow by 17.7 percent. Arts, entertainment, and recreation will grow by 25 percent and add 460,000 new jobs by 2014. Most of these new job openings will come from the amusement, gambling, and recreation sector. Job growth will stem from public participation in arts, entertainment, and recreation activities—reflecting increasing incomes, leisure time, and awareness of the health benefits of physical fitness.

Accommodation and food services is expected to grow by 16.5 percent and add 1.8 million new jobs through 2014. Job growth will be concentrated in food services and drinking places, reflecting increases in population, dual-income families, and dining sophistication.

Trade, transportation, and utilities. Overall employment in this industry supersector will grow by 10.3 percent between 2004 and 2014. Transportation and warehousing is expected to increase by 506,000 jobs, or by 11.9 percent through 2014. Truck transportation will grow by 9.6 percent, adding 129,000 new jobs, while rail transportation is projected to decline. The warehousing and storage sector is projected to grow rapidly at 24.8 percent, adding 138,000 jobs. Demand for truck transportation and warehousing services will expand as many manufacturers concentrate on their core competencies and contract out their product transportation and storage functions.

Employment in retail trade is expected to increase by 11 percent, from 15 million to 16.7 million. Increases in population, personal income, and leisure time will contribute to employment growth in this industry, as consumers demand more goods. Wholesale trade is expected to increase by 8.4 percent, growing from 5.7 million to 6.1 million jobs.

Employment in utilities is projected to decrease by 1.3 percent through 2014. Despite increased output, employment in electric power generation, transmission, and distribution and natural gas distribution is expected to decline through 2014 due to improved technology that increases worker productivity. However, employment in water, sewage, and other systems is expected to increase 21 percent by 2014. Jobs are not easily eliminated by technological gains in this industry because water treatment and waste disposal are very labor-intensive activities.

Financial activities. Employment is projected to grow 10.5 percent over the 2004–2014 period. Real estate and rental and leasing is expected to grow by 16.9 percent and add 353,000 jobs by 2014. Growth will be due, in part, to increased demand for housing as the population grows. The fastest-growing industry in the financial activities supersector will be activities related to real estate, which will grow by 32.1 percent, reflecting the housing boom that persists throughout most of the nation.

Finance and insurance is expected to increase by 496,000 jobs, or 8.3 percent, by 2014. Employment in securities, commodity contracts, and other financial investments and related activities is expected to grow 15.8 percent by 2014, reflecting the increased number of baby boomers in their peak savings years, the growth of tax-favorable retirement plans, and the globalization of the securities markets. Employment in credit intermediation and related services, including banks, will grow by 5.4 percent and add about one-third of all new jobs within finance and insurance. Insurance carriers and related activities is expected to grow by 9.5 percent and add 215,000 new jobs by 2014. The number of jobs within agencies, brokerages, and other insurance-related activities is expected to grow about 19.4 percent, as many insurance carriers downsize their sales staffs and as agents set up their own businesses.

Government. Between 2004 and 2014, government employment, including that in public education and hospitals, is expected to increase by 10 percent, from 21.6 million to 23.8 million jobs. Growth in government employment will be fueled by growth in state and local educational services and the shift of responsibilities from the federal government to the state and local governments. Local government educational services is projected to increase 10 percent, adding 783,000 jobs. State government educational services is projected to grow by 19.6 percent, adding 442,000 jobs. Federal government employment, including the postal service, is expected to increase by only 1.6 percent as the federal government continues to contract out many government jobs to private companies.

Other services (except government). Employment will grow by 14 percent. More than 1 out of every 4 new jobs in this supersector will be in religious organizations, which is expected to grow by 11.9 percent. Other automotive repair and maintenance will be the fastest-growing industry at 30.7 percent. Also included among other services is personal care services, which is expected to increase by 19.5 percent.

Goods-producing industries. Employment in the goods-producing industries has been relatively stagnant since the early 1980s. Overall, this sector is expected to decline 0.4 percent over the 2004–2014 period. Although employment is expected to decline or increase more slowly than in the service-providing industries, projected growth among goods-producing industries varies considerably (Chart 5).

Construction. Employment in construction is expected to increase by 11.4 percent, from 7 million to 7.8 million. Demand for new housing and an increase in road, bridge, and tunnel construction will account for the bulk of job growth in this supersector.

Manufacturing. Employment change in manufacturing will vary by individual industry, but overall employment in this supersector will decline by 5.4 percent or 777,000 jobs. For example, employment in transportation equipment manufacturing is expected to grow by 95,000 jobs. Due to an aging population and increasing life expectancies, pharmaceutical and medicine manufacturing is expected to grow by 26.1 percent and add 76,000 jobs through 2014. However, productivity gains, job automation, and international competition will adversely affect employment in many other manufacturing industries. Employment in textile mills and apparel manufacturing will decline by 119,000 and 170,000 jobs, respectively. Employment in computer and electronic product manufacturing also will decline by 94,000 jobs through 2014.

Agriculture, forestry, fishing, and hunting. Overall employment in agriculture, forestry, fishing, and hunting is expected to decrease by 5.2 percent. Employment is expected to continue to decline due to advancements in technology. The only industry within this supersector

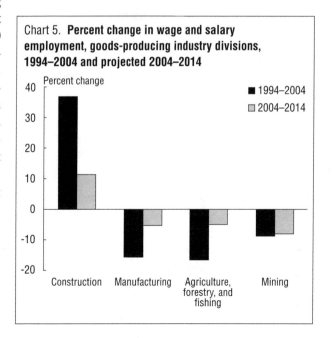

Chart 5. **Percent change in wage and salary employment, goods-producing industry divisions, 1994–2004 and projected 2004–2014**

expected to grow is support activities for agriculture and forestry, which includes farm labor contractors and farm management services. This industry is expected to grow by 18.2 percent and add 19,000 new jobs.

Mining. Employment in mining is expected to decrease 8.8 percent, or by some 46,000 jobs, by 2014. Employment in coal mining and metal ore mining is expected to decline by 23.3 percent and 29.3 percent, respectively. Employment in oil and gas extraction also is projected to decline by 13.1 percent through 2014. Employment decreases in these industries are attributable mainly to technology gains that boost worker productivity, growing international competition, restricted access to federal lands, and strict environmental regulations that require cleaning of burning fuels.

Occupation

Expansion of service-providing industries is expected to continue, creating demand for many occupations. However, projected job growth varies among major occupational groups (Chart 6).

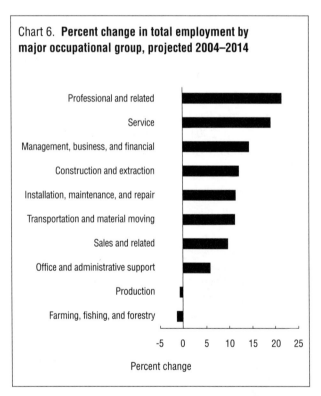

Chart 6. **Percent change in total employment by major occupational group, projected 2004–2014**

Professional and related occupations. Professional and related occupations will grow the fastest and add more new jobs than any other major occupational group. Over the 2004–2014 period, a 21.2-percent increase in the number of professional and related jobs is projected, which translates into 6 million new jobs. Professional and related workers perform a wide variety of duties, and are employed throughout private industry and government. About three-quarters of the job growth will come from three groups of professional occupations—computer and mathematical occupations; healthcare practitioners and technical occupations; and education, training, and library occupations—which will add 4.5 million jobs combined.

Service occupations. Service workers perform services for the public. Employment in service occupations is projected to increase by 5.3 million, or 19 percent, the second largest numerical gain and second highest rate of growth among the major occupational groups. Food preparation and serving related occupations are expected to add the most jobs among the service occupations, 1.7 million by 2014. However, healthcare support occupations are expected to grow the fastest, 33.3 percent, adding 1.2 million new jobs.

Management, business, and financial occupations. Workers in management, business, and financial occupations plan and direct the activities of business, government, and other organizations. Their employment is expected to increase by 2.2 million, or 14.4 percent, by 2014. Among managers, the numbers of preschool and childcare center/program educational administrators and of computer and information systems managers will grow the fastest, by 27.9 percent and 25.9 percent, respectively. General and operations managers will add the most new jobs, 308,000, by 2014. Farmers and ranchers are the only workers in this major occupational group whose numbers are expected to decline, losing 155,000 jobs. Among business and financial occupations, accountants and auditors and management analysts will add the most jobs, 386,000 combined. Employment, recruitment, and placement specialists and personal financial advisors will be the fastest-growing occupations in this group, with job increases of 30.5 percent and 25.9 percent, respectively.

Construction and extraction occupations. Construction and extraction workers construct new residential and commercial buildings, and also work in mines, quarries, and oil and gas fields. Employment of these workers is expected to grow 12 percent, adding 931,000 new jobs. Construction trades and related workers will account for more than three-fourths of these new jobs, 699,000, by 2014. Many extraction occupations will decline, reflecting overall employment losses in the mining and oil and gas extraction industries.

Installation, maintenance, and repair occupations. Workers in installation, maintenance, and repair occupations install new equipment and maintain and repair older equipment. These occupations will add 657,000 jobs by 2014, growing by 11.4 percent. Automotive service technicians and mechanics and general maintenance and repair workers will account for half of all new installation, maintenance, and repair jobs. The fastest growth rate will be among security and fire alarm systems installers, an occupation that is expected to grow 21.7 percent over the 2004–2014 period.

Transportation and material moving occupations. Transportation and material moving workers transport people and materials by land, sea, or air. The number of these workers should grow 11.1 percent, accounting for 1.1 million additional jobs by 2014. Among transportation occupations, motor vehicle operators will add the most jobs, 629,000. Material moving occupations will grow 8.3 percent and will add 405,000 jobs. Rail transportation occupations are the only group in which employment is projected to decline, by 1.1 percent, through 2014.

Sales and related occupations. Sales and related workers transfer goods and services among businesses and consumers. Sales and related occupations are expected to add 1.5 million new jobs by 2014, growing by 9.6 percent. The majority of these jobs will be among retail salespersons and cashiers, occupations that will add 849,000 jobs combined.

Office and administrative support occupations. Office and administrative support workers perform the day-to-day activities of the office, such as preparing and filing documents, dealing with the public, and distributing information. Employment in these occupations is expected to grow by 5.8 percent, adding 1.4 million new jobs by 2014. Customer service representatives will add the most new jobs, 471,000. Desktop publishers will be among the fastest-growing occupations in this group, increasing by 23.2 percent over the decade. However, due to rising productivity and increased automation, office and administrative support occupations also account for 11 of the 20 occupations with the largest employment declines.

Farming, fishing, and forestry occupations. Farming, fishing, and forestry workers cultivate plants, breed and raise livestock, and catch animals. These occupations will decline 1.3 percent and lose 13,000 jobs by 2014. Agricultural workers, including farmworkers and laborers, accounted for the overwhelming majority of new jobs in this group. The number of fishing and hunting workers is expected to decline, by 16.6 percent, while the number of logging workers is expected to increase by less than 1 percent.

Production occupations. Production workers are employed mainly in manufacturing, where they assemble goods and operate plants. Production occupations are expected to decline less than 1 percent, losing 79,000 jobs by 2014. Jobs will be created for many production occupations, including food processing workers; machinists; and welders, cutters, solderers, and brazers. Textile, apparel, and furnishings occupations, as well as assemblers and fabricators, will account for much of the job losses among production occupations.

Among all occupations in the economy, computer and healthcare occupations are expected to grow the fastest over the projection period (Chart 7). In fact, healthcare occupations make up 12 of the 20 fastest-growing occupations, while computer occupations account for 5 out of the 20 fastest-growing occupations in the economy. In addition to high growth rates, these 17 computer and healthcare occupations combined will add more than 1.8 million new jobs. High growth rates among computer and healthcare occupations reflect projected rapid growth in the computer and data processing and health services industries.

The 20 occupations listed in Chart 8 will account for 7.1 million jobs combined, over the 2004–2014 period. The occupations with the largest numerical increases cover a wider range of occupational categories than do those occupations with the fastest growth rates. Health occupations will account for some of these increases in employment,

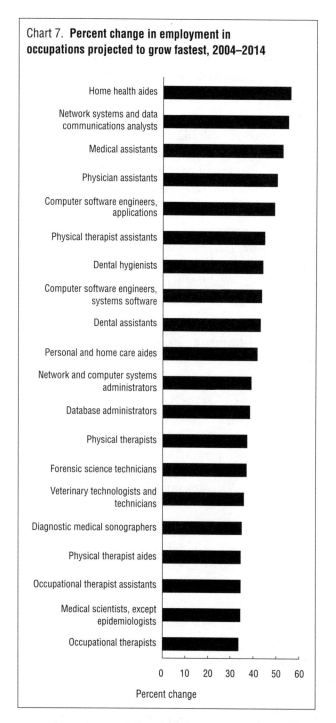

Chart 7. **Percent change in employment in occupations projected to grow fastest, 2004–2014**

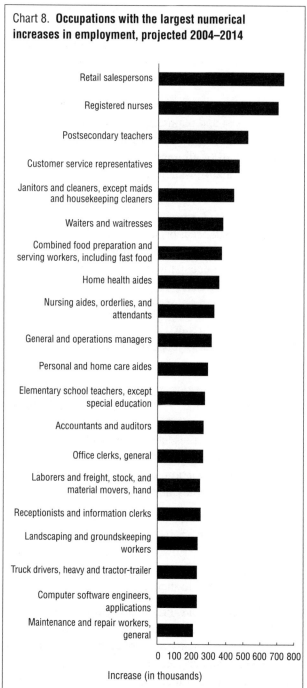

Chart 8. **Occupations with the largest numerical increases in employment, projected 2004–2014**

as well as occupations in education, sales, transportation, office and administrative support, and food service. Many of these occupations are very large, and will create more new jobs than will those with high growth rates. Only 3 out of the 20 fastest-growing occupations—home health aides, personal and home care aides, and computer software application engineers—also are projected to be among the 20 occupations with the largest numerical increases in employment.

Declining occupational employment stems from declining industry employment, technological advancements, changes in business practices, and other factors. For example, increased productivity and farm consolidations are expected to result in a decline of 155,000 farmers and ranchers over the 2004–2014 period (Chart 9).

The majority of the 20 occupations with the largest numerical decreases are office and administrative support and production occupations, which are affected by increasing plant and factory automation and the implementation of office technology that reduces the needs for these workers. For example, employment of word processors and typists is expected to decline due to the proliferation of personal computers, which allows other workers to perform duties formerly assigned to word processors and typists.

Education and Training

Among the 20 fastest-growing occupations, a bachelor's or associate degree is the most significant source of postsecondary education or training for 12 of them—network systems and data communications analysts; physician assistants; computer software engineers, applications; physical therapist assistants; dental hygienists; computer software engineers, systems software; network and computer systems administrators; database administrators; forensic science technicians; veterinary technologists and technicians; diagnostic medical sonographers; and occupational therapists assistants.

On-the-job training is the most significant source of postsecondary education or training for another 5 of the 20 fastest-growing occupations—physical therapist aides, medical assistants, home health aides, dental assistants, and personal and home care aides.

In contrast, on-the-job training is the most significant source of postsecondary education or training for 13 of the 20 occupations with the largest numerical increases; 6 of these 20 occupations have an associate or higher degree as the most significant source of postsecondary education or training. On-the-job training also is the most significant source of postsecondary education or training for all 20 of the occupations with the largest numerical decreases.

Chart 9. Job declines in occupations with the largest numerical decreases in employment, projected 2004–2014

Farmers and ranchers
Stock clerks and order fillers
Sewing machine operators
File clerks
Order clerks
Mail clerks and mail machine operators, except postal service
Computer operators
Secretaries, except legal, medical, and executive
Cutting, punching, and press machine setters, operators, and tenders, metal and plastic
Telemarketers
Word processors and typists
Credit authorizers, checkers, and clerks
Machine feeders and offbearers
Textile knitting and weaving machine setters, operators, and tenders
Textile winding, twisting, and drawing out machine setters, operators, and tenders
Meter readers, utilities
Office machine operators, except computer
Extruding and drawing machine setters, operators, and tenders, metal and plastic
Switchboard operators, including answering services
Door-to-door sales workers, news and street vendors, and related workers

-200   -150   -100   -50   0

Decrease (in thousands)

Total Job Openings

Job openings stem from both employment growth and replacement needs (Chart 10). Replacement needs arise as workers leave occupations. Some transfer to other occupations while others retire, return to school, or quit to assume household responsibilities. Replacement needs are projected to account for more than 60 percent of the

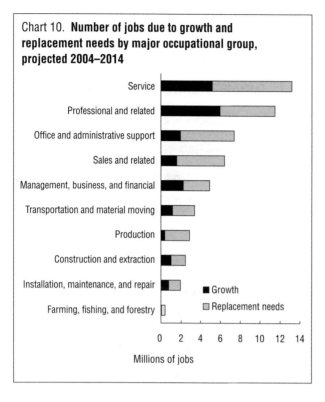

Chart 10. Number of jobs due to growth and replacement needs by major occupational group, projected 2004–2014

approximately 55 million job openings between 2004 and 2014. Thus, even occupations projected to experience slower-than-average growth or to decline in employment still may offer many job openings.

Professional and related occupations are projected to grow faster and add more jobs than any other major occupational group, with 6 million new jobs by 2014. Three-fourths of the job growth in professional and related occupations is expected among computer and mathematical occupations; healthcare practitioners and technical occupations; and education, training, and library occupations. With 5.5 million job openings due to replacement needs, professional and related occupations are the only major group projected to generate more openings from job growth than from replacement needs.

Service occupations are projected to have the largest number of total job openings, 13.2 million, reflecting high replacement needs. A large number of replacements will be necessary as young workers leave food preparation and service occupations. Replacement needs generally are greatest in the largest occupations and in those with relatively low pay or limited training requirements.

Office automation will significantly affect many individual office and administrative support occupations. Overall, these occupations are projected to grow more slowly than average, while some are projected to decline. Office and administrative support occupations are projected to create 7.5 million job openings over the 2004–2014 period, ranking third behind service and professional and related occupations.

Farming, fishing, and forestry occupations are projected to have the fewest job openings, approximately 286,000. Because job growth is expected to be slow, and levels of retirement and job turnover high, more than 95 percent of these projected job openings are due to replacement needs.

Editor's Note: This section, with minor changes, came from the *Occupational Outlook Handbook* and was written by the U.S. Department of Labor staff. Much of this section uses 2004 data, the most recent available at press time. By the time it is carefully collected and analyzed, data used by the U.S. Department of Labor is typically several years old. Because market trends tend to be gradual, this delay does not affect the material's usefulness.

Employment Trends in Major Industries

The U.S. economy can be broken down into numerous industries, each with its own set of characteristics. The Department of Labor has identified 45 industries that account for three-quarters of all workers. This section provides an overview of these industries and the economy as a whole.

Nature of the Industry

Industries are defined by the processes they use to produce goods and services. Workers in the United States produce and provide a wide variety of products and services and, as a result, the types of industries in the U.S. economy range widely—from agriculture, forestry, and fishing to aerospace manufacturing. Each industry has a unique combination of occupations, production techniques, inputs and outputs, and business characteristics. Understanding the nature of industries that interest you is important because it is this unique combination that determines working conditions, educational requirements, and the job outlook.

Industries consist of many different places of work, called establishments. Establishments are physical locations in which people work, such as the branch office of a bank, a gasoline service station, a school, a department store, or a plant that manufactures machinery. Establishments range from large factories and corporate office complexes employing thousands of workers to small community stores, restaurants, professional offices, and service businesses employing only a few workers. Establishments should not be confused with companies or corporations, which are legal entities. Thus, a company or corporation may have a single establishment or more than one establishment. Establishments that use the same or similar processes to produce goods or services are organized together into industries. Industries are, in turn, organized together into industry groups such as Information and Trade. These are further organized into industry subsectors and then ultimately into industry sectors. For the purposes of labor market analysis, the Bureau of Labor Statistics organizes industry sectors into industry supersectors. A company or corporation could own establishments classified in more than one industry, industry sector, or even industry supersector.

Each industry subsector is made up of a number of industry groups, which are, as mentioned, determined by differences in production processes. An easily recognized example of these distinctions is in the food manufacturing subsector, which is made up of industry groups that produce meat products, preserved fruits and vegetables, bakery items, and dairy products, among others. Each of these industry groups requires workers with varying skills and employs unique production techniques. Another example of these distinctions is found in utilities, which employs workers in establishments that provide electricity, natural gas, and water.

There are slightly more than 8 million private business establishments in the United States. Business establishments in the United States are predominantly small; 59.9 percent of all establishments employed fewer than 5 workers.

However, the medium-sized to large establishments employ a greater proportion of all workers. For example, establishments that employed 50 or more workers accounted for only 4.6 percent of all establishments, yet employed 56.3 percent of all workers. The large establishments—those with more than 500 workers—accounted for only 0.2 percent of all establishments, but employed 17.3 percent of all workers. Table 1 presents the percent distribution of employment according to establishment size.

The average size of these establishments varies widely across industries. Most establishments in the construction, wholesale trade, retail trade, finance and insurance, real estate and rental and leasing, and professional, scientific, and technical services industries are small, averaging fewer than 20 employees per establishment. However, wide differences within industries can exist. Hospitals, for example, employ an average of 724.9 workers, while physicians' offices employ an average of 10.1. Similarly, although there is an average of 14.3 employees per establishment for all of retail trade, department stores employ an average of 124.1 people but jewelry stores employ an average of only 5.8.

Establishment size can play a role in the characteristics of each job. Large establishments generally offer workers greater occupational mobility and advancement potential, whereas small establishments may provide their employees with broader experience by requiring them to assume a wider range of responsibilities. Also, small establishments are distributed throughout the nation—every locality has a few small businesses. Large establishments, in contrast, employ more workers and are less common, but they play a much more prominent role in the economies of the areas in which they are located.

Table 1. Percent distribution of nongovernment establishments and employment by establishment size

Establishment size (number of workers)	Establishments	Employment
Total	100.0	100.0
1 to 4	59.9	6.8
5 to 9	16.9	8.4
10 to 19	11.1	11.2
20 to 49	7.6	17.3
50 to 99	2.6	13.3
100 to 249	1.4	16.4
250 to 499	0.4	9.3
500 to 999	0.1	6.6
1,000 or more	0.1	10.7

Working Conditions

Just as the goods and services produced in each industry are different, working conditions vary significantly among industries. In some industries, the work setting is quiet, temperature-controlled, and virtually hazard-free, while other industries are characterized by noisy, uncomfortable, and sometimes dangerous work environments. Some industries require long workweeks and shift work, but standard 40-hour workweeks are common in many other industries. In still other industries, a lot of the jobs can be seasonal, requiring long hours during busy periods and abbreviated schedules during slower months. Production processes, establishment size, and the physical location of work usually determine these varying conditions.

One of the most telling indicators of working conditions is an industry's injury and illness rate. Overexertion, being struck by an object, and falls on the same level are among the most common incidents causing work-related injury or illness. In 2003, approximately 5.0 million nonfatal injuries and illnesses were reported across the various nongovernment industries. Among major industry divisions, manufacturing and construction tied for the highest rate of injury and illness—6.8 cases for every 100 full-time workers—while financial activities had the lowest rate—1.7 cases. About 5,700 work-related fatalities were reported in 2004; the most common events resulting in fatal injuries were transportation incidents, contact with objects and equipment, assaults and violent acts, and falls.

Work schedules are another important reflection of working conditions, and the operational requirements of each industry lead to large differences in hours worked and in part-time versus full-time status. In food services and drinking places, for example, fully 41.1 percent of employees worked part time in 2005 compared with only 1.7 percent in motor vehicles and motor vehicle equipment manufacturing. Table 2 presents industries having relatively high and low percentages of part-time workers.

Table 2. Part-time workers as a percent of total employment, selected industries

Industry	Percent part-time
All industries	17.4
Many part-time workers	
Food services and drinking places	41.1
Grocery stores	35.3
Clothing, accessory, and general merchandise stores	33.8
Arts, entertainment, and recreation	32.0
Child day care services	28.7
Motion picture and video industries	27.1
Social assistance	24.6
Educational services	21.9
Few part-time workers	
Pharmaceutical and medicine manufacturing	3.6
Utilities	3.2
Oil and gas extraction	3.2
Computer and electronic product manufacturing	2.8
Steel manufacturing	2.4
Mining	2.3
Aerospace product and parts manufacturing	1.9
Motor vehicles and parts manufacturing	1.7

The low proportion of part-time workers in some manufacturing industries often reflects the continuous nature of the production processes that makes it difficult to adapt the volume of production to short-term fluctuations in product demand. Once these processes are begun, it is costly to halt them; machinery must be tended and materials must be moved continuously. For example, the chemical manufacturing industry produces many different chemical products through controlled chemical reactions. These processes require chemical operators to monitor and adjust the flow of materials into and out of the line of production. Because production may continue 24 hours a day, 7 days a week under the watchful eyes of chemical operators who work in shifts, full-time workers are more likely to be employed. Retail trade and service industries, on the other hand, have seasonal cycles marked by various events that affect the hours worked, such as school openings or important holidays. During busy times of the year, longer hours are common, whereas slack periods lead to cutbacks in work hours and shorter workweeks. Jobs in these industries are generally appealing to students and others who desire flexible, part-time schedules.

Employment

The total number of jobs in the United States in 2004 was 145.6 million. This included 12.1 million self-employed workers, 141,000 unpaid workers in family businesses, and 133.5 million wage and salary jobs—including primary and secondary job holders. The total number of jobs is projected to increase to 164.5 million by 2014, and wage and salary jobs are projected to account for more than 152.1 million of them.

As shown in table 3, wage and salary jobs are the vast majority of all jobs, but they are not evenly divided among the various industries. Education, health, and social services had the largest number of jobs in 2004 with almost 28 million. Manufacturing, construction, and utilities had almost 21.9 million jobs, including 14.3 million manufacturing and 7.0 million construction jobs. The trade supersector was nearly as large, with about 20.7 million jobs, followed by professional and business services with 16.4 million jobs in 2004. Among the 45 industries, wage and salary employment ranged from only 156,200 in steel manufacturing to over 13 million in health services. The three largest industries—education services, health services, and food services and drinking places—together accounted for 34.7 million jobs, over one-quarter of the nation's wage and salary employment.

Table 3. Wage and salary employment, 2004, and projected change, 2004–14 (Employment in thousands)

Industry	2004		2014		2004–2014	
	Employment	Percent distribution	Employment	Percent distribution	Percent change	Employment change
All industries	133,478	100.0	152,093	100.0	13.9	18,615
Agriculture and natural resources	1,672	1.3	1,567	1.0	–6.3	–105
Agriculture, forestry, and fishing	1,149	0.9	1,090	0.7	–5.2	–60
Mining	207	0.2	180	0.1	–12.9	–27
Oil and gas extraction	316	0.2	297	0.2	–6.1	–19
Manufacturing, construction, and utilities	21,864	16.4	21,872	14.4	0.0	8
Aerospace product and parts manufacturing	444	0.3	480	0.3	8.2	36
Chemical manufacturing, except drugs	596	0.5	510	0.3	–14.4	–86
Computer and electronic product manufacturing	1,326	1.0	1,232	0.8	–7.1	–94
Construction	6,964	5.2	7,757	5.1	11.4	792
Food manufacturing	1,498	1.1	1,555	1.0	3.8	57
Machinery manufacturing	1,142	0.9	995	0.7	–12.8	–146
Motor vehicle and parts manufacturing	1,109	0.8	1,171	0.8	5.6	62
Pharmaceutical and medicine manufacturing	291	0.2	367	0.2	26.1	76
Printing	665	0.5	600	0.4	–9.8	–65
Steel manufacturing	156	0.1	135	0.1	–13.4	–21
Textile, textile product, and apparel manufacturing	701	0.5	380	0.2	–44.6	–321
Utilities	570	0.4	563	0.4	–1.3	–8
Trade	20,689	15.5	22,814	15.0	10.3	2,125
Automobile dealers	1,254	0.9	1,407	0.9	12.2	153
Clothing, accessory, and general merchandise stores	4,205	3.1	4,628	3.0	10.1	423
Grocery stores	2,447	1.8	2,607	1.7	6.6	160
Wholesale trade	5,655	4.2	6,131	4.0	8.4	476
Transportation	4,250	3.2	4,756	3.1	11.9	506
Air transportation	515	0.4	560	0.4	8.8	45
Truck transportation and warehousing	1,907	1.4	2,174	1.4	14.0	267

Industry	2004		2014		2004–2014	
	Employment	Percent distribution	Employment	Percent distribution	Percent change	Employment change
Information	3,138	2.4	3,502	2.3	11.6	364
Broadcasting	327	0.2	362	0.2	10.7	35
Motion picture and video industries	368	0.3	430	0.3	17.1	63
Publishing, except software	671	0.5	715	0.5	6.5	44
Software publishers	239	0.2	400	0.3	67.6	161
Telecommunications	1,043	0.8	975	0.6	–6.5	–68
Internet service providers, Web search portals, and data processing services	388	0.3	496	0.3	27.8	108
Financial activities	8,052	6.0	8,901	5.9	10.5	849
Banking	1,783	1.3	1,751	1.2	–1.8	–31
Insurance	2,260	1.7	2,476	1.6	9.5	215
Securities, commodities, and other investments	767	0.6	888	0.6	15.8	121
Professional and business services	16,414	12.3	20,980	13.8	27.8	4,566
Advertising and public relations services	425	0.3	520	0.3	22.4	95
Computer systems design and related services	1,147	0.9	1,600	1.1	39.5	453
Employment services	3,470	2.6	5,050	3.3	45.5	1,580
Management, scientific, and technical consulting services	779	0.6	1,250	0.8	60.5	471
Scientific research and development services	548	0.4	613	0.4	11.9	65
Education, health, and social services	27,973	21.0	34,399	22.6	23.0	6,426
Child day care services	767	0.6	1,062	0.7	38.4	295
Educational services	12,778	9.6	14,901	9.8	16.6	2,123
Health services	13,062	9.8	16,626	10.9	27.3	3,564
Social assistance, except child day care	1,365	1.0	1,810	1.2	32.6	445
Leisure and hospitality	12,479	9.3	14,694	9.7	17.7	2,215
Arts, entertainment, and recreation	1,833	1.4	2,293	1.5	25.1	460
Food services and drinking places	8,850	6.6	10,301	6.8	16.4	1,451
Hotels and other accommodations	1,796	1.3	2,100	1.4	16.9	304
Government and advocacy, grantmaking, and civic organizations	11,047	8.3	12,170	8.0	10.2	1,123
Advocacy, grantmaking, and civic organizations	1,231	0.9	1,410	0.9	14.5	179
Federal government	1,943	1.5	1,993	1.3	2.5	50
State and local government, except education and health	7,872	5.9	8,767	5.8	11.4	895

Note: May not add to totals due to omission of industries not covered.

Although workers of all ages are employed in each industry, certain industries tend to possess workers of distinct age groups. For the previously mentioned reasons, retail trade employs a relatively high proportion of younger workers to fill part-time and temporary positions. The manufacturing sector, on the other hand, has a relatively high median age because many jobs in the sector require a number of years to learn and perfect specialized skills that do not easily transfer to other firms. Also, manufacturing employment has been declining, providing fewer opportunities for younger workers to get jobs. As a result, one-fourth of the workers in retail trade were 24 years of age or younger in 2004, compared with only 8.2 percent of workers in manufacturing. Table 4 contrasts the age distribution of workers in all industries with the distributions in five very different industries.

Table 4. Percent distribution of wage and salary workers by age group, selected industries

Industry	Age group			
	16 to 24	25 to 44	45 to 64	65 and older
All industries	14	47	36	4
Computer systems design and related services	7	63	29	1
Educational services	9	42	45	3
Food services and drinking places	44	39	15	2
Telecommunications	8	56	34	2
Utilities	5	43	50	2

Employment in some industries is concentrated in one region of the country. Such industries often are located near a source of raw or unfinished materials upon which the industry relies. For example, oil and gas extraction jobs are concentrated in Texas, Louisiana, and Oklahoma; many textile mills and products manufacturing jobs are found in North Carolina, South Carolina, and Georgia; and a significant proportion of motor vehicle manufacturing jobs are located in Michigan and Ohio. On the other hand, some industries—such as grocery stores and educational services—have jobs distributed throughout the nation, reflecting the general population density.

Occupations in the Industry

The occupations found in each industry depend on the types of services provided or goods produced. For example, because construction companies require skilled trades workers to build and renovate buildings, these companies employ large numbers of carpenters, electricians, plumbers, painters, and sheet metal workers. Other occupations common to construction include construction equipment operators and mechanics, installers, and repairers. Retail trade, on the other hand, displays and sells manufactured goods to consumers. As a result, retail trade employs numerous retail salespersons and other workers, including more than three-fourths of all cashiers. Table 5 shows the industry sectors and the occupational groups that predominate in each.

Table 5. Industry sectors and their largest occupational group

Industry sector	Largest occupational group	Percent of industry wage and salary jobs
Agriculture, forestry, fishing, and hunting	Farming, fishing, and forestry occupations	61.1
Mining	Construction and extraction occupations	33.3
Construction	Construction and extraction occupations	66.2
Manufacturing	Production occupations	52.1
Wholesale trade	Sales and related occupations	24.7
Retail trade	Sales and related occupations	52.5
Transportation and warehousing	Transportation and material moving occupations	56.0
Utilities	Installation, maintenance, and repair occupations	25.6
Information	Professional and related occupations	29.1
Finance and insurance	Office and administrative support occupations	51.4
Real estate and rental and leasing	Sales and related occupations	22.7

Industry sector	Largest occupational group	Percent of industry wage and salary jobs
Professional, scientific, and technical services..........Professional and related occupations...................42.6
Management of companies and enterprises ....Office and administrative support occupations 33.6
Administrative and support and waste management and remediation services ....Office and administrative support occupations 23.2
Educational services, private...............................Professional and related occupations................................59.6
Health care and social assistance ....Professional and related occupations................................42.6
Arts, entertainment, and recreation ....Service occupations 57.2
Accommodation and food services ....Service occupations 84.0
Government ....Professional and related occupations................................43.7

The occupational distribution clearly is influenced by the structure of its industries, yet there are many occupations, such as general managers or secretaries, that are found in all industries. In fact, some of the largest occupations in the U.S. economy are dispersed across many industries. For example, the group of professional and related occupations is among the largest in the nation while also experiencing the fastest growth rate. (See table 6.) Other large occupational groups include service occupations; office and administrative support occupations; sales and related occupations; and management, business, and financial occupations.

Table 6. Total employment and projected change by broad occupational group, 2004–14 (Employment in thousands)

Occupational group	Employment, 2004	Percent change, 2004–2014
Total, all occupations...145,612...................13.0
Professional and related occupations ....28,544...................21.2
Service occupations...27,673...................19.0
Office and administrative support occupations ....23,907 ....5.8
Sales and related occupations..15,330 ....9.6
Management, business, and financial occupations ....14,987...................14.4
Production occupations ....10,562...................−0.1
Transportation and material moving occupations ....10,098...................11.1
Construction and extraction occupations ....7,738...................12.0
Installation, maintenance, and repair occupations...................5,747...................11.4
Farming, fishing, and forestry occupations ....1,026...................−1.3

Training and Advancement

Workers prepare for employment in many ways, but the most fundamental form of job training in the United States is a high school education. Better than 88 percent of the nation's workforce possessed a high school diploma or its equivalent in 2004. However, many occupations require more training, so growing numbers of workers pursue additional training or education after high school. In 2004, 28.7 percent of the nation's workforce reported having completed some college or an associate's degree as their highest level of education, while an additional 29.5 percent continued in their studies and attained a bachelor's or higher degree. In addition to these types of formal education, other sources of qualifying training include formal company-provided training, apprenticeships, informal on-the-job training, correspondence courses, Armed Forces vocational training, and non-work-related training.

The unique combination of training required to succeed in each industry is determined largely by the industry's production process and the mix of occupations it requires. For example, manufacturing employs many machine operators who generally need little formal education after high school, but sometimes complete considerable on-the-job training. In contrast, the educational services industry employs many types of teachers, most of whom require a bachelor's or higher degree. Training requirements by industry sector are shown in table 7.

Table 7. Percent distribution of workers by highest grade completed or degree received, by industry sector

Industry sector	High school diploma or less	Some college or associate degree	Bachelor's or higher degree
All industries	41.6	28.7	29.5
Agriculture, forestry, fishing, and hunting	64.3	21.4	14.2
Mining	60.4	21.8	17.8
Construction	64.7	24.5	10.8
Manufacturing	51.5	25.1	23.4
Wholesale trade	42.7	29.0	28.3
Retail trade	50.6	32.3	17.1
Transportation and warehousing	52.6	31.7	15.6
Utilities	38.7	34.1	27.0
Information	26.7	31.3	42.0
Finance and insurance	24.9	31.6	43.4
Real estate and rental and leasing	36.2	31.7	32.2
Professional, scientific, and technical services	14.4	25.1	60.6
Administrative and support and waste management services	55.3	28.4	16.3
Educational services	17.8	19.0	63.2
Health care and social assistance	30.6	34.8	34.7
Arts, entertainment, and recreation	39.5	31.8	28.6
Accommodation and food services	60.7	28.4	11.0

Persons with no more than a high school diploma accounted for about 64.7 percent of all workers in construction; 64.3 in agriculture, forestry, fishing, and hunting; 60.7 percent in accommodation and food services; 60.4 percent in mining; 51.5 percent in manufacturing; and 50.6 in retail trade. On the other hand, those who had acquired a bachelor's or higher degree accounted for 63.2 percent of all workers in private educational services; 60.6 percent in professional, scientific, and technical services; 43.4 percent in finance and insurance; and 42.0 percent in information.

Education and training also are important factors in the variety of advancement paths found in different industries. Each industry has some unique advancement paths, but workers who complete additional on-the-job training or education generally help their chances of being promoted. In much of the manufacturing sector, for example, production workers who receive training in management and computer skills increase their likelihood of being promoted to supervisory positions. Other factors that impact advancement and that may figure prominently in industries include the size of the establishments, institutionalized career tracks, and the mix of occupations. As a result, persons who seek jobs in particular industries should be aware of how these advancement paths and other factors may later shape their careers.

Earnings

Like other characteristics, earnings differ by industry, the result of a highly complicated process that reflects a number of factors. For example, earnings may vary due to the nature of occupations in the industry, average hours worked, geographical location, workers' average age, educational requirements, profits, and the degree of union representation of the workforce. In general, wages are highest in metropolitan areas to compensate for the higher cost of living. Also, as would be expected, industries that employ a large proportion of unskilled minimum-wage or part-time workers tend to have lower earnings.

The difference in earnings between the industries of software publishers and of food services and drinking places illustrates how various characteristics of industries can result in great differences in earnings. In software publishers, earnings of all wage and salary workers averaged $1,342 a week in 2004, while in food service and drinking places, earnings of all wage and salary workers averaged only $194 weekly. The difference is large primarily because software publishing establishments employ more higher-skilled, full-time workers, while food services and drinking places employ many lower-skilled workers on a part-time basis. In addition, most workers in software publishing are paid an annual salary, while many workers in food service and drinking places are paid a low hourly wage that is supplemented with money the workers receive as tips. Table 8 highlights the industries with the highest and lowest average weekly earnings.

Table 8. Average weekly earnings of production or nonsupervisory workers on private nonfarm payrolls, selected industries

Industry	Earnings
All industries	$529
Industries with high earnings	
Software publishers	1,342
Computer systems design and related services	1,136
Aerospace product and parts manufacturing	1,019
Scientific research and development services	1,006
Motor vehicle and parts manufacturing	925
Mining	909
Industries with low earnings	
Food manufacturing	510
Grocery stores	332
Arts, entertainment, and recreation	313
Hotels and other accommodations	302
Child day care services	299
Food services and drinking places	194

Employee benefits, once a minor addition to wages and salaries, continue to grow in diversity and cost. In addition to traditional benefits—paid vacations, life and health insurance, and pensions—many employers now offer various benefits to accommodate the needs of a changing labor force. Such benefits sometimes include childcare; employee assistance programs that provide counseling for personal problems; and wellness programs that encourage exercise, stress management, and self-improvement. Benefits vary among occupational groups, full- and part-time workers, public and private sector workers, regions, unionized and nonunionized workers, and small and large establishments. Data indicate that full-time workers and those in medium-sized and large establishments—those with 100 or more workers—usually receive better benefits than do part-time workers and those in smaller establishments.

Union representation of the workforce varies widely by industry, and it also may play a role in determining earnings and benefits. In 2004, about 13.8 percent of workers throughout the nation were union members or covered by union contracts. As table 9 demonstrates, union affiliation of workers varies widely by industry. Fully 50.0 percent of the workers in air transportation were union members, the highest rate of all the industries, followed by 37.6 percent in educational services, and 33.0 percent in iron and steel mills and steel product manufacturing. Industries with the lowest unionization rate include computer systems design and related services, 1.3 percent; food services and drinking places, 1.7 percent; and advertising and related services, 1.7 percent.

Table 9. Union members and other workers covered by union contracts as a percent of total employment, selected industries

Industry	Percent union members or covered by union contract
All industries	13.8
Industries with high unionization rates	
Air transportation	50.0
Educational services	37.6
Iron and steel mills and steel product manufacturing	33.0
Motor vehicles and motor vehicle equipment manufacturing	30.2
Industries with low unionization rates	
Banking and related activities	1.9
Advertising and related services	1.7
Food services and drinking places	1.7
Computer systems design and related services	1.3

Outlook

Total employment in the United States is projected to increase by about 14 percent over the 2004–2014 period. Employment growth, however, is only one source of job openings. The total number of openings in any industry also depends on the industry's current employment level and its need to replace workers who leave their jobs. Throughout the economy, replacement needs will create more job openings than will employment growth. Employment size is a major determinant of job openings—larger industries generally have larger numbers of workers who must be replaced and provide more openings. The occupational composition of an industry is another factor. Industries with high concentrations of professional, technical, and other jobs that require more formal education—occupations in which workers tend to leave their jobs less frequently—generally have fewer openings resulting from replacement needs. On the other hand, more replacement openings generally occur in industries with high concentrations of service, laborer, and other jobs that require little formal education and have lower wages because workers in these jobs are more likely to leave their occupations.

Employment growth is determined largely by changes in the demand for the goods and services provided by an industry, worker productivity, and foreign competition. Each industry is affected by a different set of variables that determines the number and composition of jobs that will be available. Even within an industry, employment may grow at different rates in different occupations. For example, changes in technology, production methods, and business practices in an industry might eliminate some jobs, while creating others. Some industries may be growing rapidly overall, yet opportunities for workers in occupations within those industries could be stagnant or even declining because they are adversely affected by technological change. Similarly, employment of some occupations may be declining in the economy as a whole, yet may be increasing in a rapidly growing industry.

Employment growth rates over the next decade will vary widely among industries. Agriculture and natural resources is the only sector in which all of the industries are expected to experience employment declines. Consolidation of farm land, increasing worker productivity, and depletion of wild fish stocks should continue to decrease employment in agriculture, forestry, and fishing. Employment in mining is expected to decline due to labor-saving technology while jobs in oil and gas extraction are expected to decrease with the continued reliance on foreign sources of energy.

Employment in manufacturing, construction, and utilities is expected to remain nearly unchanged as growth in construction is partially offset by declines in utilities and selected manufacturing industries. Growth in construction employment will stem from new factory construction as existing facilities are modernized; from new school construction, reflecting growth in the school-age population; and from infrastructure improvements, such as road and bridge construction. Employment declines are expected in chemical manufacturing, except drugs; machinery manufacturing; computer and electronic product manufacturing; printing; steel manufacturing; and textile, textile product, and apparel manufacturing. Textile, textile product, and apparel manufacturing is projected to lose about 321,200 jobs over the 2004–2014 period—more than any other manufacturing industry—due primarily to increasing imports replacing domestic products.

Employment gains are expected in some manufacturing industries. Small employment gains in food manufacturing are expected, as a growing and ever more diverse population increases the demand for manufactured food products. Employment growth in pharmaceutical and medicine manufacturing is expected, as sales of pharmaceuticals increase with growth in the population, particularly among the elderly, and with the introduction of new medicines to the market. Both food and pharmaceutical and medicine manufacturing also have growing export markets. Aerospace product and parts manufacturing and motor vehicle and parts manufacturing are both expected to have modest employment increases.

Growth in overall employment will result primarily from growth in service-providing industries over the 2004–2014 period, almost all of which are expected to have increasing employment. Job growth is expected to be led by health services and educational services, with large numbers of new jobs also in employment services, food services and drinking places, state and local government, and wholesale trade. When combined, these sectors will account for almost half of all new wage and salary jobs across the nation. Employment growth is expected in many other service-providing industries, but they will result in far fewer numbers of new jobs.

Health services will account for the most new wage and salary jobs, about 3.6 million over the 2004–2014 period. Population growth, advances in medical technologies that increase the number of treatable diseases, and a growing share of the population in older age groups will drive employment growth. Offices of physicians, the largest health care industry group, is expected to account for about 760,000 of these new jobs as patients seek more healthcare outside of the traditional inpatient hospital setting.

The educational services industry is expected to grow by nearly 17 percent over the 2004–2014 period, adding about 2.1 million new jobs. A growing emphasis on improving education and making it available to more children and young adults will be the primary factors contributing to employment growth. Employment growth at all levels of education is expected, particularly at the postsecondary level, as children of the baby boomers continue to reach college age, and as more adults pursue continuing education to enhance or update their skills.

Employment in one of the nation's fastest-growing industries—employment services—is expected to increase by more than 45 percent, adding another 1.6 million jobs over the 2004–2014 period. Employment will increase, particularly in temporary help services and professional employer organizations, as businesses seek new ways to make their workforces more specialized and responsive to changes in demand.

The food services and drinking places industry is expected to add almost 1.5 million new jobs over the 2004–2014 projection period. Increases in population, dual-income families, and dining sophistication will contribute to job growth. In addition, the increasing diversity of the population will contribute to job growth in food services and drinking places that offer a wider variety of ethnic foods and drinks.

Over 890,000 new jobs are expected to arise in state and local government, adding more than 11 percent over the 2004–2014 period. Job growth will result primarily from growth in the population and its demand for public services. Additional job growth will result as state and local governments continue to receive greater responsibility for administering federally funded programs from the federal government.

Wholesale trade is expected to add almost 480,000 new jobs over the coming decade, reflecting growth both in trade and in the overall economy. Most new jobs will be for sales representatives at the wholesale and manufacturing levels. However, industry consolidation and the growth of electronic commerce using the Internet are expected to limit job growth to 8.4 percent over the 2004–2014 period, less than the 14 percent projected for all industries.

Continual changes in the economy have far-reaching and complex effects on employment in industries. Job seekers should be aware of these changes, keeping alert for developments that can affect job opportunities in industries and the variety of occupations that are found in each industry.

Editor's Note: The preceding article was adapted from the Career Guide to Industries, *a publication of the U.S. Department of Labor. A book titled* 40 Best Fields for Your Career *(JIST Publishing) includes information from the* Career Guide to Industries *plus useful "best fields" lists and other helpful insights.*

Job Outlook for People Who Don't Have a Bachelor's Degree

You have skills. You have knowledge. And you can have a good career—regardless of whether you have a bachelor's degree. According to U.S. Bureau of Labor Statistics (BLS) projections, millions of job openings will be available between 2002 and 2012 for people who don't have a bachelor's degree. And many of these job openings will be in high-paying occupations.

A bachelor's degree brings many benefits, but it is not the only route to a job. In fact, most jobs are filled by workers who do not have a degree, and BLS does not expect that to change. Between 2002 and 2012, job openings for workers who are entering an occupation for the first time and who don't have a bachelor's degree are expected to total roughly 42 million. That's more than 3 times the number of job openings expected for workers who have a bachelor's degree.

Many of these jobs will require some training after high school. That could mean enrolling in vocational classes at a technical school, taking a few college courses, training on the job in an apprenticeship program, or getting an associate degree.

But which occupations should you train for? Which are expected to offer the best prospects? Read on to learn about the occupations that are projected to have the most openings for people who do not have a bachelor's degree and about high-demand occupations that pay well. Next, learn more about career fields—including construction, healthcare, education, and computer work—that are expected to provide good opportunities for new workers. Accompanying tables identify projected openings and 2002 earnings for occupations in each of these career fields.

The data in this article are estimates. They are based on the education levels of current workers and on projections of future job growth. Additionally, the results assume that future workers will have education levels similar to those of current workers. The data provided throughout the article, along with the resources listed at the end, can help you decide how to pursue a career that interests you.

Openings and Where They Will Be

Between 2002 and 2012, BLS expects about 56 million job openings to be filled. Of this total, about 42 million openings are projected to be filled by workers who do not have a bachelor's degree and who are entering an occupation for the first time. About 27 million of these openings are expected to be held by workers who have a high school diploma or less education. Another 15 million openings are expected for workers who have some college education or an associate degree but do not have a bachelor's degree.

Job openings are expected in every type of occupation. But some occupations and career fields will have more job openings and better earnings than others.

Occupations with Potential

Two main factors determine whether an occupation will have many job openings for workers entering an occupation. One factor is how many workers leave the occupation permanently. Large occupations—that is, occupations in which many jobs exist nationwide—have more workers and, therefore, also usually have more workers who leave the occupation and create openings. Occupations with few training requirements or low earnings also often have more workers who leave. And occupations with many older workers usually provide more openings because of retirements.

Another factor affecting job openings is job growth. Some occupations gain new positions faster than others, providing more openings for workers who seek to enter the occupation.

The occupations that are expected to need the most new workers between 2002 and 2012 employ workers with widely varying levels of education. Many openings are expected in occupations that people can enter right after high school. But openings in other occupations, especially higher-paying ones, often attract people who have additional training or education. People without training also enter these occupations, but they often start out earning less while they train on the job.

Occupations with the most openings. Chart 1 shows the occupations that are projected to have the most job openings between 2002 and 2012 for people who have less education than a bachelor's degree. Most of these occupations involve working with the public.

You can enter most of the occupations shown in the chart if you have a high school diploma or less education. Workers often qualify for jobs after less than 1 month of on-the-job training. But four of the occupations —truck drivers, customer service representatives, general maintenance and repair workers, and registered nurses—usually require more training. These are also the highest-paying occupations on the chart.

Truck drivers usually need 1 month to 1 year of training on the job; some attend vocational schools to learn the basics of commercial driving. Customer service representatives, who also often receive 1 month to 1 year of training, usually start their jobs by observing experienced workers. Most general maintenance and repair workers learn on the job or in vocational classes in high school or later. Registered nurses, unlike the other occupations in the chart, almost always have some college training. About two-fifths of registered nurses over age 25 have an associate degree or have taken some college courses, and nearly all of the rest have a bachelor's degree.

Chart 1 also gives the occupations' 2002 median earnings. (Median earnings show that half of the workers in the occupation earned more than that amount and half

Chart 1

Occupations with the most job openings for workers who don't have a bachelor's degree and who are entering the occupation for the first time, projected 2002-12

Occupation	Openings (thousands)	Median annual earnings, 2002
Cashiers, except gaming	2,124	$15,420
Retail salespersons	1,556	17,710
Waiters and waitresses	1,446	14,150
Combined food preparation and serving workers, including fast food	1,317	14,500
Office clerks, general	972	22,280
Laborers and freight, stock, and material movers, hand	876	19,710
Janitors and cleaners, except maids and housekeeping cleaners	844	18,250
Truck drivers, heavy and tractor-trailer	625	33,210
Stock clerks and order fillers	602	19,270
Receptionists and information clerks	595	21,150
Customer service representatives	582	26,240
Teacher assistants	541	18,660
Security guards	534	19,140
Nursing aides, orderlies, and attendants	523	19,960
Food preparation workers	473	16,330
Childcare workers	471	16,350
Landscaping and groundskeeping workers	470	19,770
Registered nurses	450	48,090
Maintenance and repair workers, general	450	29,370
Maid and housekeeping cleaners	450	16,440

■ Openings for workers with a high school diploma or less
□ Openings for workers with some college/associate degree

earned less.) All but three of the occupations had median earnings below $27,380, the median for workers in 2002.

But median earnings don't show the wide variation in pay that exists in some occupations. For example, earnings for some customer service representatives, such as those who provide help for complex computer problems, are significantly higher than the median. But these same workers are usually highly skilled and have several months of on-the-job training; some also have a bachelor's degree.

Occupations with high earnings and lots of openings. According to BLS data, about 350 of the occupations expected to provide openings for high school graduates also had higher-than-average median earnings in 2002. Chart 2 shows the high-paying occupations that are expected to have the most job openings for workers who don't have a bachelor's degree. Workers in all of these occupations have

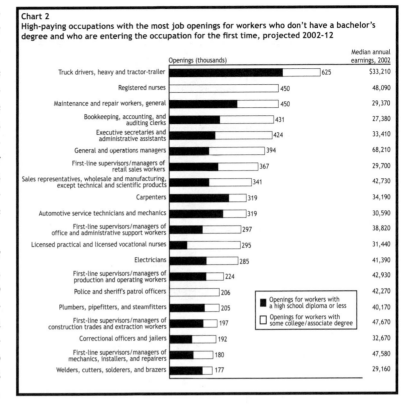

Chart 2
High-paying occupations with the most job openings for workers who don't have a bachelor's degree and who are entering the occupation for the first time, projected 2002-12

Occupation	Openings (thousands)	Median annual earnings, 2002
Truck drivers, heavy and tractor-trailer	625	$33,210
Registered nurses	450	48,090
Maintenance and repair workers, general	450	29,370
Bookkeeping, accounting, and auditing clerks	431	27,380
Executive secretaries and administrative assistants	424	33,410
General and operations managers	394	68,210
First-line supervisors/managers of retail sales workers	367	29,700
Sales representatives, wholesale and manufacturing, except technical and scientific products	341	42,730
Carpenters	319	34,190
Automotive service technicians and mechanics	319	30,590
First-line supervisors/managers of office and administrative support workers	297	38,820
Licensed practical and licensed vocational nurses	295	31,440
Electricians	285	41,390
First-line supervisors/managers of production and operating workers	224	42,930
Police and sheriff's patrol officers	206	42,270
Plumbers, pipefitters, and steamfitters	205	40,170
First-line supervisors/managers of construction trades and extraction workers	197	47,670
Correctional officers and jailers	192	32,670
First-line supervisors/managers of mechanics, installers, and repairers	180	47,580
Welders, cutters, solderers, and brazers	177	29,160

■ Openings for workers with a high school diploma or less
□ Openings for workers with some college/associate degree

technical skills or supervisory responsibilities. And all of the occupations usually employ workers who complete moderate- or long-term on-the-job training, college courses, or vocational classes.

Nearly half of the occupations in the chart relate to construction or manufacturing. Some of these occupations require physical strength, but many, such as electricians, do not. Completing a formal apprenticeship can increase your chances of getting a job in these occupations. Studying algebra and taking vocational classes in high school can also help you qualify.

Another way to a high-paying career is to work toward becoming a supervisor. Many high school graduates transfer to managerial occupations as they gain experience. According to some studies, having formal training or taking college courses can increase the chances of becoming a supervisor.

Competing with college workers. Some of the occupations shown in the charts are expected to provide jobs to workers who have a bachelor's degree, as well as to workers who do not have one. When an occupation has workers who have different levels of education, the workers with more education are often better able to compete for jobs. This is particularly true if the occupation requires complicated math, science, writing, or other academic skills.

If you do not have a bachelor's degree and are competing with people who do, you can increase your competitiveness in a number of ways. These include gaining work or volunteer experience, taking high school or college classes that relate to an occupation, and completing a certification.

Additionally, consider contacting your state's labor market information office to learn about work, volunteer, education, and training opportunities. You can also find out which training programs have high placement rates and which occupations are most in demand in your area.

Table 1
Selected office and administrative support occupations

Occupations	Net openings for workers without bachelor's degree, projected 2002-12	Median annual earnings, 2002	Most significant source of education or training	Percent of workers aged 25 to 44 with...		
				High school diploma or less	Some college/ associate degree	Bachelor's or graduate degree
Office clerks, general	972,000	$22,280	Short-term on-the-job training	41%	42%	17%
Stock clerks and order fillers	602,000	19,270	Short-term on-the-job training	65	26	9
Receptionists and information clerks	595,000	21,150	Short-term on-the-job training	50	39	12
Customer service representatives	582,000	26,240	Moderate-term on-the-job training	38	40	21
Bookkeeping, accounting, and auditing clerks	431,000	27,380	Moderate-term on-the-job training	40	44	16
Executive secretaries and administrative assistants[1]	424,000	33,410	Moderate-term on-the-job training	37	47	16
Tellers	311,000	20,400	Short-term on-the-job training	44	43	13
First-line supervisors/ managers of office and administrative support workers	297,000	38,820	Work experience in a related occupation	33	40	27
Postal service mail carriers[2]	105,000	39,530	Short-term on-the-job training	52	40	8
Legal secretaries[1]	100,000	35,020	Vocational certificate	37	47	16

[1] BLS does not have reliable education data for different types of secretaries; all secretaries were categorized as a group.

[2] BLS does not have reliable education data for this occupation specifically; data for related occupations were used.

Career Fields with Promise

Opportunities abound in almost every career field. The information that follows gives an overview of the expected job openings and common educational requirements for occupations in six widely varying fields. Career fields with the most expected openings are discussed first.

The accompanying tables show occupations that are expected to have many openings over the 2002–2012 decade. The tables also show 2002 earnings, along with the percentage of current workers aged 25 to 44 who have a high school diploma or less, some college courses or an associate degree, or a bachelor's or graduate degree. College courses or degrees may or may not relate to the occupation.

Also listed is the specific type of training, such as on-the-job training, a vocational certificate, or an associate degree, that BLS analysts deemed most significant in the occupation.

Office and administrative support. People who like business and teamwork should expect to find many opportunities in office and administrative support occupations. Between 2002 and 2012, these occupations are projected to provide several million openings for workers who do not have a bachelor's degree. Many of these openings, such as those for stock clerks, usually require little training after high school. (See table 1.) Summer jobs or high school classes in English, typing, and computer-related subjects can pave the way.

Other occupations, such as dispatchers and eligibility interviewers, often require months of on-the-job training. Many office workers also take some college courses to hone their skills, earn certifications, and increase their opportunity for advancement.

Healthcare. For workers who have an interest in science and in helping people, healthcare occupations are expected to provide some of the most plentiful and highest-paying career opportunities. Overall, healthcare occupations are projected to provide nearly 3 million job openings between 2002 and 2012 for workers who don't have a bachelor's degree. Many of these openings are expected to result from fast growth. Table 2 lists 10 of the healthcare occupations with high earnings in 2002 or a large number of expected openings over the 2002–2012 decade.

Table 2
Selected healthcare occupations

Occupations	Net openings for workers without bachelor's degrees, projected 2002-12	Median annual earnings, 2002	Most significant source of education or training	Percent of workers aged 25 to 44 with…		
				High school diploma or less	Some college/ associate degree	Bachelor's or graduate degree
Nursing aides, orderlies, and attendants[1]	523,000	$19,960	Short-term on-the-job training	63%	31%	6%
Registered nurses	450,000	48,090	Associate degree	2	40	58
Home health aides[1]	355,000	18,090	Short-term on-the-job training	63	31	6
Licensed practical and licensed vocational nurses	295,000	31,440	Vocational certificate	23	72	5
Medical assistants	282,000	23,940	Moderate-term on-the-job training	37	50	14
Dental assistants	187,000	27,240	Moderate-term on-the-job training	34	57	8
Emergency medical technicians and paramedics[2]	80,000	24,030	Vocational certificate	24	63	13
Radiologic technologists and technicians	53,000	38,970	Associate degree	11	66	24
Dental hygienists	50,000	55,320	Associate degree	5	63	32
Respiratory therapists	41,000	40,220	Associate degree	5	68	28

[1]Education data for this occupation come from the larger occupational group of which it is a part.

[2]BLS does not have reliable education data for this occupation; data for related occupations were used.

As the table shows, training varies widely within most of these occupations. For example, the most significant source of preparation for nursing aides and home health aides is less than 1 month of on-the-job training. But a large number of aides have taken college courses—either to qualify for certifications or to prepare for other, higher-paying healthcare occupations. Some aides may have college coursework unrelated to their job.

Having a job in one occupation while training for another is a common advancement strategy for healthcare workers. Emergency medical technicians and paramedics, for example, need certification and some formal training before they start work. With additional training and experience, workers can progress to higher levels of certification and new job duties. To receive the highest level of certification, most paramedics must earn an associate degree.

In part because the skills they need are becoming more complex, healthcare workers are getting more training. Often, this extra education pays off. Although many dental assistants train on the job, for example, about 25 percent of these workers aged 25 and over have an associate degree. And median earnings of dental assistants who have an associate degree are about 23 percent higher than the earnings of those who have a high school diploma or less.

For some healthcare occupations, BLS analysts were able to draw conclusions about the level of competition that future jobseekers might face. Analysts gathered anecdotal evidence and other data, including information on the number of people who have recently completed training programs. Analysts concluded that over the 2002–2012 decade, there could be excellent opportunities in the following healthcare occupations:

★ Dental assistants

★ Nursing, psychiatric, and home health aides

★ Dental hygienists

★ Registered nurses

★ Clinical laboratory technologists and technicians

★ Respiratory therapists

★ Medical records and health information technicians

These occupations usually employ people who have some on-the-job training or education after high school.

Construction. An interest in building things can lead to a career with prospects. More than 2 million job openings are projected for workers entering construction occupations between 2002 and 2012. And most of these occupations pay more than the average for all occupations.

Table 3
Selected construction occupations

Occupations	Net openings for workers without bachelor's degrees, projected 2002-12	Median annual earnings, 2002	Most significant source of education or training	Percent of workers aged 25 to 44 with...		
				High school diploma or less	Some college/ associate degree	Bachelor's or graduate degree
Carpenters	319,000	$34,190	Long-term on-the-job training	73%	22%	5%
Electricians	285,000	41,390	Long-term on-the-job training	50	44	6
Plumbers, pipefitters, and steamfitters	205,000	40,170	Long-term on-the-job training	67	29	4
First-line supervisors/managers of construction trades and extraction workers*	197,000	47,670	Work experience in a related occupation	63	27	10
Operating engineers and other construction equipment operators	127,000	35,240	Moderate-term on-the-job training	79	19	2
Painters, construction and maintenance	120,000	29,070	Moderate-term on-the-job training	77	17	6
Sheet metal workers	90,000	34,560	Moderate-term on-the-job training	69	30	2
Cement masons and concrete finishers	84,000	30,660	Moderate-term on-the-job training	85	13	2
Roofers	70,000	30,180	Moderate-term on-the-job training	85	12	3
Drywall and ceiling tile installers	58,000	33,710	Moderate-term on-the-job training	84	14	2

* BLS does not have reliable education data for this occupation specifically; data for related occupations were used.

There are many types of construction occupations. Some require outdoor work, others don't; some involve a high level of mathematics, others require math skills that are more basic. Many workers in construction occupations start as apprentices, taking vocational classes and getting paid for on-the-job training. Some workers receive college credit for the vocational classes they take.

Table 3 shows the 10 construction occupations expected to have the most job openings over the 2002–2012 decade. In 2002, all of these occupations had median earnings that were above the average for all occupations.

For three of the occupations in the table—carpenters; plumbers, pipefitters, and steamfitters; and roofers—BLS analysts had enough information to conclude that the job openings could outnumber jobseekers in some years and in some places. Prospects are considered excellent. BLS analysts also concluded that two other construction occupations—insulation workers and brickmasons, blockmasons, and stonemasons—are expected to provide good opportunities.

Police and other protective service. Workers who keep the public safe from crime, natural disasters, and fire are projected to be in high demand. Between 2002 and 2012, protective service occupations are expected to provide about 1.4 million job openings for workers who don't have a bachelor's degree. As table 4 shows, most of these openings are projected to be in three occupations: security guards, police and sheriff's patrol officers, and correctional officers and jailers.

Security guards can usually qualify for their jobs if they have a high school diploma or less. Once employed, security guards often receive some on-the-job training. Armed guards need training and licensure. Guards working in specialized fields, such as nuclear power plant security, receive extensive formal training after being hired and usually earn more than other guards. Correctional officers also train on the job, but they usually train longer and are paid more than security guards. In some states, correctional officers receive months of training and instruction, often while attending academies.

Table 4
Selected protective service occupations

Occupations	Net openings for workers without bachelor's degrees, projected 2002-12	Median annual earnings, 2002	Most significant source of education or training	Percent of workers aged 25 to 44 with...		
				High school diploma or less	Some college/ associate degree	Bachelor's or graduate degree
Security guards	534,000	$19,140	Short-term on-the-job training	52%	35%	13%
Police and sheriff's patrol officers	206,000	42,270	Long-term on-the-job training	19	53	28
Correctional officers and jailers	192,000	32,670	Moderate-term on-the-job training	43	47	10
Fire fighters	140,000	36,230	Long-term on-the-job training	26	58	16
First-line supervisors/managers of police and detectives	36,000	61,010	Work experience in a related occupation	17	54	28
Crossing guards*	36,000	18,680	Short-term on-the-job training	76	23	1
First-line supervisors/managers of fire fighting and prevention workers*	26,000	55,450	Work experience in a related occupation	18	57	25
First-line supervisors/managers of protective service workers, except police, fire and corrections	21,000	34,320	Work experience in a related occupation	31	46	23
Detectives and criminal investigators	18,000	51,410	Work experience in a related occupation	9	35	56
Private detectives and investigators	10,000	29,300	Work experience in a related occupation	18	36	46

* BLS does not have reliable education data for this occupation specifically; data for related occupations were used.

Police and sheriff's patrol officers train on the job in police academies, and many take classes in criminal justice after high school and before entering the academy. Bachelor's degrees are becoming more common among police and can make it easier to advance, but skills and character are often more important than education. Employers' requirements depend on geographic location and job type.

Education and childcare. Career opportunities in schools and daycare centers will continue to be plentiful. More than 1.2 million openings are expected in this field between 2002 and 2012 for workers who don't have a bachelor's degree. Within these occupations, workers have wide ranges of training and education. Teacher assistants, who are expected to have the most job openings among occupations in this group, are often required to have an associate degree or to pass an exam. But many others train on the job, especially if their work involves supervising children rather than helping with instruction.

Preschool teachers and childcare workers often have an associate degree, too. But the degree is not always required for workers in these two occupations; instead, workers earn an associate or bachelor's degree to learn skills and increase their advancement opportunities. A common strategy is to take courses that lead to certifications and later apply the courses toward a 2- or 4-year degree or both.

Self-enrichment education teachers often teach a hobby or skill, such as art, dance, or cooking, in which they have expertise.

Computer. Explosive growth in information technology is expected to create many openings for people who like working with computers. Openings in computer-related occupations for workers who don't have a bachelor's degree are expected to total about 444,000 between 2002 and 2012. Industry certifications and computer experience are particularly important in this field, in part because many college graduates also compete for these jobs.

According to industry experts, people who don't have a bachelor's degree may find it easiest to enter the following computer occupations: computer support specialists, network and computer systems administrators, and certain types of network systems and data communications analysts.

The computer support specialist occupation is projected to provide the most openings. Specialists who don't have a 4-year degree increase their marketability by earning certifications or getting computer experience while they are in school or are working in other jobs.

Network and computer systems administrators include workers at every educational level. Many administrators who don't have a degree begin their careers as computer support specialists, switching to more highly paid administrator jobs after they gain computer experience.

Webmasters, computer security professionals, and Local Area Network (LAN) support staff are also expected to be in high demand. All of these workers are part of the occupation of network systems and data communications analysts. Many of these workers have a bachelor's degree, but others substitute coursework, experience, or certifications.

Workers in each of these computer occupations had above-average earnings in 2002. But workers who have a bachelor's degree are included in those earnings figures; earnings might be lower for workers who have less education.

How These Numbers Were Developed

Measuring job outlook by education is complicated, and there are many ways to do it. This analysis used expected job openings as a way to measure outlook because the number of job openings helps to determine how easy it will be for workers to enter an occupation. The analysis used survey data as an objective way to separate openings by education level.

Like any analysis based on projections and estimates, however, this one has limitations. Understanding these limitations allows people to better use the results.

Methods Used

To determine job prospects, BLS analysts started by projecting the total number of job openings available between 2002 and 2012 for workers entering an occupation for the first time. Next, analysts estimated how many of those openings would be filled by workers who do not have a bachelor's degree and how many openings would be in high-paying occupations.

Job openings. Job openings come from two sources: the need to fill newly created positions and the need to replace workers who leave an occupation permanently.

To estimate the number of openings that will come from newly created positions, analysts projected how much each occupation would grow or decline between 2002 and 2012. There are many reasons that the number of jobs in an occupation might change. Sometimes, the demand for a certain type of good or service increases—for example, when an aging population creates the need for more healthcare services and, as a result, more healthcare technicians. The way a good or service is provided also can create the need for more jobs in an occupation, such as when library technicians gain jobs faster than librarians do because employment of technicians is considered to be more cost effective.

Many occupations that employ people who do not have a bachelor's degree are projected to gain jobs rapidly. In fact, for 6 of the 10 fastest-growing occupations, a bachelor's degree is not the most significant source of training. The occupation projected to be the fastest-growing of all occupations over the 2002–2012 decade, medical assistant, often employs people who train on the job.

The need to replace workers who leave an occupation permanently is expected to provide even more openings than job growth will. To estimate how many workers will need to be replaced during the 2002–2012 decade, analysts studied both past trends in each occupation and the ages of current workers. In some occupations, workers usually stay for many years. In other occupations, people tend to leave more quickly. These considerations affect replacement needs.

Openings by education. After analysts projected the total number of job openings in each occupation, they estimated how many of those openings would be filled by workers who fall into one of three different education levels: a high school diploma or less, some college or an associate degree, or a bachelor's or graduate degree.

Analysts determined which levels of education were significant in each occupation by looking at the education levels of current workers as reported in 2000, 2001, and 2002 Current Population Survey data. If at least 20 percent of workers had a particular level of education, that level was deemed significant. Expected job openings were divided among each of the significant education levels according to how common that education level was for workers in the occupation.

In addition to describing the three educational attainment categories, this article discusses specific education and training requirements for some occupations. These discussions are based on occupational analyses conducted for the *Occupational Outlook Handbook.*

Openings by earnings. The earnings data in this article are from the BLS Occupational Employment Statistics survey. The survey reflects the 2002 earnings of all workers without regard to education level or experience. Also, the survey does not include self-employed workers. In this analysis, occupations were considered high-paying if their median earnings were above the median for all workers in 2002.

Limitations of the Data

To measure total job openings and openings by education level, BLS analysts needed to make some assumptions about the future. First, analysts assumed that the education levels in each occupation would remain roughly the same over the 2002–2012 decade. In reality, the educational characteristics of some occupations change over time. Many occupations—such as registered nurses and police officers—have shown a gradual increase in the education levels of their workers.

Analysts also ignored education levels that were uncommon in an occupation; as stated previously, at least 20 percent of workers in an occupation had to have a given level of education for it to be considered significant. So, for example, even though 18 percent of current massage therapists have a high school diploma or less, none of that occupation's future openings were slated for workers with that level of education.

Another limitation of this study is that it focuses on the number of job openings expected in an occupation. Job openings give only a partial view of the prospects that workers can expect. The number of people who will compete for those openings is also important. For most occupations, BLS analysts do not have enough information about the future supply of workers to analyze the competition for jobs.

Finally, the accuracy of this study is limited by its use of survey data. Surveys are always subject to some error because not every worker is counted and because the information gathered is sometimes incorrect. In addition, many of the occupations studied here could not be counted with enough statistical accuracy because the number of workers surveyed was too small. In those cases, analysts substituted the education levels of similar occupations or groups of occupations that had larger numbers of workers.

Despite the assumptions and limitations of this analysis, there is evidence that counting future job openings using the method described here produces accurate results. When existing jobs are separated into educational categories using this method, the results closely match current numbers.

For More Information

To learn more about the occupations described here and about the hundreds of other occupations expected to provide openings for workers who don't have a bachelor's degree, see the 2006–2007 *Occupational Outlook Handbook,* available in many libraries and career centers and online at www.bls.gov/oco. The *Handbook* describes the job outlook, education and training requirements, and job duties of nearly 270 occupations.

Another BLS publication, the 2004-05 *Occupational Projections and Training Data bulletin,* explains in detail the methods used in this study and lists the projected job openings and worker education levels for every occupation studied by the BLS Office of Occupational Statistics and Employment Projections. The bulletin is available online at www.bls.gov/emp/optd/home.htm and is for sale by calling the Superintendent of Documents toll-free at (866) 512-1800.

To help workers prepare for a career, the U.S. Department of Education offers information about financial aid for people attending 2-year colleges, 4-year colleges, and vocational schools. Call the financial aid hotline toll-free at (800) 4FED-AID (433-3243); write the Federal Student Aid Information Center, P.O. Box 84, Washington, DC 20044-0084; or visit online at www.studentaid.ed.gov.

Studying potential job openings is only a starting point when deciding on a career. Many other considerations are important, including individual skills and interests, personal circumstances, and the needs of local employers. To explore these and other factors in your career decision, visit state labor market information offices and career centers. Information is available online at www.servicelocator.org or by calling the U.S. Department of Labor's toll-free helpline, (877) US2-JOBS (872-5627).

Opportunities are as varied as the workers who seek them. And when it comes to training, finding what is best for you is one of the surest routes to reward.

From the **Occupational Outlook Quarterly** *by the U.S. Department of Labor. Written by Roger Moncarz and Olivia Crosby, economists in the Office of* **Occupational Statistics and Employment Projections.**

Index